Insurance Operations

Insurance Operations

Edited by
Susan J. Kearney, MBA, CPCU, ARM, AU, AAI

1st Edition • 1st Printing

The Institutes
720 Providence Road, Suite 100
Malvern, Pennsylvania 19355-3433

Foreword

The Institutes are the trusted leader in delivering proven knowledge solutions that drive powerful business results for the risk management and property-casualty insurance industry. For more than 100 years, The Institutes have been meeting the industry's changing professional development needs with customer-driven products and services.

In conjunction with industry experts and members of the academic community, our Knowledge Resources Department develops our course and program content, including Institutes study materials. Practical and technical knowledge gained from Institutes courses enhances qualifications, improves performance, and contributes to professional growth—all of which drive results.

The Institutes' proven knowledge helps individuals and organizations achieve powerful results with a variety of flexible, customer-focused options:

Recognized Credentials—The Institutes offer an unmatched range of widely recognized and industry-respected specialty credentials. The Institutes' Chartered Property Casualty Underwriter (CPCU) professional designation is designed to provide a broad understanding of the property-casualty insurance industry. Depending on professional needs, CPCU students may select either a commercial insurance focus or a personal risk management and insurance focus and may choose from a variety of electives.

In addition, The Institutes offer certificate or designation programs in a variety of disciplines, including these:

- Claims
- Commercial underwriting
- Fidelity and surety bonding
- General insurance
- Insurance accounting and finance
- Insurance information technology
- Insurance production and agency management
- Insurance regulation and compliance

- Management
- Marine insurance
- Personal insurance
- Premium auditing
- Quality insurance services
- Reinsurance
- Risk management
- Surplus lines

Flexible Online Learning—The Institutes have an unmatched variety of technical insurance content covering topics from accounting to under-writing, which we now deliver through hundreds of online courses. These cost-effective self-study courses are a convenient way to fill gaps in technical knowledge in a matter of hours without ever leaving the office.

Continuing Education—A majority of The Institutes' courses are filed for CE credit in most states. We also deliver quality, affordable, online CE courses quickly and conveniently through our newest business unit, CEU.com. Visit www.CEU.com to learn more.

College Credits—Most Institutes courses carry college credit recommenda-tions from the American Council on Education. A variety of courses also qualify for credits toward certain associate, bachelor's, and master's degrees at several prestigious colleges and universities. More information is available in the Student Services section of our Web site, www.TheInstitutes.org.

Custom Applications—The Institutes collaborate with corporate customers to utilize our trusted course content and flexible delivery options in develop-ing customized solutions that help them achieve their unique organizational goals.

Insightful Analysis—Our Insurance Research Council (IRC) division conducts public policy research on important contemporary issues in property-casualty insurance and risk management. Visit www.ircweb.org to learn more or purchase its most recent studies.

The Institutes look forward to serving the risk management and property-casualty insurance industry for another 100 years. We welcome comments from our students and course leaders; your feedback helps us continue to improve the quality of our study materials.

Peter L. Miller, CPCU
President and CEO
The Institutes

Preface

Insurance Operations is the assigned textbook for CPCU 520, one of the four foundation courses in The Institutes' Chartered Property Casualty Underwriter (CPCU) designation program.

The goal of CPCU 520 is to enable learners to improve their operational effectiveness by increasing their knowledge of how the various property-casualty insurance functions work together to create and deliver insurance products efficiently. The eleven assignments in *Insurance Operations* support this goal.

Assignment 1 provides an overview of insurance operations, including classifications of insurers; insurers' major goals and the constraints on achieving those goals; and measurements used to evaluate insurers' success in meeting goals.

Assignment 2 discusses insurance regulation and the regulatory activities that affect insurance operations.

Assignment 3 examines the characteristics of the competitive property-casualty insurance marketplace and the marketing and distribution systems and channels that insurers use.

Assignments 4 and 5 describe the underwriting process and the major underwriting considerations for selected property-casualty lines of business.

Assignment 6 examines the risk control and premium audit functions and how they support insurance operations.

Assignments 7 and 8 describe the claim handling process and the challenges of handling specific types of property-casualty claims.

Assignment 9 examines the two most prominent actuarial functions of insurers—ratemaking and estimation of loss reserves.

Assignment 10 describes the various types of reinsurance, the design of reinsurance programs, and reinsurance regulation.

Assignment 11 broadens the functional view of insurance and examines the strategic management process insurers can use to establish goals and to determine strategies for creating a competitive advantage.

The Institutes are grateful to the following industry experts whose thoughtful review of the content and suggestions for improving it have contributed to making this content current, accurate, and relevant:

Edwin B. Barber, CPCU, ARe

Carolyn J. Bergh, FCAS, MAAA

Marsha A. Cohen, CPCU, ARe

Anne Crabbs, CPCU, CIC

Dennis Dunham, FCAS, MAAA, CPCU

Michael Goldman, MBA, CPCU, ERM

Lawrence P. Johnsen Esq., CPCU, ARe

William Kelso, APA

Daniel P. Konzen, MBA, PhD (ABD)

Michelle L. Krajewski, CPCU, ARM-E

Gerald S. Kraut

David R. Lesieur, FCAS

Gregory J. Massey, CPCU, CIC, ARM, CRM, CLCS, PMP

Claire Mead, CPCU, MBA, CPIW, AIS, ACS, PCS

Gary E. Shook, FCAS, MAAA

Jeffrey Spangler, CPCU, CSP, REM

Lynn T. Splittstoesser, PhD, CPCU, CLU, ChFC, FLMI, AFSB

Donald S. Sutton, CPCU, APA, CIPA

Sean S. Sweeney, MBA, CPCU, RPLU, ARe

Paul Walther, CPCU, ARe

Matthew T. Wulf, Esq.

The Institutes remain equally thankful to the many insurance professionals who have contributed to the development of earlier versions of this content. Although they are too numerous to name here, the current content still reflects their valuable insights.

For more information about The Institutes' programs, please call our Customer Service Department at (800) 644-2101, email us at customerservice@TheInstitutes.org, or visit our Web site at www.TheInstitutes.org.

Susan J. Kearney

Contributors

The Institutes acknowledge with deep appreciation the contributions made to the content of this text by the following persons:

Pamela J. Brooks, MBA, CPCU, AAM, AIM, AIS

Cheryl Ferguson, EdD, CPCU, AU, API, AAI, AIM

Doug Froggatt

Lynn Knauf, CPCU, ARP

Eric C. Nordman, CPCU, CIE

Judith M. Vaughan, AIM, BA

Lawrence White, ACAS, MAAA, CPCU, ARM, AIAF, ARe

Contents

Direct Your Learning ▶▶

Overview of Insurance Operations

Educational Objectives

After learning the content of this assignment, you should be able to:

▶ Explain how insurers have organized to provide property-casualty insurance.

▶ Describe the major goals of an insurer.

▶ Describe the internal and external constraints that impede insurers from achieving their major goals.

▶ Describe the measurements used to evaluate how successful an insurer is at meeting its established goals.

▶ Describe the core and supporting functions performed by insurers.

Overview of Insurance Operations

1

CLASSIFICATIONS OF INSURERS

Insurance is a system under which participants (such as individuals, families, and businesses) make payments in exchange for the commitment to reimburse for specific types of losses under certain circumstances. Insurers, which are organizations within the financial services industry, may be classified in various manners.

The insurance organization or the entity that facilitates the pooling of funds and the payment of benefits is called an insurer. Participants in this mechanism, called insureds, benefit through reimbursement of covered losses that occur, reduction of uncertainty, additional services provided by the insurer to reduce the frequency or severity of losses, and financial protection against legal liability for damages to others. Additionally, insureds can benefit from the potential availability of credit from lenders, which may help enable them to purchase property. Because the risk of loss to property is transferred to the insurer, lenders are willing to loan money to insureds with greater confidence that the loan will be repaid.

The principal function of every insurer is the same: the acceptance of risks that others transfer to it through the insurance mechanism. This task is divided into core operations consisting of underwriting, claims, and marketing, which, in turn, are supported by several other functions. These operations are described in other sections.

Property-casualty insurers can be classified in these four ways:

- Legal form of ownership
- Place of incorporation
- Licensing status
- Insurance distribution systems and channels

The exhibit shows the general classifications of insurers. An insurer might be further classified by what types of insurance it writes or its specialty. See the exhibit "Classifications of Insurers."

Legal Form of Ownership

The first classification of insurers is by legal form of ownership. The two major types of insurers in this classification are proprietary and cooperative insurers.

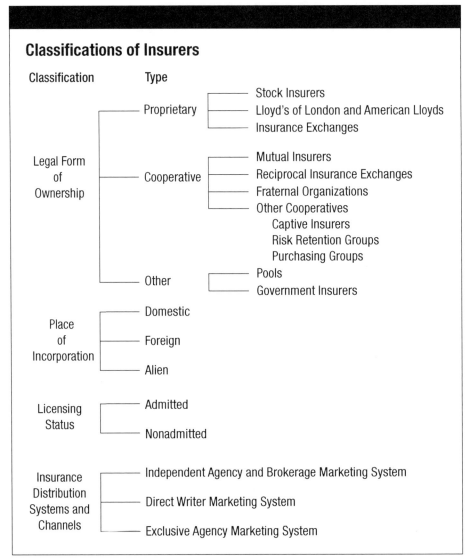

Classifications of Insurers

[DA06276]

Proprietary Insurers

Proprietary insurer

Insurer formed for the purpose of earning a profit for its owners.

Proprietary insurers include stock insurers, Lloyd's of London and American Lloyds, and insurance exchanges.

Stock Insurers

Stock insurers are the most prevalent type of proprietary insurer in the United States. These insurers are owned by their stockholders. By purchasing stock in a for-profit insurer, stockholders supply the capital needed to form the insurer or the additional capital the insurer needs to expand its operations. Stockholders expect to receive a return on their investment in the form of stock dividends, increased stock value, or both.

Stockholders have the right to elect the board of directors, which has the authority to control the insurer's activities. The board of directors creates and oversees corporate goals and objectives and appoints a chief executive officer (CEO) to carry out the insurer's operations and implement the programs necessary to operate the company.

Lloyd's of London and American Lloyds

Among the proprietary types of insurance ownership is a unique type known as Lloyds. Two types of Lloyds associations exist: Lloyd's of London and American Lloyds.

Lloyd's of London (Lloyd's) is technically not an insurer. However, it does provide the physical and procedural facilities for its members to write insurance. It is a marketplace, similar to a stock exchange. The members are investors who hope to earn a profit from the insurance operations.

In the past, all of the insurance written at Lloyd's was written by or on behalf of individual members, and the insurance each member wrote was backed by his or her personal fortune. Individual members were not liable for the obligations assumed by any other member. Today, a declining proportion of Lloyd's accounts are still underwritten and secured by individuals. A larger portion of Lloyd's members today are corporations, and the liability of each of these members is limited to the amount that the member agrees to write. Lloyd's provides coverage for many unusual or difficult loss exposures and underwrites much of the global marine and aviation insurance.

American Lloyds associations are smaller than Lloyd's of London, and most are domiciled in Texas because of the favorable regulatory climate. Most of these associations were formed or have been acquired by insurers. Like most investors of Lloyd's of London today, members (called underwriters) of American Lloyds are not liable beyond their investment in the association.

Insurance Exchanges

An insurance exchange is a proprietary insurer similar to Lloyd's because it acts as an insurance marketplace. Exchange members underwrite any insurance or reinsurance purchased on the exchange. Members can be individuals, partnerships, or corporations, and they have limited liability. Members belong to syndicates and delegate day-to-day operations to the syndicate manager.

For example, INEX (formerly the Illinois Insurance Exchange) was formed in 1979. This exchange serves as an excess and surplus lines market, writing various types of insurance. Member syndicates operate as separate businesses that focus on a particular group of loss exposures.

Cooperative Insurers

Cooperative insurers are the second type of insurer in the legal form of ownership classification. This type of insurer is owned by its policyholders and is usually formed to provide insurance protection to its policyholders at minimum cost. This classification includes mutual insurers, reciprocal insurance exchanges, fraternal organizations, and other cooperatives.

Mutual Insurers

Mutual insurer

An insurer that is owned by its policyholders and formed as a corporation for the purpose of providing insurance to them.

Mutual insurers constitute the largest number of cooperative insurers and provide low-cost insurance to their policyholders, who are the owners of the insurer. Because a traditional mutual insurer issues no common stock, it has no stockholders. Its policyholders have voting rights similar to those of a stock company's stockholders, and, like stockholders, they elect the insurer's board of directors that appoints officers to manage the company. Some profit is retained to increase surplus, and excess profit is usually returned to policyholders as dividends. Mutual insurers include some large national insurers and many regional insurers.

Although initially formed to provide insurance for their owners, who otherwise could not obtain insurance, mutual insurers today generally seek to earn profits in their ongoing operations, just as stock companies do. A mutual insurer's retained profits ensure the future financial health of the organization.

Reciprocal Insurance Exchanges

Reciprocal insurance exchange (interinsurance exchange)

An insurer owned by its policyholders, formed as an unincorporated association for the purpose of providing insurance coverage to its members (called subscribers), and managed by an attorney-in-fact. Members agree to mutually insure each other, and they share profits and losses in the same proportion as the amount of insurance purchased from the exchange by that member.

A **reciprocal insurance exchange**, also simply called a reciprocal, consists of a series of private contracts in which subscribers, or members of the group, agree to insure each other. The term "reciprocal" comes from the reciprocity of responsibility of all subscribers to each other. Each member of the reciprocal is both an insured and an insurer. Because the subscribers are not experts in running an insurance operation, they contract with an individual or organization to operate the reciprocal. This manager is called an attorney-in-fact. The subscribers empower the attorney-in-fact to handle all the duties necessary to manage the reciprocal. An insurer may be formed as a reciprocal to receive favorable tax treatment.

Fraternal Organizations

Fraternal organizations resemble mutual companies, but they combine a lodge or social function with their insurance function. They write primarily life and health insurance.

Other Cooperatives

Cooperative insurers include captive insurers, risk retention groups, and purchasing groups.

When a business organization or a group of affiliated organizations forms a subsidiary company to provide all or part of its insurance, the subsidiary is known as a captive insurer, or captive. This arrangement is sometimes referred to as "formalized self-insurance." For example, a large retail chain may decide it can insure itself at a more reasonable cost by using a captive rather than an unaffiliated insurer. The captive may also be formed to cover losses that other insurers will not cover at any price.

Captive insurers can take several forms, and their ultimate purpose is to fund the losses of their owners. Some states have enacted legislation to facilitate the formation and operation of captive insurers within their jurisdictions, while others do not permit the formation of captives.

Legislation has also allowed risk retention groups and purchasing groups to form. These cooperatives can be stock companies, mutuals, or reciprocal exchanges. They are usually organized so that a limited group or type of insured is eligible to purchase insurance from them. These types of insurers are becoming more significant in the evolving insurance marketplace.

Other Insurers

Other insurers are the third type of insurer in the legal form of ownership classification. Insurers that fall into this classification include pools and government insurers.

Pools

A pool consists of several insurers, not otherwise related, that join together to insure loss exposures that individual insurers are unwilling to insure. These loss exposures present the potential for losses that either occur too frequently or are too severe (catastrophic) for individual insurers to accept the risk. A major airplane crash is an example of such a catastrophic loss that might be insured under a pool arrangement.

Another catastrophic loss exposure that insurers may be unwilling to insure individually is a large nuclear power plant, for which losses could amount to billions of dollars for property and liability damage. Because no single insurer was willing to assume such tremendous liability, nuclear energy pools were formed. These pools allow many member insurers to spread any losses among members. Additionally, the pools buy reinsurance from nonmembers to increase their capacity.

Pools can be formed either voluntarily or to meet statutory requirements. They operate either as a syndicate or through reinsurance. A syndicate pool issues a joint (or syndicate) policy to the insured, listing all pool members and specifying the part of the insurance for which each member is responsible. Under such policies, the insured has a contractual relationship with each pool member and can sue any or all of them directly if a disagreement arises.

Under a reinsurance pool, one member of the pool issues the policy to the insured, and the other pool members reinsure an agreed proportion of the policy's insured loss exposures. The insured has a contractual relationship only with the member that issued the policy. The policyholder has no legal rights against the other members of the pool and might not even know that they exist.

Many pools are required by law. Virtually all states require some kind of pooling arrangement to provide auto liability insurance for drivers who cannot

Fair Access to Insurance Requirements (FAIR) plans

An insurance pool through which private insurers collectively address an unmet need for property insurance on urban properties, especially those susceptible to loss by riot or civil commotion.

obtain such insurance in the standard market. Similar pools are required for workers compensation coverage in most states. **Fair Access to Insurance Requirements (FAIR) plans** are required by law in at least half of the states. These pools provide property insurance to qualified property owners who are unable to obtain coverage in the standard market.

Many states in the southeastern U.S., such as Florida, have pools that provide windstorm coverage for residents in storm-prone areas who cannot obtain coverage in the standard market. Similar statutory pools for other types of insurance are required by state law. The protection that these pools provide is underwritten by private insurers and not by state governments, although state and federal governments do act as insurers in some situations.

Government Insurers

Despite the size and diversity of private insurers in the U.S., private insurers do not provide some types of insurance. Some loss exposures, such as catastrophic flooding, do not possess the characteristics that make them commercially insurable, but a significant need for protection against the potential losses still exists. Both the federal government and state governments have developed insurance programs to meet specific insurance needs of the public. Some federal government insurance programs serve the public in a manner that only the government can. For example, only the government has the ability to tax in order to provide the financial resources needed to insure some of the larger loss exposures.

The federal government offers several forms of insurance. One of the largest property insurance programs it offers is the National Flood Insurance Program (NFIP), which is administered by the Federal Insurance Administration under the Federal Emergency Management Agency (FEMA). Most property insurance policies exclude flood coverage because the catastrophic loss potential of floods would significantly raise property insurance premiums for all customers. Customers located in an area prone to flooding can obtain the needed coverage through the NFIP program.

The federal government provides a government "backstop" insurance program through the original Terrorism Risk Insurance Act (TRIA) of 2002.[1] TRIA ensures that commercial property owners can obtain reasonable and predictably priced terrorism coverage by specifying that the federal government will share the risk of loss from foreign terrorist acts. Without this backstop, financing for large commercial construction projects in high-population cities (terrorists' targets) would decline, stunting growth and hindering the economy. To qualify under TRIA, a terrorist act must be certified by the government. Federal assistance becomes available when such losses collectively exceed $5 million and when participating insurers pay a specified amount in related claims. Although originally designed to expire in three years, some form of the legislation has since been extended on each expiration date to provide continued backstop coverage.

All states offer some form of government insurance. For example, some states provide workers compensation insurance for some or all employers in the state. Most state workers compensation programs compete with private insurers. However, in some states, workers compensation insurance is offered exclusively by the state.

Most states require motor vehicle owners to have auto liability insurance before registering their vehicles. However, drivers with poor driving records or with little driving experience may have difficulty obtaining insurance from private insurers. To make liability insurance available to almost all licensed drivers, all states have implemented automobile insurance plans through a **residual market**. The cost of operating such plans is spread among all private insurers selling auto insurance in the state.

Residual market

The term referring collectively to insurers and other organizations that make insurance available through a shared risk mechanism to those who cannot obtain coverage in the admitted market.

In most states, FAIR plans make property insurance more readily available to property owners who have exposures to loss over which they have no control, such as being in a neighborhood with a high property crime rate. These state-run plans spread the cost of operating the plan among all private insurers selling property insurance in the state. Without such a program, individuals and business owners located in such areas who have exposures to loss over which they have no control would be unable to obtain property insurance for their buildings or contents.

Beachfront and windstorm insurance pools are residual market plans similar to FAIR plans. These plans, available in states along the Atlantic and Gulf Coasts, provide insurance to property owners who are unable to obtain this coverage from private insurers. The plans provide coverage for wind damage from hurricanes and other windstorms.

Place of Incorporation

The second classification of insurers is by place of incorporation and includes domestic insurers, foreign insurers, and alien insurers.

Insurance is regulated at the state level. Therefore, a domestic insurer is incorporated within a specific state or, if not incorporated, is formed under the laws of that state. An insurer is said to be operating in its own domiciled state when it is doing business in the state in which it is incorporated or was formed.

Reciprocal insurance exchanges are the only unincorporated insurers permitted in most states. Insurance exchanges and Lloyd's organizations are permitted under law in only a few states.

A foreign insurer is a domestic insurer that is licensed to do business in states other than its domiciled state. Alien insurers are incorporated or formed in another country.

Licensing Status

The third classification of insurers is by licensing status. An insurer's state license authorizes it to sell insurance in the state. A license indicates that the insurer has met the state's minimum standards for financial strength, competence, and integrity. If the insurer later fails to meet those standards or fails to comply with a state law, regulation, or rule, its license can be revoked.

A licensed insurer (admitted insurer) is an insurer that has been granted a license to operate in a particular state. An unlicensed insurer (nonadmitted insurer) has not been granted a license to operate in a given state.

Producers for primary insurance (except **surplus lines brokers**) are licensed to place business only with admitted insurers. Licensing status is also important for purposes of reinsurance.

Insurance Distribution Systems and Channels

The fourth classification of insurers is by their insurance distribution systems and distribution channels—that is, the method used to deliver insurance products to the marketplace. Insurers use many types of distribution systems and channels, designed to meet their particular marketing objectives. Most insurers use one or more of these insurance distribution systems:

- **Independent agency and brokerage marketing system**
- **Direct writer marketing system**
- **Exclusive agency marketing system**

Insurers also use these common **distribution channels** to promote products and services as well as to communicate with existing and prospective insureds: the Internet, call centers, direct response, group marketing, and financial institutions.

INSURER GOALS

Senior managers of insurers seek to meet the goals established by the insurer's owners. However, insurers' goals pose some challenges that other organizations do not face in meeting their goals.

An insurer's overall goals are similar to those of any other organization. The differences are how an insurer meets its goals and the conflicts that exist among competing goals.

Insurers have five major goals:

- Earn a profit
- Meet customer needs
- Comply with legal requirements

Surplus lines broker

A person or firm that places business with insurers not licensed (nonadmitted) in the state in which the transaction occurs but that is permitted to write insurance because coverage is not available through standard market insurers.

Independent agency and brokerage marketing system

An insurance marketing system under which producers (agents or brokers), who are independent contractors, sell insurance, usually as representatives of several unrelated insurers.

Direct writer marketing system

An insurance marketing system that uses sales agents (or sales representatives) who are direct employees of the insurer.

Exclusive agency marketing system

An insurance marketing system under which agents contract to sell insurance exclusively for one insurer (or for an associated group of insurers).

Distribution channel

The channel used by the producer of a product or service to transfer that product or service to the ultimate customer.

- Diversify risk
- Fulfill their duty to society

Earn a Profit

The profit goal is most commonly associated with proprietary, or for-profit, insurers. Cooperative insurers should also earn a profit, but doing so is not the primary goal for which they are formed.

Insurers earn money by charging insureds a "premium" for the insurance contract (policy). To be able to meet the contract terms through the payment of covered losses and to meet regulatory requirements, insurers invest the portion of premiums that is not needed to pay their operating expenses (called surplus). These investments produce income in the form of interest, dividends, and investment gains—when sold. The return on investments generates additional income to be further invested to pay future covered losses, to expand the insurer's operations, or to be returned to the insurer's investors.

A proprietary insurer must earn a profit to provide a return on the investment made by the individuals and institutions that purchased the insurer's stock (stockholders). A proprietary insurer can attract capital only as long as its profits are comparable to or better than similar insurers. If investors do not believe that they will receive an acceptable rate of return on their investment, they will seek investment opportunities elsewhere. The insurer would then be unable to raise the capital needed to run the business.

Funds from policyholders (usually premiums) are one source of capital for cooperative insurers. Growth of surplus derived from underwriting operations is another. Funds in excess of those used to pay losses and operating expenses, generally considered profits, are contributed to surplus or returned to policyholders in the form of dividends. Surplus accumulation ensures continued solvency and protects against unforeseen catastrophic losses.

Under certain circumstances, a cooperative insurer can obtain additional capital by borrowing funds using surplus notes. These notes can usually be repaid only from profits, so funds from additional capital are also likely to depend on the insurer's anticipated profitability.

An insurer's premium volume can grow through increased policy sales, resulting from marketing efforts. Additionally, when an insurer's underwriting operation evaluates risks effectively—avoiding risks that will require excessive loss payments—and prices insurance products appropriately for the risk, premium volume also increases. Increased premium volume through marketing and underwriting performance provides greater profits for an insurer.

Meet Customer Needs

To attract customers, an insurer must provide the products and services those customers seek at a competitive price. This involves determining what customers need and what price is competitive and then finding the best way to satisfy those needs.

Insurance is an intangible product; the customer receives an insurance policy, but what the customer actually purchases is a transfer mechanism. The customer pays a premium to transfer some or all of the potential financial consequences of covered loss exposures to the insurer.

As in every retail or service organization, insurance customers expect prompt service and timely responses to inquiries. When insurance customers suffer a loss, they can be upset or under considerable stress. Consequently, the insurer must provide quick and professional assistance, which requires well-trained, customer-focused personnel and automated support systems.

Meeting customers' needs can often conflict with the profit goal. In some cases, offering high-quality insurance at a price that the customer can afford may not generate the profit that the insurer needs to attract and retain capital. This is particularly true in certain heavily populated areas where risk-based pricing would not be affordable for insureds.

Providing training, operating automated call centers, and maintaining current information technology can also become costly and can conflict with achieving the profit goal in the near term. However, the long-term benefits of these expenditures can reduce costs and help reduce premiums, and the improved customer service can create a competitive advantage by encouraging policy retention and new business.

Comply With Legal Requirements

Being a responsible corporate citizen dictates legal compliance. Additionally, legal compliance promotes the insurer's good reputation in the business community and the insurer's ability to attract capital and customers. Conversely, lack of compliance can lead to fines and penalties.

One of an insurer's greatest responsibilities is compliance with state regulations. The insurance industry is highly regulated, and the expenses associated with compliance can be substantial. Insurers incur expenses for filings, record-keeping and accounting, and legal activities. Additional expenses are incurred for participation in assigned risk plans, Fair Access to Insurance Requirements (FAIR) plans, and government-required insolvency funds. To the extent that these expenses increase the cost of insurance, they create a conflict between the profit goal and the customer needs goal.

Diversify Risk

Diversifying risk is an emerging goal for property-casualty insurers because of the increased catastrophe losses that have occurred over the past decade. The Insurance Information Institute has referred to the 2000s as "a decade of disaster." Catastrophes in the 2000s increased by 117 percent as compared to catastrophes in the 1990s. Florida accounted for 19 percent of all insured catastrophe losses in the United States from 1980 to 2008.[2] This high concentration of losses in a geographic area highlights individual insurers' need to spread risk over a wider geographic area and over multiple types of insurance business, such as property-casualty insurance. Meeting this goal complements the insurer's goals of earning a profit and fulfilling its duty to society.

Fulfill Their Duty to Society

All corporations are obligated to promote the wellbeing of society. At the minimum, this obligation demands that the insurer should avoid causing any public harm. Many insurers go well beyond the minimum as responsible corporate citizens.

Many insurers contribute funds, and sometimes they volunteer employees' time to medical, educational, and other public service organizations. Additionally, many insurers establish employee benefit plans that provide for the current and future well-being of their employees. Benefits such as medical insurance, disability insurance, retirement plans, employee assistance programs, and numerous other benefits help employees and retirees to use their personal resources to meet their needs and help to minimize the use of public resources. Insurers' participation in philanthropic activities and employee benefits improves employees' job satisfaction and emotional well-being. In addition, these activities help with employee retention and attract qualified candidates to these organizations.

While fulfilling their duty to society through philanthropic activities and employee benefit programs, insurers maintain a well-qualified, knowledgeable staff, which promotes the profit and customer needs goals. However, the required use of funds for such programs also competes with the customer needs and the profit goals. Insurers must balance the use of funds to best meet all of these goals.

CONSTRAINTS ON ACHIEVING INSURER GOALS

In achieving their major goals, insurers face numerous constraints.

Insurers must contend with numerous constraints that exist within the insurer's internal operation as well as in the external environment.

Internal Constraints

Several internal constraints might prevent an insurer from meeting all of its goals. Some of these constraints are imposed only in certain circumstances or only on certain types of insurers:

- Efficiency
- Expertise

- Size
- Financial resources
- Other internal constraints

Efficiency

Some insurers operate more efficiently than others. An insurer's lack of efficiency may be caused by poor management, insufficient capital, lack of information technology, an inability to adapt to change, or other causes.

Inefficient insurers are at a disadvantage when competing with efficient ones. This competitive weakness might prevent them from meeting their profit and service goals, which can lead, in turn, to the inability to meet humanitarian or societal goals.

Inefficiency, particularly in information technology and customer service, can prevent an insurer from adequately meeting its customers' needs. In extreme cases, inefficiency can lead to insolvency and a consequent failure to meet legal and regulatory goals.

The rapid pace of technology advances makes it difficult for insurers to integrate the latest technological trends into their business processes. The need for historic information on losses and insureds often creates a dependency on core legacy systems, which require ongoing maintenance in addition to integration with new technology. Modern United States culture demands information at the touch of a button, and insurer technology tends to lag behind that of other industries in meeting that demand. Technology demands can conflict with insurers' customer needs and profit goals.

Expertise

The insurance business is complex, and considerable expertise is required to successfully operate an insurer. This is particularly true as insurers move into niche or specialty markets, both of which require expertise in underwriting, pricing, and claim settlement for unusual losses.

Lack of expertise could prevent an insurer from making a profit or meeting customers' needs, or it could eventually cause the insurer to fail to attain any of its goals. As with efficiency, in extreme cases, lack of expertise could ultimately lead to insolvency.

The insurer should make sure that the current staff has the skills needed to perform their jobs adequately. If not, then the insurer should consider necessary training or hiring staff to better fulfill job requirements. The insurer's support of ongoing training initiatives can ensure that employees maintain the skills required to perform their jobs effectively.

Size

An insurer's size affects its ability to meet its goals. A small insurer has more challenges than a large insurer in terms of available resources. Large insurers can take advantage of economies of scale and may have more financial resources to update technology or reach additional markets. Large insurers can invest more in market research and product development than small insurers can. One advantage for a small insurer is that it can be more nimble, allowing it to respond quickly to an emerging trend or a change in the external insurance environment. However, the limited resources of a small insurer might still be a disadvantage.

Financial Resources

Insufficient financial resources can pose a serious threat to an insurer. When financial resources become strained, insurers are unable to effectively train staff, make new capital investments, or reach new markets. Management must make difficult decisions about allocating scarce resources among competing priorities.

The economic strain of the past decade, and especially the recession that began in late 2007, have caused some insurers to suffer reduced financial resources through underwriting losses, investment losses, or both. Financial constraints can further inhibit insurers' ability to achieve profit and/or societal goals.

Other Internal Constraints

Other internal constraints can interfere with achieving goals. Examples include lack of name or brand recognition, or a damaged reputation.

A newly established insurer might lack the name recognition necessary to achieve its profit goals even if it has the expertise and financial resources to do so. Many established banks experienced this difficulty when they entered the insurance industry. Banks are well known in the financial services area, but they lack the brand recognition of established insurers.

Another internal constraint is a reputation damaged by past problems. Even if past problems have been corrected and the insurer is operating flawlessly and ethically, overcoming a poor reputation requires work on the part of all employees within the organization. If the brand image has been damaged, the insurer may need to develop a concerted campaign to regain customer and public confidence as well as a plan to manage that image into the future. This plan should contain an ethics component, perhaps development or adoption of a code of ethics to be applied to all internal and external business practices, and training for all employees on ethical decision-making. While a damaged reputation is also an external constraint, the insurer must address internal issues as well to communicate appropriate information to staff and avoid morale issues or other negative outcomes, and to guide staff in handling related inquiries and promote a positive image within and outside the organization. An insurer that fails to address all internal issues could develop problems retaining and hiring high-caliber managers and other staff because of its damaged image. These factors could prevent the insurer from meeting customers' needs and could jeopardize profitability.

External Constraints

In addition to internal constraints, insurers contend with several external constraints that may prevent them from meeting their goals:

- Regulation
- Rating agencies
- Public opinion
- Competition
- Economic conditions
- Insurance marketing and distribution
- Other external constraints

Regulation

Insurance operations are closely regulated, extending from incorporation to liquidation and encompassing most activities in between. Insurance regulators monitor insurers' solvency to protect the insurer's policyholders and members of the public who benefit from the existence of insurance. Regulation can also extend to the insurance rates and forms insurers use. If filed rate increases are not approved by the applicable regulator, an insurer might not achieve its profit goals. Policy form approval and the time constraints related to the filing process might keep an insurer from fully meeting customers' needs.

Insurance regulation is complex and extensive. Regulation varies by state, and federal regulation adds another layer of complexity. Products that can be offered in one state may not be approved for use in another state. The variations in property-casualty laws in different states require a broader range of staff expertise. Consequently, regulation imposes a major constraint on insurers, requiring significant personnel and financial resources that can inhibit the insurer's ability to achieve its profit goals.

Rating Agencies

Financial rating agencies, such as A.M. Best Company, Standard & Poor's, and Moody's, rate insurers based on financial strength as an indication of an insurer's ability to meet policyholder obligations. To support their current ratings, well-managed and highly rated insurers typically must maintain capitalization levels in excess of the minimum amounts required. Because favorable financial ratings help to attract and retain customers, insurers try to conduct business to achieve the required capitalization levels in order to maintain or improve favorable rating, but that also might constrain insurers from meeting their profit goals.

Rating agencies are also placing new demands when assessing insurers' financial health. While many other exposures can affect solvency, no single exposure can affect policyholder security more instantaneously than catastrophes. Catastrophic events are occurring more frequently and with greater loss potential because of significant increases in construction in heavily populated areas. To reflect this concern, rating agencies now require insurers to boost their capital to handle higher catastrophe risk. For example, A.M. Best subjects all insurers to a reduction in their reported surplus based on the greatest of a 100-year wind net **probable maximum loss (PML)**, a 250-year earthquake net PML, or a recent large loss within the calculation of Best's Capital Adequacy Ratio (BCAR)—an important financial benchmark that helps indicate whether an insurer has adequate capital to address its insurance and other risk exposures. While these boosts in capital to handle higher catastrophe risk and maintain or improve favorable ratings would help meet the insurer's customer needs and duty to society goals, they could impede the insurer's ability to achieve its profit goals.

An insurer's financial rating can also be a potential constraint for insurers whose rating has declined. Those insurers may find it very difficult to attract and retain customers, and a decrease in customers often causes financial ratings to decline further. Accordingly, a downgrade in a financial rating could adversely affect an insurer's position in the marketplace and could result in a reduction in the amount of business an insurer is able to write to achieve its profit goals.

Probable maximum loss (PML)
The largest loss that an insured is likely to sustain.

Public Opinion

Public opinion about the insurance industry as a whole can act as a constraint for individual insurers in meeting goals. While many customers are satisfied with their insurers, several high-profile issues can lead to a negative perception of the insurance industry.

For example, highly publicized legal and ethical incidents involving some insurers over recent years have tended to decrease public trust in insurers in general. Negative media coverage on questions regarding insurer contingency commissions included ethics considerations and sometimes legal implications. Insurer marketing efforts and increased emphasis—and often expenditures—on customer service were required to regain public trust. Some insurers were criticized in the 2000s for their handling of claims in the aftermath of catastrophic hurricane damage. Decisions about whether damage was caused by windstorm (which was covered) or flooding (which was not covered) caused an emotional, public outcry. In some cases, insurers resolved to pay losses that were not covered to curtail damage to their reputations.

Matters of ethics are major components in managing an insurer's reputation; therefore, efforts to manage reputation should include ethics initiatives, including ongoing training of all staff in ethical decision-making. Managing expenses to repair or protect an insurer's image or the image of the industry conflicts with the profit goal but helps attain the customer needs goal.

Additionally, affordability and lack of availability of personal auto insurance in some states, such as California, have been highly publicized and overshadow overall customer satisfaction with insurers. Dissatisfaction with insurers can lead to the involvement of legislators and regulators. Corrective action, such as California's Proposition 103 mandating rate rollbacks, can seriously constrain individual insurers from achieving profit goals.

Ultimately, such issues can constrain insurers from attaining societal goals. When the insurance industry is viewed negatively by the public, it contradicts the idea of serving in the public's best interests.

Competition

Insurance industry underwriting cycles (or market cycles) are referred to as either hard cycles or soft cycles. The property-casualty insurance industry has exhibited various hard and soft cycles as far back as the 1920s. Hard cycles are characterized by periods of decreased competition and rising rates leading to increased profitability and high rates of return. After a hard cycle ends, the industry enters a low phase, a soft cycle, when prices moderate or decline as competition increases and, eventually, profitability diminishes.

The industry entered a protracted soft cycle in the late 1980s that continued throughout the 1990s. This soft cycle resulted in many mergers and the consolidation of major insurers because of decreasing premium levels. Many insurers that existed in 1990 either no longer existed in 2000 or had significantly changed their operations because of acquisitions or mergers with competitors. The industry encountered another hard cycle from 2000 through 2003 and then settled into a soft cycle leading into the 2007 recession.

Despite the decline in the number of insurers, so many insurers remain in the market that competition is great. Competition is further fueled in personal insurance by highly standardized products that customers view as commodities.

In soft cycles, competitive pressure to decrease prices makes it difficult for insurers to achieve their profit goals. Low profits can affect insurers' ability to achieve societal goals. Excessive competition can entice some insurers to bend the rules, making insurers unable to attain their legal and regulatory goals.

Economic Conditions

Insurers' investment operations can be affected severely by economic downturns. The investment income of most insurers grew substantially during the economic expansion throughout the 1990s. Investment gain increased beginning in 2003; however, the market experienced another downturn in 2007 with the economic recession that affected the U.S.

Insurers can be adversely affected during inflationary cycles as well. Inflation affects the cost of insurance losses through increased medical costs, construction costs, and other loss-related costs. A decline in the use of automobiles during the recent recession has resulted in an overall decline in frequency of auto collision losses; however, this appears to be offset by increasing loss severity resulting from inflated medical, vehicle repair, and litigation costs. Also, in no-fault states, marked increases in no-fault claim costs resulting from abuses, such as rampant fraud and inflated claims, have tended to increase loss severity.[3] Inflation and abuses ultimately affect insurance premiums, but the effect on losses is felt more quickly than the effect on premiums. This difference in timing makes it difficult for insurers to achieve their profit goals during periods of rapid inflation.

Insurance Marketing and Distribution

Insurance marketing and distribution systems that an insurer chooses to distribute its products can affect the insurer's ability to attain its goals. Insurers distribute their products through many types of distribution systems using different types of sales and service personnel and distribution channels to promote products and services as well as communicate with existing and prospective insureds.

Recent years have seen an increase in auto insurers experimenting with multiple distribution systems and channels. Several major companies use both insurance agents and direct sale methods to reach consumers, including Internet and telephone sales. Affinity sales, or selling through special interest groups, represent a growing distribution channel. Additionally, banks are increasingly selling property-casualty insurance to their bank clients. Each distribution system or channel meets the needs of some customers, and each fails to meet the needs of others.

Other External Constraints

Other external constraints can hinder an insurer's ability to reach its goals. Some of these constraints are natural or man-made catastrophe losses, which increased dramatically in the mid-2000s; disregard for law and order, particularly in some larger cities; and legal changes that affect liability claims.

MEASURING INSURER PERFORMANCE

Insurers use measurements that are specific to their industry to determine their success at meeting established goals.

Measuring the performance of an insurer involves determining how successful the insurer is at meeting established goals, including these:

* Meeting profitability goals
* Meeting customer needs

- Meeting legal requirements
- Meeting social responsibilities

As with any assessment, some measures are objective, while others may be subjective. Financial measurements are based on statistical evidence and are considered to be more objective. Measurements of legal requirements are also objective. Measurements of how well an insurer meets customer needs and social responsibilities are more subjective.

Meeting Profitability Goals

An understanding of how insurers make a profit is crucial to understanding how they meet their profitability goals. Like any business, an insurer generates income, or profits, when its revenue exceeds its expenses. The primary sources of revenue for insurers are insurance premiums (paid by insureds) and investment income. Insurers have investments because they receive premiums before they pay for losses and expenses. Insurers invest that money in the meantime and receive investment income as a result.

When determining expenses, insurers face a special challenge compared with other organizations. The largest portion of an insurer's expenses involves losses that will occur in the future and that are, by definition, more difficult to project than past or current expenses. Estimating these future expenses and setting aside the funds to pay for them is done through reserving.

Estimating insurer profitability is generally accomplished by examining premiums and either underwriting performance (underwriting gain or loss) or overall operating performance (gain or loss from operations). A review of these topics assists in understanding insurer profitability:

- Premiums and investment income
- Underwriting performance
- Overall operating performance
- Estimation of loss reserves

Premiums and Investment Income

An insurer's profits depend heavily on the premium revenue the insurer generates. Premiums are the amounts that insurers charge insureds for insurance coverages. Insurers use rates based on the insured's loss exposures to determine the premium to charge for insurance policies.

Insurers must charge premiums to have the funds necessary to make loss payments. In fact, an insurer's total revenue (premiums and investment income) must equal or exceed the amount needed to pay for losses and to cover its costs of doing business. For example, an insurer may use eighty cents of every premium dollar to pay for losses and twenty-five cents for other expenses. If the insurer can earn an amount equal to 5 percent of its premiums on its investments, it can break even. Consequently, an insurer's profitability must consider the volume of premium the insurer writes. Investment profit also depends, in part, on premium revenue that creates the funds used for investment.

Insurance operations generate substantial amounts of investable funds, primarily from loss reserves, loss adjustment expense reserves, and unearned premium reserves. Loss and loss expense reserves are especially significant for insurers that write liability insurance because the long delay inherent in the liability claim handling process generates very large loss reserves.

Measures of insurer profitability based on premiums consider premium growth issues and the rate of growth that is sustained over time. Premium growth is not always a positive indicator of an insurer's success. An insurer should achieve premium growth by writing new policies rather than depending solely on insurance rate increases or inflation. Premium growth, or the lack thereof, must be evaluated in light of current market conditions. During periods of intense competition, significant premium growth is difficult to achieve. However, rapid premium growth may be undesirable and could indicate lax underwriting standards or inadequate premium levels. Inappropriate premium growth can eventually lead to reduced profits as losses begin to exceed premiums collected for loss exposures. To determine profitability, an insurer should consider whether growth resulted from a competitive advantage, relaxed underwriting, inadequate insurance rates, or a combination of these factors.

Evaluating the rate of premium growth sustained over time helps determine insurer profitability. Establishing reasonable rules by which to measure the adequacy, inadequacy, or excessiveness of premium growth is difficult. Growth that is slower than the industry average usually indicates a problem. Likewise, a growth rate that is substantially higher than the industry average might indicate changes that could be unfavorable in the long term.

Underwriting Performance

An insurer's underwriting performance can be measured in terms of net underwriting gain or loss. This is determined as an insurer's earned premiums minus its incurred losses and underwriting expenses for a specific period. Incurred losses include loss adjustment expenses, and underwriting expenses include acquisition expenses, general expenses, taxes, and fees. Because net underwriting gain or loss ignores investment income (or investment losses) and investment expenses, it represents the extent of the insurer's profit or loss derived strictly from the sale of insurance products.

The formula for calculating net underwriting gain or loss can be expressed as: net underwriting gain or loss = earned premiums – (incurred losses + underwriting expenses).

Three specific ratios are used to measure an insurer's underwriting performance: the loss ratio, the expense ratio, and the combined ratio (trade basis). See the exhibit "Measuring an Insurer's Underwriting Performance."

Measuring an Insurer's Underwriting Performance

The loss ratio compares an insurer's incurred losses with its earned premiums for a specific period. The figure for incurred losses includes loss adjustment expenses. The loss ratio is calculated in this manner:

$$\text{Loss ratio} = \text{Incurred losses} \div \text{Earned premiums}$$

The expense ratio compares an insurer's underwriting expenses with its written premiums for a specific period. The expense ratio is calculated in this manner:

$$\text{Expense ratio} = \text{Incurred underwriting expenses} \div \text{Written premiums}$$

The combined ratio (trade basis) combines the loss ratio and the expense ratio to compare inflows and outflows from insurance underwriting. The combined ratio (trade basis) is calculated in this manner:

$$\text{Combined ratio (trade basis)} = \frac{\text{Incurred losses (including LAE)}}{\text{Earned premiums}} + \frac{\text{Incurred underwriting expenses}}{\text{Written premiums}}$$

This can be simplified in this manner:

$$\text{Combined ratio (trade basis)} = \text{Loss ratio} + \text{Expense ratio}$$

[DA02738]

Overall Operating Performance

An alternative way to measure an insurer's profits is through overall results from operations. An insurer's overall gain or loss from operations is its net underwriting gain or loss plus its net investment gain or loss for a specific period. This overall figure gives a more complete picture of an insurer's profitability because investment income generally helps to offset any underwriting losses. The formula for overall gain or loss from operations is expressed as: overall gain or loss from operations = net underwriting gain or loss + investment gain or loss.

After an insurer pays losses, expenses, and taxes, and reserves money to pay additional incurred losses, the remainder is net operating income, which belongs to the company's owners. The owners (stockholders or policyholders) may receive a portion of this remainder as dividends. The amount that is left after dividends are paid is added to the policyholders' surplus. The increase in policyholders' surplus enables the insurer to expand its operations in the future and provides a cushion against catastrophic losses.

To obtain an accurate picture of an insurer's profitability, it is important to analyze the overall gain or loss from operations for several years because any insurer might have a single unprofitable year that is offset by a pattern of profitability over a longer period.

Insurers may lose money on their underwriting activities (that is, when the combined ratio is more than 100 percent) and yet still generate a profit on investments. Ideally, the investment profit is more than enough to offset the underwriting loss so that the insurer has an overall gain from operations, and the policyholders' surplus grows through time and generates a suitable return on equity for the insurer's owners. See the exhibit "Measuring an Insurer's Overall Performance."

Measuring an Insurer's Overall Performance

The investment income ratio compares the amount of net investment income (investment income minus investment expenses) with earned premiums over a specific period of time. The investment income ratio is calculated as shown:

Investment income ratio = Net investment income ÷ Earned premiums

The overall operating ratio, the trade basis combined ratio minus the investment income ratio, can be used to provide an overall measure of the insurer's financial performance for a specific period. Of all the commonly used ratios, the overall operating ratio is the most complete measure of an insurer's financial performance. The formula for overall operating ratio is as shown:

Overall operating ratio = Combined ratio (trade basis) − Investment income ratio

Return on equity, calculated by dividing the organization's net income by the average amount of owners' equity (policyholders' surplus) for a specific period, enables investors to compare the return that could have been obtained by investing in the insurer with the potential returns that could have been earned by investing their money elsewhere. In general, the owners' equity is invested in operations to generate income for the organization. For insurers, the policyholders' surplus is invested in underwriting activities. The formula for return on equity is as shown:

Return on equity = Net income ÷ Owners' equity

[DA02740]

The investment income ratio, overall operating ratio, and return on equity are more specific measures of an insurer's operational performance.

Estimation of Loss Reserves

One of the biggest problems in measuring insurer profitability arises from errors in estimating loss reserves. Loss reserves are generally the largest liability in the insurer's balance sheet and can have a significant effect on the insurer's overall profitability. Insurers establish loss reserves not just for reported claims, but also for losses that have occurred but that have not yet been paid (known as incurred but not reported [IBNR] losses), for losses that have been reported but for which established case reserves are inadequate (known as incurred but not enough recorded [IBNER] reserves), and for claims that have been settled and then reopened.

Errors in estimating outstanding loss amounts, by either underestimating or overestimating the final cost of claims, can distort the insurer's reported profits. This is true for both the year in which inaccurate estimates were originally made and the year in which corrections are made to the estimates. For example, if reserves are initially underestimated and subsequently increased, then net income and policyholders' surplus will decrease when the understatement is recognized. Also, because the insurer's pricing relies on historical loss data, inadequate reserves can result in reduced premium revenues. Therefore, in the long term, if an insurer does not have adequate reserves, it may not have the funds necessary to pay claims. Conversely, if the loss reserves are overestimated (higher than the ultimate loss payments), based on the artificially inflated reserve estimates, the statutory limits on premiums that could be written may be less, and the premiums may be inflated for new and existing risks. Although the reserve estimates may be decreased later, in the interim, these artificial results can cause the insurer to be less competitive in pricing, its financial strength ratings could be lowered, and the insurer's profitability may suffer. A pattern of underreserving or overreserving may ultimately lead to the insurer's insolvency.

Meeting Customer Needs

Determining how well insurers meet customers' needs is difficult because insurers are more likely to hear from customers who believe they have not been treated fairly.

Complaints and Praise

All insurers receive complaints, and each complaint should be evaluated. In some instances, a real problem exists that the insurer should address. In other instances, customers hold expectations that the insurer had not intended to fulfill.

Insurance producers can also be a source of information for evaluating an insurer's success in this area, as they are in frequent contact with customers and hear their complaints about and praise of insurers. Producers seldom keep formal records of such customer reactions, so their evaluations are likely to be subjective.

Customer Satisfaction Data

Many insurers emphasize a customer focus to maintain and raise levels of customer satisfaction with the insurer's products and services. Insurers often use response cards and phone surveys to determine whether customers feel properly treated after a transaction, particularly following a claim. Insurers can also conduct customer focus groups or interviews to determine how well a new or an existing product meets customers' needs. Additionally, insurers can survey customers to obtain an overall satisfaction rating associated with their products and services.

Insurer's Retention Ratio and Lapse Ratio

Two particularly telling measurements of customer satisfaction are the retention ratio and the lapse ratio (sometimes called the cancellation ratio). The data for developing these ratios are found in internal statistical reports. The retention ratio is the percentage of expiring insurance policies that an insurer renews, and it can be measured by policy count, premium volume, or both.

The lapse ratio is calculated by dividing the number of policies that lapse during a period by the total number of policies written at the beginning of that period. A lapse in insurance is defined as a point in time when a policy has been canceled or terminated for failure to pay the premium, or when the policy contract is void for other reasons.

These ratios can indicate the number of policies a company is losing, whether because of a service or price issue or some other issue (such as loss to competition).

Insurer-Producer Relationships

Insurers that market products through independent agents and brokers usually view this network of producers as their customers, in addition to the ultimate insurance customer. These insurers recognize that many other insurers are available to producers and that a competitive marketplace exists within their industry. Being responsive to producer requests and permitting access to insurer policy data and information systems are examples of how insurers maintain and strengthen the insurer-producer relationship. As is the case for customers, insurers can survey or meet with producers to measure their satisfaction with the insurer or to reveal unserved needs the insurer might be able to meet.

State Insurance Department Statistics

Several state insurance departments tabulate complaints they receive and publish lists showing the number of complaints received for each insurer. The number of complaints might indicate one insurer's customer relations success or failure relative to other insurers in the industry.

Consumer Reports

Consumers Union periodically surveys its membership to determine its level of satisfaction with the performance of auto and homeowners insurers. The results are published in that organization's magazine, *Consumer Reports*, including a list of the most satisfactory and least satisfactory insurers as indicated by the survey responses. Only a few of the largest insurers are included in the list because smaller insurers are not mentioned in the responses with sufficient frequency to evaluate their performance fairly.

Meeting Legal Requirements

An insurer's success or failure in meeting legal requirements is indicated by the number of criminal, civil, and regulatory actions taken against the insurer. These actions are automatically brought to the attention of management and should be evaluated carefully to see whether they result from a consistent disregard of legal requirements.

State insurance departments monitor the treatment of insureds, applicants for insurance, and claimants, and they oversee four insurer operational areas: sales and advertising, underwriting, ratemaking, and claim settlement. This regulatory oversight, called market conduct regulation, exists in addition to the role of state insurance regulation in solvency surveillance.

Most states publish a listing of regulatory actions against insurers. This information can be useful in showing how one insurer's performance in this area compares to that of its competitors.

Financial rating agencies provide summary information about insurer financial strength in the form of a financial rating. These rating agencies review all financial information presented in an insurer's balance sheet and financial statements, including any outstanding legal actions involving the organization. The prospective outcome of such actions affects the ratings that these organizations assign to insurers and are another indicator of how well an insurer meets its legal requirements.

Meeting Social Responsibilities

Meeting social responsibilities is the most difficult of the major insurer goals to evaluate. No standards exist for judging an insurer's performance in this area, and little information on an individual insurer's performance is publicly available. Of course, an insurer can get information from its own records to show its own performance, but comparisons with competing insurers are difficult to make because of the lack of available information. Many insurers use their Web sites to indicate their participation in home and workplace safety programs, support of community projects, and involvement in other social programs.

Another possible indicator of social responsibility is the benefits that an insurer provides for its employees. Some insurers have begun to promote family-friendly policies within their organization to assist employees with balancing work and family responsibilities.

Comparative information for employee benefits is available from the United States Chamber of Commerce and from various insurer trade associations. Additionally, some periodicals provide feature articles in which they rank employers according to their employee benefit programs. Although generous employee benefit plans can be construed as merely another method of competing for good employees, they can also indicate an insurer's concern for the welfare of its employees.

Expenditures on loss control activities may also indicate an insurer's level of humanitarian concern; some insurers go beyond typical efforts in loss control to improve safety conditions for their insureds. Many insurers contribute to associations that do research and raise public concern for safety. Contributions to medical, welfare, and educational institutions and programs are another indication of humanitarian efforts and social responsibility.

Additionally, "green" initiatives are emerging for many insurers as they recognize their responsibility to preserve our environment. In addition to recycling and reusing materials used in the production of policies, handling claims, and reporting, insurers are increasingly interested in auto salvage programs. Salvage programs are better for the environment and more cost-effective for insureds.

FUNCTIONAL VIEW OF INSURANCE

The functional view of insurance examines the many and varied functions an insurer performs as it conducts its business operations.

To carry out the operations of an insurer, many people are needed, all of whom perform specific functions. A function generally describes a distinct type of work or an aspect of operations or management requiring special technical knowledge. An insurer's core functions are typically marketing and distribution, underwriting, and claims. These core functions represent the lifespan of the insurer's business operations, from getting the business (marketing and distribution), to pricing the business (underwriting), and then to administering the business (claims).

Insurers perform additional functions that are designed to support these three core functions. An insurer carries out these additional functions to facilitate risk transfer, to promote efficiency, and to meet its financial and nonfinancial goals.

This section provides an overview of these categories of insurer functions:

- Core functions
- Supporting functions
- Other common functional areas

All of the functions included in these categories interact to meet an insurer's goals. Some insurers may perform only some of these functions, some may combine or separate functions, and some may use different names for them. Specific types of products might also drive an insurer's functional needs— for example, an insurer that offers surety bonds might have a surety bond function, and an insurer that offers agricultural coverages might have an agricultural support function for unique underwriting and claim issues. Regardless of these differences, each function is closely linked to all the other functions, and none is performed in a vacuum. The interaction of these core and other functions is vital to an insurer's survival and success.

Core Functions

Although insurers may use varying organizational structures, three core functions exist within the structure of a typical insurer. These core functions—marketing and distribution, underwriting, and claims—form the basis of an insurer's business.

Marketing and Distribution

Marketing and distribution involves determining what products or services customers want and need, advertising the products (communicating their value to customers), and delivering them to customers. The marketing and distribution function contributes significantly to an insurer's goals of earning a profit and meeting customers' needs. The insurer cannot make a profit if it does not provide the products and services customers need.

The goals of the marketing and distribution function must be balanced with other insurer goals. For example, the objectives of the marketing and distribution function should support the insurer's overall growth and customer retention goals. If the insurer has targeted specific regions or lines of business as growth areas, the marketing and distribution function needs to align its efforts for overall growth and customer retention. An imbalance between the marketing and distribution function's goals and the goals of any other department within the organization may reduce the efficiency of the insurer.

Underwriting

Once the marketing and distribution function has developed a relationship with potential customers, it is the job of the **underwriting** function to determine whether and under what conditions the insurer is willing to provide insurance products and services to the potential customers. The goal of underwriting is to write a profitable **book of business** for the insurer, which supports the insurer's profit goal. This is accomplished by developing appropriate **underwriting guidelines**, which underwriters use to evaluate risk. Underwriting serves both insurers and insurance buyers by helping the insurer avoid **adverse selection**. Avoiding adverse selection assists an insurer with remaining profitable and keeping premiums reasonable for insureds.

Claims

An insurance policy is a promise to make a payment to, or on behalf of, the insured if a covered event occurs. The purpose of the claims function is to fulfill the insurer's promise. To that end, the claims function is staffed by employees who are trained in the skills necessary to evaluate and settle claims

Underwriting

The process of selecting insureds, pricing coverage, determining insurance policy terms and conditions, and then monitoring the underwriting decisions made.

Book of business

A group of policies with a common characteristic, such as territory or type of coverage, or all policies written by a particular insurer or agency.

Underwriting guidelines (underwriting guide)

A written manual that communicates an insurer's underwriting policy and that specifies the attributes of an account that an insurer is willing to insure.

Adverse selection

In general, the tendency for people with the greatest probability of loss to be the ones most likely to purchase insurance.

and to negotiate or litigate the settlement of claims by or against insureds through the claim handling process.

The claim handling process is designed to achieve a fair settlement in accordance with the applicable insurance policy provisions. Claim settlements that exceed the amount payable under the policy increase the cost of insurance for all insureds. Settlements that are less than the coverage amount deprive the insured of benefits to which he or she is entitled under the insurance policy. Insurers have developed expertise in claim handling in all categories of loss exposures. Therefore, many insurance industry practitioners view claim handling as the primary service that insurers provide.

Supporting Functions

To support the core functions of marketing and distribution, underwriting, and claims, insurers provide a variety of supporting functions, including risk control, premium auditing, actuarial functions, reinsurance, and information technology. Although most insurers are able to provide these supporting functions in-house, many are available through third-party providers as well. These functions are not only necessary to the efficient operation of insurers, but are also used by a variety of other risk financing organizations, such as captives, pools, risk retention groups, and self-insurers:

- Risk control—An insurer's risk control function provides information to the underwriting function to assist in selecting and rating risks. The risk control function also works with commercial insureds to help prevent losses and to reduce the effects of losses that cannot be prevented. Insurers may also market their risk control services as a stand-alone product to third parties who have not purchased insurance policies from the insurer.

- Premium auditing—Although the premium for many types of insurance is known and guaranteed in advance, the premium is variable for some lines of insurance and cannot be precisely calculated until after the end of the policy period. For example, the premium for workers compensation insurance policies is calculated using wages paid during the policy period. Other commercial insurance policies may use rating variables such as sales or revenue to calculate the premium. Premium auditors ensure equitable treatment of insureds by reviewing the insureds' records to obtain accurate information on rating variables.

- Actuarial—Actuarial functions include calculating insurance rates, developing rating plans, estimating loss reserves, and providing predictive modeling services. The actuarial function also conducts sensitivity analysis to determine the financial security of the insurer. Furthermore, the actuarial function coordinates with the accounting and finance functions in developing reports for regulators to ensure that the insurer is adhering to all regulatory requirements.

- Reinsurance—When an insurer accepts a risk that is larger than it is willing or able to support, it can transfer all or part of that risk to other insurers through reinsurance transactions. Many insurers have a separate reinsurance department that arranges reinsurance and maintains reinsurance agreements.

- Information technology—The information technology function provides the infrastructure that supports all of an insurer's internal and external communications. Insurers use information technology to conduct their daily operations, manage marketing efforts, underwrite policies, track investments, and pay claims. Information systems are especially important to insurers because of the vast amounts of data associated with insurance operations.

Other Common Functional Areas

In addition to the core and supporting functions, insurers perform a host of other functions or outsource them to an external organization. Some common functions include investments, accounting and finance, customer service, legal and compliance, human resources, and special investigation units (SIUs).

- Investments—An insurer's investment operations enable it to earn investment income on the funds generated by its underwriting activities. This investment income enables the insurer to reduce the premium that it must charge in exchange for the risks it assumes. The nature of the insurance risks that an insurer assumes is a factor in determining the types of investments it acquires. For example, liability losses are paid out over a longer period than property losses. Therefore, liability policies can support more long-term investments, such as corporate bonds with long maturity periods, whereas property policies need to be supported by more liquid and short-term investments. An insurer that assumes only moderate underwriting risks might be able to assume greater investment risks with potentially higher investment yield, whereas an insurer that assumes high underwriting risks might need to be more conservative in its investment strategy.

- Accounting and finance—The primary responsibilities of the accounting and finance function are to ensure that the organization has funds to meet its obligations and to fairly and fully disclose the financial position of the insurer in conformance with generally accepted accounting principles (GAAP). Insurers, like all other types of businesses, use accounting to record, analyze, and summarize their financial activities and status. Once the information has been accumulated, an accountant must evaluate, interpret, and communicate the results to all stakeholders.

- Customer service—The customer service function can include an array of responsibilities that vary among insurers. Some insurers have customer service personnel assigned to specific work areas such as customer billing, claims services, underwriting support, agency relations or billing, agency technology support, customer Internet support, and information technology support services for internal users. The customer service function could apply to specific functions or to the entire organization. Customer service may be limited to telephone support, or it may include external support services, such as agency technology user support.

- Legal and compliance—The legal and compliance function provides legal counsel, support, and service to other functions within the insurer and ensures that statutory and administrative requirements are met. Large insurers may have legal counselors specifically assigned to their claim function. Activities of the legal and compliance function may include overseeing and managing litigation, managing corporate legal requirements, participating in legislative activities, and auditing all functions of the insurer for regulatory compliance and to ensure that organizational standards are met and procedures are followed.

- Human resources—The human resources function involves the selection, training, and dismissal of employees. The human resources area maintains employee records; supervises employee introduction to colleagues, performance reviews, and compensation management; conducts orientation and ongoing training; administers employee benefit programs; and performs related functions.

- Special investigation units (SIUs)—These units are established to combat insurance fraud, which includes any deliberate deception committed against an insurer or an insurance producer for the purpose of unwarranted financial gain. Fraud can occur during the process of buying, selling, or underwriting insurance, or making or paying a claim. Such fraud may be committed by applicants, insureds, claimants, medical and other service providers, and even by producers and the insurer's staff. SIU personnel investigate suspicious circumstances that affect claims such as underreporting payroll for a lower premium, overreporting square footage for the purpose of obtaining higher limits, or inflating the value on a proof of loss for a higher claim payment. SIUs collect evidence of possible fraud and may even withhold claim payments when fraud is suspected and likely.

These other functional areas may be separated into additional functions. For example, in some insurers, the human resources function is divided into human resources and training and development. Others insurers may group several of these other functional areas into one such area. For example, the actuarial, investment, and internal audit functions may be combined to form the accounting and finance function. See the exhibit "Insurance Fraud: Special Investigation Units (SIUs)."

Insurance Fraud: Special Investigation Units (SIUs)

Insurers are actively involved in the fight against insurance fraud and use various techniques, including predictive analytic tools, to detect and investigate fraudulent activity. Fraudulent activity increases insurance costs for both insurers and insureds.

According to industry estimates, fraud accounts for 10 percent of the property-casualty industry's losses.* Cases are referred to special investigation units (SIUs) based on criteria that vary by insurer. Some insurers refer every suspicious situation to SIUs; others refer cases based on the extent of the suspected fraud, the prospects of obtaining proof of the fraud, or other criteria.

Perpetrators of insurance fraud can suffer both civil and criminal prosecution. Both state and federal laws provide for the prosecution of insurance fraud and provide immunity to insurers who report information on suspected individuals. Statistics show that the number of criminal convictions and civil prosecutions continues to increase, offering evidence that SIUs have a positive effect on insurers' overall profitability.

* Insurance Information Institute, "Insurance Fraud," April 19, 2010, www.iii.org/media/hottopics/insurance/fraud (accessed July 23, 2010). [DA06351]

SUMMARY

Insurers can be classified in several ways, including legal form of ownership, place of incorporation, licensing status, and the insurance distribution systems and channels the insurer uses to deliver its products and services to the marketplace.

An insurer's overall goals differ from those of other organizations in how an insurer meets its goals and in the conflicts that exist among competing goals. Insurers' major goals are to earn a profit, meet customer needs, comply with legal requirements, diversify risk, and fulfill their duty to society.

Insurers contend with numerous constraints in achieving their goals. These constraints exist within the insurer's internal operation (efficiency, expertise, size, financial resources, and other internal constraints) as well as in the external environment (regulation, rating agencies, public opinion, competition, economic conditions, insurance marketing and distribution, and other external constraints).

Measuring the performance of an insurer involves determining how successful the insurer is at meeting established goals. Measuring how well an insurer meets its profitability goals and legal requirements is more objective, while measuring how well an insurer meets customer needs and social responsibilities is more subjective.

An insurer's core functions are marketing and distribution, underwriting, and claims. Other supporting functions include risk control, premium auditing, actuarial functions, reinsurance, and information technology. Additional common functional areas in an insurer may include investments, accounting and finance, customer service, legal and compliance, human resources, and

SIUs. While insurers vary regarding their structure and the exact role of each functional area, the interaction of the core functions and the other functions is vital to insurers' survival and success.

ASSIGNMENT NOTES

1. Each time the government extended the terrorism risk legislation, a new title (and acronym) for the Act has been developed. "TRIA" is used here to represent each rendition collectively.

2. Robert P. Hartwig, "The P & C Insurance Industry at the Crossroads: Where We Are and Where We Are Headed," March 22, 2010, www.iii.org/presentations/ The-PC-Insurance-Industry-at-the-Crossroads-Where-We-Are-and-Where-We-Are-Headed.html (accessed April 10, 2010).

3. Robert P. Hartwig, "The P&C Insurance Industry at the Crossroads: Where We Are and Where We Are Headed," March 22, 2010, www.iii.org/presentations/ The-PC-Insurance-Industry-at-the-Crossroads-Where-We-Are-and-Where-We-Are-Headed.html (accessed July 14, 2010).

Direct Your Learning ▶▶

2

Insurance Regulation

Educational Objectives

After learning the content of this assignment, you should be able to:

▶ Describe the effect each of the following had on insurance regulation:

- Paul v. Virginia

- Sherman Antitrust Act

- South-Eastern Underwriters Association Decision

- McCarran-Ferguson Act

- Insurance Services Office (ISO) and the Attorneys General Lawsuit

- Gramm-Leach-Bliley Act

▶ Explain how insurance regulation protects consumers, contributes to maintaining insurer solvency, and assists in preventing destructive competition.

▶ Identify the regulatory activities of state insurance departments and the duties typically performed by state insurance commissioners.

▶ Describe the arguments for and against federal regulation of insurance.

▶ Describe the licensing requirements for insurers and insurance personnel.

▶ Describe the methods that regulators use to maintain the solvency of insurers and to manage insolvencies, and the reasons why insurers become insolvent.

▶ Describe the goals of insurance rate regulation, the major types of state rating laws, and the reasons supporting and opposing rate regulation.

▶ Explain how the contract language contained in insurance policies is regulated.

▶ Explain how the market conduct areas in insurance are regulated and how regulatory activities protect consumers.

2

Educational Objectives, continued

▶ Explain how organizations that act as unofficial regulators affect insurance activities.

Insurance Regulation

EVOLUTION OF INSURANCE REGULATION

It is important for insurance professionals to understand the major issues in the evolution of insurance regulation and how this regulation affects the insurance industry, because issues often recur. Courts deciding future cases involving insurance regulation will continue to cite past decisions.

Insurance regulation in the United States began when the Constitution gave Congress the right to regulate commerce among the states. Six subsequent legal events significantly influenced the three major issues of insurance regulation—locus of regulatory control, extent of regulation, and collaboration among insurers:

- *Paul v. Virginia*[1]—This 1869 legal decision determined that insurance was not interstate commerce and became the legal precedent for the exemption of insurance from federal regulation.

- Sherman Antitrust Act—This 1890 Congressional act prohibited collusion to gain a monopoly. The act prevented insurers from banding together to control insurance rates and coverages.

- South-Eastern Underwriters Association decision[2]—This 1944 legal decision turned the U.S. insurance world upside down by making insurance subject to federal regulation. This decision, contrary to legal precedent, eliminated the role of state insurance regulators and made insurance subject to federal regulation that prohibits many collaborative activities that the states had previously approved and encouraged.

- McCarran-Ferguson Act—This 1945 Congressional act restored most insurance regulatory responsibilities to the states. However, federal regulation that applies to boycott, coercion, and intimidation and federal regulation that deals only with insurance (and not business in general) supersedes state regulation.

- Insurance Services Office (ISO) and the Attorneys General Lawsuit—This 1988 lawsuit alleged that insurers and industry associations conspired to draft restrictive policy language that created a liability crisis in the late 1980s. One result of the out-of-court settlement of this lawsuit was to restrict insurer collaboration in the development of insurance rates.

- Gramm-Leach-Bliley Act—This 1999 Congressional act, also known as the Financial Services Modernization Act, repealed the Glass-Steagall Act; facilitated affiliations among banks, insurers, and other financial service providers; and introduced the concept of functional regulation. The act reaffirmed the McCarran-Ferguson Act, reiterating that states would continue to have primary regulatory authority for all insurance activities.

Until the 1850s, state legislatures and various offices within state governments oversaw insurance regulation. In 1851, New Hampshire became the first state to establish an insurance board. Most other states established boards of insurance regulation by 1859, when New York created the first state insurance department. Eventually, the other states followed suit, and insurance commissioners replaced insurance boards.

Paul v. Virginia

State insurance regulation received its first legal test in 1869. Samuel B. Paul, a Petersburg, Virginia, insurance agent, wanted to be licensed in his home state of Virginia, but he wanted to represent New York insurers. According to Virginia law, insurers domiciled in another state were required to deposit a bond with the Virginia state treasurer, but the insurers Paul represented had not met this requirement. The state of Virginia therefore denied Paul's application for a license. Paul nevertheless continued to sell insurance for the New York insurers. He was indicted, convicted, and fined $50 by the Circuit Court of Virginia, and that decision was upheld by the Virginia Court of Appeals.

Paul continued to fight the charge and, in 1869, the U.S. Supreme Court reviewed the decision. Paul argued that the Virginia licensure law was unconstitutional because only Congress could regulate interstate commerce under the U.S. Constitution. The U.S. Supreme Court disagreed and upheld the lower court's ruling. The Supreme Court unanimously determined that insurance was not interstate commerce; insurance was a contract that was delivered locally. Therefore, the U.S. Supreme Court upheld state regulation of insurance, and Virginia could continue to regulate its insurance market.

For many insurers operating in more than one state, it became difficult to meet the states' varying demands. In a long line of subsequent cases, usually involving an insurer seeking to defeat state regulation, *Paul v. Virginia* was cited as the precedent for upholding state regulation of insurance. By implication, despite few explicit judicial statements, this decision came to be relied on as support for the premise that the federal government has no authority over insurance.

Problems developed for the states and for insurers in determining what areas of the insurance business needed to be regulated and how. In 1871, New York's insurance commissioner met with regulatory representatives from nineteen other states to address their common problems. By 1872, thirty states had become members of this initial regulators' association, known as the National Insurance Convention (NIC).

Sherman Antitrust Act

Before the end of the nineteenth century, insurance was considered a private, negotiated contract. Any party who did not like the price of insurance did not make the contract. The free market, not the government, determined prices.

Attitudes about general pricing methods in U.S. society changed beginning in the late 1800s and continuing into the early 1900s. During that time period, major federal legislation reflected a new business climate in the U.S. and a new role for government. A fundamental political question of the time was what to do about the "trusts." Trusts were combinations of business firms that attempted to dominate the market and control prices. The market power resulting from such combinations prompted consumer rebellions that spilled over into politics. Many believed these combinations to be an abuse of economic power.

One legislative remedy for the abuse of economic power was to outlaw collusion or conspiracy in restraint of trade. Several states passed antitrust laws. In 1890, Congress enacted the Sherman Antitrust Act (Sherman Act), which prohibits contracts, combinations, and conspiracies in restraint of trade and other attempts to monopolize the market. The Sherman Act applies to practices beyond collusive pricing activities, and it remains in effect today.

Insurance consumers hoped that these state and federal antitrust laws would limit the ability of insurers to raise rates, but applying antitrust laws to insurance was complicated because of the nature of insurance operations. In periods of intense competition, insurers cut prices to levels that had the potential to lead to insurer insolvencies. Insurers tried to organize the market to control rates and break the destructive patterns of the property-casualty underwriting cycle.

One way to organize the market was to devise a rate "tariff" listing the prescribed rates for different types of loss exposures. Insurers agreed to abide by the tariff. Over time, loss statistics helped to refine the tariffs to reflect the degree of risk inherent in the various classes of business.

By 1912, twenty-three states had passed legislation to prohibit insurer compacts or associations from controlling rates. Such associations were viewed as deterrents to open and free competition—and, in certain respects, they were. However, these associations' rate methodology also helped to prevent insurer insolvency. Eventually, states came to support insurance industry control of insurance rates through rating bureaus.

In 1923, the National Convention of Insurance Commissioners (NCIC, the renamed NIC) passed a resolution to repeal state anticompact laws. Insurance regulators had concluded that rating bureaus and insurer compacts or associations were necessary if insurers were to develop and maintain adequate and appropriate rates. By 1925, most insurance regulators were actively pursuing the repeal of their states' anticompact laws.

In a 1925 noninsurance case, the U.S. Supreme Court affirmed that sometimes public policy favors exchanging cost and pricing information in a competitive environment. With this affirmation, states continued to expand their regulation of insurance rates, and rating bureaus became the preferred organizations to gather the necessary information to disseminate information appropriate to risk classifications.

South-Eastern Underwriters Association Decision

As state anticompact laws were repealed, insurer compacts—often subject to state regulation—once again began to take hold. Among these compacts was the South-Eastern Underwriters Association (SEUA), consisting of nearly 200 private stock insurers that controlled 90 percent of the fire and allied lines insurance market in six southeastern states: Alabama, Florida, Georgia, North Carolina, South Carolina, and Virginia.

The state of Missouri wanted the federal government to challenge rating bureaus, and the SEUA seemed like an ideal target. Even though Missouri had no connection with SEUA, Missouri's attorney general tried to stop the SEUA's rate fixing and filed a complaint with the Antitrust Division of the U.S. Department of Justice. A federal investigation ensued, and criminal indictments were brought against the SEUA, twenty-seven of its officers, and all of its members for these activities:

- Continuing agreement and concerted action to control 90 percent of the fire and allied lines insurance market

- Fixing insurance rates and agents' commissions

- Using boycott and other forms of coercion and intimidation to force non-SEUA members to comply with SEUA insurance rates

- Withdrawing the rights of agents to represent SEUA members if the agents also represented non-SEUA insurers

- Threatening insurance consumers with boycott and loss of patronage if they did not purchase their insurance from SEUA members

The District Court of the U.S. for the Northern District of Georgia dismissed the case based on the U.S. Supreme Court's decision in *Paul v. Virginia*. On appeal, the U.S. Supreme Court agreed to hear the SEUA case in 1944. The Court noted that each of the activities, if performed by companies that were not insurers, would have been subject to prosecution under the Sherman Antitrust Act. The SEUA was not denying this but contended that it was not subject to the Sherman Act because of the *Paul v. Virginia* decision.

The Court decided that the Sherman Act was intended to prohibit the kinds of conduct exhibited by the interstate fire insurers and SEUA. Consequently, insurance was commerce and, as such, was subject to Congressional regulation. The Court's argument for federal regulation of insurance was essentially that no commercial enterprise of any kind that conducts its activities across state lines has been held to be wholly beyond the regulatory powers of

Congress under the Commerce Clause, and there cannot be an exception for the business of insurance.

The immediate effect of the Court's decision was that these federal acts now applied to insurance:

- The Sherman Act (1890)—This act prohibits collusion to gain a monopoly. Any activity that restrains trade or commerce and any attempt to monopolize are illegal. Insurers could no longer band together, as in the SEUA and similar groups, to control insurance rates and coverages.
- The Clayton Act (1914)—This act, together with its amendment, the Robinson-Patman Antidiscrimination Act (1936), prohibits activities that lessen competition or create monopoly power, including price discrimination, tying (requiring the purchase of one product when purchasing another product) and exclusive dealing, and mergers between competitors. The Robinson-Patman Act limited price discrimination only to price differentials that could be attributed to differences in operating costs resulting from competing "in good faith." Insurers could no longer reduce insurance rates to eliminate competition unless the insurers could prove that the reduced rates were caused by increased efficiencies in operations.
- The Federal Trade Commission (FTC) Act (1914)—This act prohibits unfair methods of competition and unfair or deceptive trade practices and therefore promotes competition and protects consumers.

Together, these federal acts would significantly change how insurers could operate. However, state insurance regulators and insurers continued to assert that some forms of cooperation, especially to establish the statistical base for adequate insurance rates, were necessary for the insurance mechanism to function effectively. The National Association of Insurance Commissioners (NAIC; the NCIC was renamed in the 1930s) worked to eliminate federal regulation of insurance.

McCarran-Ferguson Act

In 1945, Congress passed the McCarran-Ferguson Act (McCarran Act). Subject to certain conditions, the McCarran Act returned insurance regulation to the states. This act allows the states to regulate and tax the business of insurance.

One condition of the McCarran Act is extremely important because if it is not met, Congress resumes the regulation of insurance. The Sherman Act, the Clayton Act, the FTC Act, and the Robinson-Patman Act do not apply to the "business of insurance" unless the states are not regulating the activities described in the acts. This condition of the McCarran Act requires states to have their own antitrust legislation and their own unfair trade practices legislation in order to prevent the federal government from enforcing federal acts. Even then, state legislation does not supersede federal authority regarding boycott, coercion, and intimidation. The McCarran Act also prohibits states from controlling labor relations. Therefore, insurers are still subject to federal regulation regarding labor relations.

Also, if Congress passes a law that applies only to the insurance business, not to business in general, the federal law supersedes any state regulation in the areas addressed by the federal legislation. The McCarran Act did not define what constitutes the "business of insurance." Based on the court decisions that have been rendered, the "business of insurance" is defined as any activity that has one or more of these three characteristics:

- The risk of the policyholder or insured is shared and underwritten by the insurer.
- The insurer and the insured have a direct contractual connection.
- The activity is unique to entities within the insurance business.

Under the McCarran Act, the states had until 1948 to pass legislation to regulate insurance, thereby limiting federal regulation. Consequently, the NAIC and state legislatures began developing and implementing various insurance laws to allow cooperation in setting rates and to restrict the role of the federal government in insurance regulation.

In 1946, the NAIC approved two model rate regulation bills—one that applied to liability insurers and another that applied to fire, marine, and inland marine insurers. The bills had two purposes:

- To ensure that insurance rates were not excessive, were not unfairly discriminatory, and were adequate
- To allow cooperation in setting insurance rates, as long as it did not hinder competition

Most states enacted some form of rate regulation that met the requirements of the McCarran Act and therefore preempted federal legislation on cooperative ratemaking. Then, in 1947, the NAIC adopted the Act Relating to Unfair Methods of Competition and Unfair Deceptive Acts and Practices in the Business of Insurance. The NAIC's model act described certain activities that were deemed to be methods of unfair competition or unfair and deceptive practices and actions. Most states enacted laws that were similar to the NAIC model act. By the end of 1947, the NAIC and the states believed that they had succeeded in preempting federal legislation.

ISO and the Attorneys General Lawsuit

In 1971, six separate national service bureaus (then known as rating bureaus) consolidated to form Insurance Services Office (ISO). By the end of 1971, nine local or regional property bureaus also joined ISO. In 1987, ISO was a national, not-for-profit corporation that provided statistical information to insurers and insurance regulators; developed and implemented policy coverage provisions; distributed industry-wide advisory rate information; and, where appropriate, filed that information with state insurance regulators.

ISO has evolved over the years. Major changes occurred as the result of a 1988 lawsuit by seven states' attorneys general that once again raised antitrust issues. This lawsuit, filed in federal District Court in San Francisco, charged that major insurers, domestic and foreign reinsurers, and industry associations—thirty-two defendants in all—had conspired to create a global boycott of certain types of commercial general liability coverages, particularly coverage for environmental damages stemming from pollution. Twelve other states subsequently joined the federal lawsuit.

The lawsuit focused on a narrow aspect of the insurance business: the development of new policy language by ISO. The lawsuit alleged that the defendants engaged in a secret "global conspiracy" to draft restrictive policy language and that the "conspiracy" led to the mid-1980s liability insurance crisis. Six years of litigation ensued until a settlement was reached in 1994.

The settlement reorganized ISO. ISO's board was reconstituted to comprise three insurance company executives, seven executives from noninsurance companies, and ISO's president serving as chairman. Insurer committees were dissolved and replaced with insurer advisory panels, whose members make recommendations in their areas of expertise. Rate and form decisions are made not by insurer committees but by ISO staff.

ISO continued to provide insurance products and services to insurers. However, the settlement helped to eliminate a perception that ISO provided a vehicle for insurer collusion. Currently, ISO is a for-profit corporation, and the rating information it provides involves loss costs rather than advisory rates. Each insurer that subscribes to ISO services can base its insurance rates on its own experience as well as on ISO's loss cost information. ISO continues to develop insurance policy forms and coverage programs that are adopted by many property-casualty insurers and continues its role as a statistical agent for regulators in almost every state.

Gramm-Leach-Bliley Act

The issue of state versus federal insurance regulation has never been completely resolved. Many times during the last sixty-five years, it seemed likely to reappear as a major legislative concern. The issue came to the forefront during the 1990s, when affiliations between banks and insurers began to occur and questions arose about who would regulate these "bankassurance" organizations. Banking activities were traditionally regulated by the federal government and, in some cases, by the states, while insurance was regulated only by the states.

The Gramm-Leach-Bliley (GLB) Act of 1999, also called the Financial Services Modernization Act, addressed this issue. However, although the GLB Act answered some questions, it raised many others.

Under the act, each segment of the financial services business is function-ally regulated. Regarding insurance, the GLB Act makes it clear that states continue to have primary regulatory authority for all insurance activities. However, the act prohibits state actions that would prevent bank-related firms from selling insurance on the same basis as insurance producers. Meanwhile, securities activities are regulated by securities regulators, and banking activities are regulated by banking regulators. See the exhibit "Influence of Gramm-Leach-Bliley Act on Financial Services."

Influence of Gramm-Leach-Bliley Act on Financial Services

The Gramm-Leach-Bliley Act essentially repealed the Depression-era Glass-Steagall Act by permitting different types of financial services organizations, such as commercial banks, investment banks, and insurers, to merge or to diversify across functional boundaries.

The plan to merge Citibank and Travelers, a merger that was not permissible under the Glass-Steagall Act, created a legislative impetus for the Gramm-Leach-Bliley Act. Ironically, this merger did not work out well, and the two organizations have again become separate entities. The famous red umbrella logo that once covered the combined organization has now been returned to Travelers, where it originated as a symbol of the protection provided by insurance.

[DA06263]

The GLB Act also treats insurance underwriting differently from insur-ance sales and marketing. National banks are prohibited from underwriting insurance through an operating subsidiary. However, they can arrange for a financial holding company to create an insurance affiliate. This arrangement makes it more difficult for a failing bank to use insurer assets.

Information sharing among banks and insurance affiliates raises privacy concerns. However, the NAIC model privacy acts, such as the Health Information Privacy Model Act, the NAIC Insurance Information and Privacy Protection Model Act, and the Privacy of Consumer Financial and Health Information Regulation, have been adopted by many states and provide standards that meet or exceed the privacy protections granted in the GLB Act. For protected health information, insurers must have affirmative authorization to release otherwise confidential information. For other forms of insurance, the NAIC models provide for at least as much consumer protection as the GLB Act.

The GLB Act also compels states to facilitate insurance producers' ability to operate in more than one state. The GLB Act contains a provision that gave states three years to adopt full reciprocal licensing agreements. The NAIC responded to the requirements in the GLB Act by creating a Producer Licensing Model Act that requires states to establish either a system of reciprocal producer licensing or uniform licensing standards. The National

Insurance Producer Registry (NIPR), a not-for-profit affiliate of the NAIC, developed and implemented the Producer Database (PDB) and the NIPR Gateway. The PDB, an electronic database, contains information regarding producers. The NIPR Gateway provides a link for state insurance regulators to exchange producer information.

REASONS FOR INSURANCE REGULATION

Because a well-functioning insurance market is essential to society, regulation is necessary to correct market imperfections, whether those imperfections result from externalities, incomplete information, costs, or other causes. However, the reasons for regulation can differ; each market participant, each regulator, and each observer may offer different reasons for regulating a particular market.

The insurance industry is regulated primarily for three reasons:

- To protect consumers
- To maintain insurer solvency
- To prevent destructive competition

Although these purposes clearly overlap, each is examined separately.

Consumers may not have complete information about the product of insurance, yet they need the product and often are required to purchase it. Because of consumers' incomplete information, insurance regulators must ensure that the products are beneficial to consumers and available at an equitable price. In addition, inadequate information, destructive competition, and mismanagement (among other things) can threaten the solvency of insurers. Implementation and enforcement of insurance regulation is necessary to correct each of these market imperfections. If regulation can correct or reduce the effect of the market imperfections, it can encourage insurer solvency.

Protect Consumers

The primary reason insurance is regulated is to protect consumers. When consumers buy electronics, clothing, or furniture, they can usually inspect the products before purchasing them to ensure that the products meet their needs. Even if consumers inspect the insurance policies they purchase, they might not be able to analyze and understand complex legal documents.

Regulators help to protect consumers by reviewing insurance policy forms to determine whether they benefit consumers and comply with state consumer protection laws. State legislatures can set coverage standards and specify policy language for certain insurance coverages. State insurance regulators can review policy language and disapprove policy forms and endorsements that are inconsistent with state consumer protection laws.

Insurance regulators also protect consumers against fraud and unethical market behavior. Departments of insurance receive complaints about these behaviors:

- Producers have intentionally sold unnecessary insurance.
- Producers have misrepresented the nature of coverage to make a sale.
- Producers have stolen or misused insured or insurer funds.
- Claim representatives have engaged in unfair claim practices, refusing to pay legitimate claims or unfairly reducing claim payments.
- Insurance managers have contributed to the insolvency of insurers through their dishonesty.

In addition to protecting consumers against such abuses, regulators also try to ensure that insurance is readily available, especially the insurance that is viewed as a necessity. For example, all states now try to ensure that continuous personal auto insurance coverage is available by restricting the rights of insurers to cancel or nonrenew personal auto insurance policies. At the same time, regulators recognize that insurers sometimes must break long-term relationships with insureds whose loss exposures no longer match those the insurer wants to cover. Cancellation restrictions aimed at promoting availability can therefore lead insurers to reject more new-business applications, which reduces insurance availability.

Insurance regulators also provide information about insurance matters so that consumers can make more informed decisions.

Maintain Insurer Solvency

Another reason insurance is regulated is to maintain insurer solvency. Solvency regulation protects insureds against the risk that insurers will be unable to meet their financial obligations. Consumers and even some sophisticated businesspeople may find it difficult to evaluate insurers' financial ability to keep their promises. Insurance regulators try to maintain a sound financial condition of private insurers for several reasons:

- Insurance provides future protection—Premiums are paid in advance, but the period of protection extends into the future. If insurers become insolvent, future claims may not be paid, and the insurance protection already paid for may become worthless.
- Regulation is needed to protect the public interest—Large numbers of individuals and the community at large are adversely affected when insurers become insolvent.
- Insurers have a responsibility to insureds—Insurers hold substantial funds for the ultimate benefit of insureds. Government regulation is necessary to safeguard such funds.

Insurers have become insolvent despite regulatory reviews. The goal of regulation is not to eliminate all insolvencies but rather to minimize the number of insolvencies. To eliminate insolvencies would mean that regulations must be set to allow the most inefficient insurer to continue to operate which is not a desirable regulatory goal.

Prevent Destructive Competition

Insurance regulation also seeks to prevent destructive competition. Regulators are responsible for determining whether insurance rates are high enough to prevent destructive competition. At times, some insurers underprice their products to increase market share by attracting customers away from higher-priced competitors. This practice drives down price levels in the whole market. When insurance rate levels are inadequate, some insurers can become insolvent, and others might withdraw from the market or stop writing new business. An insurance shortage can then develop, and individuals and firms might be unable to obtain the coverage they need. Certain types of insurance can become unavailable at any price, such as when both products liability and directors and officers coverage became unavailable in the 1980s.

INSURANCE REGULATORS

Insurance professionals must be familiar with the entire regulatory framework for insurance, and state regulators and the National Association of Insurance Commissioners (NAIC) both play important roles in regulation.

Insurance is regulated primarily by state insurance departments. State regulators, in turn, are members of the NAIC, a nonprofit corporation that has no regulatory authority of its own but that plays an important coordinating role.

Insurers are also subject to federal regulations that affect noninsurance businesses as well. Although not discussed here, most of the state and local regulations that affect other businesses, such as zoning laws, also apply to insurers.

State Insurance Departments

Every state has three separate and equal branches of government:

- The legislative branch makes the laws.
- The judicial branch (the court system) interprets the laws.
- The executive branch implements the laws.

Day-to-day regulation of the insurance business is performed by state insurance departments, which fall within the executive branch of each state government. State insurance departments enforce insurance laws enacted by the legislature. These laws regulate the formation of insurers, capital and surplus requirements, licensing of producers, investment of funds, financial requirements for maintaining solvency, insurance rates that can be charged, marketing and claim practices, taxation of insurers, and the rehabilitation of financially impaired insurers or the liquidation of insolvent ones.

Under the insurance commissioner's direction, a state insurance department engages in a wide variety of regulatory activities that typically include these:

- Licensing insurers
- Licensing producers, claim representatives, and other insurance personnel
- Approving policy forms
- Holding rate hearings and reviewing rate filings
- Evaluating solvency information
- Performing market conduct examinations
- Investigating policyholder complaints
- Rehabilitating or liquidating insolvent insurers
- Issuing cease-and-desist orders
- Fining insurers that violate state law
- Publishing shoppers' guides and other consumer information (in some states)
- Preventing fraud

The Insurance Commissioner

Every state insurance department is headed by an insurance commissioner, superintendent, or director appointed by the governor or elected by the voting public.

The duties of a typical state insurance commissioner include these:

- Overseeing the state insurance department's operation
- Promulgating orders, rules, and regulations necessary to administer insurance laws
- Determining whether to issue business licenses to new insurers, producers, and other insurance entities
- Reviewing insurance pricing and coverage
- Conducting financial and market examinations of insurers
- Holding hearings on insurance issues
- Taking action when insurance laws are violated
- Issuing an annual report on the status of the state's insurance market and insurance department
- Maintaining records of insurance department activities

The commissioner does not personally handle most of these duties, but instead delegates them to others in the state insurance department.

Although most commissioners are appointed, some states elect their commissioners. Disagreement exists regarding which selection method better serves the public interest. Proponents of an elective system cite these reasons:

- An appointed insurance commissioner is subject to dismissal, while an elected commissioner is generally in office for a full term.

- An appointed commissioner might continue regulating in the same manner as his or her predecessor when a different approach is required, but an elected commissioner would more likely change the insurance department's stance.

- An appointed commissioner might not be aware of the public's concerns, but an elected commissioner would be keenly aware of the issues important to the public.

- An appointed commissioner might feel inclined to yield to the interests of those responsible for the appointment, while an elected commissioner is not obligated to any particular group or special interest.

Proponents of an appointing system cite these reasons:

- An appointed commissioner has no need to campaign or to be unduly influenced by political contributors.

- An appointed commissioner is less likely to be swayed by ill-informed public opinion than an elected one.

- An appointed commissioner is more likely to be perceived as a career government employee interested in regulation than as a politician interested in political advancement.

Many commissioners were employed in the insurance business before they entered public office, and many are employed by insurers or insurance-related organizations after leaving office. The expertise and understanding of insurance operations necessary to regulate effectively are most likely found in a person who has worked in the insurance business. However, some allege that such insurance commissioners have less than an objective relationship with the insurers they regulate.

In rebuttal, state insurance commissioners usually deny that they are overly responsive to insurers. Commissioners frequently issue cease-and-desist orders, fine or penalize insurers for infractions of the law, forbid insurers to engage in mass cancellations, limit insurance rate increases, and take numerous other actions that benefit policyholders at insurers' expense.

State Regulation Funding

State insurance departments are partly funded by state premium taxes, audit fees, filing fees, and licensing fees, but premium taxes are the major source of funding. Although state premium taxes are substantial, only a relatively small proportion is spent on insurance regulation. Premium taxes are designed primarily to raise revenues for the state as a whole.

The National Association of Insurance Commissioners (NAIC)

National Association of Insurance Commissioners (NAIC)

An association of insurance commissioners from the fifty U.S. states, the District of Columbia, and the five U.S. territories and possessions, whose purpose is to coordinate insurance regulation activities among the various state insurance departments.

The **National Association of Insurance Commissioners (NAIC)** coordinates insurance regulation activities among the insurance departments but has no direct regulatory authority. However, by providing a forum to develop uniform policy when appropriate, the NAIC has a profound effect on the nature and uniformity of state regulation.

The NAIC meets three times per year to discuss important problems and issues in insurance regulation. The NAIC developed uniform financial statement forms that all states require insurers to file. It collects and compiles financial information from insurers and warehouses the financial data for use by insurance regulators. It also assists state insurance departments by sharing financial information about insurers that are potentially insolvent and by developing model laws and regulations. The NAIC's Financial Analysis Working Group serves as both a coordinator and a fail safe mechanism for state insurance regulators as they oversee nationally significant insurers.

Model Laws and Regulations

The insurance laws and regulations of many states incorporate at least the primary concepts of NAIC model laws, resulting in some degree of uniformity among the states. Examples of model laws include model legislation on the regulation of risk retention groups, and a model property and liability insurance rating law.

Model law

A document drafted by the NAIC, in a style similar to a state statute, that reflects the NAIC's proposed solution to a given problem or issue and provides a common basis to the states for drafting laws that affect the insurance industry. Any state may choose to adopt the model bill or adopt it with modifications.

Model regulation

A draft regulation that may be implemented by a state insurance department if the model law is passed.

Laws are passed by the state legislature, while regulations are developed and enforced by a regulatory body such as the state insurance department. A **model law** is a draft bill that state legislatures consider; any state can choose to adopt or to adapt the model bill. A **model regulation** is a draft of a regulation that can be implemented by a state insurance department if the model law is passed.

Accreditation Program

In addition to developing model laws, the NAIC, in 1990, implemented an accreditation program to increase the uniformity of insurer solvency regulation across the states. To become accredited, a state insurance department must prove that it has satisfied the minimum solvency regulation standards required by the accreditation program.

State insurance departments must meet three criteria to satisfy the NAIC's Financial Regulation Standards and to be accredited:

- The state's insurance laws and regulations must meet basic standards of NAIC models.
- The state's regulatory methods must be acceptable to the NAIC.
- The state's insurance department practices must be adequate as defined by the NAIC.

As of June 2010, the insurance departments in fifty states and the District of Columbia had been accredited by the NAIC.[3]

Federal Regulation

The McCarran Act reverses the usual state-federal allocation of regulatory powers only for the business of insurance, and this does not include everything that insurers do. For example:

- As employers, insurers are subject to federal employment laws just like any other business.
- As businesses that sell their stock to the public to raise capital, stock insurers are subject to regulations like any other such business.

The Insurance Fraud Protection Act is part of a federal anti-crime bill titled "Violent Crime Control and Law Enforcement Act of 1994."[4] This broad legislation protects consumers and insurers against insolvencies resulting from insurance fraud.

The act prohibits anyone with a felony conviction involving trustworthiness from working in the business of insurance unless he or she secures the written consent of an insurance regulator. Moreover, it is illegal for insurers, reinsurers, producers, and others to employ a person who has a felony conviction involving breach of trust or dishonesty.

The act identifies these crimes involving the business of insurance:[5]

- Making false statements or reports to insurance regulators—including overvaluing assets—to influence regulatory decisions
- Making false entries in books, reports, or statements to deceive anyone about an insurer's financial condition or solvency
- Embezzling from anyone who is engaged in the business of insurance
- Using threats or force or "any threatening letter or communication to corruptly influence, obstruct, or impede" insurance regulatory proceedings

STATE VERSUS FEDERAL INSURANCE REGULATION

Although insurance regulation occurs primarily at the state level, the issue of federal regulation is often raised.

The question of which level of government—state or federal—should regulate insurance is far from settled. With strong arguments on both sides, the debate is likely to continue.

Proponents of federal regulation present these arguments:

- Federal regulation would provide regulatory uniformity across the states—Insurers doing business in more than one state are confronted with differing laws, regulations, and administrative rules. In theory, federal regulation would be uniform. However, many believe that Congress, because of strong opposition from the states, the legal tradition of insurance regulation in the United States, and the complexity involved, prefers not to preempt state auto reparation systems, workers compensation laws, and tort systems that result in differing insurance products across state borders.

- Federal regulation would be more efficient—Insurers doing business nationally would deal with only one government agency instead of multiple agencies. In addition, a federal agency might be less likely than state agencies to yield to pressure from local or regional insurers. Federal regulation might also be less expensive than state regulation as a result of eliminating duplicate functions performed by many different governmental agencies and extensive requirements for insurers.

- Federal regulation would attract personnel with a high level of expertise—If the federal agency were adequately funded, it would likely pay higher salaries than those paid by state agencies. Higher salaries could attract candidates with a greater degree of education and experience who may bring additional insights and skills to the regulation of insurers.

Opponents of federal regulation present these arguments:

- State regulation is more responsive to local needs—Conditions vary widely among states, and state regulators can respond quickly to local problems and needs. In contrast, federal regulation and government bureaucracy would result in considerable delay in solving local problems.

- Uniformity of state laws can be attained through the National Association of Insurance Commissioners (NAIC)—As a result of the NAIC's model laws and regulations, current state laws are reasonably uniform, with consideration given to local circumstances and conditions.

- Greater opportunities for innovation are possible with state regulation—An individual state can experiment with a new approach to regulation. If that approach fails, only that state is affected. In contrast, if a new approach to federal regulation fails, the entire country might feel its effects.

- State regulation is already in place, and its strengths and weaknesses are known—In contrast, the benefits and possible adverse consequences of federal regulation on the insurance business and consumers are unknown. Moreover, some local regulation is inevitable; thus, increased federal involvement would result in dual regulation.

- State regulation results in a desirable decentralization of political power— In contrast, federal regulation would increase the power of the federal government and dilute states' rights.

- State regulation results in multiple eyes looking at an issue—All regulators are human and make mistakes. With multiple regulators, an issue that might be overlooked by a single federal regulator is more likely to be detected by multiple state regulators reviewing and discussing an area of concern.

- State regulators have been responsive in reducing the complexity of regulation—States have worked on initiatives to create a healthy, efficient market that meets the needs of insurance buyers. Many state legislatures have enacted regulations that aim to ease restrictions on rate and form filings for larger commercial insureds. These laws typically exempt qualified commercial insurance lines from specific state review requirements, including filing policy forms, casualty insurance rating requirements, and certificate of compliance requirements.

The debate over state versus federal insurance regulation will persist. The increasing role of electronic commerce raises challenging questions about the regulation of transactions that occur in cyberspace. In addition, the changing role of banks (traditionally federally regulated) in marketing insurance (traditionally state-regulated) raises additional questions.

Large insurers, national and international businesses, and insurance trade associations increasingly favor a more centralized insurance regulatory system. The U.S. insurance regulatory system appears archaic to international businesses in light of the European Economic Community's elimination of trade barriers among European countries. Consequently, the NAIC has undertaken a Solvency Modernization Initiative to develop the framework for financial solvency insurance regulation in the U.S. and to describe the core principles underlying it. In developing the Initiative, those involved intend to review the European Union's proposed Solvency II regulatory framework and adopt any of its elements that apply to the U.S. regulatory framework.

The economic downturn in the U.S. in the first years of this century pointed out the need for more coordination among financial services regulators to identify **systemic risk**. As a result, a new Federal Insurance Office (FIO) will be created to facilitate some of the regulatory coordination and provide a source of information to Congress about the insurance industry. The FIO will have a role in negotiating agreements with other nations related to insurance.

Systemic risk

The potential for a major disruption in the function of an entire market or financial system.

INSURANCE REGULATORY ACTIVITIES: LICENSING INSURERS AND INSURANCE PERSONNEL

At the beginning of any business development plan, insurers and insurance personnel should consider insurance regulation. By anticipating regulatory requirements and processes, they can reap strategic advantages. Knowledge of insurance regulation is also important to ensure that the insurer complies with regulatory requirements. Noncompliance can lead to impeded operations resulting from regulatory intervention and more frequent examinations. It can also lead to the loss of an insurer's license or damage an insurer's reputation in the marketplace.

From the time of their formation, insurers are subject to state insurance regulation. While the review processes for insurer licensing vary from state to state, all states require property-casualty insurers to receive approval before operating within the state.

Just as departments of insurance (DOIs) have the authority to regulate insurers and related entities, state laws also give them the authority to regulate insurance producers, claim representatives, and other insurance personnel.

Licensing Insurers

By issuing a license to an insurer, a state indicates that the insurer meets minimum standards of financial strength, competence, and integrity. If these standards change later, and if the insurer fails to meet the new standards, the insurer's license can be revoked. A license indicates that the insurer has complied with the state's insurance laws and is authorized to write certain types of insurance in the state. Once licensed, the insurer is subject to all applicable state laws, rules, and regulations.

In response to complaints about the length of time regulators took to license a new insurer, regulators developed the Uniform Certificate of Authority Application (UCAA) to streamline the process. All states and the District of Columbia participate in the UCAA. The UCAA process is designed to allow insurers to file copies of the same application for admission in numerous states. While each state still performs its own independent review of each application, the need to file different applications in different formats has been eliminated.

Licensing standards vary among admitted domestic, foreign, alien, and nonadmitted insurers. Risk retention groups face yet another set of standards.

Domestic insurer

An insurer doing business in the jurisdiction in which it is incorporated.

Domestic Insurers

An insurer licensed in its home state is called a **domestic insurer**. If a domestic insurer obtains licenses in states other than its state of domicile, it is a

foreign insurer in those other states. A domestic insurer's license generally has no expiration date. Licenses of foreign insurers and **alien insurers** generally must be renewed annually.

Domestic insurers usually must meet the conditions imposed on corporations engaged in noninsurance activities as well as some special conditions imposed on insurers. An applicant for an insurer license must apply for a charter. The applicant must provide the names and addresses of the incorporators, the name of the proposed corporation, the territories and types of insurance it plans to market, the total authorized capital stock (if any), and its surplus. The state insurance commissioner reviews the application to see whether the applicant also meets the state's licensing requirements.

An insurer must be financially sound. State laws require that domestic stock insurers satisfy certain minimum capital and surplus requirements before a license is granted. Domestic stock insurers must meet **capital stock** and **paid-in surplus** requirements. Minimum initial capital and paid-in surplus requirements vary widely by state and by amounts and types of insurance written. Minimum initial capital requirements range from as little as $100,000 to as much as $15 million.

For mutual or **reciprocal insurers**, the minimum financial requirement applies only to surplus because a mutual insurer does not have capital derived from the sale of stock. When a mutual insurer is forming, its initial surplus can be derived from premium deposits paid by prospective policyholders. Also, a portion of the initial surplus can be borrowed. Most states require mutuals to have an initial surplus equal to the minimum capital and paid-in surplus requirement for stock insurers writing the same type of insurance. However, some states have set a minimum surplus requirement for mutuals that is lower than the minimum capital and paid-in surplus requirement for stock insurers. In most states, minimum surplus requirements for mutual insurers and reciprocals are the same.

Many states require the organizers of a mutual insurer to have a minimum number of applications with deposit premiums for a minimum number of separate loss exposures and aggregate premium exceeding a specific amount. These requirements help to guarantee that the insurer has a minimum book of business and hence some stability before it officially begins operations.

In addition to financial requirements, states impose other requirements on new insurers. For example, the proposed name for a new mutual insurer must include the word "mutual," and the proposed name of a new insurer must not be so similar to that of any existing insurer that it would be misleading. The commissioner might have the authority to refuse a license if he or she believes the insurer's incorporators or directors are not trustworthy.

Some states even permit the commissioner to deny a license to an otherwise worthy applicant if the commissioner believes that no additional insurers are needed in the state. Once the license has been issued, it can be revoked if the insurer operates in a manner that is clearly detrimental to the welfare of

Foreign insurer

An insurer licensed to operate in a state but incorporated in another state.

Alien insurer

An insurer domiciled in a country other than the United States.

Capital stock

A balance sheet value that represents the amount of funds that a corporation's stockholders have contributed through the purchase of stock.

Paid-in surplus

The amount stockholders paid in excess of the par value of the stock.

Reciprocal insurer

An insurer owned by its policyholders, formed as an unincorporated association for the purpose of providing insurance coverage to its members (called subscribers), and managed by an attorney-in-fact. Members agree to mutually insure each other, and they share profits and losses in the same proportion as the amount of insurance purchased from the exchange by that member.

its policyholders (for example, consistent failure to pay legitimate claims or fraudulent business conduct).

Foreign Insurers

To be licensed in an additional state (in other words, as a foreign insurer), an insurer first must show that it has satisfied the requirements imposed by its home state (its state of domicile, or the state where it is a domestic insurer). Second, a foreign insurer must generally satisfy the minimum capital, surplus, and other requirements imposed on the state's domestic insurers.

Alien Insurers

Alien insurers (insurers domiciled outside the United States) must satisfy the requirements imposed on domestic insurers by the state in which they want to be licensed. Additionally, they must usually establish a branch office in any state and have funds on deposit in the U.S. equal to the minimum capital and surplus required.

Nonadmitted Insurers

An admitted insurer is licensed by a state insurance department to do business in the insured's home state. A nonadmitted insurer is not licensed (not authorized) in the insured's home state; it may be an admitted insurer in other states, and it may even be an alien insurer.

A nonadmitted insurer is typically a surplus lines insurer. The surplus lines insurance mechanism allows U.S. consumers to buy property-casualty insurance from nonadmitted insurers when consumers are unable to purchase the insurance they need from admitted insurers. Surplus lines insurers provide a positive and legal supplement to the admitted insurance market. The business that surplus lines insurers generally accept includes distressed risks (those that have underwriting problems), unique risks (those that are difficult to evaluate), and high-capacity risks (those that require very high coverage limits). Surplus lines coverages commonly include products liability, professional liability, employment practices liability, special events, and excess and umbrella policies.

Under surplus lines laws, a nonadmitted insurer might be permitted to transact business through a specially licensed surplus lines producer if (1) the insurance is not readily available from admitted insurers, (2) the nonadmitted insurer is "acceptable," and (3) the producer has a special license authorizing him or her to place such insurance. The surplus lines producer usually must be a resident of the state.

An "acceptable" nonadmitted insurer generally must file a financial statement that the insurance commissioner finds satisfactory; supply documentation of transactions to state regulators; obtain a certificate of compliance from its home state or country; and, if an alien insurer, maintain a trust fund in the

U.S. Some states leave the determination of acceptability to the producer. A few states permit producers to use other nonadmitted insurers if the desired insurance cannot be obtained from either admitted or "acceptable" nonadmitted insurers.

The National Association of Insurance Commissioners (NAIC) maintains an International Insurers Department that helps insurance regulators evaluate the financial status of alien insurers. The International Insurers Department prepares and disseminates a quarterly listing (Non-Admitted Insurers Quarterly Listing) of alien nonadmitted insurers to assist state insurance regulators, surplus lines brokers, and the public in evaluating whether to do business with one of the insurers on the listing. An insurer that would like to be included on the quarterly listing must file an application for listing. The insurer must also agree to provide pertinent financial information to allow the International Insurers Department to determine whether the insurer meets certain capital requirements, has established the applicable U.S. trust accounts, and meets the requisite character traits such as trustworthiness and integrity. The minimum capital and surplus required is $15 million. The minimum requirements for the trust account are $100 million or an amount established by a risk-based formula, but in no event should it be less than $5.4 million. The requirement for the trust account has long been a source of discontent for alien surplus lines insurers and reinsurers.

A nonadmitted insurer writing business in the surplus lines market does not face regulatory constraints on insurance rates and forms. From the insured's perspective, a distinct disadvantage of surplus lines insurance is that it is not usually protected by the state's guaranty fund. Thus, the requirements for capital and trust accounts provide assurance for insureds that nonadmitted insurers will be able to pay their claims.

Risk Retention Groups

A risk retention group is a special type of assessable mutual insurer enabled by the 1986 Liability Risk Retention Act. Risk retention groups are often formed under state captive laws, which generally maintain lower capital and surplus requirements for captives than for traditional property-casualty insurers. Once licensed as a commercial liability insurer under the laws of at least one state, a risk retention group can write insurance in other states without a license by filing the appropriate notice and registration forms with the nonchartering state. A risk retention group can write only commercial liability insurance for its members and may not write other lines of business. However, in a nonchartering state, a risk retention group might be subject to some state laws, such as unfair claim settlement practice laws, and to premium taxes. The risk retention group might also be required to become a member of a joint underwriting association (JUA) or a similar association with which insurers share losses in such areas as assigned-risk auto insurance.

Some state regulators have expressed concerns about the financial security of risk retention groups, particularly when the group providing the insurance is licensed in another state. Congress assisted with addressing these concerns by allowing the licensing state to request and, if necessary, mandate an examination of a group's financial condition—even when the commissioner has no reason to believe that the group is financially impaired. However, some state regulators still fear abuses under the Act, while some advocates of risk retention groups remain concerned about the possibility of overregulation.

Licensing Insurance Personnel

In addition to licensing insurers, state regulators also license some categories of insurance personnel. States license many of the people who sell insurance, give insurance advice, or represent insurers, including producers, claim representatives, and insurance consultants.

Producers

Producers must be licensed in each state where they do business. To obtain a license to sell a particular type of insurance, a producer must pass a written examination. Insurance producers operating without a license are subject to civil, and sometimes criminal, penalties.

Traditionally, lack of uniformity among the states' licensing requirements has been a source of frustration and an expense for producers licensed in more than one state. Provisions in the Gramm-Leach-Bliley (GLB) Act have led to greater licensing reciprocity among states. Regulators' ultimate goal is to move beyond reciprocity and to resolve issues related to uniformity in producer licensing. Meeting this goal will streamline the licensing process while retaining state regulatory authority over it.

Much progress has been made in recent years to address producer concerns about the lack of uniformity. The development of the National Insurance Producer Registry (NIPR) has eliminated many of the inconveniences that arise from a multi-state regulatory system. The NIPR is a unique public-private partnership that supports the work of the states and the NAIC in making the producer licensing process more cost effective, streamlined, and uniform for the benefit of regulators, insurance producers, insurers, and consumers. The NIPR vision is to provide one place for producers to go to meet all aspects of the producer licensing and appointment process using an electronic communication network. The NIPR developed and implemented the Producer Database (PDB) and the NIPR Gateway.

- The PDB is an electronic database consisting of information relating to insurance producers that links participating state regulatory licensing systems into one common repository of producer information. The PDB also includes data from the NAIC Regulatory Information Retrieval System to provide a more comprehensive producer profile. Some of the key benefits of PDB are increased productivity, lower cost, reduction of paper, access to real-time information, and the ability to conduct national verification of the license and status of a producer.

- The NIPR Gateway is a communication network that links state insurance regulators with the entities they regulate to facilitate the electronic exchange of producer information. Data standards have been developed for the exchange of license application, license renewal, appointment, and termination information.

Claim Representatives

Some states require claim representatives to be licensed so that those who make claim decisions for insurers are aware of prohibited claim practices, have a minimum level of technical knowledge and skill, and understand how to handle insureds' claims fairly. Licensing of claim representatives in most states includes an examination, which is important because of the complex and technical nature of insurance policies and the claim process. The licensing process also typically involves a background check, as well as ethics requirements, to help protect consumers who file claims from unfair, unethical, and dishonest claim practices.

Public adjusters, who represent insureds for a fee, are generally required to be licensed to ensure technical competence and to protect the public.

Insurance Consultants

Insurance consultants give advice, counsel, or opinions about insurance policies. Some states require insurance consultants to be licensed, and requirements for a consultant's license vary by state. Separate examinations are usually required to be an insurance consultant in both life-health insurance and property-casualty insurance.

INSURANCE REGULATORY ACTIVITIES: MONITORING INSURER SOLVENCY

Individual consumers and most businesses do not have the skills or resources to analyze claim-paying ability when selecting an insurer. However, because insurers hold large sums of money paid by consumers for long periods of time, their financial strength must be carefully monitored to ensure their continued ability to pay covered claims, both in the present and in the future. The United States regulatory framework helps to maintain insurers' solvency and thus protect consumers.

Monitoring solvency protects insureds and the public by accomplishing two broad goals:

- Reducing the insolvency risk
- Protecting the public against loss when insurers fail

A delicate balance exists between achieving these goals and reducing the total cost of risk for society as a whole. Insurers' costs are raised by requirements that increase the amount of capital they must hold in reserve. Whether directly or indirectly, insurance consumers pay for the costs of regulation, including regulators' salaries and the costs of collecting and maintaining financial data. Other insurers must pay for the losses of an insolvent insurer, and these additional costs are passed on to insureds. Insurance regulators recognize it is important both for regulation to be efficient and for inefficient insurers to cease to operate. As a result, regulators do not regulate to completely eliminate insolvencies, but rather to effectively use their regulatory resources to keep insolvencies infrequent and manageable.

Methods to Maintain Solvency

The U.S. regulatory framework is a national system of state-based regulation where the regulatory responsibility for insurer solvency monitoring rests with the state insurance regulator. The state insurance regulators are assisted by the National Association of Insurance Commissioners (NAIC), an organization of the chief insurance regulatory official in each state, the District of Columbia, and five U.S. territories. The NAIC provides financial, actuarial, legal, technology, research, and economic expertise to state regulators to assist them in meeting regulatory goals.

The mission or purpose of U.S. insurance regulation is to protect the interests of the insured and those who rely on the insurance coverage provided to the insured, while also facilitating an effective and efficient marketplace for insurance products. To accomplish this mission, insurance regulators must have appropriate regulatory authority and be able to operate independent of undue influence from insurers or other groups. The commissioner needs to maintain adequate staffing levels of sufficiently trained personnel and be able, by law, to treat confidential information appropriately.

The U.S. regulatory framework relies on an extensive system of peer review, featuring frequent communication and collaboration to provide the necessary checks and balances needed to make the system work. Much of this collaboration occurs through the NAIC where the diverse perspectives of its members are reflected in solutions embodied in model laws and regulations. These solutions have resulted in a risk-focused approach that is constantly evolving to meet changing local, national, and international developments.

Uniformity of approach to financial regulation has been facilitated by the NAIC accreditation program. As part of the peer review process, the accreditation program subjects state insurance regulators to a thorough and comprehensive review to determine if the state has met minimum, baseline standards of solvency regulation. To become accredited, the state must submit to a full on-site accreditation review. Depending on the results of the review, the state is accredited or it is not (that is, a pass/fail system is used). To remain accredited, an accreditation review must be performed at least once every five years with interim annual reviews. The evaluation looks at these factors:

- The adequacy of the state's solvency laws and regulations to protect consumers
- The ability of the regulator to meet standards regarding effective and efficient financial analysis and examination processes based on the priority status of insurers
- The ability and willingness of the state regulator to cooperate and share pertinent information with other state, federal, or foreign regulatory officials
- The ability of a state to take timely and effective action when an insurer is identified as financially troubled or potentially troubled
- The quality of the state regulator's organizational and personnel practices
- The effectiveness of the state's processes for company licensing and review of proposed changes in control

At the present time, all fifty states and the District of Columbia are accredited. However, accreditation is not automatic. There have been several occasions when not all states have been accredited. See the exhibit "Financial Solvency Core Principles."

The U.S. regulatory framework has evolved over time into the risk-focused approach used by regulators today. There is not a single U.S. market, but rather a variety of state-based, regional, or even intrastate insurance markets that collectively are referred to as the U.S. market. A wide variety of insurers, ranging from the very small to large-sized insurer groups and some financial conglomerates, serve these markets. This wide range of regulated entities calls for a flexible and collegial approach to regulation that focuses on the risks undertaken by each regulated entity.

Financial Solvency Core Principles

Core Principle 1	Regulatory reporting, disclosure, and transparency	• Insurers are required to file standardized reports annually and quarterly to assess the insurer's risk and financial condition. • These reports contain both qualitative and quantitative information, and are updated as necessary to incorporate significant common insurer risks.
Core Principle 2	Off-site monitoring and analysis	• Assess on an on-going basis the financial condition of the insurer as of the valuation date and to identify and assess current and prospective risks through risk-focused surveillance. • The results of the off-site analysis are included in an insurer profile for continual solvency monitoring. • Many off-site monitoring tools are maintained by the NAIC (such as the NAIC Financial Analysis Solvency Tools—FAST).
Core Principle 3	On-site, risk-focused examinations	• U.S. regulators carry out risk-focused, on-site examinations in which an insurer's corporate governance, management oversight, and financial strength are evaluated, including the system of risk identification and mitigation both on a current and prospective basis. • The reported financial results are assessed through the financial examination process and a determination is made of the insurer's compliance with legal requirements.
Core Principle 4	Reserves, capital adequacy, and solvency	• Insurers are required to maintain reserves and capital at all times and in such forms so as to provide an adequate margin of safety. • The most visible measure of capital adequacy requirements is associated with the risk based capital (RBC) system. The RBC calculation uses a standardized formula to benchmark specified level of regulatory actions for weakly capitalized insurers.
Core Principle 5	Regulatory control of significant, broad-based, risk-related transactions/activities	The transactions/activities encompass these: • Licensing requirements • Change of control • The amount of dividends paid • Transactions with affiliates • Reinsurance
Core Principle 6	Preventive and corrective measures, including enforcement	• The regulatory authority takes preventive and corrective measures that are timely, suitable, and necessary to reduce the impact of risks identified during on-site and off-site regulatory monitoring. • These regulatory actions are enforced as necessary.
Core Principle 7	Exiting the market and receivership	• The legal and regulatory framework defines a range of options for the orderly exit of insurers from the marketplace. • Solvency is defined and a receivership scheme established to ensure the payment of insured obligations of insolvent insurers subject to appropriate restrictions and limitations.

"The United States Insurance Financial Solvency Framework," National Association of Insurance Commissioners, February 19, 2010, pp. 3-5, http://www.naic.org/documents/committees_e_us_solvency_framework.pdf, accessed 7/14/10 [DA06398]

The U.S. regulatory framework is built on a set of solvency requirements for insurers. States are evaluated during the accreditation process to measure the extent to which the state requires the insurer to comply with the provisions. These are examples of solvency requirements:

- Insurers must submit annual and quarterly financial statements to the domestic regulator and the NAIC using a prescribed format called the "annual statement" or the "blank." The NAIC data captures the financial statements, performs some data quality checks, and maintains a data warehouse for use by state financial regulators.

- Insurers are required to use the NAIC's Accounting Practices and Procedures Manual and the Annual Statement Blank and Instructions for consistency of accounting treatment and financial reporting.

- The accounting practices have been codified, and an insurer using a state approved permitted practice must disclose the differences so that anyone using the financial statement can make the appropriate adjustments to remove the effect of the permitted practice.

- Most insurers (excepting the very small) must submit their financial statement to a Certified Public Accountant (CPA) for audit.

- Most insurers must have their reserves evaluated by an actuary and have the actuary attest to the accuracy of the reserve estimates.

- Insurers must perform a risk-based capital calculation and report the results to regulators. The risk-based capital calculation uses a standardized formula to benchmark specified level of regulatory actions for weakly capitalized insurers. The RBC amount, based on industry experience, explicitly considers the size and risk profile of the insurer. The risk-based capital calculation provides for higher RBC charges for riskier assets or for riskier lines of business so that more capital is required as a result. Although risk-based capital results indicate when an insurer's capital position is weak or deteriorating, a ladder of intervention levels exists within the RBC system. Thus, regulators have the authority to require insurers to take some action, or the regulator may have the authority to take action with respect to an insurer when the capital level falls within certain threshold amounts that are above the minimum capital requirement. The degree of action depends upon the relative capital weakness as determined by the RBC result and the existence of any mitigating or compounding issues.

- Insurers are required to adhere to state minimum capital and surplus requirements.

- State investment laws limit the types and quantity of investments an insurer may make, encouraging insurers to maintain a conservative and diversified investment portfolio. Invested assets outside the scope are not allowed to be counted in solvency calculations.

- Insurers are required to report investment values to the NAIC Securities Valuation Office. These results are made available to regulators and used for valuing assets reported in financial statement filings. State insurance regulators are able to look up a particular CUSIP (Committee on Uniform Securities Identification Procedures) number and determine if an insurer owns a particular security and, if so, how much. Instructions are contained in the NAIC Securities Valuation Office's (SVO) Purposes and Procedures Manual.

- State laws specify limitations on the amount on any single insured risk a property-casualty insurer may underwrite.

- Treatment of reinsurance is governed by the NAIC Credit for Reinsurance Model Law, which imposes standards on credits allowed to the reporting insurer.

Liquidation of Insolvent Insurers

Insolvency

A situation in which an entity's current liabilities (as opposed to its total liabilities) exceed its current assets.

If an insurer falls into **insolvency**, the insurance commissioner places it in receivership. With proper management, successful rehabilitation might be possible. If the insurer cannot be rehabilitated, it is liquidated according to the state's insurance code. Many states now liquidate insolvent insurers according to the Uniform Insurers Liquidation Act drafted by the NAIC. This model act promotes uniformity in liquidating assets and paying claims of a failed insurer. Under this act, creditors in each state in which the insolvent insurer has conducted business are treated equally; creditors in the state where the insurer is domiciled do not receive preferential treatment. Some states prioritize claimants who are entitled to the failed insurer's assets. In 2005, NAIC members adopted the Insurer Receivership Model Act to replace the earlier model. The new model was amended in 2007 and has been adopted in only a few states at the time of this writing.

State Guaranty Funds

Guaranty fund

A state-established fund that provides a system for the payment of some of the unpaid claims of insolvent insurers licensed in that state, generally funded by assessments collected from all insurers licensed in the state.

Guaranty funds do not prevent insurer insolvency, but they mitigate its effects. All states have property-casualty insurance guaranty funds that pay some of the unpaid claims of insolvent insurers licensed in the particular state. With the exception of New York, where a pre-assessment system maintains a permanent fund, a post-insolvency assessment method is used to raise the necessary funds to pay claims. Insurers doing business in the state are assessed their share of the unpaid covered claims of the insolvent insurer. Although the amounts involved are not trivial—over the last 40 years, the state guaranty funds have paid more than $24 billion in claims[6]—they still represent a very small percentage of total premiums. Insurers can recoup all or part of the assessments by insurance rate increases, special premium tax credits, and refunds from the state guaranty fund.

Characteristics of State Guaranty Funds

State guaranty funds vary by state. However, these characteristics are common:[7]

- Assessments are made only when an insurer fails (except in New York)—The definition of "failure" varies by state. Some states regard an insolvency order from a state court as evidence of failure. Others require a liquidation order from the state. All states limit the amounts that insurers can be assessed in one year.

- Policies usually terminate within thirty days after the failure date—Unpaid claims before termination, however, are still valid and paid from the guaranty fund of the insured's state of residence if the insolvent insurer is licensed in the state. Under the NAIC's model act, if the failed insurer is not licensed in the state, an insured or claimant cannot file a claim with the guaranty fund but must seek payment by filing a claim against the failed insurer's assets that are handled by the liquidator.

- Claim coverage varies by state—No state guaranty fund covers reinsurance or surplus lines insurance (except New Jersey).

- Claims are subject to maximum limits—The maximum limit is usually the lesser of $300,000 or the policy limit. Some states have limits under $300,000, and a small number of states have higher limits, such as $500,000 or $1 million.

- Most states provide for a refund of unearned premiums—A few states have no unearned premiums claim provision. In these states, an insured with a failed insurer is not entitled to a refund of the unearned premiums from the guaranty fund.

- Most states apply a $100 deductible to unpaid claims—Many states exempt workers compensation claims from a deductible.

- Most states divide their guaranty funds into separate accounts, usually auto, workers compensation, and other types of insurance—Auto or workers compensation assessments can be limited to insurers that write only that line of insurance.

- Assessment recovery varies by state—Thirty-two states permit insurers to recover assessments by an insurance rate increase. The remaining states generally reduce annual state premium taxes, usually over a period of five years. Consequently, taxpayers and the general public, as well as insureds, subsidize the unpaid claims of insolvent insurers.

Homeowners and auto insurance claims are covered by all state funds, but some types of insurance, such as annuities, life, disability, accident and health, surety, ocean marine, mortgage guaranty, and title insurance often are not covered. Self-insured groups are not protected by guaranty funds. Risk retention groups are prohibited by federal law from participating in the state guaranty fund system. Only one state has established a special guaranty fund for surplus lines.

Reasons for Insolvency

It is difficult to state the exact reasons for an insurer's failure. Usually, there isn't a single event or mistake that causes an insurer to become insolvent; rather, poor management and adverse events combine to cause insolvencies. Increased competition among insurers, leading to lower premium prices during soft phases of the underwriting cycle, often contributes to an increase in insurer insolvencies. Some insolvencies occur when an insurer is overexposed to losses resulting from a major insured catastrophe, especially during periods when intense competition causes lower insurance prices.

Experts have identified these factors that frequently contribute to an insurer's insolvency:

- Rapid premium growth
- Inadequate insurance rates
- Inadequate reserves
- Excessive expenses
- Lax controls over managing general agents
- Uncollectible reinsurance
- Fraud

Poor management is at the root of most of these factors. A combination of inadequate insurance rates and lax underwriting standards can start deterioration in a book of business. If these problems are not detected and corrected promptly, the decay in the quality of the business accelerates.

Rapid premium growth precedes nearly all major insolvencies. Rapid growth by itself is not harmful, but it reduces the margin for error in insurers' operations. Moreover, it usually indicates lowered rates and lax underwriting standards. If insurance rates are inadequate and losses understated, net losses and capital deterioration rise quicker than management can effectively respond.

INSURANCE REGULATORY ACTIVITIES: REGULATING INSURANCE RATES

Insurers must comply with rate regulatory laws in each state in which they write insurance. Additionally, insurers are often required to satisfy social concerns that are not included in state statutes. The primary goal of rate regulation is insurer financial stability and, as a result, consumer protection.

Of the types of insurance regulation, rate regulation may well receive the most public attention. When consumers complain about lack of fairness, equity, or affordability in insurance, policymakers search for remedies through regulation.

In seeking to ensure the financial stability of insurers and protect consumers, states use a variety of approaches to rate regulation, but they all have the same broad goals relating to fairness. The proponents of different types of rate regulation present reasons to support either prior-approval systems or competitive market systems.

Insurance Rate Regulation Goals

The three major goals of rate regulation are to ensure that rates are adequate, not excessive, and not unfairly discriminatory.

Adequate

Rates for a specific type of insurance should be high enough to pay all claims and expenses for that type of insurance. This requirement helps maintain insurer solvency. If an insurer fails because its rates are inadequate, it cannot pay for losses of its insureds and third-party claimants, who would consequently be financially harmed.

Several factors complicate the regulatory goal of rate adequacy:

- An insurer usually does not know what its actual expenses will be when a policy is sold. Premiums are paid in advance, but they might be insufficient to pay all related claims and expenses that occur later. An unexpected increase in claim frequency or severity can make the rate inadequate.

- Insurers might charge inadequate rates in response to strong price competition in order not to lose business.

- State rate approval systems may not approve insurers' requests for adequate rates for public policy reasons or because of disagreement over the level of requested rates.

- Unanticipated events could lead to higher losses than those projected when rates were set.

- Regulatory actuaries and insurer actuaries may disagree about the assumptions used to determine trends or account for socioeconomic components of a proposed rate change.

Although insurance rate adequacy is a goal of insurance regulation, no method of rate regulation guarantees that rates will be adequate.

Not Excessive

Although rates should be adequate, they should not be excessive. Insurers should not earn excessive or unreasonable profits. Regulators have considerable latitude and discretion in determining whether rates are excessive for a given type of insurance, and they consider factors, such as these:

- Number of insurers selling a specific coverage in the rating territory
- Relative market share of competing insurers
- Degree of rate variation among the competing insurers
- Past and prospective loss experience for a given type of insurance
- Possibility of catastrophe losses
- Margin for underwriting profit and contingencies
- Marketing expenses for a given type of insurance
- Special judgment factors that might apply to a given type of insurance

Regulators sometimes use the fair rate of return approach in determining whether an insurer's rates are adequate or excessive. This approach is based on the premise that an insurer should expect at least some minimum rate of return on the equity invested in its insurance operations and that a fair rate of return should be similar to the rate of return of other types of businesses—especially if insurers are to attract investment capital. Regulators, insurers, and investors often disagree as to what constitutes a fair rate of return for insurers.

Not Unfairly Discriminatory

Rates that are adequate and are not excessive must also not be unfairly discriminatory. The word "discrimination" carries negative connotations, but the word itself is neutral, implying only the ability to differentiate among things. Discrimination, in the neutral sense, is essential to insurance rating. However, insurers' discrimination must be fair and consistent. This means that insureds with loss exposures that are roughly similar regarding expected losses and expenses should be charged substantially similar rates. For example, two drivers age twenty-five operating similar vehicles in the same rating territory who buy the same type and amount of auto insurance from the same insurer should be charged the same rates.

The use of sophisticated computer simulation modeling for catastrophes and the use of innovative risk classification systems, such as credit-based insurance scores, have greatly complicated regulatory evaluation of whether rates are unfairly discriminatory.

Regulation seeks to prohibit only unfair discrimination, not fair discrimination. If loss exposures are substantially different in terms of expected losses and expenses, then different rates can be charged. For example, if a woman age twenty-five and another age sixty-five are in good health and purchase the same type and amount of life insurance from the same insurer, it is not unfair rate discrimination to charge the older woman a higher rate. The higher probability of death for a woman at age sixty-five clearly and fairly justifies a higher rate.

Types of Rating Laws

A state's rating laws influence how it achieves its three major rate regulation goals and the rates property-casualty insurers can charge. Rating laws apply not only to rates for a new type of insurance, but also to rate changes. The major types of state rating laws are these:

- Prior-approval laws require rates and supporting rules to be approved by the state insurance department before they can be used. In some cases, a prior-approval law contains a deemer provision stating that filing is deemed approved if the insurer has not heard from the regulator within a given time (usually thirty to ninety days).

- File-and-use laws allow the insurer to use the new rates immediately after filing with the state insurance department. The department has the authority to disapprove the rates if they cannot be justified or if they violate state law.

- Use-and-file laws, a variation of file-and-use laws, allow insurers to use the new rates and later submit filing information that is subject to regulatory review.

- No filing laws (information filing or open competition), do not require insurers to file rates with the state insurance department. Market prices driven by the economic laws of supply and demand, rather than the discretionary acts of regulators, determine the rates and availability. However, insurers might be required to furnish rate schedules and supporting statistical data to regulatory officials, and the state insurance department has the authority to monitor competition and to disapprove rates if necessary. The goals of adequate, nonexcessive, and equitable rates still apply.

- Flex rating laws require prior approval only if the new rates exceed a certain percentage above (and sometimes below) the rates filed previously. Insurers can increase or decrease their rates within the established range without prior approval. Typically, a range of five to ten percent is permitted. Flex rating permits insurers to make rate adjustments quickly in response to changing market conditions and loss experience, but it prohibits wide swings within a short period of time. Flex rating also can restrict insurers from drastically reducing rates to increase market share. The result should be smoother insurance pricing cycles.

Variations of these filing approaches exist. For example, open competition might apply as long as insurers meet certain tests, such as evidence of competitive markets or keeping rate increases to less than 25 percent per year. Insurers that fail to meet these criteria would be subject to prior approval or another type of regulatory review.

Controversy regarding regulation of insurance rates is ongoing. Most consumer advocacy groups and regulatory agencies support prior-approval systems allowing regulators to determine the adequacy and fairness of rates. However, most insurers and economists favor competitive rating systems where the market determines rates. See the exhibit "Prior-Approval Systems Versus Competitive Rating Systems."

Prior-Approval Systems Versus Competitive Rating Systems

Arguments for Prior-Approval Systems	Arguments for Competitive Rating Systems
• Prior-approval systems require insurers to justify requests for rate increases with supporting actuarial data.	• Prior-approval systems may cause rates to be inadequate for writing profitable business by the time it is approved, because of the time required for the regulatory review and approval process. Inadequate rates may cause insurers to reduce the amount of new business written or leave a state or a market, leading to a problem with insurance availability.
• Prior-approval systems help maintain insurer solvency through regulatory review of data to analyze the adequacy of rates for reported losses.	• Competitive rating systems are less expensive to administer and allow regulators to focus their resources on other areas, such as solvency regulation and consumer affairs.
• Prior-approval systems help keep rates reasonable and fair.	• Competitive rating systems are more flexible, allowing rates to be adjusted quickly in response to changing economic and market conditions.
• Prior-approval proponents believe that without regulatory approval insurers would raise rates unfairly to earn excessive profits.	• Competitive rating proponents believe that free market forces, rather than government regulation, lead to reasonable and fair rates.

[DA06392]

INSURANCE REGULATORY ACTIVITIES: REGULATING INSURANCE POLICIES

Insurance policies are complex documents. Regulation of insurance policies helps to protect insurance consumers, who often may not understand their policies. Also, insurance policies are usually drafted by insurers, who sell them to the public on a take-it-or-leave-it basis. Regulation can protect insureds from policies that are narrow, restrictive, deceptive, or that fail to comply with state laws and regulations.

Contract language contained in insurance policies is regulated through legislation and insurance departments' rules, regulations, and guidelines.

Regulation may require certain forms, provisions, or standards, or it may prohibit certain provisions. Court decisions may arise from legal disputes regarding the language in insurance contracts and can also result in changes to policy language and forms.

Legislation

Insurance policy regulation starts with a state legislature passing laws that control the structure and content of insurance policies sold in the state. Legislative policy regulation affects these five areas: standard forms, mandatory provisions, prohibited provisions, forms approval, or readability standards.

Legislation might require insurers to use a standard policy to insure property or liability loss exposures. A standard policy is one policy all insurers must use if a coverage is sold in the state.

Legislation might also require that certain standard mandatory policy provisions appear in certain types of insurance policies. The required and optional provisions might be based on a model bill developed by the National Association of Insurance Commissioners (NAIC). For example, states usually require that workers compensation insurance, no-fault auto coverage, and often uninsured motorists coverage contain mandated policy provisions. State laws and regulations might require that the mandated policy provisions meet certain minimum standards, providing at least a basic level of protection.

State laws and regulations might list certain provisions that are prohibited in insurance contracts. For example, some states, such as South Dakota and Maryland, prohibit binding arbitration clauses in insurance contracts.

Legislation might mandate that policies be filed and/or approved by the state to protect policyholders against ambiguous, misleading, or deceptive policies. Many states require that a policy be submitted for approval before it is used. However, if a specified period elapses and the policy has not been disapproved, the policy is considered approved. (Some states permit the state insurance department to extend the review period.) The purpose of such approval is to encourage a prompt review of the policy. However, it can cause a perfunctory review.

In recent years, speed to market for insurance products has become increasingly important to insurance regulators and regulated entities. The NAIC has implemented a series of operational efficiencies along with the System for Electronic Rate and Form Filings (SERFF). SERFF has dramatically improved the timeliness of product filings. The SERFF system is designed to enable insurers to send and states to receive, comment on, and approve or reject rate and form filings. Filing volume has risen from just over 3,000 filings in 2001 to more than 500,000 filings in 2009. SERFF facilitates communication, management, analysis, and electronic storage of documents and supporting information. The system is designed to improve the efficiency of the rate and form filing and approval process and to reduce the time and cost involved in making regulatory filings. It also provides up-to-date filing requirements when they are needed.

Finally, legislation might require that insurance policies meet a readability test. Legislation may specify policy style and form as well as the size of print. Readability legislation has influenced the drafting of both personal and commercial insurance policies, but readability tests do not necessarily measure how well the policies can be understood.

Policy Rules, Regulations, and Guidelines

State insurance departments implement specific directives from the legislature or exercise the general authority they have to regulate insurance policies. Administrative rules, regulations, and guidelines can be stated in (1) regulations communicated by the state insurance department to insurers, (2) informal circulars or bulletins from the same source, and (3) precedents set during the approval process. For example, the state insurance department might require specific wording in certain policy provisions or might notify insurers that certain types of policy provisions will be disapproved.

Courts

Although the courts do not directly regulate insurers, they do influence them by determining whether insurance laws are constitutional and whether administrative rulings and regulations are consistent with state law. The courts also interpret ambiguous and confusing policy provisions, determine whether certain losses are covered by the policy, and resolve other disputes between insurers and insureds over policy coverages and provisions.

Court decisions often lead insurers to redraft their policy language and to modify provisions. For example, based on the legal doctrine of concurrent causation, certain courts ruled that if a loss under a risk of direct physical loss (formerly "all-risks") policy is caused by two causes of loss, one of which is excluded, the entire loss is covered. As a result of this doctrine, insurers were required to pay certain flood and earthquake claims they had believed were excluded by their property insurance policies. Subsequent revision of the language in many such property policies explicitly excluded coverage for flood and earthquake losses in cases in which a nonexcluded cause of loss contributed to the loss.

INSURANCE REGULATORY ACTIVITIES: MARKET CONDUCT AND CONSUMER PROTECTION

Regulation of the insurance industry's market conduct is concerned with consumer protection. By overseeing producers, sales and advertising, underwriting, ratemaking, and claim settlement procedures and activities, state departments of insurance help protect insurance consumers from such practices as unfair discrimination, insurer fraud, and excessive rates. Additionally, market conduct regulation promotes competition within the insurance marketplace.

Regulators have traditionally monitored three key areas of market conduct:

- Producer practices
- Underwriting practices
- Claim practices

While maintaining their focus on these practices, regulators are moving away from traditional market conduct examinations and toward market analysis. In addition to monitoring insurers, state insurance departments also provide information and assistance directly to insurance consumers.

Monitoring Market Conduct

Laws regarding unfair trade practices prohibit abusive practices. Currently, all United States jurisdictions except American Samoa and Guam have laws against unfair trade practices. Unfair trade practices acts at the state level regulate the trade practices of the business of insurance as required under the McCarran Act.

Unfair trade practices cases can be decided by the commissioner of the state in which the activity occurred. If an insurer is found to be in violation of the unfair trade practices act, the insurer is subject to one or both of two penalties:

- Fine per violation—The fine is often increased significantly if the activity is considered flagrant, with conscious disregard for the law.
- Suspension or revocation of license—This may occur if the practice occurred frequently and if the insurer's management knew or should have known of the unfair trade practice.

If an insurer disagrees with the commissioner's findings, generally it can file for judicial review. If the court agrees with the commissioner, the insurer must obey the commissioner's orders.

The National Association of Insurance Commissioners (NAIC) Model Unfair Trade Practices Act prohibits insurers from any activity that would restrain trade or competition in the business of insurance. The act also prohibits an insurer from misrepresenting its own or another insurer's financial status. Additionally, there are numerous provisions in the Model Act to protect insurance consumers.

The key insurer market conduct areas that are regulated by the Model Act and state-level unfair trade practices acts include producer practices, underwriting practices, and claim practices.

Producer Practices

Producers are subject to fines, penalties, or license revocation if they engage in certain illegal and unethical activities. A producer might be penalized for engaging in practices that violate the state's unfair trade practices act, such as these:

- Dishonesty or fraud—A producer might embezzle premiums paid by insureds or misappropriate some claim funds.

- Misrepresentation—A producer might misrepresent the losses that are covered by an insurance policy, which might induce a client to purchase that policy under false pretenses.

- Twisting—A producer might induce an insured to replace one policy with another, to the insured's detriment. This is a special form of misrepresentation called "twisting."

- Unfair discrimination—A producer might engage in any number of acts that favor one insured unfairly over another.

- Rebating—A producer might engage in rebating, the practice of giving a portion of the producer's commission or some other financial advantage to an individual as an inducement to purchase a policy. Rebating is currently illegal in almost all states.

Underwriting Practices

Insurance regulators attempt to prevent improper underwriting that could result in insurer insolvency or unfair discrimination against an insurance consumer. See the exhibit "Examples of Unfair Trade Practices With Respect to Underwriting."

Examples of Unfair Trade Practices With Respect to Underwriting

- Discriminating unfairly when selecting loss exposures
- Misclassifying loss exposures
- Canceling or nonrenewing policies contrary to statutes, rules, and policy provisions
- Using underwriting rules or rates that are not on file with or approved by the insurance departments in the states in which the insurer does business
- Failing to apply newly implemented underwriting and rating factors to renewals
- Failing to use correct policy forms and insurance rates
- Failing to use rules that are state specific

[DA02905]

To protect consumers, insurance regulators take actions such as these:

- Constrain insurers' ability to accept, modify, or decline applications for insurance—To increase insurance availability, states often require insurers to provide coverage for some loss exposures they might prefer not to cover.

- Establish allowable classifications—Regulators limit the ways in which insurers can divide consumers into rating classifications. For example, unisex rating is required in some states for personal auto insurance. This promotes social equity rather than actuarial equity.

- Restrict the timing of cancellations and nonrenewals—All states require insurers to provide insureds with adequate advance notice of policy cancellation or nonrenewal so that insureds can obtain replacement coverage. Insurers are typically allowed to cancel or nonrenew only for specific reasons.

Claim Practices

Regulatory controls on claim practices are intended to protect insureds and maintain public confidence in the promise of insurance to pay valid claims promptly and fairly. All states prohibit certain claim practices by law. Apart from regulatory penalties, failure to practice **good faith claim handling** can lead to claims for damages that allege **bad faith** on the insurer's part. Unfair claim practices laws prohibit unethical and illegal claim practices. The laws generally are patterned after the NAIC Model Unfair Claims Settlement Practices Act. See the exhibit "Examples of Unfair Claims Settlement Practices."

Good faith claim handling
The manner of handling claims that requires an insurer to give consideration to the insured's interests that is at least equal to the consideration it gives its own interests.

Bad faith
A breach of the duty of good faith and fair dealing.

Examples of Unfair Claims Settlement Practices

- Knowingly misrepresenting important facts or policy provisions

- Failing to properly investigate and settle claims

- Failing to make a good-faith effort to pay claims when liability is reasonably clear

- Attempting to settle a claim for an amount less than the amount that a reasonable person believes he or she is entitled to receive based on advertising material that accompanies or is part of the application

- Failing to approve or deny coverage of a claim within a reasonable period after a proof-of-loss statement has been completed

[DA02906]

In some cases, courts have ruled that an insurer's improper claim handling constitutes not only a breach of contract or a violation of regulations, but also an independent tort—the tort of bad faith. Legal remedies for bad-faith actions can lead both to first-party actions (involving the insured) and to third-party actions (involving a claimant). An insurer that violates good-faith standards can be required to honor the policy's intent (paying the claim) and pay extracontractual damages (damages above the amount payable under the terms of the insurance policy), such as emotional distress and attorney fees.

Market Analysis

Insurance regulators are moving away from traditional market conduct examinations and toward market analysis. Market analysis allows regulators to identify general market disruptions, promotes uniform analysis by applying consistent measurements between insurers, and facilitates communication and collaboration among regulators from different states. One of the fundamental components of market analysis is the collection of regulatory information from insurers using the Market Conduct Annual Statement (MCAS). In 2009, twenty-nine states participated in the MCAS project and began to assemble some baseline statistics that are used to benchmark insurer performance. As a work-in-progress at the time of this writing, regulators are engaged in these activities:

- Defining the scope of the market analysis program
- Determining minimum required skills and essential education necessary for market analysis professionals
- Developing, prioritizing, and coordinating data collection and analysis techniques
- Making recommendations regarding the expansion of the data elements for MCAS
- Developing analysis techniques to ensure states expand their focus from company-specific issues to general market problems

Ensuring Consumer Protection

In a sense, all insurance regulatory activities protect insurance consumers. However, certain activities are designed specifically to support consumers. For example, state insurance departments respond to consumer complaints, and they also provide information and education to consumers.

State insurance departments often assist with complaints about rates or policy cancellations or with consumers' difficulty in finding insurance. Although state insurance departments usually have no direct authority to order insurers to pay claims when facts are disputed (such disputes are typically resolved through the courts), most state insurance departments can investigate and follow up on a consumer complaint, at least to the extent of getting a response from the insurer involved.

Many states compute complaint ratios, and some make them readily available to consumers through the Internet. To help make consumers more knowledgeable about the cost of insurance, some states publish shoppers' guides and other forms of consumer information, and much of this information can be found on the Internet. Consumers can obtain information provided by state insurance departments by linking to each state insurance department's Web site from the NAIC Web site at www.naic.org.

UNOFFICIAL REGULATORS IN INSURANCE

Insurance regulation involves numerous entities that interact to influence insurer activities.

Only state and federal governments have the legal authority to regulate insurers. However, the National Association of Insurance Commissioners (NAIC) plays an influential role in insurance regulation, although it has no direct regulatory authority. Other entities—"unofficial regulators"—also affect insurer activities, including these four types of organizations:

- Financial rating organizations
- Insurance advisory organizations
- Insurance industry professional and trade associations
- Consumer groups

Financial Rating Organizations

Because good financial ratings help attract and retain customers—and vice versa—insurers try to conduct business in ways that maintain good ratings. Several financial rating agencies provide insurer financial ratings, including these:

- A.M. Best Company
- Duff and Phelps
- Moody's
- Standard & Poor's
- Weiss Ratings, Inc.

Generally, these organizations provide summary information about insurer financial strength in the form of a financial rating, typically a letter grade similar to those appearing on a student's report card. Corporate risk managers, independent insurance producers, consumers, and others consult these ratings when choosing an insurer. Many corporate and public entity risk managers purchase insurance only from insurers whose financial ratings meet or exceed a specific rating. Contractors and other organizations are often required to furnish a certificate of insurance in various business transactions, such as bidding on projects or applying for financing, from an insurer with a specified minimum financial rating. Banks and other lending institutions typically require **mortgagors** to provide evidence of insurance from an insurer with a specified minimum financial rating.

Mortgagor

The person or organization that borrows money from a mortgagee to finance the purchase of real property.

Insurers whose financial ratings have declined can find it difficult to attract and retain customers, and a decrease in customers can cause a financial rating to decline further. Insurers pay close attention to the factors financial rating agencies consider and endeavor to avoid an adverse rating. An insurer whose financial rating is threatened can implement remedial measures, such as purchasing more reinsurance; limiting new business; selling a portion of its book of business; selling stock to raise additional capital; or merging with another, more financially secure, insurer.

Poor financial ratings are not a widespread problem in the insurance industry. In addition, a "poor" rating does not mean an insurer will become insolvent, and a "good" rating does not guarantee that the insurer will never become insolvent. Some large insurers that have failed in recent years received high financial ratings until a year or two before they were declared insolvent. The value of financial ratings is limited because they are based on past performance. Despite this limitation, the ratings are widely used to evaluate insurers' financial strength, and insurers strive to maintain sound financial ratings.

Insurance Advisory Organizations

Advisory organization

An independent organization that works with and on behalf of insurers that purchase or subscribe to its services.

Prospective loss costs

Loss data that is modified by loss development, trending, and credibility processes, but without considerations for profit and expenses.

Insurance **advisory organizations** are companies that work with, and on behalf of, insurers. They provide services to member insurers and insurers that purchase or subscribe to their services. Advisory organizations develop standard insurance policy forms and provide data regarding rates or **prospective loss costs**. They may also file loss costs and policy forms with the state on behalf of their member and subscribing insurers. They may provide other valuable services, such as these, to participants in the insurance market and insurance regulators:

- Developing rating systems
- Collecting and tabulating statistics
- Researching important insurance topics
- Providing a forum for discussing important issues
- Educating members, the industry, insurance regulators, and the public about relevant issues
- Monitoring regulatory issues of concern to members

Insurers pay a fee for the services of insurance advisory organizations. Well-known insurance advisory organizations include Insurance Services Office (ISO), the American Association of Insurance Services (AAIS), and the National Council on Compensation Insurance (NCCI).

By developing rate information and standard insurance forms, advisory organizations provide a degree of uniformity that can benefit consumers and regulators as well as serve insurers. Relatively few insurers have the resources to independently develop the statistical data on which to base their own insurance rates or to develop policy forms, endorsements, and rating systems for many different coverages that also comply with regulations from many different states. Insurance consumers benefit from competition among insurers who base their rates on sound statistical data. Uniformity in insurance policy forms also makes it easier for consumers to compare proposals from different insurers.

Insurance Industry Professional and Trade Associations

Several national property-casualty industry professional associations and trade associations provide services to their member insurance professionals, insurers, and producers. Professional organizations' members are individuals who share a common profession; whereas the trade associations' members are companies that share a common industry. However, some professional associations also accept corporate members, and some trade associations may permit individual members. Trade and professional associations have similar activities, and their main purpose is to advance the success of members as well as uphold ethical standards.

Professional associations in the property-casualty insurance industry provide educational, leadership, and ethical development for individual members and their employers. These associations provide services either industry-wide or to specialized professional groups (such as claim representatives or actuaries), offering education and information about continuing trends and developments in the industry or a particular field. Associations may also be active in recommending or supporting industry practices or legislative initiatives. See the exhibit "Insurance Industry Professional and Trade Associations."

Trade associations serve an important function for property-casualty insurers, reinsurers, and producers. For a fee, members have timely access to legislative developments on the national level and can use association personnel to help them lobby on behalf of the industry group. Trade association members can also participate on trade association committees to help draft new legislation or to influence pending legislation. Participation in one or more major trade associations can provide insurers with information that would otherwise require a large internal staff to obtain. Individual insurers would find it difficult to match the prompt dissemination of information and the scope of coverage that the trade associations provide.

Trade associations operate not only on the national level but also at state and local levels. They report on new regulations issued by state insurance departments in response to new or modified state insurance laws. Many state and local associations focus on local issues important to their members. For insurers and producers doing business only in one or two states, membership in state or local associations may be more cost-effective than membership in a national trade association that may provide many more services than the insurer or producer needs.

Insurance Industry Professional and Trade Associations

Name	Year Founded	Members	Interests
American Insurance Association (AIA), www.aiadc.org	1964, with roots in the National Board of Fire Underwriters established in 1866	Property-casualty insurers	Provides safety and legislative services
Casualty Actuarial Society www.casact.org	1914	Insurance actuaries	Advances the knowledge of actuarial science applied to property and casualty insurance
CPCU Society www.cpcusociety.org	1944	Insurance industry professionals	Promotes excellence through ethical behavior and continuing education
Council of Insurance Agents and Brokers, www.ciab.com	1913	Commercial property-casualty insurance agencies and brokerage firms	Takes an active leadership role in crafting the commercial insurance industry's response to issues that affect members and their customers
Independent Insurance Agents & Brokers of America (IIABA), www.iiaba.net	1896	Independent insurance agencies handling property, fire, casualty, and surety insurance	Promotes education of agents and promotes regulatory and legislative issues of agents
Inland Marine Underwriters Association (IMUA), www.imua.org	1930	Member companies representing inland marine insurers	Provides its members with education, research, and communications services that support the inland marine underwriting discipline
National Association of Mutual Insurance Companies (NAMIC), www.namic.org	1895	Property-casualty insurers	Promotes governmental affairs representation; compiles and analyzes pertinent information
National Association of Professional Insurance Agents, www.pianet.com	1931	Insurance agents	Provides educational, representative, and service-oriented activities
National Association of Professional Surplus Lines Offices (NAPSLO), www.napslo.org	1975	Associate and wholesale brokers and agents	Sets standards for surplus lines industry and provides educational seminars and workshops and internships

Name	Year Founded	Members	Interests
Property Casualty Insurers Association of America (PCI), www.pciaa.net	2004, by the merger of the National Association of Independent Insurers and the Alliance of American Insurers	Property-casualty insurers	Provides a voice on public policy issues affecting property-casualty insurers before state and federal regulatory agencies and in the courts; serves as an information and education clearinghouse for consumers and the media
Reinsurance Association of America (RAA), www.reinsurance.org	1968	Property-casualty reinsurers	Promotes the interests of the property-casualty reinsurance industry to federal and state legislators, regulators, and the public
Risk and Insurance Management Society (RIMS), www.rims.org	1950	Individuals representing more than 4,000 member companies	Promotes the practice of risk management

Sources: Encyclopedia of Associations, 2000, 36th ed., vol. 1, part 1, Tara E. Sheets, ed. (Detroit, Mich.: Gale Research, Inc., 2000); The Fact Book 2001 (New York: Insurance Information Institute, 2001); and organizations' Web sites listed above. [DA02907]

Trade associations at the national, state, and local levels influence the NAIC, state and federal legislators, and state insurance regulators. Each trade association has the collective power of its membership behind it. One person speaking on behalf of a major segment of insurers affected by a proposed piece of legislation can have far more influence than the representative of a single insurer expressing the same opinion.

Proposed legislation or regulation may be based on incorrect market assumptions and misinformation or may be introduced in reaction to a crisis. Trade associations can provide accurate information to legislators and regulators about critical issues in time to influence the development of legislation, regulations, and rules. Trade associations can sometimes persuade legislators and regulators that the insurance industry can solve a problem without legislation. This type of intervention provides an important service to association members.

Consumer Groups

Consumers, through consumer groups, have had a major influence on state insurance departments, state and federal legislators, the NAIC, and insurance consumers themselves. Some consumer groups focus solely on insurance issues, while others tackle a variety of public interest issues. Some have adopted a watchdog approach, carefully monitoring insurers and their actions. Others take a more activist approach to confront issues and to work for change.

One such group, the Consumer Federation of America (CFA), is headquartered in Washington, D.C. CFA is an advocacy organization that provides information to consumers about auto insurance and works to improve the safety of household products. Another well-known consumer group that monitors the insurance industry, Public Citizen, has contributed to substantive reforms in automobile safety and seat belt laws.

Consumer complaints made to state insurance departments can trigger market conduct examinations that may lead to actions ranging from insurer warnings to revocation of an insurer's license. Additionally, regulators view multiple complaints about an insurer as a sign of potential financial trouble that may trigger a financial examination. Consumers and consumer groups often influence state insurance commissioners to hold hearings on specific issues. Such hearings can lead insurers to take corrective action or lead regulators to develop legislative proposals.

SUMMARY

In addition to the U.S. Constitution, six subsequent legal events influenced the three major issues of insurance regulation:

- Locus of regulatory control (state versus federal)
- Extent of regulation
- Collaboration among insurers

The six legal events are the *Paul v. Virginia* Supreme Court decision, the Sherman Antitrust Act, the South-Eastern Underwriters Association Decision, the McCarran-Ferguson Act, the ISO and the Attorneys General Lawsuit, and the Gramm-Leach-Bliley Act.

Insurance regulation is considered necessary to protect consumers, to maintain insurer solvency, and to avoid destructive competition.

Every state has an insurance department, headed by a commissioner that is responsible for regulating insurance in that state. Insurance regulators belong to a nonprofit association, the NAIC, which has no regulatory authority of its own but has substantial influence in coordinating the activities of various state regulators and developing model acts and regulations, as well as sharing financial information.

Federal regulation takes many forms, including the Insurance Fraud Protection Act, and a variety of regulations that affect insurers and other organizations alike.

Insurance is primarily regulated by the states. However, debate is ongoing about whether federal regulation of insurance should replace the state regulatory system. Both sides of the debate present strong arguments supporting their positions.

Insurance regulators govern the formation and licensing of insurers and the licensing of insurance personnel. By issuing a license to an insurer, a state indicates that the insurer meets minimum standards of financial strength, competence, and integrity. States also license many of the people who sell insurance, give insurance advice, or represent insurers, including producers, claim representatives, and insurance consultants.

Regulators in the U.S. have a framework to prevent insurer insolvencies and to manage those that do occur despite preventive efforts. The NAIC provides tools for uniformity and a risk-based approach in solvency regulation founded on seven core solvency principles. The NAIC has also drafted a model act for uniform procedures to liquidate insolvent insurers. State guaranty funds, financed through assessments of insurers operating in the insolvent insurer's state, provide payments for that insurer's valid claims after the insolvency. Most insurer insolvencies occur because of poor management practices.

States regulate insurance rates to help maintain insurer solvency and protect consumers. Three major goals of rate regulation are that rates be adequate, not excessive, and not unfairly discriminatory. State rating laws influence the rates property-casualty insurers can charge. The major types of state rating laws are: prior-approval laws, file-and-use laws, use-and-file laws, no filing laws, and flex rating laws. Proponents of rate regulation offer reasons to support prior-approval systems versus proponents of a competitive market system who offer reasons to oppose prior-approval systems.

Regulating contract language contained in insurance policies is necessary because insurance policies are complex documents, and they are almost always drafted by insurers, who sell them to the public on a take-it-or-leave-it basis. Insurance policy regulation starts with a state legislature passing laws regarding insurance policy form and content. State insurance departments implement specific directives from the legislature or exercise their general authority to regulate insurance policies through administrative rules, regulations, and guidelines. Courts influence insurers by determining whether insurance laws are constitutional and by interpreting insurance policy provisions.

Insurance regulators have traditionally monitored insurers' compliance with the provisions of unfair trade practices acts through market conduct examinations that focus on producers' practices, underwriting practices, and claim practices. The primary purpose of unfair trade practices laws and regulations is to protect consumers. Additionally, these laws are also intended to help maintain insurers' solvency while encouraging competition.

Regulators are moving away from the traditional market conduct examinations and toward market analysis, an approach that will allow the practices of an entire market, consisting of multiple insurers, to be reviewed.

In addition to their monitoring of insurers' conduct, regulators also protect those who purchase insurance by providing information and assistance directly to consumers.

Various types of organizations serve as unofficial insurance regulators. Financial rating organizations encourage insurers to maintain or improve their financial strength ratings. Insurance advisory organizations develop standard policy forms and provide loss cost data. Insurance industry professional and trade associations, in addition to other services, provide education, training, and information to members and act as lobbyists on issues important to their members. Consumer groups serve as watchdogs and activists.

ASSIGNMENT NOTES

1. *Samuel B. Paul v. Commonwealth of Virginia*, S.C., 8 Wall., 168–185 (1869).

2. *United States v. South-Eastern Underwriters Association*, et al., 322U.S. 533 (1944).

3. "Financial Regulation Standards and Accreditation Program," National Association of Insurance Commissioners, March 2010, http://www.naic.org (accessed June 28, 2010).

4. 18 USC Sec. 1033.

5. Ann Monaco Warren, Esq., and John William Simon, Esq., "Dishonesty or Breach of Trust" in 18 U.S.C. Section 1033: "Are You Criminally Liable on the Basis of an Associate's Record?" *FORC Quarterly Journal of Insurance Law and Regulation*, vol. X, edition III, September 12, 1998.

6. "After 40 Years the P/C Guaranty Fund System Thrives," The National Conference of Insurance Guaranty Funds, p.1, www.ncigf.org (accessed July 4, 2010)

7. www.ncigf.org (accessed July 14, 2010).

Direct Your Learning ▶▶

3

Insurance Marketing and Distribution

Educational Objectives

After learning the content of this assignment, you should be able to:

▶ Describe the following attributes of the competitive property-casualty insurance marketplace: distinguishing characteristics of insurance customers, insurer marketing differentiations, and unique factors in the insurance marketplace.

▶ Explain how typical insurer marketing activities are performed and why they are performed.

▶ Describe the main types of insurance distribution systems and channels, including the principal characteristics that distinguish one distribution system from another.

▶ Describe the functions performed by insurance producers.

▶ Describe the key factors an insurer should evaluate during the distribution-system and distribution-channel selection process.

Insurance Marketing and Distribution

3

PROPERTY-CASUALTY INSURANCE MARKETPLACE

The property-casualty insurance marketplace is the highly competitive meeting point between customers' needs and insurers' abilities to meet those needs. Competition is an important dynamic in the marketplace to provide reasonable premiums to insureds. However, the environment that influences the transactions and the price of those transactions renders the marketplace dynamic and continuously evolving.

Competition between property-casualty insurers for customers is a dynamic function of the insurance marketplace. The drivers of that competition arise from the needs and characteristics of the insurance customers. Property-casualty insurers have differentiated marketing characteristics to meet the needs of one or more customer groups.

Insurers and customers interact in an environment with factors that are unique to the insurance marketplace. These numerous factors, predictable and unpredictable, affect competition and insurers' profitability. See the exhibit "The Property-Casualty Insurance Marketplace."

Characteristics of Property-Casualty Insurance Customers

Each type of insurance customer can be distinguished in terms of insurance needs, knowledge of the insurance markets, methods of accessing the insurance market, negotiating ability, and access to alternative risk financing measures. These five distinguishing characteristics are significant to customers because they drive the demand for insurance products and services. Customers' characteristics are significant to insurers because they directly affect the products and services they supply to each type of customer group: individuals, small business, middle markets, and national accounts.

Individuals

From an insurance perspective, individuals generally share the same needs for property coverage to protect real and personal property and liability coverage for losses arising out of their personal actions and their ownership and use of property. Because so many individuals have the same insurance needs, insurers

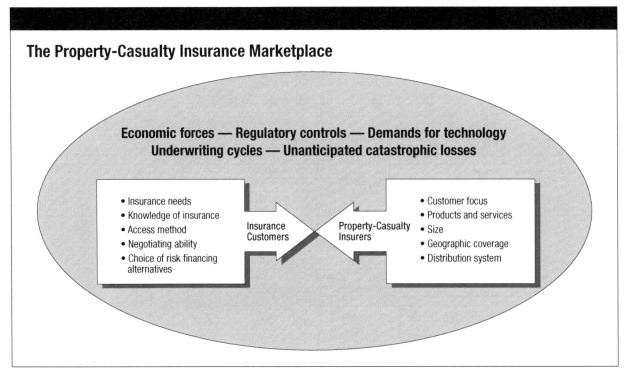

The Property-Casualty Insurance Marketplace

Economic forces — Regulatory controls — Demands for technology
Underwriting cycles — Unanticipated catastrophic losses

Insurance Customers
- Insurance needs
- Knowledge of insurance
- Access method
- Negotiating ability
- Choice of risk financing alternatives

Property-Casualty Insurers
- Customer focus
- Products and services
- Size
- Geographic coverage
- Distribution system

[DA06182]

are able to pool individual insureds' loss exposures based on relevant underwriting factors to determine the appropriate premiums for their policies.

Individuals are typically the least knowledgeable about insurance markets and the insurance mechanism. Therefore, they often need to rely on the expertise of a **producer** to help them decide which types of coverages, policy limits, and deductible levels are most appropriate for their individual circumstances. Individuals may also use direct access to insurers through Web sites or call centers to purchase their insurance products.

Individuals have few risk financing alternatives available besides retention and insurance. In addition, they are often required to purchase insurance by mortgagors and lenders. Individuals must also purchase auto liability coverage to meet state requirements because retention alternatives are financially unfeasible.

Individuals have little negotiating power in insurance transactions. Most personal lines insurance contracts are offered on an as-written basis by the insurer; therefore, very little negotiation occurs. If the individual customer is not satisfied with the policy's terms or price, typically his or her only option is to look to other insurers for coverage.

Small Business

In general, "small business" describes organizations with few employees and limited revenue. Small businesses do not usually have any employees with

Producer

Any of several kinds of insurance personnel who place insurance business with insurers and who represent either insurers or insureds, or both.

full-time risk management responsibilities. Often it is the owner, or a designated partner or manager with a limited knowledge of insurance markets, who is responsible for making risk management decisions—including the risk financing decision to purchase insurance. This decision is often made with the help of a local agent or a small local broker. Small businesses are not the typical target market for regional or national brokers because such businesses often do not generate sufficient commissions.

The insurance needs of small businesses can usually be covered by a limited number of commercial insurance policies, such as a businessowners policy, a workers compensation policy, and commercial auto policies.

Small businesses have little negotiation power with insurers and a limited number of choices when it comes to risk financing alternatives. Some small businesses have been able to join with similar organizations to form small risk retention groups or purchasing groups as alternatives to the standard commercial insurance market.

Middle Markets

Organizations that can be classified as middle markets are larger organizations with insurance needs that vary considerably according to the products or services they provide. For example, a company that manufactures airplane components will have significantly higher products liability insurance needs than a company that manufactures greeting cards.

Middle-market organizations are often large enough that their loss histories provide credible statistics for use in projecting future losses. These organizations may have a risk manager (or a small risk management department) to assist with coverage decisions. The risk managers typically use brokers to access the insurance markets and may be targeted by small (local), regional, or national brokers. They typically have some negotiating power with insurers because they have a more credible loss history, generate more premium income for the insurer, and have broker representation that can assist in their presentations to insurers.

Middle-market organizations have increasing access to risk financing alternatives such as captives, protected-cell companies, risk retention groups, and contingent capital programs.

National Accounts

The national accounts segment contains the largest organizations seeking insurance coverage. These organizations, such as Fortune 500 companies, chemical and other manufacturing organizations, and large municipalities, have the most complex insurance needs, the most comprehensive knowledge of the insurance market (with a large risk management department and regional or national broker representation), and the widest variety of risk financing alternatives.

National accounts often generate millions of dollars in premiums annually, giving national account brokers the most negotiating power with insurers. This power can be used to negotiate broader coverages, lower deductibles, higher limits, or premium reductions.

National account organizations are likely to have complex insurance programs that combine commercial insurance coverages with sophisticated retention plans and captive insurers. The use of captives by large organizations provides them with additional flexibility to bypass the standard commercial insurance market and access reinsurance markets directly. Furthermore, unique loss exposures that require extremely high limits or highly specialized underwriting consideration are often insured by a consortium of insurers that work together to provide the necessary insurance program. See the exhibit "Comparison of Insurance Consumers."

Comparison of Insurance Consumers

	Individuals	Small Business	Middle Markets	National Accounts
Insurance Needs	Least complex	Somewhat complex	Complex	Highly complex
Knowledge of the Insurance Market	Least knowledgeable	Some knowledge	Risk manager on staff—more knowledgeable	Full-time risk management department—most knowledgeable
Access Method	Direct access/ agents	Agents/small brokers	Brokers—small/ regional/national	Brokers— regional/national
Negotiating Ability	Little, if any, negotiating ability	Little, if any, negotiating ability	Some negotiating ability	Most negotiating ability
Choice of Risk Financing Alternatives	Retention only alternative	Retention/ few other alternatives	Some alternatives— rent-a-captives, risk retention groups	Wide variety of alternatives

[DA02712]

Property-Casualty Insurer Marketing Differentiations

Insurers differentiate themselves within the insurance market in various ways to meet the coverage and service needs of one or more customer groups or segments within customer groups. The level of competition for insurance customers is high. Competition is an important aspect of the functioning of insurance markets because it ensures that customers will receive competitive prices and services to meet their insurance needs.

An insurer's marketing differentiations uniquely match the characteristics of the customer groups or segments of those groups that they target for sales.

Customer Focus

To be customer focused, an insurer must understand the characteristics of specific customer groups and provide products and services that respond to those characteristics.

Customer focus is improved through **market intelligence**, which provides information that is relevant to understanding customers' current and future needs, preferences, attitudes, and behaviors. This depth of understanding leads to better customer interaction through an intensified customer-market view. Through market intelligence, the insurer understands where its insurance offer fits and discovers untapped or underserved potential markets.

Market intelligence
Information gathered and analyzed regarding a company's markets to improve competitive decision-making.

The purpose of increasing the quantity and quality of market intelligence is to accurately and confidently make decisions regarding opportunities, strategies, and market development and to assess changes in the environment that may affect the nature of the market in the future.

Products and Services

Property-casualty insurers can be further differentiated by line, for example, personal or commercial lines. Personal or commercial lines insurers may focus on property or liability insurance, package policies, or specialty lines but often sell a range of insurance products that meet the needs of their customers. Services are also tailored to respond to customers' needs identified through market intelligence.

Size

An important driver of competition is the size of the organizations in an industry. For a given number of organizations, the level of competition is usually greater if all organizations are approximately the same size than if there are two or three large organizations and many small ones. The larger companies may dominate the market, reducing competition.

An insurer's size influences its decision in the market it enters and the customer groups to which it chooses to market. If a market is dominated by a large organization, a smaller insurer might select a subsection of the market or niche market to target and tailor its product to better meet the closely defined needs of that group.

Similarly, a small insurer might avoid the national accounts market, where large written premiums must be reinsured or offset by significant reserve levels, reducing an insurer's ability to write a substantial number of other accounts.

For a small insurer that relies on a single large account, the risk of losing that account can be disproportionate to the benefits of serving a single account.

Geographic Area

Property-casualty insurers are differentiated by the geographic area they serve. Although thousands of insurers may compete in the United States, not all of them compete nationally. Many insurers are small organizations that compete in only one or a limited number of states.

An insurer's decision regarding geographic area is based on its size, its level of expertise in writing coverage in broader geographic areas, the level of competition in those areas, and its customer focus. An insurer that chooses a regional area for operation can more narrowly focus its marketing intelligence to address customers' insurance needs in the smaller area. In contrast, writing insurance nationally or internationally requires substantially more marketing intelligence to understand customers and successfully meet a wider range of insurance needs.

Distribution System

An insurer's choice of marketing system(s) is influenced by its customers' knowledge of insurance products and the risk financing alternatives available. For example, individuals generally have limited knowledge of insurance products and limited risk financing alternatives that are usually in the form of deductible selections. Insurers focused on mature customers with homes, autos, and valuable personal property may choose a distribution system based on exclusive agents or independent agents, who can assist them with coverage, limits, and deductible selections. Alternatively, an insurer targeting sales of personal auto insurance to young drivers who have a high probability of selecting the lowest-priced coverage might choose an Internet-based distribution system, which allows buyers to comparison shop in a medium in which they are comfortable.

Similar decisions regarding the selection of marketing systems are made for small-business, middle-market, and national accounts. Small businesses lack sufficient personnel to dedicate to risk management and insurance placement tasks; therefore an independent-agent distribution system is appropriate to provide that assistance. As accounts grow larger and have risk management staff to make selection decisions or work with brokers for coverage selection, broker-based distribution systems might be the selected option.

Unique Factors that Shape the Insurance Marketplace

All marketplaces are influenced by changes in the economy, such as business cycles, interest rates, and rates of unemployment as well as changing consumer demographics and social pressures, which gradually require shifts in operations, products, and distribution systems.

The property-casualty insurance marketplace is also shaped by unique economic forces, regulatory controls, and technology demands that set the parameters within which insurers must operate. Underwriting cycles, as well as the financial shock of unanticipated catastrophic losses, further shape the marketplace. Within this changing environment, insurers adjust to maintain the competitive dynamic required for the functioning of the marketplace.

Economic Forces

Property-casualty insurers manage a narrow margin of underwriting profitability to remain competitive. Inflation is a factor in increasing the costs of losses and the costs of an insurer's operations. Similarly, the availability of reinsurance influences the price and the cost of insurer operations. Investment earnings frequently offset high losses and rising costs. When investment earnings are diminished or the prospect of catastrophe losses increase, insurers must raise premiums to sustain risk-appropriate rates of return.

Many companies invest reserve funds to gain investment earnings. The importance of investment earnings to a property-casualty insurer's profitability is a key feature of the industry. Insurers operations are frequently dependant on investment earnings because premiums are held competitively low to attract customers.

Regulatory Controls

State-based insurance regulations stipulate the financial requirements that insurers must sustain to operate within a state and the marketing conduct to which insurers must adhere. In this way, insurance regulation is a stabilizing control that ensures the sustainability of insurance companies and their ability to reliably provide compensation for insureds' losses and fair treatment to insureds in business practices.

Insurance regulatory controls are a marketplace feature unique to the insurance industry creating an environment where a minimum standard of practice is required by all competitors.

Demands for Technology

The demand for technology is a powerful factor in the insurance marketplace because of the computer networks that interconnect insurers and producers as well as the technological connections between insurers and customers through the Internet. Producers complete applications and access insureds' information through computer networks to facilitate service. Customers obtain coverage information and compare premium quotations through insurers' Web sites or sites that provide quotes from multiple insurers.

The primary demand for technology in these marketing applications is ease of use. Both producers and customers are drawn to user interfaces that are easy to understand and navigate. This requires significant engineering to provide point-of-use instruction and easy user operation.

Underwriting Cycles

Underwriting cycles
A cyclical pattern of insurance pricing in which a soft market (low rates, relaxed underwriting, and underwriting losses) is eventually followed by a hard market (high rates, restrictive underwriting, and underwriting gains) before the pattern again repeats itself.

Underwriting cycles, a key feature in the insurance marketplace, create additional competitive shifts to which insurers continuously adapt. Because underwriting cycles have numerous causes, they have varying duration and depth. As a result, insurers must also adapt as the cycle patterns reveal themselves to remain competitive.

Approaches vary among companies, but insurers are collectively challenged when books of business are shuffled as competitors' premiums rise and fall. Insurers may decide to change insurance prices with the cycles or maintain a more consistent pricing philosophy throughout the cycle. In response to either decision, the underwriting cycles create dynamic balancing challenges to maintain profitability.

Unanticipated Catastrophic Losses

Insurers maintain reserves and reinsurance to pay catastrophe losses. However, catastrophes of unanticipated severity can cause losses that exceed maximum anticipated losses. These exceptional losses can result from disasters such as record-breaking hurricane losses, terrorist attacks, and oil spills, or extraordinary tort awards and class action lawsuits. Unplanned losses can result in insurer insolvencies, withdrawal of insurers from geographic markets, and reinsurance shortages.

In any year, an insurer is challenged to price a product for which the loss-cost can only be estimated. In years of extraordinary catastrophes, the market must respond with improved catastrophe ratemaking and forecasting that anticipates even greater unforeseen events.

INSURER MARKETING ACTIVITIES

Marketing is an insurer's information portal to insurance customers. Through this portal, insurers gather information about customers, make decisions about segments of customers whose needs they can address, and disseminate information to existing and prospective customers.

An insurer's marketing activities are focused on information gathering, synthesis, and dissemination. The goal is the development of products for groups of customers with results that meet the insurer's strategies and objectives.

Activities performed by marketing can be divided into these categories:

- Marketing research
- Market development
- Marketing information
- Marketing planning
- Product development
- Advertising and promotion
- Customer and public relations
- Sales fulfillment

Marketing Research

Marketing research is the systematic gathering and analyzing of data to assist in making decisions. Marketing research cannot guarantee success, but it can improve an insurer's chances of making correct decisions.

Marketing research is typically done on a project basis with a stated objective, research design, data collection, analysis, and formal report. Effective marketing research results include conclusions and implications or recommendations. Ideally, cost-benefit measures are used to track the value of information developed from the various studies. Decisions based on the research are then implemented and evaluated on a cost-benefit basis. See the exhibit "Market Research Project Examples."

Market Research Project Examples

- Test prospecting sources through wholesale clubs to determine whether the concept is worthy of prototype development and pilot testing on a larger scale
- Determine why policies lapse or are terminated by policyholders and the cost-benefit of implementing a conservation program to retain those policyholders
- Examine the insurance purchase behaviors of first-time car owners to determine what actions are needed to attract those customers
- Identify the relationship between a policyholder's claim experience and retention of the policyholder through subsequent renewals
- Use secondary data from the U.S. Government's Standard Industrial Classification (SIC) coding system combined with Metropolitan Statistical Areas (MSAs) to identify businesses within the insurer's preferred business types and geographic areas for targeted advertising

[DA06195]

Insurers use increasingly sophisticated marketing research methods to gather meaningful information, such as customer profiles, product preferences, and refinements to improve distribution channels. One important result of this research is the development of market segments in which the insurer will compete for customers.

Market Research Methods

The best marketing research is conducted as scientifically as possible. A researcher should strive for objectivity, eliminating preconceptions and bias to the extent possible. The research may consist of qualitative studies, such as **focus groups** and observer impressions, and quantitative studies that use survey research techniques and statistical analysis of the data included in corporate databases.

Focus group

A small group of customers or potential customers brought together to provide opinions about a specific product, service, need, or other issue.

The two broad categories of market data are secondary data and primary data. Research typically begins with secondary data, which is data collected by other parties, because it is immediately available at little or no cost. Many research questions can be answered at minimal expense from secondary data before the more costly primary data research is conducted, requiring the collection of data first-hand by the insurer. Primary data collection is more expensive, but it addresses issues specific to the marketing research project.

Predictive analytics

Statistical and analytical techniques used to develop models that predict future events or behaviors.

Increasingly, insurers are applying **predictive analytics** to improve the outcome of market research. The forms of predictive models applied in analytics vary depending on the behavior or event they are predicting.

Most predictive models generate a score, with the higher score indicating a higher likelihood that the given behavior or event will occur. Predictive scores are typically used to measure the risk or opportunity associated with a specific customer or transaction. These evaluations assess the relationships between many variables to estimate risk or response.

Predictive analytics models are used in many aspects of marketing. For example, insurers can use models to examine the purchasing patterns of insurance customers and can use the resulting information to increase the marketing function's hit ratio and retention ratio. An insurer could also use models to answer specific questions, such as, "What characteristics of small businesses result in the most profitable commercial insurance accounts?" Variables such as premium size, geography, business type, years in business, and form of ownership could affect the profitability of an account. A predictive model would weigh the importance of each relevant variable to provide an estimate of the likely profitability of each characteristic.

Insurers can take advantage of additional applications for predictive analytics in marketing:

- Cross-selling—identifying existing policyholder groups to whom efforts to sell additional policies will be most successful
- Target marketing—defining and refining marketing efforts on a specific group of customers
- Individualized customer support—tailoring customer support to specific customers' needs
- New agent contracting—determining which characteristics of exclusive and independent agents result in the most successful market penetration
- Designing and evaluating marketing campaigns—defining aspects of advertising efforts that result in the highest response rates from prospective customers

Market Segmentation

Insurers use **market segmentation** to differentiate themselves from other insurance providers to meet the needs of customer groups. **Target marketing** is a practice of more closely defining a group of customers within a market segment. **Niche marketing** is a well-defined, often small marketing segment of the population that has specific needs. For example, a market segmentation of small businesses can include a target market of retailers with a niche market of jewelry stores.

By identifying the characteristics of the various market segments, target market groups, and niches, insurers build a competitive advantage through designing specific marketing strategies to address their needs and characteristics. The more closely a group of customers is defined, the more closely an insurer can develop expertise regarding the customers' needs and tailor products and services to meet those needs. As groups are more closely defined, insurers are less likely to encounter competition for that group than in the open market.

- Behavioristic segmentation—the division of a total consumer market by purchase behavior
- Geographic segmentation—the division of markets by geographic units
- Demographic segmentation—the division of markets based on demographic variables, such as age, gender, education, occupation, ethnicity, income, family size, and family life cycle
- Psychographic segmentation—the division of markets by individuals' values, personalities, attitudes, and lifestyles

Marketing management defines logical market segments that provide an opportunity for success. Criteria regarding the segments, as well as the external environment and the insurer's internal environment, are considered in

Market segmentation
The process of identifying and dividing the groups within a market that share needs and characteristics and that will respond similarly to a marketing action.

Target marketing
Focusing marketing efforts on a specific group of consumers.

Niche marketing
A type of marketing that focuses on specific types of buyers who are a subset of a larger market.

the market segment selection. See the exhibit "Market Segment Selection Considerations."

Market Segment Selection Considerations

Each marketing segment should be:

- Accessible—Segments should be able to be effectively reached and served.

- Substantial—Size and purchasing power should suggest potential profitability.

- Responsive—Actions taken by the insurer should produce satisfactory results.

Internal marketing environment:

- Technical resources—What technical resources are needed to support the customers and products sold?

- Type of products sold—Do the products available meet the specific segment's needs, or do they address homogeneous needs of a larger group? What is the product fit to the market segment?

- Age of product—Do the products available meet current customer needs?

- Product mix—Do the products we will sell to this market segment help us achieve our optimum product mix?

- Distribution channels—Are our distribution channels appropriate to the characteristics of this market segment?

- Corporate ownership—Does our ownership affect our ability to obtain the sources of funds needed for growth, expansion, or financial stability to market successfully to this market segment?

- Company size and resources—Are we limited by our company size and resources to compete for customers in this market segment?

External marketing environment:

- Market segment competition—How significant is the competition within this market segment? What are the characteristics of competing insurers in this market segment (such as customer focus, size, distribution systems, and technological capabilities)?

- Economic environment—Are there issues in the current economic environment (such as inflation, investment earnings, customers' spending habits, availability and cost of employees) that affect our chances of success in this market segment?

- Social environment—What behaviors or beliefs in the population of this market segment will increase or decrease our chances of success in offering our products and services?

- Regulatory environment—Are the products and services we are proposing for this marketing segment permitted under applicable laws and regulations?

[DA06196]

Market Development

Market development activities provide leadership when an insurer enters a new market. The new market may be a new territory, a new customer type, or a new product. Other examples of major projects managed might include new approaches to selling the insurer's products or delivering Web-based applications for insurance policies.

Market development involves actions required to ensure the success of the venture, including development and implementation of a broad range of activities:

- Training programs
- Problem resolution
- Process documentation
- Funding assistance
- Technical assistance
- Public relations campaigns

The market development staff includes project managers who generate and screen ideas. Project managers are also skilled in developing project scope documents, decision grids, task outlines, progress reports, and project reports. The project manager usually handles only one or two projects at a time because of the high level of effort and responsibility involved in each project.

Marketing Information

Marketing information activities develop and maintain information needed in market planning to support management at all levels in answering specific questions concerning markets, customers, producers, and competitors. The marketing information function serves the company best when it can deliver timely and cost-effective information essential to decision making.

Marketing information is divided into two major types systems: internal accounting and market monitoring.

- The internal accounting system provides report and analysis capability based on transactions associated with sales activity. Much of the essential information on production, retention, and policies in force is available as a byproduct of the systems that keep track of commissions and billings.

- The market monitor system provides intelligence about the external environment to inform senior management about important developments and changing conditions. The market monitor should provide current, unfiltered, and unbiased information about customers, producers, and competitors. Customers and producers are monitored to determine their satisfaction levels with the service they receive from the insurer, and the resulting information helps the insurer shape decisions related to growth and profitability strategies. The market monitor also maintains up-to-date competitive intelligence about the strategies and actions of key competitors. Competitor monitoring also includes benchmark studies of competitors that excel in success factors crucial to a property-casualty insurer. Benchmark information helps management develop strategies for closing the gap between company performance and key competition.

Marketing Planning

Marketing planning provides the tools and facilitation skills to assist management in developing fact-based marketing plans. This activity also assists in the development and updating of the company's strategic plans.

Before introducing a new insurance product or service, the insurer completes a comprehensive marketing plan. The plan identifies the product or service to be promoted and the customers to be targeted, and it details the resources and strategies that will be used to create, price, promote, and sell the product or service. Because marketing plans affect many other insurer functions, representatives from other departments often participate in the creation or review of marketing plans.

Marketing plans are as varied as the products and services they promote. However, all plans serve the same fundamental purpose: they provide the "roadmaps" necessary to profitably and effectively acquaint sellers with potential buyers.

A marketing plan for a typical insurance product or service might include, but is not limited to, these items:

- Product proposal and sales goals—A summary of the new product's operation, a description of the unmet need the product is designed to fulfill, and summarized sales projections.
- Situational analysis—A SWOT (strengths, weaknesses, opportunities, threats) analysis of the current marketplace, including analyses of the competition; critical factors required for success; resource, technology, and training requirements; and an assessment of the existing legal and regulatory environment.
- Marketing goals—An outline of the proposed target market, including detailed sales projections and specifics as to how success will be measured.
- Marketing strategies—Plans and proposals for how the product will be developed, priced, promoted, and sold. These strategies include determining the appropriate distribution channels for products and services.
- Projected outcome—The pure loss ratio and ultimate loss ratio over a five-year period.

Product Development

An insurer's management team must decide which insurance products and services will be sold to which markets. There are many product decisions to be made, ranging from what product lines to offer to what coverages, limits, and deductibles will be included in the policy.

Insurers usually follow a series of steps in product development. See the exhibit "Product Development Steps."

Advertising and Promotion

The advertising function is responsible for managing the company's communications through mass media with its chosen target markets. The advertising program is developed to be consistent with strategic direction and marketing plans and supportive of distribution system efforts. Advertising is intended to build and reinforce the company's image as an acceptable choice in the minds of target customers.

Advertising is expensive. Insurers face a dilemma when trying to decide how much advertising is enough to communicate effectively with customers while staying within a reasonable budget. The effectiveness of marketing communications can be measured in several ways. For example, an insurer might pilot test advertising to determine its effectiveness or might also show proposed advertising to a focus group to obtain feedback.

Sales promotion reinforces the image and positioning created by the insurer's advertising efforts when carried down to the agency level. Sales promotion includes brochures used in the sales process, giveaway items promoting the insurer and the producer, and awards merchandise. Regular communications with producers and sales management, such as newsletters, may be part of the sales promotion function.

Customer and Public Relations

The customer relations function manages communications with individual customers from the home office. This functional area ensures that all written communications seen by customers are understandable and consistent in quality and tone.

The customer relations function also provides a forum for communications to the insurer initiated by customers, including complaints, suggestions, and questions. Insurers are often asked to respond to state insurance departments, which themselves are responding to consumer complaints about the insurer. Typically, a complaint is addressed to an insurer's CEO and must be addressed within a specified period, often ten working days.

The customer relations function also provides management with low-cost, high-value information about the evolving wants and needs of policyholders.

Public relations activities include communications with the public on behalf of the insurer to ensure a strong public image. Individuals performing these

Product Development Steps

1. Opportunity assessment

- Monitor market
- Identify opportunity
- Relate opportunities to business strategy
- Develop specifications
- Secure senior management approval to proceed

In the first step, market monitoring results in the identification of an opportunity for a new product. Marketing personnel evaluate the opportunity against the insurer's business strategies and continue the process if there is a successful match by developing specifications for the product and obtaining approval.

2. Development of contract, underwriting, and pricing

- Develop coverage and policy forms
- Develop guidelines for underwriting and claims
- Develop classifications
- Develop pricing structure
- Secure approval from functional managers to proceed

The second step is to develop the policy forms, guidelines, classifications, and prices in a cooperative effort across the insurer functions of underwriting, actuarial, claims, reinsurance, premium audit, and risk control. This step concludes with a tangible product plan.

3. Business forecast

- Review the product plan with profit center management
- Identify requirements for statistics
- Develop business forecast
- Secure senior management approval to proceed

In the third step, the product is submitted to an assessment of sales potential. The business forecast establishes benchmarks for evaluating the success of the product including expected premium volume, producers' participation, loss ratio, and methods of gathering data that can be used to analyze the product success or failure.

4. Regulatory requirements

- File with regulators
- Develop statistical information systems
- Communicate regulatory approval

The fourth step moves the development process to the regulatory arena. At a minimum, state regulators require notification of new policy forms, rating plans, and policy writing rules. Some states require regulatory approval of new products and changes in existing products to protect policyholder interests.

5. Distribution requirements

- Develop advertising and sales promotional information
- Develop sales training
- Plan roll-out strategy

In the fifth step, the insurer determines distribution requirements, which include the overall plan for effectively advertising and distributing the new product to targeted customers.

6. Introduction

- Implement sales training and promotion
- Measure and compare results to plan

The sixth step is the introduction of the product in one or more states with advertising and sales promotions. The results are monitored, and marketing management takes actions to improve the product performance or eliminates weak products in this step if the actual results do not achieve profitability objectives.

[DA06197]

activities may also be called communications or media specialists. They design and implement a consistent description of the organization and its actions.

The public relations staff provides periodic information to the insurer's community about the organization's activities. They may communicate with employees to request their participation in media or educational events, such as conferences or public speaking engagements, to ensure that the insurer's messages are included and a positive image provided. In times of crisis, the public relations staff coordinates a consolidated message to the media to provide consistent communication as well as to respond to negative publicity, if necessary.

Sales Fulfillment

Sales fulfillment is the satisfactory delivery of the products and services that result from the product development activity. Fulfillment of a product plan affects many of an insurer's functional areas. For example, the introduction of policies and services to target high-net-worth individuals as a market segment must include participation by customer service, underwriting, claims, and other functional areas. The senior management team must communicate the goals, strategies, and action plans to all areas of the organization. Each functional area must determine the impact of the plan on operations, budget, and performance standards.

Milestones should be established for the functional areas with metrics to periodically check the results of the marketing plan and take action in any area where goals are not met. If sales results do not meet projections, marketing analysis can help determine why and recommend improvements.

INSURANCE DISTRIBUTIONS SYSTEMS AND CHANNELS

Insurers are driven by competition to address customer preferences. In this environment, insurers examine the efficiency of their distribution systems and channels.

No single approach to distribution meets the needs of all insurers and all insurance customers. Insurers select one or a combination based on overall business plans and their core products and services.

Insurers use many types of **distribution systems** based on their organizational structure, business and marketing plans, growth goals, technological capabilities, staffing, and other resources necessary to support the selected system(s). The principal characteristics that distinguish one distribution system from another include the relationship to the insurer and customers, ownership of

Distribution system

The necessary people and physical facilities to support the sale of insurance products and services.

expirations, compensation methods, and functions performed. These are the main insurance distribution systems:

- Independent agency and brokerage marketing systems
- Exclusive agency marketing system
- Direct writer marketing system

Insurers use these common distribution channels to promote products and services as well as to communicate with existing and prospective insureds:

- Internet
- Call centers
- Direct response
- Group marketing
- Financial institutions

Mixed marketing systems include more than one distribution system or channel.

Independent Agency and Brokerage Marketing Systems

The independent agency and brokerage marketing system uses agents and brokers who are independent contractors rather than employees of insurers. These independent agents and brokers are usually free to represent as many or as few insurers as they want.

Independent Agents and Brokers

An independent agency is a business, operated for the benefit of its owner (or owners), that sells insurance, usually as a representative of several unrelated insurers. An insurance broker is an independent business owner or firm that sells insurance by representing customers rather than insurers. Brokers shop among insurers to find the best coverage and value for their clients. Because they are not legal representatives of the insurer, brokers are not likely to have authority to commit an insurer to write a policy by binding coverage, unlike agents, who generally have binding authority. See the exhibit "Similarities and Differences Between Brokers and Agents."

The independent agency or brokerage can be organized as a sole proprietorship, a partnership, or a corporation.

Agency expiration list

The record of an insurance agency's present policyholders and the dates their policies expire.

One of the main distinguishing features between independent agents and brokers and other distribution systems is the ownership of the **agency expiration list**. If the insurer ceases to do business with an agency, the agency has the right to continue doing business with its existing customers by selling them insurance with another insurer. The ownership of expiration lists is an

Similarities and Differences Between Brokers and Agents

In practice, despite the technical distinctions between brokers and independent agents, the differences are minimal. Both brokers and independent agents are intermediaries between insurers and insurance buyers, and both collect premiums from insureds and remit them to insurers. Both are in the business of finding people with insurance needs and selling insurance appropriate to those needs. In fact, the same person can act as an agent in one transaction and as a broker in another. A person acts as an agent when placing insurance with an insurer for which he or she is licensed as an agent but may act as a broker when placing insurance with other agents or insurers.

[DA06205]

agency's most valuable asset. An independent agency has the right to sell its expiration lists to another independent agent.

Compensation for independent agents and brokers is typically in two forms:

- A flat percent commission on all new and renewal business submitted
- A contingent or profit-sharing commission based on volume or loss ratio goals

Disclosure of the commission paid to agents or brokers enhances the transparency of the transaction for prospective insureds.

The independent agents and brokers distribution system is flexible; it can meet the needs of many different insurance customers, and it is spread geographically across the United States. In addition to insurance placement, agents and brokers may also assist their customers in establishing and managing self-insurance programs, implementing risk control measures, and determining alternatives or supplements to insurance. Some have draft authority from their insurers to settle small first-party losses.

National and Regional Brokers

National and regional brokers generally represent commercial insurance accounts that often require sophisticated knowledge and service. In addition to insurance sales, large brokerage firms may provide extensive risk control, appraisal, actuarial, risk management, claim administration, and other insurance-related services that large businesses need. These brokers are often equipped to provide services that are supported by offices in multiple states.

Large insurance brokerage firms operate regionally and nationally, and some even operate internationally. They can tailor insurance programs for customers or groups of customers who require a particular type of coverage for multiple locations. Examples of such programs are insurance marketed to attorneys, which might include professional liability coverage, and an insurance program for daycare centers that includes coverages for exposures related to child care.

The brokers receive negotiated fees for the services they provide, or they receive fees in addition to commissions, subject to state regulation.

Independent Agent Networks

Independent agent networks, also known as agent groups, agent clusters, or agent alliances, consist of independent agencies and brokerages that join together to gain advantages normally available only to large national and regional brokers. Agent networks operate nationally, regionally, or locally and, in the majority of cases, allow their agent-members to retain individual agency ownership and independence.

By combining individual agency forces into a single selling, negotiating, and servicing unit, an agent network can offer many benefits to its agent members, including these:

Countersignature laws

Laws that require all policies covering subjects of insurance within a state to be signed by a resident producer licensed in that state.

- Obtaining access to an increased number of insurers
- Meeting **countersignature law** requirements for businesses in multiple states
- Combining premium volume to meet insurer requirements for profit-sharing
- Generating additional sales income
- Receiving preferred agency contracts
- Facilitating agency succession planning
- Providing expertise in risk management services
- Offering expertise in financial planning services
- Enabling resource sharing and expense reduction
- Increasing market share

Managing General Agents (MGAs)

Managing general agent (MGA)

An authorized agent of the primary insurer that manages all or part of the primary insurer's insurance activities, usually in a specific geographic area.

Managing general agents (MGAs), also referred to as management general underwriters (MGUs), serve as intermediaries between insurers and the agents and brokers who sell insurance directly to the customer, similar to wholesalers in the marketing system for tangible goods.

The exact duties and responsibilities of an MGA depend on its contracts with the insurers it represents. MGAs can represent a single insurer, although they more commonly represent several insurers. Some MGAs can be strictly sales operations, appointing and supervising subagents or dealing with brokers within their contractual jurisdiction. That jurisdiction can be specified in terms of geographic boundaries, types of insurance, or both. A few MGAs cover large multi-state territories, although frequently only for specialty insurance.

An insurer operating through an MGA reaps several advantages:

- A low fixed cost—An insurer who writes business through an MGA does not have to staff and support a branch office. The MGA is usually compensated by a commission override on business its subagents sell. The MGA, by writing relatively small amounts of business for each of several insurers, generates enough commissions to cover its expenses and earn a profit. The MGA might also receive a contingent commission based on the profitability or the volume of business it writes.

- Specialty expertise—MGAs develop expertise in particular markets and design insurance programs in collaboration with the insurers they represent. Specialty insurance programs offered by MGAs include those for such diverse risks as petroleum distributors, fire departments, horse farms, employment practices liability, and directors and officers liability.

- Assumption of insurer activities—Full-service MGAs can provide an array of benefits to their subagents and brokers, including claim administration, information management, risk control and risk management services, underwriting and marketing services, policy issuance, and premium collection. Insurers must supervise the MGAs that represent them, and most states regulate the MGAs' activities and contracts.

Surplus Lines Brokers

Most agents and brokers are limited to placing business with licensed (or admitted) insurers. The circumstances under which business can be placed with an unlicensed (or nonadmitted) insurer through a surplus lines broker vary by state. Normally, a reasonable effort to place the coverage with a licensed insurer is required.

The agents and brokers, who must be licensed to place surplus lines business in that state, might be required to certify that a specified number (often two or three) of licensed insurers have refused to provide the coverage. In some states, agents and brokers must provide letters from the insurers rejecting the coverage. Some state insurance departments maintain lists of coverages that are eligible for surplus lines treatment without first being rejected by licensed insurers. Some states also maintain lists of eligible surplus lines insurers, requiring producers to place business only with financially sound insurers.

Surplus lines brokers have access to insurers that have the capacity to provide the needed insurance, which might not be available from insurers licensed to do business in the state. This provides a system for insuring specific customers or exposures:

- A customer that requires high limits of insurance
- A customer that requires unusually broad or specialized coverage
- An unusual or a unique loss exposure

- Loss exposures requiring a tailored insurance program
- An unfavorable loss exposure, such as a poor claim history or difficult-to-treat exposures

Surplus lines brokers work to ensure that 1) coverage is placed only with eligible nonadmitted insurers, 2) the customer's unique or unusual requirements can be met by the prospective surplus lines insurer, and 3) the financial security of the surplus lines insurer is properly evaluated.

Surplus lines brokers, like national or regional brokers, maintain their independence, can represent multiple insurers, and are compensated based on a portion of the commissions generated by the business they write.

Exclusive Agency Marketing System

The exclusive agency marketing system uses independent contractors called exclusive agents (or captive agents), who are not employees of insurers. Exclusive agents are usually restricted by contract to representing a single insurer. Consequently, insurer management can exercise greater control over exclusive agents than over independent agents. However, some exclusive agency companies allow their agents to place business with other insurers if the exclusive agency insurer does not offer the product or service needed.

Exclusive agents are usually compensated by commissions. During initial training, some of them might receive a salary, a guaranteed minimum income, or income from a drawing account. In terms of overall compensation, insurers in the exclusive agency system commonly pay one commission rate for new business and another, lower rate for renewal business. For exclusive agents, the focus is on new-business production, and a reduced renewal commission rate encourages sales and supports growth.

Exclusive agents typically do not own expirations as independent producers do. However, some insurers that market through the exclusive agency system do grant agents limited ownership of expirations. Usually, such ownership of expirations applies only while the agency contract is in force. When the agency contract is terminated, the ownership of expirations reverts to the insurer. The insurer might be obligated to compensate the agent for the expirations upon termination of the agency contract; however, the agent does not have the option of selling the expirations to anyone other than the insurer.

The exclusive agency insurer handles many administrative functions for the exclusive agent, including policy issuance, premium collection, and claim processing. Exclusive agents might offer loss adjustment services similar to those offered by independent agents and brokers; however, these agents might be restricted in their ability to offer some risk management services to their customers.

Direct Writer Marketing System

The direct writer marketing system uses sales agents (also known as sales representatives) who are employees of the insurers they represent. The sales agents sell insurance for the insurer at office locations provided by the direct writer insurer. Sales agents in the direct writer system may be compensated by salary, by commission, or by both salary and a portion of the commission generated.

Because sales agents are employees of the insurers they represent, they usually do not have any ownership of expirations and, like exclusive agents, are usually restricted to representing a single insurer or a group of insurers under common ownership and management.

Sometimes a customer needs a type of policy not available from the direct writer insurer that the sales agent represents. When this happens, the sales agent may act as a broker by contacting an agent who represents another insurer and apply for insurance through that agent, who usually shares the commission with the direct writer sales agent. Insurance sold in this manner is referred to as brokered business.

Sales agents are largely relieved of administrative functions by their employers. These insurer-assumed functions include policy issuance, premium collections, and claim functions. One key ingredient in direct writer insurer relationships with their sales agents is active encouragement to develop new business. Relieving the producer of nonselling activities and compensating at a lower renewal rate help accomplish this goal.

Distribution Channels

The distribution channels used by insurers and their representatives are conduits for contacting and establishing communication with their customers and prospective customers. Insurers' increasing use of multiple distribution channels has been driven by technology and customer preference. Customers who are familiar with the prompt, efficient delivery and service they obtain from other product providers expect the same type of response from their insurers.

Insurers and their representatives are constantly searching for ways to quote and issue policies more quickly, while keeping costs reasonable. At the same time, customers desire competitive pricing, customized insurance products, and high-quality service.

Internet

As a distribution channel, the Internet can be used to varying degrees by all parties to the insurance transaction: the insurer, its representatives, and the customer. Interactions range from exchanges of e-mail to multiple-policy quoting, billing, and policy issuance. See the exhibit "Internet Benefits and Challenges for Insurers."

Internet Benefits and Challenges for Insurers

Insurers and their representatives derive a number of benefits from having an Internet presence:

- Reduced costs for underwriting and claim processing services because of lower overhead arising from automated operations

- Streamlined business practices—the need for fewer employees to conduct direct sales

- Increased brand awareness

- Broadened marketing potential

- Lead-generation and cross-selling opportunities for all products, not just property-casualty insurance

However, Internet sales present challenges for insurers:

- Regulation requirements—Purchases transacted completely via the Internet may not meet regulatory compliance requirements that a licensed agent consummate the sale.

- Assumed cost advantage—Consumers perceive that a product bought over the Internet will be less expensive than the same product bought from a producer. These assumptions are not necessarily valid.

- Competitors are only a click away—If customers do not like what they see, they are likely to click to another, more favorable Web site.

- Quoting capabilities—An insurer's ability to quote easily and quickly is critical, because about 50 percent of users will simply move to another Web site if the quoting mechanism is too complicated.

- Availability of information—Many customers do not fully understand insurance products; the Internet largely eliminates intermediaries who would otherwise provide explanations and advice. Therefore, a Web site should maintain a frequently asked questions (FAQ) section and/or a "live contact."

- Extent of services provided—The insurer or producer must determine whether its Internet presence will be sales-only or a combination of sales and service.

- The informed consumer—Information about many insurance products and their prices is available to customers, shifting the customer's focus toward price rather than service.

- Security concerns—Some customers are unwilling to transmit personal and financial information over the Internet.

- Web site content—Information posted on the Web site must be kept fresh, interesting, and accessible.

[DA06206]

The customers' ability to access information has increased dramatically, as has the speed of the insurance transaction itself. Customers also interact with insurers on the Internet via Web-based insurance distributors, also called insurance portals or aggregators. These portals deliver leads to the insurers whose products they offer through their Web sites. Portals benefit customers by offering the products and services of many insurance providers on one Internet site, in a form of cyberspace one-stop shopping. Although the leads that portals generate must subsequently be screened and fully underwritten by the insurers accepting the coverage, those leads can increase market share and brand awareness.

Call Centers

Call centers sell insurance products and services through telemarketing. Call centers operate with customer service representatives, touch-tone service, or speech-enabled (voice response) service.

The best-equipped call centers can replicate many of the activities of producers. In addition to making product sales, call center staff can (1) respond to general inquiries, (2) handle claim reporting, (3) answer billing inquiries, and (4) process policy endorsements. In some cases, a customer can begin an inquiry or a transaction on the Internet, then have a customer service representative at the insurer's call center access the Internet activity and answer the inquiry or conclude the transaction.

Direct Response

The **direct response distribution channel** markets directly to customers. No agent is involved; rather the direct response relies primarily on mail, phone, and/or Internet sales. Although this distribution channel is also called direct mail, customers can also contact insurers via telephone and the Internet. Direct response relies heavily on advertising and targeting specific groups of affiliated customers.

With direct response, commission costs, if any, are greatly reduced. However, a disadvantage is that advertising costs are typically higher. The customer can sometimes "opt out" and speak with a call-center customer service representative or be assigned to a local servicing office.

> **Direct response distribution channel**
>
> An insurance distribution channel that markets directly to the customer through such distribution channels as mail, telephone, or the Internet.

Group Marketing

Group marketing sells insurance products and services through call centers, the Internet, direct mail response, or a producer to individuals or businesses that are all members of the same organization. Distributing insurance to specifically targeted groups is known by a number of terms, including these:

- **Affinity marketing**—Insurers target various customer groups based on profession, interests, hobbies, or attitudes. For example, the insurer, agent, or broker might decide to market personal insurance products to university alumni groups, chambers of commerce, bar associations, or users of

> **Affinity marketing**
>
> A type of group marketing that targets various groups based on profession, association, interests, hobbies, and attitudes.

a particular credit card. Coverage is sometimes offered at a discounted premium.

- Mass marketing or mass merchandising—Insurers design an offer for their policies to large numbers of targeted individuals or groups. Coverage is frequently offered at a discounted premium, and the insurer retains the right to underwrite each applicant, with guaranteed policy issuance available as an option.

- Worksite marketing or payroll deduction—Employers can contract directly with an insurer or through a producer to offer voluntary insurance coverage as a benefit to their employees. Worksite marketing (or "franchise marketing") of insurance is used frequently to offer personal insurance coverages or optional life, health, and disability coverage to employees. Premiums for employees are usually discounted and are deducted (after tax) from employees' paychecks, with an option available for employees to pay for the coverage in another way.

- Sponsorship marketing—A trade group sponsors an insurer in approaching a customer group. The sponsor participates in the profitability of the program. For example, a wholesale club sponsors an insurer to market to club members for a fee based on the success of the program.

The success of any marketing group program depends on the support of the sponsoring organization or employer, offering discounted premiums, treating the employees as a preferred group for underwriting purposes, and facilitating program operation, particularly from the employer's administrative perspective.

Financial Institutions

Insurers and producers can elect to market their products and services through a bank or another financial services institution, either exclusively or through using additional distribution channels. Marketing arrangements can range from simple to complex. For example, a small insurance agency may place an agent at a desk in a local bank, or a large insurer may form a strategic alliance with a regional or national financial holding company to solicit customers.

The prospect of diversifying into new markets appeals to many financial institutions. In fact, some financial institutions have expanded into insurance by participating in renewal rights arrangements by which they purchase only a book of business and not the liabilities of an agency or insurer.

Insurers view financial institutions as beneficial strategic partners because of these qualities:

- Strong customer base
- Predisposition to product cross-selling
- Strength at processing "transactions"
- Efficient use of technology for database mining geared to specific products and services

To sustain distribution relationships with financial institutions, insurers must focus on providing saleable products and efficient administration and support while also protecting their professional presence in financial institutions from competitors.

Mixed Marketing System

The term mixed marketing system refers to an insurer's use of more than one distribution system or channel to attract a wider range of customers. For example, some insurers that traditionally sold insurance only through independent agents are now also using direct response. Conversely, some direct writing insurers, seeking to expand their business, have entered into agency agreements with independent agents in some areas.

Similarly, insurers are using multiple distribution channels to more effectively communicate with customers.

Combining insurance distribution systems and channels requires consideration of several issues:

- Maintaining consistent customer communications—An insurer must send customers the same clear, consistent message about its products and services. In addition, the insurer's internal communications must be consistent across marketing systems and distribution channels, and workflows, data management, and underwriting standards must be communicated.

- Providing a consistent customer experience—The experience a customer has when interacting with an insurer must be consistent across all marketing distribution systems and channels. Customers' access to the Internet and its wealth of information has created knowledgeable, demanding insurance customers with distinct preferences and expectations.

- Matching the type of insurance with an appropriate distribution system and channel—Some marketing systems are more suitable than others based on the product being sold. Personal insurance and commercial insurance vary in terms of the product's level of complexity and in terms of the expertise insurers, agents, and brokers need in order to properly sell the product to consumers and service it after the sale. The combination of systems and channels selected depends on the particular type of insurance to be sold.

FUNCTIONS OF INSURANCE PRODUCERS

The functions insurance producers perform vary widely from one marketing system to another and from one producer to another within a given marketing system. Generally, producers are the initial contact with insurance customers and provide expertise and ongoing services.

Insurance producers represent one or more insurance companies. As a source of insurance knowledge for their customers, producers provide risk management advice, solicit or sell insurance, and provide follow-up services as customers' loss exposures or concerns change.

Insurance producers typically perform these functions:

- Prospecting
- Risk management review
- Sales
- Policy issuance
- Premium collection
- Customer service
- Claim handling
- Consulting

Prospecting

Virtually all producers prospect. Prospecting involves locating persons, businesses, and other entities that may be interested in purchasing the insurance products and services offered by the producer's principals. Prospects can be located using several methods:

- Referrals from present clients
- Referrals from strategic partners, such as financial institutions and real estate brokers
- Advertising in multimedia and direct mail
- Interactive Web sites
- Telephone solicitations
- **Cold canvass**

Cold canvass

Contacting a prospect without an appointment.

Large agencies and brokerages may have employees who specialize in locating prospective clients. However, a producer is typically responsible for his or her own prospecting. Insurers might also participate in prospecting, especially in the exclusive agent and direct writer marketing systems.

Risk Management Review

Risk management review is the principal method of determining a prospect's insurance needs. The extent of the review varies based on customers and their characteristics.

Individual or Family

For an individual or a family, the risk management review process might be relatively simple, requiring an interview or completion of a questionnaire that assists in identifying the prospect's loss exposures, which are often associated with property ownership and activities. Using the results of the interview or questionnaire, the producer suggests methods of risk control, retention of loss exposures, and insurance.

Businesses

The risk management review process for businesses is likely to be more complex because they have property ownership, products, services, employees, and liabilities that are unique to the size and type of organization. Substantial time is required to develop and analyze loss exposure information for a large firm with diversified operations.

A **loss run** report can guide the producer in helping the business owner develop risk management plans, track the results of current risk management efforts, identify problem areas, and project costs. Loss runs include, at a minimum, lists of losses and their total cost. More comprehensive loss runs provide details that can lead to additional questions and suggest areas of risk management improvement. For example, comprehensive workers compensation loss runs reveal lag times in reporting, creating potentially higher costs. These reports can also indicate litigation rate; a high rate can be an indication of poor communication between employers and employees or overall employee dissatisfaction.

Loss run
A report detailing an insured's history of claims that have occurred over a specific period, valued as of a specific date.

Sales

Selling insurance products and services is one of the most important activities of an insurance producer because it is essential to sustaining the livelihood of the agency or brokerage. Commission on business sold is the principal source of income for producers, and the ownership of policy expirations applicable to the business sold is the principal asset of an insurance agency.

Steps in the sales process include contacting the prospective client, determining the prospect's needs, preparing and presenting a proposal, and closing the sale.

Policy Issuance

At the producer's request, insurers issue policies and their associated forms, either mailing them directly to policyholders or sending them to the producer for delivery. In paperless environments, the policies and forms may be produced on a compact disk or placed in an Internet filing cabinet along with endorsements, bills, and loss history information.

Some producers use their own agency management systems to generate computer-issued policies on site.

Premium Collection

Producers who issue policies may also prepare policy invoices and collect premiums. After deducting their commissions, they send the net premiums to the insurers, a procedure known as the **agency bill** process. For business that is agency billed, there are three widely used methods of transmitting premiums to the insurer:

Agency bill

A payment procedure in which a producer sends premium bills to the insured, collects the premium, and sends the premium to the insurer, less any applicable commission.

- Item basis—The premium (less commission) is forwarded to the insurer when the producer collects it or when it becomes due. This is the least complex of the three methods. The producer is usually not required to pay the insurer until the premium has been collected.

- Statement basis—The insurer sends a statement to the producer showing the premiums that are due. The producer is obligated to pay the premiums indicated as due or to show that the statement is in error.

- Account current basis—The producer periodically prepares a statement showing the premiums due to the insurer, after deducting appropriate commissions, and transmits that amount to the insurer. The agency contract indicates how often the producer must submit the account current statement. The most common interval is monthly. The producer must pay the insurer when the premium is due, even if the policyholders have not paid the producer.

To give the producer some protection against policyholders' late payments, premiums are usually not due to the insurer until thirty or forty-five days after the policy's effective date. This delay also permits the producer to invest the premiums collected until they are due to the insurer. The resulting investment income can be a significant part of the producer's remuneration.

Agency billing may be used for personal insurance policies, but it is more commonly used with large commercial accounts. For small commercial accounts and the vast majority of personal insurance, the customer is usually directed to send premium payments to the insurer, bypassing the producer in a procedure known as the **direct bill** process.

Direct bill

A payment procedure in which the insurer assumes all responsibility for sending premium bills to the insured, collecting the premium, and sending any commission payable on the premium collected to the producer.

Customer Service

Most producers are involved to some degree in customer service. For independent agents and brokers, value-added services and the personalization of insurance packages are what differentiate them in the marketplace. For the producer of a direct writer, service might consist of providing advice, taking an endorsement request over the phone, providing coverage quotes, or transferring a policyholder who has had a loss to the claim department.

Producers are expected to facilitate contacts between policyholders and the insurer including these:

- Responding to billing inquiries
- Performing customer account reviews

- Engaging in field underwriting, such as obtaining loss reports, insurance credit scores, and motor vehicle reports
- Answering questions regarding existing coverage and additional coverage requirements
- Corresponding with premium auditors and risk control representatives

Claim Handling

All producers are likely to be involved to some extent in handling claims filed by their policyholders. Because the producer is the policyholder's principal contact with the insurer, the policyholder naturally contacts the producer first when a claim occurs.

In some cases, the producer might simply give the policyholder the telephone number of the claim department and possibly the name of a person to speak with. Alternatively, the producer might obtain some basic information about the claim from the policyholder, relay it to the insurer, and arrange for a claim representative to contact the policyholder. Frequently, insurers issue their policies with a "claim kit" that informs their policyholders about the proper procedures and contacts.

Some producers are authorized by their insurers to adjust some types of claims. Most often, the authorization is limited to small first-party property claims. However, a few large agencies or brokerages that employ skilled claim personnel might be authorized to settle large, more complex claims. The limitations on the producer's claim-handling authority should be specified in the agency contract.

Claim handling by qualified producers offers two major advantages: quicker service to policyholders and lower loss adjustment expenses to the insurer. Conversely, if the producer is not properly trained in how to handle claims, overpayment of claims can offset the savings.

Consulting

Many producers offer consulting services, for which they are paid on a fee basis. Such services are usually performed for insureds, but they may also be performed for noninsureds or for prospects. Services might be provided for a fee only, or the producer might set a maximum fee to be reduced by any commissions received on insurance written because of the consulting contract.

Laws in some states prohibit agents from receiving both commission and a fee from the same client. Fees are billed separately from any insurance premiums due, whereas commissions are included in the premium totals billed.

DISTRIBUTION SYSTEM AND CHANNEL SELECTION FOR INSURANCE MARKETING

Any firm that sells a product has a distribution system to carry out some of its marketing functions. Distribution systems for intangible products, such as insurance, are more flexible and adaptable than those for tangible products because they are not constrained by large investments in physical facilities. This intangibility gives insurers options to meet a wide array of customers' needs as well as their own operational needs. Distribution channels provide even more options for communicating with existing and potential customers.

Insurance distribution systems and channels provide the necessary people, physical facilities, and conduits for communication between insurers and customers.

An insurer usually selects a distribution system before it begins writing business. Changing distribution systems for existing business can be difficult and possibly expensive because of existing agency contracts and possible ownership of expirations. However, an insurer that has previously chosen one distribution system might decide to use a different one when entering a new territory or launching a new insurance product. In contrast, distribution channels selected by insurers and their representatives are more readily changeable.

The key factors in selecting distribution systems and channels are based on customers' needs and characteristics as well as the insurer's profile. See the exhibit "Distribution Systems and Conduits for Insurance Marketing."

Distribution Systems and Conduits for Insurance Marketing

Distribution systems consist of the necessary people and physical facilities to support the sale of the insurance product and services.	Independent Agency and Brokerage Marketing System • Independent agents and brokers • National and regional brokers • Independent agent networks • Managing general agents (MGAs) • Surplus lines brokers Exclusive agency marketing system Direct writer marketing system
Distribution channels are communication conduits for promoting and servicing products as well as communicating with existing and prospective insureds.	• Internet • Call centers • Direct response • Group marketing • Financial institutions

[DA06250]

Customers' Needs and Characteristics

The needs and characteristics of customers—both existing and those in target markets—are key factors in an insurer's selection of distribution systems and channels because their satisfaction drives their purchase decisions. These are examples of customer needs and characteristics:

- Products and services—What are customers' expectations regarding coverage, accessibility, price, and service? Customers with low service expectations, such as purchasers of minimum-coverage personal auto insurance, may be satisfied with the ease of comparison shopping over the Internet for direct writers' policies. Conversely, a large commercial account's risk manager will seek the expertise of an agent or broker to provide advice, assist in coverage placement, and respond to changing needs as the organization's internal and external environments change.

- Price—To what degree is the price of products and services a factor for customers? Some consumers' paramount concern is the price of insurance. Others are concerned with price to a degree, but are unlikely to make changes if they are satisfied with a product. Still others seek risk management alternatives, including insurance that will minimize the adverse effects of losses for the organization over the long term.

- Response time—How quickly can inquiries and transactions be processed? Customers routinely experience speedy financial services transactions and increasingly expect the same response from their insurance providers.

For those customers whose inquiries and transactions can be addressed by telephone or via the Internet, a variety of distribution systems and channels can meet those needs. However, speed can be an issue in attracting commercial accounts that demand extensive services if producers are not in the territory of the businesses' facilities.

Insurer's Profile

An insurer's profile—including its strategies and goals, strengths, existing and target markets, geographic location, and the degree of control over producers it requires or desires—frames the business and marketing environments within which it operates. The insurer must evaluate these key factors in selecting distribution systems and channels.

Insurer Strategies and Goals

An insurer's strategies, defined by high-level organizational goals, provide purposeful direction for the organization. These strategies and goals often address issues regarding market share size, sales, service, and the markets in which the insurer competes. They may also relate to acquisitions, strategic alliances, or mergers.

Changes in market strategies or aggressive goals can be a catalyst for an insurer to reexamine its distribution systems and channels if current approaches are inadequate to achieve required results. For example, a regional personal lines insurer that contracts independent agents as a distribution system may adopt a strategy to expand to the national market. Rather than contracting additional independent agents in the expanded geographic territory, the insurer assumes the role of a direct writer and uses the Internet as a distribution channel to reach customers through Web-based insurance distributors. This approach can reduce long-term costs and accelerate the insurer's market-share growth.

Insurer Strengths

Organizations evaluate their internal and external environments to assess their strengths and weaknesses compared to external opportunities and threats. Determining where its strengths lie, an insurer selects those distribution systems and channels that maximize its opportunities to capture market share and minimize its weaknesses. In doing so, the insurer may analyze these factors:

- Financial resources—The initial fixed cost of entering the market through the exclusive agency system or direct writer system is greater than doing so through the independent agency system. The insurer must hire, train, and financially support the direct writer and exclusive agency producers at substantial cost before they become productive. Similarly, Internet-based distribution channels have high start-up costs for supporting information systems. In comparison, the cost of conducting a direct response campaign can be much lower. Consequently, insurers with the financial resources to initiate distribution systems and channels with high start-up costs have the option of competing in markets that are best served by those marketing methods. Insurers that lack the financial resources to cover those start-up costs may be limited in the target markets they enter.

- Core capabilities—Core capabilities include the abilities of an organization's staff, processes, and technology. An insurer whose strength is successfully servicing large, complex commercial accounts can capitalize on the firm's core capabilities. Complex commercial accounts require personalized service and are well served by agents and brokers, who can provide advice and ongoing service to expand the types of businesses to which the insurer markets or its geographic market.

- Expertise and reputation of producers—Because agents and brokers are the point of contact with customers, their expertise and reputation can be a crucial strength or weakness for the insurer. The level of expertise required of a producer depends on the lines of insurance written. Specialty target markets, such as international manufacturing, high-net-worth individuals, and large public entities require knowledgeable and prominent producers to advise them. Having producers with those attributes in a direct writer distribution system allows the insurer to expand into similar or secondary markets. An insurer attempting to enter specialty markets without the skill base on staff must compete for agents and brokers who can provide the needed expertise and reputation.

Existing and Target Markets

The characteristics of an insurer's existing book of business should be considered in any change in distribution system or channel. If agents or brokers own the expirations for current accounts, the insurer must either give up that business and start over or purchase the expirations from producers. Either option might be expensive, depending on the quality of the existing business.

Disruptions in communication channels can also cause changes in communication patterns that can result in policyholder dissatisfaction and lost accounts. As a result, insurers change market systems and channels for existing customers with great caution. However, some catalysts are sufficiently threatening to cause an insurer to change marketing approaches. For example, an insurer that is losing market share to an aggressive new competitor has ample incentive to change its approach to better address customers' needs and characteristics.

Customers' needs and characteristics are driving factors for an insurer that is considering changing its marketing approach or adopting a mixed marketing approach for a new target market. If an insurer's existing distribution systems and channels do not adequately address the customers' profiles as determined through marketing research, the insurer is less likely to gain market share. To make an optimum choice, the insurer carefully balances the cost of changing its distribution systems and channels with expected benefits resulting from the new accounts it will write.

Geographic Location

The geographic location of existing policyholders or target markets is a key concern in selecting a distribution system and channels because the insurer's fixed costs of establishing an exclusive agent or direct-writer agent in a territory are substantial. Exclusive agent or direct writer marketing systems can be successful only when a sufficient number of prospects exist within a relatively small geographic area.

Because the cost of appointing an independent agent or using the direct response system is generally lower than the cost of appointing an exclusive or direct-writer agent, those systems can be used in sparsely populated areas or when the target market customers are widely dispersed. Some insurers that traditionally used either the exclusive agency system or the direct writer system have elected to use the independent agency system in rural areas and small towns because of the lower startup costs.

Degree of Control Required

The extent of control the insurer wants to exercise over its marketing operations may influence its choice of a distribution system:

- An insurer can exercise the greatest control over producers in the direct writer system. Under that system, the producer is an employee of the company, and the company can exercise control over both the results achieved and the methods used to achieve them. For example, an insurer can specify the number and type of new applications the producer must submit each month (results) as well as the marketing approaches the producer can use (methods).

- Under both the agency and brokerage system and the exclusive agency system, the producers are independent contractors; therefore, the insurer can control only the results they produce, not the methods by which they produce them. For example, an insurer can specify the number and type of new applications the producer must submit each month (results). However, the agent or broker can engage in any advertising or marketing campaign to achieve those results that do not violate insurance regulations or contractual agreements with the insurer.

- Producers are not involved in the direct response system. Consequently, the insurer has complete control of its distribution system.

Degree of control becomes important in meeting the needs of some customers. For example, pharmaceutical manufacturers require specialized risk management advice that includes a risk control recovery plan following the release of a tainted drug or defective medical device to the public. The insurer may wish to control the nature of the risk management alternatives recommended to those insureds that foster transparency and immediate response following products liability losses.

Other insurers value discretion in the producers who represent them. For example, an insurer that specializes in church insurance or distributes insurance through religious affinity groups will expect to have some control over the producers' use of social media (Web-based sites used to exchange content with selected or broad audiences through the Internet). A producer's indiscretions posted in public forums can cause an insurer to lose accounts. Therefore, the insurer might choose a direct writer distribution system under which producers are employees and subject to the insurer's guidelines for media use.

SUMMARY

The property-casualty insurance marketplace is the unique environment where insurance customers' needs and characteristics are addressed by insurers. Key features of the insurance marketplace include these:

- Insurance customers who come to the market with varying insurance needs, knowledge of insurance, access methods, negotiating ability, and choice of risk financing alternatives
- Insurers that compete in the market for customers based on differentiations in customer focus, products and services, size, geographic area, and distribution system
- Marketplace features that are unique to the industry, such as economic forces, regulatory control, demands for technology, underwriting cycles, and unanticipated catastrophic losses

An insurer's marketing activities collectively gather and analyze information so that the organization can make optimal and informed choices in market segmentation, efficient product development, and effective communication to customers to promote product sales. Marketing activities include:

- Marketing research
- Market development
- Marketing information
- Marketing planning
- Product development
- Advertising and promotion
- Customer and public relations
- Sales fulfillment

Insurance distribution systems consist of the necessary people and physical facilities to support the sale of insurance products and services. The main insurance distribution systems are these:

- Independent agency and brokerage marketing system
- Exclusive agency marketing system
- Direct writer marketing system

Insurers use distribution channels to promote products and services as well as to communicate with existing and prospective insureds. These are common insurance distribution channels:

- Internet
- Call centers
- Direct response
- Group marketing
- Financial institutions

No one distribution system or channel is best; insurers may select a mixed marketing system based on their marketing and business needs.

Insurance producers represent one or more insurance companies and perform the following typical functions:

- Prospecting
- Risk management review
- Sales
- Policy issuance
- Premium collection
- Customer service
- Claim handling
- Consulting

Insurers should evaluate various factors when selecting distribution systems and channels. These factors include customers' needs and characteristics, such as the products and services they require, the price they are willing to pay, and the response time they require.

Insurers' profiles serve as guidelines that affect their choice of distribution systems and channels. Insurers' profiles include their strategies and goals, strengths, existing and target markets, geographic location, and the degree of control required.

Direct Your Learning ▶▶

The Underwriting Function

Educational Objectives

After learning the content of this assignment, you should be able to:

▶ Describe the purpose of underwriting.

▶ Describe the underwriting activities typically performed by line and staff underwriters.

▶ Describe the importance of compliance with underwriting authority in individual account selection.

▶ Describe the constraining factors considered in the establishment of underwriting policy.

▶ Describe the purposes that underwriting guidelines and underwriting audits serve.

▶ Describe the steps in the underwriting process.

▶ Explain how an insurer's underwriting results are measured and how financial measures can be distorted.

The Underwriting Function

PURPOSE OF UNDERWRITING

Insurance companies assume billions of dollars in financial risk annually, risk that is transferred to them from individuals and businesses via the insurance transaction. Insurance underwriters, using the underwriting process and various supporting underwriting tools, are employed by insurers to assess both their new and current business. An insurance company's overall profitability can depend significantly on the quality of its underwriting.

Underwriting has multiple purposes. The overarching purpose is to develop and maintain a profitable book of business for the insurer. Underwriting is crucial to an insurer's success; underwriting goals flow directly from the insurer's corporate strategies and objectives. Favorable underwriting results are necessary for an insurer's ability to sustain profitable growth.

To achieve profitability, the underwriting function serves additional purposes:

- Guarding against adverse selection
- Ensuring adequate policyholders' surplus
- Enforcing underwriting guidelines

Guarding Against Adverse Selection

Underwriters are an insurer's guard against adverse selection. These are examples of adverse selection:

- Some property owners in areas prone to coastal storms purchase windstorm coverage or increase their limits only before a hurricane season, when they expect severe losses.
- A disproportionate percentage of property owners in an earthquake-prone zone purchase earthquake insurance, as compared to property owners in areas less prone to earthquakes.

Underwriters minimize the effects of adverse selection by carefully selecting the applicants whose loss exposures they are willing to insure, charging appropriate premiums for the applicants that they do accept with premiums that accurately reflect the loss exposures, and monitoring applications and books of business for unusual patterns of policy growth or loss.

Policyholders' surplus

Under statutory accounting principles (SAP), an insurer's total admitted assets minus its total liabilities.

Capacity

The amount of business an insurer is able to write, usually based on a comparison of the insurer's written premiums to its policyholders' surplus.

Underwriting authority

The scope of decisions that an underwriter can make without receiving approval from someone at a higher level.

Line underwriter

Underwriter who is primarily responsible for implementing the steps in the underwriting process.

Staff underwriter

Underwriter who is usually located in the home office and who assists underwriting management with making and implementing underwriting policy.

Ensuring Adequate Policyholders' Surplus

An insurance company must have adequate **policyholders' surplus** if it wishes to increase its written premium volume. An insurer's **capacity** is limited by regulatory guidelines and often by its own voluntary constraints, which are frequently more conservative than those imposed by regulators. If an insurer's underwriting practices generate policy premiums that exceed losses and expenses, the policyholders' surplus will increase, thereby increasing capacity.

Underwriters ensure the adequacy of policyholders' surplus by adhering to underwriting guidelines, making certain that all loss exposures are correctly identified, and charging adequate premiums for the applications that are accepted.

Enforcing Underwriting Guidelines

Underwriting guidelines reflect the levels of **underwriting authority** that are granted to varying levels of underwriters, producers, and managing general agents (MGAs). Exactly who has what level of underwriting authority varies considerably by insurer and by type of insurance.

Underwriting ensures that applicants accepted adhere to underwriting guidelines. If loss exposures, risks, or policy limits on an application exceed an underwriter's authority, he or she will seek approval through supervisory and management ranks within the underwriting department.

UNDERWRITING ACTIVITIES

In insurance organizations, underwriting responsibilities are delegated by members of senior management to line and staff underwriters who coordinate the day-to-day risk selection decisions and the management-level underwriting activities. This coordinated effort is crucial to the achievement of the insurer's profitability goals.

There is no standard method to organize insurer underwriting activities. However, insurers commonly distinguish between **line underwriters** and **staff underwriters**. The focus of line underwriters is evaluating new submissions and renewal underwriting. Line underwriters work directly with insurance producers and applicants. The focus of staff underwriters is managing the risk selection process. Staff underwriters work with line underwriters and coordinate decisions with other departments to manage the insurance product, pricing, and guidelines. See the exhibit "Underwriting Activities Performed by Line and Staff Underwriters."

Line Underwriting Activities

Line underwriters evaluate individual accounts for acceptability and execute underwriting policy by following practices and procedures outlined by staff

Underwriting Activities Performed by Line and Staff Underwriters

Line underwriters	Staff underwriters
• Select insureds	• Research the market
• Classify and price accounts	• Formulate underwriting policy
• Recommend or provide coverage	• Revise underwriting guidelines
• Manage a book of business	• Evaluate loss experience
• Support producers and insureds	• Research and develop coverage forms
• Coordinate with marketing efforts	• Review and revise pricing plans
	• Arrange treaty reinsurance
	• Assist others with complex accounts
	• Conduct underwriting audits
	• Participate in industry associations
	• Conduct education and training

[DA06264]

underwriters. The specific tasks line underwriters perform may vary by insurer; however, most line underwriters are responsible for these major activities.

Select Insureds

Line underwriters select new and renewal accounts that meet the criteria established in underwriting guidelines. Underwriters' effective account selection is essential to attaining these goals:

- Avoiding adverse selection
- Charging adequate premiums for accounts with a higher-than-average chance of loss
- Selecting better-than-average accounts for which the premium charged will be more than adequate
- Rationing an insurer's available capacity to obtain an optimum spread of loss exposures by location, class, size of risk, and line of business

Line underwriting selection activities are continuous. Line underwriters monitor accounts to ensure that they continue to be acceptable. A line underwriter may cancel or nonrenew an account if risk control recommendations made at the policy's inception are not implemented or if the insured fails to take corrective action to control loss frequency.

Classify and Price Accounts

Account classification is the process of grouping accounts with similar attributes so that they can be priced appropriately. Line underwriters are responsible for ensuring that all the information needed for classification is obtained and that accounts are priced properly. In many insurance companies, line underwriters do not personally perform either the classification or the pricing task. However, they are accountable for the correct accomplishment of these activities.

The price charged must not only be adequate to permit the insurer to continue to write profitable business, but also it must be competitive. A consequence of misclassification is that the premium charged is not commensurate with the risk transferred. Accounts that are misclassified and priced too low are a bargain for the policyholder, but the insurer receives premiums that are inadequate for the loss exposures they assume. In contrast, policyholders may move accounts that are overcharged, because of a misclassification, to another insurer once the policyholder discovers a better price.

Insurers submit classification plans to state insurance regulators; those who do not implement their classification plan as filed are subject to possible fines. For some lines of business and in some states, line underwriters may not have any discretionary latitude in policy pricing. In other lines of insurance, the line underwriter can use individual rating plans to apply debits and credits to the account that will adjust the premium to reflect the characteristics of the individual insured. The line underwriter must be sure that the account characteristics justify the adjustment and must document that it complies with the insurer's individual rating plan filed with regulatory authorities.

Recommend or Provide Coverage

Determining an applicant's coverage needs is generally the responsibility of the insurance agent or broker or the insured's risk manager. However, some applicants select alternative risk treatment for some exposures but choose to use insurance for other exposures. Line underwriters support the producers and policyholders by inquiring about an insured's risk management program to ensure that they are using other risk management techniques to address gaps in insurance coverage. For example, an applicant requests a Building and Personal Property Coverage Form (BPP) with the Causes of Loss—Broad Form to insure the loss exposures of a manufacturing location. While reviewing the applicant's operations as described in the inspection report, the underwriter discovers that the applicant has a loss exposure to property in transit that would not be covered adequately by these coverage forms. The underwriter discusses this loss exposure with the producer and offers to provide the coverage in an inland marine policy, thereby broadening the insured's coverage.

Sometimes an underwriter must narrow an insured's coverage. Producers often request broader coverage for the loss exposures of a particular applicant than the insurer is willing to provide. Rather than decline the application, the underwriter may offer a more limited form of coverage involving higher deductibles or covering fewer causes of loss. The producer has an opportunity to provide reduced coverage that may be acceptable to the applicant rather than reject the applicant altogether.

Line underwriters also have a role in ensuring that applicants obtain the coverage they request. The task of providing requested coverage often involves collaboration with the producer. Because each account is unique, producers and applicants often want to know how coverage will respond to a specific type of loss. Line underwriters respond to these requests by explaining the types of losses the coverage forms are designed to cover and the endorsements that must be added to provide the coverage desired.

For some complex or unique accounts, the line underwriter will draft a **manuscript policy** or endorsement that is worded to address the specific coverage needs of the insured. For most accounts, however, the line underwriter simply ensures that the policy is being issued with the appropriate forms and endorsements that provide the requested coverage.

Manuscript policy

An insurance policy that is specifically drafted according to terms negotiated between a specific insured (or group of insureds) and an insurer.

Manage a Book of Business

Frequently, line underwriters are expected to manage a book of business. Underwriting management usually reinforces departmental goals through individual line underwriters. An insurer, for example, may want to limit the number of workers compensation policies it sells that are not accompanied by an account's other insurance. The line underwriters are expected to help achieve that goal by writing workers compensation without supporting business only on a selective basis.

Some insurers also make line underwriters responsible for the profitability of a book of business accepted from a producer, or written in a territory or line of business. The line underwriter works to ensure that each book of business achieves established goals such as product mix, loss ratio, and written premium.

Support Producers and Customers

The services that line underwriters are expected to provide to producers and customers vary by insurer. Some insurers rely on customer service departments to respond to routine inquiries and requests. Insurers operating through independent agents often rely on their sales force to perform many policy service functions. Because customer service activities and underwriting are often interwoven, line underwriters have an active interest in ensuring that producers' and insureds' needs are met.

Line underwriters are usually directly involved with producers in preparing policy quotations. Producers devote significant time and expense to prospecting new accounts. This effort is lost if the insurer develops a quote that will not "win" the account.

Coordinate With Marketing Efforts

Insurer marketing efforts should conform with the insurer's underwriting policy. Producers are discouraged from submitting accounts that are clearly outside the insurer's underwriting guidelines. Likewise, line underwriters should not reject applications that meet insurer underwriting guidelines simply because of an underwriter's bias against a particular class of business.

Supporting the insurer's marketing objectives can have broader implications for the line underwriter. Some insurers rely on special agents or field representatives to market the insurer and its products to agents and brokers. Some insurers have blended the responsibilities of special agents and line underwriters into the position of production underwriter. Production underwriters usually confer personally with producers and assist them with developing accounts that are acceptable to the insurer.

Staff Underwriting Activities

Staff underwriters work closely with underwriting management to perform activities essential for profitable risk selection. These major activities are common to staff underwriters.

Research the Market

Insurers must continually research fundamental issues such as which markets the insurer should target. Staff underwriters typically share these research responsibilities with actuarial and marketing departments. Research includes an ongoing evaluation of these items:

- Effect of adding or deleting entire types of business
- Effect of expanding into additional states or retiring from states presently serviced
- Optimal product mix in the book of business
- Premium volume goals

Formulate Underwriting Policy

Underwriting policy (underwriting philosophy)

A guide to individual and aggregate policy selection that supports an insurer's mission statement.

Staff underwriters formulate and implement underwriting policy. An insurer's **underwriting policy**, also referred to as underwriting philosophy, guides individual and aggregate decision making. For most insurers, underwriting policy translates an insurer's mission and goals into specific strategies that, in turn, determine the composition of the insurer's book of business. Underwriting policy is communicated through underwriting guidelines.

Staff underwriters work with employees from other departments to formulate underwriting policy. Actuarial, claim, risk control, and marketing departments each have responsibilities so closely tied to those of the underwriting department that their involvement is needed to make most changes to underwriting policy.

No single underwriting policy is appropriate for all insurers. Insurers often develop their underwriting policy within the context of these markets they serve:

- Standard market—Better-than-average accounts for which the average premium is more than adequate

- Nonstandard market—Higher-risk applicants who are charged a higher-than-average premium

- Specialty market—Accounts that have unique needs, such as professional liability, that are not adequately addressed in the standard market

Beyond these broad market selections, the goals for an insurer's book of business and resulting underwriting policy may be established by types of insurance and classes of business to be written; territories to be developed; or forms, insurance rates (such as filed rates and surplus lines pricing), and rating plans to be used.

Revise Underwriting Guidelines

Staff underwriters are usually responsible for revising underwriting guidelines so that they accurately reflect changes in underwriting policy. The underwriting guides identify the major elements that line underwriters should evaluate for each type of insurance.

Some underwriting guides include systematic instructions for handling particular classes of commercial accounts. Such guides may identify specific hazards to evaluate, alternatives to consider, criteria to use when making the final decision, ways to implement the decision, and methods to monitor the decision. The guides may also provide pricing instructions and reinsurance-related information. Other insurers use underwriting guides that are less comprehensive. For example, they may list all classes of business and indicate their acceptability by type of insurance. Codes are then assigned to indicate the desirability of the loss exposure and the level of authority required to write the class of business.

Evaluate Loss Experience

Staff underwriters evaluate an insurer's loss experience to determine whether changes should be made in underwriting guidelines. Insurance products that have losses greater than those anticipated are usually targeted for analysis. Staff underwriters research loss data to determine the specific source of the excess losses. Part of this research includes an analysis of insurance industry loss experience that may reveal trends affecting the insurer's products. Based on their evaluation, staff underwriters, usually with the agreement of other key departments, adjust the insurer's underwriting guidelines.

Research and Develop Coverage Forms

Insurance advisory organizations have a significant role in the development of commonly used coverage forms. Insurance advisory organization-developed coverage forms are usually developed by coverage experts who consider the scope of coverage being provided, coverage provided by other policies, and legal restrictions that apply to coverage-form development.

Staff underwriters work cooperatively with the actuarial and legal departments to develop new coverages and modify existing coverage forms developed by advisory organizations. As in other businesses, insurers develop new coverages to meet changing consumer needs and competitive pressures. Additionally, insurers modify existing coverages so that the coverage being provided by the insurer will respond as anticipated. An unfavorable court decision, for example, may cause an insurer to rewrite a coverage form to limit the coverage being provided.

Review and Revise Pricing Plans

Staff underwriters review and update rates and rating plans continually, subject to regulatory constraints, to respond to changes in loss experience, competition, and inflation.

Historical loss data are gathered by the insurer or by advisory organizations to develop prospective loss costs. Then, each insurer examines its own operational profit and expense requirements. Staff underwriters combine prospective loss costs with an insurer-developed profit and expense loading to create a final rate used in policy pricing. Production efficiencies or a superior account-selection process is reflected in lower expense loadings, which can lead to a pricing plan that provides the insurer with a competitive advantage.

For those coverages for which advisory organizations do not develop loss costs, the insurer must develop its own rates. In such situations, reviewing and revising rating plans become even more crucial to ensure that the loss costs adequately reflect **loss development** and **trending**.

Arrange Treaty Reinsurance

Staff underwriters are responsible for securing and maintaining **treaty reinsurance**. Their responsibility includes determining the insurer's needs for reinsurance, selecting reinsurers, negotiating the terms and conditions of reinsurance treaties, and maintaining the insurer's relations with its treaty reinsurers.

For many insurers, treaty reinsurance limitations are directly reflected in their underwriting guidelines. For example, staff underwriters specify in the underwriting guidelines the maximum coverage limits that can be offered because

Trending
A statistical technique for analyzing environmental changes and projecting such changes into the future.

Loss development
The increase or decrease of incurred losses over time.

Treaty reinsurance
A reinsurance agreement that covers an entire class or portfolio of loss exposures and provides that the primary insurer's individual loss exposures that fall within the treaty are automatically reinsured.

higher limits of treaty reinsurance were not purchased. Additionally, some types of accounts cannot be insured because the insurer's treaty reinsurance agreements specifically exclude the account's classification. For commercial property accounts, many staff underwriters maintain a line authorization guide, which serves as a control on the property limits accepted based on the treaty reinsurance agreement.

Assist Others With Complex Accounts

Staff underwriters often serve as consultants to other underwriters. Generally, staff underwriters have significant first-hand line underwriting experience. They regularly see complex and atypical accounts, unlike most line underwriters. Staff underwriters also function as "referral underwriters"—that is, when an application exceeds a line underwriter's authority, a referral underwriter can review and approve the risk.

Conduct Underwriting Audits

Staff underwriters are often responsible for monitoring line underwriter activities and adherence to underwriting authority by conducting **underwriting audits**. The audits focus on proper documentation; adherence to procedure, classification, and rating practices; and conformity of selection decisions to the underwriting guide and bulletins.

Staff underwriters also monitor underwriting activity by analyzing statistical results by type of insurance, class of business, size of loss exposure, and territory. Statistical data show the extent to which underwriting goals are met, but they do not conclusively demonstrate whether the results are a product of implementing the insurer's underwriting guidelines.

Underwriting audit
A review of underwriting files to ensure that individual underwriters are adhering to underwriting guidelines.

Participate in Industry Associations

Many insurers are members of national and state associations that address insurance industry concerns. Additionally, insurers often share in the operating of residual market mechanisms, such as automobile joint underwriting associations and windstorm pools. Staff underwriters typically represent the insurer as a member of these organizations. Staff underwriters may also serve on an advisory organization's committees that study standard policy forms and recommend changes.

Conduct Education and Training

Staff underwriters are usually responsible for determining the education and training needs of line underwriters. Sometimes, these training needs are addressed through a formal training program that all newly hired underwriters must complete. At other times, the training need is transitory and is provided through classes that address a specific underwriting issue or procedure.

Some training needs are met through programs provided by the insurer's human resources department. However, staff underwriters often develop courses and serve as instructors in technical insurance subjects.

UNDERWRITING AUTHORITY

The levels of underwriting authority granted to underwriters reflect their experience and knowledge in risk selection decisions. Authority may also be granted to producers and managing general agencies. Compliance with levels of authority is crucial to maintaining the appropriate controls over risk selection.

Underwriters have different levels of authority. As their levels of underwriting authority increase, the responsibility for accurately applying experience and judgment also increases. Compliance with levels of authority ensures that the insurer accepts applicants within its underwriting policy.

Before accepting an applicant, a line underwriter must determine whether he or she has the necessary underwriting authority to make the decision. The underwriting authority granted typically varies by position, grade level, and experience.

Underwriting authority requirements are usually communicated to an underwriter through the insurer's underwriting guidelines. A notation next to a specific classification in the underwriting guide, for example, might indicate that a senior underwriter must review and approve an application from that classification before it is processed further. Depending on the concerns that underwriting management places on a classification, underwriting approval might be required from the line underwriter's branch manager or a staff underwriter at the home office. Another approach to controlling underwriting authority is to specify in the underwriting guidelines the policy limits at which the accounts must be submitted to a higher authority.

In addition, some rating plans, such as composite rating, might require higher underwriting authority to review the merits of the account. Similarly, certain endorsements or coverage forms named in the underwriting guidelines might require specific levels of authority for approval.

Compliance with levels of underwriting authority ensures that the individuals making application-selection decisions have the experience necessary to evaluate which risks are acceptable and the unique knowledge required to judge risk for specialized lines of insurance.

To place controls on levels of underwriting authority, insurers generally grant authority in these ways:

- Underwriters gain underwriting authority with experience and positive results.

- Producers may gain underwriting authority based on experience, profitability, and contractual arrangements. Authority, if granted, may be only for certain types of insurance within specific limits of coverage.

- Managing general agents (MGA), when appointed, assume decentralized underwriting authority, which capitalizes on an MGA's familiarity with local conditions.

Insurers with conservative internal underwriting philosophies may not grant underwriting authority to any entities beyond their own internal underwriters. Specialty insurers, such as those offering surety bonds, aviation insurance, and

Managing Underwriting Authority

Some insurers centralize their line underwriters and, consequently, their underwriting authority. Others insurers extend underwriting authority to producers, believing it to be more expeditious to empower their producers to exercise underwriting authority, as well as to pay claims, within a defined range. Normally, not all of an insurer's producers are granted underwriting authority, but those who are usually receive additional commission to compensate for the additional expenses incurred.

The primary responsibility of producers is to sell insurance. Many insurers, however, rely on their producers to "field underwrite" accounts. This means that the producer knows the types of accounts the insurer is interested in writing and submits those that are of the quality the insurer is usually willing to accept. Producers who can perform account selection before submitting the account to the insurer are often referred to as front-line underwriters. These producers save insurers from having to evaluate accounts that the insurer's underwriters will ultimately reject.

Even those producers who do not have underwriting authority know the types of accounts the insurer is actively seeking. Special agents or production underwriters, as well as periodic communication with the insurer, keep producers informed of the products the insurer wants to sell. Some insurers provide their producers with their underwriting guidelines so that issues regarding account acceptability can be determined before submission.

Many insurers use information systems to manage underwriting authority. Rather than physically submit an account for others to review, insurer information systems are able to provide those people who have approval responsibility with sufficient information to approve or disapprove the referred account. Information systems can also make it possible to identify those classifications that the insurer is making exceptions to write, despite restrictions in the underwriting guidelines, and who is requesting them. Depending on the type of insurance, insurers use automated underwriting systems to encode underwriting guidelines. This is especially common for personal lines insurance, such as auto and homeowners insurance.

livestock mortality insurance, also usually centralize underwriting authority. See the exhibit "Managing Underwriting Authority."

CONSTRAINTS IN ESTABLISHING UNDERWRITING POLICY

An insurer's underwriting policy promotes the type of insurance anticipated to produce a growing and profitable book of business. However, various factors constrain what an underwriting policy can accomplish.

An insurer's senior management formulates an underwriting policy that guides individual and aggregate underwriting decisions. Underwriting policy determines the composition of the insurer's book of business, including the lines and classes of business that the insurer will offer, the amount of business the insurer is willing to write, the rating philosophy and forms the insurer will apply, and the territories to be developed. See the exhibit "Lines of Business."

Lines of Business

The National Association of Insurance Commissioners (NAIC) Annual Statement, which is prescribed for financial reporting in all states, divides property and liability coverages into thirty-three separate lines of business. Examples of these statutory prescribed lines of business are fire, allied lines, workers compensation, commercial multiperil, and ocean marine. A complete listing appears in the NAIC Annual Statement. Insurers must report premiums, losses, and expenses by the lines of business, but related lines of business are combined to create insurance products. For example, an insurer who markets commercial auto insurance will have to offer the following NAIC Annual Statement lines of business: commercial auto no-fault (personal injury protection), other commercial auto liability, and commercial auto physical damage. When they use the term "line of business," underwriters are mentally combining several related NAIC Annual Statement lines into a single reference, such as "commercial auto."

[DA06262]

All insurers would like to obtain profitable results, and most insurers would like to expand premium writings or increase market share. However, when these changes involve the insurer's underwriting policy, major constraining factors must be considered. See the exhibit "Constraints of Underwriting Policy."

Financial Capacity

An insurer's financial capacity refers to the relationship between premiums written and the size of the policyholders' surplus, which is an insurer's net worth. That relationship is crucial in evaluating insurer solvency. The NAIC has developed a series of financial ratios that it uses in conjunction

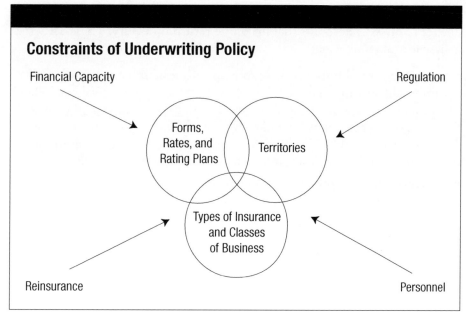

Constraints of Underwriting Policy

Financial Capacity

Regulation

Forms, Rates, and Rating Plans

Territories

Types of Insurance and Classes of Business

Reinsurance

Personnel

[DA06270]

with analytical evaluations to identify insurers that should receive additional solvency surveillance from regulators. The **premiums-to-surplus ratio** is one of those key ratios, and it is considered too high when it exceeds 300 percent, or 3-to-1.

Insurers may exceed the premiums-to-surplus ratio through the rapid growth of premiums written. Because of conservative **statutory accounting principles** used in insurance, rapid growth results in a reduction in policyholders' surplus to pay for expenses generated by that growth. This constraint often precludes premium expansion unless the insurer purchases reinsurance or obtains more capital. See the exhibit "Statutory Accounting Rules."

Premium-to-surplus ratio or capacity ratio

A capacity ratio that indicates an insurer's financial strength by relating net written premiums to policyholders' surplus.

Statutory accounting principles (SAP)

The accounting principles and practices that are prescribed or permitted by an insurer's domiciliary state and that insurers must follow.

Statutory Accounting Rules

Since the beginning of state oversight of insurance, insurance regulators have been primarily concerned with insurer solvency. The NAIC was formed in 1871 to reduce the inconsistencies and confusion caused by multiple state financial reporting requirements. The accounting system that evolved to satisfy insurance regulations is called statutory accounting principles (SAP). SAP are conservative accounting rules designed to determine whether an insurer can meet its obligations to policyholders. Most other businesses use generally accepted accounting principles (GAAP), which focus on the organization as an ongoing enterprise, for financial reporting.

[DA06271]

Return on equity (ROE)

A profitability ratio expressed as a percentage by dividing a company's net income by its net worth (book value). Depending on the context, net worth is sometimes called shareholders' equity, owners' equity, or policyholders' surplus.

Insurers recognize the limitations of their capacity and seek to write those lines of business or accounts that maximize **return on equity**. These activities help realize maximization:

- Setting return thresholds—Insurers typically establish a return-on-equity threshold against which capacity allocation proposals are evaluated. If, for example, the insurer wants a 10 percent return on equity and the sale of workers compensation insurance in a specific state is expected to generate a 12 percent return on equity, then the insurer should expand into this territory and line of business if no better opportunity is present.

- Redirecting focus on target business classes—An insurer may decide to stop pursuing one class of business and, instead, use capacity elsewhere. For example, an insurer may stop pursuing a class of general liability accounts whose losses exceed expectations and develop a marketing campaign for accounts that offer more promising returns.

- Adjusting underwriting policy based on jurisdiction—Jurisdiction can be relevant in this process. For example, inadequate rate levels and rising benefit levels for claimants in many states led some insurers to develop restrictive acceptance criteria for workers compensation submissions.

Effective account selection allows insurers to be commercially viable by rationing their available capacity to obtain an optimum spread of loss exposures by territory, business class, size of risk, and line of business. See the exhibit "Return on Equity."

Return on Equity

Return on equity is not only a benchmark for employing capacity but also a fundamental measure of insurer profitability. This financial ratio relates net operating gain (after taxes) as a percentage of prior-year capital and surplus.

The SAP and GAAP approaches to calculating return on equity differ, as shown below:

$$\text{Return on equity (SAP basis)} = \frac{\text{Net income}}{\text{Average policyholders' surplus}}$$

$$\text{Return on equity (GAAP basis)} = \frac{\text{Net income}}{\text{Average owners' equity}}$$

Stock insurers calculate both ratios since they report their financial performance using both SAP and GAAP bases. Mutual insurers calculate return on equity using only the SAP basis.

Return on equity is also a key financial ratio used by insurance regulators for solvency surveillance. An acceptable value for return on equity falls between 5 and 15 percent.

[DA06272]

Regulation

States promulgate insurance regulations that take the form of statutes enacted by state legislatures and regulations adopted by the state insurance department. Insurance is a highly regulated industry, and regulations directly and indirectly affect most insurer activities.

Regulation affects underwriting policy in several ways:

- Insurers must be licensed to write insurance in each state in which they write insurance.
- Rates, rules, and forms must be filed with state regulators.
- Some states specifically require underwriting guidelines to be filed.
- If consumer groups believe that the insurance industry has not adequately served certain geographic areas, regulatory focus on insurance availability can lead to requirements to extend coverage to loss exposures that an insurer might otherwise not write.

State regulators perform **market conduct examinations** to ensure that insurers adhere to the classification and rating plans they have filed. When a market conduct examination discloses deviations from filed forms and rates or improper conduct, the insurer is subject to penalties.

Insurance regulation is not applied uniformly across states. In some jurisdictions, insurers may be unable to get rate filings approved, or approval may be granted so slowly that rate levels are inadequate relative to rising claim costs. Some insurers have chosen to withdraw from states that impose regulations they consider too restrictive.

Market conduct examination

An analysis of an insurer's practices in four operational areas: sales and advertising, underwriting, ratemaking, and claim handling.

Personnel

Insurers require the talent of specialists to market their products effectively, underwrite specific lines of business, service their accounts, and pay claims for losses that occur. An insurer must have a sufficient number of properly trained underwriters to implement its underwriting policy. No prudent insurer, for example, would pursue the highly technical lines of aviation, surety, or ocean marine insurance without a sufficient number of experienced underwriting specialists in those lines of business.

In addition to having personnel with the necessary skills, the insurer must have the personnel where they are needed. As a general practice, an insurer should obtain premiums from a broad range of insureds to create the widest possible distribution of loss exposures. However, regulatory expenses and policyholder service requirements make it difficult for small insurers to efficiently handle a small volume of business in many widespread territories. Insurers must have a sufficient volume of premium to operate efficiently in an area. Information systems are especially important; many growth plans have been abandoned because computer support was not available.

Reinsurance

The availability and cost of adequate reinsurance can influence underwriting policy. Reinsurance treaties may exclude certain types of insurance or classes of business, or the cost of reinsurance may be prohibitive.

Reinsurers are also concerned about the underlying policy forms offered by the insurer. A reinsurer may not have any reservations about an insurer's use of forms developed by advisory organizations. However, it may expressly exclude reinsurance coverage for loss exposures covered by manuscript forms developed for a particular insured or covered by forms developed independently of an advisory organization.

IMPLEMENTING UNDERWRITING POLICY

Staff underwriters develop underwriting guidelines, which distill underwriting policies into directions for line underwriters' policy selection. Underwriting audits ensure that established underwriting standards are reasonably consistent.

Insurers convey underwriting policy through their underwriting guidelines. The guidelines describe the parameters of acceptable applicants for insurance for which the insurer has priced its insurance products.

Underwriting audits are the insurer's quality control check for uniform application of the underwriting guidelines and for continuous improvement.

Purposes of Underwriting Guidelines

An insurer's underwriting policy is communicated to underwriters through underwriting guidelines, which are continually updated to reflect changes in policy. Underwriting guidelines identify the major elements that underwriters should evaluate for each type of insurance, as well as boundaries, such as maximum coverage limits, for application selection.

Some underwriting guides include step-by-step instructions for handling particular classes of insureds. Such guides might identify specific hazards to evaluate, alternatives to consider, criteria to use when making the final decision, ways to implement the decision, and methods to monitor the decision. Some guidelines also provide pricing instructions and reinsurance-related information. Other insurers use underwriting guides that are less comprehensive. For example, they may list all classes of business and indicate their acceptability by type of insurance. Codes are then assigned to indicate the desirability of the loss exposure and the level of authority required to write the class of business.

Because underwriting guidelines usually specify the attributes of accounts that insurers are willing to insure, insurers consider them trade secrets. Disclosure of this proprietary information might cause an insurer to lose its competitive advantage over others.

Underwriting guidelines serve these purposes:

- Provide for structured decisions
- Ensure uniformity and consistency
- Synthesize insights and experience
- Distinguish between routine and nonroutine decisions
- Avoid duplication of effort
- Ensure adherence to reinsurance treaties and planned rate levels
- Support policy preparation and compliance
- Provide a basis for predictive models

Provide for Structured Decisions

Underwriting guidelines provide a structure for underwriting decisions by identifying the major considerations underwriters should evaluate for each type of insurance the insurer writes.For example, the section of an insurer's underwriting guidelines addressing contractors' equipment might indicate that equipment use is of paramount importance in determining acceptability and pricing. Contractors' equipment used in mountainous areas is more likely to be subject to upset and overturn and therefore requires more scrutiny and premium than contractors' equipment used on flat terrain.

By identifying the principal hazards associated with a particular class of business, underwriting guidelines ensure that underwriters consider the primary hazard traits of the exposures they evaluate.

Ensure Uniformity and Consistency

Underwriting guidelines help ensure that selection decisions are made uniformly and consistently by all of the insurer's underwriters. Ideally, submissions that are identical in every respect should elicit the same response from different underwriters. Guidelines facilitate uniformity because they include acceptable approaches to evaluating applicants and the overall desirability of a particular type of risk or class of business.

Synthesize Insights and Experience

Underwriting guidelines synthesize the insights and experience of seasoned underwriters. Staff underwriters, who assist with the insurer's unique or challenging accounts on a referral basis, often are able to include the approaches they have taken in underwriting particular classifications and lines of business. For many insurers, underwriting guidelines serve as a repository for an insurer's cumulative expertise.

Sample Commercial Underwriting Guidelines

I. GENERAL:

The Risk Selection Guide is a comprehensive alphabetical listing by class of business showing what the Midley Insurance Companies believe to be the desirability of insuring an average risk in the class. The Guide grades each class for Property, Commercial Automobile, Workers Compensation, Burglary and Robbery, Fidelity, Premises/Operations Liability, and Products/Completed Operations Liability. In addition, the final column titled "Form" indicates whether the General Liability coverage must be written on a Claims-Made Form (indicated by a "CM"), or whether the Occurrence Form is available (indicated by an "O"). Please remember the risk selection guide is only a guide. The company retains final authority regarding the acceptance or rejection of any specific risk.

II. CLASSIFICATION ACCEPTABILITY RATINGS:

The Risk Selection Guide is being published as a section of this agent's manual to answer the question: "Are risks within a particular class likely to be accepted by the Midley Insurance Companies"? In light of this question, the risk grades as found in the Risk Selection Guide are defined as follows:

E—Excellent

This class of business is considered to have excellent profit potential. Unless a specific risk in this class has unusual hazards or exposures, it will rarely present any underwriting problems. Risks graded as "E" may be bound by the agent without prior underwriting consent.

G—Good

This class of business is considered to have good profit potential. Normally this risk may be written before obtaining an inspection or developing additional underwriting information other than that present on the application. The agent may bind risks graded as "G" without prior underwriting consent.

A—Average

Potential for profit is marginal because of high variability of risks within the class. It is understood that the underwriter might think it is necessary to inspect the risk before authorizing binding. In all instances, it is recommended that the agent call the underwriter and discuss the risk before binding.

S—Submit

The account presents little potential for profit. These risks will require a complete written submission before binding. The underwriter must obtain a complete inspection and evaluate any other underwriting information deemed necessary before authorizing the binding of this risk.

D—Decline

Due to the lack of potential for profit, this class of risk is prohibited and will not be considered. Under no circumstances may a risk classified as "D" be bound without the prior written approval of the Vice President of Commercial Underwriting.

III. FOOTNOTES:

Footnotes sometimes are indicated as applying to an individual classification for a specific line of insurance. These footnotes are displayed at the bottom of each page and are designed to make you aware of certain hazards or exposures that are unacceptable or need to be addressed in an acceptable manner.

We hope the Risk Selection Guide will be valuable in understanding the types of business our companies want to be writing. However, please do not hesitate to call your underwriter if you are unsure as to how to classify a particular risk, or if you feel the factors associated with a specific risk make it considerably better or worse than the grading assigned by this guide.

Description	Property	Auto	Workers Compensation	Burglary and Robbery	Fidelity	Premises and Operations	Products and Completed Operations	Form
Painting—exterior—buildings or structures—three stories or less in height	A[1]	G	A	A	A	G[2]	G	O
Painting—interior—buildings or structures	A[1]	G	G	A	A	G[2]	G	O
Painting—oil or gasoline tanks	A[1]	G	D	A	A	D	D	O
Painting—ship hulls	A[1]	G	D	A	A	D	D	O
Painting—shop only	S[1,3]	G	S	A	A	G	G	O
Painting, picture, or frame stores	G	G	G	G	G	E	G	O
Paper coating or finishing	D	A	D	A	A	G	A	O
Paper corrugating or laminating—workers compensation only			D					
Paper crepeing—workers compensation only			D					
Paper goods manufacturing	D	A	D	A	A	G[4]	G[4]	O
Paper manufacturing	D	A	D	A	A	G[4]	G[4]	O
Paper products distributors	S	A	A	A	A	G[4]	G[4]	O
Paper, rag, or rubber stock dealers and distributors—secondhand	D	D	D	D	D	D	D	O
Paperhanging	G	G	G	G	G	G	G	O
Parachute manufacturing	D	A	D	D	D	D	D	O
Parades	D	D	D	D	D	D	D	O
Parking—private	A	A	S	S	S	A	A	O
Parking—public—open air	A	A	S	S	S	A	A	O
Parking—public—operated in conjunction with other enterprises	A	A	S	S	S	A	A	O
Parking—public—not open air	A	A	S	S	S	S	A	O
Parking—public shopping centers—(lessor's risk only)	G	G	S	G	G	G	G	O
Parks or playgrounds	A[5]	A	A	A	A	S[5]	S[5]	O
Paste, ink or mucilage manufacturing—workers compensation only			S					

[1] Flammable liquid storage must be minimal and controlled.

[2] A minimum property damage deductible of $250 on premises and operations coverage is mandatory.

[3] The risk is unacceptable if any painting or finishing is done inside without an approved spray booth.

[4] Acceptability will depend on the specific nature of the operation and specific types and uses of the products.

[5] This risk is unacceptable unless this classification constitutes only a small part of other properties or operations.

[DA06292]

Distinguish Between Routine and Nonroutine Decisions

Underwriting guidelines help line underwriters distinguish between routine and nonroutine decisions:

- Routine decisions are those for which the line underwriter clearly has decision-making authority according to the underwriting guidelines.
- Nonroutine decisions involve submissions that fall outside the underwriter's authority.

Underwriting guides usually indicate that the classifications and lines of business must be either declined or submitted to a higher level of authority for approval.

Avoid Duplication of Efforts

Many underwriting situations recur. If the problems inherent in a particular situation have been identified and solved, the solution should apply to all similar situations that might arise in the future. Underwriting guidelines contain the information necessary to avoid costly duplication of effort.

Ensure Adherence to Reinsurance Treaties and Planned Rate Levels

Compliance with underwriting guidelines ensures that coverage limits and accepted loss exposures will not exceed the insurer's treaty reinsurance, because staff underwriters reflect those treaty limitations in the guidelines.

Compliance with underwriting guidelines also ensures selection of loss exposures in an overall book of business commensurate with the planned rate levels for those policies. The importance of compliance with underwriting guidelines as it affects the profitability of a book of business is illustrated by an example of the outcome when compliance with guidelines fails. Many homeowners policy underwriting guidelines require property to be insured to within a percentage (such as 100 percent) of the replacement cost of the dwelling. Because most property losses are partial losses, rates are developed with the expectation that total losses will be rare. If property insured in a portfolio is significantly undervalued, average losses will equal a larger percentage of the average dwelling-coverage limits. The portfolio might also experience a greater number of losses equal to the total dwelling-coverage limit. Overall, the profitability of the book of business will decline as losses exceed expectations.

In resolving this profitability problem, one alternative is to increase the rates charged. However, that does not resolve the underlying problem of undervaluing the property insured, and the increased rates might not be competitive in the market. A better alternative is to enforce compliance with underwriting guidelines, ensure adequate coverage to replacement cost at the time of the initial application, and implement a program to increase dwelling coverage to keep pace with inflation and building cost increases. See the exhibit "Undervalued Homes Statistics."

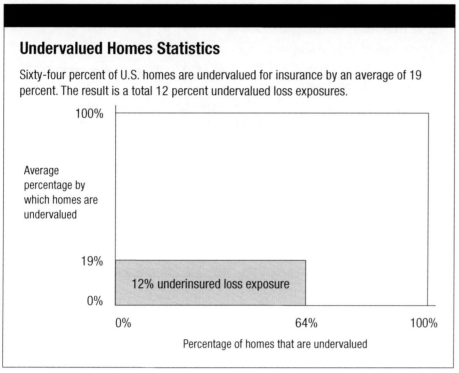

Undervalued Homes Statistics

Sixty-four percent of U.S. homes are undervalued for insurance by an average of 19 percent. The result is a total 12 percent undervalued loss exposures.

Adapted from Marshall & Swift/Boeckh, "Degree of Home Undervaluation Shifts in 2008," News, June 17, 2009, www.msbinfo.com/Company/News/17 (accessed July 2, 2010). [DA06293]

This illustration can be applied to other situations in which the failure to comply with underwriting guidelines results in inadequate premiums for loss exposures accepted that are not anticipated in the insurer's planned rate levels.

Support Policy Preparation and Compliance

Underwriting guides provide information to assist underwriters and support staff in policy preparation. Rules and eligibility requirements for various rating plans are also included. Specialized information, such as eligibility for experience and retrospective rating together with appropriate rating formulas, often appears in the underwriting guide. Underwriting guidelines also support compliance with state regulatory requirements, as staff underwriters incorporate applicable regulations in the guidelines.

Provide a Basis for Predictive Models

Underwriters use **predictive modeling** to identify applications that present lower underwriting risk. Predictive modeling incorporates underwriting thought processes with underwriting guidelines by assigning a rank or score to

Predictive modeling

A process in which historical data based on behaviors and events are blended with multiple variables and used to construct models of anticipated future outcomes.

all of the variables presented by an account and its loss exposures. Predictive models function in this way:

- Multiple data variables of individual risks are developed to rank the relative likelihood of insurance loss.
- Data variables are based on underwriting guidelines along with the insurer's loss experience, loss data collected from external sources, and underwriting expertise.
- The ranking or score developed from the data variables is a predictive measure of future profit potential based upon the account's characteristics.

Predictive modeling can provide a consistent way to review individual applications that improves the overall profitability of a book of business. It can also help in managing a large book of business for which conducting an in-depth underwriting review on every account would be too costly.

Purposes of Underwriting Audits

Staff underwriters conduct periodic audits to monitor line underwriters' adherence to the practices and procedures outlined in the underwriting guidelines. Audits are a management tool used to achieve uniformity and consistency in the application of underwriting standards.

Underwriting audits are typically conducted on-site at the branch or regional office being audited. A typical underwriting audit may involve selecting accounts at random or reviewing files that had experienced notable claims. These accounts are then scrutinized to determine whether prescribed procedures were followed and whether the underwriter acted in accord with the insurer's underwriting policy. Feedback from the audit of individual files provides individual line underwriters with strategies to improve future underwriting decisions.

Underwriting audits can also be used to monitor statistics for books of business. This can provide indications of applications written in excess of underwriting guidelines. For example, an excessive number of workers compensation applications accepted with hazardous classification codes in one territory could indicate an imbalance of product mix. It can also indicate inconsistent adherence to underwriting guidelines.

An underwriting audit provides staff underwriters with information on the effectiveness of the underwriting guidelines. Underwriting guidelines that are not being following may be either outdated or considered unrealistic. This could indicate that a critical review for updates is required. Line underwriters, for example, might ignore the underwriting guidelines when changes in the insurance marketplace have occurred without corresponding changes having been made to the underwriting guidelines. As a result, staff underwriters might learn that producers are not receptive to complying with the insurer's underwriting guidelines. If compliance with underwriting guidelines is not leading to the desired results, such information is valuable in the ongoing effort of developing or revising effective underwriting guidelines.

UNDERWRITING PROCESS

Whether relying on independent judgment or the guidance of expert systems, underwriters engage in a series of steps and tasks designed to ensure that, ultimately, insurers are able to reach their business goals.

The underwriting process incorporates these underlying concepts into a series of steps and tasks:

- The purpose of underwriting is to develop and maintain a profitable book of business.
- Underwriting activities include line underwriting activities, which are focused on evaluating new applications and renewal policies, and staff underwriting activities, which are focused on managing the risk selection process.
- Levels of underwriting authority are based on experience and knowledge.
- Underwriting policy should support an insurer's mission.

After a producer submits an application for insurance to an insurer, the application must be qualified for acceptance. **Underwriters** qualify an application through following the steps in the underwriting process. If the application is accepted, the policy will be issued, and both the policyholder and insurer must adhere to the conditions of that contract for coverage to apply in the event of a loss.

In addition to applications, the underwriting process is also applied to renewal policies as well as certain policy changes, such as a request to add a new location to a property policy. For ease of discussion, applications, renewals, and policy changes to which the underwriting process is applied are referred to as **underwriting submissions**.

Typically, an insurance company underwriter makes decisions regarding underwriting submissions for commercial lines. Underwriters increasingly use **expert systems**, which help them make better and more consistent underwriting decisions. Expert systems, also known as knowledge-based systems or rules-based systems, are most frequently used in personal lines and small commercial lines insurance, but their ability to handle larger commercial accounts is growing.

The underwriting process is a series of steps with related tasks applied to determine what submissions will be insured, for what amount of insurance, at what price, and under what conditions. In addition to considering the merits of an individual submission, underwriters consider how a submission fits into the insurer's business portfolio mix and whether a submission provides the best available opportunity for profitability, as compared to other submissions.

Underwriter

An insurer employee who evaluates applicants for insurance, selects those that are acceptable to the insurer, prices coverage, and determines policy terms and conditions.

Underwriting submission

Underwriting information for an initial application, or a substantive policy midterm or renewal change.

Expert systems, or knowledge-based systems

Computer software programs that supplement the underwriting decision-making process. These systems ask for the information necessary to make an underwriting decision, ensuring that no information is overlooked.

Although experienced underwriters do not always follow each of these steps in strict order, the sequence of steps provides a sound framework within which underwriters can make decisions. See the exhibit "Underwriting Process."

Evaluate the Submission

The first step in the underwriting process is evaluating a submission's **loss exposures** and associated **hazards**. Underwriters must understand the activities, operations, and character of every applicant. However, tradeoffs are necessary to control underwriting expenses and to handle a reasonable number of applications.

To evaluate a submission, underwriters perform two tasks: weighing the need for information and gathering the necessary information.

Weigh the Need for Information

Underwriters apply **information efficiency** to weigh the need for information against the cost to obtain it. For example, an underwriter is likely to investigate a chemical manufacturer extensively. However, the underwriter may require much less information to underwrite a gift shop. Sometimes the account's premium size drives the decision regarding the amount of information gathered or the resources used to gather it. An account with a small premium volume may not justify expensive research.

Underwriters may also use these categories intuitively or consciously when determining whether the additional information should be obtained:

- Essential information—information that is absolutely necessary to arrive at the decision and is often specified in the underwriting guidelines
- Desirable information—information that is not absolutely necessary but would be helpful in evaluating the account if the information can be obtained at an acceptable cost and without any undue delay
- Available information—information that may or may not be helpful and is not worth making any special effort to obtain

Gather the Necessary Information

Underwriters compile information from a number of sources to develop a profile of a submission. Underwriters pay close attention to a submission's hazards to determine whether those hazards are typical of similarly classified accounts. See the exhibit "Hazard Categories."

Loss exposure

Any condition or situation that presents a possibility of loss, whether or not an actual loss occurs.

Hazard

A condition that increases the frequency or severity of a loss.

Information efficiency

The balance that underwriters must maintain between the hazards presented by the account and the information needed to underwrite it.

Underwriting Process

Steps	Tasks	
1. Evaluate the submission	• Weigh the need for information	Categories of information: • Essential • Desirable • Available
	• Gather the necessary information	Resources: • Producers • Applications • Inspection reports • Government records • Financial rating services • Loss data • Field marketing personnel • Premium auditor • Claims files • Production records • Consultants' reports
2. Develop underwriting alternatives		Alternatives: • Accept • Reject • Modify–require risk control measures • Modify–change insurance rates, rating plans, or policy limits • Modify–amend policy terms and conditions • Modify–use facultative reinsurance
3. Select an underwriting alternative		Factors to consider: • Underwriting authority • Supporting business • Mix of business • Producer relationships • Regulatory restrictions
4. Determine an appropriate premium		
5. Implement the underwriting decision	• Communicate the decision • Issue documents • Record information	
6. Monitor underwriting decisions	Monitor individual policies Monitor books of business	Triggering events: Substantive policy changes Significant and unique losses Preparation for renewal Risk control and safety inspections Premium audits

[DA06324]

Hazard Categories

- A physical hazard is a tangible characteristic of property, persons, or operations to be insured that increases the frequency or severity of loss. Physical hazards can be attributes of the applicant, of the property to be insured, or of the environment in which the property is located. An untrained driver, damageability of cargo being shipped, and the quality of public fire protection are all examples of physical hazards.

- A moral hazard is a condition that increases the likelihood that a person will intentionally cause or exaggerate a loss. Although most information that suggests a moral hazard is subjective, objective data such as history of financial difficulties, criminal records, or other public records may be available. Underwriters try to recognize symptoms of a moral hazard, such as property that is grossly overinsured. An insured facing serious financial difficulty may present a moral hazard because such difficulty might give the insured an incentive to commit insurance fraud.

- A morale hazard is a condition of carelessness or indifference that increases the frequency or severity of loss. Careless driving, failing to lock an unattended building, or failing to clear an icy sidewalk to protect pedestrians are examples of attitudinal hazards. While difficult to detect, morale hazards may be indicated by an applicant's behavior, poor management, or weak financial condition.

- A legal hazard is a condition of the legal environment that increases loss frequency or severity. For example, people in some geographic areas are much more litigious than those elsewhere.

[DA06330]

These are the principal sources of underwriting information:

- Producers—Underwriters rely more on the producer than on any other source for information about the account. Typically, the producer has personal contact with an applicant, has firsthand knowledge of the applicant's business operations, and knows the applicant's reputation in the community. The producer usually determines the applicant's coverage needs and "pre-qualifies" or field-underwrites applicants. The degree to which an insurer depends on the producer to evaluate the applicant varies by producer and by type of business and may differ based on the insurer's distribution system and distribution channels.

Application

A legal document that provides information obtained directly from an applicant requesting insurance and that an insurer can use for underwriting and claim handling purposes.

- Applications—Insurance **applications** provide general information required to process, rate, and underwrite loss exposures of the applicant. The application requires specific information necessary to evaluate the acceptability of an applicant's loss exposures for a particular type of insurance. Each insurer develops its own applications or uses standard ACORD applications. In addition, insurers often use supplemental applications or questionnaires for certain coverages or classes of business to obtain more pertinent information in evaluating the submissions.

- Inspection reports—Independent inspections or risk control reports provide underwriting information about the property's physical condition, the business operations' safety record, and the policyholder's management. Most inspection reports in commercial insurance contain mandatory and suggested recommendations. The underwriter should follow up to determine the applicant's degree of compliance, which provides insight into management's attitude toward safety.

- Government records—Government records that provide underwriting information include motor vehicle reports; criminal court records; and civil court records, including records of suits filed, mortgages and liens, business licenses, property tax records, United States Securities and Exchange Commission (SEC) filings, and bankruptcy filings. Motor vehicle records (MVRs) are a fundamental information source for auto underwriting. Most underwriters use independent services to obtain civil and criminal information, even though they can obtain it directly from court records. Civil and criminal reports show any previous bankruptcies or judgments that are on record.

- Financial rating services—An applicant's financial status provides important underwriting information. Dun & Bradstreet (D&B), Standard & Poor's, and Experian are some of the major financial rating services that underwriters use. These services provide data on the credit ratings of individual businesses, together with industry averages for comparison. Using a financial rating service is almost universal in surety bond underwriting and is common with many other types of commercial insurance. Services can verify an applicant's financial statements and provide an overall picture of the applicant's financial status. A financially weak business might present an unacceptable moral or morale hazard.

- Loss data—Loss data are a significant underwriting tool for predicting future losses. The loss experience of a commercial policyholder might be extensive enough to be statistically significant on its own. The policyholder's loss runs provide information on loss frequency and severity, types of losses, possible seasonality, trends in loss experience, and indications of management's attention to prompt loss reporting. Loss data also provide important information for policy pricing.

- Field marketing personnel—Insurers often employ field marketing personnel (such as marketing representatives or special agents) who can provide both specific and general underwriting information. Field marketing personnel often obtain information that a producer omitted from an application. In sparsely populated areas or in other situations in which qualified risk control personnel are not available, many insurers use field marketing personnel to make simplified inspection reports.

- Premium auditor—A premium auditor examines the policyholders' operations, records, and books of account to determine the actual loss exposure for the coverage already provided. Premium audit reports provide information about the policyholders' operations that may have underwriting implications, including moral and morale hazards.

- Claim files—When renewing existing policies, an underwriter can obtain insights into the policyholder's character by reviewing the policyholder's claim files. The claim representative is one of the few insurer employees who get a firsthand view of insured locations. Claim representatives typically accumulate a significant amount of underwriting information during their investigations. Some insurers have a process for claim representatives to e-mail or call underwriters about their concerns regarding hazards. For example, a claim representative investigating a small fire loss at a machine shop might uncover evidence of poor housekeeping and the policyholder's disregard for risk control.

- Production records—Records on individual producers, indicating loss ratio, premium volume, mix of business, amount of supporting business, length of service, and industry experience, help underwriters make decisions about the quality of the applicants that the producer is submitting. In personal auto underwriting, for example, the mix of business indicates whether a particular producer is submitting an inordinately large percentage of young drivers or drivers with poor driving records. In commercial insurance, production records indicate the producer's familiarity with complex or unusual classes of business. For example, the producer's background and experience might be a concern to the underwriter evaluating a complex manufacturing submission. If the producer's business involves mostly personal insurance, the underwriter might question the producer's familiarity with commercial coverages and his or her ability to service those accounts properly.

- Consultants' reports—Large and specialized commercial accounts may require special expertise to fully underwrite loss exposures and hazards from emerging issues. These issues involve new or little-known exposures that could change the evaluation profile for a particular submission. Consultants who are experts in the business classes can bring insights to issues of concern that have not yet manifested as actual losses. Such concerns can arise from changing accounting standards, manufacturing failures in similar businesses, and trends in tort litigation.

Many tools are available to help underwriters evaluate, select, and price submissions. Underwriters choose and balance the tools available to make the decision, which requires a holistic understanding of all of the information available in evaluating submissions. See the exhibit "Underwriting Evaluation Tools."

Develop Underwriting Alternatives

The second step in the underwriting process is developing underwriting alternatives. The underwriter must consider each alternative carefully and choose the optimal one for the circumstances. The underwriter may accept a submission as is, reject the submission, or accept the submission subject to certain modifications. Determining the modification that best meets the needs of the

---

Underwriting Evaluation Tools

- Telematics—The use of Global Positioning Systems (GPS) tracking to collect and analyze data regarding driver behavior and vehicle use.

- Predictive analytics—Statistical and analytical techniques used to develop models that predict future events or behaviors.

- Predictive modeling—A process in which historical data based on behaviors and events are blended with multiple variables and used to construct models of anticipated future outcomes.

- Catastrophe (CAT) modeling—A type of computer program that estimates losses from future potential catastrophic events.

[DA06331]

insurer, producer, and applicant can be a challenge. There are four major types of modifications:

- Require risk control measures
- Change insurance rates, rating plans, or policy limits
- Amend policy terms and conditions
- Use facultative reinsurance

Require Risk Control Measures

The first type of modification for an unacceptable submission is a **counteroffer** with a requirement for the applicant to implement additional risk control measures.

Risk control measures such as installing an automatic fire-extinguishing sprinkler system, adding guard service, and improving housekeeping and maintenance can reduce physical hazards. Installing machinery guards can reduce the frequency of employee bodily injuries. Some risk control measures are relatively inexpensive and simple to implement, while others, such as sprinklers, require considerable capital investment.

Some applicants welcome an insurer's recommendations and understand that implementation reduces ultimate business costs. Other applicants view risk control requirements unfavorably and consider them unnecessary expenses. Underwriters should make sound recommendations accompanied by well-reasoned and convincing explanations.

Underwriters must follow up to ensure that required risk control measures are implemented and that submissions meet underwriting guidelines. Insurers generally establish controls to verify that required modifications have been implemented.

Counteroffer

A proposal an offeree makes to an offeror that varies in some material way from the original offer, resulting in rejection of the original offer and constituting a new offer.

Change Insurance Rates, Rating Plans, or Policy Limits

The second type of modification for a submission is a counteroffer to change insurance rates, rating plans, or policy limits. A submission that is not desirable at standard rates may be desirable if the underwriter can charge a different rate, use a different rating plan, or provide a different limit of coverage.

A rate modification could either increase or decrease the premium. An increase in rate would compensate the insurer for potential increases in loss severity or frequency. In private passenger auto underwriting, for example, an applicant might not be eligible for the requested preferred-risk program but might qualify for another program at higher, standard rates. Alternatively, the underwriter might offer a preferred-risk program to a desirable applicant who applies for coverage at standard rates. By offering a lower price, the underwriter might keep that applicant from buying coverage from a competitor.

Underwriters have greater price discretion in commercial insurance than in personal insurance. For example, an underwriter can use a range of rates for an **(a) rated classification** or **estimated loss potentials (ELP)** for general liability policies, for which no manual loss cost is published. Good judgment plays an important role in selecting a rate that earns a reasonable profit and is competitive enough to obtain the account.

In addition to changing rates, this type of modification also includes changing rating plans. Several rating plans are available for commercial applicants:

- **Experience rating** uses the policyholder's past loss experience to develop a premium modification factor to adjust the manual rate upward or downward. Experience rating is available for submissions that have a specific premium level (which varies by insurer) and at least one year of experience. The experience rating plan uses three years of past loss experience, when available, and a credibility factor based on the size of the policyholder's premium to determine the modification. In comparison to other rating plans, experience rating has a formal methodology that must be applied without discrimination to all submissions that meet experience-rating eligibility requirements. Selectively applying experience rating to some risks and not to others can be considered unfair discrimination between applicants and policyholders.

- **Schedule rating** awards debits and credits to a submission based on categories of business characteristics, such as the care and condition of the premises and the selection and training of employees. Credits and debits vary by insurer, are limited by insurance statute (usually between 25 and 40 percent of the premium), and reflect the underwriter's judgment of the account's loss exposure. Insurance statutes require that insurers apply schedule rating plans to all eligible submissions without discrimination and that adequate documentation be kept on file to justify the pricing decision.

- **Retrospective rating** is an individual rating plan that uses the current year as the experience period to develop the experience modification

Estimated loss potentials (ELP)

Rate development factors used for operations with unique characteristics or for which inadequate statistical experience exists. ELPs are multiplied by loss cost multipliers to develop rates.

(a) rated classification

The rate classifications provided by the ISO Commercial Lines Manual that describe operations with unique characteristics or for which inadequate statistical experience exists.

Experience rating

A ratemaking technique that adjusts the insured's premium for the upcoming policy period based on the insured's experience for the current period.

Schedule rating

A rating plan that awards debits and credits based on specific categories, such as the care and condition of the premises or the training and selection of employees, to modify the final premium to reflect factors that the class rate does not include.

Retrospective rating

A ratemaking technique that adjusts the insured's premium for the current policy period based on the insured's loss experience during the current period; paid losses or incurred losses may be used to determine loss experience.

factor. Under this rating plan, a provisional premium is charged at the beginning of the policy period. At the end of the policy period, the actual loss experience for that same period is determined, and a final premium is calculated. The premium is then adjusted, after the end of the policy period, to reflect the account's expenses and losses during the policy period. The premium is subject to a specified minimum and maximum. This rating plan has several variations that protect the policyholder from fluctuations in the final premium.

Changing policy limits also falls into this type of modification. An insurer's underwriting guidelines usually specify the maximum limits of insurance that an underwriter can approve. The limits usually reflect reinsurance limitations or reinsurance availability and possible catastrophic loss from a single loss exposure. If high policy limits are requested, the underwriter may suggest lower limits or may use **facultative reinsurance**.

When dealing with property insurance, the underwriter must be alert for overinsurance that could indicate a moral hazard and might lead to a fraudulent loss. Underinsurance, however, is a more common problem. Adequate insurance limits are essential to collect a premium commensurate with the loss exposure. From the policyholder's standpoint, adequate limits also meet coinsurance requirements and ensure an adequate loss recovery.

Facultative reinsurance

Reinsurance of individual loss exposures in which the primary insurer chooses which loss exposures to submit to the reinsurer, and the reinsurer can accept or reject any loss exposures submitted.

Amend Policy Terms and Conditions

The third type of modification for an unacceptable submission is a counteroffer to amend policy terms and conditions. An unacceptable submission may become acceptable by modifying the policy to exclude certain causes of loss, add or increase a deductible, or make another coverage change. An insurer might be unwilling to provide replacement cost coverage on a poorly maintained building but might be willing to provide a more limited coverage form. Increasing a deductible might make coverage more viable for a small commercial account in which a large number of small losses has caused unsatisfactory loss experience in the past.

The underwriter's flexibility varies by type of insurance. If policies have been approved by state regulators, coverage modifications are seldom possible. When the requested coverage cannot be provided, the underwriter might suggest alternative coverage.

Use Facultative Reinsurance

The fourth type of modification for an unacceptable submission is an insurer's internal decision to use facultative reinsurance if treaty reinsurance is not available. The underwriter may be able to transfer a portion of the liability for the applicant's loss exposure to a facultative reinsurer. An alternative to purchasing facultative reinsurance is to ask the producer to divide the insurance among several insurers—an approach sometimes called "agency reinsurance."

Select an Underwriting Alternative

The third step in the underwriting process is selecting an underwriting alternative. An underwriter must decide whether to accept a submission as offered, reject it, or accept it subject to modifications. Rejection is sometimes unavoidable; however, rejections produce neither premium nor commission, only expense. Therefore, underwriters try to make the submission acceptable because one of an insurer's goals is to produce profitable business.

Selecting an alternative involves weighing a submission's positive and negative features, including loss exposures contemplated in the insurance rate, risk control measures, and management's commitment to loss prevention. These additional factors need to be considered before selecting an underwriting alternative:

- Underwriting authority—Before accepting a submission, an underwriter must determine whether he or she has the necessary underwriting authority. If the underwriter lacks authority, the submission must be referred to a higher underwriting authority.

- Supporting business—A submission that is marginal by itself might be acceptable if the other insurance components of the applicant's account— the supporting business—are desirable. For example, the underwriter might decide to accept a marginal workers compensation submission if the insurer already provides the applicant's commercial general liability, commercial property, and automobile policies. The **account underwriting** approach evaluates all lines together, as a total risk.

- Mix of business—The underwriting policy determined by management and specified in the underwriting guidelines frequently indicates the insurer's mix-of-business goals. The mix of business is the distribution of individual policies that constitute the book of business of a producer, territory, state, or region among the various types of insurance and classifications of insureds. Particular classes, such as youthful drivers in private passenger auto insurance or restaurants in commercial property coverage, might be overrepresented in the book of business. Consequently, the insurer might decide to change the acceptability criteria or prohibit new business in a particular class. When underwriting an individual new application, the underwriter must consider whether accepting the application supports the insurer's goals for mix of business.

- Producer relationships—Some producers pressure underwriters to accept a marginal submission as an accommodation. The relationship between the underwriter and the producer should be based on mutually shared goals. Differences of opinion are common, particularly because some of the goals of producers and underwriters conflict when producers focus on production and underwriters focus on strict adherence to selection standards. Nevertheless, the long-term goals of producers and underwriters

Account underwriting

A method of underwriting in which all of the business from a particular applicant is evaluated as a whole.

are growth and profit. Collaboration and a willingness to see the other's viewpoint are essential to building a satisfactory working relationship.

- Regulatory restrictions—State regulations restrict underwriters' ability to accept or renew business. Additionally, federal and state privacy laws restrict the type and the amount of information about an applicant that an underwriter can obtain. Underwriters must know these restrictions, which are usually codified within the state's **unfair trade practices** laws. If regulation limits reasons for cancellation or refusal to renew, then new submissions should be evaluated carefully because eliminating undesirable business after it has been written can be difficult. Many states also limit the time within which an underwriter can decline a submission or provide notice of refusal to renew. Therefore, underwriters should make timely decisions to avoid mandatory acceptance or renewal of an otherwise unacceptable submission.

Unfair trade practices
Methods of competition or advertising or procedures that tend to deprive the public of information necessary to make informed insurance decisions.

Determine an Appropriate Premium

The fourth step in the underwriting process is determining an appropriate premium. Underwriters must ensure that each loss exposure is properly classified so that it is properly rated.

Insurance loss costs are typically based on an elaborate classification system in which similar loss exposures are combined into the same rating classification. Combining loss exposures into rating classifications enables the insurer to appropriately match potential loss costs with an applicant's particular loss exposures. Consequently, the insurer can develop an adequate premium to pay losses and operating expenses and to produce a profit.

Accurate classification ensures a pooling of loss exposures whose expected loss frequency and loss severity are similar. Misclassification can produce adverse results, including insufficient premium to cover losses and expenses, inability to sell policies because prices are higher than competitors' prices, and charges that the insurer has violated regulations prohibiting unfair trade practices.

For most types of personal insurance, workers compensation, and some other commercial insurance, proper classification automatically determines the premium. For major types of commercial insurance, such as general liability, the underwriter might have the option of adjusting the premium based on the characteristics of the account's loss exposures.

Many insurers operate subsidiary insurers with different rating plans that reflect the loss exposures of different groups of insureds. Insurers typically have subsidiary companies for insureds with loss exposures that fall into the preferred-risk, standard-risk, and high-risk categories. Underwriters can place each applicant with the subsidiary considered most appropriate. The underwriter must be certain in each case that the characteristics of the applicant's loss exposures justify the placement and must document that any adjustment is consistent with the insurer's rating plan.

Implement the Underwriting Decision

The fifth step in the underwriting process is implementing the underwriting decision. Implementing underwriting decisions generally involves three tasks:

- Communicate the decision—The underwriting decision is communicated to the producer. If the decision is to accept the submission with modifications, the reasons must be clearly communicated to the producer and applicant, and the applicant must agree to accept or implement any modifications made as a counteroffer. In addition, the insurer must establish controls to verify that modifications, such as risk control measures, are implemented. If the underwriter decides to reject the application, he or she must communicate the rejection to the producer in a positive way to preserve their long-term relationship. Underwriters must provide clear and logical reasons as to why a particular applicant does not meet the insurer's underwriting requirements. Effective communication of both positive and negative decisions clarifies the insurer's standards and helps the producer understand what kinds of business the insurer wants to write.

- Issue documents—In accepting a submission, the underwriter might need to issue a **binder**. For some types of business, the underwriter might also need to prepare **certificates of insurance**.

- Record information—Information about the policy and the applicant are recorded for policy issuance, accounting, statistical, and monitoring purposes. Data entry personnel enter essential information into the insurer's information system. Data about a policyholder include location, limits, coverages, price modifications, and class of business. Those data must be coded so that the insurer and the industry can accumulate information on all accounts for ratemaking, statutory reporting, financial accounting, and book-of-business evaluations. Those data are also used to monitor the account, trigger renewals, and flag situations requiring special attention. For example, expiring policies are identified so that updated information can be obtained. A good policy information system, containing accurate data, also alerts underwriters to claim activity during the policy period, problems, or substantial changes regarding the policyholder. A claim referral system can immediately refer the file to the underwriter if the loss frequency exceeds a predetermined limit or if a severe loss occurs.

Monitor the Underwriting Decisions

The sixth step in the underwriting process is monitoring the underwriting decision. After an underwriting decision has been made on a new-business submission or a renewal, the underwriter has two tasks to ensure that satisfactory results are achieved: monitor activity for individual policies, and monitor books of business.

Binder

A temporary written or oral agreement to provide insurance coverage until a formal written policy is issued.

Certificate of insurance

A brief description of insurance coverage prepared by an insurer or its agent commonly used by policyholders to provide evidence of insurance.

Monitor Individual Policies

Underwriters must be alert to changes in insureds' loss exposures. Changes in the nature of an insured's business operation, for example, could significantly raise or lower the policyholder's loss potential. Underwriters do not have the resources necessary for constant monitoring of all policies while they underwrite new submissions. Monitoring existing policies usually occurs in response to these triggering events:

- Substantive policy changes—Adding a new location to a property policy or a new driver to an auto policy can cause the underwriter to investigate whether the additions significantly change the loss exposures.

- Significant and unique losses—A notice of loss provides the underwriter with another opportunity to review the account and to determine whether that loss is the type the underwriter expected. Summary information about the claim or a review of the claim file provides valuable information about the nature of the loss and the insured's operations.

- Preparation for renewal—As a policy's expiration date approaches, the underwriter may need to repeat the underwriting process before agreeing to renew the policy for another term. Renewal underwriting can generally be accomplished more quickly than new-business underwriting because the insured is already known to the underwriter and more information might be available if claim reports or risk control reports have been added to the file. However, the underwriter must determine whether any changes to the account have occurred, and, if so, carefully go through the underwriting process again.

- Risk control and safety inspections—A risk control and safety inspection might have contained recommendations that were requirements for policy issuance. A follow-up investigation could reveal that only some of the requirements were met. The underwriter can contact the inspector, who will have first-hand knowledge of the insured, to obtain detailed information.

- Premium audits—Premium audits usually lag behind a renewal policy by several months. The audit report could disclose larger loss exposures than originally contemplated, unacceptable operations, new products, new operations, or financial problems. The underwriter can contact the auditor for information on new loss exposures, additional hazards, or operations that help the underwriter reevaluate the account and determine its continued acceptability.

Monitor Books of Business

In addition to monitoring individual policies, underwriters must monitor books of business. Monitoring a book of business means evaluating the quality and profitability of all the business written for any group of policies. The evaluation should identify specific problems for each type of insurance, which can be subdivided into class of business, territory, producer, and other policy subgroups. Additionally, the insurer is concerned that the premium volume covers fixed costs and overhead expenses for each book of business.

Underwriters use premium and loss statistics to identify aggregate problems in a deteriorating book of business. Reviewing the book of business can also help determine compliance with underwriting policy and detect changes in the type, volume, and quality of policies that may require corrective action.

Special attention is given to some books of business when they are defined by these characteristics:

- Class of business—A poor loss ratio in a particular class of business can indicate inadequate pricing or a disproportionate number of high-hazard policyholders relative to the average loss exposure in the classification. Classes with poor or deteriorating loss experience can be identified and corrected through rate increases, coverage restrictions, or more stringent selection standards. Changes in technology, materials, and operations, as well as changes in the social and legal environment, can significantly affect the loss ratio of a class of business.

- Territories or geographic areas—A territory can be defined in various ways to reflect an insurer's operations. For example, a territory could encompass a single state or the three-state area serviced by a branch office. Territories can also be the geographic areas within a state used in pricing policies. Monitoring territorial underwriting results can help the insurer to target areas for future agency appointments in profitable regions. Poor results could indicate areas from which the insurer might withdraw or in which the insurer might raise rates, if permitted by regulators. The regulatory and legal climate for insurance varies by state. Regulation can have a major effect on the desirability of conducting business in a state and the possibility of achieving a profit. Other factors to consider in monitoring territorial underwriting results include the degree of urbanization, physical differences in terrain, and the potential for natural disasters.

- Producers—Ideally, each producer's book of business should be evaluated annually. The producer's premium volume, policy retention, and loss ratio are evaluated both on an overall basis and by type and class of business. That evaluation should include the balance or mix of business desired between personal and commercial insurance and the projected growth factor. Key considerations are the goals that the insurer and producer established and the progress made toward achieving them. If the producer has a small premium volume with the insurer, one large loss can distort the loss ratio. A similar situation can occur in a small class of business. For example, a producer might appear to have unprofitable workers compensation experience based on loss ratio when the producer actually had only one policy with an unsatisfactory loss ratio.

MEASURING UNDERWRITING RESULTS

An insurer's underwriting results are a key indicator of its profitability. Without a clear understanding of their underwriting performance, insurers may not be able to respond to conditions that adversely affect them or recognize opportunities to improve their performance.

Insurers typically track their underwriting results through the use of financial and nonfinancial measures. The most common financial measure of underwriting results over a specific time period—typically one year—is the insurer's combined ratio. Proper underwriting should produce an underwriting profit or perhaps a small underwriting loss that is more than offset by investment profits. However, financial measures are not always reliable indicators of underwriting success in the short term.

Nonfinancial measures can be used to evaluate the actions of individual underwriters and underwriting departments, rather than their results.

Financial Measures

Many insurers use the **combined ratio** (or combined loss and expense ratio) to measure the success of underwriting activities. See the exhibit "Combined Ratio."

Combined ratio

A profitability ratio that indicates whether an insurer has made an underwriting loss or gain.

Combined Ratio

$$\text{Combined ratio (or trade-basis combined ratio)} = \frac{\text{Loss and loss adjustment expenses incurred}}{\text{Premiums earned}} + \frac{\text{Underwriting expenses incurred}}{\text{Premiums written}}$$

When the combined ratio is:

Exactly 100 percent	Every premium dollar is being used to pay claims and cover operating costs, with nothing remaining for insurer profit.
Greater than 100 percent	An underwriting loss occurs: more dollars are being paid out than are being taken in as premiums.
Less than 100 percent	An underwriting profit occurs because not all premium dollars taken in are being used for claims and expenses.

Most insurers consider any combined ratio under 100 percent to be acceptable because it indicates a profit from underwriting results, even before income from an insurer's investment activity is considered in its overall financial performance.

[DA06399]

From an insurer's perspective, the lower the combined ratio, the better. For example, a combined ratio of 95 percent means that an insurer has an outflow of $0.95 for every premium dollar, while a combined ratio of 115 percent means that the insurer has an outflow of $1.15 for every premium dollar. Therefore, a lower combined ratio reflects a higher level of profitability for an insurer.

Although the combined ratio is the most often cited measure of underwriting success, the results that it produces are generally subject to an additional analysis of its components. For example, individual categories of insurer expenses may be compared to those of other insurers or to industry norms, or the specific lines of business that exceeded anticipated losses may be examined. An in-depth analysis permits an insurer to make changes to its underwriting guidelines that yield desired results in the future. See the exhibit "Property-Liability Insurance Combined Ratio—All Lines Combined for the United States."

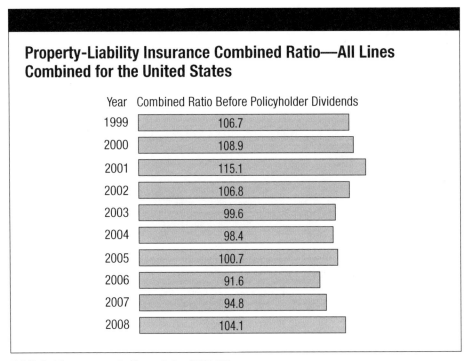

Property-Liability Insurance Combined Ratio—All Lines Combined for the United States

Year	Combined Ratio Before Policyholder Dividends
1999	106.7
2000	108.9
2001	115.1
2002	106.8
2003	99.6
2004	98.4
2005	100.7
2006	91.6
2007	94.8
2008	104.1

© A.M. Best Company - used with permission. [DA06400]

Changes in premium volume, major catastrophic losses, and delays in loss reporting can distort the combined ratio, making it difficult to evaluate the effectiveness of underwriting. Additionally, any discussion of insurer underwriting profitability needs to be considered within the context of the underwriting cycle.

Distortions Created by Changes in Premium Volume

An insurer's combined ratio must be evaluated, taking into consideration fluctuations in premium volume and the distortions that they can create. Premium volume and underwriting policy are related. Restrictive underwriting policy usually reduces premium volume. Conversely, a less restrictive underwriting policy generally increases premium volume.

Changes in underwriting policy, however, often do not have the immediate effect desired. For example, an insurer that becomes more restrictive in its underwriting criteria will usually see a reduction in premiums written. Because incurred losses remain outstanding from the prior period that had a less restrictive underwriting policy, the loss ratio component of the combined ratio will likely deteriorate. With this reduction in premiums written, the expense ratio will increase, even though the insurer's underwriting expenses might have remained relatively unchanged. Similarly, a significant relaxation of underwriting standards, at least in the short term, can make an insurer appear profitable and even cost conscious when its book of business is underpriced.

Distortions Created by Major Catastrophic Losses

Underwriting results are usually evaluated annually. However, major hurricanes, major earthquakes, and other natural catastrophes occur too irregularly to be predicted annually. Floods, for example, are typically predicted over a hundred-year period. Certain flood plains are predicted to have a flood, on average, once every one hundred years or, in lower-elevation areas, once every ten or twenty years.

Catastrophes such as industrial explosions, airplane crashes, nuclear reactor breakdowns, or terrorist activities likewise occur with too little regularity to create a predictable pattern. Ideally, insurance rates allow for unpredicted losses. Still, a major catastrophe is likely to cause an underwriting loss for that year for most if not all affected insurers. However, failure to predict the unpredictable does not necessarily indicate inadequate underwriting.

Distortions Created by Delays in Loss Reporting and Loss Development

Delays in loss reporting reduce the value of the information provided by the combined ratio. If premiums and losses could be readily matched, an insurer could determine whether its book of business was underpriced and then make corrections in its pricing structure. This information is valuable to insurance regulators as well, because an inadequately priced book of business is a significant threat to an insurer's solvency.

Insurers establish a loss reserve amount when a claim is reported. Reserved losses are included in incurred losses and reflected in the combined ratio. The type of loss usually determines how quickly the insurer is notified of a claim and how quickly the reserve is replaced with the amount of final payment.

With certain types of insurance, particularly liability insurance, a considerable amount of time can elapse between when a loss is reported and when a claim is settled. Reserves are established as soon as the loss is reported, but significant inaccuracy exists in estimating ultimate loss costs that will be paid at some future date. The longer the time between the estimate and the ultimate claim settlement, the greater the inaccuracy is likely to be.

These delays in loss reporting and loss settlement can result in an understatement of losses in one year and an overstatement in another year that appear in the combined ratio. However, these misstatements do not reflect changes in actual underwriting results.

Distortions Created by Underwriting Cycle

Historically, insurance industry underwriting cycles have consisted of a period of underwriting profits followed by a period of underwriting losses, as measured by the combined ratio. When insurers earn underwriting profits, they may use those profits to reduce their premium rates and offer broader coverage to increase their market share.

At times of underwriting losses, insurers may need to increase premium rates and restrict the availability of coverage to increase underwriting profits. These tactics may be necessary for the insurer to maintain the policyholders' surplus it needs to support its level of business.

Because insurance premium levels, capital allocation strategies, investment strategies, and insurer profitability are affected by this market phenomenon, insurers have tried to better understand what factors cause the underwriting cycle to shift to a different phase. Insurers essentially want to be able to maintain their competitive advantage and market share regardless of the cycle phase.

In addition, insurance regulators are concerned about the effects of the underwriting cycle on insurance availability and affordability. Although most of the factors affecting the underwriting cycle have been identified through examination of past cycles, changes in the insurance marketplace have reduced the predictive value of these factors. This increases the difficulty of determining when the next cycle phase will begin.

Individual insurers cannot change the underwriting cycle. However, effective underwriting and financial management can enable an insurer to periodically reposition itself through changes in its underwriting guidelines and allocation of capital to underwriting. This allows the insurer to maximize profits and market share growth during the cycle phases. See the exhibit "Phases of the Underwriting Cycle."

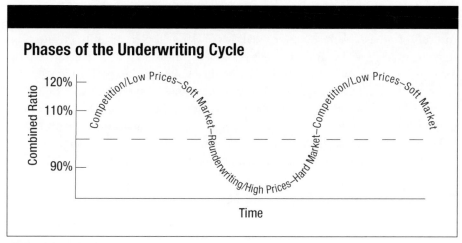

Phases of the Underwriting Cycle

[DA02639]

Nonfinancial Measures

The success of an insurer depends on the ability of every underwriter to attain and maintain profitable results over the long term. This profitability goal is accomplished in part by using nonfinancial measures to assess performance.

Nonfinancial measures link an organization's business strategy and its outputs to its performance. These measures evaluate individual underwriters and underwriting departments based on their actions rather than on their results. If underwriters adhere strictly to underwriting guidelines, underwriting should produce favorable financial results over the long term, barring uncontrollable variables. Underwriting performance standards include these areas of underwriting:

- Selection
- Product or line of business mix
- Pricing
- Accommodated accounts
- Retention ratio
- Hit ratio
- Service to producers
- Premium to underwriter

Some of these nonfinancial measures apply only to commercial lines underwriting departments. Others apply to both personal and commercial lines. Portions of both types may be automated using expert systems. Some measures can be evaluated during an underwriting audit. Insurer management and underwriting staff typically work together to agree on the nonfinancial measures or standards that constitute underwriting goals.

Selection

Insurers often establish selection goals for underwriters in order to ensure that the quality of the underwriter's book of business does not deteriorate. For example, an underwriter might be required to have specific percentages of its book of business be considered "highly desirable," "average," and "below average." For this type of performance standard to be effective, the insurer's underwriting guidelines need to clearly delineate among account categories. Selection standards for individual underwriters usually support overall underwriting goals and are evaluated during an underwriting audit.

Product or Line of Business Mix

Measuring product or line of business mix is one way to evaluate an underwriter's contribution to a profitable book of business. Building a proper mix in a book of business requires that underwriters have a thorough knowledge of the insurer's business goals, including the types of products it prefers to write and the "appetite" the insurer has for certain types of risks. For example, if product liability losses are causing an adverse effect on the insurer's entire book of business, the product mix standard might require a reduction in manufacturing classes and a concerted effort to increase the writing in the contractor, service, and mercantile classes.

This performance measure requires a statement in the insurer's underwriting guidelines of the desired product or line of business mix for new and renewal business. Underwriters are often held accountable for supporting product or line of business mix goals, provided the goals are clearly stated in the insurer's underwriting guidelines.

Pricing

Insurers generally establish pricing standards as a nonfinancial measure. Pricing standards enable insurers to determine levels of premium adequacy by comparing premiums charged to the established pricing standards. For example, in commercial insurance, underwriters typically modify rates for each account being underwritten to reflect specific features of that account. Pricing standards indicate the extent to which these modifications depart from the insurer's regular or "standard" pricing. If one or more underwriters continually apply excessive premium credits to accounts to obtain new business or to retain it on renewal, an underwriting audit might reveal that profitability is being sacrificed in return for short-term growth.

Insurers also track through information systems the extent to which their underwriters deviate from the insurer's established pricing for specific classifications. This information might be useful in determining the extent to which the underwriter's book of business is underpriced or overpriced and where pricing adjustments might be made, should market conditions change.

Accommodated Accounts

Making an underwriting accommodation usually means accepting substandard exposures in return for other, more profitable accounts. Some insurers require that underwriters note the accommodation in the file for the account. Other insurers require underwriters to keep a log in which all accommodated risks are entered, along with the reasons for the accommodations. Evaluating the accommodation notes in the files or the log as part of underwriting audits and reviews can reveal whether the underwriter is making excessive accommodations and can ensure that the producer has increased volume or has fulfilled some other promise in exchange for the accommodations.

Retention Ratio

The retention ratio is the percentage of expiring policies that an insurer renews. Retention can be measured by policy count, premium volume, or both. Because most, if not all, of the underwriting investigation work has been completed for existing policies, retaining those policies offers more profit potential than acquiring new business, which involves acquisition costs.

A low retention rate might indicate serious deficiencies in the way insurers do business, including poor service to producers, noncompetitive pricing, or unfavorable claim service. This standard of performance requires careful monitoring of the renewal rate and evaluation of any trends detected.

Hit Ratio

Increasingly, underwriters have dual responsibilities. They are responsible not only for underwriting a profitable book of business, but also for meeting any new business sales goals the insurer makes applicable to their book of business, which is often referred to as **production underwriting**. The **hit ratio**, sometimes called the "success ratio," is a nonfinancial measure used to determine how well underwriters (or the insurer as a whole) are meeting their sales goals.

Underwriting management usually monitors this performance measure more closely than the other standards of performance because the success ratio provides information about the insurer's competitiveness in the current insurance market. Ratios that are either inordinately high or low might require further investigation. A high success ratio might indicate any of these conditions:

- Competition is easing.
- Rates are inadequate or lower than other insurers' rates.
- Coverage is broader than other insurers'.
- The underwriter has the skill set for production underwriting.
- Underwriting selection criteria are deteriorating.
- An extremely good relationship exists between the insurer and the producer.

Production underwriting

Performing underwriting functions in an insurer's office as well as traveling to visit and maintain rapport with agents and sometimes clients.

Hit ratio

The ratio of insurance policies written to those that have been quoted to applicants for insurance.

A low success ratio might indicate one of more of these conditions:

- Competition is increasing.
- Rates are higher than other insurer's rates.
- Coverages or forms are too restrictive.
- The underwriter does not have the skill set for production underwriting.
- Selection criteria are too stringent.
- Service is poor.
- A poor relationship exists between the insurer and the producer.

Service to Producers

Producers work most frequently with insurers who work most cooperatively with them. Because producers usually rank insurers on the basis of service received, an insurer must be able to evaluate its own performance.

This standard requires establishing a set of minimum acceptable standards for certain types of service to producers. The actual performance of each underwriter, branch, or region being evaluated is then compared with the targeted level of performance. See the exhibit "Example of "Service to Producers" Underwriting Standards."

Example of "Service to Producers" Underwriting Standards

Category	Minimum Acceptable Standard
1. Quotations	3 working days
2. New policies	3 working days
3. Replies to correspondence	2 working days
4. Cancellations, endorsements, certificates	5 working days
5. Direct cancellation notices	Same-day service
6. Renewals	No later than 10 days before expiration

[DA06401]

Premium to Underwriter

The volume of premium an underwriter is able to handle is an often-used measure of performance. Underwriting management uses this measure to determine whether individual underwriters are assuming their share of work compared with other underwriters in the same company handling similar accounts.

SUMMARY

The overarching purpose of underwriting is to develop and maintain a profitable book of business for the insurer. To accomplish this, underwriting serves additional purposes:

- Guarding against adverse selection
- Ensuring adequate policyholders' surplus
- Enforcing underwriting guidelines

Line underwriters are primarily responsible for making day-to-day risk selection decisions, which include these activities:

- Select insureds
- Classify and price accounts
- Recommend or provide coverage
- Manage a book of business
- Support producers and insureds
- Coordinate with marketing efforts

Staff underwriters assist underwriting management with making and implementing underwriting policy, which includes these activities:

- Research the market
- Formulate underwriting policy
- Revise underwriting guidelines
- Evaluate loss experience
- Research and develop coverage forms
- Review and revise pricing plans
- Arrange treaty reinsurance
- Assist others with complex accounts
- Conduct underwriting audits
- Participate in industry associations
- Conduct education and training

Underwriting authority reflects an insurer's underwriting policy. Compliance with levels of underwriting authority is important because it ensures that people with the proper experience and knowledge are making risk selection decisions.

An insurer's senior management formulates an underwriting policy to guide underwriting and the composition of the insurer's book of business. These major constraining factors are considered in establishing an underwriting policy:

- Financial capacity
- Regulation

- Personnel
- Reinsurance

Underwriting guidelines describe the parameters of acceptable applicants for insurance for which the insurer has priced its insurance products. Underwriting guidelines serve these purposes:

- Provide for structured decisions
- Ensure uniformity and consistency
- Synthesize insights and experience
- Distinguish between routine and nonroutine decisions
- Avoid duplication of effort
- Ensure adherence to reinsurance treaties and planned rate levels
- Support policy preparation and compliance
- Provide a basis for predictive models

Underwriting audits are a quality control check for uniform application of underwriting guidelines. Continuous improvement results from audits in the form of feedback to underwriters and from enhancements to the underwriting guidelines.

The underwriting process is a series of steps with related tasks applied to determine what submissions will be insured and for what amount of insurance, at what price, and under what conditions.

The underwriting process consists of six decision-making steps:

- Evaluate the submission
- Develop underwriting alternatives
- Select an underwriting alternative
- Determine an appropriate premium
- Implement the underwriting decision
- Monitor the underwriting decisions

An insurer's underwriting results are a key indicator of its profitability. However, the combined ratio, a widely used measurement, can be distorted by these factors:

- Changes in premium volume
- Major catastrophic losses
- Delays in loss reporting and loss development
- Underwriting cycles

Nonfinancial measures are useful in evaluating individual underwriters' and underwriting departments' performance. Such measurements include these:

- Selection
- Product or line of business mix

- Pricing
- Accommodated accounts
- Retention ratio
- Hit ratio
- Service to producers
- Premium to underwriter

Direct Your Learning ▶▶

Underwriting Property and Liability Insurance

Educational Objectives

After learning the content of this assignment, you should be able to:

▶ Describe in detail each of the COPE factors used to evaluate property loss exposures.

▶ Explain how insurable interest, policy provisions for valuing losses, and insurance to value affect a loss payment amount under property insurance.

▶ Explain how underwriters use policy amount, amount subject, normal loss expectancy (NLE), probable maximum loss (PML), and maximum foreseeable loss (MFL) to measure potential loss severity.

▶ Describe the underwriting considerations for business income and extra expense coverage.

▶ Describe the underwriting considerations and risk control techniques associated with employee dishonesty and crimes committed by others.

▶ Describe the loss exposures and the underwriting considerations for commercial general liability insurance.

▶ Describe the underwriting considerations for personal and commercial auto insurance.

▶ Describe the underwriting considerations for workers compensation insurance.

▶ Describe the underwriting considerations for umbrella and excess liability insurance.

5

Underwriting Property and Liability Insurance

UNDERWRITING PROPERTY INSURANCE USING THE COPE MODEL

Because fire is generally the most significant cause of loss for most forms of property insurance involving buildings and personal property, most of the tools that property underwriters use to evaluate loss exposures are related to the fire cause of loss. However, these tools are also beneficial in evaluating exposures from other causes of loss, such as lightning, explosion, collapse, windstorm, hail, water damage, flood, and earthquake.

The COPE model is a common tool underwriters use to evaluate exposures related to fire and other causes of loss. COPE is an acronym that stands for the four property risk characteristics an underwriter reviews when evaluating a submission for property insurance:

- Construction
- Occupancy
- Protection
- External exposure

While underwriting property insurance typically focuses on physical hazards, moral and morale (or attitudinal) hazards are also important.

Construction

The construction of the covered building, or the building that contains insured property, is a key factor in underwriting property insurance. The building's construction characteristics relate directly to its ability to withstand damage by fire and other causes of loss and to protect its contents.

The insurance application and an inspection report provided by the producer or risk control representative identify a building's construction. Advisory organizations publish building construction information for buildings subject to specific rating. If an underwriter needs additional information, independent inspection companies can be hired to conduct a property survey.

Construction Classes

Insurance Services Office (ISO) defines six classes for building construction.[1] Construction classes reflect the construction materials' ability to resist fire damage. Ratings consider the vertical load-bearing members that ultimately support the building's weight and the materials used in the roof and floors, which spread the weight across the vertical load-bearing members.

These are the six ISO construction classes:

- Class 1—Frame
- Class 2—Joisted Masonry
- Class 3—Noncombustible
- Class 4—Masonry Noncombustible
- Class 5—Modified Fire Resistive
- Class 6—Fire Resistive

Frame construction

A class of construction that has load-bearing components made of wood or other combustible materials such as brick or stone veneer.

ISO Class 1 is **frame construction**. In addition to the direct damage caused by a fire, frame construction can suffer structural damage because the weight-bearing supports are combustible. Frame construction is used in many dwellings and small mercantile buildings. Buildings of mixed construction, such as wood frame with brick veneer, stone veneer, aluminum siding, or stucco, are classified as frame buildings.

Joisted masonry construction

A class of construction that has load-bearing exterior walls made of brick, adobe, concrete, gypsum, stone, tile, or similar materials; that has floors and roofs of combustible materials; and that has a fire-resistance rating of at least one hour.

ISO Class 2 is **joisted masonry construction**. Joisted masonry construction is also called ordinary construction, ordinary masonry, brick, wood joisted, and brick joisted. Exterior walls can be fire-resistive construction with a fire-resistance rating of at least one hour, or they can be masonry construction. The walls are self-supporting, meaning that they stand without support from the building's frame. Because the exterior walls are load bearing (a load-bearing wall is a wall that runs at a right angle to the joists and bears the weight of the structure), many underwriters regard them as part of the building's frame. Interior columns and floors are of combustible material, usually wood.

Joisted masonry buildings are found in most major metropolitan areas, especially in northern states. The need for the exterior walls to support the structure's weight limits the height to which these structures can be built. Joisted masonry construction is rarely used for buildings higher than five stories and is typically used for buildings of three stories or fewer.

When a joisted masonry building suffers an intense fire, only a shell is left—the bare exterior walls. Walls can even fall or be pulled or pushed down by collapse of the roof or wooden support beams. The bricks in brick walls can be damaged beyond use by heat of sufficient intensity and duration. In the more frequent, less intense fires, the exterior bearing walls usually remain in usable, or nearly usable, condition; they continue to support the roof, and the walls and roof provide some protection for the interior.

Mill construction

A subclassification of joisted masonry construction that uses heavy timber for columns, beams, supports, and ties; has a minimum two-hour fire-resistance rating on bearing walls; and has an absence of floor joists.

Mill construction, also known as heavy timber construction, is a type of joisted masonry construction in which no concealed areas exist under the roof and floors that might permit a fire to go undetected. The heavy wood floors serve as a firestop, slowing the spread of fire. The size of the wood members used in mill construction gives these buildings structural strength. Fires that would consume the light joists used in typical joisted masonry might only char the heavy timber beams used in mill construction. This type of construction, though once commonly found in cotton and wool mills, is rarely used today.

ISO Class 3 is **noncombustible construction**. Although these buildings are noncombustible, they are not fire resistive. The buildings' unprotected steel structural supports twist and bend when subjected to the heat of a typical fire. If this type of building is filled with combustible contents, structural failure is extremely likely in a serious fire. See the exhibit "Light Noncombustible Building After Fire."

Noncombustible construction

A class of construction in which the exterior walls, floor, and roof of a building are constructed of, and supported by, metal, gypsum, or other noncombustible materials.

Light Noncombustible Building After Fire

Photo by Kim Holston. [DA03349]

Even though these structures are constructed of noncombustible material and do not provide fuel for a fire, their susceptibility to damage makes them only marginally safer from a fire underwriting perspective than joisted masonry or frame construction.

ISO Class 4 is **masonry noncombustible construction**. In masonry noncombustible construction, the building's exterior walls are made of self-supporting masonry materials, and the floors and roof are made of metal or some other noncombustible or slow-burning material. The exterior walls are made of construction with a fire-resistive rating of not less than one hour.

Masonry noncombustible construction

Masonry construction or construction that includes exterior walls of fire-resistive construction with a fire-resistance rating of not less than one hour.

A typical masonry noncombustible building has a masonry nonbearing wall surface, a concrete floor, a metal deck roof, and an unprotected metal frame. Low initial cost and low maintenance have made this type of construction extremely popular.

Modified fire-resistive construction

A class of construction that has exterior walls, floors, and roofs of masonry or other fire-resistive materials with a fire-resistance rating of one to two hours.

Fire-resistive construction

A class of construction that has exterior walls, floors, and roofs of masonry or other fire-resistive material with a fire-resistance rating of at least two hours.

ISO Class 5 is **modified fire-resistive construction**. It is similar to fire-resistive construction, except that the material's fire-resistance rating is one to two hours.

ISO Class 6 is **fire-resistive construction**. In a building of fire-resistive construction, the structure's load-bearing members can withstand fire damage for at least two hours. The construction materials are either (1) noncombustible with a fire-resistance rating of at least two hours or (2) protected by a noncombustible covering such as concrete, masonry, plaster, or gypsum that provides at least a two-hour fire-resistance rating. Fire-resistive ratings are assigned to construction material based on laboratory evaluations in test furnaces. Evaluations certify that materials can withstand fire damage under certain weight loads regardless of whether materials can be repaired or reused. The performance of such materials can differ significantly under actual fire conditions.

The load-bearing components of a fire-resistive building do not buckle or collapse as readily as those of other construction types. This is a higher standard than requiring that the structure not burn, because even though a structure does not burn, the fire's intense heat can still cause a building's load-bearing components to collapse. Fire-resistive construction is superior to other types of building construction, but it is not "fireproof."

From an underwriting standpoint, fire resistive is the best type of construction to prevent damage from most causes of loss. In addition to resisting fire damage, the strength of a fire-resistive structure gives it superior resistance to causes of loss such as windstorm, earthquake, and flood.

Construction Materials

The construction of a building's weight-bearing members is a basic underwriting consideration for the fire cause of loss. The interior finishing materials used on walls, floors, and ceilings; the insulation; and the roofing also affect a structure's combustibility and underwriting desirability.

Interior finish includes paint, paneling, and other wall coverings, as well as floor and ceiling materials. Underwriters must consider several interior finish characteristics, including their ability to spread fire, the fuel provided for a fire, and the smoke and noxious gases emitted while burning. Each of these characteristics affects the structure's overall property loss potential and the occupants' safety.

Fuel load (fire load)

The expected maximum amount of combustible material in a given area of a building, including both structural elements and contents, commonly expressed in terms of weight of combustibles per square foot.

Relatively noncombustible interior finishes include plaster, gypsum, and wallboard. Combustible interior finishes include wood or plywood, fiber ceiling tiles, and plastic wall coverings. Even fire-resistive buildings can have an interior finish that is highly combustible, such as an office with elaborate furnishings, draperies, and wall coverings. Certain paints, varnishes, wallpapers, and other surface coatings, when added to other combustible finishes, could contribute significantly to the building's **fuel load** (also called the fire load). Even the adhesives used in floor or ceiling tile can substantially affect a building's capacity to sustain or fuel a fire.

Interior finishing materials might be not only a property hazard but also a threat to life safety. A fire that consumes combustible interior finishes can generate highly toxic gases that circulate quickly throughout a building. See the exhibit "The Influence of Interior Finishes."

The Influence of Interior Finishes

A 1980 fire that started in a first-floor restaurant of the MGM Grand Hotel in Las Vegas involved highly combustible finishing materials on the walls and ceilings. As they burned, these materials generated hot smoke and gases that seeped into stairwells and elevator shafts. These toxic gases were then dispersed throughout the building's twenty-six floors, killing eighty-four occupants, many on upper floors. These deaths occurred not only because the interior-finish fumes were toxic, but also because vertical openings were not properly protected.

Another example of the influence of interior finishes is a Rhode Island nightclub fire that took place in February 2003. In this case, pyrotechnics used as part of a musical act ignited soundproofing materials, starting a fire that engulfed the building in less than five minutes and caused almost 100 deaths.

[DA06358]

Insulation is another construction material that can be problematic. Whether insulation is installed to conserve heat or to suppress sound, underwriters should try to determine its flame spread, fuel contribution, and smoke contribution characteristics. This information should be available from the insulation manufacturer. Insulation can contain the heat of a fire within a building, concentrating it on structural members. Such an insulated building could, therefore, weaken and collapse more quickly than anticipated.

In addition to considering the construction materials used for interior finishes and insulation, underwriters should consider the construction materials used in roofing. A roof's exterior surface not only keeps out the weather but also provides a barrier against fires in adjacent or nearby buildings, as sparks and embers falling from fires outside the building can make contact with roofs.

Roof coverings vary in the fire resistance they provide. Asphalt shingles are probably the most common roof covering for residential buildings. Although they are somewhat combustible, they are excellent barriers to severe fire exposures when properly constructed and installed. Conversely, combustible materials such as wood shake shingles or tar paper afford almost no protection. Consequently, many municipalities prohibit using untreated wood shingles in congested sections of major metropolitan areas.[2]

In addition to analyzing a building's construction type and construction materials, underwriters must consider additional characteristics such as age, building height, fire divisions, building openings, and building codes.

Building Age

The age of a building is the first additional construction characteristic that underwriters should consider. These age factors should be noted:

- A different building code might have been in effect when the building was constructed. Consequently, the building might lack protective features and systems generally considered essential today.

- Complying with current building codes might increase the cost of making repairs after a loss.

- Heating, cooling, electrical, and fire protection systems might be obsolete.

- The building might have been intended for a different occupancy and might not be suitable for its current use.

- Conversion and remodeling might have created concealed spaces in which fire could burn undetected and spread rapidly.

- Alterations and repairs made over the years might have left unprotected openings in vertical and horizontal firestops.

- The building's condition might have deteriorated for numerous reasons, including normal wear and tear, hard use, or lack of maintenance.

- The value of an older building might be difficult to determine, especially if the builder used construction techniques and materials that are no longer available.

Although proper maintenance mitigates the effects of age and deterioration, all buildings eventually wear out. The degree of obsolescence or deterioration is directly related to the type of construction, the occupancy, the physical abuse of the building, and the quality of the owner's maintenance. A frame structure normally shows its age more quickly than a joisted masonry building. However, an office occupancy in a frame structure with good maintenance might be preferable to a fire-resistive building with minimal maintenance occupied by a foundry, for example.

Construction methods and materials have changed over time. For example, building materials used in the 1930s have long been abandoned. Forty years ago, electrical systems were designed primarily for lighting, whereas modern wiring systems are designed to handle space heating, air conditioning, computer systems, and heavy appliances.

A building that was designed for a particular commercial occupant fifty years ago might be inadequate for the business that occupies the building today. The weight of equipment and stock associated with a business might have increased since the building was designed and built. In addition to the increase in hazard that occurs because of the change in occupancy, the building's structural integrity has probably deteriorated over time.

Building Height

Building height is the second additional construction characteristic that underwriters should consider. Buildings present unique problems when their height restricts the capability of the local fire service to fight fires from outside. The tallest extension ladders can reach 120 feet, but many municipal fire services are not capable of fighting a fire from the exterior of a building that exceeds 100 feet high (eight or nine floors). The National Fire Protection Association (NFPA) defines a high-rise building as one that is at least 75 feet tall.

In a high-rise building, the fire department has to fight the fire from inside—if possible. In one high-rise fire, the fire department could not approach the building because of flying glass caused by heat-shattered windows. Firefighters were forced to enter the building through a parking garage that provided access to the basement.

Controlling combustible contents in high-rise buildings is crucial. Such buildings should not contain occupancies that create a high fire hazard or a heavy fuel load. High-rise structures are commonly used as offices, apartments, and hotels—occupancies that present a low fire hazard. However, offices often store highly combustible paper files that create a high fire hazard.

High-rise structures sometimes have restaurants or bars on upper floors. Restaurants are a hazardous occupancy, and, when located on upper floors without adequate control or private protection, they constitute a significant fire hazard.

Property underwriters must realize that the fire department's first priority is the safety of a building's occupants. When lives are endangered, firefighters concentrate on human safety before fighting the fire.

When evaluating a high-rise structure, underwriters must consider the structure's fire-resistive characteristics and also the presence or absence of approved horizontal and vertical barriers designed to confine a fire to its area of origin.

Fire Divisions

A building's fire divisions are the third additional construction characteristic that underwriters should consider. While vertical integrity is the solution to many fire problems in high-rise structures, **fire divisions** are the analogous solution for fires in buildings with large horizontal areas. Many structures have a total horizontal area approaching one million square feet, making fire divisions critical.

A **fire wall** restricts the spread of fire by serving as a fire-resistive barrier. Interior walls might not be of sufficient fire resistance to qualify as a fire wall. Generally, fire walls must consist of at least eight inches of masonry material; however, fire wall adequacy also depends on the combustibility of building contents. A fire wall must also be free standing, which means that it must

Fire division

A section of a structure so well protected that fire cannot spread from that section to another, or vice versa.

Fire wall

A floor-to-roof wall made of noncombustible materials and having no open doors, windows, or other spaces through which fire can pass.

support its own weight without assistance from other building components. A load-bearing wall might not be a fire wall.

Fire walls are not effective if fire could easily spread over or around them. To prevent fire from spreading, fire walls must extend above a combustible roof and through exterior walls. Building codes typically specify that fire walls have a **parapet** eighteen to thirty-six inches above a combustible roof.[3] Extensions of the fire wall through the outer walls are known as fender walls. They are common in frame construction that uses masonry interior fire walls to create fire divisions. In many frame apartment structures, fender walls also provide privacy to terraces and patios. See the exhibit "Fire Divisions."

Parapet

A vertical extension of a fire wall that extends above a roofline.

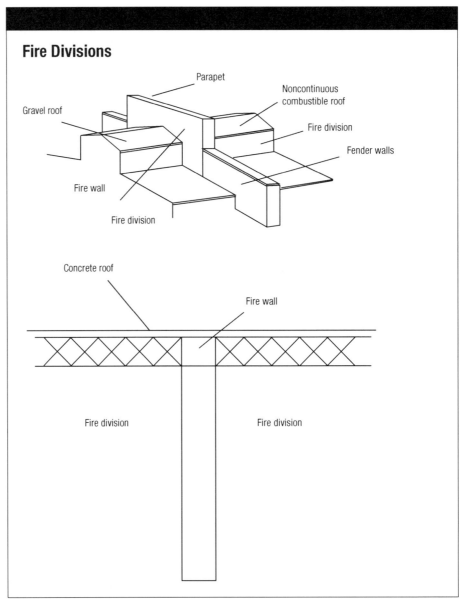

[DA06380]

A firestop is an element of fire-resistant construction, inserted in concealed spaces or between structural elements of a building, either a floor, wall, or roof area, that prevents the passage of flame from one point to another. Firestops may contain a fire for a time, thereby increasing the chance that the fire can be extinguished before it spreads further. Firestops are used to restore the entire structure, via each individually penetrated partition, to its original fire-rated integrity.

Building Openings

Building openings are the fourth additional construction characteristic that underwriters should consider. Openings that pierce fire walls or firestops increase fire loss potential. Although the building's original construction might have been appropriate, electricians and heating and air conditioning contractors, for example, might have installed equipment (such as electrical conduits and ductwork) that penetrates vertical and horizontal firestops or firewalls. See the exhibit "Consequences of Unplanned Building Openings."

Consequences of Unplanned Building Openings

A high-rise structure nearing completion in New York City had noncombustible structural components that were adequately protected and had originally been adequately protected to provide at least a two-hour fire rating. Installation work by subcontractors subsequently diminished that protection. The effect was to expose the structural steel components. The building was completed without those structural components having been resurfaced with a protective coating. When a fire occurred, the steel components were weakened and required replacement. Although the damage to those components was minimal, the cost of replacing the major building supports in this structure resulted in a multimillion-dollar loss.

[DA06381]

In addition to containing ducts and passageways, buildings contain many openings that, without additional protection, can compromise the integrity of a fire division. These openings include doors between fire walls, floor openings for stairs between floors, elevators, dumbwaiters, and conveyor belts. In most circumstances, fire doors can protect these openings. The most common causes of unprotected openings are oversight and poor risk control.

A vertical opening such as an elevator or a stairwell is protected only when it is completely segregated into a separate fire division. A properly constructed elevator shaft or stairwell constitutes a building within a building. If this design is achieved, a fire cannot spread from one floor to another unless it moves horizontally through one floor, through a barrier door, into the stairwell, up the stairwell, and through a second barrier door.

Fire doors are classified based on their ability to resist fire. To be most effective, a fire door in a fire wall must be capable of withstanding the same fire as the wall itself. Even with a fire door and other fire protection devices in operation, an opening will likely have less resistance to fire than a fire wall that has not been compromised by an opening. For example, a one-hour fire door in a two-hour fire wall reduces the fire protection rating of the entire wall to one hour.

Fire doors are approved when they meet NFPA design specifications. The NFPA's classification scheme ranges from doors that withstand fire for three hours to those that withstand fire for one-third of an hour. Approved doors have a rating seal that is usually placed on the door's edge.

An approved fire door cannot be effective if it is propped open or blocked. Each door must be automatically self-closing and unobstructed. Doors that must be left open to permit efficient industrial operations are fitted with fusible links that melt and release the door when the temperature reaches a predetermined level. This permits the doors to close automatically when exposed to the heat of a fire.

Building Codes

Building codes
Local ordinances or state statutes that regulate the construction of buildings within a municipality, county, or state.

Building codes are the fifth additional construction characteristic that underwriters should consider. Building codes can provide the underwriter with information regarding the construction of buildings erected under the provisions of those codes. For example, older buildings might have been constructed according to the provisions of a code that differs from the one in effect. Well-designed and properly enforced building codes can reduce insured losses, especially from such causes of loss as windstorm and earthquake.

A tool that underwriters can use to evaluate the effectiveness of building codes in general and in a particular community is ISO's Building Code Effectiveness Grading Schedule (BCEGS). The BCEGS program includes grades from 1 to 10, indicating the effectiveness of a community's building code. The schedule emphasizes mitigation of losses resulting from natural hazards, such as wind and earthquakes. A BCEGS grade of 1 indicates a municipality with exemplary commitment to building-code enforcement.[4]

Occupancy

Occupancy
The type or character of use of the property in question.

Occupancy is another prime consideration in property underwriting. The underwriter needs to know information about the activities and operations taking place in the building. Like construction, a building's occupancy affects property loss frequency and severity.

Occupancy Categories

Underwriters have traditionally grouped occupancies into six categories to help analyze their hazards:

- Habitational
- Office

- Institutional
- Mercantile
- Service
- Manufacturing

Habitational occupancies include apartments, hotels, motels, and nursing homes. Habitational occupancies are often in the control of someone other than the building owner, so detecting or controlling hazards can be difficult. Often, superior habitational occupancy results when the owner performs most of the building maintenance. Such maintenance demonstrates to the underwriter that the owner cares about the building's condition. In addition, regular maintenance permits the owner regular access to occupant-controlled areas that might have deteriorated because of tenant neglect. Unfavorable conditions that are identified can then be corrected.

Habitational occupancies, especially those in the hospitality industry, are often affected by fluctuations in the economy. The owner's financial stability correlates directly with the business's vacancy rate. An account's vacancy rate can be evaluated by comparing it with the average vacancy rate of similar operations in the area.

Office occupancy is a relatively low-hazard category. Materials found in offices are usually of limited combustibility and are relatively less susceptible to damage than those found in other occupancies. Buildings used primarily for office occupancies can have unusual features, such as restaurants or heliports. Likewise, office occupancies can exist in any type of structure and often share the building with other occupancies.

Institutional occupancies include schools, churches, hospitals, and property owned by governmental entities. Governmental entities often operate habitational properties such as public housing and nursing homes. Institutional occupancies also include special-purpose facilities such as prisons and police and fire stations. Risk retention groups, municipal pools, and other alternative risk-transfer programs are commonly used to insure public entities. To avoid adverse selection, an underwriter might sometimes need to determine why institutional property is being submitted for a traditional insurance program.

Mercantile occupancies include businesses that buy and sell goods and merchandise, whether wholesale or retail. Department stores, clothing stores, hardware stores, specialty shops, and grocery stores are examples of mercantile occupancies. The combustibility of a mercantile operation's contents varies by type of stock sold. A sporting goods store might stock ammunition and camping-stove fuel. Hardware stores and home centers normally have large quantities of flammables and combustibles, such as paints, varnishes, solvents, lumber, curtains, and wallpaper. The stock of mercantile occupancies is usually of significant value and is susceptible to fire, smoke, and water damage. Clothing is especially subject to severe loss from smoke and water damage, and a hardware store's stock can rust from the water used in fighting a fire. Health authorities usually require food exposed to fire and smoke to be withdrawn from sale. Therefore, a small fire can produce a large loss in this occupancy category.

Service occupancies include businesses that perform an activity or a service for the customer rather than create or sell a product. This category includes a long list of service businesses such as dry cleaners, auto service stations, barbers, and car washes and contains a diverse assortment of occupancies. The hazards presented by a service occupancy are usually specific to the service being performed. Dry cleaners, for example, have several occupancy hazards. Lint accumulation presents a fire and an explosion hazard. Dry cleaners also have large boilers for the hot water used in cleaning, and irons and presses could serve as ignition sources. Many of the solvents used in dry cleaning are flammable and need to be handled and stored properly.

Manufacturers' operations involve converting raw stock into finished products. The hazards of occupancies in this category vary widely according to the product being manufactured. Each occupancy must be considered on its own merits, with the underwriter's evaluation based on any special hazards in that occupancy. For example, a steel manufacturer has blast furnaces, rolling mills, and associated steel processing equipment, while a pasta manufacturer has an extensive drying process that creates a severe dust hazard.

Characteristics of Contents

Different types of occupancies present different types of underwriting concerns based on the characteristics of the contents at the insured location. The loss potential of a particular occupancy can be evaluated by examining the contents' ignition sources, combustibility, and susceptibility.

Ignition sources are the first characteristic of contents that underwriters should evaluate. Ignition sources provide the means for a fire to start. Underwriters must know the principal sources of ignition associated with the occupancy or the use of the covered building. Potential ignition sources include these:[5]

- Friendly fires that escape containment—Hostile fires can result from "friendly" open flames (such as in a fireplace) and heaters, smoking, lamps, furnaces, and ovens and space heaters, as well as from welding and cutting torches.
- Friction that generates enough heat to ignite nearby combustible material—Sources of friction include hot bearings, rubbing belts, grinding, shredding, picking, polishing, cutting, and drilling.
- Electricity that produces sparks or heat that can ignite exposed combustibles—Static electricity frequently causes sparks. Lighting fixtures, overloaded circuits, and worn wiring can release potentially damaging amounts of heat.
- Certain chemical reactions, called exothermic reactions, that produce heat sufficient to cause ignition—Sources of exothermic reactions include

substances such as magnesium or phosphorus, resulting in fires that are difficult to contain and extinguish.

Many industrial occupancies have obvious ignition sources as well as other, more subtle hazards.

Combustibility of content is a second characteristic of contents that underwriters should evaluate. The contents' combustibility determines how quickly the material ignites, the rate at which a fire spreads, and the intensity or amount of heat a fire generates. Gasoline, for example, ignites easily, spreads fire quickly, and burns with explosive intensity. Materials that are highly combustible include these:

- Light combustible materials such as thin plywood, shingles, shavings, paper, cotton, and other fibers
- Combustible dusts such as those produced when refinishing bowling alley lanes or refining flour
- Flammable liquids
- Combustible gases such as hydrogen
- Materials subject to spontaneous combustion
- Explosive materials, acids, and oxidizing agents

The combustibility of a building's contents affects the underwriting desirability of the building. Regardless of the contents' combustibility, the insured's management practices in controlling its hazards can make a significant difference in the acceptability of the account.

Susceptibility of content is a third characteristic of contents that underwriters should evaluate. Susceptibility measures the extent to which fire and its effects, either direct or resultant, will damage personal property—either merchandise or materials—typical of the occupancy. Contents that do not burn can also sustain damage from the heat of the fire, from smoke, or from water used to extinguish the fire. The susceptibility of contents is also a major underwriting consideration when determining the probable maximum loss. Even a small and quickly extinguishable fire can cause a severe loss due to highly susceptible contents such as expensive clothing, furniture, or electronic equipment.

Occupancy Hazards

The physical hazards that any occupancy presents can be classified into three categories: common hazards, special hazards of the class, and special hazards of the risk.

Common hazards exist in almost every occupancy. For example, housekeeping practices hazards are a concern for all occupancies. Sources of hazards include improper handling and disposal of waste and trash. An accumulation of greasy soot in vents and flues, particularly over cooking stoves, is also a significant hazard. Another source of common hazards is heating equipment. Furnaces and other heating equipment present a hazard because they are potential sources of ignition. Some sources of heat present greater hazards than others. Wood-burning stoves and salamanders (portable heaters), for example, present a greater hazard than gas furnaces, because fuel cannot be controlled or withdrawn once added to the fire. Typical electrical equipment found in occupancies, such as appliances and computers, and smoking also represent common hazards.

In addition to common hazards, occupancies have special hazards of the class and special hazards of the risk.

Special hazards of the class

A characteristic typical of all occupancies in a given class that can cause or aggravate a loss. An example is the hazard of cooking, common to the restaurant class.

Special hazards of the risk

A condition that can cause a loss but that is not typical of an occupancy. An example is the use of a welding torch in an auto repair shop.

Hazards that increase the probable frequency or severity of loss but that are typical for the type of occupancy are called **special hazards of the class**. Examples include cooking in a restaurant or using volatile chemicals in a manufacturing plant. Almost every class of occupancy has a hazardous activity that can reasonably be expected based on the nature of the occupancy. Underwriters must be familiar with the operations and hazards that are typical of the classes they handle.

Some businesses engage in activities that are not typical of other businesses in their class. Those activities create **special hazards of the risk**. These hazards are neither contemplated by the underwriter nor considered in standard rates for that class. A maintenance garage for a large fleet of trucks or taxicabs, for example, might contain a small body shop with welding equipment. The garage creates special hazards of the class, but the auto body work, typically performed by an auto body shop, creates special hazards of the risk. Identifying special hazards of the risk usually requires a physical inspection of the insured's business.

Protection

Protection

Measures taken to prevent or reduce the damage done by fire.

Protection is the third area in the COPE model that underwriters analyze. The quantity and quality of fire protection available to individual properties vary widely. Fire protection is of two types:

- Public or municipal fire protection provided by towns and cities
- Private fire protection provided by the property owner or occupant

Public Fire Protection

Public fire protection

Fire protection equipment and services made available through governmental authority to all properties within a defined area.

The organization of **public fire protection** varies by community. Municipalities and sometimes counties often provide protection to all properties within their political boundaries. However, fire district boundaries are sometimes drawn where they make the most effective use of available equipment and personnel.

Public fire protection consists primarily of the fire department that serves the community. The quality of protection varies. Because fire department quality is such a critical factor in insurance, public fire protection is a crucial underwriting consideration.

The American Association of Insurance Services (AAIS) personal and commercial insurance fire rates recognize these fire protection classifications:[6]

- Protected—This classification is divided into five tiers (Protected 1, Protected 2, Protected 3, Protected 4, and Protected 5) based on how far the building is from a responding fire department. To qualify for this classification, a building must be within 1,000 feet of a fire hydrant and within five road miles of a responding fire department.

- Partially protected—Building is located more than 1,000 feet from a fire hydrant and is within five road miles of a responding fire department.

- Unprotected—Building is located in an area that is classified as neither protected nor partially protected.

ISO independently collects and evaluates information on a community's public fire protection using its Fire Suppression Rating Schedule (FSRS) . The schedule measures the major elements of a community's fire suppression system and develops a numerical grading called a public protection classification (PPC) for each community. The PPC is an integral part of the ISO property insurance rating process. Most underwriters need only a basic understanding of the municipal grading system, but more extensive knowledge permits them to evaluate the relationship between private and public protection.

The PPC classification system rates the quality of a public fire service on a scale of 1 to 10. The scale measures the adequacy of the equipment available to the public fire service, the water supply, and response time available for property in a particular area. Class 1 represents the ideal; it is not reasonable to expect any community to achieve this rating. Classes 1 through 8 apply to properties in protected communities, while Classes 9 and 10 apply to unprotected communities. Properties located too far from a water supply adequate for fire suppression fall into Class 9. Properties that have no public fire protection service available fall into Class 10.

A single public protection class does not always apply to the property in an entire municipality or fire district. Geographic features sometimes prevent prompt fire service response to property in some areas, and water mains and hydrants in some areas might not extend to all properties that a given fire service protects. These considerations produce a higher public protection class number (indicating lower-quality public fire protection).

A given property might also have a public protection class inferior to the community as a whole, for two principal reasons. First, the property might present a loss exposure to fires that are more challenging than the fire service is equipped to handle, such as flammable metals or large quantities of flammable liquids. Second, the fire service might lack adequate year-round access to the property, especially when the property owner maintains private access roads. The owners of some seasonal properties in cold climates make no arrangements for snow plowing because they are closed for the winter. Snow accumulation on the roads periodically makes such properties inaccessible to fire services. The PPC considers this and assigns a class of 9 or 10 for those properties.

Property insurance underwriting evaluates not only public fire protection systems but also private fire protection systems. Fire protection systems consist of prevention, detection, and suppression measures.

Private Fire Protection: Prevention

Many measures can be taken to prevent fires from occurring or to minimize the damage that fires cause. Fires can be prevented by controlling heat sources and by separating fuel and heat. Fires can also be prevented by controlling arson. Various building design features can limit or slow the vertical or horizontal spread of fire or reduce the damageability of property exposed to fire.

Heat sources can sometimes be reduced or eliminated. Sometimes furnaces, forges, or kilns are larger or hotter than necessary, or the number of heating devices can be reduced. Sometimes hot water, for example, can be used instead of an open flame. When heat is a byproduct, various options, such as fluorescent lighting, can sometimes reduce heat sources. Cooling systems can dissipate heat energy. Electrical energy can be controlled with circuit breakers and adequate grounding.

Fuel and heat can often be separated by ensuring that flammable or combustible materials are kept away from fixed-location heat sources. For example, trash, paper, and flammable liquids should not be stored in the furnace room. Restaurant cooking stoves and their vent systems should be cleaned periodically to prevent the buildup of greasy deposits. Mobile heat sources, from equipment such as welding torches and portable heaters, present a special challenge because the hazards continually change. Such equipment is taken where it is needed and is not necessarily restricted to use in areas free of fuels or combustible materials.

Private Fire Protection: Detection

Early fire detection is important because the size of a fire increases exponentially with time, and large fires are more difficult to suppress than small fires. Major detection systems include a guard service with a clock system, a private patrol service, smoke and heat detectors, a local fire alarm system, a central station system, and a remote station system or proprietary alarm system. Sprinkler systems often have a local or central station alarm that is triggered by the flow of water within the system. The major detection systems are described here:

- Guard service with a clock system—The effectiveness of a guard service depends on its guards' alertness. A clock system verifies that the guard makes regular rounds. Guards carry devices that time-mark their routes through the premises. The disadvantage of a basic clock system is that the watchperson's alertness cannot be determined until the device is reviewed. Many businesses have connected certain locations to a central station. If these locations are not checked by the watchperson, central-station personnel follow up.

- Private patrol service—Small merchants or businesses often employ private patrol services to check for break-ins. In many areas, business and industry associations provide private patrol services as a member benefit. A guard visits each business several times during the night to ensure that all doors and windows are secure and that fire has not broken out. Some private patrol services employ a clock system to verify that guards complete their assigned rounds on schedule. Although they provide some security, private patrols are unlikely to discover a fire on a timely basis.

- Smoke detectors—The use of smoke detectors in private residences and businesses has increased significantly with the development of inexpensive, battery-powered smoke detectors. NFPA standards require that smoke detectors be wired directly to an AC power source in all newly constructed dwellings or buildings. The NFPA also recommends that residential smoke detectors be located outside each sleeping area, on each floor serving as living quarters, and in the basement. Most smoke detectors perform independently, sounding an alarm only at the location of the detected smoke. More advanced systems connect the smoke detectors so that all the alarms sound simultaneously. Often, these advanced systems also serve as burglar alarms by sounding a different alarm tone to indicate break-ins.

- Heat detectors—Heat detectors can be operated independently of suppression devices but are most frequently combined with devices like automatic sprinkler systems. Heat detectors are slow to activate, which makes them less desirable than smoke detectors. Heat detectors are used when other detection devices are not effective or are triggered too easily. Small storage rooms in which heat buildup would be rapid or kitchens in which some smoke is a usual byproduct might be better protected by heat detectors. Heat detectors activate when heat causes a physical or an electrical charge in a material or gas. They can also respond to a specific temperature or to a predetermined rate of increase in the ambient temperature.

To perform their intended function, smoke and heat detectors must be connected to an alarm, which can be local, central station, remote station, or proprietary:

- Local fire alarm system—A **local fire alarm system** is a type of automatic fire detection system that relies on occupants or passersby to report the alarm to fire or police officials. Such an approach depends on unreliable assumptions, such as the notion that someone will hear and report the alarm. Consequently, local alarms are not considered effective at report-

Local fire alarm system

A detection system, triggered by smoke or heat, that sounds a bell, siren, or another audible alert at the premises only.

ing fires; however, they do provide basic protection and are better than having no system at all.

Central station system

A private detection service that monitors the systems of multiple businesses and/or residences and that calls appropriate authorities or dispatches its own personnel when an alarm is activated.

- Central station system—A **central station system** is a private service with personnel who monitor the systems of commercial establishments and, sometimes, residences. When an alarm is activated, the service either calls the appropriate authorities or dispatches its own personnel to investigate. Central station alarm systems eliminate the need for human intervention at the scene and offer a better solution to fire detection than local alarms. A central station alarm, with or without sprinklers, greatly increases the likelihood of a rapid response to a fire, which should significantly reduce both insured and uninsured losses. The disadvantage of this method is its relative cost.

- Remote station system and proprietary alarm system—These are similar to central station systems, except that they do not signal a commercially operated central station. A remote station alarm directly signals the local police and fire stations. A proprietary alarm directly signals a receiving station located on the protected premises, notifying on-site personnel.

Private Fire Protection: Suppression

Fire detection devices can alert people to evacuate the property, but for property underwriting purposes, prompt fire detection does no good unless the fire that has been detected can then be suppressed. Private fire suppression systems consist of equipment and personnel that the insured uses to suppress a fire before the municipal fire service arrives. For isolated commercial properties, a private suppression system could be the only fire service available. Private fire suppression methods fall into four categories: (1) portable extinguishers, (2) standpipes and hoses, (3) automatic sprinkler systems, and (4) private fire brigades.

Portable fire extinguishers should be available in every business and residence. To be effective, extinguishers must be maintained regularly, and users must be trained to operate them. Most fire extinguishers are classed as "ABC," meaning they can be used on all types of fires. Class "D" extinguishers are designed for fires involving flammable metals. Class "K" extinguishers are designed for fires involving cooking oils or fats. NFPA publishes standards that indicate the number and type of portable fire extinguishers that a property should have based on size and occupancy.

Standpipe and hose systems consist of water supply pipes located inside buildings and equipped with standard fire department connections at regular intervals. In a multistory structure, standpipes are commonly located in stairwells or fire towers with a hose connection at each floor landing. When the building covers a large horizontal area, standpipe hose connections are typically spaced at regular intervals throughout the floor. Standpipe systems usually have fire hoses attached so that both the fire service and the building's occupants can use them. A valve at the standpipe station controls water flow to the hoses. Even without attached hoses, standpipes are an invaluable aid to firefighters. By delivering water to the interior areas and upper floors of a building, they eliminate the need for firefighters to drag charged hoses across long distances to reach a fire. Standpipe systems can draw their water from the building water supply, but they do not always contain water. All standpipe systems have a fire department connection, sometimes called a "Siamese connection," outside the building. This allows the fire service to pump additional water into wet standpipe systems for more effective fire suppression.

Automatic sprinkler systems are the most effective means of suppressing a fire. Automatic sprinkler systems consist of a series of interconnected valves and pipes with sprinkler heads. Commonly, each sprinkler head contains a heat-sensing element that responds individually to the heat generated by a fire. Contrary to what is depicted in some television shows and movies, only the sprinkler heads directly exposed to the fire's heat release water. The exception is a deluge system, which is used only under special circumstances. Automatic sprinkler systems respond more quickly than any other fire suppression system and deliver water where it is needed. Sprinkler systems always require their own water supply, but they also come equipped with an external fire department connection to supplement water and pressure.

There are a variety of approaches to delivering fire extinguishment materials through sprinkler systems. The most common types of automatic sprinkler systems that rely on water as an extinguishing agent are wet pipe sprinkler systems, dry pipe sprinkler systems, pre-action sprinkler systems, and deluge sprinkler systems.

Most automatic fire sprinkler systems are **wet pipe sprinkler systems**. In areas in which the sprinkler lines are exposed to temperatures below freezing, a dry pipe system might be more appropriate. The pipes in **dry pipe sprinkler systems** respond more slowly to fire than wet pipe systems because the gas must leave the system before water can flow through the sprinkler heads. However, a dry pipe system is not advisable if water damage to sensitive property is a concern.

Pre-action sprinkler systems are used where property is highly susceptible to water damage from damaged sprinklers or piping. The sprinkler system valve remains closed until the smoke or heat detector opens it in response to fire conditions. Before the system discharges water, the detection component must sense a fire, and heat must activate a sprinkler head.

Deluge sprinkler systems are similar to pre-action systems, except that sprinkler heads are always open. When a fire activates a detection device, water is simultaneously discharged from all sprinklers in the system, flooding or "deluging" the protected areas.

Depending on the occupancy, and where water damage to sensitive property is a concern, it may be appropriate to have specialized sprinkler systems that use gas extinguishing agents—typically halon, carbon dioxide, or environmentally friendly agents such as Inergen. The gas disrupts the chemical reaction in a fire and eliminates the extensive damage to contents caused by water

Wet pipe sprinkler systems
Automatic fire sprinkler systems with pipes that always contain water under pressure, which is released immediately when a sprinkler head opens.

Dry pipe sprinkler systems
Automatic fire sprinkler systems with pipes that contain compressed air or another inert gas that holds a valve in the water line shut until an open sprinkler head releases the gas and allows water to flow through the previously dry pipe to the sprinkler head.

Pre-action sprinkler systems
Automatic fire sprinkler systems with automatic valves controlled by smoke or heat detectors.

Deluge sprinkler system
A type of sprinkler system in which all the heads remain permanently open; when activated by a detection system, a deluge valve allows water into the system.

from other kinds of sprinkler systems. These specialized systems are also used when a fire can be expected to involve flammable liquids or live electrical equipment—cases in which the gas extinguishants are more appropriate and effective than water. For example, properly protected restaurants use a wet chemical extinguishing system, often called Ansul systems (Ansul is the leading manufacturer of such systems), to protect hoods over cooking equipment and ducts that disperse the heated air and combustion products. Water is not an appropriate extinguishing agent where heavy accumulations of grease are common.

Both sprinkler and standpipe systems can be connected to an alarm that alerts a monitoring station to the flow of water through the pipes. An alarm can be connected directly to the fire department. Both sprinkler and standpipe alarms can be connected to a central station that monitors them constantly and responds to any water flow. Sprinkler and standpipe alarms provide early notification of both fires and sprinkler leakage. Some alarms can still be connected only to a local alarm outside a building.

Fire brigade

A fire service in which building personnel in establishments located far from municipal fire services respond to fire situations.

Private **fire brigades** are found only in the largest industrial complexes, such as petrochemical plants, and rural areas in which municipal fire protection is unavailable or considered inadequate. Underwriters should evaluate private fire brigades in the same way that they evaluate public fire departments. They should gather information about the number and training of personnel, about the amount and type of equipment and its location within the industrial complex, and about the size and reliability of the water supply.

External Exposure

External exposure

A loss exposure outside the area owned or controlled by the insured.

External exposure is the fourth major element property underwriters analyze. External exposure refers only to fires that originate outside the insured premises. This source of loss is significant, because a fire in one building often spreads to adjacent buildings.

External exposure is much more difficult to analyze than construction, occupancy, and protection. Lack of information is the biggest problem. Because the underwriter usually has no direct contact with the owner of the exposing property, the information needed for analysis is difficult to obtain. Underwriters obtain some of the needed information by asking the producer specific questions or by ordering a risk control report. Single-occupancy loss exposures and multiple-occupancy loss exposures present different underwriting challenges.

Single-Occupancy Loss Exposures

A single-occupancy loss exposure exists when the property being underwritten consists of a single building, fire division, or group of buildings, all owned or controlled by the insured. The external exposures come from adjoining properties. One example is the loss exposure created by buildings situated close enough to permit a fire in that exposing building to spread to the insured (exposed) building. Another example is the loss exposure created by combustible materials such as brush, woodlands, or trash surrounding the open areas of the exposing building.

An exposing building is one that significantly increases the possibility of a fire in the insured building. A fire that erupts in an exposing building is an exposure fire. External exposures are by definition outside the insured's control. Often, little can be done from a risk control standpoint to reduce external exposures. However, fire walls, fire doors, special barriers, and parapets can reduce the probability that an external fire will spread to the insured property. Clear space between buildings, good water supply, quick response from the fire department, and internal and external automatic sprinkler systems are additional methods of controlling external loss exposures.

Multiple-Occupancy Loss Exposures

In a multiple-occupancy building, persons other than the insured own or control portions of the fire division that contains the insured property. If the insured occupies part of a building that is divided from the rest of the building by an approved fire wall, that part is considered a single occupancy; the rest of the building is then treated as an exposing fire division. However, if the insured occupies part of a building with combustible walls separating the insured property from the other occupancies, a multiple-occupancy loss exposure exists. For example, shopping centers commonly have walls that can be moved to resize store areas to meet the needs of new occupants. Most office buildings occupied by more than one tenant are also multiple-occupancy buildings.

When evaluating a multiple-occupancy building, underwriters consider the occupancy class of the other occupants. In a typical commercial shopping center of brick construction, for example, a shoe store could be exposed by a restaurant or a paint store in adjacent portions of the same fire division.

Another factor to consider is the amount of protection available against fire originating in exposing occupancies. Even when no fire wall separates occupancies, a noncombustible wall provides some protection. However, the walls separating some occupancies could be no more than drywall partitions, and the entire fire division might have one continuous attic. See the exhibit "Practice Exercise: Using the COPE Model for Risk Analysis."

Practice Exercise: Using the COPE Model for Risk Analysis

An application has been received for commercial property with basic form causes of loss (includes fire, lightning, explosion, vandalism, sprinkler leakage, windstorm, hail, smoke, aircraft, vehicles, riot or civil commotion, sinkhole collapse, and volcanic action) from Music, Inc., an electronics company that produces a well-known line of stereo equipment. The relevant hazards include these:

- Building construction—All operations are located in a one-story structure that is 25 percent joisted masonry construction and 75 percent masonry noncombustible construction.

- Fire safety—The risk has three major fire divisions: the warehouse, the manufacturing area, and the office and laboratory. The sprinkler system was installed in 1968 when the building was constructed and covers 75 percent of the total area. In the warehouse, a dry pipe sprinkler system is used; in all other sprinklered locations, a wet pipe sprinkler system is in operation.

- Vandalism—The building is protected by guards on duty between 4:30 PM and 7:30 AM. A local burglar alarm system covers all door openings (exterior and interior) of the warehouse portion of the building.

- Location—The property is located in an industrial park and is flanked by a four-story, multiple-occupancy manufacturing building and a warehouse. Asphalt parking lots are on the other two sides.

- Operations—All metal stamping, bending, and forming operations for component casings are carried out in an area completely separated from the rest of the plant. The dip tank for painting metal parts is located in the sprinklered portion of the building. The highest concentration of values is in the drying rooms, where dipped items are stored after passing through drying ovens.

Use the COPE model to perform a risk analysis of these hazards.

Answers

Use of the COPE model results in this risk analysis of the hazards:

- Construction—Construction appears to be acceptable. Masonry noncombustible will sustain less fire damage than the joisted masonry areas. It is important to determine which operations are being conducted in the 25 percent of the building that is joisted masonry construction. Fire divisions will assist in limiting the horizontal spread of fire from one section of the building to another.

- Occupancy—The areas of greatest concern are the exposures and hazards related to the manufacturing operations. Potential hazards include heat treatment, welding, soldering, electrical and wiring systems, and drying ovens. Improper storage of flammables or other hazardous materials may increase the likelihood of a property loss. Housekeeping and maintenance are also important considerations. The contents of this occupancy include finished stereo equipment, unfinished components, and work in progress. These are all highly susceptible to damage from either fire or accidental sprinkler leakage.

- Protection—No information is provided as far as public protection. The underwriter would need to determine the Public Protection Class and the availability of fire department service and proximity to fire hydrants. Private protection is adequate and includes partial sprinkler protection, overnight guard service, and a local fire alarm.

- Exposure—The property is located in an industrial park with similar-type occupancies as exposing properties. The immediate exposing structure is the adjacent four-story manufacturing and warehouse building. A possible concern would be any hazardous manufacturing occupancies in surrounding buildings. The asphalt parking lots are a positive factor and provide clear space, which reduces the possibility of damage to the covered building as the result of a loss at an exposing structure.

[DA06382]

PROPERTY POLICY PROVISION UNDERWRITING CONSIDERATIONS

Determining the quality of a property claim submission begins with assessing the amount that the policy will obligate the insurer to pay in the event of the loss.

For property underwriters, how much an insurer will be obligated to pay when a loss occurs is a significant consideration. The factors that determine the amount include the insurable interest of all persons insured, policy provisions for establishing the value of insured property, and the relationship of the amount of insurance to that value.

Insurable Interest

Underwriters must consider how each type of ownership will affect the amount of loss paid by the policy. Subject to the limits of coverage, coinsurance provisions, and the deductible, standard commercial property forms limit the insured's recovery to the amount of its insurable interest at the time of the loss. The most common interest in property comes from outright ownership. Other forms of ownership exist in which the insured may have something less than an insurable interest in the entire property or may have an insurable interest for only a period of time. For a given property, several persons or entities may have insurable interests that, in total, may exceed the value of the property.

Policy Provisions for Valuing Losses

The method prescribed by the policy provisions for placing a value on covered property at the time of loss is important when determining the acceptability of a new submission or a renewal and for properly underwriting property coverage. The underwriter must understand how the policy provisions for placing

Replacement cost

The cost to repair or replace property using new materials of like kind and quality with no deduction for depreciation.

Actual cash value

A method in valuing property which is calculated as the cost to replace or repair property minus depreciation, the fair market value, or a valuation determined by the broad evidence rule.

Coinsurance clause

A clause that requires the insured to carry insurance equal to at least a specified percentage of the insured property's value.

a value on insured property affect the amount the insurer will have to pay in the event of a loss.

The most common property valuation methods are **replacement cost** and **actual cash value**. Other valuation clauses may be appropriate for some accounts and used in some insurance contracts. While actual cash value is the standard valuation approach in many commercial property forms, most underwriters regard replacement cost as the valuation most appropriate to property insurance in general and to commercial property coverage in particular. The replacement cost option in commercial property forms typically reimburses the insured fully for any losses sustained, eliminates uncertainty in loss adjustment, and creates a contract that fulfills a reasonable customer's expectations.

Insurance to Value

Underwriters use the value of the covered property to determine whether the insured carries an adequate amount of insurance. An underinsured property owner (one who has not purchased insurance to value) will not be completely indemnified if the property is destroyed. Although this is the most obvious reason to purchase insurance to value, total losses are relatively uncommon and lower limits of insurance have lower premiums. Therefore, to encourage purchasing insurance to value, insurance policies include **coinsurance clauses** and other insurance-to-value provisions.

Insurance to value provides better policyholder protection against a total loss, and policyholders who are insured to value will not face a coinsurance penalty at the time of loss. The insurer benefits when underwriters encourage insurance to value because these results are then promoted:

- Higher limits of property insurance—Insurance to value promotes higher limits of property insurance, which in turn generate higher property insurance premiums that properly reflect the insurer's loss exposures.

- An adequately insured book of business—An underinsured book of business generates inadequate premiums that, in turn, can contribute to an underwriting loss.

- Competitive status for the insurer—An underwriting loss caused by underinsurance can indicate the need for higher property insurance rates, which, in turn, make the insurer less competitive.

When working to prevent underwriting losses, it is preferable to insure to value with rates that reflect the loss exposure than to underinsure property at inflated rates. Underwriters can confirm insurance to value on new business by using various appraisal tools, including those that might be available from the insurer's risk control department. In addition, various vendors offer building and contents valuation services for a fee.

At policy renewal, the underwriter should reassess the values exposed to loss and adjust limits accordingly. Due to external forces such as inflation, having adequate limits of insurance on new business does not necessarily ensure ongoing insurance to value.

MEASURES OF POTENTIAL LOSS SEVERITY

An important consideration in evaluating property loss exposures is their potential severity.

Underwriters use several measures to determine the potential severity of a loss:

- Policy amount
- Amount subject
- Normal loss expectancy (NLE)
- Probable maximum loss (PML)
- Maximum foreseeable loss (MFL)

Each measure is the sum of separate values for every type of coverage the policy provides. The calculations of amount subject, NLE, PML, and MFL include subjective elements. General agreement on precisely what each means does not exist. Different underwriters arrive at different estimates of amount subject, NLE, PML, and MFL for the same or similar risks. Estimates by any two underwriters with a common employer, however, should be consistent if not identical because insurers ordinarily establish rules for determining both values.

Policy Amount

The amount of insurance the policy provides (or its limit of liability) is the easiest to calculate and is the only measure of potential severity on which underwriters tend to agree. However, the amount of insurance is also the least useful figure for determining potential loss severity, because the amount of insurance purchased could have little bearing on the amount of the loss. Blanket insurance can complicate the calculation by providing a single amount of insurance for multiple properties at one or more locations.

Amount Subject

Amount subject measures the exposure to a single loss and varies by cause of loss. Because their perspectives differ, the insurer and the insured might have differing opinions about the amount subject.

For fire insurance, the amount subject is almost always the value of all insured property exposed within a single fire division. This could be part of a building, an entire building, or several buildings. Underwriters often use the expression "within four walls" to explain the concept of amount subject. This description is generally accurate, but it implies that the calculation is more precise than it actually is. It requires subjective judgment to measure the boundaries of a fire division. Where no firewalls are present, adjacent buildings of frame, masonry, or noncombustible construction might constitute a single fire division. Not all underwriters agree about what constitutes an acceptable firewall. Not all insurers apply the same rules concerning how much distance between buildings is enough to create separate fire divisions.

To create separate fire divisions between adjoining buildings, some underwriters insist on firewalls with parapets (a parapet is a vertical extension of a firewall that extends above a roofline) that extend at least four feet above the roof. Others accept firewalls that extend only to the underside of a noncombustible roof. An insurer may or may not accept a lower parapet height when there is clear space between exposing buildings. The amount of clear space needed between buildings also varies from one insurer to another. At one extreme, an insurer might insist that any building close enough to generate an exposure charge in the rate schedule constitutes part of the same fire division. Others may divide two buildings into separate fire divisions with much less clear space between them. The insurer's underwriting policy reflects the values individual insurers apply to make these judgments. Two insurers looking at the same account may arrive at very different estimates of the amount subject.

Internal firewalls can also divide a single building into several separate fire divisions. Underwriters typically apply the same standards to firewalls within a building as they do to firewalls between structures that adjoin one another and have no intervening space. Firewalls within structures that incorporate fire-resistive construction need not extend through the roof, which acts as a full fire stop. Effectively partitioning a modified fire-resistive building into multiple fire divisions might require parapets. But the parapets generally do not need to be as high as those for **noncombustible**, masonry, or frame structures.

Underwriters must also consider how ventilating systems and electrical conduits affect the ability of a fire to spread from one part of a building to another. Heat and products of combustion can spread very quickly through the ducts of ventilating systems. Ventilation ducts that pass through firewalls should be equipped with automatic dampers. Conduits for electrical wires and telephone lines pose a similar threat, although their smaller size restricts their ability to transmit heat. The primary concern when conduits pierce firewalls is having firestopping to prevent heat from penetrating the firewall.

When determining the amount subject, the underwriter must consider all insurance that the insurer writes within a single fire division. The insurance company might insure the owner of a building and its tenant separately or separately insure several tenants in a multiple-occupancy structure. The insurer might have to pay the face amount of all policies that insure property within a single fire division.

Noncombustible construction

A class of construction in which the exterior walls, floor, and roof of a building are constructed of, and supported by, metal, gypsum, or other noncombustible materials.

Normal Loss Expectancy

Normal loss expectancy (NLE) is defined as the loss expected under normal operating conditions with all fire protection services working. In determining the NLE for a risk, several elements are used for consideration:

- Construction
- Protection (positive pressure ventilation/sprinklers)
- Business interruption contingency plans
- Fire divisions
- Susceptibility of contents to damage and combustibility
- Operational hazards

Probable Maximum Loss

Probable maximum loss (PML) is the underwriter's estimate of the largest loss likely to occur. PML calculations are subjective estimates. To many underwriters, PML is meaningful only for fire-resistive buildings and their contents. For other types of construction, such as frame, underwriters consider PML equal to the amount subject and make only one calculation. Some underwriters assign a PML equal to the maximum value exposed in any two adjacent fire divisions that are separated by firewalls breached by protected openings. Other underwriters might calculate a PML at less than the full value exposed within a single fire division. Amount subject considers the benefit of horizontal fire divisions, but PML includes the effects of building features that impede the vertical spread of fire from one floor to the next. Underwriters disagree on the best method for determining PML and on whether to modify the PML calculation to reflect differences in the quality of various types of fire-resistive construction.

Underwriters often calculate PML based on the assumption that anything that can go wrong will go wrong. For example, an underwriter might assume that the automatic fire sprinklers will not be maintained and fully functional to actuate when a fire occurs and that firefighters will not respond to the alarm in a timely manner. Underwriters often refer to the protection available to a property as "lines of defense." Insurer underwriting guidelines might specify that PML be calculated presuming that the first two lines of defense have failed (the sprinkler system and the fire service, in the example). Insurer underwriting guidelines vary considerably on this issue, and many insurers ask their underwriters to consider worst-case scenarios but permit their underwriters considerable flexibility in determining what those scenarios are.

For fire-resistive construction, insurer underwriting guidelines might establish PML as the value of a certain number of floors, expressed as maximum and minimum values. One insurer, for example, established a PML that ranged from three to five floors for full (not modified) fire-resistive construction in which all walls, floors, and roofs had at least a two-hour fire-resistive rating.

The insurer reserved the lower end of the fire-resistive rating scale for less hazardous occupancies or properties protected by a sprinkler system with a higher grading. The insurer also regarded two or more floors connected by unprotected openings as a single floor for PML calculations but accepted automatic fire sprinklers installed only at the vertical openings as adequate protection. For modified fire-resistive construction (one-hour fire-resistive rating), the PML ranged from five to eight floors. In divided masonry and noncombustible construction, the insurer established a basic PML at two fire divisions, assuming that at least one fire door would fail. While these underwriting guidelines are specific, underwriters at this insurer were granted some flexibility in calculating PML, based on individual risk conditions.

To establish an accurate PML for a fire-resistive building, the underwriter must also consider how a fire can spread vertically from floor to floor and how fire can damage property on the floors that it never reaches. It is sometimes helpful to think of fire-resistive floors as horizontal firewalls that inhibit the vertical spread of fire, similar to the way in which firewalls contain the horizontal spread of fire. Vertical conduits and ducts for ventilating systems can spread fire from floor to floor in a high-rise building in the same way in which they can allow fire to travel horizontally from one fire division to another. Fire can also travel up the outside of a fire-resistive building, moving from floor to floor by radiating heat through the windows to floors above the fire. This is a significant cause of damage in most severe high-rise fires.

The fact that a fire is contained within one or two floors of a fire-resistive building does not limit damage to property on those floors. Water used to suppress a fire will flow to floors below the fire floor by gravity, carrying soot and debris with it. All the ensuing damage from smoke and water is part of the fire loss. In setting the PML, the underwriter must allow for smoke and water damage on floors the fire never reaches.

Accurately calculating the amount subject and PML is also important for complying with state insurance codes and satisfying reinsurance arrangements. Statutes generally prohibit an insurance company from exposing more than 10 percent of its policyholders' surplus to a single loss net of authorized reinsurance. Because amount subject measures this single loss exposure for property insurance, a liberal calculation of a high-value property could endanger the insurer's financial condition. Most insurers are of sufficient financial size or have adequate reinsurance programs so that writing too large an account and violating regulatory constraints are not problems. For some weakly capitalized insurers, this constraint would be a concern because insurance regulators will penalize insurers that exceed what is considered a prudent risk retention on any one account. Because underwriting guidelines typically adopt a conservative net line, expressed as limits of liability that fall within the underwriter's authority, a line underwriter would have to exceed his or her own authority by a considerable amount before violating the 10 percent rule.

PML also influences the availability of both treaty and facultative reinsurance. Reinsurers have designed many property treaties to facilitate writing large amounts of insurance on a single risk while limiting the reinsurer's exposure within the PML.

PML is a concept that can accommodate a wide range of definitions. Faced with the same account, different underwriters will assign different values to the PML. Underwriters might often legitimately use other terms to convey the concept of a loss larger than the probable maximum loss, but the difference is often only semantic. One underwriter, for example, may assign a PML to an account and then proceed to calculate a higher maximum foreseeable loss. A more conservative colleague might ignore the concept of maximum foreseeable loss entirely but assign a PML higher than the first underwriter's PML. Thus, PML is a concept that each insurer will apply according to its own underwriting policy. By its nature, PML produces different values when applied by different underwriters. Several terms have emerged to express refinements of the concept that individual insurers consider important.

Maximum Foreseeable Loss

PML is not the only term underwriters use to describe the largest loss that can reasonably be expected. It is simply the term used most often and accepted most widely. To clarify their own statement of this concept, some underwriters will use other similar terms, such as maximum possible loss and maximum probable loss (both abbreviated "MPL"). Underwriters can also expect to encounter the term "maximum foreseeable loss" (MFL). Generally applied to fire losses, MFL is an estimate of the financial cost of the loss that would occur if all protection measures (automatic and manual) were to fail and no effective fire department response occurred. It assumes that only passive protection measures, such as separation and barrier walls, limit the loss.[7] Some insurers underwrite to the MFL only and do not consider the PML. Others underwrite to the PML only and limit losses through policy limits.

UNDERWRITING BUSINESS INCOME AND EXTRA EXPENSE COVERAGE

When a business sustains an insured loss, the financial ramifications extend beyond simply the loss itself. Coverage for income lost and associated expenses the business incurs as it recovers is a significant consideration for underwriting business income and extra expense coverage.

Business income coverage forms provide compensation for reductions in income or profits resulting from a necessary interruption of the policyholder's business operations arising from direct physical damage to property by a covered cause of loss. Both versions of the Insurance Services Office (ISO) business income coverage form also include coverage for extra expenses. One version adds extra expense coverage to compensate the policyholder for the additional expenses incurred to minimize the interruption of operations even when the extra expenses do not reduce the loss of business income. Insureds who are more concerned with uninterrupted business operations than with loss of business income can purchase extra expense coverage separately. Various coverage options are available.

Businessowners policies (BOPs) usually include business income coverage on an actual loss sustained basis, often with fewer conditions or restrictions than separate business income or extra expense policy forms. Because of the broad coverage, underwriting information in the application must be accurate. Underwriters must also recognize situations in which the business income loss exposure is more severe than contemplated by the simplified businessowners rate structure. See the exhibit "BOP Business Income Coverage: Time Limit Consideration."

BOP Business Income Coverage: Time Limit Consideration

While BOPs' business income coverage with an actual loss sustained (ALS) coverage feature typically does not have a coverage dollar limit, it usually does have a time limit (such as twelve, eighteen, or twenty-four months) that may ultimately prove inadequate for some businesses. For example, catastrophes such as Hurricane Katrina, taught small business owners that they should be concerned not just about the catastrophe itself, but the aftermath. Effects of natural and man-made catastrophes can be so devastating and far reaching that businesses with business income coverage written on an ALS basis do not always receive complete compensation for their losses because the period of business interruption exceeds the specified policy time limit. Situations other than catastrophes can also extend the period of business interruption past the specified policy time limit. For example, if a fire destroys specialized, made-to-order equipment that takes eighteen to twenty-four months to replace, a business may find itself without adequate coverage.

[DA06259]

A covered loss of use, loss of business income, or extra expense loss cannot occur without direct damage to property at the insured premises. For underwriting purposes, analysis of the physical, moral, and morale (or attitudinal) hazards therefore begins with an analysis of the direct damage loss exposure. If business income or extra expense coverage is written separately, analysis of the **COPE** factors is required. With homeowners or dwelling property insurance, or when the business income coverage form is added to a direct damage policy, presumably this analysis has been made. Additionally, the underwriter must consider both the probable maximum loss and factors affecting the business interruption period.

COPE

Four interdependent elements that are analyzed by commercial property underwriters when evaluating submissions for property insurance; construction, occupancy, protection, and external exposures.

Probable Maximum Loss

Determining the amount of coverage an insured should carry and the probable maximum loss (PML) for business income coverage can be a complicated task for an underwriter. Underwriters can estimate the PML for business income coverage in three steps:

1. Determine the most serious direct loss that is likely to occur. The direct PML is the logical starting point for estimating the business income PML. When the direct PML is used to estimate future business income losses, the dollar amount of the direct loss is not important. The extent of the damage and its location will determine how much time is necessary for repairs and how long the time element loss will continue. The direct PML might, for example, assume total loss to a single fire division plus 25 percent of each adjoining fire division.

2. Calculate the longest period of restoration that this loss can reasonably be expected to cause.

3. Compute the largest loss of business income that the insured is likely to sustain during a period of this length.

Factors Affecting the Period of Interruption

The severity of a business income loss is not necessarily related to the underlying direct damage loss severity. A relatively minor fire destroying only 5 percent of the insured's building and personal property might result in a total business income loss up to the policy limit if, for example, the destroyed property included a custom-made piece of machinery, vital to the manufacturing process, that could not be replaced in less than one year.

Underwriters must consider the time frame when underwriting time element coverages. Any factor that would lengthen the likely period of interruption increases the insured's potential loss amount. To evaluate the time frame, the underwriter must consider these elements: the time required to rebuild the insured premises, the seasonality of the business, bottlenecks, computer systems, long production processes, availability of substitutes, and business continuity and disaster recovery planning.

Rebuilding Time

The time required to repair, replace, or rebuild the insured's building or the building containing the insured's premises is a major factor in determining loss exposure. Specialized structures requiring long construction periods, lengthy delays in obtaining permits, severe climatic conditions inhibiting construction during certain times of the year, and congested urban locations are all factors that increase loss exposure. The absence of these characteristics makes a loss exposure more desirable to underwriters.

Seasonality

A seasonal business such as a toy store or ski resort with, for example, 80 percent of its business concentrated in a three-month peak season, could suffer a severe business income loss from a relatively short shutdown at an inopportune time of year. Conversely, the time of year when a loss occurs has little effect on a nonseasonal business whose income stream is spread evenly across the year.

Bottlenecks

A bottleneck can apply to a machine, process, or building that is essential to the continued operation of an entire facility or manufacturing plant. For example, several products manufactured on different assembly lines might all flow through the same oven; if that oven is out of operation, no product can be completed. A flowchart of the production process often reveals one or more bottlenecks through which every product must pass.

A relatively minor direct damage loss involving a bottleneck can lead to a severe business income loss. If a vital process is duplicated on machines in separate fire divisions, the loss exposure is greatly reduced. Although bottlenecks usually result from manufacturing processes, a congested area or an unusual building configuration can also create them.

Computer Systems

Computer systems play a central role in many business operations. Relatively minor damage to a computer system can halt an entire operation. This is obviously a concern for manufacturing or processing plants operated by a central computer system. Many other businesses could be similarly affected, although the effect might not be as obvious. A large hotel, for example, might be virtually unable to operate when its computer system is inoperable, because clerks cannot tell what rooms are occupied, make reservations, or produce bills.

Long Production Processes

If the insured's normal manufacturing or processing operation takes an unusually long time to complete, the underwriter must consider the time required to get stock in process back to the point at which it had been before the loss. For example, if a product must be aged or seasoned, destruction of the facility could lead to a lengthy interruption, because the aging or seasoning period would be added to the period necessary to restore the facility and its machinery to operating condition. Examples of such operations include wineries, leather processing, or cheese processing.

Availability of Substitutes

When replacing damaged or destroyed property takes a long time, the insured might not have to wait to resume full operations. In many cases, other property can be substituted. The substitute can be permanent or temporary.

Business Continuity and Disaster Recovery Planning

The existence of an operational plan for business continuity management is a positive underwriting factor. A business continuity plan (BCP) allows an organization to anticipate its response to potential disruption and determine the critical functions that must continue so that it survives, recovers, and resumes growth. A crucial element of a BCP is a disaster recovery plan, which includes detailed written plans to restore the production process if part or all of the facility and equipment were destroyed. The disaster recovery plan should indicate what would be necessary if each part of the process were destroyed. The plan could also indicate whether continuation of the operation is feasible following certain types of damage. If it is, extra expense insurance might be indicated, either instead of business income coverage alone or in a combined form.

UNDERWRITING COMMERCIAL CRIME INSURANCE

Crime is a significant cause of loss for commercial insureds. It is important for underwriters to assess crime loss potential by examining both the characteristics of the property subject to loss and the characteristics of the account itself.

Commercial crime loss exposures and their associated underwriting considerations fall within two broad categories: employee dishonesty and crimes committed by others.

Employee Dishonesty

Employee dishonesty loss exposures have unique characteristics:

- Employees have ready access to money and other valuable property. They learn the company's routines and schedules and the habits of fellow employees. They can discover the controls employers have to prevent crime and how well those controls work.

- Losses can be hidden from discovery. Unlike burglary and robbery, which by definition are visible crimes, employee theft involves stealth and can often be concealed for months or years.

- Once losses occur, they are often large. A thief's access to property continues until the crime is discovered. The length of time of access, in turn, contributes to the size of the loss.

- Employers are often reluctant to believe that employees may steal from them. That reluctance leads to practices that create opportunities for theft, greatly increases exposures to loss, and creates a problem of adverse selection for the insurer.

- Employers might be reluctant to prosecute employees who steal. Many employers will not sign complaints or testify at criminal proceedings against their employees. They might want to avoid negative press coverage; to accept the culprit's hard-luck story; or to quickly resolve the situation, especially when the employee promises restitution.

- Incidents of employee theft might be frequent, but they are usually hidden until large losses have accumulated. For example, an embezzler typically steals small sums of money over a long time period and is caught only when the sum is so large that the embezzler cannot continue to conceal it.

Many commercial insureds overlook the employee dishonesty loss exposure, and only a small percentage of mercantile establishments purchase employee dishonesty coverage. Employee dishonesty losses are significant, and they are estimated to cost businesses more than any other form of crime. Nonetheless, employee dishonesty insurance is profitable for insurers and available for most types of insureds.

Underwriting Employee Dishonesty Loss Exposures

Employee dishonesty insurance does not usually receive specific attention in the underwriting process, but is often included in businessowners policies and commercial package policies. However, before issuing a policy, underwriters should be satisfied that certain conditions exist:

- There is no evidence of a moral hazard. (If there is, other coverages probably should not be written either.)
- Burglary and robbery risk control systems should be in place and maintained. Defenses against external crime also deter employee crime.
- As with other coverages, amounts of insurance should fall within the limits prescribed by the insurer's underwriting guidelines.
- The organization should be managed soundly. Management controls provide evidence of management's care and concern.

Controlling Employee Dishonesty Losses

Minimizing employee dishonesty losses requires strict adherence to management controls. These controls, applicable to almost all organizations, improve underwriting acceptability:

- New hires are screened for prior criminal activity, and their references are checked.
- Seasoned employees are evaluated before they are promoted, especially for moves into sensitive positions.
- A substance-abuse screening program is in place. Underwriters regard this as a positive sign because substance dependency creates potential for employee dishonesty.
- The rate and level of employee turnover is appropriate given the insured's business (employee turnover can increase the insured's loss exposure).

- Termination procedures are well defined. The computer passwords of employees who had worked in sensitive areas are revoked, and keys or access cards are returned upon termination.

- Management is sensitive to dramatic changes in employee behavior, such as sudden or drastic lifestyle changes, which might indicate employee dishonesty.

- Periodic audits are conducted to evaluate accounts receivable, cash accounts, inventories, and disbursements.

- Bank reconciliations are done to ensure that company records and bank records agree.

- Employees monitor one another through a division of authority among employees.

- Annual vacations of a minimum length of time are required. This acts as a control because some embezzlement methods require a daily adjustment of records.

- Duties are rotated, a practice that helps to uncover irregularities or embezzlement.

- Two-person or dual control systems are in place on some items, such as the vault, cash, and other items susceptible to theft.

Crimes Committed by Others

Crime committed by others includes acts such as robbery, burglary, and theft. Definitions used in crime insurance policies often differ from those generally used. Underwriters must be aware of the crime coverage form definitions, whether they involve cause of loss (for example, robbery, burglary, theft, or disappearance) or personnel (for example, watchperson, custodian, or messenger).

Underwriting Crimes Committed by Others Loss Exposures

Underwriters analyzing crimes committed by others loss exposures consider six factors:

- Susceptibility and marketability
- Property location
- Nature of the occupancy
- Moral and morale hazards
- Public protection
- Coverage and price modifications

The first factor that underwriters consider when analyzing crime committed by others loss exposures is an item's susceptibility to being stolen and its marketability. These characteristics are usually considered together, but an underwriter should be able to recognize them separately.

The size, weight, portability, visibility, and accessibility of property determine how susceptible it is to being stolen. The property's size or weight does not in itself reduce its susceptibility to being stolen. For example, a forty-ton steel truss bridge was stolen from a West Virginia creek in the late 1950s. However, large or bulky items generally have a lower susceptibility to being stolen. Jewelry, clothing, small electrical appliances, precious metals, books, and hand tools are highly susceptible. The higher the property's value relative to its bulk and weight, the more susceptible it is to being stolen.

A combination of factors determines an item's marketability. Property that is widely used has more potential customers, and property that is difficult to trace is more marketable. Economic conditions also may render a particular property highly marketable for some time.

The second factor that underwriters consider when analyzing crime committed by others loss exposures is property location. Topography, neighborhood, climate, and the local crime rate can tell underwriters what kind of losses to expect. Seasonal occupancy, typical of a resort, for example, makes loss from an off-season burglary more likely. Urban areas have a higher crime rate than suburban and rural areas, but that gap seems to be narrowing.

The third factor that underwriters consider when analyzing crime committed by others loss exposures is the nature of the occupancy. A reporter once asked Willie Sutton, a notorious bank robber of the 1940s and 1950s, why he chose to steal from banks when there were easier targets. Sutton answered, "Because that's where the money is." Some occupancies generally have a great deal of cash or other valuable property on hand. Those occupancies include banks, savings and loans, credit unions, check-cashing services, grocery stores, stadiums, arenas, churches, and buildings where charitable events are held.

Some businesses are conducted in obscure locations where criminal activity might not be readily detected, or they operate during hours when few people are around to deter criminals (for example, public warehouses and twenty-four-hour convenience stores).

The fourth factor underwriters consider when analyzing crime committed by others loss exposures is moral hazard and morale hazard. These can be present for any peril, but they are particularly important with regard to crime. A dishonest insured can readily dispose of inventory and arrange a fraudulent claim. Likewise, a lax attitude toward loss might mean that precautions and protective measures are not consistently adhered to, thereby creating an environment in which a loss is more likely to occur.

The fifth factor underwriters consider when analyzing crime committed by others loss exposures is public protection. The quality of police protection varies by community. It is unlikely that an underwriter would have the knowledge needed to make a judgment on the caliber of the police protection in the area in which an insured is located. The FBI does maintain crime statistics by city, but these statistics do not address specific areas within a city. Producers or claim adjusters who live in a particular area can probably provide anecdotal information about the need for police protection in their community and the ability of the community to meet that need.

The sixth factor underwriters consider when analyzing crime committed by others loss exposures is coverage and price modifications. Underwriters usually have some latitude in handling commercial crime insurance applications. Sometimes applicants know what coverage they want and will turn to another insurer if the requested coverage is not provided. Often, however, the applicant simply requests the broadest coverage available at the lowest cost. Insureds requesting crime insurance are often willing to accept counteroffers made by an underwriter who is trying to write the account. Possible modifications include changing coverage, limits, pricing, deductibles, and adding endorsements requiring protective safeguards.

For most other types of insurance, the insured purchases a policy limit close to the value of the exposed property. With crime insurance, the policy limit more often reflects the probable loss amount. Total crime losses are rare; most insureds assume that only partial crime losses will occur. This assumption, the absence of a coinsurance requirement, and the desire to minimize premiums tend to reduce the policy limit and to increase problems associated with underinsurance. However, underinsurance can lead to underpricing, so underwriters must consider the amount subject when pricing crime coverage.

For most property insurance, underwriters encourage insurance to value. With crime insurance, however, an underwriter is usually satisfied with policy limits much lower than the amount of the values insured. Because too much insurance can create a moral hazard, most underwriters do not want to provide crime insurance to full value even if the insured requests it.

Because policy limits tend to be low relative to the amount at risk, the probable maximum loss per occurrence usually equals the amount subject. More than one covered crime loss can occur during the policy period, so underwriters who provide commercial crime coverage should recognize that total losses might exceed the policy limits.

Deductibles in crime insurance serve the same purposes as they do in other types of insurance. They eliminate small, more predictable losses, and they tend to make the insured more conscious of the benefits of risk control. The deductible for crime insurance should at least equal the deductible amount that applies to other types of losses to the insured's business personal property.

A protective safeguards endorsement warrants that certain safeguards are in place. If the insured fails to protect the property as promised, the insurer is not contractually obligated to pay any resulting losses. Some courts dismiss such warranties in insurance policies, but courts are more likely to rule that breach of warranty negates coverage in crime insurance because the insured's promise is clearly material to the underwriting decision. However, underwriters cannot assume that courts will require the insured's full warranty compliance. A good faith effort to comply is almost always sufficient. For example, the failure of a central station alarm service solely because of a power or telephone service outage does not breach the warranty. The situation is different, however, if the utility cuts off electrical service because the insured has failed to pay its bills. A warranty's intent is not to create a loophole through which an adjuster can deny liability. Rather, the warranty in a protective safeguards endorsement requires the insured to make a good faith effort to maintain the specified level of protection.

Warranties ensure that the loss exposure is appropriately rated. Insurers almost always require a warranty for any protective system that earns a rate credit. Underwriters might also regard a system as essential even when it does not qualify for a reduced rate. If the underwriter demands that protective systems be installed, the protective safeguard endorsement should be added to the crime policy to enforce the system's maintenance throughout the policy period.

Controlling Crime Committed by Others Loss Exposures

A good prospect for crime committed by others coverage implements risk control measures and uses them diligently. Crime loss exposures respond well to risk control efforts. Private protection systems to prevent or reduce loss include these:

- Safes and vaults
- Cages, special rooms, and limited-access areas
- Indoor and outdoor lighting
- Fences and walls
- Protection of openings on the premises (gates, doors, windows, and skylights)
- Guard services
- Alarm systems
- Electronic surveillance systems
- Inventory control and other management activities

Private protection systems generally serve two important functions: to prevent crime losses and to reduce losses that do occur. Safes, vaults, fences, and so on rarely prevent access for a criminal who is strongly motivated, because even the best protection systems do not eliminate loss, but their value as a deterrent cannot be overemphasized. They can frustrate, confuse, and delay criminal activity, thereby reducing losses or causing a criminal to seek an easier target. After moral hazard, private protection is the most important consideration in crime insurance underwriting.

Underwriting guidelines should indicate the protection level that a particular class or location requires. The two main categories of private protection devices are: detection devices and barriers to criminal access. Detection devices are guards, alarms, and surveillance systems. Barriers include devices that protect the premises, safes, and vaults.

UNDERWRITING COMMERCIAL GENERAL LIABILITY INSURANCE

When evaluating a commercial general liability submission, an underwriter must consider a variety of loss exposures and hazards.

The loss exposures covered under Insurance Services Office (ISO) Commercial General Liability (CGL) insurance that an underwriter must consider when evaluating a business for coverage fall into these categories:

- Premises and operations liability
- Products and completed operations liability
- Personal and advertising injury liability
- Premises medical payments liability

Premises and Operations Liability Underwriting Considerations

The primary loss exposures facing most businesses are those for either their premises or their operations. General liability insurance covers the loss exposures of the insured's business premises and operations.

Premises liability loss exposures arise from the insured's ownership or possession of real property. Operations liability loss exposures arise from an insured's business operations conducted away from its own premises and from uncompleted work. To distinguish operations loss exposures from completed operations loss exposures (liability for damage or injuries arising from finished work), underwriters frequently refer to the former as operations in progress (injuries arising while work is being performed).

Liability underwriters tend to evaluate a business's loss exposures in terms of its "premises risks" or "operations risks." For example, underwriters consider a retail store a premises risk and a building contractor an operations risk. This does not assume that the loss exposures of the risk are exclusively premises or operations. Underwriters recognize that insureds whose loss exposures are primarily related to their premises also face incidental liability for the loss exposures of their operations in progress. Likewise, when the operations-in-progress loss exposures are primary, underwriters recognize the existence of incidental premises loss exposures.

Extent of Public Exposure

Underlying an underwriter's evaluation of an account for general liability insurance is the extent of its liability exposure to the public. The public includes customers, representatives of suppliers, anyone else associated with the business, and the general public. Although all businesses have this exposure, the extent of the exposure can vary widely. Underwriters should determine whether the account's exposure is common for the classification and how much variation in the exposure is likely.

In many cases, the hazards inherent in the insured's operations bear little or no relation to the extent to which the public is exposed to them. For example, a very hazardous manufacturing operation may present minimal exposure to the public for bodily injury or property damage.

The differences in exposure between two premises may be a result of location, type of business, or time in business, or a combination of the three. Consider a retail store, for example—a typical premises risk. A long-established store with a good reputation and a steady business is more likely to attract customers than a new or declining store.

A higher level of customer traffic suggests higher premises loss exposures. A store's location may create a similar increase in traffic and thus increase the extent of public exposure. For example, a downtown consumer electronics store may open a new branch in a suburban shopping mall. A mall usually has several large, well-known stores that attract traffic to the other small stores in the mall. People are in the mall to shop and are much more likely to enter the electronics store premises than pedestrians on city streets would be. In addition, because of differences in store hours and customers' shopping habits, malls are likely to have many customers at night or on weekends. Even if the total number of customers is average for the class, the mall electronics store will have a relatively high concentration of customers at certain hours. The fire exposure increases as well, because the setup of a mall and more customer traffic make it less likely that customers will be able to exit the premises safely in an emergency. In contrast, most weather-related exposures would decrease for a store located in a fully enclosed shopping mall, and mall maintenance services usually help to eliminate premises hazards such as icy walkways or sidewalks.

The presence of heavy traffic does not necessarily mean that a premises has excessive exposure. Heavy traffic may create an underwriting problem for an electronics store, but not for a theater. For example, the store's general liability rate may not be adequate to cover unanticipated heavy traffic, while the theater's rate, which anticipates heavy traffic, is adequate. In addition, customers in a store may be moving about more than those in a theater, which could increase the store's exposure.

Underwriters must also consider the legal status of persons likely to be on the premises. What is the insured's legal duty to these persons, and what standards of care are expected? The insured must demonstrate behavior that is consistent with the standard of care required. The underwriter can compare the insured's required degree of care with that of an average risk in the same classification. For example, a retail store with mostly adult customers might need to exercise reasonable care, but a toy store attracting many children might need to exercise a higher degree of care.

Because bodily injury claims tend to produce larger losses, bodily injury loss exposures are usually a primary underwriting concern. An underwriter cannot, however, ignore the potential for property damage losses. Property damage losses include claims not only for the value of the damaged property but also for the loss of its use.

Physical Hazards

The physical hazards relating to premises and operations liability loss exposures fall into three categories:

- Common hazards—Physical hazards common to many premises, such as those that induce slips and falls. Common hazards can include uneven stairs, tears in carpets, inadequate lighting, congested aisles, poor housekeeping, and defective heating or electrical equipment. The underwriter tries to determine what hazards or conditions increase the likelihood of bodily injury or property damage for which the owner or lessor of the premises would be held liable.

- Special hazards of the class—Physical hazards, such as chemicals, dust, and explosives, that occur only in certain types of businesses.

- Special hazards of the risk—Physical hazards found in businesses that conduct operations that are not typical of the class to which they belong. Underwriters must identify any special hazards of the risk and decide whether they present unacceptable liability loss exposures. These hazards could evolve from an incidental operation, a gradual diversification of operations, or an assumption of operations not contemplated when the loss exposure was originally insured and rated. When special hazards of the risk exist, the business has loss exposures beyond those anticipated by the standard rates for the class.

To properly evaluate the physical hazards of premises loss exposures, underwriters consider the entire premises. When the primary loss exposures arise from the premises' interior, underwriters cannot overlook the exterior loss exposures. Injuries can be caused outside the premises by broken or icy sidewalks, parking lots in poor condition, falling signs, playground equipment, swimming pools, and other features of the premises. Forklift trucks or other mobile equipment could cause injury inside or outside the premises, depending on the equipment's type and use.

In addition to evaluating bodily injury loss exposures, an underwriter considers the physical hazards that can cause property damage losses. Fire has one of the greatest potentials for causing severe losses. Operations-oriented accounts generally have a greater potential for causing property damage losses than do premises-oriented risks. A plumber can damage a customer's house with equipment or solvents, cause water damage, and possibly cause fire damage from using a soldering torch. Leased equipment can damage a customer's property if it is not kept in good repair or if the customer misuses it. Use of heavy equipment may cause serious property damage, but the major sources of property damage losses are fire, collapse, water damage, and, in some cases, pollution.

Generally, businesses with substantial premises loss exposures, such as apartment houses and office buildings, have minimal operations loss exposures. Businesses with small premises loss exposures, such as service businesses and contractors, have substantial operations loss exposures. An electrical contractor will usually have a place of business, but it is not likely to present a substantial premises loss exposure affecting risk selection. A store and shop where electrical fixtures are sold and repaired, on the other hand, would present premises loss exposures that an underwriter would have to assess separately. Typically, contractors have few premises loss exposures, but they have substantial operations loss exposures because of installation and repair work. An electrical contractor who has a sales and repair operation on the premises has both premises loss exposures and operations loss exposures.

The hazards related to operations loss exposures vary more than those related to premises loss exposures. Some service or contracting risks have heavy machinery or mobile equipment; some use flammables and blowtorches; some rent or lease equipment; and some blast, excavate, or erect. The builders of ranch-style residences and high-rise apartments do similar work, use similar tools, and create loss exposures at construction sites, but the similarity ends there. The high-rise building contractor uses steel girders, land-leveling equipment, and cranes, often in heavily populated areas.

Contractors and Subcontractors

General contractors performing construction work often hire subcontractors to complete a portion of a job. A contractor is covered by its CGL policy for its **vicarious liability** for the acts of its subcontractors. Employing subcontractors on a construction site thus creates additional hazards for the general contractor because the general contractor may be held vicariously liable for injury or damage caused by the subcontractor. A subcontractor must purchase its own CGL policy to cover itself against liability claims arising out of its work for the general contractor.

Ideally, contractors would engage only adequately insured subcontractors, however defined, and underwriting information about them would be available. In reality, contractors use subcontractors so frequently that they are evaluated based on the quality of work, timeliness, and availability—not by the adequacy of their insurance. Often, when the insured realizes the difference in premium between treating its subcontractors as employees and treating them as independent contractors, the insured either acquires the information the insurer needs or stops using "inadequately insured" subcontractors. Accounts that use inadequately insured subcontractors or that consistently dispute premiums are seldom desirable accounts. Premium payment disputes may be isolated incidents, but they could also be symptomatic of the contractor's poor management of the operation.

Vicarious liability

A legal responsibility that occurs when one party is held liable for the actions of a subordinate or associate because of the relationship between the two parties.

Underwriting subcontractors is nearly impossible. The insured might not know at the outset of the policy term exactly which subcontractors will be used. Depending upon the number of subcontractors used, it is often not feasible for a contractor to notify its insurer every time a new subcontractor is hired. Even if this information is provided, it is unlikely that the underwriter would be able to investigate every subcontractor before the work is performed. This inability to evaluate subcontractors before a policy is written places the underwriter at a disadvantage. The underwriter must rely on the insured's reputation in hiring competent subcontractors. At the least, the underwriter can convey its requirements for adequate insurance to the insured and insist that certificates of insurance be obtained from each subcontractor.

Products and Completed Operations Liability Underwriting Considerations

Products liability and completed operations liability are considered together because both address exposures to accidents or damage caused by a defect in finished work that is away from the insured's premises and over which the insured has relinquished control. Any business that makes, sells, distributes, or even gives away products has loss exposures that can lead to products liability. Many service businesses, such as builders and repair shops, have completed operations loss exposures from the work they perform for others.

Sources of Products Liability

Liability for sale, manufacture, or distribution of products can arise from three areas:

- Breach of warranty
- Negligence
- Strict liability in tort

Plaintiffs frequently assert all three causes of action in a products liability suit.

Breach of warranty is the first source of products liability. A warranty can be an explicit guarantee of safety, for example, or it can be an assurance that a product has a particular feature or characteristic. Every sale, even a routine one, involves a contract, and warranties expressed or implied in the sale are part of the contract. If the seller or manufacturer produces a product that fails to meet the standards expressed in the contract terms or warranties and if the customer suffers economic consequences, the law holds the seller or manufacturer liable to pay damages or make restitution.

Breach of warranty
The failure to meet the terms of a promise or an agreement associated with a product.

An express warranty is a statement or representation about a product's quality or suitability for its intended use. An implied warranty is an obligation that the courts impose on a seller to warrant certain facts about a product.

Implied warranty of merchantability

An implied warranty that a product is fit for the ordinary purpose for which it is used.

Implied warranty of fitness for purpose

An implied warranty that a product is fit for a particular purpose; applies if the seller knows about the buyer's purpose for the product.

Negligence

The failure to exercise the degree of care that a reasonable person in a similar situation would exercise to avoid harming others.

Strict liability (absolute liability)

Liability imposed by a court or by a statute in the absence of fault when harm results from activities or conditions that are extremely dangerous, unnatural, ultrahazardous, extraordinary, abnormal, or inappropriate.

In all states, common law and the Uniform Commercial Code recognize two implied warranties in any contract of sale:

- The **implied warranty of merchantability** represents that the product is reasonably fit for the ordinary purpose for which it was intended.
- The **implied warranty of fitness for a particular purpose** applies when the buyer relies on the seller's knowledge in selecting a particular product for a particular purpose.

Because breach of warranty has limitations as an effective basis for products liability, the courts also recognize two other grounds for products liability:

- **Negligence** can occur at many different steps in the product process, from the design, manufacture, or inspection of the product to the instructions or warnings that accompany it. Regardless of the source of negligence, the result is a defect in the product. Negligence may cause harm to a broad range of persons who have no contractual relationship with the seller, and negligence is often difficult to prove. A plaintiff can rarely point to a specific act of negligence in a products liability suit. Many products cannot be manufactured free of danger, and their hazards are not always obvious. The manufacturers of such products have a duty to warn potential consumers of any danger that is not public knowledge. Failure to give adequate warning is the most common ground for negligence in products liability suits.
- **Strict liability** in tort is the most common basis for products liability suits; it imposes liability on any person who produces an unreasonably dangerous product.

Underwriting Products Liability Loss Exposures

Underwriting generally focuses on the product itself. The underwriter is concerned about the product's potential to harm the public—that is, the product's loss frequency and severity.

Determining the inherent hazards of a product is, therefore, the first and most important step in underwriting a product. A product that is not inherently hazardous has a relatively minor loss exposure. The reverse is also true. Consider two products: a power lawnmower and a metal chair. The lawn mower is a much more hazardous product than the chair because the mower's inherent characteristics increase the likelihood of loss.

The applicant's business, the limits of liability, and the business's size and scope are important in underwriting both types of products. However, the quantity of underwriting information needed varies with the type of product. In fact, most business insurance application forms have a section (or the insurer has a separate questionnaire) that requires specific information about products liability loss exposures. See the exhibit "Underwriting Products Liability Loss Exposures—Checklist of Considerations."

Underwriting Products Liability Loss Exposures—Checklist of Considerations

- ☑ What are the product's inherent hazards?
- ☑ What representations or promises are made to the consumer in the sales material and advertising?
- ☑ Do technical manuals for complex products accurately reflect the safety precautions required in the product's assembly and repair?
- ☑ Does the product's packaging adequately protect the product so that it will operate properly when used?
- ☑ Are the instructions easy to read and understand?
- ☑ Does the product's warranty overstate the capability of the product?
- ☑ Are risk control efforts introduced into the product's design and production phases?
- ☑ Is a complaint-handling system in place to identify flaws and prevent injury and damage?
- ☑ Are quality-control checks incorporated into the product's manufacture?
- ☑ Are accurate records kept of products and components so that defective products can be identified and recalled?
- ☑ Have product lines changed to increase the inherent hazards?
- ☑ What is the applicant's position in the channel of distribution?
- ☑ Who is the product's ultimate consumer?

[DA06322]

Plaintiffs increase their chances of winning a products liability lawsuit when they assert more than one ground for recovery, thereby increasing underwriting losses. For example, the owner of a sport utility vehicle (SUV) is injured when the vehicle overturns on a road. A court may find that the vehicle's propensity to overturn is a reasonable hazard for an SUV. Consequently, the plaintiff could lose the strict liability claim in a tort suit. However, if the SUV manufacturer's advertising had portrayed the SUV as a suitable family car, a jury could infer that the manufacturer had breached an express warranty of fitness for a specific purpose and render a judgment against the manufacturer on those grounds.

Underwriting Completed Operations Loss Exposures

Completed operations loss exposures include construction, service, repair, and maintenance activities. The characteristic that distinguishes completed operations loss exposures from products loss exposures is the insured's completed work, which can cause injury or damage.

Generally, businesses that perform services primarily have operations loss exposures rather than premises loss exposures. Businesses with operations loss exposures are likely to have completed operations loss exposures. Underwriting focuses on the applicant's activities or operations that could cause a loss, particularly those performed off-premises.

How work is performed is important to the underwriter in evaluating loss exposures of both operations in progress and completed operations. Quality of workmanship and equipment, supervision of employees, technical skill, reputation, and experience are all areas the underwriter considers when evaluating operations loss exposures. An underwriter who finds significant shortcomings in any of these areas might conclude that the operations loss exposures are significant. These same areas are important in evaluating completed operations loss exposures. For example, faulty workmanship may cause a loss while the work is being performed and also after the work has been completed.

Careless or faulty work could damage customers' premises and could even cause a fire. If such losses occur after the work has been completed and the workers have left the premises, the resulting injury or damage falls within completed operations loss exposures. Careless or faulty work is likely to increase loss frequency to the same degree for both operations in progress and completed operations.

The completed operations loss exposures the underwriter should consider vary by class of business. Consider, for example, the loss exposures faced by a contractor building high-rise apartments. While constructing a building, workers can cause extensive property damage from fire, collapse, or water, as well as bodily injury from falling objects, the operation of equipment, and the use of construction materials and tools. After the apartments are inhabited, fire or collapse could cause even more serious injuries and damage. If the cause of such a fire or collapse could be traced to the contractor's faulty workmanship, the insurer that underwrote the completed operations loss exposures would be responsible for the loss.

At the other extreme, a piano tuner could damage the customer's property while performing his or her work, but it is extremely unlikely that injury or damage resulting from this work would occur after the work has been completed. Logically, piano tuning is an operations classification in which completed operations loss exposures are included in the premises and operations insurance rate.

When evaluating an applicant for completed operations coverage, the underwriter must determine the likelihood and severity of potential losses by evaluating the applicant's business. Completed operations loss exposures for a given business can be considerably different from the completed operations loss exposures for other businesses in the same class.

Personal and Advertising Injury Liability Underwriting Considerations

Personal and advertising injury is automatically included as Coverage B in the ISO CGL coverage form, unless it is specifically excluded by attaching an endorsement to the policy. Because it is a part of the coverage form, underwriters do not usually evaluate this loss exposure closely unless the insured's operation is one for which personal injury or advertising injury losses might occur frequently. Based on this evaluation, the underwriter can decide to exclude both personal injury and advertising injury or to eliminate coverage for advertising injury only.

Personal injury loss exposures include the insured's legal liability arising out of libel; slander; false arrest; wrongful eviction; invasion of the right of private occupancy; and infringement of copyright, trade dress, or slogan. Underwriters would evaluate the personal injury loss exposure for department or other retail stores because of potential false arrest of suspected shoplifters. Likewise, hotels, motels, or apartment occupancies could present a personal injury loss exposure for wrongful eviction or invasion of privacy.

The coverage provided under the CGL form for advertising liability excludes personal injury and advertising injury committed by an insured whose business is advertising, broadcasting, publishing, or telecasting. This coverage is intended for businesses that purchase advertising to sell their own products or services, not for a company that is in the advertising business.

Premises Medical Payments Liability Underwriting Considerations

Medical payments coverage is also automatically included as Coverage C in the CGL coverage form. Underwriters do not individually underwrite this loss exposure but do consider the medical payments loss exposure as part of the premises or operations loss exposures.

Medical payments coverage applies to medical expenses of persons other than the insured who are injured on the insured's premises or because of the insured's operations. Medical payments coverage does not, however, require the insured to be legally liable to pay for them. Because of this, the limits for medical payments coverage are usually much lower than those for bodily injury or property damage, typically $5,000 or $10,000 per person. Medical payments coverage can be excluded by attaching an endorsement to the policy, but this is rarely done.

UNDERWRITING PERSONAL AND COMMERCIAL AUTO INSURANCE

Motor vehicles provide essential transportation for both personal and commercial insureds. They also cause the death and disability of thousands of people each year. Therefore, an underwriter must carefully analyze several factors when considering auto insurance policies.

The Insurance Services Office (ISO) personal auto policy (PAP) covers the ownership and operation of vehicles by families and individuals; however, it does not address all types of persons, vehicles, activities, and uses. Insurers usually evaluate the loss exposures presented by an applicant by evaluating factors related to the driver and to the insured vehicle.

In commercial auto underwriting, underwriters typically use the same factors to evaluate the loss exposures of insurance applicants as they do to determine appropriate rates. Thus, information that is key to policy pricing is essential to the underwriting of commercial auto exposures. Factors relating to both the driver and the vehicle are considered, as well as whether the insured has a fleet safety program or is willing to work with the insurer's risk control representative in developing one.

Personal Auto Underwriting Considerations

The desirability of individual personal auto policyholders is usually determined by specific characteristics of the individual drivers. The insurer's underwriting guidelines reflect management's evaluation of the factors related to the driver, most of which are also used to classify and rate the application. However, various systems are used to evaluate the loss potential of personal auto applicants. The major underwriting factors that are considered in most private passenger auto underwriting guidelines include these:

- Age of operator
- Age and type of auto
- Auto use
- Driving record
- Territory
- Gender and marital status
- Occupation
- Personal characteristics
- Physical condition of driver
- Safety equipment

Age of Operator

Vehicle operator age is an important determinant of the likelihood of auto losses, because a disproportionate number of young drivers are involved in motor vehicle accidents relative to the driving population as a whole. In fact, according to data compiled by the National Highway Traffic Safety Administration, motor vehicle crashes are the leading cause of death among fifteen- to twenty-year-olds.[8] Accordingly, rating plans in virtually all states consider the age of the operator and charge considerably higher rates for young drivers. Whether the higher rate completely offsets the increased loss potential remains for the underwriter to judge.

Although young drivers are involved in a higher number of accidents and fatalities than older drivers, more attention is being paid to the driving records of older drivers as the proportion of drivers over age sixty-five continues to increase. The ability of older drivers to drive safely may be compromised by age-related physical and mental impairments.

Age and Type of Auto

The age of an auto generally indicates its mechanical condition. Although some old autos are in outstanding mechanical condition, a correlation exists between age and mechanical condition.

The type of auto also affects underwriting acceptability. The loss experience for specific types of autos in areas such as bumper-impact results, damage-ability, repairability, and likelihood of vehicle theft are considered when underwriting or pricing an account. For example, the manner in which sports cars and sport utility vehicles may be driven (that is, recreationally and/or aggressively) classifies them as more likely to sustain damage than station wagons and sedans, depending partly on the geographic area in which they are operated. The physical damage premium should reflect the damageability and cost of auto repairs.

Auto Use

Generally, the longer an auto is in use, the greater the probability of its being in an accident and incurring a loss. A long commuting distance or business use of an auto would affect rates because those factors increase loss potential. Rates reflect these classifications of auto use:

- Cars driven for pleasure use only
- Cars driven to work in a carpool in which drivers rotate driving responsibility
- Cars driven to work more than three miles but fewer than ten miles one way
- Cars driven to work more than ten miles one way
- Cars driven for business use

The classification for pleasure use only includes driving to work fewer than three miles one way. Underwriters must determine whether the driving mileage indicated is excessive in view of the rate that applies and should consider this when pricing the policy.

Driving Record

Driving experience is a crucial component of an underwriter's review of a driver, because driving experience is a likely indicator of a driver's future actions and the chance of loss. Underwriters evaluate a driver's prior accidents and prior moving violations. The driver's prior loss history may indicate poor driving habits, recklessness, or simply a lack of skill. Certain moving violations indicate a disregard for safety, while others indicate carelessness. The applicant or insured, index bureaus, and motor vehicle records are sources of underwriting information, though these sources often provide incomplete information.

Territory

Liability and physical damage losses vary based on the driver's principal garaging location and where the vehicle is used. For example, a driver may garage her car in a rural area but drive it every day through dense traffic to her job in a city.

Theft and vandalism occur more frequently in congested urban areas with on-street parking than in less-populated areas where cars are generally parked in driveways or garages. Drivers are more likely to be involved in auto accidents in urban areas but more likely to be involved in fatal accidents in rural areas.

Other territorial considerations are unrelated to population density. Some areas in the United States have severe winter weather that causes slippery roads. Other areas have sandstorms that frequently cause other-than-collision losses to paint and windshields.

Gender and Marital Status

Underwriters have long recognized the correlation between gender, marital status, and loss experience. Although statistics indicate that the gap between male and female motor vehicle crash deaths is diminishing, more men than women die in motor vehicle accidents. This disparity is attributable to the greater number of miles men drive and the greater likelihood that they will engage in risky behavior such as speeding and driving under the influence of alcohol.[9]

The marital status of younger drivers is both a rating and an underwriting factor, and it relates directly to stability. From the underwriter's point of view, the effect is most pronounced at younger ages because marriage tends to enhance maturity. In addition, being married also may suggest that the driver spends more time at home.

Some states regulate the use of gender and marital status for underwriting purposes. A few states prohibit price discrimination based on gender or marital status; in these states, both men and women pay the same rates.

Occupation

Occupation is rarely used overtly in evaluating personal auto exposures, but it is sometimes a factor in making an underwriting decision on a particular submission. Occupation is sometimes considered when determining whether a business-use surcharge is appropriate. For example, self-employed artisans (carpenters, plumbers, electricians, and so forth) often use their vehicles for business to travel to and from job sites, as well as for personal use. In addition, certain occupations, such as traveling salespersons, require extensive driving and increase the probability of loss. Some insurers make accommodations for vehicles used in such occupations by rating them as personal autos with a surcharge to reflect the additional exposures. Other insurers require such accounts to be submitted under their commercial auto programs.

Personal Characteristics

Underwriters often order consumer investigation reports to provide information on the personal characteristics of applicants and other drivers. This information is subjective and must be evaluated carefully.

Many insurers use **credit scoring** to evaluate the stability of insurance applicants. Studies have demonstrated a positive correlation between a poor insurance score (developed using information in a credit report) and higher insurance losses. Critics of insurers' use of credit scores suggest that the connection between the two factors is nonspecific and that it could mask factors that are prohibited for evaluation purposes, such as race.

Credit scoring
A decision-making tool that uses credit report information to develop a predictive score on the creditworthiness of an applicant for additional credit.

Physical Condition of Driver

Physical impairments may be a problem if allowances for the impairment have not been made. Auto modifications made to accommodate a driver with physical impairments and the driver's demonstrated driving mastery usually make the applicant acceptable.

Safety Equipment

Many new cars come equipped with advanced safety systems, and these are considered in pricing and evaluating an account. For example, rate discounts are frequently offered for antilock braking systems and side air bags. Vehicles that incorporate global positioning system technology and wireless communication technology for safety purposes have also earned rate credits from some insurers.

Commercial Auto Underwriting Considerations

The analysis of a commercial auto risk should closely follow the characteristics used in rating the policy. As such, information that is key to policy pricing is essential to the underwriting of commercial automobile exposures.

Factors that underwriters consider for commercial vehicle drivers include their motor vehicle record, especially if it indicates any violations; accident history; and experience with operating commercial motor vehicles. See the exhibit "The Federal Commercial Motor Vehicle Safety Act (CMVSA) of 1986."

The Federal Commercial Motor Vehicle Safety Act (CMVSA) of 1986

The federal Commercial Motor Vehicle Safety Act (CMVSA) of 1986 requires drivers of large vehicles (trucks with a gross vehicle weight of 26,000 pounds or more, buses that can carry more than sixteen passengers, and vehicles that transport hazardous materials) to hold a commercial driver's license (CDL).The Act requires that drivers pass both written and road tests. Drivers are forbidden from holding more than one CDL, which makes concealing a history of accidents and violations more difficult.

[DA06383]

Underwriters also consider factors relating to the vehicle. The physical condition and age of, and the existence of a regularly scheduled maintenance program for, the insured's vehicles are important factors in evaluating the desirability of a commercial auto risk.

Private passenger vehicles owned or operated by a business would be covered under a commercial auto policy. However, the underwriting considerations are similar to those of a personal auto loss exposure.

Class rate

A type of insurance rate that applies to all insureds in the same rating category or rating class.

Commercial auto policies are **class rated**. A policy that develops a large enough premium is also eligible for experience rating. Schedule rating is used to modify the premium for characteristics not reflected in class rates. Trucks, tractors, and trailers, as well as truckers hauling exclusively for one concern, are classified and rated using these four factors:

- Vehicle weight and type
- Vehicle use
- Radius of operation
- Special industry classifications

Vehicle Weight and Type

The damage resulting from an auto accident is related to the size, weight, and speed of the vehicles involved. Commercial tractor-trailer rigs can weigh

80,000 pounds or more when loaded, and they often travel at or above the maximum posted speed; hence, these vehicles are more likely than others to cause severe damage when an accident occurs. Large trucks are also difficult to maneuver in heavy traffic or on small inner-city streets, a factor that increases loss potential.

Vehicle Use

Commercial vehicles vary significantly in their amount of road exposure and in how they are used. Some vehicles may be used almost continually to haul goods, while others may be used only to travel to and from job sites, remaining parked most of the time.

The ISO *Commercial Lines Manual* (CLM) classifies trucks and tractor-trailers into service, retail, and commercial use. Each of these classifications is described in the *CLM* and is reflected in determining the primary classification to which the vehicle is assigned. The use classification reflects the extent to which the vehicle is used:

- Service use applies to vehicles that are used principally to transport personnel or material to job sites. These vehicles are often driven to job sites at the start of a shift and remain there until the shift is over. Because they are used to the least extent, service vehicles receive the lowest rate.

- Retail use means that the vehicle is used primarily for deliveries to and pickups from households. Drivers frequently follow unfamiliar routes and operate on tight schedules. This use class receives the highest rate.

- Commercial use applies to any vehicle that does not fall into one of the preceding two classes.

The underwriter verifies that vehicles are properly classified to ensure that sufficient premium is charged for the loss exposure. The *CLM* also provides classifications for public use vehicles. Public use vehicles include taxis, public livery vehicles, van pools, school and church buses, and charter and sightseeing buses. These classifications and rating factors reflect the unique characteristics of these loss exposures involving multiple passengers in a single vehicle.

Radius of Operation

Radius of operation is another measure of road exposure. The distance traveled, as well as the nature of that travel, can affect accident frequency. Trucks operated over long distances may be more likely to have more severe accidents than those operated locally. There are two reasons for this. First, a driver who operates a truck over long distances may not be as familiar with the route and its hazards as drivers who operate trucks locally. Second, long-distance trucking is more likely to be more strictly scheduled. If drivers are rushing to meet a delivery deadline, the resulting fatigue and excessive speeds can increase accident frequency.

Special Industry Classifications

Special industry classifications, or secondary classifications, consist of seven major industry classifications, each of which is further divided into subclassifications. The numerous classifications permit the capture of meaningful data by specialized use, even though most of the subclassifications within a classification have the same rate:

- Truckers—Vehicles used to transport the goods or materials of others; this does not include moving household goods, office furniture, or fixtures and supplies.
- Food delivery—Vehicles that wholesale food distributors and food manufacturers use to transport raw and finished products.
- Specialized delivery—Delivery vehicles such as armored cars or autos for delivering film, magazines or newspapers, mail and parcel post, and similar items.
- Waste disposal—Vehicles transporting waste material for disposal or resale.
- Farmers—Vehicles owned by farmers and used in farming operations.
- Dump and transit mix trucks and trailers—Vehicles that have no other appropriate classification and that have an incidental dumping operation.
- Contractors—All vehicles used by contractors, other than dump trucks.
- Not otherwise specified—Vehicles that cannot be classified into any other group.

From an underwriting perspective, trucks or tractor-trailers with special industry classifications can present additional concerns and require the underwriter to gather more information. For example, trucks with a food-delivery secondary classification may operate under tight timetables or require specialized equipment, such as refrigerated units. Although the application of a special industry classification should result in a premium that reflects any increase in loss exposure, the underwriter needs to ensure that all necessary controls are in place. The risk control department can provide valuable assistance to the underwriter with this assessment.

Underwriting Use of Risk Control Services

An insurer's risk control activities are important to achieving and maintaining the underwriting profitability of an account. Risk control representatives can assist the insured with making drivers and managers more safety conscious. Risk control can also aid the insured with developing fleet safety programs that address problems identified in risk control reports and with creating a positive approach to safety through safety programs.

Risk Control Reports

Risk control reports, a first-hand evaluation of an account by the insurer's risk control representative, can be valuable but generally are used only for accounts that meet premium size or other specific criteria. Risk control reports confirm and supplement information on the application, such as determining how well the insured adheres to its fleet safety program. Underwriting guidelines might specify that a risk control report be ordered when the account carries liquefied petroleum gas, acids, corrosive chemicals, flammable materials, explosives, or other hazardous materials.

Some insurers rely on the expertise of their risk control representatives to provide services to their commercial auto accounts. A risk control representative might be asked to make recommendations to improve unsafe conditions at an account and follow up to ensure that those conditions have been corrected. Many insurers involve risk control representatives in analyzing claim information to determine whether underlying conditions exist that could be corrected to reduce future losses. The risk control representative might determine that a few drivers are the source of the bad loss experience and suggest training programs that would improve their driving skills. Additionally, a risk control representative who is familiar with many commercial auto accounts will likely be able to share risk prevention and risk reduction measures with accounts that demonstrate a need.

Fleet Safety Programs

A fleet safety program consists of the written policy and procedures that an account uses in the management of its drivers and vehicles. For accounts in the transportation business, a fleet safety program is essential and is usually a significant part of their overall operational guidelines. Such accounts usually must satisfy extensive state and federal transportation guidelines for safety. Most accounts insured under the Business Auto Coverage Form have only an incidental auto exposure. Nevertheless, a fleet safety program can serve to communicate the importance of responsible driving behavior to employee-drivers. A fleet safety program is also the hallmark of the better-than-average account that underwriters seek to insure. A fleet safety program generally indicates that the account's management understands the value of risk management and is working to prevent and control losses.

Although the content of fleet safety programs varies, most programs include provisions specifying vehicle use, driver selection, vehicle maintenance, and accident reporting. The vehicle-use section, for example, might specify the limits of liability an employee must maintain while using a personal auto for business use. The driver-selection section might explain that on-the-road performance will be evaluated and disclose the criteria the company uses to eliminate high-risk drivers. The vehicle-maintenance section might list the maintenance tasks that are the responsibility of the vehicle's regular driver. The driver, for example, might be required to check the oil level every time the vehicle is refueled and check that the tires are properly inflated once a week. The fleet manager is usually responsible for overseeing the entire fleet and ensuring that more extensive vehicle maintenance is performed when needed. The accident-reporting section might describe the procedure to report accidents and the process that company management will use to review them.

Copies of the fleet safety program are usually given to employees who have permission to operate company-owned vehicles. Employees are asked to read the program manual and sign a statement agreeing to adhere to the program requirements.

Good fleet safety programs are clear, concise, and written at a level appropriate for the program user. They should contain practical procedures that employees can follow and the account's management can support. See the exhibit "Restrictions on Cancellations and Nonrenewals."

Restrictions on Cancellations and Nonrenewals

In response to public pressure, most states have enacted laws that restrict the reasons for which insurers can cancel or nonrenew auto policies. In most states, the restrictions apply to both personal and commercial policies. In some states, requirements for personal auto policies are more restrictive. Some statutes specify the acceptable reasons to cancel or nonrenew. Others rely on the insurance department to establish the restrictions.

Laws also specify the time period required for insurers to notify policyholders that their policy will be canceled or will not be renewed. In most cases, this notice ranges from thirty to sixty days before the policy's cancellation date or expiration date.

Cancellation and nonrenewal restrictions have important underwriting implications. It can be difficult or impossible to cancel a policyholder's insurance once it is in effect. Underwriters must also make certain that they review pending renewals well before the policies' expiration date so that they can comply with the nonrenewal notification period imposed by law. Although legislators generally restrict cancellation and nonrenewal rights with the intention of improving insurance availability, these restrictions often make underwriters more selective.

[DA06384]

UNDERWRITING WORKERS COMPENSATION INSURANCE

Underwriting workers compensation insurance is similar to underwriting general liability insurance because general liability and workers compensation insurance, to a large extent, present many of the same hazards. The difference, however, is that general liability underwriting concerns itself with injuries to the general public while workers compensation underwriting focuses on injuries to the insured's employees.

Workers compensation insurance protects employers against statutory liability losses incurred under workers compensation statutes, and is essentially a benefits delivery system that includes death benefits, disability income, medical expense, and rehabilitation expense as required by applicable workers compensation laws. Workers compensation benefits are compulsory in all states except New Jersey and Texas, and even in those states most employers have workers compensation insurance.

The workers compensation and employers liability policy also provides employers liability coverage for employers whose employees are killed, injured, or have acquired an occupational disease in the course of their employment. For legal liability to an employee for bodily injury arising out of and in the course of employment that is not covered under the workers compensation law, employers may find coverage through employers liability insurance.

The standard workers compensation and employers liability policy provides complete coverage for employee bodily injury, except for specified exclusions. The policy provides both blanket coverage for obligations imposed by the state workers compensation law and broad coverage for other employers liability. This broad coverage and the additional flexibility provided by endorsements spare policyholders the necessity of revising their insurance program when a new location is established or some other business change occurs.

Workers compensation benefits vary by state, but the same policy can be used for basic coverages in various states because the compensation laws of those states, not the policy provisions, control the conditions of coverage. Workers compensation laws are specifically incorporated into the policy contract by policy reference. Therefore, an underwriter must read applicable statutes in order to interpret the policy. Workers compensation insurance loss experience is closely related to changing economic, regulatory, and political environments, which often vary by state.

Underwriting Guidelines for Individual Classes and Applicants

Beyond the physical hazards, general liability and workers compensation lines of business differ drastically in how they are perceived by insurers. Not all insurers offer workers compensation insurance coverage, and of those that do, many insurers have fairly strict underwriting guidelines to the classifications approved by underwriting management.

A conservative insurer might want to avoid high-hazard classes of business such as steeplejacks or window washers. This same insurer might be willing to write some contractors while avoiding roofing and insulation contractors. Other insurers might target their marketing efforts to high-hazard classes. As with other types of insurance, there is no single right way to underwrite workers compensation.

If an applicant is in a classification written by the insurer, specific underwriting criteria are used to evaluate the acceptability. The primary underwriting consideration is the existence or nonexistence of on-premises and off-premises hazards. The underwriters may decide to investigate an applicant further based on certain factors, such as the experience modification factor, number of temporary or leased employees, the existence of uninsured subcontractors, potential maritime exposure, the size of the workers compensation premium relative to the premium for the entire account, and employee concentration.

Experience Modification Factor

Experience modification factor

A factor that tailors manual rates to an insured's experience based on the insured's payroll and loss record of certain prior years.

The **experience modification factor** serves as an index of the account's desirability within a particular class. An experience modification factor greater than 1.00 may require further investigation, but a potential insured may still be considered if its high modification factor resulted from an unusually large loss or if risk control procedures have been implemented to reduce the occurrence of similar losses in the future. If an experience-rated policy develops adverse results during the year, the experience rating mechanism ensures that the policyholder will be penalized in future policy periods. It does not matter who provides coverage because experience modifications are calculated by the applicable state's workers compensation rating organization. This provides a financial incentive for effective loss control. Experience rating provides an accurate method to capture statistics about an applicant. Loss records indicate both past losses and future trends.

Some insurers restrict their writings to those accounts that are eligible for experience rating. The National Council on Compensation Insurance's (NCCI's) experience rating plan is used in the majority of states. If an applicant is eligible, the experience rating program is mandatory. Experience rating can not be used as a competitive tool.

Temporary and Seasonal Employees

Many businesses use temporary employees, seasonal employees, or both. These employees are generally not as well trained as full-time employees and, therefore, have a greater risk of being injured. These workers also present a potential moral hazard because they could fake an injury while on the job and receive workers compensation benefits.

An important consideration for an underwriter regarding leased employees relates to whether the company that leases workers is considered the employer for workers compensation purposes or the organization that hires them. This is an important consideration when attempting to segregate payrolls to calculate experience modifications and to collect other statistical data for a particular group of employees. NCCI has developed several endorsements for use with workers compensation policies covering leased workers. These endorsements clarify whether coverage applies to leased workers, non-leased workers, or both.[10]

Subcontractors

Most workers compensation laws hold a contractor responsible for workers compensation benefits to employees of its uninsured subcontractors. Because the standard workers compensation policy automatically insures this loss exposure, the underwriter must ascertain whether a subcontractor loss exposure exists and, if it does, evaluate it and charge the appropriate premium charge. The policyholder must either prove that the loss exposure has been insured by the subcontractor or pay a premium based on the subcontractor's payroll as well as the insured's own payroll.

Maritime Occupations

Maritime loss exposures are those related to occupations involving work on vessels while at sea or in close proximity to bodies of water, such as on docks, on piers, or in terminals. It is important for underwriters to understand the policyholder's operations before including any endorsement to the workers compensation policy when maritime loss exposures are involved, because different coverage applies for different occupations.

The principal federal laws covering on-the-job injuries for maritime occupations are the United States Longshore and Harbor Workers' (USL&HW) Compensation Act and the Merchant Marine Act. The latter is more commonly known as the Jones Act and is intended to cover masters and crew members of vessels. Some insurers avoid any workers compensation loss exposures falling under federal jurisdiction because they require specialized underwriting expertise or because reinsurance agreements may contain restrictions for maritime loss exposures.

Maritime loss exposures can be overlooked when certain occupations or employees conduct occasional tasks that fall outside their regular duties, creating a "gray area" for coverage. These are employees who are not regular masters or crew members of vessels who usually clearly fall under the Jones Act or dockworkers who are covered under the USL&HW Act. Underwriters often discover this type of loss exposure only when a claim is presented.

Underwriters must always be alert to the existence of potential maritime loss exposures. Maritime loss exposures can be assessed by reviewing certificates of insurance, the type of equipment owned, a list of jobs in progress, and previous loss experience. Some producers may request a USL&HW endorsement on every workers compensation application or as part of every request for insurance proposal, even when no obvious maritime loss exposure exists. In those situations, the underwriter must discuss the operations with the producer to determine whether a maritime exposure exists and then must determine what coverage can and should be provided.

An underwriter can discover USL&HW Act exposures in many typical construction and erection operations. Too often, the discovery results from a claim. They can be indicated in many ways, including persons to whom certificates of insurance are issued, the type of equipment owned, a list of jobs in progress, and claims under other coverages. Some producers located near navigable waters attach a USL&HW Act coverage endorsement to every workers compensation policy, even if such exposures are not contemplated when the policy is issued. In those situations, the underwriter must instruct the producer to indicate clearly when a maritime exposure is anticipated.

Relative Premium Size

Even otherwise acceptable applicants may be rejected if the workers compensation premium is too high relative to other coverages. An underwriting guideline may be to accept the insured's account only if the workers compensation premium is less than 50 percent of the total premium developed by the account. A comparable guideline for an insured contractor may be 70 percent.

Employee Concentration

Workers compensation underwriters have placed more emphasis on the concentration hazard since the terrorist attacks of September 11, 2001, which demonstrated that an employer with a large number of employees at a single location faces the possibility that a single incident could result in many injuries or deaths. A catastrophic loss could arise from many causes, but the loss exposure could be greatest for employees working in prominent properties that might be terrorism targets.

Management Attitude and Capability

In evaluating management of an insured, the underwriter should consider the willingness and ability of management to minimize hazards and reduce losses. If an insured does not have a safety program, or if the program exists only theoretically, managerial indifference can usually be assumed.

Employee morale and claim consciousness often reflect management's attitude toward workers compensation and industrial safety. If employee morale is low, grievances against management might motivate workers to file false or exaggerated claims for workers compensation to escape an unpleasant work environment. A poorly managed insured is likely to have worse-than-average workers compensation loss experience.

When assessing management, underwriters also should perform a wage analysis, which could reveal whether its salaries are attracting high-quality employees and minimizing turnover, which could generate a higher premium to hold losses. They also should consider whether management provides healthcare benefits for its employees, which could reduce the possibly of injuries occurring outside of the workplace being inappropriately claimed under a workers compensation policy.

On-Premises Hazards

A variety of on-premises hazards affect workers compensation loss experience. On-premises hazards relating to housekeeping and maintenance are found in almost all occupations, while special hazards of the class are related to a particular operation or industry. Special hazards of the risk must also be considered where applicable.

Housekeeping

From an underwriting standpoint, housekeeping refers to a workplace's physical layout, its cleanliness, and its operating efficiency. Efficiency includes such factors as the arrangement of machinery, aisle placement and adequacy, stair cleanliness, freight-elevator opening and stair marking, and general cleanliness.

Maintenance

Poorly maintained machinery presents an inherent danger. A good program of plant and machinery maintenance indicates a positive attitude toward work safety. The absence of such a program indicates carelessness or a lack of awareness, which can have a severe impact on future work injuries because poorly maintained machinery presents an inherent danger.

Although general hazards are present in all types of firms, specific hazards might be present as a result of the type of machines, equipment, materials, and processes used in a particular firm's operation. These specific hazards require controls such as machine guards, exhaust systems, and materials-handling devices designed to meet the requirements of the particular situation.

Specific hazards vary widely but can be placed in these categories:

- Machinery and equipment
- Material-handling
- Electrical
- Occupational
- Fire and explosion
- Slips, falls, and poor working conditions
- Dangerous processes, resulting in burns from heat and chemicals
- Flying and falling material, resulting in eye and head injuries
- Miscellaneous hazards, resulting in cuts, punctures, bumps, bruises, and abrasions

Occupational Disease

Workers compensation laws provide benefits for some diseases in addition to injuries from accidents on the job. The definition varies by state, but an occupational disease is generally one resulting from causes the worker faces on the job and to which the general public is not exposed. Some of the occupational diseases covered by the various state workers compensation laws are silicosis (from exposure to silica dust); asbestosis (caused by inhalation of asbestos fibers); radiation (including ionizing radiation); tuberculosis; pneumoconiosis (black lung); and heart or lung disease for certain groups, such as police or firefighters.

It is more difficult to predict the frequency and severity of occupational diseases than of work-related accidents. Exposure to unfavorable conditions at work does not always cause occupational disease. The factors that could cause accidents, on the other hand, are more readily identifiable.

In an industrial setting, hazard analysis also includes monitoring the work environment for the presence of industrial poisons that can enter the body by ingestion, inhalation, or skin absorption. Analyzing the toxicity of the various chemical compounds used in a particular process provides a means of evaluating the related occupational disease hazards.

Cumulative Trauma Injuries

Cumulative trauma disorders, sometimes referred to as repetitive strain injuries (RSI), arise from a series of minor stresses over a period of time. These relatively minor injuries accumulate until they require medical treatment and can result in a disability. Examples of cumulative trauma include back strains from repetitive lifting and shoulder strains from repetitive pushing or pulling on pipes or hoses. Also, the increased use of computer keyboards has caused some office workers to experience numbness or pain in their hands and wrists. This injury, called carpal tunnel syndrome, results from cumulative trauma.

The major difficulty associated with determining compensability for these injuries is distinguishing between normal aging conditions, or conditions to which the general public is subject, and those that are truly job related. However, most states now recognize cumulative trauma disorders as compensable injuries.

Analysis of On-Premises Hazards

Most accidents occur as a result of either an unsafe act or an unsafe condition. Unsafe acts or practices on the part of employees include failing to use the proper personal protective equipment. Workers might, for example, fail to wear dust masks or air-supplied respirators in dust-laden atmospheres or fail to use safety glasses when their use is indicated. Management can influence employee behavior through its hiring policy, safety program, and enforcement of safety rules. Premises inspections can indicate the extent to which the insured tolerates unsafe actions. Unfortunately, there is always the danger that employees may act differently during an inspection than at other times or that supervisors may not enforce safety rules continuously.

Unsafe conditions are generally easier to identify than unsafe acts. Routine practices that usually are safe can become unsafe in particular circumstances, creating more likely hazards than those that are more apparent. For example, an office usually has minimum loss exposure to dangerous conditions such as those involving machinery, chemicals, and similar hazards. Depending on the premises, the office might be a place where workers can slip and fall, or develop back strain from improperly lifting files, boxes of paper, and similar heavy objects. Each of those hazards is easy to identify and control. However, the pace of business and the demands placed on workers has increased the frequency of stress-related workers compensation claims. Emerging technologies and increased use of computers have led to claims for cumulative trauma and claims related to radiation emitted by video display terminals (VDTs). Long periods of work with a VDT can also cause eye fatigue and other physical ailments.

In a factory, the manufacturing process and the type of materials used are important to underwriters. The loss history of the policyholder and others in the same industry provides information on the types of losses that might occur. In woodworking, for example, operating sharp cutting tools at high speeds can result in serious lacerations. In other processes, there is an inherent potential for burns.

Advisory loss costs or rates take into account the difference in relative hazards among occupational classes. A machine shop is more hazardous than an office, for example. The underwriter must determine to what extent the policyholder is typical of its class. The machine shop must be evaluated relative to some guidelines that indicate the conditions usually found in a typical machine shop. The presence of additional hazards not found in other machine shops or the heightening of typical hazards because of poor maintenance or housekeeping would indicate a less desirable exposure.

Off-Premises Hazards

Employees in some organizations fulfill all their employment duties on the premises, while employees in other organizations have a great deal of travel or off-premises work. Three aspects should be considered when evaluating off-premises hazards: (1) the duration of travel, (2) the mode of transportation, and (3) the hazards at remote job sites. Contractors, for example, are subject to a constantly changing work environment as they move from one job site to another. The hazards faced by a residential building contractor vary significantly from those of a commercial building contractor. See the exhibit "Off-Premises Hazards Illustration."

The use of corporate aircraft can result in a multiple-fatality workers compensation loss in the event of a crash. The potential for multiple losses is also present when several employees share the same vehicle when traveling on business.

Off-Premises Hazards Illustration

A comparison of two accounting firms with identical payrolls illustrates the first two aspects of off-premises hazards. Accountants for Firm A do all their work on the firm's premises, while accountants for Firm B travel when performing audits for construction firms. This travel is done in private autos as well as in commercial and corporate aircraft. Traffic accidents or plane crashes could result in serious workers compensation losses for Firm B, whereas the off-premises transportation hazard is not present for Firm A.

[DA06323]

The same techniques for evaluating on-premises hazards can be used for off-premises hazards.

UNDERWRITING UMBRELLA AND EXCESS LIABILITY INSURANCE

Because they are designed to cover large, infrequent losses, umbrella and excess liability insurance policies entail unique underwriting considerations.

Many policyholders find that they need high limits of liability coverage not offered in standard liability policies, especially due to the increasing size of lawsuits and jury verdicts. Businesses and individuals often have significant assets that need protection from potentially catastrophic liability claims. Severe losses can result from multiple-passenger auto accidents, gasoline truck explosions, building collapses, hotel fires, and defective products. The need for higher liability limits combined with the relatively low limits of insurance available from primary liability insurers creates the market for umbrella and excess liability policies. Underwriting such policies requires accounting for considerations related to the risks the policies cover, examining the underlying policies, and considering the underlying insurer.

Umbrella and Excess Liability Insurance

Umbrella liability insurance, both personal and commercial, is designed to cover large, low-frequency losses. They do not provide primary insurance in most cases, nor do they cover all losses. Most umbrella policies have a deductible or self-insured retention that the policyholder must pay. The retention for a commercial policy is usually $10,000, and the retention for a personal policy is usually $250.

Umbrella liability insurance

Liability insurance that provides excess coverage above underlying policies and may also provide coverage not available in the underlying policies, subject to a self-insured retention.

Umbrella policies are not standardized. Policy language, as well as underwriting rules and guidelines, vary by insurer. Most umbrella policies are designed to serve three functions:

- Provide excess liability limits above all specified underlying policies
- Provide coverage when the aggregate limits of the underlying policies have been exhausted
- Provide coverage for gaps in the underlying policies

An umbrella policy requires that liability insurance with agreed limits of liability be maintained on the underlying policies. If this is not done, the umbrella will respond as though the required underlying coverage exists.

Excess liability insurance increases the limits of liability on one or more underlying policies but does not generally broaden coverage. Umbrella policies, in contrast, provide coverage in some situations when underlying coverage does not exist. Excess policies are frequently written on a layered basis, with several policies providing successively higher limits.

Excess liability insurance
Insurance coverage for losses that exceed the limits of underlying insurance coverage or a retention amount.

Underwriting the Risk

For umbrella and excess liability policies, loss severity, as opposed to loss frequency, is the primary underwriting concern. Because these types of policies usually have a long tail, the underwriter must approach loss severity by using a longer and broader underwriting perspective. So instead of three to five years of loss experience, ten or more years of loss information may be more appropriate, if required.

The underwriter should also consider any catastrophe loss exposures, such as the potential for a major explosion that could cause many injuries and serious damage to adjacent property. The underwriter also should examine issues that could affect liability claims in the future, such as trends related to emerging technologies, environmental concerns, and litigation.

Another important underwriting concern is whether the underlying coverage is written on an occurrence or claims-made basis, and how closely the umbrella or excess coverage corresponds to the primary layer. Underwriting acceptability is a more important issue if the potential for significant **drop-down coverage** is present.

Drop-down coverage
Coverage provided by many umbrella liability policies for (1) claims not covered at all by the underlying policies and (2) claims that are not covered by an underlying policy only because the underlying policy's aggregate limits have been depleted.

Underwriting the Underlying Policies

Underwriting umbrella or excess policies requires a careful analysis of the same loss exposures covered by the underlying policies, as well as additional loss exposures covered by the umbrella (and in some cases excess) policies but not by underlying coverage. Underwriters must be thoroughly familiar with not only what coverage is provided by underlying policies but also how the applicant's underlying policies have been modified through endorsements. These elements of the underlying insurance can affect underwriting:

- Type of insurance
- Name of insurer
- Applicable limits and deductibles
- Premium for bodily injury liability coverages
- Premium for property damage liability coverages
- Details of extensions of coverage beyond standard policy provisions

---

Underwriting a Straight Excess Policy

Underwriting a straight excess policy that covers over only one primary policy is essentially the same as underwriting the primary coverage. Usually, the excess rate is a percentage of the primary rate, but there are no standard rates, and the underwriter uses judgment rating. If the straight excess liability policy is used over automobile insurance, the excess liability underwriter requires the same information as the primary underwriter. This information may be found on the application submitted to the primary insurer. An excess underwriter usually can rely on the primary underwriter's judgment about any drivers insured for the automobile fleet. Also, the excess underwriter will ask for loss history only on losses in excess of $5,000 or $10,000. When the excess liability policy includes more than one type of coverage, underwriters need more information about the insured.

[DA06373]

Underwriting the Insurer

Because the umbrella or excess insurer must assume defense of a claim if the underlying insurer cannot, underwriters should consider the underlying insurer's financial condition. An insurer's solvency may be assessed based on the rating it receives from a recognized service such as A.M. Best or Standard & Poor's. An underwriter may also judge an insurer's financial stability based on the length of time it has been in existence.

SUMMARY

Property insurance underwriters use the COPE model to remind them of the four basic areas that should be analyzed for every application: construction, occupancy, protection, and external exposure.

For property underwriters, how much an insurer will be obligated to pay when a loss occurs is a significant consideration. Insurable interest, policy provisions for establishing the value of insured property, and the relationship of the amount of insurance to that value all affect the amount an insurer must pay in the event of a loss. Underwriters must consider how each type of property ownership will affect the amount of loss paid by the policy, how the policy provisions for placing a value on insured property affect the amount the insurer will have to pay in the event of a loss, and whether the insured carries an adequate amount of insurance.

Underwriters usually use several measures to determine the potential severity of a loss:

- Policy amount
- Amount subject
- Normal loss expectancy (NLE)
- Probable maximum loss (PML)
- Maximum foreseeable loss (MFL)

When determining business income and extra expense coverage, the underwriter must consider both the probable maximum loss and factors affecting the business interruption period following a loss. To evaluate this coverage aspect, the underwriter should examine the time required to rebuild the insured premises, the seasonality of the business, bottlenecks, computer systems, long production processes, availability of substitutes, and the extent to which the insured has prepared for a business income loss through business continuity and disaster recovery planning.

Underwriting considerations for commercial crime coverage stem from two general areas: employee dishonesty and crimes committed by others. Employee dishonesty loss exposures have unique characteristics related to employees' access to company property and the employer-employee relationship. Analysis of crimes committed by others considers susceptibility and marketability, property location, occupancy, public protection, and coverage and price modifications.

When evaluating a commercial general liability submission, an underwriter must consider premises and operations loss exposures, which include those associated with public exposure, physical hazards and exposures that stem from the work of contractors and subcontractors. Products liability loss exposures, which include potential sources of products liability such as breach of warranty, negligence, and strict liability in tort, also must be considered, along with completed operations exposures from the insured's completed work. Other considerations include those related to personal and advertising injury and premises medical payments, though loss exposures in these categories are automatically included in the CGL coverage form and generally are not individually underwritten.

Effective personal auto underwriting requires an analysis of factors such as age of operator, age and type of auto, auto use, driving record, territory, gender and marital status, occupation, personal characteristics, physical condition of driver, and safety equipment. When assessing commercial auto coverage, underwriters should consider the characteristics used in rating the policy that relate to both the driver and the vehicle. Additional underwriting factors for trucks, tractors, and trailers include vehicle weight and type, vehicle use, radius of operation, and special industry classifications. Insurer risk control activities, such as making drivers and managers more safety conscious through fleet safety programs, can contribute to an account's underwriting profitability.

There are many considerations associated with underwriting workers compensation insurance, including various underwriting guidelines for individual classes and applicants, management attitude and capability, on-premises hazards, and off-premises hazards.

Umbrella and excess liability policies offer higher coverage limits than those provided by primary insurance policies. Underwriting considerations associated with such coverage include: the severity of the risks the policies are intended to address, elements of the underlying policies that could affect coverage, and the solvency of the insurer providing the underlying coverage.

ASSIGNMENT NOTES

1. Insurance Services Office, "Construction Briefs," www.isopropertyresources.com/Training-Education/Construction-Briefs/Construction-Briefs.html (accessed July 7, 2010).

2. National Fire Protection Association, Fire Protection Handbook, 20th ed. (Quincy, Mass.: National Fire Protection Association, 2008), p. 19-23.

3. Fire Protection Handbook, 20th ed., p. 18-14.

4. Insurance Services Office, "ISO's Building Code Effectiveness Grading Schedule," www.isomitigation.com/bcegs/0000/bcegs0001.html (accessed July 16, 2010).

5. Fire Protection Handbook, 20th ed., p. 2-17

6. "AAIS Revises Fire Protection Classifications," American Association of Insurance Services, February 6, 2008,www.aaisonline.com/press/2008/Press020608.html (accessed July 30, 2010).

7. Thomas F. Barry, "Developing Fire Risk Tolerance Profiles; An Overview," www.fireriskforum.com/RiskTOOLS/whitepapers/RISKTOOLS%20Developing%20Fire%20Risk%20Tolerance%20Profiles;%20An%20Overview.pdf (accessed July 1, 2010).

8. "Traffic Safety Facts: 2008 Data, Young Drivers," NHTSA National Center for Statistics and Analysis, www-nrd.nhtsa.dot.gov/Pubs/811169.PDF (accessed July 12, 2010).

9. Insurance Institute for Highway Safety, "Fatality Facts 2007," www.iihs.org/research/fatality_facts_2007/gender.html (accessed July 13, 2010).

10. "Professional Employer Organizations Frequently Asked Questions," National Council on Compensation Insurance, www.ncci.com/nccimain/IndustryInformation/PEO/Pages/PEO_General_FAQs.aspx#Q6 (accessed Jul 20, 2010).

Direct Your Learning ▶▶

Risk Control and Premium Auditing

Educational Objectives

After learning the content of this assignment, you should be able to:

▶ Describe the goals of insurer risk control activities.

▶ Describe the risk control services provided by insurers.

▶ Explain how risk control cooperates with other insurer functions.

▶ Explain why premium audits are conducted.

▶ Describe the premium auditing process.

▶ Explain why premium audits must be accurate.

▶ Explain how premium auditing contributes to other insurer functions.

Risk Control and Premium Auditing

6

INSURER RISK CONTROL GOALS

The primary purpose of an insurer's risk control function is to evaluate loss exposures to assist with underwriting decisions. Another important risk control function is to recommend strategies to customers to prevent or mitigate losses.

Insurers conduct risk control activities to achieve several goals:

- Earn a profit
- Meet customer needs
- Comply with legal requirements
- Fulfill duty to society

Earn a Profit

Risk control activities can help insurers reach their profit goals in several ways:

- Improving underwriting decisions—By inspecting the premises and operations of insurance applicants, risk control representatives can improve the information on which the underwriting department bases its decisions about which applicants to accept and how to price coverage. Better underwriting information enables the insurer to do a better job of selecting insureds and pricing its coverage at a competitive level to produce an underwriting profit.

- Improving premium volume—Risk control personnel often recommend risk control measures that can change a marginal account to an acceptable account, thereby increasing the insurer's premium volume while meeting underwriting guidelines. In addition, risk control personnel and the services they offer can be instrumental in winning new business by helping producers demonstrate added value to their prospective clients.

- Encouraging insureds to improve risk control—Risk control representatives can influence insureds to implement more effective risk control initiatives by working with them to identify risk control opportunities and safety improvements.

- Reducing insureds' losses—Risk control representatives can continue to monitor insureds and suggest appropriate risk control measures as the nature or extent of the insureds' loss exposures change. Consequently, risk control representatives can reduce losses that the insurer must pay, thereby helping to keep the insurer's book of business profitable.

- Providing an additional revenue source—Traditionally, insurers provided risk control services only to their insureds and did not charge a fee in addition to the policy premium. Now, many insurers also sell unbundled risk control services to firms that have chosen to retain, or self-insure, their losses. Some insurers also provide their insureds with supplemental risk control services for a fee in addition to the policy premium. Several major insurers offer access to a variety of experts, such as nurses, ergonomic specialists, industrial hygiene specialists, engineers, attorneys, and chemists.

- Reducing errors and omissions claims against the insurer—Competent risk control service reduces the possibility of errors and omissions claims by insureds or others alleging injury because of the insurer's negligence. In addition, the errors and omissions liability loss exposure can influence an insurer's decision about what types or levels of risk control services to provide.

Meet Customer Needs

Some insurers offer risk control activities in response to the needs of insurance customers—usually their commercial and industrial customers.

These needs have resulted partly from the pressures of legislation such as the Occupational Safety and Health Act, the Consumer Products Safety Act, the Comprehensive Environmental Response Compensation and Liability Act, and the Americans with Disabilities Act. The threat of large liability judgments in certain areas has also contributed to the demand for risk control services.

By exercising sound risk control, organizations make their accounts more attractive to underwriters (especially during a hard market); help control their insurance premiums and possibly even lower them; reduce disruption to operations following accidents; remain socially responsible; comply with occupational safety and health standards; comply with local, state, and federal laws; and improve their financial performance.

Insurers who rely on the independent agency system to market their products often provide risk control services to help agents develop their relationships with insureds and potential accounts. By providing risk control services, the insurer can also experience these additional benefits:

- Enhance its relationship with the producers, staff, and customers of the independent agency
- Increase its own market share as well as that of the agency
- Attract and retain higher-quality accounts
- Help the agency and its customers accomplish their goals

By satisfying customer needs for risk control services, insurers can attract new customers, retain satisfied customers, and gain a competitive advantage over insurers that do not provide these services.

Comply With Legal Requirements

Some states require insurers to provide a minimum level of risk control service to commercial insureds. This requirement applies most often to workers compensation insurance but may also exist for other lines of coverage. Some insurers charge an additional fee for providing risk control services that exceed what the law requires. Charges for services often depend on the premium volume associated with the account. Insurers comply with these laws to not only meet the state's legal requirements and avoid financial penalties, but also to minimize the possibility of errors and omissions claims by insureds.

Fulfill Duty to Society

Insurers benefit society by providing financial resources to help individuals and businesses recover from accidental losses. However, preventing accidental losses is clearly preferable. An occupational injury can cause pain, suffering, and loss of income for an individual and his or her family. A fire at a large factory can cause loss of business income, employee layoffs, and contingent business income losses for the firm's suppliers. Accidental losses collectively have a profound adverse effect on society.

Insurers have an ethical obligation to use their expertise wisely. By assisting insureds in preventing or reducing accidental losses, insurers pursue humanitarian goals and benefit society. This is true even when the insurer derives no direct financial benefit from its risk control services.

RISK CONTROL SERVICES PROVIDED BY INSURERS

Many insurers employ individuals who specialize in risk control. Insurance personnel who perform risk control activities have varying titles, such as safety specialist, risk control specialist, loss control representative, or loss control engineer. The term "risk control representative" refers to all risk control personnel, regardless of job title. Risk control representatives are often members of an insurer's risk control department, which might be centralized in the home office or decentralized in field offices.

Insurers provide three types of risk control services:

- Conducting physical surveys
- Performing risk analysis and improvement
- Developing safety management programs

An insurer with the necessary resources might provide services in all three categories for some of its insureds. Insurers' decisions regarding the risk control services they provide to their insureds are influenced by several factors, including line of insurance, commercial insured size, types of loss exposures insured, and potential legal liability.

Some insurers employ a limited number of risk control staff, or none at all. These insurers often choose to contract with private firms to provide risk control services on an as-needed basis. An insurer that has its own risk control department might also contract with private firms to provide services in geographically remote areas, for highly specialized risks, or to augment its in-house staff during busy times or major underwriting initiatives.

Conducting Physical Surveys

Conducting physical surveys consists mainly of collecting underwriting information on a customer's loss exposures, such as building construction type(s), worker occupations, site diagrams, and fire protection systems. Less-experienced risk control representatives are often assigned to this type of work, particularly with property-only risks.

On a typical survey, a risk control representative inspects the customer's premises on a walking tour and interviews the customer's management to discover details that might not be apparent from the tour. The risk control representative evaluates loss exposures and associated hazards relating to these factors:

- Fire, windstorm, water damage, burglary, and other causes of property loss
- Legal liability arising out of premises, operations, products, completed operations, automobile, mobile equipment, environmental impairment, and other sources of liability
- Employee injuries relative to working conditions, machinery hazards, and employee safety practices

In addition to evaluating loss exposures and physical hazards, the risk control representative evaluates management's ability to control exposures effectively. Their ability to control exposures depends on the experience of the management team, the consistent use of rules and procedures, the use of engineering controls and protective clothing, and the use of safety systems such as safety committees and job safety analysis. Two key components of the success of risk control measures are management's commitment to risk control and employee attitudes about safety. By carefully evaluating management's approach to accident prevention, the risk control representative can obtain important insight into the possibility and extent of **moral hazards** and **morale hazards**.

At the tour's conclusion, the risk control representative meets with management to ask questions, discuss loss exposures and hazards, and provide recommendations for controlling hazards identified during the survey. After leaving the customer's premises, the risk control representative organizes the information in a formal report, which is sent to the insured along with

Moral hazard

A condition that increases the likelihood that a person will intentionally cause or exaggerate a loss.

Morale hazard (attitudinal hazard)

A condition of carelessness or indifference that increases the frequency or severity of loss.

any applicable resource information to help implement the recommendations. Resource information might include training materials, an example of a written safety program, a self-inspection checklist template, or regulatory compliance information. Risk control correspondence is typically shared with underwriting and with the producer, and it might also be shared with claims and other insurer departments. See the exhibit "Risk Control Report."

The written recommendations made by the risk control representative can help the customer eliminate or control loss exposures. They also help the underwriting department and the producer to follow up on the customer's progress in addressing the identified hazards. Typically, recommendations are generated when a risk control representative identifies a loss exposure that falls below a satisfactory level. With mercantile loss exposures, for example, a common recommendation is to control slip-and-fall hazards by improving the maintenance program for aisles, steps, and stairwells.

Recommendations should be as practical as possible, conform to industry and regulatory standards, and be explained in enough detail to allow successful implementation by the insured. The potential cost of addressing a particular hazard should be considered when a recommendation is made but should not determine whether the recommendation is actually made. When the cost of addressing a hazard in the traditional manner is high or even prohibitive, alternatives should be offered to accomplish risk control in a more cost-effective manner. A simple cost-benefit analysis can be done to help ensure that recommendations are not unnecessarily burdensome. Too often, recommendations are limited to fixing what is broken or upgrading the item in question to meet regulatory standards. It is in the best interest of the insured and the insurer to offer recommendations that are not merely minimum requirements but "best practices."

A survey report might also include information about a property valuation (appraisal) that has been done by others. This can be important if the actual values differ from the coverage limits requested by the customer. For example, if a customer has requested $500,000 insurance coverage (actual cash basis) on an older building, and a professional appraisal then values that building at $750,000 (functional replacement cost basis), a coverage gap can be avoided. The underwriter, and even the producer, might determine the current estimated value of a property using commercially available software. However, most insurers choose to avoid making an official determination of property values for policy-limit purposes, as doing so can subject them to errors and omissions claims. Risk control representatives generally do not participate in determining actual property values, but their observations and experience can help to identify situations in which the stated values or requested policy limits should be examined more closely. By accurately determining a building's actual cash value, functional value, or full replacement cost, the correct limit of insurance can be determined and the most appropriate basis of coverage used.

Risk Control Report

Midley Insurance Companies
429 Smithtown Rd., Anywhere, PA 22484

INSURED
Terry's Casual Wear

MAILING ADDRESS
4814 Hwy. 17 South, N. Myrtle Beach, S.C.

LOCATION SURVEYED
SAME

PERSON INTERVIEWED
Theresa Mason

SURVEY DATE
6/28/X3

RISK CONTROL REPRESENTATIVE
John Henderson

POLICY NUMBER
CR07234525

EXPLAIN OR MAKE RECOMMENDATIONS FOR ALL CIRCLE ○ ANSWERS

A. RISK OVERVIEW

OVERALL RISK	LOSS CONTROL	PREMISES CONDITION	HOUSEKEEPING	PRIOR LOSS	OPINION OF RISK
☐ Low	☑ Good	☑ Good	☑ Good	○ Yes	☑ Good
☑ Medium	☐ Fair	☐ Fair	☐ Fair	☑ No	☐ Fair
○ High	○ Poor	○ Poor	○ Poor		○ Poor

B. DESCRIPTION OF OPERATIONS

1. Description of business and/or operations:
    Retail clothing store

C. GENERAL DATA

1. Insured is: ☑ Owner ☐ Tenant ☐ Lessee
2. Insured is: ☑ Corporation ☐ Partnership ☐ Individual
3. Yrs. in business: 5 At this location 3
4. Business hours: 10 to 11
5. Estimated gross annual sales: $225,000
6. Neighborhood is: ☑ Commercial ☐ Rural ☐ Residential ☐ Industrial

7. Neighborhood is: ☑ Stable ○ Other
8. Does business appear successful? ☑ Yes ○ No
9. Management attitude satisfactory? ☐ Yes ○ No
10. Other occupants in building? ☐ Yes ◉ No
    If YES, describe:

BUILDING

1. Year built: _____ 20X0 _____

2. Building height (stories & ft./story): _____ 1 _____

3. Exterior wall construction: Frame _____ Wood _____ Cover: _____ Wood shingle _____

4. Floor construction: _____ Wood _____

5. Roof const.: Support: _____ Wood _____ Deck: _____ Metal _____ Cover: _____ Metal _____

6. Area (include basement only if finished): sq. ft. _____ 1,320 _____

7. ☐ Fire Resistive   ☐ Ordinary
    ☐ Non-Combustible   ☑ Frame

8. Vertical openings:

    Stairways protected?   ☐ Yes   ○ No   ☑ None

    Elevators protected?   ☐ Yes   ○ No   ☑ None

    Elevators: # of passengers: _____ # of freight: _____

9. Int. finish: _____ Walls: _____ Wood _____ Ceiling: _____ S/R _____

10. Building condition satisfactory?   ☑ Yes   ○ No

11. Basement in building?   ○ Yes   ☑ No

    If YES,   ☐ Full   ☐ Partial _____ %
    ○ Finished   ☐ Unfinished

HAZARDS

1. Heating type: _____ FA central loc elsewhere

    A. Fuel   ☐ Gas   ☑ Electric   ☐ Wood/Coal   ☐ LP Gas   ☐ Oil

    B. Appears safely arranged? _____ not seen _____ ☐ Yes   ○ No

2. Air conditioning?   ☐ Yes   ○ No

    Type: ☑ Central   ☐ Package   ☐ Portable   ○ Other _____

3. Electrical type: ☐ Conduit   ☑ Romex   ☐ _____

    A. Overcurrent Protection: ☑ Cir. Brkrs.   ☐ Fuses

    B. Appear safely arranged?   ☑ Yes   ○ No

4. Are the following satisfactory?

    A. Housekeeping   ☑ Yes   ○ No
    B. Maintenance   ☑ Yes   ○ No
    C. Trash Removal   ☑ Yes   ○ No
    D. Smoking Control   ☑ Yes   ○ No
    E. Flam./Combust. liquids   ☐ Yes   ○ No   ☑ None noted
    F. Welding/hot work   ☐ Yes   ○ No   ☑ None noted
    G. Other special hazards   ☐ Yes   ○ No   ☑ None noted

FIRE PROTECTION

1. Risk within city limits?   ☑ Yes   ○ No

2. Fire department: ☐ None   ☑ Paid   ☐ Volunteer

3. Distance to fire dept.: _____ 1/3 _____ Miles

4. Number of hydrants and distance: 1 at 50'; 1 at 370'

5. Adequate fire extinguishers?   ☑ Yes   ○ No

    Size and type: _____ 2A _____

6. Extinguishers properly tagged and serviced?   ☑ Yes   ○ No

7. Sprinkler system?   ◉ Yes   ☐ No

    A. Coverage: ○ Partial _____ %   ☐ Full

    B. Alarm: ☐ Local   ☐ Central Station

8. Fire detection/alarm system?   ◉ Yes   ☐ No

9. Watchman service?   ◉ Yes   ☐ No

10. Fire dept. name and class: _____ N. Myrtle Beach _____

Operations

Your insured is a corporation that has been in business for five years. It has been in business at the present location since the shopping mall was constructed three years ago. The mall has numerous small shops and restaurants built up on a boardwalk over a small inlet, approximately 3,000 feet from the Atlantic Ocean. Insured leases this space for a clothing store, selling ladies' moderately priced casual wear and a few accessories, such as purses, belts, etc. Also, a small line of costume jewelry is in one case at the counter.

Building

The building is three years old, of wood frame construction, and found to be in good condition and well maintained. The building is on wood pylons, and a portion of the building is above the water (see diagram and photo).

Heating and Air Conditioning

Heat and air conditioning are ducted from elsewhere in the mall and are said to be water-controlled and thought to be electric; however, the unit was not located. The insured said she believes the units are near Hwy. 17, several hundred feet from the building.

Wiring

Wiring is Romex with breaker protection. This appears to be in good condition and is three years old.

Protection

Insured is located in North Myrtle Beach, and the North Myrtle Beach fire department will respond there. No unusual fire department obstructions were noted.

Portable extinguishers were posted all around the mall area, and these were properly tagged and serviced. Also, a Z100 Moose digital alarm system protects the shop. This has heat detectors as well as infrared motion detectors, and insured states she believes this is directly monitored by the fire department. The alarm system was installed by the owners of the mall, and apparently these are present in every location.

Much of the mall is sprinklered, and there is a PIV valve fifty feet outside the insured's location; however, this particular shop is not sprinklered.

Security guards are employed by the mall, and the insured said that they patrol this area twenty-four hours a day.

Liability

The shop was in good condition from a liability standpoint. Stock is neatly stored and arranged in a clutter-free manner. Floor covering, lighting, and egress are good, and there are marked exits. All parking is controlled by the mall.

Losses

Contact states no losses have occurred under these coverages. They did have one business interruption loss during Hurricane Hugo in 1989.

Comments

Because of premises and building conditions, as well as good controls and the nature of insured's operation, this risk rates "good" for all coverages surveyed.

Note

Initially, we visited insured on 6/20; however, the contact was not in. We phoned back on several occasions before she contacted us on 6/28 to obtain loss and other information.

Recommendations

None are deemed necessary at this time.

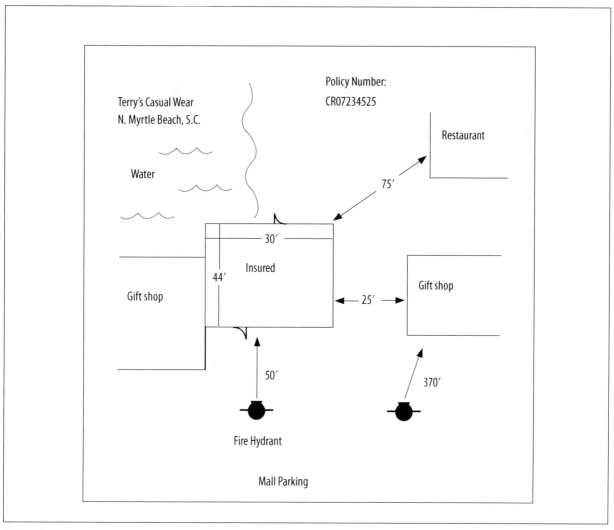

[DA03354]

Physical surveys provide benefits to both the underwriter and the insured:

- The survey report helps the underwriter gain a better understanding of the loss exposures being insured. Underwriters often provide an insurance quotation with the condition that various risk control recommendations in the survey report be implemented.

- The insured can gain a better understanding of its loss exposures and the steps that could be taken to prevent or reduce losses, comply with applicable laws and regulations, and provide a better working environment for employees, all of which can increase employee morale and productivity.

- If a property valuation is part of the survey, the insured can be more confident of an adequate recovery in the event of a total loss and less likely to incur a coinsurance penalty in the event of a partial loss.

Performing Risk Analysis and Improvement

In addition to completing a physical survey and loss exposure and hazard evaluation, the insurer's risk control representative might analyze the customer's loss history (risk analysis) and submit written recommendations (improvements) to the business owner or manager about how to reduce hazards that have led to previous losses. A risk control representative or the producer usually contacts the insured within sixty to ninety days to follow up on the insured's progress in complying with the recommendations. Some insurers' risk control departments follow up on all recommendations on a scheduled basis—for example, sixty to ninety days from when the recommendations were made. Depending on the procedures of the particular insurer, follow-up might occur at intervals or as part of the renewal process. Some insurers require that the producer conduct the follow-up. Ideally, underwriting will have written confirmation from the insured that the recommendations have been implemented.

To support the risk analysis and improvement effort, the insurer's risk control representatives can provide training, information, or counseling services, such as these:

- Coordinated safety programs
- Technical risk-control information resources
- Workers compensation risk management strategies
- Fire protection systems testing and evaluation
- Preconstruction counseling

A safety training program includes a series of presentations on safety-related subjects to raise workers' awareness of loss exposures and appropriate safety behaviors. Typical subjects are fire safety, driver safety, and machine operation safety. Subjects are selected based on an analysis of the insured's loss exposures or trends in loss experience. Priority is given to subjects that could significantly improve the insured's loss experience. Films, slide shows, and videotapes can be shown in conjunction with training programs or can be loaned to insureds as requested.

Safety programs can help to develop positive safety attitudes among all workers, improve workers' understanding of safety-related matters, and help workers accept responsibility for their role in the organization's safety program. To prepare the insured's managers for assuming a leadership role in risk control, the insurer might also conduct supervisory safety training sessions.

A written safety program is a collection of policies and procedures the insured uses in its operations to facilitate risk control. Written safety programs generally include information on awareness and training, life safety, accident reporting and investigation, reporting of safety concerns, employee responsibilities, supervisory responsibilities, and regulatory compliance.

Many insurers also serve as a source of technical risk control information. Information sought by the insured might relate to specific hazards and appropriate controls, the interpretation of standards, or particular safety management products or suppliers. By providing this information, the insurer helps the insured save time and effort in obtaining information needed to make informed risk-control decisions. The insurer also builds a working relationship with the insured that can help to retain the account in the future.

The risk control departments of some larger insurers enter into service contracts with their insureds or other clients to provide periodic testing and maintenance for fire protection and detection systems. The insurer's concerns include whether the system will respond in an emergency and whether the system is designed properly for the insured's current loss exposures. However, most insurers rely on the insured property owner to contract for these services directly with outside service providers.

When business owners expand existing facilities or build new structures, they often overlook the connection between construction features and insurance rates. Generally, rating credits can be given for noncombustible or fire-resistive construction, sprinkler systems, smoke detectors, burglar alarms, security hardware, and other features. A pre-construction review by the insurer of the drawings and specifications allows the insured to see how insurance rates and underwriting acceptability will be affected by the new construction. Any plan alterations can be made more cost effectively before construction begins.

Developing Safety Management Programs

The development of safety management programs is often coordinated by senior risk control staff, who generally have the advanced technical and communication skills needed for more in-depth consultation work.

Developing safety management programs begins with a complete evaluation of the insured's operations, just as in risk analysis and improvement risk control services. After reviewing the evaluation, the more experienced risk control representative or risk control consultant assists the insured in establishing risk control goals, selecting appropriate risk control measures, organizing the resources necessary to implement the chosen risk control measures, and establishing procedures to monitor the program.

Because of several concerns, the insured is ordinarily responsible for implementing the program on a daily basis without direct assistance from the risk control consultant. These concerns include errors and omissions liability, lack of authority to exercise a management role in the insured's business, and the need for management to have program ownership.

After being implemented, the program must be monitored to determine whether adjustments are needed. The risk control consultant can provide a great deal of technical assistance in the monitoring phase of the program.

The consultation process normally requires several visits to the insured's premises to gather initial information, plan the review with management, and follow up to monitor the program. Depending on the needs, abilities, and preferences of the insured, ongoing risk control visits may occur on a semi-annual, quarterly, or monthly basis.

Factors Affecting Service Levels

Every insurer must decide what levels of risk control service to provide and to which insureds. Several factors influence insurers' decisions.

Line of Insurance

One of the factors that will influence an insurer's decision about the level and type of risk control service to provide is the line of insurance. An insurer that writes only personal insurance is unlikely to provide extensive risk control services. The relatively small premium for a typical personal auto or home-owners account does not justify the expense necessary to conduct on-site safety inspections.

During personal insurance underwriting, insurers sometimes request that their agents or salespeople photograph a house or an auto (the latter to verify a car's vehicle identification number). Insurers might provide producers with checklists to ensure that certain items are either requested specifically of the applicant or identified during the producer's drive-by inspection. See the exhibit "Personal Insurance Property Report."

Producers can effectively implement risk control programs when insurers provide explicit instructions. When insuring exceptionally high-valued property, such as a mansion or a yacht, the insurer might use specifically trained risk control representatives to develop underwriting information or recommendations for reducing physical hazards.

In addition to conducting on-site inspections, an insurer can promote risk control among its personal lines insureds by publishing educational bulletins or by offering rate discounts for home security systems, deadbolt locks, automobile anti-theft devices, driver education, or other risk control measures. An insurer might also support industry associations that disseminate information, conduct research, lobby legislators, or otherwise support risk control efforts to benefit society. Fire safety and highway safety are two major areas addressed by such associations.

Commercial Insured Size

The large premiums generated by commercial insureds and the increased values at risk often make it economically feasible to provide such insureds with risk control services. The level of service rendered to a commercial insured can depend on the size of the account. Typically, an insurer devotes more resources to accounts that generate a substantial premium. Some insurers make some or all of their risk control services available to smaller accounts who request them.

Sometimes, insureds might not want a higher level of service than the insurer normally provides with its insurance. Insurers may provide options for insureds to purchase supplemental risk control services. By not including the cost for such supplemental services in the premium, insurers allow insureds

Personal Insurance Property Report

PERSONAL INSURANCE PROPERTY REPORT

DATE   November 1, 20XX
POLICY NUMBER   PCA 123 4579
NAME   Willis Bethea
MAILING   Providence Road
ADDRESS   Malvern, PA 19355
PROPERTY
LOCATION
(IF OTHER THAN ABOVE)

PHOTOS
☑ ATTACHED
PHOTOS _____ (IF MORE THAN ONE)
☐ NOT AVAILABLE

AMT. OF COVERAGE $ 194,000

OBSERVATIONS	VALUES

OBSERVATIONS

1. Apprx. Year Built: ___1977___   OTHER:

2. Number of Stories: ☐ 1   ☑ 2   ☐ 3   ☐ _____

3. Occupancy:
   ☑ Single Family   ☐ Two Family   ☐ _____

4. Predominant Constr. Material:
   A. Dwg.   ☑ Frame   ☐ Brick   ☐ Solid   ☐ _____
              Veneer   or Stone   Brick
   B. Roof   ☑ Comp.   ☐ Tar &   ☐ Wood   ☐ _____
              Shingle   Gravel   Shingle
   C. Outbuildings   ☐ None   ☑ Frame
                     ☐ Masonry   ☐ Metal   ☐ _____

5. Condition:
   A. Dwg.   ☑ Good   ☐ _____
   B. Roof   ☑ Good   ☐ _____
   C. Outbuildings   ☐ None   ☑ Good   ☐ _____

6. Neighborhood:
   A. Type   ☑ Residential   ☐ Commercial
             ☐ Rural   ☐ _____
   B. Status   ☐ Improving   ☑ Stable   ☐ _____

7. Protection:
   Approximate Distance in Feet to Nearest Hydrant   100 ft
   Approximate Distance in Miles to Nearest
   Responding Fire Department   1-1/2 mi

8. Liability Hazards:
   ☑ Outside Pool   ☑ Fenced   _____
   ☐ Horses   ☐ Unfenced
   ☐ Large Dogs   ☐ Business use

9. Hazards Noted: ☐ None
   ☐ Vacant or   ☐ Isolated or   ☐ Difficult Access
     Seasonal   Hidden   for Fire
     Property   ☐ Wood Stove   Department
   ☐ Dead Trees   ☐ Combustible   ☐ Open
     or Limbs   Brush or Debris   Foundation
   ☐ Adjacent   ☐ Flooding or
     Property   High Water   ☐ Other

VALUES

DIAGRAM—SHOW DIMENSIONS

Utility shed

Deck

Covered porch   Two-car garage

Estimated replacement cost using:

☑ Room count method

☐ Square foot method

$ 210,000

CUSTOM HOME FEATURES:
_____
_____
_____
_____

Date of Report   9/1/20XX
Agency: F.A. Smith, West Chester
Inspector: Bill Smith

REMARKS—RECOMMENDATIONS
FOR IMPROVEMENT
_____
_____
_____
_____
_____
_____

[DA03355]

who do not want or need these additional services to avoid subsidizing the costs associated with them.

Types of Loss Exposures Insured

The risk control services an insurer provides depend to some degree on the types of loss exposures the insurer is willing to cover. An insurer that covers large and complex industrial firms needs skilled personnel and sophisticated equipment to meet the risk control requirements of such firms, including these examples:

- Testing and evaluating the effects of noise levels on employees
- Assessing the hazards to employees from solvents, toxic metals, radioactive isotopes, and other substances
- Assisting in the design of explosion suppression systems or fire extinguishing systems for dangerous substances or easily damaged equipment
- Evaluating products liability loss exposures and preparing programs to minimize such loss exposures
- Consulting on complex and specialized risk control problems

An insurer that deals primarily with habitational, mercantile, and small manufacturing loss exposures might be able to maintain a less-sophisticated risk control department.

Potential Legal Liability

Making recommendations to existing insureds is an important risk management tool for insurers. However, the threat of being named in a lawsuit for negligence in providing risk control services may lead some insurers to choose not to offer risk control services at all or to limit their risk control activities in order to avoid or minimize their exposure.

Some states have enacted statutes that protect insurers by preventing insureds, their employees, and third parties (including applicants) from bringing suit against an insurer for injuries or damages sustained as a result of providing, or failing to provide, risk control services. Although relatively infrequent, negligent inspection claims do occur. If an insurer's underwriting department chooses to require certain controls as a prerequisite to providing coverage, such controls should be expressed as conditions of the insurance quote and the subsequent insurance agreement rather than as risk control recommendations, in order to avoid unnecessary exposure to potential legal liability.

COOPERATION BETWEEN RISK CONTROL AND OTHER INSURER FUNCTIONS

An insurer's risk control efforts are most effective when they complement the activities of its other departments and various external organizations.

Cooperation between risk control representatives and the representatives of other insurer functions can improve the quality of information available to an insurer and the services it offers. Insurers and insureds can also benefit from cooperative relationships between the risk control function and various external organizations, particularly producers. Other external organizations include reinsurers; trade associations that engage in risk control activities; the Occupational Safety and Health Administration (OSHA) and other regulatory agencies; law enforcement and codes enforcement agencies; and public safety entities such as fire departments.

These are the principal opportunities for risk control cooperation:

- Underwriting
- Marketing and sales
- Premium auditing
- Claims
- Producers

Underwriting

The risk control function provides information to underwriters that enables them to make better underwriting decisions. This information consists primarily of field inspection reports on the premises and operations of new applicants and existing insureds renewing their policies. Inspection reports should provide a clear profile of the applicant's loss exposures and related hazards. Additionally, an insurer's risk control department can provide technical support to its underwriting department in many areas, such as fire hazards of new building materials, health hazards of materials or production processes, and new techniques or equipment for materials handling.

The risk control function can also help underwriters modify a new applicant's loss exposures to meet eligibility requirements. After an applicant has been accepted, risk control can help the insured to remain within underwriting guidelines and qualify for policy renewal. Risk control can even help "rehabilitate" a marginal account that underwriting has accepted because of competitive considerations.

Risk control representatives also play an important role in communicating effectively with insureds. Often, a risk control representative is the main communications link between the underwriter and the insured.

Marketing and Sales

The risk control function also can be instrumental in helping the insurer's marketing and sales staff meet its goals. By evaluating an applicant's premises and operations, interviewing management staff, and evaluating the nature of historical losses, risk control representatives can help determine if an applicant's current risk controls are acceptable or if there are ways to improve an accepted applicant's risk controls. The risk control representative's evaluation can make the difference between an applicant's acceptance or rejection.

By making marginal accounts acceptable, risk control helps marketing reach its sales goals. Risk control can also help marketing by proving to applicants and insureds that the insurer understands their business operations and associated hazards, and is prepared to help them protect their interests. The risk control representative can offer crucial advice on improving safety.

After applicants become insureds, risk control can play a key role in retaining them as customers. In fact, a commercial insured might have more regular contact with the insurer's risk control representatives than with any other employee of the insurer. By providing professional and courteous service, risk control personnel can create customer goodwill.

Finally, through their direct contact with insureds, risk control representatives can learn the insurance coverages or services insureds need or want. By conveying this information to the appropriate marketing or sales personnel, risk control representatives can assist the marketing department in either meeting an insured's specific needs or developing product enhancements that will appeal to many insureds.

For example, a risk control survey might reveal that the insured has acquired new property that is not adequately covered under their existing policy. If conveyed to the appropriate marketing staff, this information might lead to the sale of additional coverage to that insured. If several insureds experience the same problem, that information could lead to a decision to revise the insurer's policy forms to provide better coverage for newly acquired property.

Premium Auditing

In one respect, the roles of risk control representatives and premium auditors are similar, because both visit the insured's premises and have direct insured contact. However, risk control representatives typically visit the insured at the beginning of the policy period and as needed throughout the policy period, while premium auditors visit at the end of the policy period. Premium auditors often visit the insured after the point at which recordkeeping deficiencies resulting from the insured's lack of knowledge or misunderstanding can be corrected. Risk control personnel can use the opportunity provided by their own inspections, as well as information from recent premium audits, to help improve insured documentation and the accuracy of premium audits. During the premium auditing process, a new exposure or an increase in exposure that is discovered by an auditor can prompt risk control involvement.

To take advantage of this opportunity, however, premium auditors must communicate their needs to risk control representatives so that they can, for example, note the location of the accounting records and the name of the person to contact at audit time. They can also record the names, titles, and duties of executive officers.

Their description of operations could be a starting point for the auditor's classification of loss exposures. Risk control representatives might help estimate the payroll by classification or at least the number of employees per department. They can report the existence of any new operations. If properly informed, they can also advise the insured about recordkeeping requirements and the need for good risk transfer practices, including certificates of insurance with additional insured-specific language and written contracts that include hold-harmless language.

Finally, risk control representatives can offer the assistance of the insurer's premium auditors to deal with any complex questions about an audit. Problems such as a gap in coverage, a burdensome charge for additional premium at the end of a policy year, or a significant return of premium can be prevented.

Claims

A partnership between risk control and claims can be just as valuable to an insurer as the partnership between risk control and underwriting, marketing, or premium auditing. The risk control department needs claim experience information to direct risk control resources and efforts to crucial areas. The claims department relies on risk control for loss exposure data and background information that can support the loss adjusting process. Claims and risk control personnel should discuss common concerns and review loss cases regularly. The claim experience information that can be useful to the risk control function includes frequency and severity of losses by type of insurance, by cause of loss, by the kind of business the insured engages in, and by worker occupation.

Regarding individual accidents, particularly in the workers compensation area, risk control can also benefit from information about the type of accident, the body part injured, how the accident occurred, and perhaps other details from the adjuster's report. Risk control staff can use this information for these purposes:

- Identifying areas for research
- Targeting loss exposures for additional attention
- Identifying characteristics associated with particular types of losses
- Developing alternatives to control losses

Risk control representatives are usually well informed in engineering, mechanical, and technological areas with which claims personnel might be unfamiliar. Therefore, the risk control department can provide codes, standards, technical advice, laboratory analyses, valuable insight based on experience, and other assistance to the claims department when investigating and settling claims. A risk control specialist can design product recall procedures to assist claims personnel and insureds in controlling specific product losses. Risk control representatives can also support the claims function by reviewing and emphasizing the importance of thorough loss documentation and proper claim reporting procedures.

Producers

Traditionally, producers encouraged the insured's risk control activities and coordinated the efforts of the insurer's risk control representatives with the insured. Producers still perform this role, which might be the only role played by many small to medium-sized agencies or brokerage firms. However, many large agencies and brokerages maintain their own risk control departments, and some can furnish services equivalent to those offered by insurers. If an insured is receiving risk control services from both the insurer and its producer, the risk control entities of both organizations should strive to coordinate their efforts for the mutual benefit of all parties involved, particularly the insured.

REASONS FOR PREMIUM AUDITING

The premium auditing function plays a vital role in the insurance mechanism. With knowledge of insurance principles, accounting procedures, and particular state regulations, premium auditors can obtain the information needed to calculate premiums accurately and collect the data used to establish future insurance rates. By safeguarding the accuracy of information on which insurance premiums are based, premium auditing helps make the insurance mechanism work as intended and support the insurer's profit goal by ensuring that appropriate premiums are charged for policies provided.

Insurers conduct premium audits for these reasons:

- To determine correct premiums
- To collect ratemaking data
- To meet regulatory requirements
- To deter and detect fraud
- To reinforce confidence of insureds
- To obtain additional information

Premium audit

Methodical examination of a policyholder's operations, records, and books of account to determine the actual exposure units and premium for insurance coverages already provided.

Exposure unit (unit of exposure)

The unit of measure (For example, area, gross receipts, payroll) used to determine an insurance policy premium.

The need for a **premium audit** arises because some insurance policies have adjustable premiums. For these kinds of insurance policies, loss exposure varies substantially by individual insured. A standard premium rate might be far from reflecting an insured's actual exposure to loss. When entering an adjustable premium contract, the insured pays a standard premium, which is adjusted the following year based on the actual loss exposure. Adjustable premium policies include a clause that allows the insurer to perform premium audits to determine the actual amount of **exposure units** on which the premium will be based.

For many commercial insurance policies, the premium paid at the beginning of the policy period is a provisional premium based on an estimate of the extent of operations to be insured. At the end of the policy period, typically one year, the insured's records are examined, or audited, by a premium auditor to determine the exposure units. After the auditor reports the data, the audit processors apply the rates and various factors, such as experience modification and premium discounts, to determine the final earned premium. If the insured's operations were more extensive than estimated, an additional premium is charged. If less extensive, the insured receives a partial refund.

Premium auditing is performed for many coverages, including workers compensation, which is rated per $100 of payroll, and general liability, which is rated per $1,000 of payroll or sales. Commercial auto policies for large fleets are rated based on the vehicles that are exposed to loss during the policy period. Although premium auditing most often involves liability insurance, some property insurance policies, such as those covering fluctuating inventory values, are also subject to premium audit. These premium bases are also called exposure units. An exposure unit is the fundamental measure that is used to calculate the policy premium.

Determine Correct Premiums

The primary reason for premium auditing is to determine the correct premium for the policy period. The insurer bears a responsibility to determine the premium correctly. Unless premiums are sufficient for the loss exposures covered, the insurer cannot operate profitably. If, however, the insurer overcharges the insured, it will certainly encounter negative reactions when the error is discovered and will probably lose the business. The insurer's interest and obligation, therefore, require as much certainty and precision in the premium determination as possible. A premium audit provides that accuracy.

When a policy is written subject to audit, the actual premium can be calculated only after the end of the policy period when the exact exposure units or premium bases during the policy period are known. In most cases, the applicable manual for the type of insurance involved has rules that strictly define the procedure to be followed, specifying inclusions and exclusions in the premium base and defining distinct rating classifications. For example, for workers compensation coverage, manual rules specifically indicate how to assign payroll for clerical or construction employees. Mastering these rules requires considerable effort and practice.

Insureds have the accounting information or other data that are used to determine the premium base, but they rarely understand insurance manual rules well enough to present the information in the necessary form. A skilled premium auditor, employed by the insurer, usually assembles the information and determines the actual earned premium. Even if the insured can provide the necessary premium data, having a premium auditor inspect the original books of account makes the insurer more confident that the data are accurate.

However, due to staff shortages, heavy workloads, expenses, or company policies, some insurers do not have their own premium auditors and may rely on voluntary audit reports or external premium auditing consultants.

A premium audit is also important to provide the insurer with current and accurate information to determine whether the renewal premium estimate is in line with the audited exposures. This allows the insurer to collect sufficient premium in advance in the event that the insured experiences financial problems during the policy period, which could make collection of a retrospective premium adjustment difficult.

Collect Ratemaking Data

Loss costs

The portion of the rate that covers projected claim payments and loss adjusting expenses.

Insurance advisory organizations collect ratemaking data and, in most cases, project the costs of future losses, or **loss costs**. To these loss costs, insurers add their own expense component to determine a final insurance rate.

Calculating actuarially credible rates begins with data about claim payments, earned premiums, and insured exposure units for each rating classification. Although claim reports provide the necessary information on claims for a given period, the premium volume and total insured loss exposures by class cannot be determined with any degree of certainty without compiling data from premium audits.

A detailed classification breakdown of exposure units obtained by a premium audit is necessary for the insurer's statistical report to the advisory rating organizations (rating bureaus), as well as for billing purposes. When an advisory organization has credible statistics showing premium volume, loss experience, and total insured exposure units for each rating class, its actuaries can calculate appropriate loss costs that are used to establish rates. These data usually must be filed with state regulators to support rate increases or other rate filings.

Meet Regulatory Requirements

Although requirements vary by state, premium audits are often required to meet workers compensation insurance regulations. Compared with other types of insurance, workers compensation regulation tends to be more restrictive because of the compulsory nature of its coverage. It can be argued that in requiring such insurance coverage, the state has also assumed an obligation to guarantee its availability and to administer the coverage equitably. Therefore, uniform workers compensation rules and rates are usually prescribed even in states allowing open competition on other types of insurance. As an added protection for insureds, the rules prevailing in some states stipulate that the insurer must audit the records of insureds that meet certain criteria, usually related to premium size or type of business, within specific time frames, such as every three years.

Deter and Detect Fraud

Premium auditing tends to deter fraud. Insureds are less likely to submit false or misleading information to an insurer when they know the information might be checked and independently verified by a premium auditor. Although uncovering fraud is not the primary purpose of premium auditing, premium auditors have often uncovered deceptive business practices during routine audits. Such discoveries can lead to a maze of falsified or missing records. The insurer's usual recourse is not to renew the policy; however, any such decision depends on accurate and precise information from the auditor. Therefore, even when performed randomly, premium audits are an effective control on the integrity of the premium computation and collection process.

Reinforce Confidence of Insureds

Most insureds want to deal fairly with insurers and to be dealt with fairly by insurers. Competent premium audits can contribute to insureds' confidence that they are receiving fair treatment. A premium computed from a meticulous audit has credibility when the insured knows the auditor exercised due care in collecting and verifying the data. Observing the audit process counters the notion that premium adjustments are arbitrary and conveys the impression that all insureds are, and in fact must be, treated according to uniform and equitable standards. A good premium auditor also explains the audit procedure to the insured so that any premium adjustment does not surprise the insured.

The benefits of a competent audit extend beyond the premium audit itself. An insured with a favorable impression of the insurer is less likely to look for another insurer at renewal time or when the need for additional coverage arises. Having gained from the audit procedure a greater understanding of how the premium is determined, an insured might improve record keeping, especially when having properly organized records reduces the premium charges. The insured might also be more receptive to risk control advice or other services the insurer can provide after a well-conducted premium audit.

Obtain Additional Information

A premium audit might generate additional underwriting information about the insured, such as an incorrect classification or a new loss exposure that the underwriter had not previously identified. A premium audit can also identify all named insureds on the policy to make sure all exposures from additional entities are included in the exposure. Such information can be extremely useful to the underwriter in determining whether to renew a policy. Premium audit information can also identify marketing opportunities and assist the claim department in adjusting certain types of losses. Finally, a premium audit is a source of feedback on the insurer's image and effectiveness.

PREMIUM AUDITING PROCESS

Premium auditors follow a systematic process for each audit to ensure that their information is accurate and complete and that others can rely on their work.

At each stage of the auditing process, premium auditors make judgments and decide how to proceed. Sometimes they need more information about the insured's operations, additional records, or an explanation of an apparent discrepancy. These judgments are necessary because premium auditors must be satisfied that the information they receive is reasonable and reliable.

These stages in the premium auditing process provide a framework for organizing the many decisions premium auditors must make:

- Planning
- Reviewing operations
- Determining employment relationships
- Finding and evaluating books and records
- Auditing the books and records
- Analyzing and verifying premium-related data
- Reporting the findings

As with many other processes, each stage of the premium auditing process is not necessarily a clearly defined step. The process is a continuum, and many of the stages blend.

Planning

Because insurers cannot afford the expense of auditing every auditable policy every year, they must decide which policies to audit. In some cases, an insurer might determine that an audit is not worth the cost and elect to waive it, if permissible by regulators, after considering the policy and its endorsements, prior audit reports, and the potential reliability of a voluntary report from the insured.

A voluntary report (also called a policyholder's report) is a form the insured completes and returns to the insurer's premium audit department. The insurer includes instructions to assist the insured in compiling the exposure unit information required to adjust the premium for the expired policy period. Once the insurer receives the voluntary report, it might choose to accept it (to perform a two-year audit at the end of the next policy period) or to initiate an immediate field audit to confirm the voluntary report. See the exhibit "Voluntary (Policyholder's) Report."

Field audits (also called physical audits) consist of examinations of the insured's books and records at the insured's premises. Field auditors must judge how long each audit will take and decide how to schedule audit appointments

Voluntary (Policyholder's) Report

POLICYHOLDER'S REPORT

Your Insurance Policy was issued on an **estimate** of the premium bases listed below. We now need the **actual amounts** so we can figure the premium. Please fill in the amounts for the period of time shown in the section called **Reporting Period**. If you have any questions, **please contact your agent**. We will appreciate your response by the **due date**. Thank you.

NAME AND ADDRESS OF AGENT		NAME AND ADDRESS OF COMPANY	
Elliott B. Arnold Agency P. O. Box 1224 Atlanta, GA 30301	AGENCY CODE 3207	Midley Insurance Company P. O. Box 1000 Springton, PA 19809	

NAME AND ADDRESS OF INSURED	POLICY NUMBER	KIND OF POLICY
	WC 1234	Workers Compensation

NAME AND ADDRESS OF INSURED

John's Sporting Goods, Inc.
1972 Olympic St.
Atlanta, GA 30301

POLICY PERIOD MONTH–DAY–YEAR TO MONTH–DAY–YEAR	DATE
6-6-X5 TO 6-6-X6	6-7-X6
REPORTING PERIOD	**DUE DATE**
6-6-X5 TO 6-6-X6	7-6-X6

CODE	DESCRIPTION/LOCATION	PREMIUM BASE	AMOUNT	RATE	PREMIUM
8017	Retail Stores N.O.C.	Remu-neration		3.73 per $100	

☐ COMPLETE   ☐ DO NOT COMPLETE THIS SECTION   EXECUTIVE OFFICERS/PARTNERS/PROPRIETORS

TITLE	NAME	SPECIFIC DUTIES	EARNINGS
			DO NOT INCLUDE IN UPPER SECTION

Who keeps your records? __David Schneider__   Signature _David Schneider_   Title __Treasurer__
NAME

Where are they kept? __178 Trimmings Ct.__   Phone Number __522-3054__   Date __7-1-X6__
ADDRESS

RETURN TO   ☑ COMPANY   ☐ PRODUCER

[DA03359]

efficiently. For each audit, auditors must anticipate the classification and loss exposure concerns and must determine the premium base and any necessary allocations. They must then plan how to approach the audit, what records to use, where to locate the records, whom to contact, and which questions to ask. Planning greatly improves the efficiency and quality of the premium audit.

The decision about whether to conduct a field audit is influenced by legal requirements, premium size, the insured's operations, prior audit experience, nature of the policy, cost of auditing, geographical factors, and staffing requirements. For example, a workers compensation audit might be legally required. Advisory organization rules usually require audits of all policies involving a premium above a certain amount and might restrict audit waivers to no more than two in a row. Advisory organization rules also restrict classification changes, except under specific circumstances.

Some audit teams use predictive modeling in planning both mandatory and discretionary audits. The model can help with strategies for mandatory audits by scheduling the order of audits within contract terms to achieve the optimal effect on the insurer's earned premium. A wider variety of strategies is available for discretionary audits, including determining which insureds to audit and whether to conduct a survey, telephone, or field audit.[1]

Reviewing Operations

Before they look at the books, skilled premium auditors determine the nature of the operations insured; observe the nature of the operation and compare it to similar businesses, looking for classifications that might not be shown on the policy; assess management quality and cooperation to determine how to proceed with the audit; and report any significant information to the underwriting department. Additionally, auditors note organizational changes and are always alert to other clues about the nature and direction of the insured's business.

The process the premium auditor uses is also known as auditing the risk, rather than auditing the policy. By reviewing the operations, organization, and business processes, the premium auditor notes what exposures exist and reports any changes or additional exposures, both new and not previously identified, to the underwriter. The underwriter may request additional information from the insured or have a risk control representative inspect the operations and make recommendations. Newly identified exposures could result in the underwriter's deciding to cancel or not to renew the policy or to propose additional coverage options.

The insured often does not communicate changes or new operations to the producer or the insurer. Even if such information is reported, it might be incomplete, faulty, or otherwise insufficient for underwriting purposes. A premium auditor should supply the underwriting department with details about ownership and operations that are sufficient for rating purposes.

The auditor should also indicate the proper classifications for any new loss exposures. Other items of interest to the underwriting department include the experience of a new operation's management, the financing of the operation, the marketing of its product(s), the derivation of its income, and any information about unusual hazards.

The Insurance Services Office (ISO) Premium Audit Advisory Service (PAAS) offers numerous guides and publications to assist premium auditors as they review insureds' operations. Classification guides, which are available in electronic format, provide detailed descriptions of all ISO general liability classifications and National Council on Compensation Insurance (NCCI) workers compensation classifications, as well as state exceptions to these classifications. PAAS also publishes a series of electronically distributed bulletins to provide current information and updates for premium auditors.

Determining Employment Relationships

After analyzing the insured's operations, premium auditors must determine those employees covered by the types of insurance for which premiums are based on payroll. These determinations are not always simple. Employees' payroll might constitute the premium base for both workers compensation and general liability policies, but the definition of "employee" is not necessarily the same for both coverages.

The premium basis of workers compensation policies includes the payroll of every person considered an employee under workers compensation laws. Therefore, the premium auditor must distinguish between employees and independent contractors (who are not covered under workers compensation). Moreover, applicable workers compensation laws vary by state. Many insureds do not realize that they must obtain certificates of insurance from their subcontractors; otherwise, premium auditors must include the subcontractors' payroll in the premium base.

Each state also has regulations regarding workers compensation for corporate officers, sole proprietors, and partners. Most states exclude sole proprietors and partners from workers compensation coverage, although coverage may be extended to them under the voluntary compensation endorsement. Some states allow exclusion of corporate officers, and all states have rules regarding the payroll amount to be used in determining premium for the corporate officers listed in the corporate charter.

Many of the state workers compensation **Test Audit** programs also review the claims filed under workers compensation policies to verify that the injured employees were valid employees or under the insured's direction and control, subject to coverage, and that the employee's class assignment is proper. This process was developed to substantiate the ratemaking process as well as the experience modification calculation. As a result, many insurers require their premium auditors to review and verify the claims for each workers compensation audit.

Test Audit

An audit conducted by an insurance advisory organization or bureau to check the accuracy of insurers' premium audits.

Finding and Evaluating Books or Records

Premium auditors can examine all books or records of the insured related to insurance premiums. Auditors must decide, however, which records provide the necessary information most efficiently and reliably. They must evaluate the accounting system to determine record accuracy and to identify any alternative sources to confirm the data. The quality of the insured's accounting system and records can reflect the quality of the management. Poor quality of the accounting records will reduce the auditor's confidence in their reliability and accuracy, and the auditor should take special care to verify the information obtained from those records.

Premium pay (shift differential)

A payroll system that increases the regular hourly wage rate for the night shift or other special conditions.

In addition to meeting accounting standards, insureds should set up their records to take full advantage of insurance rules and requirements. Producers can assist in this process. For example, insureds should separate their payroll records by classification and arrange their records so that auditors can easily identify previously unreported classifications. Payroll records should identify the overtime **premium pay**, which is not typically included in the premium basis. Severance and per diem pay are excludable in all states. The basis of premium includes other forms of remuneration, such as vacation pay, tool allowances, bonuses, commissions, sick pay, the value of board and lodging, and other types of nonmonetary compensation.

The premium auditor's role includes determining what benefits and compensation are included or excluded in the workers compensation premium base for each, as well as what is included for the general liability premium base. The PAAS Chart of State Exceptions can assist the premium auditor in making these determinations. See the exhibit " Example of Premium Auditor's Determination of Excludable Benefits."

Example of Premium Auditor's Determination of Excludable Benefits

For nonunion construction companies that are required to pay prevailing wage rates, fringe benefits (additional benefits paid by employers in addition to wages), that are usually paid to the union at union companies, may be deducted for workers compensation premium calculation. These fringe benefits, however, would not be deducted for general liability premium calculations.

[DA06137]

For large accounts, auditors frequently visit a prospective insured before the insurer accepts the account or shortly after acceptance. During this pre-audit survey, the premium auditor confirms the information on the application. The auditor can also assist in setting up appropriate bookkeeping procedures.

Auditing the Books and Records

The auditor's job involves not only counting the loss exposures but also classifying them correctly. Classifying an account properly can be a complex task. Rating manuals contain numerous rules and exceptions, and insureds' operations change over time. Particularly when a policy does not generate premium sufficient to justify an on-site inspection or a risk control report, a premium audit can uncover any classification changes necessary to revise coverage.

The premium auditor's expertise with classification questions can help underwriters maintain the proper classifications of the insured's operations and align the **deposit premium** with the loss exposures covered by the policy. Proper classifications are important for two reasons.

Deposit premium
The amount the primary insurer pays the reinsurer pending the determination of the actual reinsurance premium owed.

- If the classification is incorrect and the rate on the policy is too high, the insured is being overcharged and consequently might be placed at a competitive disadvantage when bidding for jobs or pricing products. Such a situation could have serious legal ramifications if the insurer has acted negligently.
- If the classification is incorrect and the rate on the policy is too low, an account is less likely to be profitable for the insurer. Premiums might decrease, but claims and expenses do not decrease when an insured is classified incorrectly.

When premium auditors examine the insured's accounting records, they must decide how much evidence is sufficient to determine the loss exposures and classifications with a reasonable degree of confidence. If evidence is not readily available, they must balance the time and expense of obtaining it against its potential effect on the audit.

When the insured uses an automated accounting system, the premium auditor must evaluate the system's capabilities and the accounting process's reliability and must decide what output to accept for premium determination purposes and what additional data to request. If the output does not include all the necessary information, the premium auditor must determine the steps to take to obtain the information. Time spent at the beginning of the audit arranging for the computer to produce the necessary data can save significant overall auditing time.

Analyzing and Verifying Premium-Related Data

Once premium auditors have obtained the data necessary for calculating the premium, they must decide whether the data are reasonable. These are some of the questions the premium auditor might ask:

- Are the data logical?
- Do the data seem complete?
- Do the data reflect enough detail for the insured's operations?

- Are the data consistent with industry averages? For example, are the ratios of payroll to sales or labor to materials reasonable considering the nature of the insured's operation?
- Can deviations from expected amounts be explained?

Premium auditors should verify premium-related data against the general accounting records and reconcile any discrepancies. If a risk is misclassified, the auditor should attempt to correct the error and notify the underwriter as soon as possible when the error involves a lower-rated class. The NCCI *Basic Manual* rules require an insurer to add or change a classification at the audit or during the policy period if the addition or change results in a premium decrease. If the appropriate class is higher rated, the correction may not be applied until the next renewal. There are exceptions in some states, such as Delaware and Pennsylvania, which are independent from NCCI and use only authorized classes regardless of the effect on rate.

Usually, the rates for workers compensation policies are based on an exposure unit of $100 of payroll. However, there are other premium bases, such as per capita for domestic workers, "upset payroll" (factors based on wood production) for loggers, and per shift for taxi drivers. General liability policies may use a number of different premium bases, such as units, area, frontage, payroll, sales, costs, or gallons. Sales and payroll are usually based on exposure units of $1,000 or gallons of 10,000. Because they are not regulated by any bureaus, general liability policies may also be written on a composite-rated basis, using whatever was agreed when the policy was written. The most important fact is that all parties should understand the premium basis being used for all policies and how records should be maintained to develop the final premium.

Verification and analysis ensure that the audit is appropriate in relation to the insured's actual loss exposures and should confirm expectations developed in the audit planning and operations review. Considerable judgment is required of auditors when analyzing and verifying premium-related data to ensure the validity of the audit findings.

Reporting the Findings

No premium audit is complete until the results are submitted. The premium-related data should be recorded and the billing information clearly summarized so that the audit can be processed and billed immediately. In addition, premium auditors must show in their reports how they obtained the data to enable others to retrace their audit steps.

The premium auditor should succinctly describe the insured's operations and explain any deviations from the usual operations for that type of business. Premium auditors must also identify other significant information obtained during the audit and communicate it effectively to the appropriate people, such as underwriters.

IMPORTANCE OF ACCURATE PREMIUM AUDITS

A premium audit error can have lasting and far-reaching effects. It is important that premium audits be accurate for the sake of the insured, the insurer, and insurance rates.

The insurance mechanism relies on each insurer to measure and classify loss exposures correctly. Premium audit errors can distort the insurer's rating structure and cause significant problems for both the insured and the insurer.

Importance for the Insured

If audit errors slip past insurers and insureds undetected, insureds may end up paying the wrong premium for their insurance. Some insureds may pay more than their proportional share for the loss exposures covered; others may pay less than their share. Insureds who pay excessive insurance premiums are placed at a competitive disadvantage and can experience financial problems. Other insureds are placed at a competitive advantage; they might continue to operate despite unusually hazardous working conditions because audit errors can lead to a subsidy in the form of underpriced insurance coverage. Insureds can also experience problems if their financial planning decisions are based on erroneous past audits. A recent, more accurate audit can result in a substantial difference in premium.

Errors in audits also result in incorrect **experience modifications**. Experience rating bases an insured's current premium on the insured's past experience (exposure units and losses). If those exposure units and losses are incorrect, the experience modification is incorrect, and so are any future premiums. In addition, if an error in an audit is detected, the rating bureau cannot calculate the correct experience modification until it receives the correct audit data. Depending on whether the modification is higher or lower than the current premium, the insured is either overpaying or underpaying for insurance until the rating bureau calculates the final, correct modification.

Experience modification
A rate multiplier derived from the experience rating computation.

Errors in premium can also reduce insureds' confidence in premium auditors, in the insurer, and in the insurance mechanism in general. This loss of confidence can reduce insureds' cooperation with the insurer and their perception of insurance as an appropriate risk management option.

Importance for the Insurer

Incorrect or incomplete premium audits negatively affect the insurer in a variety of ways. Each audit error impairs the efficiency of an insurer's operations even when the errors are corrected. Timely and correct premium audits can significantly benefit the insurer's financial position, customer relations, operational efficiency, and collections.

Financial Position

The premium audit function significantly affects the insurer's balance sheet. A prompt and accurate premium audit can benefit the insurer's financial position in three ways:

- Accurate classification of loss exposures is important to ensure equitable and accurate insurance rates. Misclassifying hazardous business into a lower-rated classification results in loss of premium volume, which might make an otherwise profitable policy unprofitable. Similarly, the insurer could unintentionally insure additional loss exposures because of errors in a premium audit.

- Timely premium audits directly affect an insurer's cash flow management. The premium audit is the foundation of the premium collection process for auditable commercial businesses. Delay in audits and the resulting billing delay can have a negative effect on the insurer's cash flow. Even more important is the effect of increasing the deposit premium for a renewal policy based on the premium audit. Keeping the deposit premium at a realistic level provides additional cash at policy inception and prevents any later collection problems.

- Premium that has been developed by audit is fully earned and, consequently, has an immediate effect on profit and policyholders' surplus. Policyholders' surplus determines the insurer's ability to write new business.

The accuracy of premium audits is critical to an insurer's financial position. Repeated premium auditing errors can undermine the profitability of an insurer.

Customer Retention

Undetected premium audit errors can cause some insureds that are overcharged to switch to another insurer to obtain coverage at a lower premium. Insureds that are undercharged are likely to remain with their insurers. Consequently, the insurer loses premium volume, and underwriting results deteriorate.

Goodwill

When insureds are informed of errors in the premium audit, the insurer's image suffers. Insureds could lose confidence in the insurer's competence and might consider switching to another insurer. Insureds who continue their coverage with the insurer despite an incorrect premium audit might be less cooperative in claim investigations or in implementing risk control recommendations. Perhaps the biggest cost, however, is the marketing and underwriting effort expended to replace business that is lost because of premium audit errors.

Efficiency

In addition to the extra work required to replace lost business, incorrect or incomplete audits can cause extra work for several insurer departments. Redoing the audit drains the resources of the premium audit department. Other departments may become involved in attempting to explain the error and reassure the insured. Underwriters may have to correct records and may be drawn into controversy. The accounting department may have to adjust entries and issue a corrected bill. The marketing department may also have additional work to try to regain the insured's confidence.

Collections

Insureds are less likely to pay premium bills they suspect to be incorrect. For example, suppose that a prompt audit of a policy expiring December 31 leads to a January 23 billing for an additional premium of $14,000, payable within forty-five days. On March 25, the producer reports significant errors in the premium audit, requiring a re-audit of the insured's records. The insured refuses to pay until the errors are corrected. The re-audit, conducted on April 2, reveals a correct additional premium of $11,000. That amount is billed on April 20. The insured expresses doubts about the accuracy of the re-audit. Because the initial audit was incorrect, the insured has no confidence in the revised premium and continues to refuse to pay the bill. The insurer's premium collection department has to spend a great deal of time and effort with the producer and the insured before the billing issues are resolved.

Importance for Insurance Rates

An equitable insurance premium requires that similar loss exposures be priced similarly. Therefore, all insureds presenting similar loss exposures belong in the same rate classification. Lack of consistency in audit classification of loss exposures causes inequity not only in the level of the current premium paid but also in the resulting distortion of the classification loss results, which determine the future insurance rates.

Particularly in workers compensation insurance, in which a large volume of the business is audited, the results of premium audits substantially affect insurance rate equity and accuracy. No matter what ratemaking method is used to develop the rates for the various workers compensation classifications, the accuracy of the underlying classification rate can be no better than the data provided by the premium audits.

Premium audits affect the equity and accuracy of rates in two ways:

• Consistency and accuracy of classification determinations—If premium auditors in one area of a state consider a particular industrial class to be in classification X, while the premium auditors in another part of the state consider it to be in class Y, then the inconsistency distorts the resulting loss data from both classes and leads to inequitable rates for all insureds in the state for those two classes. Equally important in the ratemaking procedure is accurately classifying claims. By notifying the claim department when additional classifications are assigned and by reviewing the classification of past claims at the time of an audit, premium auditors can assist the claim department in accurately classifying losses as well as loss exposures.

- Measurement of the exposure unit base—An audit error, not in classification but in determining the exposure units, also distorts the rate structure. However, rate distortions resulting from misreporting of exposure units are likely to be minor relative to distortions resulting from misclassification. Either underreporting or overreporting the exposure units affects the rate for that class.

PREMIUM AUDITING CONTRIBUTIONS

Effective insurer management capitalizes on the opportunities for premium auditing to contribute to other insurer functions.

Premium auditors may be the only insurer representatives to meet insureds, see their operations, and review their financial records. This direct contact not only significantly influences the insured's impression of the insurer, but also provides a channel to communicate relevant information to other insurer functions, including these:

- Underwriting
- Marketing and sales
- Claims
- Risk control

Underwriting

Premium auditing contributes most directly to underwriting. Premium audit reports constitute a valuable source of information for underwriters, and effective cooperation between underwriters and premium auditors is essential to ensuring that existing accounts remain profitable. Premium auditing can contribute significant information to many areas of underwriting. These examples are some of the more important and common ones. The premium auditor should develop an underwriter's perspective of an account and use the premium auditor's report, or an acceptable substitute, to communicate the desired information.

A crucial responsibility of the premium auditing function is to classify insured exposures correctly. Often, the audit is the only source of information for proper classifications. Although underwriting must establish the classifications when the policy is issued, the information submitted is occasionally incomplete or inaccurate. Properly classifying an account can be complex, and the operations of insureds can change. The premium audit, conducted at the end of the policy period, can reveal any classification changes necessary to update the policy. Premium auditors notify underwriting of any discrepancies between the classifications on the policy and those classifications that are proper for the operation.

Another important contribution of the premium auditing function to underwriting is the identification of inadequate exposure estimates. When the insured exposure has been underestimated or incorrectly classified, an inadequate deposit premium for a renewal will result. Although the premium audit will help to develop the proper exposure, it is possible that additional premium charged after the end of the policy period will never be collected.

A premium audit report can also provide a comparison of anticipated loss exposures to actual loss exposures. In a well-managed insurance operation, anticipated loss exposures should not differ significantly from actual loss exposures. Unless the insured has changed its business operations, the premium audit assessment at the end of the policy period should correspond with the underwriting assessment at the beginning of the policy period.

For large accounts, advance audits—or pre-audit surveys—can be used to support underwriting decisions by ensuring that insurers issue policies based on correct business classifications and exposure bases. During these advance audits, the premium auditor can classify the operation, verify the estimated premium base, and observe the operation. These visits can also contribute to greater efficiency in conducting the audit at the end of the policy period.

New exposures are another important area in which underwriting information might be deficient. New exposures can result from a change in operations or a new venture. The insured often does not communicate such changes or new operations to the producer or the insurer, and, even if reported, the information might not be sufficient for underwriting purposes. Premium auditing can assist underwriting by identifying new exposures during review of the insured's operations. The premium auditor can also indicate the proper classifications for the new exposures.

Premium auditors are also in a position to provide underwriting with information on the desirability of an account. Premium auditors visit the insured's premises, meet with management, review business records, and observe the employees and operations. These activities provide valuable insight that can assist the underwriter in determining an account's desirability and can help guide underwriting decisions about the most appropriate coverage options and amounts.

While on the insured's premises, a premium auditor can become aware of physical, moral, and morale hazards. Examples of physical hazards include construction, hazardous materials, and poor safety or hygiene practices. Moral hazards can be indicated by questionable business practices or a failing business. Indicators of morale hazards include indifference to proper maintenance or poor financial records. Any of these hazards noted in the premium auditing process should be promptly communicated to underwriting.

Premium audits can also assist in underwriters' evaluation of producers. Comparing premium audit reports with producers' applications might reveal a pattern of inaccurate or deficient information from a particular producer, which, when corrected, can improve future underwriting decisions.

Marketing and Sales

Premium auditing can also play a significant role in the area of marketing and sales. It is important that premium audits be conducted in a timely manner. A delay of a return premium due to an insured could adversely affect the insurer's future marketing efforts. The auditor's professional conduct and skill are also important factors in retaining an account. Auditors must often be able to convince an insured of the accuracy of an audit when the audit results in additional premium owed by the insured. This additional premium might significantly affect the profit margin and thus the insurer's decision about retaining the account.

During a premium audit, insureds may mention plans to expand operations or erect new buildings. They may be considering an employee benefits plan or business interruption insurance, or they may have gaps in present coverage observed during the audit. All of these situations may present new marketing opportunities for the insurer, and the auditor can benefit both the insured and insurer by referring the insured to marketing or sales.

Advance audits or pre-audit surveys can have significant public relations value. Insureds appreciate visits prior to the actual audit, especially if the auditor can help the insured with recordkeeping to take advantage of manual rules that might save the insured money.

Claims

Claims information can be valuable to premium auditing in the verification of employment classifications. However, premium auditing provides an even more valuable contribution to the claims function by verifying or correcting the classification codes assigned to an insured's claims. Various insurance regulators have emphasized the importance of improving claims-coding accuracy. This review also ensures that claims and premiums are matched in the same classifications, thus improving the credibility of rates.

Premium auditors can also verify that injured employees in workers compensation claims were employees of the insured when their injuries occurred. The premium audit can assist in verifying the earnings of injured employees. If there are any discrepancies in employment dates or wages, the premium auditor can notify claims.

Additionally, premium auditors can provide values of inventories, contractors' equipment lists and values, automotive equipment values, and other facts that are important to the claims function. For example, the claims department might request that the auditor review crime and fidelity losses during the premium audit. Although this line does not usually have auditable exposures, the premium audit can help determine that the amount claimed was accurately calculated from the insured's books and records.

Risk Control

Risk control also has an interest in the premium auditor's observations. Since risk control representatives cannot visit every insured, the premium auditor can serve as a source of information for risk control. The premium auditing process can contribute information about unsafe procedures or working conditions, observations of insureds' vehicles, and any hazards that provide opportunities for further risk control investigation and recommendations..

SUMMARY

The primary purpose of an insurer's risk control function is to evaluate loss exposures to assist with underwriting decisions and to help the insured prevent losses or reduce their effect. Insurers conduct risk control activities to achieve several goals: earn a profit, meet customer needs, comply with legal requirements, and fulfill their duty to society.

Insurers provide three types of risk control services: conducting physical surveys, performing risk analysis and improvement, and developing safety management programs.

Every insurer must decide what levels of risk control services to provide to which insureds. Several factors that influence insurers' decisions regarding the type and extent of risk control services they provide to insureds include the line of insurance, the size of commercial insureds, the types of loss exposures insured, and potential legal liability.

An insurer's risk control function is most effective when performed in cooperation with other insurer functions, such as underwriting, marketing and sales, premium auditing, and claims. Additionally, both insurers and insureds can benefit from risk control cooperation with external organizations, such as producers, reinsurers, OSHA and other regulatory agencies, law enforcement and codes enforcement agencies, and public safety entities.

Premium auditing plays an important role in the insurance mechanism because of the number and size of policies now written with a variable premium base. Premium audits are used to determine correct policy premiums; to meet regulatory requirements; to collect ratemaking data; to deter and detect fraud; to reinforce confidence of insureds; and to obtain additional information about the insured that may be useful to other insurer functional areas such as underwriting, marketing, and claims.

A systematic process for conducting premium audits is important to provide complete, accurate reports and to effectively use premium audit resources. The stages in the premium auditing process include planning, reviewing operations, determining employment relationships, finding and evaluating books or records, auditing the books and records, analyzing and verifying premium-related data, and reporting the findings.

Accurate premium audits are important for the financial positions of both the insured and the insurer, and the accuracy of audits has a significant effect on the insurer-insured relationship. It is also essential that premium audits be accurate for the insurance ratemaking process to determine equitable insurance rates.

Because premium auditors are often the only insurer representatives with direct insured contact, premium auditing can provide important contributions to other insurer functions, such as underwriting, marketing and sales, claims, and risk control.

ASSIGNMENT NOTE

1. Sharon Carney, "Using Predictive Analytics to Optimize the Premium Audit Process," ISO Review, Insurance Services Office, Inc., December 2009.

Direct Your Learning ▶▶

Overview of the Claim Function

Educational Objectives

After learning the content of this assignment, you should be able to:

▶ Identify the goals of the claim function, the users of claim information, and the parties with whom claim personnel interact.

▶ Describe the claim department structure, types and functions of claim personnel, and claim personnel performance measures.

▶ Describe the following activities in the claim handling process:

- Acknowledging and assigning the claim
- Identifying the policy and setting reserves
- Contacting the insured or the insured's representative
- Investigating the claim
- Documenting the claim
- Determining the cause of loss, liability, and the loss amount
- Concluding the claim

▶ Explain how the law of bad faith relates to an insurer's duty of good faith and fair dealing and how the legal environment affects the law of bad faith.

▶ Describe the elements of good-faith claim handling.

Overview of the Claim Function

7

THE CLAIM FUNCTION

An insurer's claim function must fulfill its responsibility to the insured and pay covered claims, while also supporting an insurer's financial goals.

Proper, efficient performance of the claim function greatly influences the insurer's success. When the two goals of the claim function are attained, success results. An outcome of the claim function is a vast amount of information that is essential to an insurer's marketing, underwriting, and actuarial departments. From the perspectives of the insured and the public, claim personnel are among the most visible of insurer employees; consequently, they must be able to interact effectively with individuals within and outside the insurance organization.

Claim Function Goals

When establishing goals for the claim function, senior management should recognize the effect the claim function has on both the insurance customer and the insurer itself. The claim function has these two primary goals:

- Complying with the contractual promise
- Supporting the insurer's financial goals

Complying With the Contractual Promise

The first goal of the claim function is to satisfy the insurer's obligations to the insured as set forth in the insurance policy. Following a loss, the promise of the insuring agreement to pay, defend, or indemnify in the event of a covered loss is fulfilled.

The insurer fulfills this promise by providing fair, prompt, and equitable service to the insured, either (1) directly, when the loss involves a first-party claim made by the insured against the insurer, or (2) indirectly, by handling a third-party claim made by someone against the insured to whom the insured might be liable.

From the insurer's perspective, claims are expected, and claim representatives must deal with them routinely. For the individuals involved, the loss occurrence and its consequences are not routine and can be overwhelming. Claim representatives, therefore, routinely deal with insureds and claimants in stressful situations. A claim representative should handle a claim in a way that treats all parties involved fairly and equitably, and do so in a timely manner. Were it not for insurance, administered through the claim handling process, recovery would be slow, inefficient, and difficult.

Supporting the Insurer's Financial Goals

The second goal of the claim function is supporting the insurer's financial goal. Achieving this goal is generally the responsibility of the marketing and underwriting departments. However, it would be shortsighted not to recognize the role of the claim function in helping insurers achieve an underwriting profit by controlling expenses and paying only legitimate claims.

By managing all claim function expenses, setting appropriate spending policies, and using appropriately priced providers and services, claim managers can help maintain an insurer's underwriting profit. Similarly, claim staff can avoid overspending on costs of handling claims, claim operations, or other expenses. Finally, by ensuring fair claim settlement, claim representatives prevent any unnecessary increase in the cost of insurance and subsequent reduction in the insurer's underwriting profit.

Insureds and other claimants are entitled to a fair claim settlement. By overcompensating an insured or a claimant, the insurer unnecessarily raises the cost of insurance for all of its insureds. Overpaid claims can lower insurer profits and result in higher policy premiums.

Conversely, underpaid claims can result in dissatisfied insureds, litigation, or regulatory oversight. Insureds and claimants who believe they are being treated fairly are likely to accept the claim representative's settlement offer, but if insureds and claimants are treated unfairly, they might sue the insurer or file a complaint with their state insurance department. Mishandled claims can lead to litigation or regulatory oversight, both of which erode goodwill and generate increased insurer expenses, thereby reducing the insurer's profitability.

An insurer's success in achieving its financial goal is reflected in its reputation for providing the service promised. A reputation for resisting legitimate claims can undermine the effectiveness of insurer advertisements or its goodwill earned over the years. Consequently, the two goals of the claim function work together to help bring about a profitable insurance operation.

Claim Information Users

The claim function provides valuable information to other insurer departments. The three primary recipients of claim information are the marketing, underwriting, and actuarial departments.

Marketing

The marketing department needs information about customer satisfaction, timeliness of settlements, and other variables that assist in marketing the insurance product. The marketing department recognizes that the other services the insurer performs for the insured are forgotten quickly if the insurer fails to perform well after a loss occurrence.

Many insurers that market commercial policies have developed "niche" products to address the needs of specific types of insureds. The intent of these insurers is to become the recognized expert in certain business classes, providing a product and service that cannot easily be equaled elsewhere. The claim handling process can be a source of new coverage ideas and product innovations for niche marketers.

Producers must be prepared to explain any premium changes and changes to policy provisions to their insureds. Producers must have insured loss information to prepare renewal policies properly because many commercial policies are subject to rating plans that affect the policy premium, based partly on the insured's loss experience. In personal insurance, personal auto policies might be surcharged when property damage claims are paid during the policy year. Additionally, claim personnel often inform producers of court rulings that affect the insurer's loss exposures or pricing, such as interpretations of policy exclusions or application of limits.

Underwriting

The insurance business operates effectively if underwriters accept loss exposures that are likely to experience only the types and amounts of losses anticipated in the insurance rates. If underwriters accept loss exposures that experience more losses than anticipated, the rates charged by the insurer will be inadequate, and the insurer could become financially insolvent. Claim personnel help underwriters in this regard by ensuring that claims are paid fairly and according to the policy. Proper, consistent, and efficient claim handling enables underwriters to evaluate, select, and appropriately price loss exposures based on consistent claim costs.

When claim representatives inspect accident scenes in homes or at work sites as part of the claim investigation, they sometimes notice loss exposure characteristics, either negative or positive, that were not readily apparent in the insurance application. When claim representatives report such findings to the underwriter, the underwriter may adjust the premium or take other actions to accommodate the difference in the exposure. For example, based on information from the claim representative, the underwriter may cancel coverage or renew it only if the insured implements corrective measures. Alternatively, the underwriter may grant a premium credit based on a claim representative's report of an above-average loss exposure.

A number of similar claims may also alert underwriting management to a problem for a particular type or class of insured. These claims might be the result of new processes or technologies being used by the class of insureds as a whole. For example, some roofing contractors might have tried to speed the process of replacing composite roofs by moving the tar smelter to the roof of the structure being repaired. This practice might have caused a number of fire losses. An adverse court ruling could also cause the loss experience of a class of business to deteriorate or could increase the number of claims presented.

Claim representatives' interaction with underwriters is not limited to providing loss information. Although claim personnel are typically the final authority on coverage interpretation, underwriters can provide insight into the intentions of the two parties to the insurance policy using the insurance application and producer's notes, which may affect coverage interpretation. When claim representatives explain their interpretations of coverage to underwriters, the underwriters can reassess coverage forms and endorsements and make any needed changes to clarify the coverages.

Actuarial

Actuaries need accurate information not only on losses that have been paid but also on losses that have occurred and are reserved for payment, collectively called incurred losses. Loss reserves can be increased or decreased as the claim develops, and reserve change reports help actuaries more accurately predict loss development. Incurred loss information helps actuaries establish reserves for incurred but not reported (IBNR) losses and project the development of open claims for which the reserves might change substantially before the claim is finally settled.

In addition to incurred loss information, actuaries need accurate information on loss adjusting expenses and recoverable amounts associated with claims, such as salvage and subrogation, any ceded reinsurance recoverable, and deductibles (when the insurer pays an entire claim and then asks the insured to reimburse the deductible amount).

All of the claim information that actuaries collect from claim personnel must be accurately represented through appropriate reserving methods in the insurer's financial statements. Actuaries must update these statements for reporting at various times during the year. When claim payments are recorded accurately and realistic reserves are set in the insurer's claim processing system, then the raw data that actuaries use to develop rates will be accurate and the rates will reflect the insurer's loss experience.

Claim Department Contacts

Other than the producer, claim department personnel are the contacts within the insurer who are most visible to the public. Therefore, the claim department must interact effectively with outside contacts, such as the public, lawyers, and state regulators.

The Public

Although many insurers have a public relations department that handles advertising, the insurer's public image is determined largely by the claim department's behavior.

Because the claim representative is an insured's and a claimant's primary contact with the insurer, claim service significantly affects an insured's or a claimant's (referred to as "claimant" through the remainder of this section) satisfaction with an insurer. The claim representative's skill at communicating directly with claimants influences their satisfaction with the insurer.

Claim representatives' first contact with a claimant occurs after the claimant has sustained a loss. Most claimants suffer some type of emotional reaction to a loss, which may include anger, depression, frustration, or hopelessness. Claim representatives must empathize with claimants to interact effectively with them.

Most claimants' knowledge of insurance is less sophisticated than that of an insurance professional. Claim representatives must be prepared to explain the policy's claim provisions to the claimant as those provisions apply to the claimant's property damage or injury. A well-prepared, professional claim representative who empathizes with the claimant will gain the claimant's confidence and increase the likelihood of reaching a mutually agreeable settlement.

Claim representatives must recognize that claim handling requires a high degree of integrity, involving honesty and diplomacy. If the claim representative is concerned that coverage will not apply to the damage or injury, he or she must explain those concerns to the claimant and preserve the insurer's right to deny a claim that is not covered. Even when a claim is denied, a claim representative who carefully explains the issues and empathizes with the claimant might be able to avoid costly litigation.

Technological improvements have allowed many insurers to improve the quality and speed of their claim service. Starting with the growth of cell phones and the Internet and progressing to improvements in wireless technologies, claim departments have found new ways to streamline the claim process and improve customer satisfaction.

Technology facilitates communications among field personnel, regional or local claim offices, claimants, vendors, and service providers. In catastrophe losses, floods, tornadoes, hurricanes, and earthquakes can cause significant damage to the infrastructure used for traditional communication systems. Satellite transmissions and other modern communication devices used in wireless technology may overcome these problems to enable continued electronic communications for claim personnel and, ultimately, faster and better customer service for claimants when they need it most.

Lawyers

For some types of claims and in certain areas of the United States, claimants are more likely to hire lawyers, often leading to costly litigation. Although legal representation can result in a higher payment by the insurer, representation does not necessarily result in higher settlements for claimants, because claimants must pay expenses and legal fees from settlements. Legal representation also does not guarantee a faster settlement. Even if litigation ensues, claim representatives should continue to interact in a cordial, professional manner with claimants' lawyers.

When an insurer needs a lawyer either to defend the insured or to defend itself, it will typically hire a lawyer from the jurisdiction in which the claim is submitted. The lawyer will provide advice regarding specific losses and legal issues. Claim representatives will assist the insurer's lawyers as needed by sharing claim details and assembling information that supports the insurer's legal position.

State Regulators

State insurance regulators monitor insurers' activities in the claim handling process. Regulators exercise controls by licensing claim representatives, investigating consumer complaints, and performing market conduct investigations. Enforcement is usually handled through the Unfair Claims Settlement Practices Act or similar legislation.

Not all states currently license claim representatives, and no standard procedure or uniform regulation exists for those that do. Some states require licensure only for independent adjusters, who work for many insurers, or for public adjusters, who represent insureds in first-party claims against insurers. Other states require staff claim representatives to be licensed.

State insurance regulators also handle customer complaints made against an insurer. Most states have a specific time limit within which the insurer must answer or act on inquiries from the insurance department. Failure to respond can result in expensive fines and even in the loss of the claim representative's—or his or her employer's—license.

Insurance regulators periodically perform market conduct investigations either as part of their normal audit of insurer activities or in response to specific complaints. The typical market conduct audit includes more than just claim practices; it audits all departments that interact directly with insureds and claimants.

CLAIM DEPARTMENT

An insurer's claim department can be organized in many different ways. No ideal organizational structure exists for the claim function. A particular claim department's structure reflects the insurer's overall organization, its size, its growth, and its willingness to use outside claim service providers.

Insurers have claim departments; however, claim departments can also be found in large business entities that self-insure, in third-party administrators (TPAs) that handle the claims of others, and in agents' or brokers' offices. The claim representatives in a large business or at an agent's or a broker's office may or may not investigate and pay claims, as a claim representative working at an insurer would. If claim representatives do not investigate and pay claims directly, their role is often that of an examiner, monitoring the actions of the insurer or third-party administrator.

A **third-party administrator** contracts to provide administrative services to other businesses and is often hired to handle claims by organizations that have self-insurance plans. Claim representatives at a third-party administrator perform many, if not all, of the same claim-related activities as an insurer's claim representatives.

Examination of a sample structure of an insurer's claim department and its various parties, policies, and performance measures helps explain how an insurer fulfills its promise to pay covered losses.

Claim Department Structure

An insurer's claim department can be organized in several different ways. A sample departmental structure can illustrate the various claim positions within the department. See the exhibit "Claim Department Organization Chart."

Usually a senior claim officer heads the claim organization and reports to the chief executive officer, the chief financial officer, or the chief underwriting officer. The senior claim officer may have a staff located in the same office. This staff is often called the home-office claim department. Within the home-office claim department, any number of technical and management specialists can provide advice and assistance to any remote claim offices and claim representatives.

The senior claim officer may have several claim offices or branches country-wide or worldwide. Staff from remote claim offices can all report directly to the home-office claim department, or regional/divisional claim officers may oversee the territory. Regional claim officers may have one or more branch offices reporting to them. Each branch office may have a claim manager, one or more claim supervisors, and a staff of claim representatives. Similar department structures are adopted by TPAs, large organizations that self-insure, and large agents and brokers.

Third-party administrator (TPA)

An organization that provides administrative services associated with risk financing and insurance.

Claim Department Organization Chart

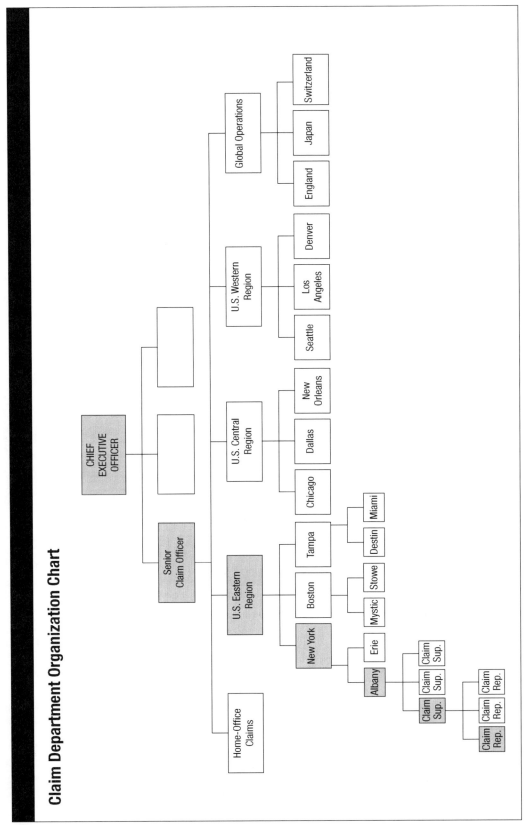

[DA02262]

Claim Personnel

A claim representative (a generic title that refers to all who adjust claims, except for public adjusters) fulfills the promise to pay the insured or to pay on behalf of the insured by handling a claim when a loss occurs. People who handle claims may be staff claim representatives, independent adjusters, employees of TPAs, or producers who sell policies to insureds. In addition, public adjusters also handle claims by representing the interests of the insureds to the insurer.

Staff Claim Representatives

Staff claim representatives are employees of an insurer, and they handle most claims. They may include inside claim representatives, who handle claims exclusively from inside an insurer's office, and field claim representatives, who handle claims both inside and outside the office. Field claim representatives, also called outside claim representatives, handle claims that require such tasks as investigating the scene of the loss; meeting with insureds, claimants, lawyers, and others involved in the loss; and inspecting damage. Staff claim representatives usually work from branch or regional offices rather than at the insurer's home-office. If the branch or region covers a large territory, the insurer may set up claim offices in areas away from the branch office to enable the claim representative to serve insureds efficiently.

Independent Adjusters

Certain insurers may not find it economically feasible to set up claim offices in every state where insureds are located. In this case, insurers may contract with **independent adjusters** to handle claims in strategic locations.

Some insurers use independent adjusters for all field claim work. These insurers employ claim personnel in their home-office or branch offices to monitor claim progress and settle claims but use independent adjusters to handle all the field work.

Some insurers use independent adjusters when their staff claim representatives are too busy to handle all claims themselves. For example, staff claim representatives may need assistance when a disaster strikes to handle the large number of claims quickly enough to satisfy the insurer and its insureds. Insurers may also use independent adjusters to meet desired service levels or when special skills are needed. For example, some independent adjusters are experts in highly specialized fields, such as investigating aircraft accidents.

Some independent adjusters are self-employed, but many work for adjusting firms that range in size from one small office with a few adjusters to national firms with many offices employing hundreds of adjusters.

Independent adjuster

An independent claim representative who handles claims for insurers for a fee.

Third-Party Administrators

Businesses that choose not to purchase insurance but to self-insure do not use agents, underwriters, or other typical insurer personnel. However, they do need personnel to handle the losses that arise. Self-insured businesses can employ their own claim representatives or contract with TPAs who handle claims, keep claim records, and perform statistical analyses. TPAs are often associated with large independent adjusting firms or with subsidiaries of insurance companies. Many property-casualty insurers have established subsidiary companies that serve as TPAs.

Producers

The term "producer" is used to describe anyone who sells insurance. This can include agents, brokers, employees of insurers, or intermediaries. Insurers may give some producers the authority to pay claims up to a certain amount, such as $2,500. Those producers can issue claim payments, called drafts, directly to insureds for covered claims, thus reducing the time an insured waits for payment. In this capacity, producers function much like inside claim representatives.

Public Adjusters

If a claim is complex, or if the settlement negotiations are not progressing satisfactorily with the insurer, the insured may hire a public adjuster to protect his or her interests. A public adjuster is an organization or a person hired by an insured to represent the insured in a claim in exchange for a fee.

Some states have statutes that govern the services public adjusters can provide. In general, the puble adjuster prepares the insured's claim and negotiates the settlement with the staff claim representative or independent adjuster. The insured, in turn, pays the public adjuster's fee, which is usually a percentage of the settlement.

Claim Performance Measures

Because a claim department staff can be diverse and may be spread over a wide geographic area, insurers face special issues in evaluating and measuring their performance.

Insurers are businesses, and, as such, they must make a profit to survive. Although claims may be considered to reduce an insurer's profit, claim departments play a crucial role in insurer profitability. They do so by paying fair amounts for legitimate claims and by providing accurate, reliable, and consistent ratemaking data. Because fair claim payment does not conflict with insurer profit goals, an insurer measures its claim and underwriting departments' performance using a loss ratio, which is a profitability measure. The quality of a claim department's performance can be measured using best practices, claim audits, and customer satisfaction.

Profitability Measures

The insurer's loss ratio is one of the most commonly used measures of evaluating the insurer's financial well-being. An increasing loss ratio could indicate that the insurer is improperly performing the claim function. Increasing losses could also mean that underwriting failed to select above-average loss exposures or that the actuarial department failed to price the insurer's products correctly.

The **loss ratio** is an insurer's **incurred losses** (including loss adjustment expenses) for a given period divided by its **earned premiums** for the same period. The **expense ratio** is developed using underwriting expenses plus other, nonclaim-related expenses divided by the written premium.

$$\text{Loss ratio} = \frac{\text{Incurred losses} + \text{Loss adjustment expenses}}{\text{Earned premium}}$$

$$\text{Expense ratio} = \frac{\text{Incurred underwriting expenses}}{\text{Written premium}}$$

Loss adjustment expenses usually include these:

- Salaries and expenses for an insurer's claim staff
- Legal fees for defending insureds in lawsuits
- Fees charged by service providers (for example, doctors' fees for independent medical examinations or engineers' fees to inspect damaged property)
- Costs of obtaining medical, police, and other types of reports

The loss ratio and expense ratio are the two components of the combined ratio, which represents an insurer's underwriting profitability. The combined ratio is calculated in this fashion:

$$\text{Combined ratio} = \text{Loss ratio} + \text{Expense ratio}$$

Because claims usually do not occur immediately after a policy is issued and because they take some time to be paid, insurers can invest premiums to gen¬erate additional income until the premiums are needed to pay claims. Insurers select stocks, bonds, Treasury bills,and other securities to buy and sell. They seek to earn the highest possible return from investments while making sure that funds are available to meet their financial obligations. Insurers typically spend slightly more on operations (claims and other expenses) than they collect in premiums. Managing investments wisely enables insurers to earn a profit despite a loss on operations.

This example illustrates all of the performance ratios and their implications. In fiscal 20XX, the Atwell Insurance Company ended the year with $25 million in earned premiums and $35 million in written premiums. Atwell incurred $16 million in losses and loss adjustment expenses and incurred

Incurred losses

The losses that have occurred during a specific period, no matter when claims resulting from the losses are paid.

Loss ratio

A ratio that measures losses and loss adjustment expenses against earned premiums and that reflects the percentage of premiums being consumed by losses.

Earned premiums

The portion of written premiums that corresponds to coverage that has already been provided.

Expense ratio

An insurer's incurred underwriting expenses for a given period divided by its written premiums for the same period.

underwriting expenses of $7 million. Therefore, Atwell's combined ratio is 84 percent.

$$\text{Loss ratio} = \frac{\$16 \text{ million}}{\$25 \text{ million}} = 0.64 \text{ or } 64\%$$

$$\text{Expense ratio} = \frac{\$7 \text{ million}}{\$35 \text{ million}} = 0.20 \text{ or } 20\%$$

$$\text{Combined ratio} = 64\% + 20\% = 84\%$$

When an insurer's loss ratio and combined ratio increases, the claim department, along with other functions, is pressured to reduce expenses. Claim representatives could quickly reduce loss adjusting expenses in the short term by offering insureds and claimants the settlement demanded rather than the settlement deserved. However, to reduce loss adjusting expenses in the long term, inflated settlement demands should be resisted; researched; negotiated; and, if necessary, litigated.Loss adjustment expenses can also be reduced by following claim procedures. By managing losses and controlling expenses associated with handling losses, the claim department plays an important role in an insurer's profitability.

Quality Measures

Even though claim handling is more art than science, there are measures that can be used to evaluate the performance of a claim department. Three of the more frequently used quality measures are best practices, claim audits, and customer satisfaction.

Best practices can mean different things to different people. In the context of a claim department, best practices usually refers to a system of identified internal practices that produce superior performance. Best practices are usually maintained electronically or in written form and shared with every claim representative. An insurer can create best practices by studying its own performance or by studying the performance of similar successful insurers.

Claim department best practices are often based on legal requirements specified by regulators, legislators, and courts. For example, a claim department may have a best practice that states "every claim will be acknowledged within twenty-four hours." This time frame may have been selected because of a regulation, law, or court decision that requires insurers to acknowledge a claim within twenty-four hours of receipt. Other best practices may relate to these factors:

- Timely initial contact with the insured and claimant
- Timely responses to outside communications
- Timely and accurate loss reserving
- Standards and procedures for file documentation

- Timely payment of or denial of claims
- Thorough explanation of payment or denial

Insurers use claim audits to ensure compliance with best practices and to gather statistical information on claims. A claim audit is performed by reviewing a number of open and closed claim files and evaluating the information contained in those files. Claim audits can be performed by the claim staff who work on the files (called a self-audit), or they can be performed by claim representatives from other offices or by a team from the home-office. Claim audits usually evaluate both quantitative and qualitative factors. See the exhibit "Quantitative and Qualitative Audit Factors."

Quantitative and Qualitative Audit Factors

Quantitative	Qualitative
Timeliness of reports	Realistic reserving
Timeliness of reserving	Accurate evaluation of insured's liability
Timeliness of payments	Follow-up on subrogation opportunity
Number of files opened each month	Litigation cost management
Number of files closed each month	Proper releases taken
Number of files reopened each month	Correct coverage evaluation
Percentage of recovery from subrogation	Good negotiation skills
Average claim settlement value by claim type	Thorough investigations
Percentage of claims entering litigation	
Percentage of cases going to trial	
Accuracy of data entry	

[DA02267]

The quality of a claim department's performance is also measured by customer satisfaction. Claim supervisors and managers will usually keep track of any correspondence they receive about the performance of individual claim representatives. While compliments are usually acknowledged, supervisors or managers must respond to complaints, and most claim departments have procedures for doing so. Complaints may come directly from the insured, claimant, or vendor, or they can be submitted by a state insurance department on behalf of an insured, a claimant, or a vendor. However received, the complaint must be investigated by management and responded to in a timely manner. Complaints about issues such as not receiving a return phone call may indicate legitimate service issues. Other complaints can simply indicate dissatisfaction with an otherwise-valid claim settlement. Review of complaints received in a claim office can show whether problems exist with a particular claim representative, supervisor, or manager.

CLAIM HANDLING PROCESS

The claim representative is responsible for thoroughly investigating a claim to determine how coverage applies. However, investigation is only one activity in the claim handling process. To ensure that every claim is handled in good faith from beginning to end, the claim representative must follow a systematic claim handling process.

The claim handling process consists of a series of typical activities. The activities are not always sequential. Some can be performed concurrently, and others may need to be repeated as new facts are uncovered. Depending on the severity and complexity of the claim, the process may be completed quickly, or it may take months or even years to complete.

The claim handling process is important because it creates consistency in claim handling and helps ensure that claims are handled in a manner that conforms with legal and ethical standards.

Although some claims may require unique treatment, the same basic activities are performed with every claim. These activities provide a framework for handling all types of property, liability, and workers compensation claims:

- Acknowledging and assigning the claim
- Identifying the policy and setting reserves
- Contacting the insured or the insured's representative
- Investigating the claim
- Documenting the claim
- Determining the cause of loss, liability, and the loss amount
- Concluding the claim

The claim handling process begins when the insured reports the loss to the producer or directly to the insurer's claim center. IIf the loss is reported to the producer, the producer enters the loss information into the agency's claim information system, which then transmits the appropriate loss notice to the insurer. Some producers prepare a hard copy of the loss notice and fax it to the insurer. If the loss is reported directly to the insurer, claim personnel enter the loss information into the insurer's claim information system.

Losses can be reported using a loss notice form, which varies by type of loss. One of the most commonly used loss notice forms is the ACORD form. ACORD forms include basic information about the loss, such as the loss date and time, policy number, insured name and address, covered property, and loss description. For injury claims, the loss notice also includes the accident location, witness names and addresses, and the names and addresses of any injured persons.

However, not all losses are reported using a loss notice. Some losses may be reported in a letter or as part of a lawsuit. But regardless of how a loss is reported, the same information must be entered into the insurer's claim information system. If the first notice of the loss is a lawsuit, the claim representative must be aware of the deadline by which to respond. The time allowed for response varies by state. The claim representative must turn the lawsuit over to legal counsel to answer, even while the initial investigation is underway.

Once a loss notice has been received and the information has been entered into the insurer's claim information system, the insurer begins the claim handling process.

Acknowledging and Assigning the Claim

Generally, the first activity of the insurer in the claim handling process involves two functions, acknowledging receipt of the claim and assigning the claim to a claim representative. The purpose of the acknowledgment is to advise the insured that the claim has been received. The acknowledgment also provides the name and contact information of the assigned claim representative and the claim number.

Some insurers acknowledge claims immediately upon receiving the loss notice by contacting the insured. Others acknowledge the claim after it has been assigned to a claim representative. Many insurers transfer claim files to a claim manager for assignment to a claim representative. Insurers acknowledge claims in this timely manner to comply with insurance regulations.

Insurers use different methods of assigning claims to claim representatives. Some insurers assign claims based on territory, type of claim, extent of damage, workload, or other criteria contained in the insurer's claim information system. But no matter what the method, the goal is to assign the claim to a claim representative who possesses the appropriate skills to handle it.

Some states require claim representatives who handle claims in the state to have an adjuster license. These licensing requirements must also be considered when assigning a claim to a claim representative.

After receiving the claim assignment, the claim representative contacts the insured, and possibly the claimant (if it is a third-party claim), to acknowledge the claim assignment and explain the claim process. For insurers that do not make contact immediately after receiving the loss notice, this contact serves as the claim acknowledgment. For some types of losses, the claim representative may give the insured instructions to prevent further loss, such as to cover roof damage with a tarp. If the claim involves property damage, the claim representative may arrange a time with the insured to inspect the damage or the damage scene. As an alternative, the claim representative may advise the insured or claimant that an appraiser or an independent adjuster will be in contact to inspect the property damage. If the claim involves bodily injury, the claim representative should get information about the nature and extent of the injury.

Identifying the Policy and Setting Reserves

Another early activity in the claim handling process involves two functions, identifying the policy and setting reserves. Some insurers do both before they acknowledge the claim. Other insurers identify the policy in force before the claim representative begins the claim investigation.

Identifying the Policy

Usually, the claim representative first identifies the policy in force upon receiving the assignment. Regardless of the sequence of these functions, once the claim is assigned, the claim representative must thoroughly read the policy, using the framework for coverage analysis, to determine what types of coverage apply to the loss.

If it is apparent from the loss notice that coverage may not be available for the loss, the claim representative must notify the insured of this concern through a **nonwaiver agreement** or a **reservation of rights letter**. Both of these documents reserve the insurer's rights under the policy.

Setting Reserves

Claim representatives will establish claim or case (loss) reserves, often in conjunction with identifying the policy. This can occur at almost any point in the claim handling process; however, it depends on the insurer's internal guidelines. While the exact timing may differ among insurers, the setting of an initial reserve(s) usually occurs early in the claim handling process.

The insurer's claim information system often determines the types of reserves that are established. For instance, there may be one reserve for property damage and another for bodily injury. Some systems require separate reserves for each claimant in a claim. Other systems require separate expense reserves for the costs of handling the claim. For example, in a claim for an auto accident, an individual reserve may be set up for damage to the insured's vehicle, damage to the other party's vehicle, medical expenses for the insured, and bodily injury for the claimant.

Setting accurate reserves is an important part of the claim representative's job. Establishing and maintaining adequate reserves is important for the insurer's financial stability because reserves affect the insurer's ability to maintain and increase business.

Nonwaiver agreement
A signed agreement indicating that during the course of investigation, neither the insurer nor the insured waives rights under the policy.

Reservation of rights letter
An insurer's letter that specifies coverage issues and informs the insured that the insurer is handling a claim with the understanding that the insurer may later deny coverage should the facts warrant it.

Insurers can use different methods of setting reserves, including these six common methods:

- Individual case method
- Roundtable method
- Average value method
- Formula method
- Expert system method
- Loss ratio method

The individual case method and the roundtable method rely on the claim representative's judgment. The other methods rely on statistical analysis.

Under the **individual case method**, claim representatives set an individual or a case reserve for each claim or cause of loss. This is based on the claim representative's expectation of what the insurer will pay. Because of the subjective nature of the evaluation, reserves can vary widely by claim representative. Certain factors should be considered when using the individual case method for a bodily injury claim. See the exhibit "Individual Case Method Considerations."

Individual case method
A method of setting reserves based on the claim's circumstances and the claim representative's experience in handling similar claims.

Ideally, under the **roundtable method**, the claim personnel at the roundtable discussion should not initially know the reserves set by the others participating in the roundtable. After the evaluation and a discussion, a consensus reserve figure may be reached, or an average of all the figures may be calculated. Because this method is time consuming, it is not appropriate for setting initial reserves. However, for serious or prolonged claims, it is a suitable method to review reserves.

Roundtable method
A method of setting reserves by using the consensus of two or more claim personnel who have independently evaluated the claim file.

The **average value method** is useful when there are small variations in loss size for a particular type of claim and when claims can be concluded quickly. The average values are usually based on data from past claims and adjusted to reflect current conditions. For example, auto physical damage claims may be initially reserved at $1,500 based on an insurer's previous loss experience with those claims. That figure may remain the same until the claim has been concluded. For some claims, the initial reserve is set based on the average value method; however, claim representatives are required to modify the initial reserve within a specified number of days to reflect each claim's circumstances.

Average value method
A case reserving method that establishes a predetermined dollar amount of reserve for each claim as it is reported.

Under the **formula method**, a formula may be developed based on the assumption that a certain ratio exists between certain costs, such as the medical cost and the indemnity (or wage loss) in a workers compensation claim. Based on an insurer's loss history with many similar claims, the indemnity reserve may be set at a certain percentage of the medical reserve.

Formula method
A method of setting claim reserves by using a mathematical formula.

The formula method may also be used to set the additional living expense reserve under a homeowners policy if the home is destroyed by fire. The reserve may be set as a certain percentage of the coverage limit. The formula

Individual Case Method Considerations

Considerations a claim representative may use when setting reserves on a bodily injury claim using the individual case method include the following:

1. Claimant profile (factors in calculating economic loss)
   a. Age
   b. Gender
   c. Occupation
   d. Level of education
   e. Dependants, if any, their ages, and to what extent they rely on the claimant financially and for companionship

2. Nature and extent of the injury (factors in calculating general damages)
   a. Whether the injury is permanent
   b. Extent of pain and suffering
   c. Extent of disruption the injury creates in the individual's lifestyle

3. Special damages (factors in calculating special damages)
   a. Anticipated medical bills incurred to date and for future care
   b. Type of medical care that has been or is being provided; whether it includes diagnostic care or treatment
   c. Whether the claimant will lose any wages

4. Claimant representation (factors in determining the likelihood of a lawsuit and predicting general damages that could result)
   a. Whether the claimant is represented by a lawyer
   b. If so, the lawyer's reputation
   c. Typical value of local court verdicts

5. Liability factors (factors in calculating compensatory and/or punitive damages)
   a. Whether the case involves ordinary negligence or gross negligence
   b. Whether the case involves any comparative or contributory negligence
   c. Any legal limits to recovery, such as a cap on certain types of damages
   d. Any other parties' contribution to the loss or responsibility for contributing to the settlement

6. Miscellaneous factors
   a. General economic conditions in the geographic area (factor in calculating economic loss)
   b. Whether the insured's conduct in causing the loss was outrageous (factor in calculating compensatory damages)
   c. Whether drinking or drug use contributed to the loss (factor in calculating liability)
   d. The insured's credibility as a witness (factor in determining likelihood of successful lawsuit)
   e. The claimant's credibility as a witness (factor in determining likelihood of successful lawsuit)

[DA2310]

is determined by the insurer and is automatically created for the claim representative based on the facts of the claim.

Under the **expert system method**, the details of a particular claim are entered into the computer, and the program applies the appropriate rules to suggest reserves for the loss. An expert system can provide greater consistency in reserving than the individual case method. Although it is similar in operation to the formula method, the expert system includes more subjective information, such as loss location or the name of the treating physician, in creating the loss reserve and the loss adjusting expenses (LAE).

Expert system method
A method of setting reserves with a software application that estimates losses and loss adjustment expenses.

The **loss ratio method** is used to suggest standard reserves for similar types of claims or for a class of loss exposures. The actuarial department uses this method when other methods of establishing claim reserves are inadequate. For example, in medical malpractice insurance for physicians and surgeons, claims are often reported long after the expiration date of the policy that provided the coverage. To ensure that the insurer has adequate reserves for those claims, the actuarial department may project reserves using the loss ratio method.

Loss ratio method
A loss reserving method that establishes aggregate reserves for all claims for a type of insurance.

Additionally, insurers are required by law and accounting practices to establish reserves for losses that have been incurred but not reported (IBNR). Although the name refers only to incurred but not reported losses, in many cases unreported losses account for only a part of the reserve. Often, the IBNR reserve also includes an amount for reported losses for which the case reserves are judged to be inadequate. A reserve for claims that have been closed and then reopened may also be included in the IBNR reserve.

Actuaries analyze the insurer's experience by comparing paid losses to case reserves to determine whether the insurer typically under-reserves or over-reserves claims. If the insurer typically under-reserves claims, the IBNR reserve will be set at an amount to cover the ultimate cost of the claim.

Causes of Reserve Errors

Reserve adequacy and accuracy are important to an insurer's continued solvency and ability to write new business (its capacity). Claim representatives can negatively influence solvency and capacity by undervaluing claim reserves. Although an occasional reserve may be inadequate or inaccurate with little or no effect on the insurer, consistently inaccurate or inadequate reserves on thousands of claims can distort the ratemaking process. This may eventually affect an insurer's ability to write business competitively and ultimately affect solvency.

Reserving errors can be caused in several ways. Initial reserves may be inaccurate because they are determined based on limited information. Thus, many insurers require that initial reserves be reviewed and adjusted for accuracy within a short time frame. In addition, most insurers require reserves to be evaluated whenever a claim file is reviewed. That evaluation ensures that reserves reflect the most current information contained in the claim file.

Stairstepping

Incremental increases in claim reserves by the claim representative without any significant change in the facts of the claim.

Reserve inaccuracy can also be the result of the claim representative's poor planning, lack of expertise in estimating claim severity, or unwillingness to re-evaluate the facts. In these cases, the claim representative may set a modest initial reserve, but then raise the reserve by a few thousand dollars to issue payments. Later, the reserve is increased again when more bills arrive. This process is called **stairstepping** the reserve. On a claim that concludes in thirty, sixty, or ninety days, stairstepping has little effect. But if the claim remains open for several years, as many liability and workers compensation claims do, the incremental increase in reserves during those years is not properly reflected in the insurer's ratemaking process.

Stairstepping can be avoided if proper claim handling practices and reserving methods are used. For example, the roundtable method or expert system method may result in a realistic reserve that would prevent frequent stairstepping. This does not mean that claim representatives cannot adjust a reserve up or down during the course of a claim. However, they should make those adjustments because of new information or changes in the circumstances of the claim.

Because reserves should reflect the ultimate cost of a claim and not the claim's present value, the reserve should account for the claim's future settlement value. For example, a catastrophic injury claim may take years to settle. During that time, inflation may increase the cost of medical care, or new and expensive medical technology may be developed. The reserves for such claims should anticipate those increased costs.

Claim representatives may underestimate the future settlement value of a claim if they are overconfident of their ability to conclude the claim for a lesser amount. Reserves should always be based on the value of a claim, never on the perceived likelihood of successful negotiation and settlement. Analysis of verdicts rendered in similar cases helps to show the potential value of a claim and discourages the tendency to base reserves on negotiation expertise.

Some inadvertent errors in setting reserves can be detected by using computer software that stores claim information. Some claim information systems provide a data entry check. For example, the software might require that the reserve amount be entered twice to give the person entering the data an opportunity to verify the amount. Additionally, claim managers can review reports of reserves for unusual entries or reserves established in excess of authority. For example, a report listing all reserves of $100,000 or more might uncover a $10,000 reserve incorrectly entered as $100,000.

As claim representatives proceed with claim investigations and evaluations, they should increase or decrease the reserve amounts to reflect new information received. For example, if the estimate for car repairs is $5,000, the claim representative would set up a reserve of $5,000. If hidden damage is then found and the estimate is revised to be $10,000, the claim representative should change the reserve to reflect this increase in the repair estimate. Likewise, if an estimate to repair is lowered, the reserve should be changed to reflect the decrease. Because these changes are based on changes in the facts of the claim, they are not considered stairstepping.

Contacting the Insured or the Insured's Representative

Another activity in the claim handling process, which occurs soon after the loss is assigned to a claim representative and initial reserves are established, is contacting the insured or the insured's representative. This initial contact with the insured serves several purposes. It can reassure the insured that the claim will be investigated. It also provides the claim representative with an opportunity to explain the claim process and to begin the claim investigation.

For some insurers (or in certain claims as specified in the insurer's guidelines) this contact occurs at the same time as the claim acknowledgment. Generally, the claim representative reviews the initial loss report and policy and then contacts the insured and schedules a time to speak with the insured or a party representing the insured about the facts of the loss. This can be a face-to-face meeting at the insured's location or the loss location, or it can be a telephone discussion. If the loss involves a third-party claimant, then the claim representative also contacts the claimant and schedules a meeting with the claimant or a party representing the claimant to discuss the facts of the loss.

For some claims, the insured is represented by a public adjuster or an attorney. Public adjusters are active in some states and metropolitan areas. Usually this is the case in property damage claims. Such adjusters charge a fee to help insureds present claims to insurers. The claim representative should discuss claim-related issues with the public adjuster or attorney until advised not to do so by the insured.

Not every claim requires a face-to-face meeting with the insured or claimant. Some claims can be handled by phone and supplemented by an exchange of documents. Most insurers have guidelines for claim representatives to determine which claims can be handled by phone.

Before making initial contact with any of the parties, the claim representative should prepare a list of questions for the insured or claimant. A set of instructions on how the claim will be handled and what actions the insured or claimant will have to complete as part of the claim process should also be prepared.

The first meeting or discussion with the insured sets the tone for the claim. For the insured or the claimant, the loss has most likely created a disruption resulting in strong emotions, such as anger or grief. Those who have never filed an insurance claim may be apprehensive or confused about how the claims will be handled. The claim representative should be aware of these factors and take them into consideration when initially meeting or speaking with the insured or the claimant. See the exhibit "Apply Your Learning: Adjusting Tip."

Apply Your Learning: Adjusting Tip

Claim representatives should be aware that their words and actions set the insured's or claimant's expectations about the claim. If the claim representative promises that something will be done by a certain date, the insured or claimant will expect it to be done by that date. Therefore, claim representatives demonstrate good-faith claim handling practices by meeting these deadlines.

[DA06187]

At the initial contact, claim representatives frequently find that many insureds do not fully understand the details of their insurance coverages. The claim representative must be prepared to explain the policy terms and their meanings in relation to the loss. The claim representative must explain possible policy violations, exclusions, or limitations that can affect coverage. Withholding such information can be considered a breach of the claim representative's or insurer's duties. The claim representative must be careful not to give the insured or claimant the impression that a claim will be paid if possible grounds exist to deny a claim.

Once contact is made, the claim representative should take these actions:

- Tell the insured what is required to protect damaged property and to document the claim. Be specific about what the insured must do, and provide deadlines.
- Describe the inspection, appraisal, and investigation the claim representative will be conducting.
- Tell the insured what additional investigation is needed to resolve potential coverage issues. If the insured must provide additional information, be certain to give complete and clear instructions.
- Explain potential coverage questions or policy limitations or exclusions, and obtain a nonwaiver agreement when necessary.
- If medical and wage loss information is part of the claim, obtain the necessary authorizations.

Apply Your Learning: Adjusting Tip

When speaking with the insured, discuss all potential coverage issues, not just the ones most likely to apply. If the insured or claimant can overcome the first potential coverage issue and then is told of another that may apply, it can appear that the claim representative is trying to avoid paying the claim.

[DA06188]

- Explain the amount of time it will take to process and conclude the claim.
- Supply the insured with a blank proof of loss form for property damage and any necessary written instructions so that the insured can document the claim.

In some cases, the claim representative may conduct a recorded interview with the insured during the initial meeting or discussion. Claim representatives must be aware of the legal implications of their words and actions when communicating with insureds. They must be careful not to mislead the insured or the claimant about the potential coverage for the claim or the amount of the claim payment. To avoid such pitfalls, claim representatives must understand three legal concepts: good faith, waiver, and estoppel.

Good Faith

Insurance policies are contracts of utmost good faith. When conducting a good-faith investigation, a claim representative must attempt to correctly and promptly resolve coverage issues. Many situations that present coverage issues require further investigation to determine whether the claim should be paid or denied. Until the coverage issues are resolved, the claim representative and insurer must avoid any conduct that would lead insureds or claimants to believe that the claim will be paid. Otherwise, the insurer may waive its right to legitimately deny coverage.

While attempting to resolve the coverage issues, claim representatives must focus on the facts and decide whether the facts support coverage. Claim representatives must also quantify the loss so that payment is not delayed if coverage is confirmed.

Waiver and Estoppel

Waiver is the voluntary or intentional relinquishment of a known contractual right, such as one contained in a policy condition or exclusion. For example, a claim representative can waive a right contained in a policy condition or exclusion by telling an insured that a loss is covered before confirming that by checking the policy. The claim representative has waived the insurer's right to deny the claim if the facts later prove there is no coverage.

Estoppel is a legal bar to asserting certain contractual conditions because of a party's previous actions or words to the contrary. Estoppel results when one party's action causes another party to rely on that behavior or those words with detrimental results. For example, a claim representative who tells an insured that damaged goods can be discarded before they are inspected cannot later deny the claim on the grounds that the damaged goods were not available for inspection. The claim representative is estopped from denying the claim on that basis. See the exhibit "Example of Case Involving Both Waiver and Estoppel."

Example of Case Involving Both Waiver and Estoppel

An insured calls the claim service center of Atwell Insurance and reports that a large tree fell into her yard during a windstorm. The customer service representative who answers the call tells the insured to have a contractor remove the debris and send the bill to the insurer.

Two weeks later, the insurer receives a bill from the contractor for $1,200. The customer service representative is authorized to settle claims only up to $500, so she takes the bill to her supervisor. Her supervisor indicates that the policy does not cover this type of loss unless the tree damages the insured's house, fence, or other covered structure. The supervisor further explains that when a falling tree damages property, a $500 limit on debris removal applies.

The insured's policy does not cover this loss. However, the customer service representative waived this coverage defense by telling the insured to arrange for the debris removal and to send the bill to the insurer without first explaining the coverage under the policy. Because the insured relied on what the customer service representative told her and incurred expenses, Atwell Insurance may be estopped from denying coverage. Even though coverage does not apply to the original loss, Atwell may have to pay the $1,200 bill. The insurer's failure to notify the insured at the beginning of the claim process that coverage did not apply estopped it from later denying coverage.

[DA02308]

Claim representatives use two common methods to avoid waiver and estoppel: nonwaiver agreements and reservation of rights letters.

Nonwaiver agreements and reservation of rights letters serve these purposes:

- To advise the insured that any action taken by the insurer in investigating the cause of loss or in ascertaining the amount of loss is not intended to waive or invalidate any policy conditions.
- To clarify that the agreement's or the letter's intent is to permit a claim investigation and that neither the insured nor the insurer will thereby waive any respective rights or obligations.

Apply Your Learning: Adjusting Tip

Claim representatives have a reasonable amount of time, usually specified in state unfair claim practices acts, in which to conduct an investigation and advise the insured of a coverage decision without waiving any of the insurer's rights. Thus, claim representatives should not obtain nonwaiver agreements and reservation of rights letters on every claim because most claims will not require them. If in doubt, claim representatives should proceed cautiously and obtain guidance from supervisors or managers.

[DA06190]

A nonwaiver agreement, which must be signed by both parties, protects the insurer from estoppel by reserving the right to deny coverage based on information developed during the investigation. It also alerts the insured to a potential coverage problem. The nonwaiver agreement is usually used when the claim representative is concerned about investigating a claim before the insured has substantially complied with the policy conditions or when there appears to be a specific coverage problem or defense. Such concerns can be identified from the initial claim report, during initial contact with the insured, or at any point during the claim investigation. See the exhibit "Example of Use of Nonwaiver Agreement and Reservation of Rights Letter."

Example of Use of Nonwaiver Agreement and Reservation of Rights Letter

A claim representative may offer a nonwaiver agreement when the insured reports the theft of an auto but refuses to make a police report about the theft. If the insured refuses to sign the nonwaiver agreement, the claim representative can use a reservation of rights letter to protect the insurer's rights.

[DA06191]

A reservation of rights letter serves the same purpose as a nonwaiver agreement but is in letter form, and it is a unilateral document; it does not require the insured to sign or agree to the contents of the letter. It simply advises the insured of the potential coverage issue. Nevertheless, a reservation of rights letter can be as effective in protecting the insurer's rights to policy defenses as a nonwaiver agreement if the insurer has drafted the letter carefully and can show that the insured received it. Nonwaiver agreements and reservation of rights letters are usually sent by certified mail with a return receipt requested. The insurer then has evidence that the insured received it.

Nonwaiver agreements and reservation of rights letters are used only with the insured and can be used with any type of first-party claim. They are not sent to third-party claimants because third parties have no obligations under the policy.

The claim representative must take steps to ensure that the insured understands why an investigation is necessary to determine coverage and how the reservation of rights letter or nonwaiver agreement will facilitate the investigation. The legal strength of a reservation of rights letter or a nonwaiver

Apply Your Learning: Adjusting Tip

The language in a nonwaiver agreement or a reservation of rights letter is often mandated by case law. The claim representative should consult with counsel to obtain the language for a specific state.

[DA06192]

agreement in protecting the insurer's policy defenses in court depends on the circumstances. See the exhibit " Apply Your Learning: Adjusting Tip."

Investigating the Claim

The next activity in the claim handling process is investigating and documenting the claim. Investigation and documentation occur throughout the life of the claim. However, the investigation can take many different forms, and all aspects of it must be documented to create a complete claim file.

Claim representatives begin investigating a claim as soon as it is assigned. They can develop an outline or notes to logically organize the investigation and to ensure that information that may be available only for a short time is investigated first (such as accident scenes or damaged property that may be destroyed or discarded). Claim representatives should contact any third-party claimant early in the investigation. Doing so establishes rapport with claimants, facilitates the investigation, and leads to a timely settlement.

Claim representatives must also know when they have sufficient information on which to base a decision. Investigations should be geared to obtain information that will help determine the cause of loss, the amount of loss, and liability. The insurer's claim handling guidelines help claim representatives determine the types and extent of investigation needed for a satisfactory claim settlement. Once sufficient information is obtained to make a reasoned determination, the claim representative does not need to continue the investigation, unless the determination is disputed.

Claim Investigations

This section provides a basic outline for the claim representative to follow to investigate any type of claim. Claim representatives must use good-faith claim handling practices and insurer guidelines to ensure a thorough investigation. Several types of investigations, including these examples, are common to many types of claims:

- Claimant investigation—In a first-party property claim, the claimant is the insured. In an automobile or liability claim, the claimant may be a third party injured in the accident or a third party whose property was damaged. In a workers compensation claim, the claimant is the injured worker. To determine the claimant's version of the incident, claim representatives conduct a claimant investigation, usually by taking the claimant's statement. This information helps the claim representative determine the value of the injury or damage, how it was caused, and who is responsible.

- Insured/witness investigation—Claim representatives often take statements (either written or recorded) from the insured and witnesses because they can provide valuable information about the circumstances surrounding the loss. The insured is always the party named as the insured in the policy. Witnesses are any persons who have personal, first-hand knowledge of the incident that resulted in the claim. The witness investigation can support or refute an insured's version of an incident. This can affect the liability determination. A statement can also be used to attack the witness's credibility if later testimony differs from the information given in the original statement.

- Accident scene investigation—The accident scene offers crucial clues in automobile, third-party liability, and workers compensation claims. By observing details such as tire tracks, curves in the roadway, and objects or conditions that may interfere with a driver's view or that may cause an accident (such as a pothole in the road), the claim representative can determine whether accounts of the accident are plausible or questionable. Claim representatives also consult weather or traffic reports in certain accident scene investigations to identify external factors that may have contributed to the loss.

- Property damage investigation—An investigation of the scene where property was damaged can be useful in automobile and property coverage claims to confirm the cause of loss and the extent of damage. For business income claims, a property damage investigation is useful for determining lost profits or loss of business use resulting from covered property damage. The investigation can also help confirm the need to move operations to an alternate site or to temporarily replace damaged equipment with rented equipment so that business operations can continue while repairs are being made.

- Medical investigation—Claim representatives conduct medical investigations in all bodily injury claims, including workers compensation claims. A medical investigation helps the claim representative determine the costs of the medical treatment, the expected duration of medical treatment and disability, the need for rehabilitation, and the suitability of medical care for the type of injuries the claimant suffered. This information is also used to evaluate the amount of pain and suffering that resulted from the accident or injury.

- Prior claim investigation—Claim representatives conduct prior claim investigations on all claims to avoid paying for property damage or bodily injury that has been paid through prior claims by the same insurer or by other insurers.

A prior claim investigation may reveal that the claimant has a history of lower-back injuries or that the insured's vehicle had sustained similar damage from a prior accident. By conducting a prior claim investigation, the claim representative ensures that the insurer pays only new claims for which the insurer has legal responsibility. The prior claim investigation is usually performed by comparing the facts of the current claim to an industry database containing information from many different insurers. Insurers subscribe to these databases and also furnish them with claim information. The databases provide a quick way to check for similar prior claims.

If the prior claim check returns a likely match, the claim representative should investigate the prior claim history in more detail to determine whether the current claim is for the same injury or damage. If this is the case, the claim representative may have a basis for denying the claim or may adjust the investigation.

Subrogation Investigation and Recovery

Subrogation

The process by which an insurer can, after it has paid a loss under the policy, recover the amount paid from any party (other than the insured) who caused the loss or is otherwise legally liable for the loss.

During the course of an investigation, the claim representative may discover that the insured was not at fault and that a third party caused the accident. When an insurer pays a claim to an insured for a loss caused by a negligent third party, the insurer can recover that payment amount from the negligent third party through the right of **subrogation**. Subrogation rights are established by insurance policies and by law. When claim representatives investigate any loss, they must be alert to any subrogation possibilities; they should be looking for ways to recover any money paid out on the claim. Claim representatives investigate subrogation possibilities concurrently with other investigations. These examples describe losses for which a claim representative should investigate subrogation possibilities:

- Losses caused by the negligent operation of an automobile or a piece of construction equipment
- Fire, explosion, or water losses caused by the negligence of tenants
- Fire, explosion, or water losses caused by construction workers at a building site
- After work is completed, losses that result from poor workmanship of contractors
- Losses caused by defectively manufactured or poorly designed products

The subrogation clauses in most insurance policies require the insured to cooperate with the insurer by assigning the rights of subrogation to the insurer through a subrogation agreement. The subrogation agreement could be included in another form, such as a proof of loss form that the insured completes for a property damage claim. Most subrogation agreements require the insured to give testimony and appear in court, when necessary, so that the insurer can establish the legal basis to recover from the negligent third party.

An insured may breach the subrogation agreement by impairing or interfering with the insurer's right of subrogation. This can occur if the insured fails to cooperate in preserving evidence, gives or fails to give testimony, or releases the responsible party from any liability after the loss. If an insured breaches the subrogation agreement, the insurer has the right to collect from the insured the amount that could have been recovered from the responsible third party.

When subrogating, the insurer has the right to recover only the amount that it has paid on the claim. The insurer has no right of recovery for losses that the insured has absorbed because of lack of coverage, exclusions, or coverage limitations under the policy. Therefore, both the insurer and the insured may have rights to recover from the responsible third party. When the insured has absorbed only the deductible amount, however, the insurer usually pursues recovery of that amount as well, as a courtesy to the insured.

Claim representatives must consider the costs required to pursue subrogation as well as the likelihood of success. They must also be alert for any contract that may deny the right of subrogation (such as a lease agreement). Subrogation can be costly to pursue if litigation is required. In some cases the insurer may decide that pursuing subrogation is not cost-effective. However, the insurer's decision does not affect the insured's right to pursue payment from the responsible party for the unpaid portions of the claim.

When the subrogation action is against a negligent third party who is responsible for a loss, the insurer can present a subrogation claim for payment to the third party's liability insurer. Usually, the liability insurer pays the entire loss or offers a compromise settlement on the claim, depending on the assessment of liability. When the two insurers cannot agree on the liability, they can agree to arbitrate the dispute, often through intercompany arbitration.

Intercompany arbitration is conducted by having one or more arbitrators review written submissions from both parties. The insurer submits the claim representative's claim file, usually with highlighted details or tabs on specific documents for the arbitrator's benefit. The file should be legible and in chronological order. An arbitration statement that outlines the insurer's position in the case should accompany the file. The decision of the arbitrator(s) is final and binding on both insurers.

Documenting the Claim

Along with the investigation, claim personnel's documentation of the claim must be ongoing throughout the life of the claim. All aspects of a claim must be documented to create a complete claim file. Three crucial parts of the claim documentation are diary systems, file status notes, and file reports.

Diary Systems

Because claim representatives simultaneously handle many claims, they must have a system for working on and reviewing each claim. Whether this system is called a diary system, a suspense system, or a pending system, the purpose is the same. The system allows the claim representative to work on a claim one day and then diary it or calendar it for review. For example, the claim representative may send a letter to the insured requesting a repair estimate and diary that file for review on a date two weeks in the future. During that time, the claim representative would expect to receive the requested estimate. If the estimate has not been received by then, the review prompts the claim representative to follow up.

Diary systems are usually maintained by the insurer's claim processing system. This may automatically set diary dates for the file based on the type of claim. Most systems allow claim representatives to override system-generated diary dates and set a review date manually. Claim representatives who set dates manually must ensure that their handling of the file meets the requirements of any applicable unfair claims practices acts. For example, a state law may require that the insured receive a status letter on the claim every thirty days. The automated system would set the diary dates to meet this requirement. But claim representatives should not reset dates that cause them to miss this requirement or any others.

File Status Notes

File status notes (or an activity log) must accurately reflect and document investigations, evaluations of claims, decisions to decline coverage, or decisions to settle the claims. Because lawyers and state regulators can obtain copies of claim files, the file status notes and other file documentation must reflect these elements:

- Clear, concise, and accurate information
- Timely claim handling
- A fair and balanced investigation considering the insured's and the insurer's interests
- Objective comments about the insurer, insured, or other parties associated with the claim
- A thorough good-faith investigation

A claim file must speak for itself through the file status notes. The file status notes should include a chronological account of the claim representative's activities and can also include notes regarding activities of the claim supervisor and claim manager that relate to the claim. Ideally, an entry should exist for anyone who works on the file. Additionally, the file status notes should contain short summaries of reports and information received from outside sources. File status notes should be objective; they should not leave the reader with the impression that the claim representative is taking sides, such as in this statement: "The claimant obviously wasn't paying attention." File notes should not express prejudice of any sort, avoiding any remarks about race, religion, weight, or sex. Humor is also out of place in file notes. A note that seems innocuous when written can be devastating when read to a jury. See the exhibit "Example Status Note Entries."

Some file status notes can be lengthy because they continue for as long as the claim remains open, which can be years in some cases. They can also be very detailed, outlining why reserves are set at a particular dollar amount or how settlement figures are determined. File status notes should not be cryptic or written in personal shorthand because the claim representative who writes them may not be available to interpret them later. Claim representatives should determine from their company guidelines whether there are abbrevia-

Example Status Note Entries

4/5/XX Received new assignment. Called insured at work and spoke to Mr. Smith. Took a recorded statement from Mr. Smith about the accident. He indicates that his car was struck from behind while stopped at a stop sign. No injuries reported. Assigned appraiser to inspect the vehicle, which is currently located at Sam's Auto Body, 123 Main Street, Anytown, Any State. Phone number is 555-1234. Requested police report.

4/6/XX Called adverse driver, Mr. Jones, and took his statement. He indicates he was traveling east on Main when he was blinded by the sun and struck Mr. Smith's car, which was stopped at the intersection.

4/10/XX Received and reviewed police report. Report states that vehicle 1 (Mr. Smith's) was stopped at a stop sign eastbound on Main at the intersection of Broad, when struck in the rear by vehicle 2 driven by Mr. Jones. Report confirms statement of the insured. Awaiting estimate from appraiser.

4/15/XX Received repair estimate from appraiser. The body shop agrees with the estimate. The amount of the damages is $5,250. Called Mr. Smith and advised him of the amount and that it was an agreed price with the body shop. Reached agreement with Mr. Smith and processed a payment for $5,000, which is the repair estimate, less the $250 deductible. Confirmed no lien-holder or other payee to be on the payment. Referred file to subrogation unit.

[DA06194]

tions for terms that are acceptable, such as "PR" for police report or "s/s" for stop sign.

File Reports

File reports to various parties are developed by claim representatives to document claim activity. The reports include various types of internal and external reports.

Claim representatives prepare and distribute internal reports to parties within the insurance organization who have an interest in large losses or loss of a specific nature, such as death, disfigurement, or dismemberment. Most insurers have guidelines outlining when and under what circumstances internal reports should be prepared. These reports are prepared while a claim is open and may have attachments such as estimates, police reports, diagrams, photos, statements, and correspondence. If the claim is handled by in-house claim representatives, these attachments may already be included as images in the electronic claim file or included in the paper claim file. Often these reports are typed directly into a claim entry system (the electronic claim file) using an electronic form; distributed electronically to claim supervisors, managers, or underwriters; and then printed for any necessary outside distribution (such as lawyers).

An insurer may require preliminary reports within the first twenty-four hours, within seven days of the claim assignment, or only if the file remains open after thirty days. Preliminary reports acknowledge that the claim representative received the assignment, inform the insurer about initial activity on the claim, suggest reserves, note coverage issues, and request assistance, if needed. For small, uncomplicated claims that claim representatives settle quickly, the preliminary report may be the only report in the claim file.

Status reports tell the insurer how the claim is progressing on a periodic basis, generally every fifteen to thirty days. In these reports, claim representatives record the progress of the claim, recommend reserve changes, and request assistance and settlement authority when the amount payable exceeds their authority. Status reports are one way to confirm that the claim representative is working on a claim and progressing in a timely manner.

Summarized reports are often detailed narratives that follow an established format with captioned headings that give them structure. Claim representatives usually file a summarized report within thirty days of the assignment date. Insurers may require summarized reports for specific claims that require review by managers at regional or home offices. For example, suspected arson and insurance fraud claims are typically reported to the regional and home offices because of their potential for litigation. Managers may also review a file when the reserve exceeds a specified amount. Some insurers require summarized reports on certain types of claims because they want to track trends in certain types of business.

IInsurers also document claim activity using external reports containing information collected by claim representatives. External claim reports inform interested parties about the claim and inform the public of the insurer's financial standing. These reports are prepared for producers, some states' advisory organizations, and others who have an interest in the claim. Because insurers often write business through producers, losses are reported to the producer who sold the insurance. These reports provide details about the losses, such as the amount paid and the amount in outstanding reserve.

Determining the Cause of Loss, Liability, and the Loss Amount

Claim representatives use the information gained during their investigation to determine the cause of loss, liability, and the loss amount. The facts of the loss determine the cause of the loss. For example, in a fire loss, the claim representative may find that a toaster caused the fire.

The claim representative also determines the liability for the loss based on the facts of the case. For example, in an auto accident, the claim representative applies statutory and case law on negligence to determine liability of the parties involved.

Concurrent to the determination of the cause of the loss and the liability for the loss, the claim representative may determine the amount of the loss. For a property claim, the claim representative investigates the amount of damage to the property and the cost to repair or replace it and may also investigate the amount of business income lost.To determine a loss amount in a bodily injury claim, the claim representative investigates the extent of the injury, the residual and lasting effects of the injury, and the amount of pain and suffering the individual has endured.

The procedures required to investigate and to determine the cause of loss, liability, and damages depend on the type of claim. Having determined the cause of loss, liability, and loss amount, the claim representative can apply the policy coverages to the loss. Claim representatives can use the framework for coverage analysis to assist them in this application.

Concluding the Claim

When the investigation has been completed and all documentation has been received, the claim representative must decide whether to pay the claim or deny it.

If the claim is to be paid, the claim representative often must negotiate the amount with the insured or the claimant. Negotiation involves discussing disputed matters and mutually agreeing on a settlement. In some cases, alternative dispute resolution (ADR) methods may be used to resolve a disagreement and, ultimately, the claim. When an agreement on the settlement amount is reached, the claim representative secures the necessary final documents so that payment can be made. If the claim is denied, the insured or claimant may accept the denial or may choose to file a lawsuit to challenge the denial. Litigation may also be started if no agreement on the claim can be reached.

Payments

When a covered claim is concluded through negotiation or other means, the claim representative or claim personnel must issue a claim payment. Claim payments can be made by check, draft, or electronic transfer of funds A check creates a demand for payment on the insurer's bank account and can be presented for payment without further insurer authorization. A draft is similar to a check. However, when the claimant presents the draft to the insurer's bank (often through the claimant's bank transaction), the bank must verify that the insurer has authorized payment before disbursing any funds. Because of this required authorization, a claimant cannot present a draft at a bank for immediate payment. This delay in disbursing funds allows the insurer to confirm that the payment is proper.Funds can also be electronically transferred into an account of the insured's choosing.

When issuing claim payments, claim personnel must ensure that the proper parties are paid. Many other parties, such as mortgagees on homes and loss payees on autos and personal property, can have a financial interest in the property. Parties named in the policy have rights, described in the policy, to be included as a payee under certain circumstances, such as for property that has been destroyed. For third-party liability claim payments, the claim representative must determine whether an attorney or a lienholder, such as a medical service provider, should be named as an additional payee on the payment. The claim representative is responsible for including all required payees when issuing a claim payment.

Claim representatives must also check databases to ensure that the claim payment complies with federal and state laws. The Office of Foreign Asset Control, an agency of the United States Department of the Treasury, requires all claim payors (insurers, self-insureds, and third-party administrators [TPAs]) to check the master list of potential terrorists and drug traffickers before making a claim payment. Claim payors may be prohibited from paying a claim to an individual or entity appearing on this list. Many insurers and TPAs have contracted with third parties to provide an automated means of performing this check. Failure to comply with this requirement can result in substantial penalties to the payor.

Insurers and other claim payors must also be aware of state child support enforcement initiatives that can affect claim payments. Many states have statutes that require a claim representative to check a database to determine whether a claimant or beneficiary owes unpaid child support. If child support is owed, the claim representative must follow specific procedures when issuing the payment because the unpaid child support has priority. The claim payment goes toward reducing the amount of the child support in arrears rather than to the injured party. For example, Massachusetts law requires that an insurer licensed to do business in Massachusetts check the database before making payment on a claim of $500 or more. Failure to comply can result in financial consequences to the insurer. Many insurers and claim payors have created ways to automate the process.

Claim representatives must ensure that all of these checks have been completed before issuing payment. If they have not, the insurer can be subject to fines, penalties, and possibly additional payments.

Claim Denial

A claim may conclude with a denial rather than a payment. When claim investigations reveal that a policy does not provide coverage for a loss or when an insured fails to meet a policy condition, the claim representative must make a timely claim denial. Insurers often have strict guidelines that claim representatives must follow when denying claims, and some insurers require a claim manager's approval to issue a claim denial.

Before denying a claim, the claim representative must analyze the coverage carefully, investigate the loss thoroughly, and evaluate the claim fairly and objectively. Courts often favor insureds when a claim denial fails to meet these requirements, and the insurer can be assessed penalties in addition to the loss amount.

Once claim management gives authority to deny a claim, the claim representative must prepare a denial letter as soon as possible. Some denial letters are drafted by lawyers to ensure that they comply with the jurisdiction's legal requirements. For example, a denial letter must usually state all the known reasons for the claim denial. Specific policy language should be quoted, and the location of the language in the policy should be cited. The policy provisions should be described in relation to the facts of the loss. Also, an insured who disagrees with the denial should be invited to submit additional information that would give the insurer cause to re-evaluate the claim. The denial letter should be signed and sent by the claim representative, even if it is drafted by a lawyer.

Insurers usually send denial letters by certified mail with a return receipt requested to be signed by the addressee. Some insurers also send a copy of the letter by regular mail, marked "personal and confidential," in case the certified mail is not claimed. These procedures help ensure that the denial letter reaches the correct party, and they provide documentation that it was received.

Alternative Dispute Resolution

If an insurer and an insured or a claimant cannot agree on the claim value or claim coverage, they may resolve the disagreement in court. However, court costs and delays in the court system have encouraged insurers, insureds, and claimants to seek alternative ways of resolving their disputes about claims that are less expensive and time consuming than litigation. Such processes also help relieve the courts of the burden of handling such disputes. ADR refers to methods for settling disputes outside the traditional court system. These are the most common ADR techniques:

- Mediation
- Arbitration
- Appraisals
- Mini-trials
- Summary jury trials

Mediation is an ADR method by which disputing parties use a neutral outside party to examine the issues and develop a mutually agreeable settlement. The mediator, often a retired judge or an expert in the field under dispute, manages the process. The mediator may be appointed by the court or selected by the parties.Each party presents its case to the mediator, who leads the parties through in-depth settlement discussions. The mediator points out the weaknesses in each argument or in the evidence presented. Then the mediator proposes solutions, and helps the participants reach a mutually agreeable settlement. If mediation does not resolve the dispute, the parties may consider another ADR method or litigation.

Mediation

An alternative dispute resolution (ADR) method by which disputing parties use a neutral outside party to examine the issues and develop a mutually agreeable settlement.

Arbitration

An alternative dispute resolution (ADR) method by which disputing parties use a neutral outside party to examine the issues and develop a settlement, which can be final and binding.

Arbitration is an ADR method by which the disputing parties use a neutral outside party to examine the issues and develop a settlement. The arbitrator acts as a judge, weighing the facts of the case and making a decision based on the evidence presented. The advantage of arbitration is that someone other than the insurer and the claimant decides the case.

The type of arbitration determines whether the decision is binding on the parties. Under binding arbitration (required by some states' laws for arbitrated claim disputes), the parties must accept the arbitrator's decision. Under non-binding arbitration, neither party is forced to accept the arbitrator's decision. However, the decision provides the "winner" with leverage for future negotiations. This method of ADR is cost-effective for all parties and relieves the courts of the burden of handling such disputes.

When two policies issued by different insurers cover the same loss, arbitration can be used to settle a dispute about which insurer should pay the claim and how much should be paid. Generally, one insurer settles with the insured. The case is then submitted to an arbitration service to determine what each insurer owes. Insurers may use an organization such as Insurance Arbitration Forums, Inc. or the American Arbitration Association. Insurer trade associations also offer arbitration services and other forms of ADR to member companies.

The appraisal provision is included in property insurance policies as a form of ADR used to settle disputes between insurers and their insureds over the amount owed on a covered loss before litigation. It is not used to settle coverage disputes, only the amount of damages. Almost all property insurance policies contain an appraisal provision. For example, the HO-3 provides that the insurer or the insured can demand an appraisal if they disagree on the loss amount. Each party chooses an appraiser. Then the two appraisers choose a third appraiser to act as an umpire. Each party pays its own appraiser, and the two parties share the cost of the umpire. The appraisers can hear evidence that is typically excluded from trial. The two appraisers estimate the property damage separately. If their estimates match, the insurer pays the insured that amount. If the estimates are different, the umpire offers a binding decision on the loss amount.

Mini-trial

An alternative dispute resolution method by which a case undergoes an abbreviated version of a trial before a panel or an adviser who poses questions and offers opinions on the outcome of a trial, based on the evidence presented.

Mini-trials are another form of ADR. A mini-trial enables parties to test the validity of their positions and continue negotiations. Parties can terminate the process at any time. The parties agree not to disclose in future litigation anything that occurs during the mini-trial, in order to preserve their rights in litigation if the negotiation fails.

The parties select an impartial adviser, often a retired judge, an executive, or an expert. They also decide on the role of the adviser. The adviser can be a passive participant, an arbitrator, or a judge. The adviser has no authority to make a binding decision. However the adviser can ask questions that test the validity of each side's case and can offer an opinion based on the evidence presented.

Before the mini-trial, parties can exchange information about their anticipated testimony and documents that they plan to introduce as evidence. That
information may also be given to the adviser. Witnesses and experts may testify during the mini-trial. Lawyers are allotted a limited time to present their
cases. The main advantage of mini-trials is that claimants and insurers can
learn the likely outcome of their cases without having to contend with delays
in the legal system.

A **summary jury trial** offers a forum for deciding the merits of cases for court
proceedings. It may also assist in negotiations. A summary jury trial is staged
much like a regular jury trial, except that only a few witnesses are used to present the case. Mock jurors are pulled from a pool of persons selected to serve as
possible jurors in an actual court case. Evidence and witnesses' testimony may
be presented in both oral and written format. Lawyers present summarized
information. The mock jurors decide the case based on the limited, though
representative, presentation of evidence.

Summary jury trial

An alternative dispute
resolution method by which
disputing parties participate
in an abbreviated trial,
presenting the evidence of
a few witnesses to a panel
of mock jurors who decide
the case.

A summary jury trial can be concluded in a relatively short time, so legal costs
are significantly reduced. Fewer witnesses mean less expense for witness fees.
Although lawyers are required, the time necessary to develop the case and
prepare for trial is considerably less. Summary jury trials can produce effective
settlements and control legal expenses.

Litigation

Even with the variety of ADR methods available, many cases are concluded
through litigation. Litigation can occur at almost any point during the life of a
claim. However, it occurs most often when the parties to the claim are unable
to reach an agreement by negotiation or ADR, or when a claim is denied.
ADR reduces, but does not eliminate, the possibility that a claimant will sue
and take a case to trial. Accordingly, insurers must be prepared to litigate
some claims.

Many insurance policies require insurers to defend their insureds at trial. The
duty to defend usually ends when the amount the insurer has paid in settlements or judgments on the claim reaches the insurer's limit of liability.

When litigation cannot be avoided, claim representatives participate in developing a litigation strategy for the insured's defense and for litigation expense
control. Claim representatives must carefully select and direct defense lawyers. The lawyer's role is to be the insured's advocate. To mitigate the claim
against the insured and to encourage the claimant to settle out of court,
the lawyer must address every aspect of the claimant's case, from liability to
damages.

Closing Reports

When a claim is resolved, the claim representative may complete a closing
or final report, which can include the claim representative's recommenda-

tions on subrogation, advice to underwriters, and other suggestions. In some instances, subrogation claim representatives use these reports to evaluate the likelihood of a successful subrogation action.

Claim supervisors and managers may use the reports to audit the claim representative's performance. These reports can also be submitted to reinsurers for reimbursement of loss payment. Claim representatives should be aware of claims that should be referred to reinsurers and must complete reports on those claims based on the insurer's internal guidelines and reinsurance agreements.

LAW OF BAD FAITH

A primary function of insurers is to pay valid insurance claims. Claim representatives should strive to handle claims with utmost good faith and in an ethical and professional manner. Because interactions with claim representatives are often the only personal contacts that the general public has with an insurer, the claim representative's actions may be closely scrutinized and are often criticized. These criticisms, whether or not legitimate, can result in bad-faith allegations against an insurer.

To avoid bad-faith allegations, claim representatives must understand the law of bad-faith claims. Bad faith law evolved from the special relationship between insurers and insureds based on the implied duty of good faith and fair dealing.

No single widely-accepted definition of bad faith exists. However, Black's Law Dictionary (Eighth Edition 2004) defines "bad faith" in insurance as:

> An insurance company's unreasonable and unfounded (though not necessarily fraudulent) refusal to provide coverage in violation of the duties of good faith and fair dealing owed to an insured. Bad faith often involves an insurer's failure to pay the insured's claim or a claim brought by a third party.

Although some state laws define bad faith differently or more specifically, the Black's definition is useful for discussion of the issue because it is broad enough to encompass actions that courts nationwide have determined to constitute bad faith.

Development of the Law of Bad Faith

The law of bad faith developed in response to the perception that insurers were placing their own interests ahead of their insureds' interests. In some cases, insureds became personally liable for losses or damages they believed were covered by their insurance, and they sued their insurers for **breach of contract**. The insureds alleged that, by wrongfully denying or mishandling their claims, the insurers had failed to fulfill their contractual promise.

Breach of contract
The failure, without legal excuse, to fulfill a contractual promise.

However, in some of these cases, breach of contract remedies were perceived to be inadequate. The legal remedy for breach of contract is damages in amounts up to the contract's terms, or the policy limits. Consequently, if an insurer wrongfully denied or mishandled a claim, the policyholder would have to go through the expense, stress, and delay of a lawsuit to get the insurer to pay what it should have rightfully paid under the policy. Furthermore, if the insurer's actions caused the insured to be liable to a third party for damages above the policy limits, the insured would be responsible for those damages as well.

Because contract remedies were considered inadequate in such cases, insureds brought lawsuits against insurers for alleged torts, such as fraud and intentional infliction of emotional distress. However, such cases often failed because of the difficulty of proving in court that the insurer's behavior was either fraudulent or outrageous enough to award damages for emotional distress.

Eventually, some courts decided that insurers have an implied duty of good faith and fair dealing when settling claims, requiring insurers to value their insureds' interests at least as much as their own. This duty applies by extension to claim representatives. Insurers' failure to comply with this duty can result in a bad-faith claim. Therefore, bad-faith law evolved from the special relationship between insurers and insureds based on the implied duty of good faith and fair dealing.

Insureds and claimants continue to seek new bases for bad faith claims, such as invasion of privacy, defamation, libel, or slander based on letters or documents in the claims files. In addition, the standard of conduct for proving bad faith continues to evolve.

Duty of Good Faith and Fair Dealing

Most bad-faith claims for breach of the implied duty of good faith and fair dealing arise under insurance-related contracts rather than other types of contracts. Why have bad-faith claims developed to such an extent in insurance? Insurance contracts involve the public interest and require a higher standard of conduct because of the unequal bargaining power between the parties. The insured has less "bargaining power" than the insurer because the insurer not only dictates the terms of the contract (the policy), but also usually controls the claim investigation, evaluation, negotiation, and settlement.

Public Interest

States regulate insurers to protect consumers against illegal business practices and against insurer insolvency because it is in the public interest that insurers have the financial resources to pay claims. Courts also want to protect the public interest by ensuring that insurers pay claims they owe. In cases in which insurers have acted in bad faith and have harmed the public interest, courts require them to pay damages beyond their contractual obligations.

Higher Standard of Conduct

In comparison to other contracts, insurance contracts require a higher standard of conduct—utmost good faith. Because of the nature of insurance contracts, both the insured or applicant and the insurer must disclose all pertinent facts. The insurer must disclose all the terms of the insurance policy, and the applicant must disclose all the information needed to accurately underwrite the policy.

The parties to insurance contracts have unequal bargaining power. Insurers are often perceived as powerful corporations with vast resources. Even if the insured is a large, financially strong corporation, insurers are considered to have greater bargaining power because they develop the insurance contract and settle the claims. When individual consumers purchase an insurance policy, they generally must accept the policy terms written by the insurer.

In addition, many insurance policies specifically state that the insurer controls the investigation and settlement of a claim. For example, Section II—Liability Coverages of Insurance Services Office's (ISO's) homeowners policy states the following: "We may investigate and settle any claim or lawsuit that we decide is appropriate."[1] Because insurers control how claims are resolved, courts reason that insurers should be responsible for the outcome of their claim handling if they have acted in bad faith. Thus, courts hold insurers to a higher standard of conduct to discourage insurers from abusing their position of power. Consequently, filing and defending bad-faith lawsuits has become a specialty in the legal community.

To conclude that an insurer has acted in bad faith, courts must determine the standard of conduct to which the insurer should be held. Can an insurer be guilty of bad faith for unintentional mistakes or errors in judgment? Or, must an insurer's behavior be intentional, wanton, or reckless to constitute bad faith? Courts differ about whether bad faith should be based on negligence or on gross or intentional misconduct. In many cases, the results are the same regardless of the standard because insurers' actions can be considered both negligent and reckless or intentional.

Some courts use a negligence (sometimes called due care) standard in determining whether a claim representative's (and, by extension, the insurer's) actions constitute bad faith. Some courts may use negligence as a basis to award compensatory damages but award punitive damages only when the insurer has exhibited gross misconduct.

Many courts have rejected a negligence standard for bad faith. They hold insurers liable only if their behavior is found to be intentional or to constitute gross misconduct. To prove intentional misconduct, a complainant must show that the claim representative intended both the misconduct and the consequences, for example, denying coverage with the knowledge that coverage applies under the policy.

When applying a gross misconduct standard, courts have historically looked for signs of "dishonest purpose, moral obliquity, conscious wrongdoing… some ulterior motive or ill will partaking of the nature of fraud."[2] Bad faith may fall somewhere between simple error and outright fraud. Other courts have used terms such as "arbitrary, reckless, indifferent, or intentional disregard"[3] of a party's interests to describe bad-faith behaviors. Because these behaviors are judged on a subjective basis, courts attempt to determine the claim representative's state of mind at the time that bad-faith acts are alleged to have occurred.

Claim representatives should understand the subjective interpretation of negligence and gross misconduct. The difference between negligence and gross misconduct is determined by the court's or jury's interpretation of the facts. For example, a claim representative issues a coverage denial after performing an incomplete investigation. One court might consider the incomplete investigation to be the result of an oversight or of mere negligence. Another court might conclude that deciding coverage without being fully informed is clearly reckless and arbitrary and, therefore, constitutes gross misconduct on the part of the claim representative. Although the standard of care required varies by jurisdiction, some areas of bad faith, such as the parties to a bad-faith claim, remain stable.

Legal Environment of Bad Faith

Bad faith litigation is becoming more common, and the bases on which bad-faith claims can be brought are expanding. In this constantly changing climate, claim representatives must make an effort to stay informed about the bases of bad-faith claims so that they can provide good-faith claim handling in every instance. Although charges of bad faith are often unfounded, they drain insurer resources. Allegations of bad faith, legitimate or not, continue to proliferate. See the exhibit "A Word of Caution."

A Word of Caution

Even if a lawyer's initial letter to an insurer regarding a claim makes an allegation of bad faith, that does not mean that the insurer is guilty of bad faith. However, responses to such letters should be timely and carefully crafted. The claim representative may wish to consult with a supervisor or manager and possibly an attorney when drafting this response.

[DA03021]

Although most bad-faith law is case law, state legislatures can pass laws that affect bad-faith claims. For example, in October 1999, the governor of

California signed the California Fair Insurance Responsibility Act to take effect January 1, 2000. This Act would have allowed claimants to sue insurers for unfairly or fraudulently delaying or denying claim payments. The legislation was put to a popular vote as Propositions 30 and 31 in March 2000 and was defeated. Similar legislation was defeated by a Wyoming legislative committee in December 1999. These examples illustrate why claim representatives must be aware of the status of bad-faith laws in the states in which they handle claims and of additional circumstances that can put them and their employer at increased risk of bad-faith claims.

ELEMENTS OF GOOD-FAITH CLAIM HANDLING

To use the defenses to bad-faith claims, the insurer and the claim representative must be able to show they acted in good faith.

Good faith is broadly defined as consideration given to the insured's interests that is at least equal to that given to the insurer's interests in handling the claim. This broad definition allows courts great leeway in deciding what constitutes good faith in a given situation. As a result, common sense and good judgment must underlie all claim handling.

Good-faith claim handling involves these elements:

- Thorough, timely, and unbiased investigation
- Complete and accurate documentation
- Fair evaluation
- Good-faith negotiation
- Regular and prompt communication
- Competent legal advice
- Effective claim management

Thorough, Timely, and Unbiased Investigation

Investigations that are thorough, timely, and unbiased are the foundation of good-faith claim handling. If claim representatives investigate claims adequately, they will have sufficient evidence of their good-faith efforts to conclude claims. That evidence is helpful in defending bad-faith lawsuits.

Thorough Investigation

Claim representatives should thoroughly investigate claims and collect all relevant and necessary evidence. Investigation should continue as long as new facts develop or become available. Claim representatives should develop the information and documentation necessary to determine liability and damages and should make decisions once they believe they have sufficient information to do so. They should not delay decisions while trying to uncover or investigate what could be construed by a jury as unnecessary information.

A claim file must be organized so that the information is readable and easy to follow. For example, medical bills, doctors' reports, and other information on each claimant should be in a logical order. Photographs, police reports, and other documentary evidence should be sorted for easy reference.

In a thorough investigation, the claim representative is alert for new information that may change the course of the claim. For example, a homeowner files a claim for an injury to a visitor who fell on his front step. This may appear to be a simple claim. However, a claim representative may discover from the homeowner's statement that the visitor was actually a resident of the household or was on the premises as a business customer. Either situation may exclude coverage under the homeowner's policy. Without the additional investigation, the claim representative may have paid a claim that was not covered by the policy.

Claim representatives often determine when an investigation is sufficiently thorough, using their own judgment. For example, the insurer's claim handling guidelines offer guidance about which claims require statements and from which parties. However, a claim representative may decide a statement is necessary for a specific claim, even if the guidelines do not require it. In any case, an investigation should be thorough enough to satisfy a judge and jury that the claim representative followed good-faith claim handling procedures. Evidence of compliance with company procedures or best practices used in investigation helps convince the court or jury.

Timely Investigation

An insured who makes a claim expects prompt contact from the claim representative. Most insurers have guidelines requiring the claim representative to contact the insured and the claimant within a specific period, such as twenty-four hours after the claim has been submitted. Timely contact with the parties to the claim benefits the insurer in several ways. First, parties are more likely to remember the details of the loss accurately. Memory fades quickly over time; therefore claim representatives are most likely to get complete, accurate information from insureds and claimants if they contact them promptly. Second, the parties are more likely to share information if contacted promptly; prompt contact reassures insureds and claimants that their claims are important and makes them less likely to accept the advice of others who may encourage them to retain a lawyer or pursue unnecessary litigation. Documentation of timely contact in the claim file can help prove an insurer's use of good-faith claim handling procedures and/or the insurer's compliance with the provisions of the Model Act.

Unbiased Investigation

When investigating claims, claim representatives should pursue all relevant evidence, especially evidence that establishes the claim's legitimacy, without bias. They should avoid asking misleading questions that slant the answers toward a particular outcome, such as "The light was red when you saw it, wasn't it?" In addition, claim representatives should work with service providers that are unbiased and have no conflict of interest. As mentioned previously, courts and juries may not look sympathetically on medical providers or repair facilities that always favor insurers. Investigations should seek to discover the facts and consider all aspects of the claims so that decisions are impartial and fair.

Federal Statute

When conducting a good-faith claim investigation, claim representatives must comply not only with state unfair claim practices acts, but also with federal statutes. These statutes, designed to ensure the privacy of confidential information, include the Health Insurance Portability and Accountability Act of 1996, the Gramm-Leach-Bliley Act, the Sarbanes-Oxley Act, and the Fair Credit Reporting Act.

Health Insurance Portability and Accountability Act of 1996

Claim representatives must be careful in handling confidential information learned about an insured or a claimant during the course of a claim investigation. Several statutes and regulations govern the handling of information. Congress established the Health Insurance Portability and Accountability Act of 1996 (HIPAA)[4] to address the use and disclosure of individual health information. HIPAA applies to health plans, healthcare clearing houses (that process health information), and healthcare providers, termed "covered entities" in the act. Its major goal is to protect individuals' health information while allowing the flow of information to provide and promote high quality healthcare. A major aspect of the primary rule in this act concerns the disclosure of medical information in connection with claims or potential claims.

HIPAA describes permitted uses and disclosures of protected information. A covered entity is permitted, but not required, to use and disclose protected health information, without an individual's authorization:

- When the information is disclosed to the individual
- When the information is used in treatment, payment, and healthcare operations, such as sending a patient's medical records to another doctor
- When the individual is given the opportunity to agree or object to certain disclosures
- When the information is incident to an otherwise permitted use and disclosure
- In the interests of public health
- As limited data for the purpose of research, public health, or healthcare operations

A covered entity may rely on professional ethics and best judgment in deciding which of these uses are permitted. Claim representatives must be aware of HIPAA restrictions and obtain the necessary authorizations to obtain HIPAA-protected information.

Gramm-Leach-Bliley Act

Congress enacted the Gramm-Leach-Bliley Act of 1999 (GLB)[5] to protect the security and confidentiality of customers of financial institutions. GLB sets forth requirements for protecting and using customer information. GLB applies to financial institutions such as banks, securities firms, insurers, and others who provide financial services and products to consumers and protects both current and prior customers of these institutions. The act includes requirements for handling confidential information and a disclosure provision, which requires companies to advise consumers of the company's information-sharing practices.

The protected information ranges from general biographical background information to information revealed in connection with a transaction. The act also provides several exceptions, including information required to be shared in administering a financial transaction authorized by a customer or made in connection with fraud prevention. Claim representatives must be aware of GLB because it may restrict their access to financial information obtained by their company for a purpose other than a claim, but which would be useful to the claim investigation.

Sarbanes-Oxley Act

Congress enacted the Sarbanes-Oxley Act[6] in 2002 in response to the financial and accounting scandals of the 1990s. This act requires publicly traded companies to meet and certify certain financial disclosure requirements. It requires commercial insureds and many insurers to conduct more intense investigations of their claims from an accounting standpoint to make sure they comply with the law. This requires more extensive reporting of claim information, greater accuracy in setting claim reserves, and more extensive audits of claims and claim files.

Fair Credit Reporting Act

Congress enacted the Fair Credit Reporting Act[7] in 1970 to promote the accuracy and privacy of personal information assembled by credit reporting agencies. The personal information includes credit reports, consumer investigation reports, and employment background checks.

The act requires reporting agencies to follow "reasonable procedures" to protect the confidentiality and privacy of personal information. To this end, procedures are established to handle personal information that includes the right to access and correct credit information.

Claim representatives should be aware of the restrictions imposed by the Fair Credit Reporting Act should they find it necessary to obtain or disclose an insured's or a claimant's financial information during a claim investigation. Claim representatives should check with their supervisors or managers to determine what "reasonable procedures" are in place to protect the confidentiality of this information.

While a violation of these statutes may not lead to a bad-faith claim, it may lead to a claim for extracontractual liability because the violations fall outside the scope of the policy but have occurred during the course of claim handling.

Complete and Accurate Documentation

A common saying among claim representatives is that if an activity, action, or event is not written in the claim file, it did not happen. A claim file must provide to anyone who reads the claim file a complete and accurate account of all the activities and actions taken by the claim representative. Claim representatives must remember that a claim file may be read by many different people, each with a different purpose. The claim representative's supervisor or manager may read the file to provide assistance to the claim representativeA home-office examiner or an auditor may review the file for compliance with claim handling guidelines. Claim department peers may review the file as part of a roundtable discussion of reserving. The underwriter, the agent, or the broker may review the file to determine whether the coverage determination or valuation is appropriate. A state insurance department may review the file in response to a complaint or during a market conduct study. Defense counsel, and maybe even the claimant's counsel, will review the claim file during the course of litigation. Mediators and arbitrators may review the file as part of a dispute resolution process. Regardless of who reads the file, no reader should be left wondering why something did or did not happen or how a conclusion was reached.

Fair Evaluation

Another aspect of good-faith claim handling is the fair evaluation of the claim. This is particularly important in liability claims. A fair approach to evaluating liability claims is to evaluate them as if no coverage limit existed. This approach helps claim representatives avoid the mistake of unfairly attempting to settle a claim for less than the policy limit when it may be worth more.

A crucial element of fair claim evaluation is a prompt evaluation. The evaluation of a claim usually takes place at the conclusion of the investigation, when the claim representative has received all supporting documentation. Unfair claims settlement practices acts often specify time limits within which evaluations of coverage and damages must be completed. Claim representatives' compliance with these requirements helps reduce the insurer's exposure to bad-faith claims.

Promptness is also important in responding to the claimant, the insured, or their respective lawyers' demands. If a letter specifies a time limit for reply, the claim representative should make every effort to respond within that limit or should respond by telephone and explain why more time is needed. The call should be confirmed promptly in a follow-up letter or e-mail. Any time extension agreed on should be documented by a letter and a copy should be placed in the claim file.

Courts have dismissed bad-faith claims based on unreasonable time limits. In some cases, the opposing side may set intentionally unreasonable limits to raise the inference of bad faith or to pressure a claim representative into settling before thoroughly investigating the claim. Prompt handling and constant attention help avoid these situations.

If a letter or another communication contains a demand that is at or near the policy limits, a prompt reply is particularly important. The lawyer may contend that the case is worth much more than the policy limits but that the client will accept the policy limits if the claim is settled quickly. If the claim representative has properly evaluated and documented the claim file, this time demand should pose no problem.

Claim representatives can perform a fair evaluation if they have conducted a thorough, timely, unbiased investigation and understand the jurisdiction of the claim. In addition, to assist in making a knowledgeable evaluation, they can consult with sources inside and outside the insurance company, including these:

- Co-workers
- Supervisors and managers
- Defense lawyers who are already involved in the case
- Other defense lawyers who are not involved in the case
- People who represent a typical jury
- Computer-generated damage or injury evaluations
- Jury verdict research companies

Information about settlements or trial results from similar cases gained from any of these sources can help claim representatives knowledgeably evaluate the claim. However, each claim is unique and should be evaluated on its own merits.

Fair evaluations are based on facts, not opinions. A claim representative's statement in the file that "I think the case is worth $50,000" is of little value unless the investigation and file documentation substantiate that amount. Claim representatives determine a range of claim amounts based on the facts of the claim, the credibility of the evidence, and applicable laws. This is not an exact science. File documentation showing that the claim representative used best practices to evaluate a claim is evidence of good-faith claim handling. Of course, the amount of the eventual verdict or damages will be used to argue for or against a bad-faith claim.

Good-Faith Negotiation

Good-faith negotiations flow naturally from thorough, timely, unbiased investigations and prompt, fair evaluations. Courts in some jurisdictions have held that an insurer cannot be liable for bad faith for not settling a claim unless the claimant has made a settlement demand. However, claim representatives should take the initiative in making realistic offers when doing so is likely to promote a settlement. Such offers may include an offer to settle before a demand is ever made.

Although claim representatives must make realistic offers and carefully consider all demands, lawyers are not held to the same standard. They can make exaggerated demands in a vigorous representation of their clients, and their clients often expect them to do so, in the hope of obtaining the best settlement possible. Claim representatives should evaluate each claim fairly and respond to such demands by offering a settlement that is consistent with the evidence and documentation in the claim file. They should not trade unrealistic offers and demands with lawyers, as such behavior may result in an unrealistic settlement. All responses to demands should be reasonable and made in a courteous and professional manner.

Claim representatives should not allow their emotions or egos to affect negotiations. Unchecked emotions or egos can stop negotiations and prompt arguments. Judgment becomes clouded and the spirit of fair dealing can be replaced with bad feelings. When this happens, everyone loses, and it is more difficult for an insurer to prove that it has followed good-faith claim handling procedures.

Claim representatives should use policy provisions, such as arbitration clauses, when applicable, to resolve disputes over the settlement amount. Adherence to the policy provisions and payment of the amount determined through arbitration places the insurer in a better position to defend a bad-faith lawsuit.[8] Claim representatives should consider all possible forms of voluntary alternative dispute resolution, including mediation or a series of face-to-face negotiations to resolve claims.

Regular and Prompt Communication

Communicating with all parties to a claim (for example, the insured, the defense attorney, and the excess insurer) is a crucial aspect of good-faith claim handling and resolving claims. Keeping insureds informed is especially important because they expect it, they are most likely to make a bad-faith claim, and they may have the most important information about an accident.Regular and prompt communication with the insured achieves several important results, including these:

- The insured feels like a part of the defense and can offer assistance.
- The insured can participate in discussions about the possibility of settlement and the handling of the claim.
- The correspondence with the insured documents the insurer's good-faith claim handling and the basis for its judgment about settlement.
- The correspondence establishes that the insured gave the insurer informed consent to take on the defense of the case and to decide how to defend it.

The defense attorney should regularly and promptly inform the insured of all major events in the defense. Any request by an insured not to be informed of these events should be confirmed in writing. Claim representatives and lawyers should document telephone and personal communication in writing and confirm what they learn in such communications if it is crucial to the claim.

If defense lawyers fail to communicate promptly and regularly, claim representatives should contact them to solicit information and correct any misunderstandings. Claim representatives cannot abandon claims to defense lawyers and still meet good-faith claim handling standards.

Written communication from the defense lawyer to the insured may include these:

- A letter advising that the insurer has received a demand for policy limits with an explanation of the insurer's planned course of action
- A letter indicating that negotiations have stalled, that the claimant has retained a lawyer, and what the insured should do if he or she receives a summons
- If suit is filed, a letter stating the defense lawyer's name, address, and phone number; identifying coverage questions or reservations of rights that result from the lawsuit; advising the insured of a possible excess verdict or punitive damages; and advising the insured of the right to hire a lawyer at the insured's own expense
- A letter stating that the claim has been settled without trial
- A letter stating that the court's decision is being appealed

If the insured has excess insurance, the claim representative should notify the excess insurer of the claim and provide the insured with copies of all communications. The excess insurer may request a copy of the claim file and may or may not want to be actively involved in the claim thereafter to protect its interests. Additionally, if the insured hires a lawyer, that lawyer will want to be kept advised of significant claim activity.

Competent Legal Advice

Following the advice of competent lawyers can be considered evidence that an insurer acted in good faith. Lawyers who defend the insured should be selected based on their experience, knowledge of the law, and success in the courtroom. Lawyers have an ethical obligation to be loyal to the insured first and the insurer second, because the insured is the lawyer's client, regardless of who is paying the lawyer's fees. Defense lawyers who are overly optimistic about their chances of successfully defending a case may not be good choices, because their optimism may be unproven and can expose the insured and insurer to an excess verdict. Claim representatives should provide lawyers with all information and documentation necessary to reach a complete and accurate opinion and should avoid any attempts to influence the lawyer's independent judgment.

When resolving a coverage question, insurers should avoid conflicts of interest by using lawyers other than the defense lawyers hired to defend an insured. Asking a lawyer who defends an insured a coverage question creates an ethical dilemma for that lawyer because the answer may not be in the insured's best interest. Insurers that use in-house or staff lawyers (lawyers who are the insurer's employees) to defend insureds should be especially sensitive to the possibility of a conflict of interest and, if any appearance of such a conflict exists, should use outside lawyers.

Effective Claim Management

An insurer's claim management directly affects a claim representative's ability to handle claims in good faith. Claim management in this context refers to how claim departments are managed by claim managers and claim supervisors. Claim management involves many duties. Although every duty is important, these three are crucial to good-faith claim handling:

- Consistent supervision
- Thorough training
- Manageable caseloads

Consistent Supervision

Supervisors and managers should work with claim representatives frequently and consistently to ensure that claims are investigated, evaluated, and resolved promptly and accurately. Supervisors and managers are responsible for quality control and for ensuring that claim representatives follow proper claim handling practices. They should make notes in files to document their reviews and to provide instruction and guidance. If a supervisor recognizes delays or improper claim handling practices, he or she must act to correct the problems and document those actions.

Managers also have a responsibility to maintain proper claim handling standards and practices. They develop guidelines for claim handling and are ultimately responsible for ensuring that the guidelines are followed.

Supervisors and managers have more settlement authority (the authority to settle a claim up to a specified dollar amount) than claim representatives. Therefore, they should become involved in the settlement evaluation and strategy when the claim representative's settlement authority is exceeded.

Thorough Training

Insurers should provide continuous and consistent training for claim representatives relating to all necessary claim handling procedures and best practices as well as to good-faith claim handling. Training is essential when a claim representative handles a new type of claim or a more complex, serious claim for the first time. Claim representatives should make an effort to continually improve their competence in handling claims, and training is one way to improve.

Manageable Caseloads

Supervisors and managers must monitor the number of claims assigned to a claim representative (referred to as caseload or pending) to ensure that the work is manageable. Situations arise when caseloads increase, such as when one or more claim representatives leave the company or are out of the office for an extended period. At some point, a claim representative's caseload may become unmanageable and increase the possibility of a bad-faith claim. Supervisors and managers must monitor caseloads to identify potential problems and reassign claims or provide support to ensure good-faith claim handling.

Claim representatives who practice good-faith claim handling know their job is to properly and expeditiously resolve claims according to the facts, law, and policy language. They do not delay or minimize claim payments. Some insurers summarize good-faith claim handling as "doing what is right." Claim representatives who adopt this attitude are likely to avoid or reduce the occurrence of bad-faith claims.

SUMMARY

Two primary goals of the claim function are complying with the contractual promise and supporting the insurer's financial goals. The insurer fulfills its contractual promise to the insured through the claim handling process. Claim departments provide claim information that is used by marketing, underwriting, and actuarial departments to perform their functions. Additionally, the claim department must interact effectively with outside contacts, such as the public, lawyers, and state regulators.

Insurers and other insurance organizations have claim departments. Claim departments may be structured in various ways, but the structure should best serve the organization's needs. Claim personnel who handle claims may be staff claim representatives, independent adjusters, employees of TPAs, or producers. In addition, public adjusters handle claims by representing the interests of the insureds to the insurer.

Claim department performance can be measured by mathematical means such as loss ratio and combined ratio. It can also be measured qualitatively through the use of best practices, claim audits, and customer service comments. These performance measures are often tied to insurance regulations.

Claim representatives must be able to apply the information contained in the policy to the activities in the claim handling process. This process creates consistency in claim handling and helps ensure that claims are handled in a manner that conforms with legal and ethical standards.

Through the claim handling process, these activities are performed on every claim, to some degree:

• Acknowledging and assigning the claim
• Identifying the policy and setting reserves
• Contacting the insured or the insured's representative
• Investigating the claim
• Documenting the claim
• Determining the cause of loss, liability, and the loss amount
• Concluding the claim

Insurers and the claim representatives who work for them have a duty of good faith and fair dealing in claim handling. This requirement is imposed on insurers and claim representatives because of (1) the public interest in ensuring that insurers have the financial resources to pay claims and that they pay claims fairly and promptly, (2) the unequal bargaining power of the parties to the insurance contract, and (3) the insurer's control over the investigation and resolution of the claim. If insurers or their claim representatives do not live up to the standard of good faith and fair dealing, they are said to be acting in bad faith.

The definition of bad faith varies by state but can be generalized as any unfounded refusal to pay a claim. Courts have interpreted this definition in many ways, so claim representatives must be aware of the bad-faith law in every state in which they handle claims. Generally, a bad-faith lawsuit can be based on the claim representative's negligence or gross or intentional misconduct.

To use the defenses to bad-faith claims, the insurer and the claim representative must be able to show they acted in good faith. The claim file must contain documentation of a thorough investigation; a fair, prompt, and knowledgeable evaluation of the claim; and a documentation of good-faith negotiation. The file should reflect prompt and adequate communication among the parties to the claim, the insurer's consideration of legal advice, and adherence to the insurer's claim management practices. The file should also show compliance with federal statutes such as the Health Insurance Portability and Accountability Act of 1996, the Gramm-Leach-Bliley Act, the Sarbanes-Oxley Act, and the Fair Credit Reporting Act.

ASSIGNMENT NOTES

1. Form ISO HO 00 03 05 01, Copyright ISO Properties, Inc., 1999.

2. *Slater v. Motorists Mut. Ins. Co.*, 174 Ohio St. 148, 187 N.E.2d 45 (1962).

3. *Commercial Union Ins. Co. v. Liberty Mutual Ins. Co.*, 393 N.W.2d 161, 164 (Mich. 1986).

4. Quoted and/or adapted from Department of Health and Human Services, *OCR Privacy Brief*, available at the department's Web site: www.hhs.gov/ocr/hipaa/ (accessed October 17, 2005).

5. 15 U.S.C. § 6801 et seq. (2005).

6. 15 U.S.C. § 7201 et seq. (2005).

7. 15 U.S.C. § 1681 et seq. (2005).

8. "Bad Faith in the 90's: Successful Tactics & Strategies for Defending the Insurer," sponsored by The CPCU Society's Golden Gate Chapter, presented by Ropers, Majeski, Kohn & Bently, a Professional Corporation, San Francisco, p. 33.

Direct Your Learning ▶▶

8

Adjusting Property and Liability Claims

Educational Objectives

After learning the content of this assignment, you should be able to:

▶ Explain how and why the activities in the framework for handling property claims are accomplished.

▶ Describe the challenges of adjusting the following types of property claims:

- Residential dwelling claims
- Residential personal property claims
- Commercial structure claims
- Business income claims
- Merchandise claims
- Transportation and bailment claims
- Catastrophe claims

▶ Explain how and why the activities in the framework for handling a liability claim are accomplished.

▶ Describe the challenges of handling each of the following types of claims:

- Auto bodily injury liability claims
- Auto property damage claims
- Premises liability claims
- Operations liability claims
- Products liability claims
- Workers compensation claims
- Professional liability claims

▶ Given a claim, determine coverage for a loss using the framework for coverage analysis and the activities in the claim handling process.

Adjusting Property and Liability Claims

8

PROPERTY CLAIM HANDLING PROCESS

Claim representatives generally work mostly in either first-party property damage claims or in third-party bodily injury claims. Claim representatives apply a framework for handling claims, regardless of claim type.

Property claim representatives are primarily concerned with applying detailed insurance policy provisions to specific loss situations. Property claim representatives evaluate and settle primarily objective, quantifiable losses.

Claim representatives must answer these general questions as part of the property claim handling process:

- Who has an insurable interest? Who is an insured?
- What property is insured? Where is it insured? When is it insured?
- What are the covered causes of loss?
- What is the dollar amount of loss?
- What are the insured's duties after a loss?
- What procedures are used to conclude a claim?

The answers to these questions are determined by applying the insurance policy provisions to the specific facts of the loss. Answering these questions provides a framework for property claim representatives to use for all kinds of property damage claims.

Who Has an Insurable Interest? Who Is an Insured?

The first questions a claim representative must answer about a property claim are "Who has an insurable interest?" and "Who is an insured?" Property insurance protects people or organizations from loss of the value of their interest in property. Accordingly, an insurable interest in property is a prerequisite to asserting a claim under an insurance policy.

Interests in Property

Generally, anyone who would be financially harmed by the destruction of property has an insurable interest in that property. The simplest and most obvious example of an interest in property is ownership. A sole owner has complete interest in the property. However, numerous other interests, in addition to sole ownership, can exist, often simultaneously.

More than one person can own property simultaneously. Under joint owner-ship, two or more owners each have a complete, indivisible interest in the property. If one joint owner dies, ownership need not be transferred, because the other owner already has a complete interest in the property. Joint owner-ship between husband and wife is known as tenancy by entirety. Ownership in common involves two or more owners, each with an identifiable fractional financial interest in the property. Ownership in common is typical among partners.

A person or an organization can also have an interest in property that is not an ownership interest. Lessees of property have an interest in the use of the property for the life of the lease. Custodians of property, such as bailees, warehouse employees, and carriers, have an interest in the property to the extent of their fees and for their legal liability for the property's safe return to its owner.

Finally, security interests can exist in almost any property. Security interests are created by contractual agreement or by law. The secured party is generally a creditor of the property owner. A security interest is usually not evident by inspecting property. The secured party usually does not have possession of the property, and the property is not marked physically to show the interest.

Policy Requirements for an Insurable Interest

Rather than listing the existence of an insurable interest as a precondition to coverage, insurance policies simply limit payment on any claim to the extent of the insured's interest. For example, the HO-3 policy states the following under Section I—Conditions, A:

> ...we will not be liable in any one loss:
>
> 1. To an "insured" for more than the amount of such "insured's" interest at the time of loss; ...

The Business and Personal Property Coverage Form, under Loss Conditions, Loss Payment, Paragraph 4.d., states:

> d. We will not pay you more than your financial interest in the Covered Property.

Limiting claim payments to the extent of an insured's insurable interest and requiring all interests existing in the property to be specified are essential claim handling practices. Allowing the insured to collect more than its insur-able interest in the insured property would provide a great incentive for the insured to deliberately destroy the property.

Identifying all insurable interests in the property enables the claim representa-tive to treat every party fairly without compromising the insurer's rights. This also helps the claim representative identify other coverage on the same prop-erty. Whenever there are multiple insurable interests in property, each party might have its own insurance protecting its own interest. Parties with different interests who commonly have separate insurance policies are landlords and tenants, bailors and bailees, and mortgagors and mortgagees. Another party's property or liability insurance might reduce the claim payments of the investigating insurer. Policies contain provisions to uphold the indemnification concept, such as the "other insurance" and "subrogation" clauses.

Identification of Insureds

Claim representatives must carefully distinguish among a variety of people with rights and duties under a policy. A policy might identify a "first named insured," "named insureds," spouse of a "named insured," "insureds," and people whose property might be covered under a policy.

Generally, only the first named insured, named insured, or spouse of the named insured is entitled to make a claim. These specified individuals are likewise responsible for paying premiums and performing the insured's duties in the event of loss.

In the event of the named insured's death, a claim representative can settle claims with the named insured's legal representative, either the executor or the estate administrator. These legal representatives are included in most policies' definitions of "insured." Loss payees are parties, such as owners of leased office equipment, who do not have any rights greater than or independent of the insured, but the loss payee's name must be included on any claim settlement check.

Claim representatives must deal with the right parties to avoid paying the claim to the wrong person and to avoid invalidating any legal notices the insurer has given. Claim representatives can determine which parties to deal with because the policy declarations identify the named insureds. The policy also indicates who can make claims and who must perform the insured's duties in the event of loss.

For cases in which the insurer can deny coverage to the first named insured or to the named insured's spouse, the claim representative must carefully check the policy for the rights the other insureds might have. If the policy language is unclear about such rights, the claim representative should consult legal counsel.

What Property Is Insured? Where Is It Insured? When Is It Insured?

The second set of questions a claim representative must answer about a property claim includes these: "What property is insured?" "Where is it insured?" and "When is it insured?" Policy provisions about what property is covered, where it is covered, and when it is covered are straightforward and usually do not cause disagreement between the insured and the claim representative.

Property Type and Location

As part of determining what property is covered, claim representatives must understand the difference between real and personal property. The two types of property might be valued differently (actual cash value versus replacement cost), might have different limits of coverage, and might have different coinsurance requirements. Real property is land and everything attached to it, such as buildings. Personal property is everything not considered real property.

Fixtures are items of personal property that have become attached to and part of real property. In the event of a loss, the claim representative must determine whether a given fixture is real or personal property. Claim representatives can determine whether fixtures are real property by asking these three questions:

- How permanently attached to the real property is the fixture? (For example, a furnace is a fixture, but a window air conditioner is not.)
- Is the fixture well adapted to the real property? (For example, draperies that have been selected to match the interior decor of a particular room are real property, but non-custom window treatments are not.)
- What was the intent of the owner? (For example, the owner would expect that shelves bolted to the wall would be removed when a tenant moved, but that built-in shelves would not be removed.)

Policy Period

In addition to verifying the type of property and its location, claim representatives must also verify that the loss occurred during the policy period. All property policy conditions state that coverage applies only during the policy period stated on the declarations page.

What Are the Covered Causes of Loss?

The third question a claim representative must answer about a property claim is, "What are the covered causes of loss?" Most property insurance policies provide coverage only for direct physical loss. Claim representatives must, therefore, recognize indirect or nonphysical types of losses.

Direct and Indirect Loss

Direct loss concerns the amount of financial loss that is covered by the policy. Direct loss is damage to property caused by a covered cause of loss with no intervening cause. Examples include the failure of electrical components (refrigerator compressor, air conditioning unit, satellite system, and telephone) caused by a lightning strike to the home wiring or damage to the roof of an office building and its exposed contents caused by a windstorm. Often, the direct loss results in an indirect loss.

The most important type of indirect loss is loss of use of property. Coverage for loss of use is provided as part of the package of coverages in the typical homeowners policy. In contrast, some commercial property policies do not automatically provide loss of use coverage; in these policies, loss of use of property is covered only if the insured purchases such coverage.

Even when loss of use is covered, direct physical loss to property is required to trigger such coverage and to measure its duration. For example, coverage for loss of business income applies only when the loss is caused by a direct loss to covered property resulting from a covered cause of loss or when civil authorities close the business because of a hazardous situation nearby. Such coverage begins following a brief waiting period after the covered property suffers direct loss and usually ends when the same property should be repaired or replaced.

Physical and Nonphysical Loss to Property

Physical loss to property occurs when the property can no longer be used for its intended purpose because it has been destroyed or damaged, or has disappeared. Physical loss is tangible; it can be observed through the senses (seen, touched, and so forth). Physical loss to property that results from a covered cause of loss is generally covered by property insurance.

Nonphysical loss is intangible and includes loss of value to property not caused by physical damage or destruction, such as obsolescence, loss of market, investment loss, and financial fraud. Loss of market is a significant problem for claim representatives. Insureds who operate seasonal businesses and suffer losses at the busiest time of year frequently expect compensation for the diminished value of inventory that has not been sold because of their losses. Assuming such inventory has not suffered physical loss, its diminished value is generally not covered by property insurance.

Exclusions and Verification of Causes of Loss

Verification of some causes of loss can be complicated by several exclusions, including these:

- Gradual causes of loss—Gradual causes of loss include wear and tear, rust, decay, deterioration, latent defect, and rot. Property that has suffered loss from any of these excluded causes of loss might suffer a subsequent loss that is covered. A claim representative must determine how much damage was caused by gradual causes as compared to damage caused by a direct loss. For example, if a windstorm caused damage to a roof, but the joists on one corner of the roof had deteriorated from a leak in the aged roofing material, then the claim representative must determine the value of the property damaged by the leak as well as the value of the property damaged by the wind, and then handle the loss according to the terms of the policy.

- Ordinance or law—Local ordinances or laws might require the demolition of a damaged structure. The cost of demolition might be more than the cost to rebuild the structure. Additionally, local ordinances or laws might require construction plans, methods, or materials that are different from, and more expensive than, those originally used in the damaged structure. Generally, property policies do not cover these additional costs unless a special endorsement has been added to the policy.

- Faulty design, construction, or material—Losses caused by faulty design, construction, or materials are generally excluded from first-party property coverage. The additional coverage for collapse actually "gives back" coverage for faulty construction in limited circumstances, such as when the collapse occurs during construction, remodeling, or renovation.

- Intentional acts of the insured—The most obvious type of loss that is excluded from coverage is loss caused intentionally by the insured. Fires are the most common type of intentionally caused loss. Intentionally set fires are arson, whether committed by the insured or not. Arson can also be committed for revenge, in the commission of a crime, or by vandals. In those cases, innocent property owners are entitled to insurance coverage.

What Is the Dollar Amount of Loss?

The fourth question a claim representative must answer about a property claim is, "What is the dollar amount of loss?" Insurance policies do not specify how claim representatives should determine the amount of loss. For property claim representatives, this question begins the step in the claim handling process that determines damages.

Policies usually value property at replacement cost or actual cash value. However, policies do not explain how "replacement cost" can be determined or what "actual cash value" might mean (for example, does it differ from "cash value" or "value"?).

Replacement Cost

Replacement cost settlement provisions spare claim representatives the difficulties of determining actual cash value and convincing the insured to agree with that value.

The claim representative and the insured must identify the property precisely using these details:

- For personal property, the manufacturer's name, product description, and exact model or style numbers must be determined.

- For real property, the exact measurements and descriptions and an exact specification of the type and quality of materials are necessary.

Once the property has been fully identified and described, the claim representative must determine the cost to replace it at the time of loss. The amount the insured originally paid for the property (which is generally less than the replacement cost) is irrelevant. The cost at the time of loss should be the amount at which the insured can buy the item of personal property.

If the exact type of property damaged or destroyed is no longer available, the claim representative can make settlement based on property of like kind and quality. Specific models and styles of goods are frequently discontinued. However, similar items are usually available, often from the same manufacturer. Settlement on the basis of such goods is rarely a problem with the insured, as long as the goods are of similar quality.

Determining replacement cost for building damage requires construction estimates. Proper estimates are based on these factors:

- Specifications—Specifications state precisely what must be done, including whether to repair or replace the property, the exact type of materials, and the quantity of materials in exact dimensions or count.

- Materials—The total quantity of materials is determined based on the specifications. Material prices are based on prevailing material costs for projects similar to that required by the insured's loss. Bulk discounts cannot be considered unless such quantities are needed.

- Labor—The hours of labor required for a particular job depend on the amount and type of material to be installed and the working conditions. Skilled estimators can calculate labor amounts fairly accurately. Additionally, published "standard" work rates are generally regarded as fair. For example, such rates might indicate that wallpaper can be hung at 200 square feet per hour.

- Overhead—Overhead represents the contractor's fixed costs of doing business or fixed specific costs attributable to the job. Examples include office space, telephones, insurance, permits, and job site offices. Generally, overhead is calculated as a percentage of the cost of the job, usually 10 to 15 percent, depending on a contractor's circumstances. Costs that are specific to the job, such as permits, might simply be added in.

- Profit—Contractors are in business to earn a profit. The amount computed for overhead is not profit. Overhead represents real costs for the contractor. Once overhead costs have been added to the job costs, profit is calculated as a percentage of total costs.

Computer software is available to help claim representatives or contractors prepare estimates. The claim representative or contractor specifies the work to be done, the measurements, and the quantities, and the computer calculates the total cost of materials and the total hours and cost of labor, and determines the total estimate.

Insurance policies generally do not permit replacement cost settlements until the property has been repaired or replaced. Such policy provisions exist to prevent unjust enrichment of the insured and to discourage intentional losses. Nevertheless, the insured might need funds to pay a contractor or merchant before repair or replacement is complete.

The claim representative will either (1) release an actual cash value settlement to the insured, with the balance paid upon complete repair or replacement or (2) parcel out a replacement cost settlement as repair or replacement is gradually accomplished. Either of these approaches should be satisfactory to the insured.

Actual Cash Value

Actual cash value (ACV) is usually calculated as replacement cost minus depreciation. Claim representatives applying this formula must have a sophisticated understanding of depreciation. Although the formula is generally appropriate, claim representatives must realize when it is not.

Depreciation

The reduction in value caused by the physical wear and tear or technological or economic obsolescence of property.

Depreciation represents loss of value. It is not limited to physical wear and tear, although physical wear and tear is obviously an important consideration in determining the depreciation of certain property, such as carpeting. When physical wear and tear is the chief cause of depreciation, claim representatives usually apply straight-line depreciation, by which a fixed percentage of the property's value is deducted for every year of the property's useful life that the owner has enjoyed.

Aside from physical wear and tear, obsolescence is the main cause of depreciation. Obsolescence is caused by changes in technology and fashion and can have much more sudden and dramatic effects on the value of property than physical wear and tear. Clothing in last year's styles, even if untouched by wear and tear, has lost significant value. Property for which technology advances rapidly, such as electronics and computers, also loses value quickly.

Claim representatives frequently rely on published guides to determine depreciation. Individual insurers have created such guides based on their experience. Trade groups have published guides for items such as clothing and household furnishings. Guidebooks are primarily useful as a starting point for discussing depreciation caused by wear and tear. In many situations, the published rate of depreciation is perfectly appropriate; in others, it might not be.

As long as depreciation is understood to represent loss of value of any type, the "replacement cost minus depreciation" approach for actual cash value is usually appropriate. However, it is not appropriate in all circumstances.

Application of the "replacement cost minus depreciation" approach requires an ascertainable figure for replacement cost. Sometimes, no such figure exists. For example, antiques cannot be produced and sold new. Old buildings may feature construction methods that are no longer used. Finally, many claim representatives mistakenly infer that the "replacement cost minus depreciation" approach allows only for deductions from the replacement cost. Certain property, such as some collectibles, is known to appreciate in value.

Some courts have defined actual cash value to mean fair market value. The fair market value of an item reflects both the "replacement cost minus depreciation" approach and the possibility that an item is irreplaceable. The market valuation of antiques and objects of art is generally regarded as fair. Additionally, a well-functioning market considers obsolescence and any other factor that affects value.

A well-functioning market for a type of property determines market valuation. Unfortunately, no substantial secondary market exists for many common items of property, such as used clothing, which most people regard as relatively valueless. This situation is evolving with the advent of online outlets that deal in used items. Claim representatives should not apply market valuation unless a well-functioning secondary market exists.

Other courts have avoided definitions based strictly on a formula of actual cash value. These courts have required claim representatives to consider numerous factors that affect the value of the property, including physical wear and tear, obsolescence, market value, and any other relevant factors. This approach is known as the **broad evidence rule**.

Broad evidence rule
A court ruling explicitly requiring that all relevant factors be considered in determining actual cash value.

Deductibles

Applying a deductible is a simple matter when a loss is otherwise fully covered. The deductible amount is subtracted from the amount of the loss, and the insured is paid the remainder. However, applying deductibles to a loss that is not fully covered is more difficult.

When a coinsurance penalty reduces the recoverable amount of loss, the insured benefits by having the deductible applied first.

Deductible Illustration With Coinsurance Penalty

Loss = $10,000

Actual Amount of Coverage = $60,000

Required Amount of Coverage = $80,000

Deductible Applied First

$10,000 − $100 deductible = $9,900

$$\frac{\$60,000}{\$80,000} \times \$9,900 = \$7,425.$$

Coinsurance Applied First

$$\frac{\$60,000}{\$80,000} \times \$10,000 \text{ loss} = \$7,500$$

$7,500 − $100 deductible = $7,400.

Claim representatives should apply the deductible before coinsurance unless the policy explicitly states otherwise. The commercial building and personal property (BPP) form is an example of a policy that states otherwise. A loss might also not be fully covered because of the application of a sublimit.

Stated Values and Agreed Amounts

Some property policies are written on a scheduled basis, such as personal articles floaters and homeowners policy endorsements designed for scheduled property. Individual property items might be listed separately with a value assigned for each, or the property might be listed by class, such as cameras, furs, or jewelry. Some coverages provided on personal articles floaters are on a stated amount basis. The stated amount is typically determined by appraising the insured's property or reviewing a sales receipt for the property in question. In the event of a loss, the insured is entitled to no more than the least amount of (1) the property's actual cash value, (2) the cost to repair or replace, or (3) the applicable amount of insurance.

Agreed amount

A method of valuing property in which the insurer and the insured agree on the property's value at the time the policy is written and that states the amount in the policy declarations as the amount the insurer will pay in the event of a total loss to the property.

Fine arts and valuable papers are usually insured on an **agreed amount** basis. In the event of a loss, the insurer agrees to restore the property to its condition before the loss or to pay the agreed amount. The distinction between these types of property and those covered on a stated amount basis is that the more valuable property is typically impossible to replace.

Repair or Replace Option

Claims are generally settled with money. Occasionally, claim representatives prefer to settle claims by repairing or replacing the property as the policy allows. Claim representatives might prefer not to repair or replace property because doing so opens a new area for potential disagreement with the insured. The insured might expect the insurer to guarantee the repairs or certify the quality of a replacement item.

Claim representatives choose the repair or replace option whenever it is significantly less expensive to do so. It might be less expensive to perform repairs or provide a replacement item when the insurer has discount purchasing arrangements through local contractors and retailers. Insurers frequently replace jewelry through wholesale channels. Repairing or replacing the property enables insurers to eliminate the financial incentive some insureds have to file unfounded claims. Insurers can also settle the claim with money based on the insurer's cost to replace the item.

Appraisal Clause

The appraisal clause found in every property insurance policy is used solely to settle disputes over the value of the property or the amount of loss. Claim representatives who work for years in property claims might never participate in an appraisal, but this does not mean that the clause is unimportant.

The appraisal clause prompts the insured and the claim representative to meet the requirements of the appraisal procedure. The claim representative provides the insured with estimates from contractors and other supporting documentation. The insured provides similar information to the claim representative. The claim representative and the insured, or the contractors working for them, negotiate their differences and usually reach an agreement. The possibility of an appraisal procedure in which an impartial umpire settles the dispute gives both sides an incentive to negotiate in good faith.

What Are the Insured's Duties After a Loss?

The fifth question a claim representative must ask about a property claim is, "What are the insured's duties after a loss?" Every property insurance policy indicates the duties the insured must perform after a loss. These duties are policy conditions. An insured is not entitled to loss payment unless these duties have been performed. The insured's performance of duties following a loss helps the claim representative to verify the extent and the dollar amount of the loss and to protect against fraudulent or exaggerated claims.

Provide Prompt Notice

Obviously, nothing can be done with a claim until the insured notifies the insurer of the loss. The insured need not provide notice in any special form or in any special wording. The insured does not even have to give written notice; a telephone call suffices.

Although policies do not require the insured to give notice in any particular form, they do require that the notice be "prompt." A claim representative cannot properly investigate and evaluate a loss after too much time has passed. The prompt notice requirement rarely becomes an issue between insureds and insurers. Nevertheless, lack of prompt notice (as well as breach of other policy conditions) is an issue, for example, when the insured repairs or replaces property before ever notifying the insurer of the loss.

In case of loss by theft, the insured is required to notify the police. In most states, it is a felony to submit false reports to the police, so the insured's duty to report thefts and other criminal violations discourages fraudulent claims. The BPP requires the insured to notify the police if a law is broken, which includes the occurrence of a possible theft. The common-sense interpretation of the BPP limits this duty to violations of *criminal law* only.

Homeowners policies provide coverage for lost or stolen credit cards. The insured must, however, notify the credit card or funds transfer card company. Thereafter, the insured is not liable for improper and unauthorized charges. Should the insured fail to notify the credit card company, the insurer is not liable for any charges incurred after a reasonable time during which notice could have been given.

Protect Property

The insured is required to protect the property from further loss by making emergency repairs (such as covering a damaged roof with a tarpaulin) and by implementing emergency safeguards. Such measures are a reimbursable part of the loss (subject to policy limits) as long as they are "reasonable" and "necessary."

The insured usually seeks pre-approval of such measures from the claim representative. Claim representatives agree to approve these requests because they limit the loss. Nevertheless, the insured is obligated to take "reasonable" and "necessary" measures regardless of whether the claim representative's approval has been obtained. Failure to do so might void coverage for any subsequent loss that results.

Assist With the Loss Adjustment Process

Insureds have several duties that help expedite and conclude the claim settlement process. They must inventory all damaged property and, under certain policies, all undamaged property as well. The inventory must include quantities, values, and amounts of loss and might be required as part of, or independently of, the proof of loss. Without such an inventory, the claim representative would have difficulty organizing and analyzing the loss to personal property and would have to deal with continual additions to the claim for personal property.

The insured must show the damaged property to the claim representative. The purpose of this requirement is to preclude claims based on photographic or verbal evidence and to discourage exaggerated or fraudulent claims.

The insured must also allow books and other records to be inspected. The claim representative might personally inspect the insured's books or hire an accountant to do so. The evidence in an insured's books and records is often essential to verify the existence and value of property. For example, property is often destroyed in all-consuming fires or as a result of theft.

Some insurance policies require the insured to cooperate. For example, among the insured's duties in the event of loss, the BPP lists the duty to "cooperate with us in the investigation or settlement of the claim." The absence of such a duty in other policies means that the insured has no general duty of cooperation, although the lack of such a duty does not usually create any problems for the claim representative. The specifically listed duties—and, in particular, the duty to submit a proof of loss—are sufficient for the claim representative to obtain whatever is necessary from the insured.

Provide Proof of Loss

The proof of loss is a powerful adjustment tool, yet it is often not used, or is misused, by claim representatives. It is the insured's official version of the loss. Because the proof of loss is signed and sworn to, all statements it contains are material and, if false, are grounds to void the coverage. The formality of the proof of loss impresses insureds with the importance of the statements made within it.

In a proof of loss, the insured is typically required to specify the time, place, and cause of loss; the interests in the property; any other insurance on the property; and detailed estimates, inventories, bills, and other documentation that prove the loss. The proof of loss should contain all of the information necessary for the claim representative to settle the claim, including an exact dollar figure for the loss.

Once a proof of loss has been submitted, the claim representative must respond promptly. Many states have laws specifying the number of days following receipt of a proof of loss that a claim representative has to either accept or reject the proof of loss or to tell the insured specifically what is further required.

A claim representative who rejects a proof of loss should do so in writing and should state specific reasons for the rejection. The rejection letter should explain that the claim cannot be settled without a proper proof of loss and should ask the insured to submit a new proof if possible and still timely.

Many insurers routinely waive the proof of loss. On uncomplicated claims, doing so expedites settlement. The danger to insurers of routinely waiving proofs of loss on simple, straightforward losses is that claim representatives might not spot nonroutine cases soon enough to implement the proof of loss requirement, waiving valuable rights.

Some claim representatives require the insured to complete a proof of loss only at the claim's conclusion. At that point, the claim representative has presumably already agreed with the insured about the amount of settlement. However, to be most effective, the proof of loss should be required early in the adjustment process. On the other hand, a proof of loss that is completed after settlement is still a sworn statement of material fact and therefore could be the basis of a fraud defense.

Submit to Examination Under Oath

Insurers rarely require an examination under oath, but when they do, they usually suspect insured fraud.

The examination under oath is a policy condition that the insured must fulfill, if required by the insurer. The insurer might require an examination even though the claim is not being litigated. The insured might have counsel present, but such counsel cannot interrupt, object, or ask questions. Although claim representatives can conduct examinations under oath themselves, they are almost invariably conducted by a lawyer working for the insurer and helping the insurer prepare its fraud case.

An examination under oath is usually conducted after the insured completes and submits a proof of loss. The proof of loss commits the insured to a certain story, and the examination under oath allows the insurer to clarify that story.

What Procedures Are Used to Conclude a Claim?

The sixth question a claim representative must ask about a property claim is, "What procedures must be followed to settle the claim?" This determination is the final step in the claim handling process. Regardless of how a claim is investigated, it involves doing three things:

- Determining the cause of the loss
- Determining the amount of the loss
- Documenting the cause and amount of the loss

Claim representatives perform one or some combination of these actions when they receive a new claim:

- Accept the insured's word and settle the claim accordingly
- Hire experts to investigate the claim or refer it to a special investigative unit (SIU)
- Personally investigate the claim

Determining the Cause of Loss

A claim representative may accept the insured's word and settle the claim accordingly if there were no extenuating circumstances, there was no question that the said loss occurred and that fraud was not a factor, and the loss was properly documented. However, circumstances and the amount of the claimed loss may require a full investigation.

For some claims, the claim representative might hire an expert to complete the claim investigation. For example, when extenuating circumstances appear in an auto accident, such as when discrepancies between witness statements are apparent, when accident scene reconstruction is required, or when special evidence investigation is needed. In these cases, an expert in accident reconstruction may be better able to investigate and ascertain the events that led to or contributed to the accident. Some insurers use SIUs in similar cases and when circumstances are suspicious or fraud is suspected. SIUs have special training and resources available to detect suspicious behaviors, evidence tampering, and fraud. In many cases, the claim representative recognizes the need for an expert or SIU after personally beginning the claim investigation.

A claim representative may personally investigate the cause of a loss by inspecting the damaged property, taking the insured's statement, or both.

By personally inspecting the damaged property, the claim representative determines how the property has been damaged and identifies the property for purposes of verifying coverage. The effects of causes of loss such as fire, smoke, lightning, windstorm, hail, explosions, and vandalism are usually obvious, and a brief inspection can verify coverage.

When a claim representative takes the insured's statement, it is recorded even though a statement is informal compared to the proof of loss or examination under oath. In some states, taking the insured's statement might preclude a subsequent proof of loss or examination under oath. When taking the insured's statement, the claim representative asks about the cause of loss, any other interests in or liens on the property, other insurance, steps taken to mitigate loss, documentation of the extent of loss, and any subrogation possibilities.

Determining the Amount of Loss

A claim representative who personally determines the amount of a loss must take careful, detailed inventories of personal property to specify the exact quantities and types of property and must prepare estimates for losses to buildings.

Most claim representatives leave the item-by-item preparation of a personal property inventory to the insured. The claim representative spot-checks the physical property or verifies the information using the insured's books and records. The claim representative must check the physical property sufficiently to determine appropriate depreciation.

A claim representative who prepares estimates must have extensive knowledge of construction practices, material prices, and labor allowances. Such claim representatives usually have their own library of materials catalogs, manufacturers' price lists, and construction trade association guides.

A claim representative also develops a methodology for taking thorough specifications at a loss site. For example, a claim representative might take all outside measurements first; then go inside to take room measurements; and, finally, determine all mechanical and electrical specifications. Completed estimates are usually organized by room or by trade, such as demolition, frame carpentry, finish carpentry, drywall, painting and decorating, plumbing, and electrical.

Documenting the Cause and Amount of Loss

When claim representatives investigate and gather the information necessary to determine the amount of settlement checks, they should simultaneously create files that enable others to understand the claim, including the cause and amount of loss. All pertinent information should be in the file. Insurers need complete and accurate claim files to justify settlement payments, to audit claim procedures and claim-handling quality, and to transfer cases among claim representatives. Insurers, state insurance regulators, and reinsurers require complete and accurate claim files.

Determining Salvage Value and Subrogation Rights

Claim representatives can minimize the insurer's losses by salvage and subrogation activities. Whenever an insurer pays the insured the full value of personal property that has suffered a loss, the insurer is entitled to take ownership of the property and can subsequently resell it. Any amount realized in the sale reduces the cost of the claim. Taking the salvage value of property that has been "totaled" is the insurer's option. The insured cannot require the insurer to pay full value for damaged property and then keep the salvage. Claim representatives do not reduce the amount of a loss settlement because of the value of expected salvage. Instead, if salvage value is apparent, insurers usually pay full value to the insured and handle the salvage themselves.

Ordinarily, claim representatives do not directly market salvage. They either sell or consign the property to professional salvage companies. The markets for salvaged property are specialized, variable, and irregular. Even insurers that frequently sell salvageable property from their losses find that they cannot compete in salvage markets. Salvage companies typically sell property on consignment for expenses incurred plus a percentage commission.

An insurer might have subrogation rights when a party other than the insured is responsible for causing the loss. When an insurer pays an insured for a loss under a policy, the insurer is substituted (subrogated) for the insured and obtains the insured's rights against any responsible party. Handling a claim involving potential subrogation is no different for a claim representative than handling any other claim, except that the claim representative must be especially thorough in establishing and documenting the cause of loss and might notify the responsible party of the liability claim.

If the responsible party has liability insurance, the claim representatives for the respective insurers can negotiate a settlement. However, if the two insurers cannot agree on a settlement amount, a subrogation claim is likely to be handled through the nationwide arbitration system operated by Arbitration Forums, Inc. Although an arbitrated agreement applies only to claims between signatory parties and amounts of $100,000 or less, the agreement keeps many claims out of court. Settlements under this agreement are fair and are far less expensive than court settlements.

When an insurer obtains a recovery through subrogation efforts, it must first pay the attorneys' fees and other expenses of subrogation, and then reimburse the insured for any deductible or any other amount of loss not covered. The insurer receives the remaining recovery amount.

HANDLING SPECIFIC TYPES OF PROPERTY CLAIMS

Handling losses for damage to particular types of property can be challenging. What is important in handling claims for residential structures may be unimportant when settling claims for commercial structures or common carriers, and vice versa.

Claim representatives deal with different challenges when handling losses involving different types of property. Each type of property loss raises specific issues that must be addressed through the claim handling process. Additionally, certain types of claims require special considerations that can present claim handling challenges.

Each of these types of property claims poses unique challenges for a claim representative:

- Residential dwelling claims
- Residential personal property claims
- Commercial structure claims
- Business income claims
- Merchandise claims
- Transportation and bailment claims
- Catastrophe claims

Residential Dwelling Claims

Handling losses on people's homes may be the most rewarding job in the property-casualty industry. Protecting people from the financial and emotional devastation that can follow the destruction of a home is perhaps the insurance industry's most crucial task.

Claim representatives who handle losses to homes have two goals: (1) to address the insured's concerns and (2) to enforce policy provisions and protect the insurer's rights. Generally, little conflict exists between these goals, provided the loss is not suspicious and the claim representative and insured continually communicate and cooperate.

Insured's Concerns

Most insureds who suffer a loss to their home have never experienced such a loss before. As a result, the emotional trauma of seeing their home damaged is compounded by uncertainty and anxiety about their insurance and the claim handling process. Many insureds fear that an inadvertent error on their part might somehow void their coverage.

Following a serious loss to a home, a claim representative should have three priorities:

- Assisting the insured in ensuring the physical safety of the insured's family
- Assisting the insured in ensuring the safety and security of the damaged home and its contents to prevent further damage
- Explaining the coverage and the claim handling process to the insured

If doubts about coverage exist, the claim representative can issue a reservation of rights letter and begin to address these priorities immediately.

Sometimes insureds escape from their burning home with nothing but the clothes on their backs, which might be pajamas. A claim representative who deals with the insured at such a time can provide reassurance that the coverage extends to living expenses and replacement of personal property and issue an advance on the settlement amount on the spot.

Once the insured's family and property are secure, the claim representative should thoroughly explain the coverage and the claim handling process and answer any questions. This communication should take place at the first contact with the insured after the loss. The claim representative should immediately communicate the existence or non-existence of coverage for living expenses and emphasize the importance of the insured's good-faith compliance with policy conditions. The claim representative should address the insured's questions so that the insured knows what he or she should do the next day, the next week, and the next month.

Additional Living Expense

In the time immediately following a loss to a residence, insureds appreciate additional living expense coverage because it helps to normalize their condition by paying for increased living expense after a loss.

The claim representative should explain the scope of additional living expense coverage, if the policy provides for it, and emphasize to the insureds that they must obtain and keep receipts. Furthermore, although it is best to have receipts for everything, the insured must understand that compensation is only for *additional* living expense. Most insureds can quickly grasp that normal living expenses for which they would be responsible even without the loss are not compensable. The claim representative explains that coverage is limited to the insured's normal standard of living. Insureds should be encouraged to check with the claim representative before making a doubtful expenditure.

The insured's residence must be uninhabitable (because of a covered loss) before additional living expense coverage is available. With large (total) losses, the inhabitability of a residence is obvious. With other losses, whether a home is inhabitable might be harder to judge. Claim representatives can best answer this question by asking themselves whether they would expect their own family to live in a place damaged as badly as the insured's home. For example, the stench of smoke might make a home uninhabitable, at least until it can be ventilated or fumigated. The loss of only a refrigerator or a stove probably does not make a home uninhabitable, but the loss of an entire kitchen or a sole bathroom probably would. Loss of a furnace (during a cold season) or a water heater might also make a home uninhabitable, depending on the specific circumstances.

Contractors

Damage to the insured's home is determined based on estimates. The insurance policy obligates the insured to provide proof of damages.

Contractors engaged by the insured should prepare detailed estimates that clearly show specifications; material costs; hours; costs of labor; and additional expenses, such as overhead, permits, and demolition and debris removal. Estimates that show only grand-total costs or trade-by-trade total costs are not suitable for claim settlements because it is impossible to see how such estimates differ from other estimates and to negotiate those differences.

Most claim representatives prefer to negotiate differences in estimates directly with contractors because these individuals routinely handle construction issues. Estimates are likely to differ regarding specification of the work to be done, quality of materials, or hours of labor. Once the quality and hours have been specified, the costs of materials and labor can be determined.

Some insurers allow claim representatives to recommend contractors to insureds. Such recommendations help insureds who might otherwise not know honest, competent contractors who are interested in insurance repair work. However, making such recommendations creates some real dangers for the insurer. The insured might interpret the claim representative's recommendation as a guarantee that the contractor's estimate will be accepted or that his or her work will be of good quality. Furthermore, some insurers fear that allowing claim representatives to make recommendations might lead to claim representatives' receiving kickbacks and gratuities from contractors. Usually, if the claim representative is going to recommend contractors, he or she will recommend two or three and let the insured make the final decision. This is appropriate because the contract will be between the insured and the contractor.

Restoration and Cleaning Services

Initially, many losses, especially losses caused by smoke and water damage, look far worse than they actually are. Although many types of water damage are not covered, water damage resulting from fire-fighting activity is covered (under the fire cause of loss) and is often a significant problem. Both smoke and water can cause increasingly worse damage to property the longer they remain untreated. Furthermore, smoke and water cause little or no damage to certain types of property if they are removed quickly. Professional cleaning and restoration services are available for such removal.

Although the claim representative can take an "arm's-length" approach to the insured's selection of a contractor, the claim representative must quickly become involved in hiring a professional cleaning and restoration service. Claim representatives and insurers typically have contacts with such services, so arrangements can be made quickly for them to work at the scene of a loss.

The claim representative may agree on the scope of the work needed and the price with the service providers and then obtain the insured's authorization for those providers to begin work immediately. Rapid work by such services can save a great deal of property, minimize additional living expense, and reduce repair costs. Sometimes, cleaning alone is sufficient, even though early observations may have indicated that repainting would be necessary, and, sometimes, repainting alone is sufficient, even though it was thought that replacement would be necessary.

Residential Personal Property Claims

Claims for loss to residential personal property present claim representatives with some difficult challenges. Frequently, proof that the property existed and that it was lost is scarce. Evaluation is difficult to do with any confidence or accuracy. Policy sublimits apply for certain types of property. The dollar amount of such claims is often small, so the claim representative must constantly be aware of the adjustment costs relative to the value of the damaged property.

Inventory

Damaged personal property is usually available for the claim representative's inspection unless fire or theft caused the loss. Unfortunately, fire and theft are two of the most common causes of loss affecting personal property. The insured must prepare an inventory, even when personal property is burned beyond recognition or is stolen.

Most homeowners do not have written records of their personal property. Few people can provide an accurate account of all the clothes they own. Often they cannot remember where or when various items were bought. Despite the often minimal evidence of personal property, claim representatives cannot refuse to settle such claims.

In most instances, the claim representative can jog the insured's memory by going through a checklist of types of property. Included in such a checklist might be major furniture in each room, clothes (by category) for each person in the household, drapes, rugs, towels and linens, kitchen appliances and utensils, food and liquor, pots and pans, dishes, televisions, radios, stereo equipment, tapes and compact discs, telephones, power tools and hand tools, gardening equipment, office supplies and books, home computers, toys, framed pictures and art objects, sports equipment, bicycles, firearms, and jewelry.

Depreciation

Homeowners generally can produce no better evidence of their property's depreciation than of its existence. Sometimes they can remember where they made major purchases, and those stores might have exact records to provide evidence of purchase dates.

In the absence of specific evidence of the age or condition of property, certain assumptions can be made. Clothes wear out and are subject to fashion obsolescence at a predictable rate. Carpets become threadbare after a certain number of years. Kitchen appliances have a limited lifespan; kitchen utensils and pots and pans last longer. Major furniture can last a long time if it is not subject to abuse and is of classic styling. Insureds and claim representatives can usually agree on reasonable assumptions of depreciated value.

Sublimits

The claim representative should explain the rationale of **sublimits**: some property is especially vulnerable to theft (for example, cash, jewelry, and firearms), and large coverage limits for such property would greatly increase the exposure to loss and the insurance premium. Other property (boats, valuable papers, and business property) is often covered by specialized policies.

Sublimit

A policy provision that imposes smaller limits for certain kinds of property or lines of insurance.

Scheduled Property

When the insured has special coverage for individual items of property, the claim representative often has more loss settlement flexibility than with ordinary personal property.

Insureds often schedule coverage for individual property because the property is valuable, and insureds want the broader causes of loss or risks of direct physical loss typically associated with scheduled items. Scheduled coverage usually identifies the property precisely. Consequently, the claim representative can contact merchants and appraisers who specialize in such property to determine whether it can be repaired, whether it can be replaced through a secondary market, how much its value has decreased because of a loss, and whether the insurer can buy replacements at discount. Jewelry, camera equipment, and firearms are the types of property for which the insurer is likely to exercise its "repair or replace" option, because the insurer might be able to buy an exact replacement for less than the insured originally paid. The high value of these items also makes their repair far more feasible than for lower-value property.

Commercial Structure Claims

Handling claims for losses to commercial structures is usually limited to highly skilled and experienced claim representatives because the value of commercial structures can easily reach millions of dollars. Additionally, experienced claim representatives are needed to deal with complex issues such as alternative methods of property repair and the value of depreciated property. Rarely can a claim representative handle losses to commercial structures without expert assistance. Investigating arson and considering the loss of use coverage for commercial structures is also more complex than it is for residential dwellings.

Architects and Contractors

Claim representatives with substantial experience and expertise in estimating residential losses are not necessarily able to estimate losses for commercial structures. Construction principles, methods, materials, and available contractors differ for commercial and residential structures. For commercial construction, the claim representative may have to employ an architect to review building specifications.

Architectural plans dating from the building's construction may still be available. Those plans can provide valuable information about a building's details if a serious loss has occurred. They can also serve as the basis of reconstruction of the destroyed building. Even with such plans, claim representatives might have to hire an architect to identify changes in building codes or suggest alternatives to obsolete construction features and building techniques. An architect can develop precise cost estimates or hire professional estimators to do so.

Local contractors might not be adequate for reconstructing certain commercial structures. They might lack sufficient expertise, equipment, or staff for a large or complicated structure. The insured or his or her architect might have to solicit bids from contractors throughout the region or the country. The claim representative cannot necessarily settle the claim based on the lowest bid for the work. The low bidder might be lowest because the contractor's lack of experience caused a faulty estimate. The architect can help the claim representative identify which bidders are responsible, capable, and reasonably priced.

The claim representative must remember that the insurer's duty is to settle the claim with the insured, not to engage a contractor to perform the actual reconstruction. The claim representative solicits bids from contractors to help evaluate the loss. Only the insured should enter into contracts for the construction work.

Property's Actual Cash Value

The value of commercial structures is more variable than that of residences. Additionally, commercial structures are more likely than residences to significantly depreciate because of factors other than wear and tear.

The principle of supply and demand determines the value of a commercial structure. A portion of a structure's value depends on the profit a business derives from its use, or demand. The remainder of the structure's value depends on the cost of rebuilding that structure or of obtaining an alternative location, or supply. When demand is strong and supply is low, the value of commercial structures rises significantly. Alternatively, when demand is weak and supplies are high, values decline.

The demand for commercial structures fluctuates with the overall economy and with business conditions in particular industries. The more specialized a building is, the more the demand for its use parallels economic conditions in a particular industry. For example, the value of an auto assembly plant corresponds more to the demand for autos than to the value of other commercial structures.

The supply of commercial structures is characterized by frequent shortages and oversupplies. This phenomenon is caused by the amount of time required to build commercial structures. In times of shortage, buildings are planned that might not be completed until an oversupply of similar buildings exists.

A claim representative evaluating the actual cash value (ACV) at the time of loss of a commercial structure must consider market conditions. The market might be such that the replacement cost of a structure has appreciated significantly since the structure was built. If so, the insured should be compensated appropriately. Alternatively, the value of a structure might have depreciated significantly.

Although commercial structures experience wear and tear, other significant causes of depreciation exist. Commercial structures are more susceptible than residences to economic and technological obsolescence. For example, an old warehouse might still be useful but less desirable than a new warehouse because its floor space is divided by pillars, its lighting is inadequate, its access roads and parking lots are in poor condition, its loading dock is not well designed, and its heating and ventilation are obsolete. Though still in use, the older, obsolete structure has far less value per square foot than a new structure. This difference is usually easy to document through commercial realtors. Realtors can quote the likely rental values of an old property and a new property. The difference in rental rates is a good gauge of depreciation.

The extent of depreciation an insured has taken in its financial records is irrelevant. Because financial depreciation reduces taxes, insureds take it as fast as the tax laws allow. Therefore, most buildings have less actual depreciation than the amount recorded in the insured's financial records.

Problems With Mortgageholders

Commercial mortgage agreements usually make the mortgage amount completely due and payable upon the destruction of the structure.

During depressed markets for commercial properties, mortgageholders might see an insurance claim as their opportunity to collect the remaining mortgage. Therefore, the mortgageholder might ignore the owner's desire to rebuild the structure and want to be paid in full. The claim representative cannot resolve this problem because it is between the structure's owner and the mortgageholder. This is often more of a problem for commercial structures than it is for residential dwellings. The claim representative must include the names of both the owner and the mortgageholder on the claim settlement check and keep both parties advised of the settlement. Beyond these actions, the claim representative has no obligation to either party.

Contamination and Pollution Cleanup

Serious losses at commercial structures, especially at manufacturing and storage sites, might result in contamination and pollution. Claim representatives should be concerned about such losses for these three reasons:

- The claim representative's own health and safety might be at risk from exposure to pollutants at the loss site. Firefighters might be obligated to notify the Environmental Protection Agency (EPA) or state environmental agencies of contaminated loss sites. When such agencies are involved, the claim representative should avoid the site until notified that entry is safe.

- The coverage for pollution cleanup is extremely limited in most policies. The claim representative must be familiar with these limitations and communicate them to the insured. Nevertheless, pollution caused by a covered cause of loss is often covered.

- The claim representative should have contacts with specialized technical services that can help the insured to decontaminate a site. The claim representative should not recommend such a service unless its cost is covered or unless the insured provides clear acknowledgment (preferably in writing) of being responsible for such costs. Although these technical services are expensive, they can often devise solutions that might be more practical, less expensive, and faster than EPA solutions.

Arson Investigation

Arson is the intentional burning of property, either by the property's owner or by someone other than the owner. If a third party is responsible, it may or may not be at the owner's direction. The claim representative must prove three things to establish arson of an insured structure: (1) incendiary fire, (2) motive, and (3) opportunity.

When arson is suspected, the claim representative will engage an origin and cause expert to prove the incendiary nature of the fire. Motive and opportunity can be investigated by a special investigative unit (SIU).

The main focus in cases of suspected arson is on the arsonist's motive. Such motive is usually economic, especially if the insured is a suspect. Economic motive might exist even for a structure used regularly, provided the insured would be better off financially with the insurance settlement and vacant real estate. However, arson can also be motivated by anger or revenge, which is often the case when the arsonist is not the property owner.

Often in cases of suspected arson, the insured structure is owned by a failing business in need of cash. Such need can be established by having an accountant examine the insured's financial records. Indeed, considering the seriousness of the matter and the amount of money at stake, a claim representative should not consider asserting an arson defense without a solid accounting report that establishes motive.

Business Income Claims

Claim representatives regard business income claims as highly complex. Proper settlement of cases involving them requires detailed analysis of financial records. Nevertheless, claim representatives can organize and simplify their task by remembering their goal of returning insureds to essentially the same financial position they would have been in had the loss not occurred and concentrating on these issues:

- Identifying the best loss settlement approach
- Determining business income loss
- Determining the period of restoration
- Determining extra expense amounts
- Consulting accountants to determine amounts

When settling business income claims, claim representatives may also have to determine extra expense amounts and use accountants to analyze data.

Identifying the Best Loss Settlement Approach

Business income claims can be settled prospectively or retrospectively. **Prospective settlements** are desirable when the insured does not intend to repair the property or intends to make significant alterations. The insured can request a prospective settlement and is not required to wait until the property is repaired and operations resume before concluding the settlement. Provided the insured and the claim representative agree on all relevant loss data, settlement can be made immediately.

Prospective settlements
Settlements made before property has been repaired.

Retrospective settlements are probably more common. Once the property has been repaired and the insured has resumed operations, the amount of time taken to make repairs and the expenses incurred during the interruption are known. Furthermore, during the interruption of business, the insured is probably so preoccupied with reopening that the business income loss settlement becomes a secondary concern. Disagreements between the insurer and the insured on the period of restoration are also more likely with retrospective settlements. Insurance covers only the time in which repairs should be made, not necessarily the amount of time taken to complete the repairs.

Retrospective settlements
Settlements made after property has been repaired and the policyholder has resumed operations.

Determining Business Income Loss

Business income is most easily understood when placed within the framework of business accounting. A business determines its profit (or loss) by subtracting its expenses from its revenue. Revenue consists mainly of sales. Expenses consist of the cost to acquire the goods the business sells plus all other costs. For retailers, the cost of goods is called "cost of goods sold" and represents the cost to the retailers of acquiring goods from their suppliers. For manufacturers, the cost of goods is their own manufacturing cost.

Business income
Sum of (1) net profit or loss that would have been earned or incurred if the suspension had not occurred and (2) normal operating expenses, including payroll, that continue during the suspension.

A business that completes a Business Income Report/Work Sheet, which lists projected figures, can determine the likely amount of its business income. This amount can be understood as either (1) revenue minus cost of goods sold minus discontinued operating expenses or as (2) net profit (or loss) plus operating expenses that continue. These two amounts should be equivalent. Typically, both claim representatives and insureds find it easier to approach a loss settlement based on the first formula.

A claim representative cannot directly use the Business Income Report/Work Sheet to settle a claim because the work sheet lists projected amounts, but the claim should be settled based on actual loss data. Using the actual loss principle might seem to conflict with the prospective approach to settlement. For a prospective settlement, the claim representative and the insured make new projections of what the insured's loss of business income is likely to be for the expected period of restoration. Any actual experience that has developed since the insured completed the work sheet should be used to make the best projection of the actual loss of business income.

Determining the Period of Restoration

Period of restoration

The period during which business income loss is covered under the BIC forms; it begins seventy-two hours after the physical loss occurs and ends when the property is (or should have been) restored to use with reasonable speed. (With regard to extra expense coverage, it begins immediately after the physical loss occurs.)

The **period of restoration** is defined to compel the insured to make repairs and resume operations with due diligence and to allow for settlement when the insured neither makes repairs nor resumes operations.

The time in which repairs should be made can be determined by consulting with the contractors hired to do the work. Claim representatives must remember that any such estimate from a contractor, even if made in good faith, is still an estimate. Contractors cannot control weather, interruptions in the availability of supplies or of subcontractors, or subcontractor behavior.

Many claim representatives and insureds prefer to settle business income claims only after the repairs have been completed. However, at that point, the claim representative and insured might disagree over whether the insured used due diligence to complete the work. Generally, claim representatives do not penalize insureds for delays caused by factors beyond their control. Claim representatives also do not penalize the insured for any delays caused by the settlement of the underlying property damage claim because such delays could be caused by the insured, the claim representative, or both.

Determining Extra Expense Amounts

Claims for extra expense can be settled only retrospectively. For coverage to apply, extra expenses must be incurred to avoid or minimize the suspension of business. For example, a retailer might lease a temporary selling location to maintain sales. An insured could profit if a claim representative paid extra expense based on projections. In addition, claim representatives cannot adequately monitor whether insureds use the payments appropriately.

Extra expense might also be incurred to repair damaged property and is covered *to the extent it reduces the business income claim*. A claim representative can authorize expedited construction methods or relatively expensive contractors if doing so reduces the business income loss.

Consulting Accountants to Determine Amounts

Probably no type of claim requires as much use of accounting assistance as business income claims. Most claim representatives are not trained to analyze the hundreds of entries that record individual transactions of an ongoing business. Claim representatives cannot review historic data and determine the insured's "normal" operating expenses.

Consequently, some accounting firms specialize in claim work. These firms understand the policy coverages and can explain them to the insured's accountant. Claim representatives find that business income claims run smoothly when one of these accounting firms is hired to work with the insured's accountant.

Merchandise Claims

Merchandise that an insured holds for sale is a special type of business personal property. Its valuation raises unique issues: it offers the best opportunities for salvage and use of salvor services, and its claims must be settled in special ways.

Merchandise Valuation

The replacement cost of merchandise is the insured's cost to replace that merchandise. The insured usually has ongoing relations with its suppliers and can provide accurate information about their prices. If the insured regularly obtains discounts from its suppliers, the effective cost to the insured is less than what appears on supplier invoices. Replacement cost of a manufacturer's finished goods is the cost of manufacture.

Actual cash value standards can be difficult to apply to merchandise. Often, the goods have not depreciated, and actual cash value is equivalent to replacement cost. Depreciation caused by ordinary wear and tear is uncommon, but many goods suffer "shop wear." They are picked over and handled by so many people that they are no longer presentable as first-quality goods.

Merchandise is also subject to significant depreciation caused by obsolescence. Fashion changes, technological changes, and seasonal selling patterns can all cause an inventory to become obsolete. Insurance is not designed to reimburse for such loss of value. A claim representative can identify obsolete merchandise even if he or she is unfamiliar with the product. If, before the loss, the insured was offering the product to the public at a discounted price or had stopped offering it altogether, the product has likely suffered obsolescence. In fact, good accounting practice requires that the inventory value of merchandise be reduced whenever its listed retail price is reduced. The claim representative can note such an accounting approach by the insured and can cite it as justification for settling claims at the reduced inventory figure.

Salvage

Other than vehicles, merchandise is the only significant source of salvage for the insurance industry. Claim representatives and insurers rarely try to sell salvaged merchandise themselves; they employ professional salvage firms.

Salvage proceeds from the sale of damaged merchandise can be significant. Some merchants refuse to deal in damaged goods, no matter how superficial the damage. These merchants refuse to consider a loss settlement based on a percentage of the goods' value because in those merchants' markets, the goods are "worthless." Claim representatives find it easiest to settle with such merchants for 100 percent of the goods' value and to take the merchandise for salvage.

Professional salvage firms can act quickly to protect goods from further damage, inventory and separate goods, and give advice to claim representatives about the likely amount of residual value in damaged goods.

Reporting Form Losses

Inventories of merchandise are often insured under reporting form policies that require the insured to submit regular reports of value. Claim representatives who handle claims for such merchandise must know what to do when the insured underreports its values or fails to report the values promptly. These rules are based on Insurance Services Office, Inc.'s value reporting form.

Following a loss to merchandise insured under a value reporting form, the claim representative must determine the value of the insured's inventory as of the date of the last report. The claim representative is not concerned with the inventory's value on the date of loss unless the inventory is totaled. Inventory analysis for a past date might require an accountant's assistance. If the insured underreported its inventory's value, the insured cannot recover the full loss amount. The insured can recover only the percentage of the loss that is equal to the percentage of inventory value it reported.

If the insured fails to submit a report when due, then the claim representative does not pay more than the amount last reported, which might penalize the insured. However, should the insured fail to submit even the first required report, the claim representative pays only 75 percent of the original reported value of the inventory, which always penalizes the insured.

Importance of Negotiation

Claim representatives sometimes settle merchandise losses based on a percentage of their value. Under these settlements, the merchant keeps the merchandise and is reimbursed for its decreased value. The claim representative is not required to pay full value for the merchandise or to dispose of salvage. Claim representatives should try to negotiate such settlements with insureds because they are mutually beneficial.

For example, suppose that following a merchandise loss, the claim representative believes that salvage of the damaged merchandise would yield about 35 percent of its insured value. However, because the merchant is already organized to sell such merchandise, it may be able to sell the merchandise for a much higher percentage of value, perhaps 55 percent. In such a case, the claim representative has two options. He or she could total the merchandise and sell it as salvage for a net loss of 65 percent, or the claim representative could try to negotiate a settlement with the insured for some percentage less than 65 percent. The insured might be willing to take as little as 45 percent, because the insured believes it can still realize 55 percent by selling the merchandise itself. Any settlement figure between 45 percent and 65 percent is fair to both parties.

This situation is common in merchandise losses. Each party must assess the situation accurately to negotiate effectively. The claim representative can get advice from a salvor or negotiate based on personal experience with similar losses. Sound negotiating by the claim representative does not disadvantage the insured. An insured who is knowledgeable of the value of the merchandise can refuse unfavorable settlement proposals. The insured can invoke the appraisal clause or challenge the claim representative to total the merchandise and try to realize the expected salvage value.

Transportation and Bailment Claims

Property is frequently in the possession of someone other than its owner. Losses to such property create complicated legal and insurance policy coverage issues. Claim representatives might have to handle claims for either the property owner or the party in possession of the property. A claim representative must carefully review the coverage, the law, and the contracts between the parties in these situations.

The most common circumstances in which property is in the possession of someone other than its owner are transportation and bailment situations. Carriers such as trucking companies, railroads, and air freight companies are in the business of transporting other people's property. Bailments include situations in which owners entrust their property to bailees such as cleaners, repairers, and warehousers. Bailment relationships are contractual, and the applicable contracts can affect both insurance coverage and legal liability.

Insurance Coverages

Claim representatives handling transportation and bailment claims must orient themselves to the applicable insurance policy. Insurance policies exist for both the owner and the other party involved. Policies written for motor truck carriers, bailees, warehouse workers, and others might provide certain coverage for other parties. Therefore, claim representatives might settle a claim for one party under a policy that names another party as the insured. For example, a claim representative might settle losses under a dry cleaner's policy for the dry cleaner's customers rather than for the named insured—the dry cleaner.

Policies for carriers and bailees typically protect the interests of both the owner and the carrier/bailee. A claim representative handling claims under a carrier/bailee policy must usually settle two claims arising out of the same property loss: the owner's and the carrier/bailee's. The carrier/bailee has an interest in the property to the extent of its earned fees. Additionally, the carrier/bailee might be legally liable to the owner for the property's return.

A carrier/bailee's insurance policy that extends liability for the owner's property requires the claim representative working for the carrier/bailee's insurer to settle the owner's claim. Most policies of this sort allow the claim representative to deal directly with the owner and allow the insurer to defend the carrier/bailee against the owner's claim rather than to pay it. Some carrier/bailee policies protect the owner regardless of the carrier/bailee's legal liability. Such policies are purchased to maintain customer goodwill. Owners expect to be reimbursed for damage to their property without hairsplitting over legal liability. This quasi-first-party coverage allows the claim representative to deal immediately with the owner before conducting an investigation of legal liability.

Legal Liability

Because the relationship between the owner and the carrier/bailee is contractual, the terms of the contract between the parties also affect legal liability between them. In the absence of an agreement to the contrary, the law makes common carriers liable for damage to an owner's goods. The only exceptions to this liability are for acts of God, war, negligence of the shipper, exercise of public authority, and inherent vice of the goods.

Bill of lading

A document acknowledging receipt of goods from the shipper, given by the carrier which includes the terms of the contract of carriage for the goods.

Released bill of lading

A bill of lading that limits the carrier's liability for cargo loss in return for charging a lower freight rate than would be charged for carrying the cargo subject to full valuation.

Carriers usually specify the dollar amount of their liability in their **bill of lading**. An owner or a shipper with a large loss exposure can use a **released bill of lading** to avoid paying high insurance rates for the carrier's increased liability. Claim representatives handling losses in shipment must review the applicable bill of lading.

Other bailees are generally liable to the owner only for their own negligence. Should a loss occur without any negligence on the bailee's part, the owner must bear the loss. Therefore, owners with significant off-premises loss exposures must obtain special coverage. A bailee's coverage might not apply.

As with a transportation contract, a bailment contract can modify the parties' respective legal rights. A bailment contract might limit the dollar amount of a bailee's liability or might make the bailee strictly liable. A claim representative handling an owner's claim against a bailee for legal liability must read and understand the bailment contract. To the extent that the bailee's liability is limited, so, too, is any coverage for the owner that is based on liability.

Furthermore, the subrogation rights of the owner's insurer might be limited. Most property insurance policies allow the insured to waive subrogation before a loss occurs. A claim representative who has paid a claim under an owner's insurance might find that the insured/owner has waived the bailee's liability beyond a certain dollar amount. Such a waiver likewise limits the insurer's subrogation rights.

Catastrophe Claims

Hurricanes, floods, tornadoes, earthquakes, and fires or explosions causing widespread damage affect entire communities. The insurance industry's response in helping communities recover from catastrophes provides an opportunity to gain goodwill. Property claim representatives' response to catastrophes includes pre-loss and post-loss planning.

Pre-Loss Planning

Claim departments would be overwhelmed by catastrophes if they did not plan for them. They must respond to catastrophes by having a sufficient number of claim representatives in potential disaster areas while maintaining acceptable service throughout the rest of the country.

Certain areas of the United States, such as the Gulf and Atlantic coasts during hurricane season, are most likely to "host" disaster recovery teams. Claim offices in these areas should prepare kits that include forms, maps, telephone directories, temporary licenses, tape measures, clipboards, calculators, and anything else a visiting claim representative needs to operate in a disaster area. Although state insurance regulators vary as to how strictly they enforce licensing requirements following a catastrophe, every claim representative who is likely to be called into an area should be licensed.

The insurer's administrative departments must be prepared to rent office space; have telephones, copy machines, desks, and other equipment installed; and procure temporary living quarters and rented cars on short notice.

Local agents or the underwriting department must establish a system by which claim representatives can confirm coverage simply and reliably.

Post-Loss Planning

Claim representatives on "storm duty" must work long hours and be separated from their families and normal lives for lengthy periods. Additionally, catastrophes cause the claim representative to modify normal claim handling procedures. Claim representatives often pay claims with less documentation than usual. They might also reimburse the insured for the insured's own labor in cleaning up the property, a circumstance that is especially common following catastrophes. Claims that would normally require an in-person inspection might be handled by telephone.

Local agents should be familiar with the insurer's claim practices so they can advise insureds on how to begin loss recovery. The agents should advise insureds of what documentation they must maintain and what actions they should take immediately after a loss.

Contractors' services might be offered at a premium after a catastrophe. However, contractors from around the country flock to the disaster area to help mitigate the shortage. Insureds should be advised to be very careful about paying advanced fees to unknown contractors. Unscrupulous persons might take advantage of people who are shocked, confused, and suddenly holding cash.

LIABILITY CLAIM HANDLING PROCESS

Liability claim handling differs so significantly from property claim handling that many insurer claim operations are organized separately into either property or liability coverage units.

For personal insurers, liability claim handling might consist primarily of handling third-party auto, homeowners, or personal umbrella liability claims. Insurers servicing commercial customers might have the same claim department personnel handle auto liability and general liability claims, while workers compensation and auto physical damage claims are organized into separate units within the claim department.

Claim personnel usually specialize in handling property or liability insurance claims. Once coverage has been established, resolving liability claims depends more on determining legal liability and damages than on an insurance policy's terms. Legal liability and damages exist apart from insurance policy terms.

Liability insurance policies protect the insured against the financial consequences of legal liability. Therefore, liability claim representatives spend most of their time and effort investigating and evaluating the legal aspects of liability and damages and relatively less time than property claim representatives enforcing and evaluating insurance policy terms.

In liability claims, the insured is not the person making the claim. The party making a liability claim against the insured is the claimant. This party is also referred to as the third party. The insurer has no contract with, and the liability claim representative has no contractual obligations to, the third-party claimant. Although most insurers consider it to be both ethical and in their own best interests to deal with claimants promptly and responsively, the claim representative has more leeway in dealing with a third-party claimant than with the insured.

Liability claims include both property damage and bodily injury liability. Although liability claims for property damage exist, they represent a relatively minor percentage of the total dollars paid on all liability claims. The predominantly injury-oriented nature of liability claims distinguishes their settlement from property damage claim settlement. The evaluation of bodily injuries by both claimants and claim representatives is more subjective and uncertain than the evaluation of property damage, and, therefore, negotiation plays a greater role in settling bodily injury claims than it does in settling property damage claims.

Handling a liability claim entails four steps, which are not necessarily completed sequentially:

• Determining coverage
• Determining legal liability
• Determining damages
• Negotiating and settling the claim

Because all claims cannot be negotiated successfully, claim representatives must know how to guide a claim through the courts as part of the litigation process, and they must understand their role in the insurer's duty to defend its insureds.

Determining Coverage

The first step in the liability claim handling process is determining coverage. The essential coverage clause of most liability insurance policies is simple. For example, Coverage A of the Commercial General Liability (CGL) form states, "We will pay those sums that the insured becomes legally obligated to pay as damages, because of 'bodily injury' or 'property damages' to which this insurance applies."[1] Therefore, any type of bodily injury or property damage for which the insured is allegedly liable is covered, unless it is specifically excluded.

When determining coverage, claim representatives are primarily concerned with the possible application of exclusions. Nevertheless, the essential coverage clause raises important issues. Under Coverage A of the CGL, the claim must be for "bodily injury" or "property damage." Under most auto liability coverages, the claim must also arise out of the use of certain autos by certain individuals. Therefore, a claim that is not for "bodily injury" or "property damage" or that does not arise out of the use of certain autos or autos being used by specified individuals is not within the essential coverage provisions.

Claimant's Allegations

When a liability claim is first presented to a claim representative, the facts might be unknown or disputed. Without knowing the facts, how can a claim representative determine coverage?

The claimant's allegations determine coverage, even if those allegations are disputed and even if they are eventually proved untrue. Liability policies protect the insured against legal claims and the cost to defend them, regardless of whether the claims are valid or groundless. Protection against false, unproved, and unprovable claims is a crucial part of the protection provided by liability insurance policies. A claim representative determining coverage must first consider the claimant's allegations at face value even if those allegations might not be covered or if coverage might be doubtful.

Coverage Problems

Claim representatives face difficulty whenever coverage for a claimant's allegations is doubtful. This difficulty occurs when some aspects of a claim are covered and others are not, and when coverage for the entire claim is questionable. Clear communication with the insured and prompt action by the claim representative are essential to protect both the insured's and the insurer's interests. Whenever coverage is doubtful or not applicable to part of a claim, the claim representative must explain to the insured clearly, in writing, why this is so and what both the claim representative and the insured must do.

If part of a claim is clearly not covered, the claim representative must explain to the insured why it is not, with reference to specific policy provisions. The claim representative must explain that the insurer will continue handling the claim but that the insured might have to contribute to an eventual settlement or judgment. The claim representative should invite the insured to engage a private lawyer in the claim. Usually in these situations the insured neither involves a private lawyer nor contributes to a settlement. This is so because part of the claim is covered, and the insurer must continue to defend the claim and must pay any applicable settlement unless part of the claim is clearly not covered. Because most liability claims are settled without clearly specifying the basis of liability or the elements of damages, the insurer usually pays the entire settlement.

When coverage for the entire claim is doubtful, the claim representative must explain to the insured why, in writing, and must explain what the claim representative will do. The claim representative usually investigates further. Pending this investigation, the claim representative reserves the insurer's right to deny coverage should the facts so indicate. After issuing a letter advising the insured of a coverage problem and reserving the insurer's rights, the claim representative must promptly investigate and make a coverage determination. If coverage is found to apply, the insured is informed. If coverage does not apply, a prompt letter of denial is forwarded to the insured.

Insurers can resolve coverage questions through declaratory judgment actions in court. These actions result in a court declaration of the rights of parties. Many jurisdictions allow courts to declare rights of parties whenever a controversy arises in the investigation of a claim. However, declaratory judgment actions have drawbacks. They are likely to generate thousands or tens of thousands of dollars of legal expense; therefore, they are not feasible for small and moderately sized claims. Furthermore, in many jurisdictions, declaratory judgment actions do not move through the courts any faster than other cases. A declaratory judgment that takes years to attain does not serve its purpose. The insurer has to pay to defend the insured throughout that time and might have had to settle the claim in the meantime. Filing a declaratory action, if unsuccessful, also complicates the defense of the underlying action.

Whenever coverage does not apply to a claim, the insured should receive a written explanation, and a copy should be sent to the producer. If a lawsuit has been filed, the insured must be told exactly how much time he or she has to file a response with the court. Additionally, a claim representative should direct the insured to engage a private lawyer.

Bodily Injury and Property Damage

As noted, liability insurance policies usually apply only to claims for bodily injury or property damage. The most likely exception is the personal injury coverage of the CGL, which extends to damages that are not limited to bodily injury and property damage. Lawyers often use the term "personal injury" to refer to bodily injury claims as defined in insurance policies. In insurance, "personal injury" refers to specific policy coverage for defamation, false arrest, advertising injury, and malicious prosecution.

Generally, insureds submit claims only for bodily injury or property damage. However, not all insureds have a clear understanding of what their insurance covers, and so they often submit any claim in the hope that it might be covered. Therefore, claim representatives occasionally encounter claims for damages other than bodily injury or property damage.

Money damages are an appropriate remedy for both bodily injury and property damage and are normally included in the relief sought in a lawsuit. Lawsuits that seek only injunctions, and not money damages, are generally not for bodily injury or property damage. A claim representative must be careful not to deny coverage too hastily in a lawsuit seeking injunctive relief. This is true especially for claims of interference with use of property and claims of ongoing bodily injury. Because loss of use of property is included within the definition of "property damage," a lawsuit based on such alleged damage might be covered.

Lawsuits alleging breach of contract resulting only in financial harm or lawsuits alleging financial fraud are more clearly not covered, because they do not concern claims for bodily injury or property damage. Likewise, regulatory fines or minor criminal fines are not property damage and are not covered.

Claims for emotional injury only, without physical bodily injury, present more difficult coverage issues. Generally, if the court cases of the applicable jurisdiction allow a tort claim based on emotional injury only, then an emotional injury would constitute bodily injury for coverage purposes. Increasingly, more jurisdictions accept emotional injury as bodily injury.

Intentional Acts

Because insurance is designed to cover accidental events, liability insurance policies generally exclude coverage for the insured's intentional acts. This is an important exclusion for claim representatives because claimants often allege that the insured acted intentionally.

Applying this exclusion is difficult because claim representatives must uncover the answers to two questions: (1) Did the insured intend the result of his or her action or merely intend to commit the action without contemplating the injurious outcome? and (2) Can intentional acts be excluded when the claimant also alleges negligence or strict liability on the insured's part? An additional question can be, "Is the insured liable for the intentional acts of an agent or a servant, if the insured is vicariously liable?"

Claim representatives cannot rely on the intentional act exclusion unless they are familiar with the law in their state regarding its meaning. For example, in some states, an assault might not be excluded as an intentional act unless the insured intended the resulting harm. This standard makes the exclusion much harder to apply than in states that consider an intentional assault covered as long as the insured intended to commit the assault. States that require an indication that the insured intended the harm do not require that the insured intended the precise harm that occurred. Furthermore, the intent to cause harm might be inferred from the commission of the assault. Unfortunately, an insurer cannot deny coverage, hoping that a court infers intent.

Applying the intentional act exclusion is difficult when the claimant also alleges negligence or strict liability on the insured's part. Based on the claimant's allegations, part of the claim is covered, and part is not. In such situations, the insurer must defend the insured. If the opportunity arises, the claim representative might also have to settle the claim completely. Upon settlement, no distinction is made between which parts of the settlement are for which allegations. The case is settled as a whole, and coverage issues cannot be resolved in a settlement.

The same problem exists even when a case is litigated to a verdict. In a few states, courts require juries to identify damages awarded count by count. Otherwise, the verdict is expressed as a single sum of money and does not resolve any coverage issues. Sometimes the insurer can prove through a lawsuit's discovery process that the insured must have intended the behavior, and this evidence could be the basis for denying coverage. However, an insurer taking this approach is acting contrary to the insured's best interests and must do so through a separate lawyer. The lawyer hired by the insurer to defend the insured cannot simultaneously work for the insurer to prove that the insured acted intentionally.

Contractual Obligations

Generally, liability insurance does not guarantee that insureds will perform their contractual agreements. However, claim representatives cannot deny coverage for all claims based on breach of contract. Contractual obligations are frequently involved in covered claims.

The consequences of a breach of contract might be covered even if the breach itself is not. For example, a contractor might be hired to erect a wall. Should the contractor do the work negligently and the wall collapse on a person, the cost of rebuilding the wall (the contract's subject) would not be covered, but bodily injury to the person would be. Claim representatives frequently encounter this type of claim.

Certain contractual obligations might be directly insured by liability policies. For example, the CGL excepts from its contractual exclusion (therefore provides coverage for) contractual liability assumed in a lease and contractual liability assumed for another's torts for bodily injury or property damage. Both of these contractual obligations affect coverage.

As with claims involving alleged intentional acts, claims of contractual breach might be combined with claims of negligence or strict liability. Such claims generally involve products or professional liability. The breach of contract aspect of these claims is usually incidental. Claim representatives handling such claims often realize that they will not differentiate between the intentional act and the contractual breach so they do not inform the insured that part of the claim should technically not be covered. Failure to so advise the insured is equivalent to granting coverage for the entire claim. Claim representatives should follow good-faith claim handling practices in deciding whether the insured should be notified of the part of the claim that is not covered.

Property Under the Insured's Control

Insureds often submit claims for property damage to another's property that has been damaged while in the insured's care, custody, or control, possibly while the insured was working on it. Such property damage is clearly excluded from coverage by the typical liability insurance policy.

Insureds are usually not aware of what is or is not covered. Claim representatives can identify care, custody, or control situations with minimal investigation. They can then usually direct the insured to the first-party coverage that deals with these situations.

Property damage to the insured's product itself, to the insured's work itself, or to property that the insured has sold or given away is likewise excluded from typical liability policies. However, claims for consequential bodily injury and damage to another's property are usually covered. Claim representatives frequently encounter these situations and must carefully distinguish between bodily injury and property claims that are covered and those that are not.

Determining Legal Liability

The second step in the liability claim handling process is determining legal liability. This section describes the procedures a claim representative follows to determine legal liability. Proper investigation is essential in determining legal liability. The ability to conduct a complete and proper investigation is one of the core skills of claim handling.

The claim representative's investigation is guided by the facts that must be established to determine legal liability. These facts are dictated by the legal principles applicable to the situation. Many legal principles are relevant to claim handling, including tort liability, criminal liability, contractual liability, statutory liability, and vicarious liability. This section describes these principles as they apply to claim handling and describes the defenses that can be asserted against liability claims.

Investigation

A claim's initial report usually states nothing more than, "Insured involved in auto accident at 10th and Washington," or "Claimant fell at insured's store." The claim representative must gather the additional facts.

The claim representative organizes the investigation according to what information is needed and what is most important. For example, regarding the loss reports previously cited, the claim representative would want to know the potential claimants' names, addresses, and telephone numbers and whether any of them were injured. After learning these facts, the claim representative would want to know each claimant's account of the accident. When a claimant's account of an accident is committed to a statement, he or she cannot easily change it later.

A claim representative should also obtain the insured's account of the accident. The insured is required to cooperate and usually is eager to do so. The claimant might exaggerate, embellish, or falsify his or her account if not questioned promptly. In addition to preserving evidence, prompt contact reassures the claimant about the insurer's responsiveness and greatly reduces the chance that the claimant will hire a lawyer.

Taking statements from witnesses is standard practice with liability claims. A good statement has a proper introduction of both the witness and the claim representative and systematically covers all relevant facts. A claim representative should even cover areas with which the witness is likely to be unfamiliar. Having a witness respond "I don't know" prevents that witness from later inventing evidence on the same point. As long as a witness is available to testify, a statement given out of court cannot be used as evidence, except for impeachment.

Claim representatives also collect evidence in other forms, such as police reports, photographs and diagrams of accident scenes, and products or objects involved in claims. Evidence should be collected promptly to preserve the accident scene or the product before changes occur. For example, skid marks wear away quickly. Such evidence is useful for checking the credibility of witness statements and to provide direct evidence of what happened. A police report should never substitute for the claim representative's own investigation unless all parties agree about the facts of the accident.

Obtaining all of the relevant evidence is the most important aspect of any investigation. Once all evidence has been gathered, the claim representative must evaluate its credibility and must decide what most likely happened. Claim representatives should continually evaluate the credibility of evidence as it is received.

Claim representatives quickly learn that in many cases, the "truth" is never known for sure. All that is available is evidence, and one piece of evidence can contradict another. The best the claim representative can do is to evaluate the relative credibility of the evidence. Although the evidence credibility might not be the same in every case, it is the basis for decisions on the outcome of claims.

Tort Liability

A tort is a civil wrong not arising out of breach of contract. Some torts, such as assault, can also be crimes, and others, such as professional malpractice, can also be breach of contract. Generally, though, the law provides a remedy for torts because the wrongdoer (called a tortfeasor) has behaved in a manner that falls below acceptable legal standards and has caused bodily injury to another or damaged another's property.

Negligence is the usual basis of tort liability. Claim representatives and lawyers use the term "negligence" to refer both to negligent behavior and to a cause of action in negligence. A cause of action in negligence requires a legal duty owed to the claimant, a breach of that duty that causes harm, a causal connection between the breach and the harm, and actual bodily injury or damage on the claimant's part.

When a person has failed to behave carefully and prudently, that person has likely breached a duty of care. Negligent behavior is common. A claim representative investigating a claim involving potentially negligent behavior usually proceeds by investigating what the insured could have done differently to prevent the accident. If the insured could have reasonably avoided the accident, the insured is probably negligent. Violations of certain laws, such as traffic laws, are deemed negligence per se. These laws are designed to fix the standard of care for all people subject to the law. Anyone who drives must observe the traffic laws, and failure to do so is negligence.

It is not enough for the bodily injury of a person to be "caused by" another for compensation to result; **proximate cause** (or legal cause) must also exist. This legal concept requires that an unbroken chain of events must link the "cause" and the injurious "event." Although "proximate" means close, a proximate cause is not necessarily physically close or close in time to its outcome. The

Proximate cause

A cause that, in a natural and continuous sequence unbroken by any new and independent cause, produces an event and without which the event would not have happened.

proximate cause requirement protects a wrongdoer from responsibility for remote, unforeseeable consequences. Proximate cause is most likely questioned when the injurious outcome is also caused by intervening negligence. The intervening negligence could eliminate proximate cause between the original negligence and the injurious outcome.

Damages are an essential part of an action in negligence. Unless negligent behavior causes bodily injury or property damage to another party, the wrongdoer escapes any legal consequences.

Tort liability can also be based on behavior other than negligence. Intentional torts include assault, battery, false arrest, false imprisonment, conversion (theft), defamation, trespass, and fraud. Although many of these torts are crimes and all involve intentional conduct, a claim representative cannot assume they are excluded. Indeed, personal injury coverage includes many of these torts. Convicting the insured of a crime is generally conclusive evidence that a tort was committed.

Torts can also be based on strict liability (or "absolute liability"), which is liability that exists regardless of whether the insured was negligent. The term strict liability is often used in regard to products liability claims and is imposed because some defense, such as improper use of the product, might be available. Strict liability is generally imposed for activities such as operating aircraft, storing explosives, or having wild animals on premises, even if they have been tamed—such as in a zoo or circus. For such hazardous activities, the possibility of a loss is almost inevitable, and persons who engage in these activities are held liable for damages regardless of fault.

A claim representative investigating tort liability must know all of the elements of the tort(s) in question so that tort liability can be recognized. Claimants are unlikely to say, "I have an action in negligence against your insured." Instead, they say, "I fell and was injured at your insured's store."

Criminal Liability

Criminals are legally liable in civil courts to their victims. As noted, criminal acts are generally intentional, but that does not automatically mean they are excluded by insurance.

Anyone, including a convicted criminal, who seeks insurance coverage for a victim's claim is required by the insurance policy to cooperate with the insurer. Claim representatives frequently find that convicted criminals are not cooperative even though they have a duty to be so. Those accused of crimes are often unable to cooperate with the claim representative if doing so jeopardizes their Fifth Amendment rights.

A convicted criminal's lack of cooperation might have little practical significance. A conviction is conclusive evidence that the crime was committed. Therefore, the criminal's cooperation would not help to defend the claim. A claim representative handling a claim filed against a convicted criminal must often concede liability, but not necessarily coverage. In the case of an accused insured, the claim representative can usually wait until the criminal proceedings have concluded before demanding the insured's cooperation. Criminal cases generally proceed much faster than civil cases, so the insurer is usually not prejudiced by the claim representative's waiting.

Contractual Liability

A party who breaches a contract is legally liable to the other party to the contract. If such breach causes bodily injury or property damage, the breaching party's liability insurance might cover the claim. As noted, certain contractual obligations might be covered by liability insurance.

In cases of alleged breach of contract, the claim representative must thoroughly review the entire applicable policy. The claim representative must investigate the insured's behavior to determine whether it constitutes a breach of contract. Finally, the claim representative must investigate all potential contractual defenses. Did the claimant breach the contract first, thereby excusing further performance by the insured? Did a precondition for the insured's contractual obligations not occur or fail to be met? Did the insured and the claimant substitute a new contract for a previous one?

In cases of contractual **hold-harmless agreements** and **assumptions of risk** clauses the claim representative must scrutinize the contract to determine whether it applies to the situation in question. Courts interpret such contracts narrowly, and a claim representative should do so as well. For example, a hold-harmless agreement must specifically state the circumstances under which the insured is not legally liable for a loss and the situation must fall within those circumstances or the contract would be disregarded and the insured would be liable.

Statutory Liability

Except for workers compensation, insurance is generally not designed to cover an insured's statutory obligations. (Workers compensation laws create an obligation for employers even when negligence is not an issue.) Nevertheless, should a statute violation cause bodily injury or property damage, the insured's liability coverage might apply. For example, violating a traffic law and injuring someone is covered by auto liability insurance.

Not all statutory violations that cause bodily injury or property damage are covered by liability insurance. For example, intentionally dumping pollutants is excluded. A claim representative handling a case involving an alleged statute violation must determine what the statute requires, what the insured did, and whether any insurance policy exclusion applies.

Hold-harmless agreement (or indemnity agreement)
A contractual provision that obligates one of the parties to assume the legal liability of another party.

Assumption of risk
A defense to negligence that bars a plaintiff's recovery for harm caused by the defendant's negligence if the plaintiff voluntarily incurred the risk of harm.

Vicarious Liability

Frequently, claim representatives must investigate the possibility of vicarious liability, which is liability imposed on a party because of that party's relationship to a wrongdoer. For example, employers might be liable for the acts of their employees, and principals might be responsible for the acts of their agents. Most claims against commercial insureds involve vicarious liability because corporations are legal entities that act through their employees.

For claim representatives, the most important issue regarding vicarious liability is the scope of employment or agency. An employer is liable for the acts of its employees only while they are acting within the scope of their employment. For example, if an employee goes home and assaults a neighbor, the employer is not liable. Unfortunately for claim representatives, the scope of employment is not always clear cut. For example, employees often make brief deviations from their employer's business to attend to personal matters. Whether such deviations occurred and when they ended are difficult to determine. A claim representative handling such situations must thoroughly investigate such deviations.

Another difficult situation for determining scope of employment arises when an employee attempts to conduct the employer's business by prohibited means, such as driving at illegally high speeds from one appointment to another. Usually, the law deems these situations to be within the scope of employment. The claim representative handling such situations often faces difficulty because the employer might overstate the extent to which it made its rules and prohibitions known to the employee.

Defenses to Liability Claims

Claim representatives must be aware of possible defenses to any claim they handle. As they investigate liability, claim representatives also investigate possible defenses. The most useful defenses are comparative or contributory negligence, assumption of risk, and statute of limitations. Absence of any one of the elements necessary to prove negligence also serves as a type of defense.

Comparative negligence

A common-law principle that requires both parties to a loss to share the financial burden of the bodily injury or property damage according to their respective degrees of fault.

Contributory negligence

A common-law principle that prevents a person who has been harmed from recovering damages if that person's own negligence contributed in any way to the harm.

Comparative or contributory negligence—This exists whenever a claimant's own fault contributes to causing his or her bodily injury. Such negligence is common. Under **comparative negligence** laws, the claimant's recovery may be reduced in proportion to the claimant's share of fault. Two primary forms of comparative negligence are the "pure" form and the "modified" form. Under the pure form, no matter how great the degree of the claimant's own negligence, as long as it is not 100 percent, a claimant may still recover for an amount reduced by his or her own negligence. Two thresholds exist under the "modified" form of comparative negligence: the "50 percent rule" and the "49 percent rule." Under the 50 percent rule, recovery is permitted if the liability of the claimant is not more than that of the other party. Under the 49 percent rule, the claimant may not recover if he or she was 50 percent or more at fault. In the few states that recognize **contributory negligence**, any fault on the claimant's part completely bars the claimant from recovery. See the exhibit "Applications of Comparative Negligence."

Applications of Comparative Negligence

Application of comparative and contributory negligence can vary among states based on their laws. For example:

- "Pure" comparative negligence—When a claimant is 20 percent at fault and the other party is 80 percent at fault, if damages were $10,000, then the claimant's recovery would be $8,000 (10,000 × 0.80).

- "Modified" comparative negligence, 50 percent rule—When a claimant's share of negligence is 50 percent and the other party's negligence is 50 percent, if the claimant's damages were $20,000, then the claimant's recovery would be $10,000 (20,000 × 0.50). However, if the claimant's negligence was over 50 percent, then he or she would not recover any amount.

- "Modified" comparative negligence, 49 percent rule—When a claimant's share of negligence is 50 percent and the other party's negligence is 50 percent, if the claimant's damages were $20,000, then the claimant's recovery would be $0.

- Contributory negligence—When a claimant's share of negligence is 1 percent or more, the claimant cannot recover.

[DA06297]

Assumption of risk—This defense applies whenever a claimant knows of a risk and voluntarily assumes it anyway. For the defense to be valid, the claimant's behavior must be both knowing and voluntary. Assumption of risk is frequently confused with comparative negligence. For example, participating in sports such as downhill skiing includes a risk of injury, but it is not negligent to participate. Knowing that risk, many people choose to participate anyway.

Statute of limitations—Each state has statutory time limitations on the right to file lawsuits. The amount of time varies by state and by the type of legal claim; time limits can range from two to fifteen years, depending on the circumstances. Failure to file a lawsuit within the allotted time waives any obligation on the tortfeasor's part so that an expired statute of limitations can serve as an absolute defense.

Absence of negligence—Many accidents occur through no one's fault. Claimants often assert claims believing that the mere occurrence of the accident entitles them to compensation. See the exhibit "Application of the Absence of Negligence Defense."

Application of the Absence of Negligence Defense

A claimant who twists an ankle while walking through undeveloped land might expect compensation from the landowner. However, the surface of undeveloped property is naturally uneven, so the land owner is not negligent in the claimant's injury. Nature does not provide smoothly paved walkways, and anyone walking through natural terrain should be wary of the hazards.

[DA06299]

Determining Damages

The third step in the liability claim handling process is determining damages. Claim representatives must determine and document damages before settling a claim. Doing so usually takes more time than determining liability. Determining liability often takes a few days, whereas determining damages can take weeks, months, or longer. Claim representatives usually rely on outside experts for damage information, such as doctors for bodily injury; appraisers, contractors, or repairers for property damage; and accountants or economists for financial factors.

Damages in bodily injury liability claims are usually proved with medical reports and bills, hospital records, and employer information. The claim representative must assemble this documentation throughout the time in which the claimant continues to receive treatment. So, settling a bodily injury claim often does not occur until treatment has concluded or until a clear prognosis and course of future treatment are known.

Damages in property damage claims are proved with repair estimates or with actual bills for repair and rental. Most of this section concerns damages in bodily injury claims because those claims account for the majority of liability claim dollars spent.

Bodily Injury Claims

To investigate and document claims properly, claim representatives must understand every element of damages for which the law provides compensation. The claimant has the burden of proving the damages. Nevertheless, the claim representative must investigate the nature and value of damages.

Damages can be classified as either special damages or general damages. Special damages are established for losses that can be quantified, such as loss of earnings. General damages are for intangible losses, such as pain and suffering. These damages are highly subjective, but they are the largest and most important element of damages in bodily injury claims. Claim representatives, claimants' lawyers, and claimants often do not agree about how to evaluate general damages. Nevertheless, those involved are regularly required to negotiate and settle claims involving general damages.

Medical expenses include expenses for emergency care, physicians' services, hospital care, nursing and rehabilitation treatment, medications, medical devices and equipment, and even transportation to receive medical care. Medical expenses must be related to the bodily injury, necessary to heal the bodily injury, and reasonable in amount.

Although unrelated medical expenses should not be compensable, they are often submitted for payment. Many claimants have preexisting medical conditions for which they were already or should have been receiving treatment. Bills for these treatments are often included with bills for accident-related treatment. Preexisting problems and unrelated problems that develop after an accident are not the liability insurer's responsibility unless the bodily injury exacerbates a preexisting condition.

Medical treatment must be necessary to be compensated. Medical treatment is usually controlled by the claimant and the claimant's physician. Insurer arguments against the prescribed treatment are fruitless after the fact. Second-guessing the treating physician is not easy, but, with a solid case, an insurer can avoid payment for unnecessary treatment.

Finally, medical treatment must be reasonable in amount and cost. Although insurers do not have any statutory, regulatory, or contractual controls over physicians and hospitals, they are neither required to reimburse a course of treatment nor to pay bills that they can show are excessive.

Claim representatives use utilization review services to evaluate the necessity and frequency of medical treatment. These services represent a recognized specialty within the medical field. By assessing medical treatment and bills, they can advise when a course of treatment is unnecessary, unrelated to the specific injury, or redundant with other treatment.

In addition to medical expenses, damage can include lost earnings. Any amount that a claimant would have earned during a disability period is recoverable. Lost wages are established by verifying the extent and period of disability and the claimant's earnings. The extent and period of disability are medical issues that must be determined by a physician familiar with the physical demands of the claimant's job. A physician who expresses an opinion about disability without knowing the demands of the claimant's job cannot be reliable, unless the claimant's condition disables the claimant from any work at all.

The issue in every case is what the claimant would have earned during the disability period, not what was earned just before disability. It might be necessary to contact the claimant's customers and clients or to hire an accountant to review the claimant's books. The lost time of a claimant who is a businessowner is especially difficult to verify because the business can often carry on temporarily without the owner.

Pain and suffering is an intangible factor in every bodily injury case and is usually the largest component of damages. The amount awarded in a suit, or

Pain and suffering

Compensable injuries that are difficult to measure, such as physical and mental distress and inconvenience associated with a physical injury.

agreed on in a claim settlement, depends on the medical expense amount, the disability's length, the severity and nature of the bodily injury, the locale where the lawsuit is tried, the lawyers' respective skill at creating sympathy and favorable impressions, the sympathies created by the parties, and many other factors.

In addition to having chronic pain, claimants sometimes suffer scarring or loss of bodily function that might not cause pain but that reduces the quality of life. Permanent bodily injuries and scars are evaluated similarly to pain and suffering—unscientifically. For example, burns or other scars on the face would be considered differently if they were on the claimant's back or another less visible area. However, damages for permanent bodily injuries that reduce earning capacity can be determined more accurately.

Loss of consortium is an element of damages that generally belongs to the injured party's spouse. Some states permit payment to other family members such as a parent or grandparent. Other states limit consortium payments only to the spouse. Consortium traditionally consists of sex, society, and services. Sex means the loss of sexual relations because of the bodily injury. Society means the loss of enjoyable companionship because of the bodily injury. Services mean the loss of useful services that the injured party formerly performed for the spouse, such as housekeeping, home repairs, or childcare. This element of damages is also difficult to evaluate, and sometimes it is estimated as a percentage of the underlying injury damages.

Any of the previous elements of damages that can be expected to continue into the future should be included in a settlement or jury verdict. With serious bodily injury, future damages—such as future medical expenses, future lost earnings and future pain and suffering—can exceed the damages incurred.

Because of inflation, future damages can be larger in their face amount than present damages. However, any future damages that can be specified in amount should be adjusted to their present value. This procedure recognizes that a dollar received in the future is worth less than a dollar received today.

Property Damage Claims

In some respects, determining damages in third-party property damage liability claims is easier than in first-party property damage claims. The claim representative need not worry about deductibles, special sublimits, coinsurance, or damages caused by both covered and noncovered causes.

However, in third-party claims, the law allows a deduction for depreciation from replacement cost. Determining depreciation in these claims can be as complex as it is in first-party claims. The claim representative must consider physical wear and tear; obsolescence because of fashion, seasonal, and technological changes; market value; and any other relevant factors. However, as in first-party claims, depreciation can be negligible, and a replacement cost settlement can be appropriate in many cases.

One important difference between first-party and third-party property damage claims is that the property owner's own negligence is irrelevant in first-party claims, but it can be a major factor in settling third-party claims. In contributory negligence states, the owner's fault in causing the loss is a complete bar to recovery. In comparative negligence states, the owner's fault reduces the recovery by a proportionate percentage or might even completely bar recovery.

Many property damage liability claims first appear as subrogation claims from other insurers. The claim representative for the liability insurer should respond to the claim as he or she would respond to a claimant. Should the claim representatives for the respective insurers be unable to negotiate a settlement, the claim can be resolved by intercompany arbitration.

Negotiating and Settling Claims

The fourth step in the liability claim handling process is negotiating and settling claims. Everything a claim representative does on a claim should be directed toward settlement. The vast majority of liability claims are settled without resulting in a lawsuit. The vast majority of claims that do result in lawsuits are settled before trial.

Settling liability claims is the most valuable service liability claim representatives perform for insureds, claimants, insurers, and society. The courts would be overwhelmed if even a small percentage of claims that are settled were tried. It is in the insurers' best interests for claim representatives to settle liability claims. Insurers would pay more in legal fees and verdict amounts than they would pay in settlements if they were to try all the claims that they could settle. Therefore, negotiating to settle claims is a crucial responsibility of claim representatives. Negotiation involves discussing all issues and arriving at a mutually satisfactory disposition of the claim.

Liability insurance policies usually give insurers the right to settle claims, but they do not impose a duty to settle because insurers might want to litigate a claim. The insurer must have the right to litigate to protect itself against frivolous, fraudulent, or unfounded claims. The threat that a claim might be litigated helps keep many dubious claims from ever being asserted.

When the value of a claim approaches or exceeds the insured's policy limit, making settlement becomes a legal obligation and is no longer just good judgment. The insurer, rather than the insured, controls the defense and claim settlement. If a verdict exceeds the insured's policy limit, however, the insured has to pay the excess. This situation creates a potential conflict. Absent a duty to settle the claim and once the claim's value approaches or exceeds the policy limit, the insurer would have little to lose by going to trial because the insurer might face the payment of a relatively low award. However, the insured could end up paying damages exceeding the policy limit.

To prevent insurers from exploiting this situation, courts require them to make reasonable efforts to settle within policy limits and to accept settlement offers within policy limits whenever the value of the claim exceeds policy limits. An insurer that rejects a settlement offer within policy limits does so at its own risk. Although courts have not made insurers absolutely liable for excess verdicts following the rejection of a settlement, convincing a court that the excess verdict was unforeseeable after it has been rendered is difficult. If a court thinks that an insurer unreasonably rejected settlement, it would probably hold the insurer responsible for the damages exceeding policy limits. This is one type of **bad-faith claim** against the insurer.

Most claims are settled using a general release, in which the claimant releases the insured of all liability for the claim and the insurer agrees to pay the claimant the agreed settlement amount. Specialized releases address particular situations, such as those involving joint tortfeasors and minors.

For claims by married individuals, the claimant's spouse should also be a party to the release to dispose of his or her consortium claim. For claims in which a lawsuit has been filed, the settlement must include the lawsuit's dismissal by the claimant. The claimant's lawyer files a simple notice in the court records stating that the claim has been settled.

Liability claims are usually settled with a lump-sum payment. Sometimes, the settlement requires both a lump-sum payment at the time of settlement and a series of payments into the future. These are called **structured settlements**. Although structured settlements are usually made on high-value claims, such settlements have no minimum-size claim. Structured settlements are especially useful when the claimant is likely to experience regular damages into the future, such as loss of income, or when the claim representative suspects that the claimant might be unable to effectively manage a lump-sum payment.

Structured settlements are attractive to insurers because they enable them to offer a larger total settlement at a lower present cost than with a lump-sum payment. Insurers can fund their future obligations with annuities purchased from other insurers, usually life insurance companies. The present cost of an annuity is less than what the annuity will pay in the future.

Many insurers also use **advance payments** to discourage claimants from hiring lawyers. Advance payments are made as the claimant incurs medical or other expenses. Payments are paid without receiving a release in return, but the claimant must sign a receipt acknowledging payments and that the advance payments count toward final settlement.

Some insurers practice **walk-away settlements**. These settlements are most appropriate for small claims. Insurers that advocate this practice say it promotes excellent public relations, enhances assertive claim handling, and encourages claimants to refrain from bringing suit. In claims in which the claimant does sue, the insurer is entitled to credit for what it has paid.

Bad-faith claim

A claim that implies or involves actual or constructive fraud, a design to mislead or deceive another, or a neglect or refusal to fulfill some good-faith duty or some contractual good-faith obligation.

Structured settlement

An agreement in settlement of a claim involving specific payments made over a period of time.

Advance payment

A payment made to a claimant following a loss to cover the immediate expenses resulting from that loss.

Walk-away settlement

A settlement that involves lump-sum payments made by insurers to settle claims and that does not require a release from the claimant.

Litigation Process

All liability claim representatives should be familiar with litigation. Ultimately, courts determine both liability and damages for any claim that is not settled. Claimants might have to go to court to obtain compensation. Insurers and claim representatives must understand how courts operate and how courts balance the rights and interests of plaintiffs and defendants.

Defending lawsuits is a significant part of the protection insureds buy through liability insurance policies. Insurers have both the right and the duty to defend the insured. Claim representatives must understand and properly handle this right and duty.

Role of Courts in Resolving Claims

Although the majority of claims are settled before suit is filed and the majority of suits are settled before trial, courts play an essential role in settling claims. Courts provide an incentive to negotiate. An insured could not be held legally liable without a court determination. Insurers would not need to protect insureds without the threat of legal liability.

Nevertheless, courts are not fast, inexpensive, or predictable. Claimants who might otherwise rely on courts to determine their rights against insureds have an incentive to negotiate. Claimants who do rely on courts find that they wait many years, spend considerable money on legal expenses, and often end up with a result no better than they could have achieved in settlement.

The adverse psychological effects of litigation tend to mount as time progresses, a circumstance that increases incentives to settle. Just before the trial, the pace of depositions and motions usually increases. These pretrial activities place great stress on the parties and their lawyers and indicate what trial will be like. Following pretrial activities, many parties conclude that they prefer a settlement for a definite amount, with relief from the aggravation and stress of litigation, to the difficulty and uncertain outcome of a trial.

The values that lawyers and claim representatives place on claims are derived from actual results of claims litigated to conclusion. Claims that are litigated to conclusion therefore have important effects on all other claims. Although only a small percentage of claims are decided by court verdicts, those verdicts influence the price of all claims.

Duty to Defend

In addition to paying amounts for which the insured is legally liable (up to policy limits), insurers are also obligated to defend their insureds against lawsuits. This obligation is a valuable aspect of liability insurance. Many times, the insurer's duty to defend is more important to the insured than the duty to indemnify.

Many claims take a long time and a great deal of effort to settle. Other claims cannot be settled at all and are concluded by a trial and verdict. In both of these cases, legal expenses can be extraordinary. Thousands and then tens of thousands of dollars in legal expenses can quickly accumulate on ordinary claims, such as auto liability and premises liability claims. Complex claims can result in legal expenses well into six figures.

The insurer's duty to defend is especially important in frivolous, fraudulent, or meritless claims. Absent the insurer's duty to defend, plaintiffs would be in a strong position to coerce settlements from defendants who lack the resources or the ability to resist lawsuits.

For liability insurance claims, plaintiffs face an opponent with tremendous resources and experience in defending lawsuits: the insurer. When insurers defend frivolous lawsuits to a verdict, they spend far more on defense than on claim indemnification. When insurers settle frivolous lawsuits, they usually do so because settling saves an equal or a greater amount of legal expenses.

The insurer's duty to defend is also its right. The insurer can select the defense lawyer, and the insured is then obligated to cooperate with that chosen lawyer. As long as it is solely liable for the claim, the insurer can dictate defense strategy. The insurer can unilaterally decide to settle or to continue a claim's defense. Although the defense lawyer is professionally obligated to serve the insured's interests above all, the insurer pays the defense lawyer and therefore dictates all defense decisions.

The insurer's right and duty to defend suits is complicated for claims in which coverage is doubtful or in which part of the claim is clearly not covered. Generally, an insurer must defend an entire claim whenever a plaintiff's allegations for any part of the claim are covered. Coverage applies according to the plaintiff's allegations, not according to the claim's merits. Otherwise, insureds would be without coverage when they need it most—when faced with unfounded claims.

However, plaintiffs often assert claims that are clearly not covered (such as intentional wrongdoing) in the same lawsuit as claims that are covered (such as ordinary negligence) or assert claims that might not be covered at all (such as a claim in which it is doubtful whether the bodily injury or property damage occurred during the policy period). In these claims, the insurer must defend the entire lawsuit, but the insured has a right to involve a lawyer of the insured's choosing at the insured's expense.

When two defense lawyers are involved, the insurer's lawyer has the right to control the case as long as the insurer's money is at stake. The insurer's lawyer attempts to involve and obtain the approval of the insured's private lawyer in all major decisions. Should the insurer's lawyer ever disagree with the insured's private lawyer, the insurer is likely to be financially responsible for any consequences.

HANDLING SPECIFIC TYPES OF LIABILITY CLAIMS

Liability insurance is designed to protect the insured party from liability claims brought by third parties. Claim representatives face many challenges when handling various types of liability.

The claim representative's general duties to determine coverage, legal liability, and damages, and to negotiate and settle claims, exist in all liability claims. The challenges of performing these duties vary by claim. General principles of liability and damages apply somewhat differently to different situations.

Auto bodily injury and physical damage claims are not traditional liability-based claims but are covered by the auto policy, which is a liability coverage form. Claims arising out of premises, operations, and products are typically covered by general liability insurance. Specialized areas of workers compensation claims, and professional liability claims, derive from various liability coverages.

Auto Bodily Injury Liability Claims

Auto accidents generate the most common type of liability claim. Nevertheless, auto accidents can cause some of the worst bodily injuries and the most expensive claims. New claim representatives often begin work in auto claims because a majority of relatively minor auto claims exists and because the liability principles are well established.

Although auto claims are a traditional training ground for liability claim representatives, auto claims can be complicated regarding coverage determination; accident reconstruction; and coordination with no-fault, workers compensation, and uninsured or underinsured motorists claims.

Coverage Determination

Coverage determination is simple only when the accident involves the named insured as the driver and a vehicle specifically listed on the policy. Situations in which the named insured, or another insured, has coverage while driving a vehicle not listed on the policy or when someone other than the named insured is using a covered vehicle are more complicated.

Usually, when an insured is driving another's vehicle, the coverage on that other vehicle covers any loss. However, the other vehicle's coverage sometimes does not apply or is inadequate. In the event of the insolvency of the vehicle's insurer or the exclusion of coverage for any reason, the driver's insurer must take over the handling of the claim.

Cases of inadequate policy limits are more common than cases in which vehicle coverage does not apply. The claim representative working for the driver's insurer can adopt different strategies, depending on the circumstances. If the underlying coverage is far less than the value of the claim, the claim representative for the driver's insurer should become heavily involved in the claim or ensure proper handling of the underlying claim. If the underlying coverage is adequate to pay the claim, the claim representative for the driver's insurer is likely to take a less active role.

Accident Reconstruction

The facts of most auto accidents are not difficult to ascertain. The points of impact on each vehicle involved in the accident indicate at what angle and from what direction the vehicle came into contact with other vehicles or objects. The extent of damage to a vehicle provides some indication of its speed and that of other vehicles.

The parties to an auto accident usually differ more about who was at fault than over what happened. Fortunately for claim representatives, clear right-of-way rules apply when two vehicles converge on the roads. Also, whenever the parties disagree about what happened, claim representatives or accident reconstruction experts might be able to determine the facts. Accident reconstruction experts are most helpful in determining vehicle speed and what a driver should have been able to see at the time of an accident.

Vehicle speed is determined by examining skid marks and vehicle damage. Skid marks are reliable indicators of speed because once the brakes are fully applied, vehicles stop according to their weight, the road grade, the road surface, and speed. All of these factors except speed are known or can be measured precisely after an accident. When, instead of coming to a complete stop, a vehicle collides with another vehicle, an accident reconstruction expert can determine that the vehicle was traveling no slower than a certain speed based on the skid marks. This information can be sufficient to disprove a party's statements or establish liability. The point at which skid marks begin can establish when and where the driver first reacted to a hazard, an essential piece of evidence when driver inattention is an issue.

Accident reconstruction experts can also determine what a driver should have been able to see just before impact. The exact time of day and weather conditions at the time of the accident can usually be established. The driver's lines of sight can be determined according to vehicle type and driver height. The effects on visibility of curves or hills in the road are also considered. All of this information can be combined to determine whether a driver reacted promptly to a hazard or was slow and inattentive. That determination is essential in claims in which the driver alleges a sudden and unavoidable hazard or in which the claimant's comparative negligence is at issue. Comparative negligence is frequently an important issue in auto accident claims. For example, the insured could be primarily at fault, but the claimant could also be substantially negligent for failing to respond to a hazard.

Coordination With Auto No-Fault and Workers Compensation

A claim representative handling auto liability claims must frequently deal with other insurers that provide auto no-fault or workers compensation benefits to an injured claimant.

The no-fault or comp insurer will establish a subrogation claim against the auto liability insurer for the medical expense amount and must, therefore, provide medical information. In jurisdictions in which subrogation is possible, the no-fault or comp insurer is obligated to submit medical information to any insurers involved with the claim. This enables the claim representative to stay abreast of the claimant's bodily injury to ensure that the liability claim reserves for the claim are adequate.

However, difficulties can arise between the claim representative and the other insurer when subrogation rights do not exist or when comparative negligence is a crucial issue. In the absence of subrogation rights, the no-fault or comp insurer should not release any medical information about the claimant to the claim representative without authorization from the claimant or his or her representative.

Eventually, the claimant must release medical information to the other party's claim representative, but the claimant is likely to want control over any such release. As a professional courtesy, the claimant's claim representative might be willing to comment on the adequacy of the liability claim reserves, but the other claim representative might be accused of invading the claimant's privacy should any medical information be revealed.

Uninsured Motorists Coverage

Insureds purchase uninsured motorists (UM) coverage to protect themselves against motorists who do not have liability insurance. Under this coverage, the insured becomes the claimant. Denying a claim under UM coverage might have immediate legal ramifications for the insurer because lawyer representation in a UM claim is almost inevitable in many parts of the United States. Once an insured realizes that the opposing driver is uninsured, the insured assumes that legal representation is essential. Unfortunately, dealing with the insured as a claimant leaves the claim representative with no favorable witness because the uninsured driver is usually unavailable or uncooperative. A person who drives without insurance or who causes hit-and-run accidents is usually not a credible witness, even if that party is available and cooperative. Therefore, UM claims are extremely difficult to defend with respect to liability or on the basis of comparative negligence.

The claim representative has limited powers to defend UM claims. In the event of any disagreement over the settlement amount, the insured can require arbitration. Arbitration is less expensive and less time consuming than litigation. Furthermore, arbitrators are usually lawyers who are aware that the claim involves the insured versus the insurer. Arbitrators tend to give the insured the benefit of every doubt. Unfortunately, fraud and exaggeration can be at least as common in UM claims as they are in third-party liability claims.

Underinsured Motorists Coverage

Because states' minimum liability-limit requirements have not kept pace with rising medical costs, insurers have offered underinsured motorists (UIM) coverage to help counter that problem.

UIM coverage varies by state and by UIM endorsement. Court decisions in UIM coverage cases are not consistent, so claim representatives are advised not to base claim decisions on prior court decisions. The major point of contention in UIM coverage is the definition of an underinsured motor vehicle, which triggers coverage. Some states apply a "limits trigger," while other states apply a "damages trigger."

In states that apply a limits trigger, the UIM endorsement applies when the negligent driver carries liability insurance limits that are lower than the limits provided by the injured party's UIM coverage. States using the limits trigger do not consider the extent of the injury claim in determining whether UIM coverage applies.

In states that apply a damages trigger, the UIM endorsement applies when the negligent driver carries liability insurance limits that are lower than the insured party's damages. See the exhibit "UIM Limits and Damage Trigger Illustrations."

UIM Limits and Damage Trigger Illustrations

UIM "Limits Trigger" Illustration

Tom has an auto liability policy with a $100,000 UIM limit, and Lynn has an auto liability policy with a $50,000 liability limit. Lynn's limit exceeds the minimum financial responsibility limits in her state. Tom and Lynn have an auto accident, and Lynn is liable for Tom's damages. If Tom's damages are $60,000, he will collect $50,000 from Lynn's liability insurer and $10,000 under his UIM coverage. His UIM coverage applies even though the limits of Lynn's policy are greater than the minimum required by the state, as long as Lynn's liability limits are less than Tom's UIM limits.

UIM "Damages Trigger" Illustration

Anne has UIM coverage with a $50,000 limit. Randy has auto liability coverage with a $100,000 limit. Randy causes an accident in which Anne is injured. If Anne's damages are $150,000, then her UIM coverage will be triggered because Randy's liability limit is less than Anne's damages; both policies will pay the damages. However, if Anne's damages are $75,000, her UIM coverage will not be triggered because her damages are less than Randy's limit; Randy's policy will pay the damages.

[DA06295]

Another variation among states' UIM laws relates to stacking limits, which is the application of two or more limits to a single auto accident. Stacking can involve two or more separate policies (called interpolicy stacking). In stacking, the UIM policy limit of one policy is added to the UIM limit of another policy. Some states allow interpolicy stacking by endorsement. See the exhibit "UIM Interpolicy Stacking Limits Illustration."

UIM Interpolicy Stacking Limits Illustration

John and Nancy are married and have separate auto policies. Both policies may apply when either or both of them are injured by an underinsured motorist. If the UIM limit of John's policy is $25,000 and the UIM limit of Nancy's policy is $50,000, with stacked policy limits, the injured insured will be able to collect up to $75,000 for damages.

[DA06296]

Stacking can also occur when a single policy covers more than one vehicle (called intrapolicy stacking). Some states allow intrapolicy stacking by endorsement. In some of these states, the insured can choose between stacking or nonstacking limits but must pay a higher premium for a policy that allows stacking. Other states prohibit stacking and require that the maximum amount to be paid for an accident is the single (unstacked) UIM limit shown on the declarations page, regardless of the number of insureds, claims made, vehicles involved, or vehicles or premiums shown on the declarations page.

Auto Property Damage Claims

In addition to bodily injury, auto accidents can also result in the insured's becoming legally liable for damage to property such as buildings, appurtenant structures, landscaping, contents of over-the-road shipments, or other vehicles. These third-party losses are covered under auto property damage liability.

Because damage to other vehicles is the most frequent damage in auto accidents, claims for such damage are handled similarly to first-party property damage losses. First-party property damage losses are covered under the physical damage section of the auto policy. Such losses might involve damage resulting from collision, fire, flood, or theft of the vehicle. Damaged autos are usually first inspected by an appraiser, who writes a damage estimate that is forwarded to the claim representative assigned to the claim. Auto damage appraisers have expert knowledge of auto body repair methods and costs.

Once the appraisal has been received, the claim representative verifies coverage and pays the covered loss. As part of these procedures, the claim representative should explain the claim process to the insured and remain in contact with the insured to resolve any problems. The insurer will pursue subrogation, if appropriate and, if successful, will promptly reimburse any deductible paid by the insured.

Handling third-party property damage liability claims correctly is an essential part of good relations with both insureds and third-party claimants. As with first-party claimants, a claim representative should provide prompt service to third-party claimants. If the third-party claimant is injured, courteous and professional service in handling the property damage can hasten the settlement of any bodily injury claim that might be asserted. A claim representative is permitted to make good-faith comparative negligence arguments but should be willing to negotiate an equitable settlement.

Constructive Total Losses

Constructive total loss

A loss that occurs when the cost to repair damaged property plus its remaining salvage value equals or exceeds the property's pre-loss value.

When the cost to repair a vehicle plus its remaining salvage value equals or exceeds the vehicle's pre-loss value, the vehicle is a **constructive total loss**. It does not make sense financially to repair a constructive total loss, even if it is possible to make satisfactory repairs. By paying the vehicle's pre-loss value and taking the salvage, the insurer pays less overall. For example, assume an auto worth $3,500 before the loss suffers $3,000 of damage and retains $1,000 of salvage value. Rather than pay $3,000 for repairs, the insurer should pay $3,500 for the title to the auto and obtain $1,000 in the salvage market, for a net loss of $2,500. Insurers are in a better position to dispose of salvage efficiently than is the average person.

Neither insureds nor claimants, however, are required to "sell" their autos to insurers, as the preceding example might imply. Should the insured want to keep the auto, the claim representative is entitled to pay the claim based on the actual cash value (ACV), adjusted for salvage value. For example, using the values in the preceding paragraph, the vehicle's actual cash value before the loss ($3,500) minus the vehicle's ACV after the loss ($1,000) equals the amount of the loss ($2,500) paid to the claimant or insured.

Agreed Repair Prices

If a vehicle can be repaired, the claim representative should obtain an agreed repair price from the body shop selected by the insured or claimant. This agreement demonstrates that the claim representative's evaluation of the loss is legitimate and prevents disputes between the insurer and the claimant or between the auto owner and the body shop.

Although the claim representative should try to agree on a repair price, the choice of a body shop should be left to the claimant. Many states have enacted "anti-steering" laws that restrict an insurer from directing a claimant to a particular repair shop. These laws prevent collusion between an insurer and a body shop and discourage any unethical behavior or the appearance of unethical behavior.

Premises Liability Claims

Businesses that regularly have members of the public on their premises, such as retail stores, restaurants, banks, and hotels, probably experience more premises liability claims than any other type of liability claim. Premises liability claims are usually relatively minor slip-and-fall claims; nevertheless, they are important to the claimant and the insured. Responsively handling such claims can reduce their cost to the insurer and can preserve goodwill with the insured.

Claim representatives who handle premises liability claims must establish good rapport with the claimant, both to establish the cause of the accident and to determine comparative negligence. Witnesses and employees of the insured can often help the claim representative in these efforts.

Determining the Cause of the Accident

Legal liability in premises liability claims is determined by negligence theories. Typically, the claimant asserts that the insured failed to maintain the premises in a reasonably safe condition. Under the law of negligence, the insured should be judged by how a reasonably prudent person would behave under the same circumstances.

The standard of care for property owners is traditionally qualified by the claimant's status on the premises. An owner owes only a slight level of care toward a trespasser, primarily a duty not to inflict intentional injury. An intermediate level of care is owed to licensees, a group that includes social guests, letter carriers, and solicitors. A property owner owes a high level of care to business invitees, those who are on the premises at the owner's invitation to do business with the owner. This group of claimants includes customers of the business. Some jurisdictions have eliminated this level of care classification, requiring instead that a reasonable level of care is the duty owed to all.

On learning that a customer has had an accident on the premises, most insureds are genuinely solicitous toward the injured person, out of human decency and a sense of self-protection. Most insureds want to preserve their customers' goodwill and forestall possible legal actions against them. Injuries to pride and dignity are as common as bodily injuries, and insureds find that injured customers respond well to genuine concern. Some insureds in these circumstances insist that the customer be seen by a physician and promise to pay whatever medical expense is incurred.

Medical payments coverage is usually obtained for exactly this situation: taking care of a customer regardless of fault. Insureds who do not have medical payments coverage probably violate their liability insurance policy conditions by making promises of payment, yet such promises do not usually cause trouble with insurers. If doing so settles the claim, claim representatives are usually willing to pay for minor medical expenses, regardless of fault, under liability coverage.

When premises liability claims cannot be settled quickly and easily, liability issues are important. For business invitees, the insured owes a high level of care. Therefore, almost any factor in the environment of the insured premises contributing to the accident could indicate negligence on the insured's part.

When investigating premises liability claims, claim representatives should solicit statements from the claimant and all witnesses who can testify about either the accident or the condition of the accident scene. If the scene is substantially the same as when the accident occurred, the claim representative should take photographs.

The claim representative should also determine the insured's cleaning, maintenance, and inspection practices and should obtain copies of any logs or other records of such activities. If the insured uses an independent contractor for cleaning or maintenance work, the claim representative should determine the scope of that contractor's duties, obtain copies of the contracts, and determine what role the contractor might have played in the accident.

Determining Comparative Negligence

Regarding liability for their accident, claimants in premises liability claims are often in a difficult position. Unless their accidents were caused by a hidden hazard, claimants usually provide one of these three reasons for the accident:

- They have no idea what caused their accident. A common example of this situation is a fall down smooth, even, well-lighted stairs. Most insureds that have the public on their premises maintain their stairways well, and the insured's defense is that the fall on the stairs is the claimant's own fault.

- They knew of the causes but failed to observe and avoid them. An example of this situation is a claimant who falls on an obvious hazard, such as debris on the floor. The defense of claims of this sort is challenging whenever something in the environment, such as a sales display, was a conspicuous distraction or whenever the insured should have known of the hazard and eliminated it before the accident.

- They were aware of and observed the causes before the accident but encountered them anyway. An example of this situation is a claimant who voluntarily walks across an obvious hazard, such as a torn-up or an icy sidewalk.

An assessment of liability applicable to these three reasons, respectively, is as follows: (1) no negligence exists on the insured's part, (2) comparative negligence exists on the claimant's part, and (3) in most cases, the claimant assumed the risk, so the insured was not negligent. Concerning the third reason, the assumption of risk defense is weakened if the claimant had no choice. The assumption of risk defense cannot be applied unless the claimant acted voluntarily.

Operations Liability Claims

Claims arising out of an insured's operations are similar to premises claims with regard to liability theories and applicable defenses. The primary difference is that operations liability claims usually focus on an unsafe act rather than an unsafe condition. Additionally, the insured in operations liability claims is typically a contractor rather than an establishment open to the public.

Bases of Liability

An insured's operations are alleged to be responsible for an accident whenever the accident results from an unsafe or improper act by the insured or the insured's employees, whenever the insured fails to provide proper supervision of another party for whom it is responsible, or whenever the insured has contractually assumed liability.

When investigating operations liability claims, the claim representative should begin by investigating exactly how the claimant's accident occurred. Questions to resolve include these:

- Exactly where did the accident occur?
- What workers were in the vicinity?
- Who employs and supervises these workers?
- Exactly what were these workers doing at the time of the accident?
- What equipment were the workers operating?
- What did each worker see?

Even in the face of evasion and reluctance from witnesses, a claim representative can usually establish what happened through a thorough and methodical investigation.

A contractor may be responsible for its employees as well as for the supervision of others. Under many construction contracts, a general contractor has a duty to ensure workplace safety, and individual contractors might be responsible for their own subcontractors. The duty to supervise might be an explicit contractual obligation, a custom of the trade that is implied in the contract, or a requirement under general tort principles.

When faced with a case of potential improper supervision, a claim representative usually assumes that the primarily responsible party is the workers' employer. Nevertheless, the claim representative should thoroughly investigate what supervisory steps the insured actually took and determine whether the insured communicated with its subcontractors about safety, and whether the insured conducted inspections, gave warnings, or otherwise enforced safe practices.

Contractual Assumptions of Liability

In addition to their direct responsibility for their workers and their duty to supervise others, contractor-insureds are often liable for the property damage and bodily injury caused by others because they have assumed contractual liability. Liability assumed by contract is different from liability for failure to supervise. When a contractor assumes liability for another, it is responsible for that other party's liabilities. In contrast, liability for failure to supervise is based on the contractor's own failure, not the liabilities of another.

The legal interpretation of contractual liability can be complex. Generally, courts recognize contractual assumptions of liability as valid but interpret them narrowly. A claim representative examining an assumption of liability clause must determine whether it requires defense and indemnity or just indemnity. Questions to answer are, "Does the assumption of liability extend to all liabilities of the indemnified party or just to liabilities that arise out of the indemnifying party's behavior?" and "Does the assumption of liability extend to the owner of the project site or to the indemnified party's subcontractors?"

Insurance coverages for contractual assumptions of liability vary. Therefore, claim representatives who handle contractual liability claims must check policy wording carefully. If coverage is unclear or doubtful, claim representatives should seek opinions from their superiors or staff advisers and should issue a reservation of rights letter to the insured to be effective until the matter has been resolved.

Preservation of the Accident Scene

For a claim involving contractor operations, the claim representative should immediately try to preserve the accident scene through photos, diagrams, and detailed measurements. Construction sites change rapidly, and witnesses' memories can become confused and vague.

In addition to preserving the precise scene of an accident, photos can provide many important incidental details. Photos can show the exact stage of the project at the time of the accident, including the exact stage of each subcontractor's work. Photos can show which contractors were on the scene on the day of the accident, and they can show the presence or absence of safety measures and precautions. On large or well-organized projects, the owner, architect, or general contractor may have daily records of progress, including photos.

Products Liability Claims

Any party that manufactures or sells a product that harms another can be liable for that harm. A claim representative who handles products liability claims must investigate all possible bases of liability and all applicable defenses.

Bases of Liability

In addition to traditional negligence theories, products liability can be based on breach of warranty or strict liability in tort.

A **warranty** is any contractual promise about the product that accompanies the sale. The warranty that guarantees performance or durability is one type of warranty. An alleged breach of warranty can be based on an express warranty or on an implied legal warranty. Many written sales contracts explicitly disclaim any warranties, express or implied, unless included in the written contract.

An **express warranty** is advertising material that describes the product or its uses. For example, a statement that reads, "These hedge clippers can easily cut through branches up to one-quarter-inch thick" could be the basis of liability if the hedge clippers failed to perform and caused bodily injury or property damage. Express warranties can allow a claimant to assert a products liability claim that might not be sustainable on negligence or strict liability grounds. In the absence of an express warranty, a longer statute of limitations usually applies in a products liability claim based on a warranty, compared to a strict products liability claim based on tort. Consequently, the claimant is more likely to assert products liability based on a warranty.

Strict liability in tort differs from negligence, yet the claim investigations for both are similar. Under strict liability, the nature of the product is the issue, not the defendant's behavior. Specifically, the issue is whether the product is defective in a way that makes it unreasonably dangerous, not whether the defendant was negligent.

Warranty
A written or oral statement in a contract that certain facts are true.

Express warranty
An explicit statement about a product that often accompanies the sale of a product.

Product and Manufacturer Identification

The product in question must be carefully identified for subsequent identification of the manufacturer. Many retailers sell products that are manufactured elsewhere but that carry their store label. Many products have component parts from sources other than the assembling manufacturer. Unless the manufacturer can be identified, the retailer is responsible to the claimant. A retailer can usually verify whether it sold a particular type of product at a particular time. The retailer can usually also identify the source from which it bought its merchandise.

Defending products liability claims is significantly different for manufacturers than for wholesalers or retailers. If a wholesaler or retailer resells a product in the same condition in which it left the manufacturer, the manufacturer is responsible for indemnifying the wholesaler or retailer from any products liability claims. A claim representative handling a wholesaler or retailer products liability claim can usually withdraw from the claim once the manufacturer's insurer is involved. Nevertheless, because the wholesaler or retailer is liable as far as the public is concerned, a claim representative for a wholesaler or retailer should be prepared to handle the claim in the event that the manufacturer goes out of business or is unidentifiable; insolvent; uninsured; or unwilling, for any reason, to handle the claim. Usually, however, manufacturers want to defend their products and their retailers for business reasons.

Use of Experts

Once a product has been identified, the issue of liability depends on whether the product could have been made safer and still perform its intended function. Some products are inherently dangerous. For example, power tools cannot perform their intended function without simultaneously being capable of severe bodily injury.

Determining liability in products claims often involves redesigning the product after an accident. The feasibility of redesign can be determined only through expert opinion. Both the claimant and the insurer must hire an engineer or another expert who can provide an opinion in a court case. Therefore, handling products liability claims is expensive. Most manufacturers consider the expense of having an engineer or expert worthwhile because manufacturers face potentially millions of claims from product users. Because the insured has often been in business for years, the insured can frequently provide the claim representative with the names of engineers and experts in the appropriate field. However, claim representatives must consider any financial stake such people might have in their relationships with the insured and whether they are defending their own designs.

Review of Warnings and Instructions

Often, in products liability claims, the product itself cannot realistically be redesigned, so the plaintiff alleges that the warnings and instructions that accompanied the product were inadequate and that the product was defective.

When faced with such an allegation, the claim representative must review all information accompanying the product. He or she should determine whether the warnings and instructions provided, if followed, would have prevented the claimant's accident. If not, the claim representative should try to determine what additional warning would have been necessary to prevent the claimant's accident.

The claim representative should also investigate whether the claimant read the instructions. If the claimant asserts that he or she did, the claim representative should ask the claimant to repeat whatever he or she remembers. Should it appear that the claimant never read the instructions, or forgot everything that he or she read, the claimant will have a difficult case to prove. Any alleged shortcomings in the manufacturer's instructions cannot be a cause of the claimant's accident if the claimant failed to read them or cannot remember them.

Improper Use

Claimants are often injured while using products in ways that are not intended or foreseeable. For example, claimants can suffer bodily injuries by using a lawn mower to trim hedges or by using prescription drugs for conditions other than those for which they were prescribed.

Claim representatives who suspect improper use should obtain detailed statements from the claimants. If the claimant is not available for a statement, the claim representative might be able to obtain an account of what happened from the claimant's emergency-room records or from an initial report by the claimant to a state or federal consumer products regulatory agency.

Workers Compensation Claims

The workers compensation system operates differently from the liability system. The majority of work-related bodily injury claims are compensated regardless of fault and usually without judicial intervention. These claims are covered under Part One of the Workers Compensation and Employers Liability Insurance policy. Part One of this policy theoretically provides the exclusive remedy for bodily injury claims caused or aggravated by conditions of employment. A small percentage of bodily injury claims fall under Part Two of the Workers Compensation and Employers Liability Insurance policy, which is the Employers Liability coverage part.

Employers liability is a liability-based third-party coverage under which the employee must prove negligence. It is an exception to the exclusive remedy approach used for workers compensation coverage. Employers liability coverage applies to employees who are excluded from workers compensation laws by employment exemptions, such as agricultural workers, or to employees who have rejected compensation benefits under elective statutes in certain states.

Employers liability also provides coverage for care and loss of services to a spouse and to family members of an injured employee who suffer bodily injury as a consequence of the employee's bodily injury. Two additional types of claims would not be covered under workers compensation coverage but would be covered under employers liability coverage:

- Third-party-over claims—for example, when an employee of the insured sues a third party, such as a machine manufacturer, for a work-related bodily injury, and the third party then sues that employee's employer.

- Dual capacity claims—for example, when an injured employee sues his or her employer in a capacity other than as employer, such as in a products liability suit, while also asserting a workers compensation or employers liability claim.

The claim handling process used for employers liability is similar to the process used for other third-party claims. Because these claims are uncommon, this discussion focuses on handling workers compensation claims rather than on employers liability claims. Although the compensability of work-related bodily injuries is usually straightforward, claim representatives handling workers compensation claims must investigate them diligently. Additionally, the medical aspects of workers compensation claims can be extraordinarily complex and expensive.

Investigating Compensation Cases

Workers compensation claims that involve only medical expenses, such as a single visit to the emergency room, are usually processed with no investigation. The insured's word is accepted as proof that the accident occurred on the job and that the injury is work related.

Should an accident involve lost time from work, the claim representative is likely to conduct an investigation. Statements are obtained from the claimant, the employer, and any witnesses. The purpose of these statements is to establish that the bodily injury is work related, that the bodily injury was not preexisting, what the likely period of disability will be, and whether relations between the employee and employer are such that the claimant might have staged the claim or might be inclined to exaggerate the disability. The claim representative must document the employee's earnings so that the employee's disability compensation can be calculated properly.

Controlling Medical Expenses

Workers compensation medical expenses are potentially unlimited. The law requires the employer (or its insurer) to pay all necessary and reasonable medical expenses related to the bodily injury sustained on the job. Consequently, workers compensation policies have no policy limits. A small percentage of workers compensation claims account for an enormous percentage of the medical expenses paid by workers compensation insurers.

Workers compensation claim representatives have limited tools with which to challenge medical expenses. The employee-patient is not required to co-pay any portion of the expenses, as is common with health insurance expenses. Workers compensation insurers often do not have the bargaining power that health insurers have with medical providers. Furthermore, many states do not have fee schedules or other controls over medical expenses. Consequently, workers compensation medical expenses have risen faster in the past decade than healthcare expenses in general.

Preferred provider organization (PPO)

An administrative organization that meets the common needs of healthcare providers and clients and that identifies networks of providers and contracts for their medical services at discounted rates.

To control medical expenses, some workers compensation insurers have entered into agreements with **preferred provider organizations (PPOs)**, through which the insurer receives a discount on the usual medical expenses in exchange for a volume of referrals. This type of agreement is feasible only in states that allow the employer or insurer to select the treating physician.

As with liability claims for other types of bodily injury, insurers also control workers compensation medical expenses by conducting medical bill audits.

Most workers compensation insurers conduct bill audits to identify charges that are excessive, fabricated, or redundant. Specialized bill auditing firms can perform this service for workers compensation insurers. Bill audits usually result in more than enough savings to justify the expense of the audit.

Utilization review services are another valuable tool to control medical expenses by determining whether medical treatment is necessary. However, before an insurer can deny reimbursement for medical treatment, the insurer must be certain that experts from the utilization review service are willing and able to testify on its behalf. Because workers compensation laws are designed to protect workers regardless of fault, insurers should not deny claims without strong grounds for doing so.

Workers compensation claims can also include claims for psychological conditions, which are very expensive. The causes of psychological conditions are complex and can include a combination of work-related and nonwork-related factors. Furthermore, the recovery from and cure of psychological conditions are often difficult to verify. Therefore, claims for psychological conditions are expensive to investigate and difficult to terminate.

Claims for work-related stress disability can involve a complex interaction of employer-employee difficulties, preexisting personality disorders, and difficulties outside the workplace. Claim representatives generally do not have the expertise to evaluate these claims. However, experts in the fields of psychology and psychiatry specialize in defense evaluations of psychological conditions.

The most sophisticated form of medical expense control is **medical management**. Medical management controls medical expenses on the small percentage of claims that involve high medical expenses. Those claims usually involve permanent bodily injuries that require tens of thousands of dollars of medical expenses annually for the remainder of the claimant's life.

Medical management
A medical expense control measure that involves directing and coordinating efforts of healthcare providers to meet patient and insurer needs.

Medical management ensures that the claimant receives care in appropriate facilities with appropriate specialists. Rehabilitation facilities can specialize in certain bodily injuries, such as brain trauma, quadriplegia, burns, or blindness. Medical management can enable an injured claimant to live independently rather than in an institution. By specializing in the care of serious permanent bodily injuries, medical management specialists can ensure both optimum treatment for claimants and medical expense control for insurers.

Controlling Disability Expenses

Controlling disability expenses is probably the foremost challenge for workers compensation claim representatives. Claims in which the claimant loses no time from work and claims in which the claimant returns to work promptly are relatively simple and straightforward. Claims in which disability extends over a long or an excessive period present the biggest challenges and expense for workers compensation insurers.

Workers compensation insurers generally do not have the legal power to stop claim payments when they believe the disability has ended. Once a claim has been accepted as compensable, the insurer can end disability payments only by agreement with the claimant or by order of the compensation commission. If the claimant does not agree, cases before the compensation commission can take months to resolve.

Claim representatives can control disability expenses by insisting that the treating physician explain why the claimant cannot perform his or her job responsibilities. Many treating physicians certify disability without any real understanding of the physical demands of the claimant's job responsibilities. For almost any physical impairment, some jobs, or aspects of jobs, can be performed by someone with that impairment. Therefore, physicians cannot simply assume that certain impairments prevent employees from performing their jobs.

When handling disability claims, a claim representative can also work with the employer to modify the employee's job by removing its most physically demanding parts. Claim representatives can encourage claimants to think in terms of returning to work by constantly asking them what aspects of their work they are still incapable of performing. Claim representatives can then suggest job modifications to the employer that will enable the employee to return to limited-duty work. Claimants who return to limited-duty work are usually on the road to recovery.

Professional Liability Claims

Liability claims for professional malpractice are generally handled by specialized insurers and claim representatives. These claims require a specialized determination of liability and a complex determination of damages. Because of the importance of these claims to the insured's professional reputation, the insured is usually involved in his or her own defense, and these claims are likely to be litigated to verdict rather than settled.

Professional liability claims can be asserted against people who provide professional services, such as physicians, engineers, architects, lawyers, accountants, or insurance producers.

Determining Standard of Care

Professionals are not necessarily at fault for negative outcomes. Physicians cannot guarantee a complete cure for every patient. Lawyers cannot win every case. Accountants cannot guarantee the financial health of a business or an investment. Professionals are required to exercise the standard of care accepted in their profession. In other words, professionals should perform their services competently.

Malpractice claims are usually proved by experts who testify that the defendant should have behaved or decided differently, given the facts and circumstances when the professional services were rendered. A claim representative investigating a malpractice claim should ask what could have and should have been done differently at every point.

Many physicians are found at fault for failing to obtain a patient's informed consent. Physicians are required to explain their care to their patients; they should explain the treatment options and risks associated with each option. Should a physician fail to explain the risks of treatment, he or she might be liable to the patient, even if the adverse outcome is an unavoidable risk. Physicians must exercise judgment in how much they tell patients, because exhaustive explanations would confuse most patients. Nevertheless, a physician who fails to fully inform a patient of the risks of treatment could be responsible for any negative outcome. After a negative outcome, patients often claim not to have understood the risks they faced, and the physician cannot prove otherwise.

Determining Damages

Damages in medical malpractice claims are similar to those in other bodily injury cases, except that the physician is not liable for the underlying condition that initially prompted treatment. Determining damages requires expert testimony about how much the patient's condition would have improved or progressed with proper treatment. Often these determinations are only matters of probability.

For alleged attorney malpractice, the underlying legal matter from which the malpractice claim arose must be relitigated or reconsidered in the professional liability claim. The damages in the malpractice claim depend on how much better the result obtained in the underlying legal matter should have been.

Determining damages in other types of malpractice claims is similar. Expert testimony is used to establish what the claimant's condition would have been had proper professional services been rendered.

Defending Malpractice Claims

Generally, malpractice claims are litigated by only the most sophisticated plaintiff and defense lawyers. The insured is also likely to be heavily involved in the claim's defense.

As malpractice suits became more common, the insurers that handled them resisted easy settlement. Often, the insured had to consent in writing to any settlement. Absent such consent, the verdict had to be litigated. As the strength of the defense became obvious, only the most talented plaintiff lawyers accepted these cases. To match the skills of the plaintiff lawyer, insurers increasingly relied on specialized defense lawyers. Currently, a general practice lawyer rarely handles a malpractice case.

Many professional malpractice insurance policies require the insured's consent to settle. The insured is more personally concerned about the outcome of the professional malpractice claim than about the outcome of other claims because the insured's professional reputation is at stake. Some policies require the insured who rejects a proposed settlement to be responsible for any verdict in excess of the proposed settlement.

A claim representative involved in a professional malpractice claim must investigate any possible defenses. In medical malpractice claims, for example, the patient could be responsible for failing to divulge all relevant information to the physician, for failing to follow the prescribed course of treatment, or for failing to report complications. Contribution on the part of the patient could decrease the damage award.

THE FRAMEWORK FOR COVERAGE ANALYSIS AND THE CLAIM HANDLING PROCESS CASE STUDY

To ensure good-faith handling of property and liability claims, insurers' claim departments adopt specific procedures and guidelines.

Claim representatives can use the claim handling process and apply the framework for coverage analysis as a guide for every claim they handle. Specific information about handling property, liability, and bodily injury claims will help dictate the procedures for each claim handling activity. Ultimately, the language of the policy and the facts of the claim provide the details to enable the claim representative to settle the loss in a timely and professional manner.

Case Facts

Susan and Thomas Reed live at 104 Fremont Street in Malvern, Texas. They have two children: Ann, age 16, who lives at home, and John, age 19, who lives at home when not attending Columbus College in New Mexico. Susan's mother, Marie, also lives with them. Susan is a schoolteacher. Thomas is the owner of a small company called Universal Widgets.

Susan and Thomas own their home and three cars. The ABC Loan Company holds a mortgage on their home. They also have a car loan, from Union Trust Company, on their 2010 Lexus. They do not have lienholders for their other two cars (a 2007 Toyota Camry and a 2006 Honda Civic).

Susan and Thomas have an HO-3 (2000) policy covering their home. They have a Personal Auto Policy (PAP) covering all three cars.

On April 12, 20XX, Susan and Thomas received a phone call from John's roommate informing them that John had been in an auto accident while driving the Honda Civic. John suffered minor injuries after failing to obey a stop sign and then hitting another car. The driver of the other car, Karen Jones, was hospitalized.

Case Analysis Tools

To handle a claim such as the one provided in this case study, a claim representative would need to have an understanding of the coverages provided in the HO-3 policy form and in the PAP form. However, to resolve the case study, only a thorough understanding of the activities in the claim handling process and specific knowledge about handling auto property and liability claims is required.

Activities in the Claim Handling Process

A thorough understanding of these activities in the claim handling process will lead to the conclusion described in the Correct Answer section and other possible conclusions to this case study:

- Acknowledging and assigning the claim
- Identifying the policy and setting reserves
- Contacting the insured or the insured's representative
- Investigating the claim
- Documenting the claim
- Determining the cause of loss, liability, and the loss amount
- Concluding the claim

Acknowledging and Assigning the Claim

After talking with John, Thomas called his insurance agent and reported the claim. The agent then reported the claim to the insurer. Claim Representative Jim Smith was assigned to handle all aspects of the claim.

After he received the claim assignment, Jim acknowledged receipt of the claim to the agent. Then he entered the claim information into the insurer's claim-processing system.

Identifying the Policy and Setting Reserves

Jim identified the Reeds' auto policy and performed an initial review. He established that the 2006 Honda Civic had liability coverage, collision coverage with a $1,000 deductible, and Personal Injury Protection coverage. Based on the limited information on the first notice of loss, Jim set up these parts of the claim with preliminary reserves:

- Bodily injury liability claim from Karen Jones—reserve $5,000
- Property damage claim from Karen Jones—reserve $2,500
- Collision coverage for the 2006 Honda—reserve $2,500
- PIP coverage for John's injuries—reserve $1,000

Contacting the Insured or the Insured's Representative

Jim contacted Susan and Thomas Reed. They gave him a brief description of the accident and asked Jim to contact John for all of the details about what happened. While talking with Susan and Thomas, Jim confirmed that they are the registered owners of the car, that the car is registered in Texas, and that John was using the car with their permission.

Jim called John and took a recorded statement that provided these facts:

- John is a full-time college student in New Mexico. He lives in a dormitory on campus. He has had the Honda at school since the beginning of the semester and parks it on a campus parking lot.
- The accident occurred at 11:30 AM on a Saturday morning. John was driving to a sandwich shop. He did not see a stop sign or the car on his right because of sun glare, so he entered the intersection without slowing down or stopping.
- John's car struck the car driven by Karen Jones on the driver's side door. John was wearing his seatbelt at the time of the accident. His air bag deployed on impact. He was taken to the emergency room, treated for minor cuts, and released.
- Karen Jones was also taken to the emergency room. John believed she had a concussion and a deep laceration on her forehead. John received a ticket for careless driving.
- The Honda was taken to Sam's Auto Body Shop in Columbus, New Mexico.

Investigating the Claim

After concluding his conversation with John, Jim requested a police report and reviewed the PAP to answer some questions he had regarding coverage for this claim. Jim had already confirmed that the Honda is listed on the Reeds' policy and that it has collision coverage. *(Is the damaged property covered? Is the cause of loss covered?)* He also confirmed that the accident date occurred within the policy period. *(Did the loss occur during the policy period?)*

Jim determined who is covered by the PAP. According to the liability coverage part, "insured" is defined in this manner:

1. You or any "family member" for the ownership, maintenance or use of any auto or "trailer".

According to the definition of insured, John is covered by the policy. *(Is the person involved covered?)* The insuring agreement states that the insurer will pay damages for bodily injury or property damage for which any insured becomes legally responsible because of an auto accident. The insuring agreement also states that the policy will pay defense costs in addition to the limit of liability. *(Is the type of loss covered?)*

Jim then checked the Part A exclusions. None of the exclusions appear to apply. *(Do any exclusions apply?)*

Next, Jim examined the policy period and territory provision of the PAP. The loss occurred during the policy period and within the policy territory of the U.S. *(Is the location where the loss occurred covered?)*

Based on the information obtained from Thomas Reed and John Reed, no other auto policies are applicable to this accident because all of the Reeds' cars are insured under this policy. *(Does other insurance apply?)*

The PAP provides out-of-state coverage, so the policy complies with New Mexico's financial responsibility laws. New Mexico does not have no-fault laws, so the liability portion of the Reeds' coverage will apply to Karen's bodily injury and property claims. *(Do any other policies apply to the loss?)* Based on the limited medical information available at this time concerning Karen, Jim believes that the liability limit on the Reeds' policy is sufficient to cover the bodily injury and property damage that Karen sustained. *(Are the amounts of loss or damages covered?)* However, Jim will have to review this portion of the claim frequently as more information about Karen and her injuries becomes available

Jim confirmed that Karen was released from the hospital after she received treatment for her injuries and was kept for 24 hours of observation because of blood loss. He called her the next day to take her claim statement, which confirmed John's account of the accident. Karen's statement also revealed these details:

- Karen is 38 years old and single, and lives at 2227 North Casa Avenue, Apt. 215, Pueblo, New Mexico.

- Karen received sixty stitches for the wound in her forehead. While in the hospital, she received blood to replace blood she lost because of the laceration to her forehead. The emergency staff confirmed through an X-ray that she had suffered a minor concussion, and the physician prescribed a pain reliever for her headaches.

- Karen was placed under observation for one week to monitor any problems that might ensue because of the concussion.

- Karen's 2008 Buick Lucerne was taken to Roy's Auto Damage, where an estimate for $3,800 was prepared to cover repairs to the driver's-side door and front fender. Karen agreed to mail the estimate to Jim.

- Based on the estimate, Jim adjusted the property damage reserve for Karen's auto to $3,800.

Documenting the Claim

Jim recorded all of the information he learned through the investigation in his file status notes for this claim. He included the police report with a diagram of the scene (that matched John's and Karen's accident descriptions), Karen's auto estimate, and the recorded statements of the two claimants with the claim file documents.

The claim diary system created an automatic entry for follow-up two weeks after the date of Jim's initial entry. Jim changed the diary date to two weeks from the date he completed this phase of the investigation. Documentation of changes in the claim information, reserves, and settlements will be ongoing. Jim will also have to continue his investigation to determine who is liable for the accident.

Determining Cause of Loss, Liability, and Loss Amount

As part of his analysis of liability coverage, Jim answered some of the questions that needed to be asked when analyzing coverage for the damage to the Reeds' Honda:

- Did the loss occur during the policy period?
- Is the loss location covered by the policy?
- Do any other auto policies apply to this loss?

Based on the police report, the ticket issued to John, and John's own admission of fault, Jim determined that John was liable for the damages in the accident through tort liability. Because John is an insured under Susan and Thomas's policy, the policy will cover the damages up to the policy limits.

This investigation resolved the questions to which answers are required to ensure coverage under auto liability. (*Did the claim arise out of the use of certain autos by certain individuals? Was the claim for bodily injury or property damage?*) The investigation also addressed the PAP exclusion for intentional acts, as John did not intend the result of his actions or intend to commit the action that caused the injurious outcomes.After reviewing Part D—Coverage for Damage to Your Auto of the PAP, Jim confirmed that there is collision coverage on the Reeds' Honda. Based on the facts currently known, Jim reviewed the exclusions to Part D coverage and determined that none of the exclusions apply.

Property Damage Claims

Jim assigned an appraiser to assess the amount of damage to the Reeds' Honda and to Karen's Buick and to prepare estimates to repair the damages. Based on the description of the accident that John gave in his statement, Jim decided that the $2,500 reserve for the Honda is adequate. He will review the reserves after he receives the appraiser's estimates.

Jim changed the diary date to two weeks after the date he requested the estimate from the appraiser, so that he can follow up if he does not receive the reports. He also updated the file status notes with the cause of loss, liability, and coverage information.

Two days later, Jim received the appraiser's estimate for $3,700 in damages to the Reeds' Honda and an estimate for the damage to Karen's Buick that was $5 less than the estimate Karen submitted. He also received photos of the damage to both autos. Jim adjusted the reserve for this expected damage amount on the Reeds' auto to $2,700 (after application of the $1,000 deductible). The difference in the estimates for Karen's Buick was negligible, so he made no change to that reserve. Jim updated his file status notes and added the estimates and photos to the claim file.

John's Medical Claim

Jim reviewed the Personal Injury Protection (PIP) endorsement attached to the Reeds' auto policy. This endorsement provides unlimited medical expenses coverage to covered persons. Jim confirmed that the definition of insured applies to a family member. The insuring agreement states that PIP benefits will be paid to an insured who sustains bodily injury caused by an accident and resulting from the use of an auto. The medical expenses must be reasonable and necessary.

John had indicated that he suffered a laceration above his eye, which was treated at the emergency room. He also received treatment from a chiropractor for his sore neck and back. John will give his medical bills to Jim for review and reimbursement.

Jim also reviewed the exclusions in the endorsement and determined that none of them apply. Jim decided to raise the reserve on John's PIP claim to $2,500 to cover the emergency room bill and three months of chiropractic treatment.

Four months after the accident, Jim verified that John's treatment for his injuries had ended. John submitted medical bills and medical mileage expenses totaling $2,400. Jim examined the bills and mileage figures and determined that they were reasonable and necessary for John's injuries.

Karen's Medical Claim

Six weeks after the accident, Jim reviewed the medical receipts and medical mileage records he received from Karen for treatment of her injury. He determined that they were reasonable and necessary for the injuries she sustained. He reviewed an early photo of Karen's injured forehead and a recent photo showing that scarring was minimal.

Jim submitted a query in an injury database to which his employer subscribes. It showed that Karen had never sustained any injuries that were submitted to a workers compensation or liability insurer. This indicated that her injuries from this accident were new injuries.

Jim totaled the medical receipts and medical mileage claim at $4,200. Because she was hospitalized over a weekend and was able to report to work the following Monday, Karen incurred no loss of income. Jim added 10 percent to the total to compensate Karen for her "pain and suffering." Jim then confirmed that the total of $4,620 plus $3,800 for Karen's Buick, or $8,420, was within the Reeds' PAP liability policy limit.

Concluding the Claim

Before issuing any payments, Jim checked the federal and state databases to ensure that neither Karen nor any of the Reeds had any outstanding legal obligations that would require payment before they could receive any payment for their claims.

After Karen's auto was repaired, Jim issued a check payable to Roy's Auto Damage and to Karen Jones for $3,800. He then closed Karen's property damage reserve. After the Reeds' Honda was repaired, Jim issued a check payable to Sam's Auto Body and Thomas and Susan Reed for $2,700 and closed the Reeds' property damage reserve.

Jim arranged a settlement review with Karen, in which he offered her the calculated total of $4,620 for her medical expenses. Jim explained how he arrived at that amount and that he believed it was a reasonable settlement. He also showed Karen the total amount of the bodily injury and property damage claims paid by the Reeds' insurer for Karen's damages. (At this time, Jim noted that the scar on Karen's forehead was barely visible). Karen accepted Jim's settlement offer. He issued her a check for her medical expenses and obtained a full release from liability for the claim, which Karen signed. Later, Jim closed Karen's bodily injury claim reserve.

Jim contacted the Reeds and offered to pay $2,400 for John's PIP claim. Because John was at fault for the accident, no "pain and suffering" compensation was warranted. Jim noted that they had already paid $2,700 ($3,700 less the $1,000 deductible) for repairs to the Honda. The Reeds accepted Jim's settlement offer. He mailed them a check for $2,400, along with full releases for their property damage claim and for John's PIP claim. The Reeds signed the forms and returned them to Jim's office the following day. Jim closed John's PIP reserve.

Jim included the signed releases in the claim file and completed his file status notes to indicate the outcome of Karen's settlement meeting and the Reeds' settlements. Then he marked the claim file as closed on the insurer's claim information system. See the exhibit "Correct Answer*."

Correct Answer*

Claim Payments for Reed/Jones Accident, DOL: 04/12/20XX

- Bodily injury liability claim payment for Karen Jones-Final payment, $4,620
- Property damage claim for Karen Jones's 2008 Buick-Final payment, $3,800
- Collision coverage for the Reeds' 2006 Honda-Final payment, $2,700
- PIP coverage for John Reed's injuries-Final payment, $2,400

*This solution might not be the only viable solution. Other solutions could be exercised if justified by the analysis. In addition, specific circumstances and organizational needs or goals may enter into the evaluation, making an alternative action a better option.

[DA06275]

SUMMARY

Several questions must be answered about every property claim. Answering these questions forms a framework for property claim representatives to use for all kinds of property damage claims:

- Who has an insurable interest? Who is an insured?
- What property is insured? Where is it insured? When is it insured?
- What are the covered causes of loss?
- What is the dollar amount of loss?
- What are the insured's duties after a loss?
- What procedures are used to conclude a claim?

Claim representatives must adapt their claim handling process for different types of property losses because of challenges faced in each type of property claim. Each of these types of property claims poses unique challenges for a claim representative:

- Residential dwelling claims—The emotional devastation of insureds and the need for alternative shelter and living arrangements are special challenges to claim representatives in these claims.
- Residential personal property claims—Lack of personal property inventories, valuation issues, and depreciation pose challenges for handling such claims.
- Commercial structure claims—High property values, the need for architectural and construction expert advice, and difficulties determining ACV often pose challenges in handling these claims.
- Business income claims—These complex claims often require a detailed analysis of financial records by an accountant for proper claim handling.
- Merchandise claims—Merchandise that the insured holds for sale is a special type of business personal property requiring special valuation and salvage considerations.

- Transportation and bailment claims—These losses can create complicated legal and coverage issues.
- Catastrophe claims—The widespread damage caused by catastrophes, affecting entire communities, requires pre-loss and post-loss planning and deployment that creates challenges for insurers and their claim representatives.

Liability claim representatives are primarily concerned with the laws of liability and damages, which exist apart from the insurance policy.

Handling a liability claim entails four steps, which are not necessarily completed sequentially:

- Determining coverage—Liability coverages generally require that the insured pay sums the insured is legally obligated to pay.
- Determining legal liability—The basic law of negligence applies to most liability claims that claim representatives handle, but claim representatives must also consider strict liability for products and specific statutory liability for certain auto accidents.
- Determining damages—Determining and evaluating general damages are essential skills for liability claim representatives because general damages are often the main element of the claim.
- Negotiating and settling the claim—Negotiation involves discussing all issues and arriving at a mutually satisfactory settlement of the claim, usually within the policy limits. Should negotiations prove unsuccessful, liability claim representatives must know how to guide claims through the courts as part of the litigation process, and they must understand their role in the insurer's duty to defend its insureds.

Specific types of liability claims present their own distinct challenges. Experienced liability claim representatives are familiar with the difficulties that can arise for various types of claims. These types of liability claims pose unique challenges for claim representatives:

- Auto bodily injury liability claims—These claims can be complicated and might require accident reconstruction experts and coordination with auto no-fault, workers compensation, UM, and/or UIM claims. Subrogation issues can further complicate auto liability claims.
- Auto property damage claims—These claims usually require an appraisal and can involve issues with third-party claimants, constructive total losses, and agreed repair prices.
- Premises liability claims—In these claims, the claim representative must first determine the cause of the accident according to negligence theories to establish whether the insured is liable for the injuries arising from the accident.
- Operations liability claims—Handling operations liability claims generally focuses on an unsafe act rather than on an unsafe condition within the premises.

- Products liability claims—In these claims, the claim representative must investigate all possible bases of liability and applicable defenses before settling the claim.

- Workers compensation claims—These claims are compensated regardless of fault and are, therefore, an exception to the liability system. Controlling medical and disability expenses each pose different challenges in workers compensation claims.

- Professional liability claims—These claims are usually handled by claim representatives who specialize in liability claims against professional service providers such as physicians, engineers, architects, lawyers, accountants, and insurance producers.

Claim representatives can use the framework for coverage analysis and the claim handling process as guides for every claim they handle. The language of the policy and the facts of the claim will provide the details.

ASSIGNMENT NOTE

1. Commercial General Liability Coverage Form, CG 00 01 12 01 © ISO Property, Inc., 2006, p. 1.

Direct Your Learning ▶▶

Actuarial Operations

Educational Objectives

After learning the content of this assignment, you should be able to:

▶ Describe the actuarial function in insurer operations and the actuarial services required by insurers.

▶ Describe the insurer goals of ratemaking and the ideal characteristics of rates.

▶ Describe the components of an insurance rate and common ratemaking terms.

▶ Explain how the following factors can affect ratemaking:

- Estimation of losses
- Delays in data collection and use
- Change in the cost of claims
- Insurer's projected expenses
- Target level of profit and contingencies

▶ Describe the following ratemaking methods:

- Pure premium
- Loss ratio
- Judgment

▶ Describe each of the following steps in the ratemaking process:

- Collect data
- Adjust data
- Calculate the indicated overall rate change
- Determine territorial and class relativities
- Prepare and submit rate filings to regulatory authorities as required.

9

▸ Describe the policy-year, calendar-year, accident-year, and report-year data aggregation methods.

▸ Explain how the following ratemaking factors vary by type of insurance:

- Experience period
- Trending
- Large loss limitations
- Credibility
- Increased limits factors

▸ Describe the purpose and types of loss reserves, the importance of accurate estimation of loss reserves, and techniques used by actuaries in their analysis.

Actuarial Operations

9

THE ACTUARIAL FUNCTION

Actuaries are professionals who evaluate the financial consequences of future events. As such, they play a critical role in the fields of insurance and risk management.

The actuarial function is responsible for ensuring that the insurer operates effectively and conducts its operations on a financially sound basis. The two most prominent actuarial functions for an insurer involve ratemaking and estimation of unpaid liabilities and adequacy of loss reserves. Actuaries are also instrumental in developing an insurer's predictive models, and they perform other important functions for insurers, including analyzing reinsurance structure and participating in corporate planning and budgeting.

What is an Actuary?

There are many definitions of what an actuary is. The American Academy of Actuary succinctly states, "actuaries put a price tag on risk."[1] A more encompassing definition states, "an actuary is a business professional who deals with the financial impact of risk." The latter definition includes several terms that describe actuaries and their work.

First, actuaries are professionals; they have a formal educational process, a set of standards for performance, and a code of conduct. Focusing on the financial effects of risk, actuaries are found throughout the business world, often employed by either insurance companies or firms supplying services to insurers. Actuaries often rely heavily on mathematical models and statistical techniques, but their examination process also covers insurance operations, accounting, insurance law, and financial analysis.

In the United States, actuaries have several specialties, including life insurance, health insurance, pension, and property/casualty insurance. This discussion focuses on property/casualty actuaries specific to insurer operations.

Actuarial Functions

One of the major functions of actuaries is to direct insurer ratemaking operations. Actuaries also develop factors that are applied to loss costs in order to reflect individual insurer experience and expenses. The ratemaking process involves estimation of trends that will affect claim costs during the future effective period of the rates. Thus, the actuary must consider economic and regulatory factors that will affect the potential cost of coverage.

Another major function of an actuary involves the estimation of an insurer's unpaid liabilities and adequacy of its loss reserves. Insurers are required by both accounting standards and law to set aside funds for the future payments on claims for which they are liable. Actuaries use various methods to estimate the amount of these liabilities. In the U.S., insurers are required to submit, with their statutory annual statement, a statement of opinion by a qualified actuary as to whether the carried reserves make a reasonable provision for this liability. The actuary providing this statement must have been approved by the insurer's board of directors and is named individually in the statement.

Data mining

The process of extracting hidden patterns from data that is used in a wide range of applications for research and fraud detection.

Actuaries are also instrumental in developing insurer's predictive models using **data mining** tools. Predictive modeling is increasingly being applied in areas such as ratemaking, underwriting, claims analytics, customer segmentation, and target marketing, which can lead to increased profits for an insurer.

Because of their quantitative background and familiarity in dealing with uncertain events, actuaries often perform other tasks, primarily related to assessment of insurer risks, including these:

- Analyzing reinsurance needs to determine the level and concentration of risk the insurer can retain versus the cost of reinsurance
- Estimating future cash flows so that assets will be available when claims are to be paid
- Assessing corporate risk by testing the adequacy of surplus under potential adverse conditions (catastrophe, sudden change in asset values, soft pricing, and inflation, for example)
- Providing financial and statistical information to regulators and applicable statistical agents (with accounting and finance areas)
- Participating in corporate planning and budgeting

Actuarial Services

Many large insurers employ a number of actuaries. Although small insurers may have a few actuaries on staff, most tend to rely on actuarial consultants. Some actuaries are concentrated in specialized departments, such as reserving. Insurers may also use actuaries within regional offices or in other functional areas, such as underwriting.

Insurers that employ staff actuaries may also retain actuarial consultants. Outside actuaries can supplement staff knowledge with specialized expertise, provide independent opinion when needed, and ease workload peaks. Regulatory authorities and reinsurers sometimes require insurers to provide a consulting actuary's opinion verifying the accuracy and reasonableness of the staff actuaries' work.

Insurers with limited data for ratemaking rely on rates or loss costs prepared by actuaries at advisory organizations, such as Insurance Services Office (ISO), American Association of Insurance Services (AAIS), or the National Council on Compensation Insurance (NCCI). The actuaries at these organizations collect premium and loss data from many insurers to use in calculating expected loss costs for various types of insurance. Advisory organizations also maintain contact with regulatory authorities to facilitate approval of rate filings. Advisory organizations also provide some services that are not actuarial, such as drafting insurance policies.

INSURER RATEMAKING GOALS

Insurance ratemaking is challenging, because when rates are developed, the amounts of fortuitous future losses and their associated expenses are unknown. In light of this uncertainty, insurers try to develop rates that meet their goals.

With the ratemaking process, insurers strive to be profitable while also meeting all insurance policy obligations. An ideal insurance rate has a number of different characteristics, including some that are contradictory.

Ratemaking Goals

From the insurer's perspective, the primary goal of **ratemaking** is to develop a rate structure that enables the insurer to compete effectively while earning a reasonable profit on its operations. To accomplish this, the rates must result in premiums that adequately cover all losses and expenses and that leave a reasonable amount for profits and contingencies.

Ratemaking
The process insurers use to calculate insurance rates, which are a premium component.

This ratemaking goal complements the underwriting goal, which is to develop and maintain a profitable book of business. To be profitable, the insurer must have adequate rates. However, to maintain its book of business, the insurer's rates must be competitive. These goals can easily conflict with each other. The rate chosen by an insurer is often a compromise between maximizing profit and maintaining (or expanding) market share.

To be approved, rates must comply with applicable regulations. Rate regulation is generally based on having rates that are adequate, not excessive, and not unfairly discriminatory.

Ideal Characteristics of Rates

Ideally, rates should have five characteristics:

- Be stable
- Be responsive
- Provide for contingencies

- Promote risk control
- Reflect differences in risk exposure

Rates do not always have all of these characteristics. Also, some characteristics conflict with others, and compromises are often necessary. For example, rate stability could conflict with the characteristic of responsiveness, which suggests that rates should change promptly in response to external factors that affect losses.

Stable

Stable rates are highly desirable because changing rates is expensive. It takes a fair amount of time and expense to calculate rate indications, get needed approval, and implement them. Generally, rates are changed no more than annually. Rates should also be stable in the sense of not changing drastically from one rate change to the next. Sudden large rate changes cause dissatisfaction among customers and sometimes lead to regulatory or legislative actions.

Responsive

Rates should include the best possible estimates of losses and expenses that will arise from the coverage. Because external conditions change over time, the most recent claim experience ought to predict future experience better than older experience. For this reason, most insurers and advisory organizations review their rates at least annually.

Provide for Contingencies

Future events cannot be predicted accurately, and the insurer has a responsibility to pay all valid claims even if costs are higher than estimated. Rates should provide for contingencies, such as unexpected variations in losses and expenses. This provision will also provide greater security that the insurer will be able to meet its obligations to potential claimants.

Promote Risk Control

Ratemaking systems help to promote risk control by providing lower rates for policyholders who exercise sound risk control. For example, policyholders who install burglar alarm systems receive a reduction in their crime insurance rates. Lower fire insurance rates are charged to policyholders who install automatic sprinkler systems at their premises. However, policyholders who engage in activities that tend to result in more losses, such as persons who use their cars for business, generally pay higher rates.

Reflect Differences in Risk Exposure

A rate is a charge for the exposure to risk. If insureds have attributes that make them more or less susceptible to a risk, using a flat rate means that some will be overcharged and others will be undercharged. For example, the fire insurance rate should not be the same for a wood-frame building as for a steel and concrete building; an ideal rate reflects these differences. Moreover, if the rate could not reflect differences in exposure, the insurer would end up with only higher-risk insureds, a process called anti-selection. Using the preceding example again, owners of wood-frame buildings would gladly pay an "average" rate for fire insurance, while owners of steel buildings would find another insurer who would credit them for the lower risk. The first insurer would end up with only wood-frame insureds, and the average rate would be insufficient for that group. Because insurers have the ability to collect and analyze detailed data on each insured, they can incorporate exposure differences into the rates more accurately.

RATE COMPONENTS AND RATEMAKING TERMS

A rate is the basis for the premium charged by an insurer. To understand why a certain premium or rate is charged, the components that make up a rate must be understood. Knowledge of the components and terminology used in ratemaking will serve as a foundation to understanding the ratemaking process.

This section reviews the components of an insurance rate and discusses common ratemaking terms.

Rate Components

An insurance **rate** consists of three components:

- An amount needed to pay future claims and loss adjustment expenses (prospective loss costs)
- An amount needed to pay future expenses, such as acquisition expenses, overhead, and premium taxes (expense provision)
- An amount for profit and contingencies (profit and contingencies factor)

The first component of an insurance rate is related to the prospective loss costs developed by advisory organizations or by insurers with large pools of loss data. The second and third components are related to an expense multiplier. Once the insurance rate is calculated, it is multiplied by the appropriate number of exposure units to produce a **premium**.

Ratemaking Terms

These are common terms used in the ratemaking process:

- Exposure base (sometimes just exposure) is a variable that approximates the loss potential of a type of insurance. For property coverage, the expo-

Rate
The price per exposure unit for insurance coverage.

Premium
The price of the insurance coverage provided for a specified period.

sure base is the value being insured; for product liability, the exposure is sales.

- Earned exposure unit is the exposure unit for which the insurer has provided a full period of coverage. The periods are typically measured in years.

- **Pure premium** is the amount included in the rate per exposure unit required to pay losses. This component is also sometimes called the loss cost.

- **Expense provision** is the amount added to the pure premium required to pay expenses. Such expenses include acquisition expenses; general expenses; premium taxes; and licenses and fees paid to government, regulatory, and advisory organizations. This component is sometimes referred to as **underwriting expenses**.

- **Loss adjustment expenses (LAE)** are the expenses associated with adjusting claims. These expenses are often split into either **allocated** or **unallocated LAE**. Some allocated loss adjustment expenses, such as legal fees to defend a claim, may be included in the pure premium instead of in the expense provision. An example of loss adjustment expenses included in the expense provision is the cost of an insurer's in-house claims adjusters.

- Insurers add a loading for profit and contingencies. This loading protects the insurer against the possibility that actual losses and expenses will exceed the projected losses and expenses included in the insurance rate. If excessive losses or expenses are not incurred, the funds generated by the loading produce additional profit for the insurer.

Investment Income

A property-casualty insurer performs two distinct operations: insurance operations and investment operations. The insurance operations write policies, collect premiums, and pay losses. The result of the insurance operations is called **underwriting profit**. The investment operations use the funds generated by the insurance operations to buy or sell bonds, stocks, and other investments to earn an investment profit. The return from these investments is called investment income.

Historically, property-casualty insurers did not consider their investment returns directly when calculating insurance rates. They may, however, have considered investment returns informally when determining allowances for profits and contingencies. Today, insurers commonly consider investment results explicitly in their rate calculations. Some states even require that investment income be considered explicitly. Sophisticated models are available that can be used to include investment returns in the insurance rate.

The investment return earned by an insurer depends largely on the types of insurance written, the loss reserves, and associated unearned premium reserves. Property losses are usually paid relatively quickly, while liability

Pure premium

The average amount of money an insurer must charge per exposure unit in order to be able to cover the total anticipated losses for that line of business.

Expense provision

The amount that is included in an insurance rate to cover the insurer's expenses and that might include loss adjustment expenses but that excludes investment expenses.

Underwriting expenses

Costs incurred by an insurer for operations, taxes, fees, and the acquisition of new policies.

Loss adjustment expense (LAE)

The expense that an insurer incurs to investigate, defend, and settle claims according to the terms specified in the insurance policy.

Allocated loss adjustment expenses (ALAE)

The expenses an insurer incurs to investigate, defend, and settle claims that are associated with a specific claim.

Unallocated loss adjustment expenses (ULAE)

Loss adjustment expenses that cannot be readily associated with a specific claim.

Underwriting profit

Income an insurer earns from premiums paid by policyholders minus incurred losses and underwriting expenses.

losses often are not paid until years after losses occur. Consequently, an insurer's loss reserves for liability insurance are usually much greater than its loss reserves for an equivalent amount of property insurance. Because the assets that support the loss reserves are invested to produce income for the insurer, investment returns have a much larger effect on liability insurance rates than property insurance rates.

FACTORS THAT AFFECT RATEMAKING

Various factors have considerable effect on the rate that is set for a particular insurance coverage.

Estimating future events and costs in the real world is subject to uncertainty. These areas of uncertainty affect ratemaking:

- Estimation of losses
- Delays in data collection and use
- Change in the cost of claims
- Insurer's projected expenses
- Target level of profit and contingencies

Estimation of Losses

The key to developing insurance rates that are adequate to pay future claims is estimating the amount of losses for those claims. Past loss experience is generally used as a starting point to estimate future losses. Ratemaking is based on estimating losses from past coverage periods and then adjusting those losses for future conditions. For example, adjustments could be made to past loss experience for anticipated future inflation or for changes in benefits mandated by legislation.

However, past loss experience may not be completely known because not all covered losses are paid immediately. At any point in time, many claims have been incurred but not yet paid. The difference between the estimated amount that will ultimately be paid for claims and the actual loss amount paid to date is the loss reserves. Insurers face the challenge of estimating **ultimate losses** for past experience as accurately as possible because of the difficulty of estimating future payments.

Ultimate loss

The final paid amount for all losses in an accident year.

Insurance rates are based partly on incurred losses. Incurred losses include both paid losses and outstanding loss reserves. Loss reserves are estimates of future payments for covered claims that have already occurred, whether the claims are reported or not. Insurers are legally required to set aside funds for these future payments; these are shown as liabilities on their balance sheets. Because loss reserves are estimates of future events, they are somewhat imprecise. Nonetheless, rates are based partly on such estimates. Therefore, if loss reserve estimates are too low, rates will probably be too low. If loss reserves are too high, rates will probably be too high.

To illustrate, assume that rates for auto liability insurance are calculated based on losses that occurred in the most recent three-year period. The insurer's past experience indicates that 25 percent of losses are paid in the year the accident occurs, 50 percent are paid in the second year, and 25 percent are paid in the third year. The exhibit shows the losses for each year in the three-year period, with Year 1 being the earliest year and Year 3, the most recent year. See the exhibit "Hypothetical Auto Liability Loss Experience at Year 3 End."

Hypothetical Auto Liability Loss Experience at Year 3 End

Year	(1) Paid Losses	(2) Loss Reserves	(3) Incurred Losses
1	$10,000,000	$0	$10,000,000
2	7,500,000	2,500,000	10,000,000
3	2,500,000	7,500,000	10,000,000
Total	$20,000,000	$10,000,000	$30,000,000

[DA03362]

The exhibit shows this information:

- The paid losses in Column (1) are the amounts paid from January 1 of Year 1 up to and including December 31 of Year 3. The insurer has already paid this money to claimants.

- The loss reserves shown in Column (2) are the insurer's best estimates, as of December 31 of Year 3, of the amounts it will pay in the future for losses that occurred during each one-year period. Because all losses that occurred in Year 1 have been paid, no loss reserve exists for Year 1.

- Column (3), which is incurred losses for a given period, is the sum of Columns (1) and (2).

If the insurer in this exhibit insured 100,000 cars each year during this three-year period, it provided 300,000 car-years of protection. A car-year represents the loss exposure of one car insured for one year. If the 300,000 car-years are divided into the $30 million of incurred losses, the insurer needs a pure premium—the amount needed to pay losses—of $100 per car per year ($30,000,000 ÷ 300,000 = $100) to pay its losses during this past three-year period. This example includes not only paid losses but also loss reserves.

If the pure premium indicated by this experience period were used to develop rates for a future year, any inadequacy in past loss reserves would also make future rates inadequate. Using the preceding example, assume that the loss reserves were underestimated by 15 percent; that is, the company had only $8,500,000 in loss reserves at the end of Year 3 instead of $10,000,000. The total incurred losses for the years would then be $28,500,000, and the calculated pure premium would be only $95 per car per year ($28,500,000 ÷ 300,000). Rates based on underestimated losses could lead to underwriting losses and possibly even insolvency.

In theory, an insurer could avoid this problem by waiting for all claims to be paid before using loss experience to calculate rates. When all claims incurred during a given period have been paid, there is no need for loss reserves. In practice, however, waiting would create problems. If the rate filing were delayed for several years to permit all claims to be settled, then factors such as inflation, changes in traffic conditions, and so forth would have a greater chance of changing the loss exposure. The effects of these factors might be greater than the effects of errors in estimating loss reserves.

Delays in Data Collection and Use

Responsiveness is a desirable ratemaking characteristic. Because conditions are constantly changing, any delay between when data are collected and when they are used tends to reduce rate accuracy. A delay inevitably occurs between when losses are incurred and when they are reflected in rates charged to customers. The delay can span several years. During this period, economic or other factors can increase or decrease the rates the insurer should charge if the premium is to reflect the expected losses.

The delay in reflecting loss experience in rates stems from several sources, including these:

- Delays by insureds in reporting losses to insurers
- Time required to analyze data and prepare a rate filing
- Delays in obtaining state approval of filed rates
- Time required to implement new rates
- Time period during which rates are in effect, usually a full year

When a rate is in effect for a full year, the last policy issued under that rate could be issued 365 days (one year) after the effective date of the rate filing, and the policy's coverage under that rate continues until policy expiration, yet another year later. See the exhibit "Policy Year Timeframe."

Policy Year Timeframe

1/1/X1 ----------------- 12/31/X1 ----------------- 12/31/X2
Beginning of Policy Year First Policies Issued	Last Policies Issued for This Policy Year	Policies Issued 12/31/X1 Expire

[DA03368]

Experience period

The period for which all pertinent statistics are collected and analyzed in the ratemaking process.

The "Chronology of a Rate Filing" exhibit shows a reasonably typical schedule for developing, approving, and implementing new rates for auto insurance. The exhibit assumes that the insurer is basing its new rates on its loss experience for a prior three-year period, called the **experience period**. Data from the experience period are collected and analyzed in the ratemaking process. See the exhibit "Chronology of a Rate Filing."

Chronology of a Rate Filing

1/1, Year 1	Start of experience period, first loss incurred
12/31, Year 1	
12/31, Year 2	
12/31, Year 3	End of experience period
3/31, Year 4	Start of data collection and analysis
7/1, Year 4	Rates filed with regulators
9/1, Year 4	Approval of rates received
1/1, Year 5	New rates initially used
12/31, Year 5	Rates no longer used
12/31, Year 6	Last loss incurred under this rate filing

[DA03369]

The experience period in the exhibit begins on January 1 of Year 1. Data are collected for the three-year period beginning on that date and ending on December 31 of Year 3. The analysis phase of the ratemaking process begins three months after the end of the experience period. Some insurers wait longer to start the ratemaking process in order to permit loss data to mature because many claims incurred during the experience period would not yet have been reported to the insurer within three months.

The exhibit assumes that the new rates will become effective on January 1 of Year 5, one year after the end of the experience period. They will remain in effect until December 31 of Year 5, two years after the end of the experience period. However, the policies issued on December 31 of Year 5 will remain in force until December 31 of Year 6. Consequently, the last claim under these rates will be incurred three years after the end of the experience period, and six years after the beginning of the experience period, when the first losses on which the rate calculation was based occurred.

Some insurers shorten this process slightly by filing new rates every six months or issuing six-month policies. Others follow a longer cycle.

Change in Cost of Claims

Both loss severity and loss frequency affect an insurer's loss experience during any given period. Economic inflation or deflation during the inevitable delay also affects the average cost of a loss (severity). Finally, legislative or regulatory changes such as modification in rules governing claim settlement can affect the number of losses (frequency). Rates calculated without regard to these factors could prove to be grossly inadequate or grossly excessive.

These factors are difficult to quantify, but they clearly affect losses. Some factors that affect the size and frequency of losses cannot be identified or measured directly, but their aggregate effect on losses can be determined with reasonable accuracy by trending. The effects of historical changes can be used to adjust the experience used in the ratemaking analysis. In addition, the rates must include a provision for changes that may arise during the period rates will be in effect. For example, in the "Chronology of a Rate Filing" exhibit, the end of the experience period used is December 31, Year 3. However, the claims under the new rates will not start occurring until January 1, Year 5, and may occur as late as December 31, Year 6. Therefore, the filing made on July 1, Year 4 must make allowance for as much of two and a half years of additional (estimated) trend.

Insurer's Projected Expenses

Insurance rates are also based on the insurer's projected expenses. Like losses, expenses can change over time, and any projected changes must be considered in the ratemaking process. Rather than past expenses, it is sometimes more relevant to use judgment or budgeted expenses, especially when conditions change dramatically. For example, if a new agent commission plan was introduced, past commission expense would not necessarily be a good estimate of the costs for new policies.

Ratemakers are also challenged to allocate general administrative expenses properly among different types of insurance. Changes in the allocation of these expenses may need to be reflected in the rates.

Target Level of Profit and Contingencies

The insurer must decide what provision for profit and contingencies should be included in the rate. Consideration is given to the overall desired rate of return, including likely returns from **investment income** versus underwriting profit, respectively. An insurer's target profit may also depend on other factors. For example, an insurer may initially accept a lower profit (and thus charge lower rates) for a new insurance product in order to build a customer base.

Investment income

Interest, dividends, and net capital gains received by an insurer from the insurer's financial assets, minus its investment expenses.

RATEMAKING METHODS

While there can be myriad data, adjustments, and other inputs to the rate-making process, there are actually just a few methods for adjusting an existing rate or developing a new rate.

Insurers commonly use three ratemaking methods:

- Pure premium method
- Loss ratio method
- Judgment method

The three methods are compared in the exhibit. See the exhibit "Ratemaking Methods."

Ratemaking Methods

Method	Data Required	Uses
Pure premium method	• Incurred losses • Earned exposure units • Expense provision • Profit and contingencies factor	To develop rates from past experience (Cannot be used without past experience)
Loss ratio method	Actual loss ratio, calculated from: • Incurred losses • Earned premiums Expected loss ratio, calculated as: 100% - Provision for expenses, profit, and contingencies	To modify existing rates (Cannot be used without existing rates; cannot be used to determine rates for a new type of insurance)
Judgment method	Rates based on experience and judgment	To develop rates when data are limited (Requires skilled judgment)

[DA03381]

Pure Premium Ratemaking Method

The first ratemaking method is the **pure premium method**. This method uses loss per exposure based on past experience as the basis for the rate. While this method relies on past experience, it is independent of any current rates.

The pure premium method has four steps. The first step is to calculate the pure premium. The pure premium (the amount needed to pay losses and, depending on the line of business, allocated loss adjustment expenses) is calculated by dividing the dollar amount of incurred losses by the number of earned exposure units.

Pure premium method

A method for calculating insurance rates using estimates of future losses and expenses, including a profit and contingencies factor.

$$\text{Incurred losses} = \$4 \text{ million}$$
$$\text{Earned car-years} = 100{,}000$$
$$\text{Pure premium} = \frac{\text{Incurred losses}}{\text{Earned car-years}}$$
$$\text{Pure premium} = \frac{\$4{,}000{,}000}{100{,}000} = \$40$$

The second step in the pure premium method is to estimate expenses per exposure unit based on the insurer's past expenses (except investment expenses and possibly loss adjustment expenses). Whatever loss adjustment expenses are included in the pure premium are excluded from the expenses. Investment expenses are not directly reflected in rate calculations. If expenses are $1.7 million, then expenses per exposure unit are:

$$\frac{\$1{,}700{,}000}{100{,}000} = \$17$$

The third step is to determine the profit and contingencies factor. In this example, a factor of 5 percent is used. A provision for net investment income is generally included within the profit provision.

$$\text{Rate per exposure unit} = \frac{\text{Pure premium} + \text{Expenses per exposure unit}}{1 - \text{Profit and contingencies factor}}$$
$$= \frac{\$40 + \$17}{1 - 0.05}$$

The final step is to add the pure premium and the expense provision and divide by one minus the profit and contingencies factor. For example, if the pure premium is $40, the expenses per exposure unit are $17, and the profit and contingencies factor is 5 percent, the formula would be:

$$\text{Rate per exposure unit} = \frac{\text{Pure premium} + \text{Expenses per exposure unit}}{1 - \text{Profit and contingencies factor}}$$

$$= \frac{\$40 + \$17}{1 - 0.05}$$

$$= \frac{\$57}{0.95}$$

$$= \$60$$

The rate per exposure unit of $60 is equal to the pure premium of $40 (the amount required to pay losses) plus an additional $17 (the amount required to pay expenses) and $3 (for profit and contingencies).

Fixed and Variable Expenses

Some insurers separate their expenses into two components: fixed expenses and variable expenses. Fixed expenses are stated as a dollar amount per exposure unit. Variable expenses are stated as a percentage of the rate. For example, the insurer in the preceding example might decide that its cost for issuing a policy and collecting the premium is $2.50 per car-year, regardless of premium size, rating class, or rating territory. Its other underwriting expenses, such as commissions and premium tax, vary by premium size. The variable expenses equal 12 percent of the final premium. The rate per exposure unit in this case would be:

$$\text{Rate per exposure unit} = \frac{\text{Pure premium} + \text{Fixed expenses per exposure unit}}{1 - \text{Variable expense percentage} - \text{Profit and contingencies factor}}$$

$$= \frac{\$40 + \$2.50}{1 - 0.12 - 0.05}$$

$$= \frac{\$42.50}{0.83}$$

$$= \$51 \, (\text{rounded}).$$

The new rate per exposure unit of $51 is equal to the sum of pure premium of $40 (the amount required to pay losses or loss costs), fixed expenses of $2.50, variable expenses of $6 (rounded), and $2.50 (rounded) for profit and contingencies.

Loss ratio method

A method for determining insurance rates based on a comparison of actual and expected loss ratios.

Loss Ratio Ratemaking Method

The second ratemaking method is the **loss ratio method**. In its simplest form, the loss ratio method uses two loss ratios—the actual loss ratio and the expected loss ratio of the insurer during the selected experience period:

1. $\text{Actual loss ratio} = \dfrac{\text{Incurred losses}}{\text{Earned premiums}}$

2. $\text{Expected loss ratio} = 100\% - \text{Expense provision}$

In this method, profit and contingencies are included in the expense provision because the method modifies a current insurance rate. The expected loss ratio plus the provision for expenses, profit, and contingencies always add up to 100 percent.

This is the loss ratio ratemaking equation in its simplest form:

$$\text{Rate change} = \frac{\text{Actual loss ratio} - \text{Expected loss ratio}}{\text{Expected loss ratio}}$$

If the rate change percentage is negative, it indicates a rate reduction. If positive, it indicates a rate increase. For example, if the actual loss ratio equals 54 percent and the expected loss ratio equals 60 percent, then the rate change is a decrease of 10 percent.

$$\frac{\text{Actual loss ratio} - \text{Expected loss ratio}}{\text{Expected loss ratio}} = \frac{(0.54 - 0.60)}{0.60}$$

$$= \frac{-0.06}{0.60}$$

$$\text{Rate change} = -0.10 = -10\%$$

In this case, the insurer's actual loss ratio was better than expected. Based only on this information, it appears that the insurer could lower its rates and still make the desired profit on business subject to these rates. Lower rates would probably also attract additional business, which would produce greater profits.

The loss ratio ratemaking method cannot be used to calculate rates for a new type of insurance, because neither an actual loss ratio for the calculation nor an old rate to adjust is available. For a new type of insurance, either the pure premium method or the judgment method must be used.

Judgment Ratemaking Method

The third and oldest ratemaking method is the **judgment ratemaking method**. Though its use is no longer as widespread as it once was, this method is still used for some types of insurance, such as ocean marine insurance, some inland marine classes, aviation insurance and situations when limited data are available, as with terrorism coverage. Although the judgment ratemaking method might use limited or no loss experience data, an experienced underwriter or actuary generally has a sense of what rates have produced desired results in the past.

Judgment ratemaking method

A method for determining insurance rates that relies heavily on the experience and knowledge of an actuary or an underwriter who makes little or no use of loss experience data.

RATEMAKING PROCESS OVERVIEW

Ratemaking can involve a number of complex technical issues. An understanding of the process involved reveals the importance and contribution of each step in the ratemaking process.

When creating or revising insurance rates, an insurer's staff, or an advisory organization on behalf of the insurer, follows a series of steps:

1. Collect data
2. Adjust data
3. Calculate overall indicated rate change
4. Determine territorial and class relativities
5. Prepare rate filings and submit to regulatory authorities as required

An insurer follows a similar process when reviewing loss costs, rather than rates. The provisions for expense and for profit and contingencies are excluded from the process, but all other adjustments and parts of the process are unchanged.

For companies that rely on loss cost filings made by advisory organizations, the ratemaking process involves calculating and filing an appropriate **loss cost multiplier**.

Loss cost multiplier

A factor that provides for differences in expected loss, individual company expenses, underwriting profit and contingencies; when multiplied with a loss cost, it produces a rate.

Collect Data

To obtain and maintain usable data, each insurer must code data when transactions occur. Some coding is prescribed by advisory organizations, but many insurers collect more data than advisory organizations require. Information about specific policies is collected most conveniently when policies, endorsements, and invoices are issued. Claim data are collected when claims are reported, reserves are established or changed, checks or drafts are issued, or claims are closed.

Before collecting ratemaking data, the insurer must determine the kinds of data needed. The data fall into three general categories:

- Losses, both paid and incurred (including any loss adjustment expenses to be included in the pure premium)
- Earned premium and/or exposure information
- Expenses, including a profit and contingencies factor

If rates are to vary by rating class and/or territory, data must be identified for each class and territory. For example, if an insurer is considering establishing a new class of business, it would first identify experience for this class separately so there would be data to calculate a separate class rate.

Ideally, the incurred losses, earned premiums, and earned exposure units should be based on the same group of policies. Because this is not always practical, approximation techniques are used. For example, sometimes it is most practical to compare premiums during one twelve-month period with losses for a slightly different twelve-month period, even if these two periods do not involve exactly the same policies.

Different aggregations of data may be used, depending on the line of business. For example, loss payments for a single claim could be made over several successive calendar years. Consequently, the **calendar-year method** is unsuitable for collecting ratemaking data for liability and workers compensation insurance, because the delay in loss payment can be long and the loss reserves can be large relative to earned premiums. For those types of insurance, either the **policy-year method** or **accident-year method** should be used.

For fire, inland marine, and auto physical damage insurance, losses are paid relatively quickly, and loss reserves tend to be small relative to earned premiums. Consequently, the calendar-year method may be satisfactory for ratemaking data collection, although it is still not as accurate as the other two methods.

Adjust Data

After data have been collected, they must be adjusted. Adjustment is necessary because the raw exposure, premium, and loss data reflect conditions from present and past periods, whereas the rates being developed will be used in the future.

Actuaries use several ways of adjusting premium and loss data:

- Adjust premium to current rate level
- Adjust historic experience for future development
- Apply trending to losses and premium

Adjust Premiums to Current Rate Level

If rates charged in the experience period were written at different rate levels, premiums will need to be adjusted to the current level.

The ideal way to adjust premiums to current rate level is to calculate the premium for each policy in the experience period at current rate level. For example, the 20X1 personal auto premiums at 20X4's rate level would be calculated by pricing each auto insured in 20X1 at 20X4 rates. However, re-rating every exposure requires storing, retrieving and using every rating factor for each policy of each exposure, possibly making this method economically unfeasible. An alternative is to adjust historic premiums in total to current levels.

As an illustration of this approach, assume that a book of business has $100 of losses each year. In Year 1, a premium of $200 is charged, but the insurer decreases rates by 20 percent in each of the next two years. Therefore, an

Calendar-year method

A method of collecting ratemaking data that estimates both earned premiums and incurred losses by formulas from accounting records.

Policy-year method

A method of collecting ratemaking data that analyzes all policies issued in a given twelve-month period and that links all losses, premiums, and exposure units to the policy to which they are related.

Accident-year method

A method of organizing ratemaking statistics that uses incurred losses for an accident year, which consist of all losses related to claims arising from accidents that occur during the year, and that estimates earned premiums by formulas from accounting records.

insured that paid $1,000 premium in the first year would pay only $640 after the two rate decreases. If the insurer had a 50 percent loss ratio the first year, 63 percent the second year, and 78 percent the third year, it would be inappropriate to project the coming year's loss ratio as the average of those loss ratios. The 50 percent loss ratio in Year 1 was based on premiums that would not be charged as of Year 3, so it should not be used directly for ratemaking. The premium that had been charged must be adjusted to what would be charged in Year 3, the most recent year. See the exhibit "Effect of On-Level Premium Adjustment."

Effect of On-Level Premium Adjustment

	(1)	(2)	(3) = (1)/(2)	(4)	(5)	(6) = (2)×(5)	(7) = (1)/(6)
Year	Developed Losses	Collected Premium	Collected Loss Ratio	Rate Level Index	On-Level Factor	On-Level Premium	On-Level Loss Ratio
1	$100	$200	50%	1.00	0.64	$128	78%
2	$100	$160	63%	0.80	0.80	$128	78%
3	$100	$128	78%	0.64	1.00	$128	78%

[DA06289]

On-level factor

A factor that is used to adjust historical premiums to the current rate level.

Column 4 in the table shows the rate level relative to Year 1. This rate level index reflects the assumption that rates decreased 20 percent from the prior year in both Year 2 and Year 3. The **on-level factor** in Column 5 adjusts rate levels for each year to the most recent period's rate levels. It equals the rate level index for the most recent period (Year 3) divided by the rate level index for each year. At the most recent year's rate level, each year's losses would have produced a 78 percent loss ratio.

Premiums may also have to be adjusted for different levels of coverage purchased. For example, an automobile liability insurer finds that it is now selling much more of its $100,000 per accident limits than the $25,000 limit it had in the past. The premiums (and perhaps losses) need to be adjusted for this change in coverage provided.

Adjust Historic Experience for Future Development

When policy-year or accident-year experience is used to predict future results, one must remember that the experience might not be complete. There may still be open claims that require future payment or the possibility of a late-reported claim for which the insurer is liable. The insurer must estimate the values of these future payments and add it to the payments to date in order to estimate the ultimate losses of each period.

For example, at the end of a year, payments for medical malpractice claims that occurred during that year may be only 10 percent of the ultimate payment. Because of the complexity and long discovery period of such claims, even the incurred losses tend to increase over time. Conversely, for automobile physical damage, an insurer's net loss payments might decrease over time as it collects salvage and subrogation recoveries on claims it has paid.

The future development of the losses can be estimated by several actuarial methods. The most common method used is applying **loss development factors** to the current experience. With any method, the goal is to estimate the final, total cost to pay all the claims within each year. These projections are then used as the basis for estimating the losses that will be incurred in the proposed policy period.

Loss development factor
An actuarial means for adjusting losses to reflect future growth in claims due to both increases in the incurred amount for reported losses and incurred but not reported (IBNR) losses.

Apply Trending to Losses and Premium

Another way losses are adjusted for ratemaking is through trending. Trending is the review of historic environmental changes and projecting such changes into the future. Examples of such changes would be inflation of claim costs, the increasing safety of newer cars, or changes in legal liability.

Trend adjustments can come from various sources. In some instances, external indexes such as the Consumer Price Index or one of its components may be used in trending. The most frequently used source of trends is historical experience. This experience can be reviewed by an insurer using its own data or by a statistical agent, such as Insurance Services Office (ISO) or the National Council on Compensation Insurance (NCCI), using the combined experience of numerous companies. The trend adjustment commonly uses historical experience to project past trends into the future. Loss trending is usually reviewed in separate severity and frequency components.

These trends can be projected into the future using an exponential trending method. **Exponential trending** assumes that data being projected will increase or decrease by a fixed percentage each year as compared with the previous year. For example, claim frequency will increase 1.3 percent each year, or claim severity will increase 8.2 percent each year. Exponential trends have a compounding effect over time. For example, price inflation would be expected to follow an exponential trend. See the exhibit "Claim Severity Trend Calculation."

Exponential trending
A method of loss trending that assumes a fixed percentage increase or decrease for each time period.

Losses may need to be adjusted to current conditions if other significant external changes have affected loss payouts in recent years. For example, workers compensation insurance benefits are established by statute. If legislation or a court decision changes these benefits, past losses must be adjusted to current benefit levels.

Premiums may also need to be trended to reflect changing conditions. For example, the amount of homeowners insurance purchased tends to change with the value of the home. If home prices have risen, more premiums might be collected on the same house just because of its increase in value. Trending

Claim Severity Trend Calculation

(1) Accident Year	(2) Developed Losses	(3) Developed Number of Claims	(4) = (3)/(2) Average Claim Severity	(5) Change From Prior Year
20X1	$11,000,000	9,167	$1,200	
20X2	$10,287,750	7,913	$1,300	8.3%
20X3	$11,112,000	7,880	$1,410	8.5%
20X4	$10,659,000	6,995	$1,524	8.1%
20X5	$11,275,000	6,860	$1,644	7.9%
			Average	8.2%

The losses and claims are the estimated final values for each accident year, projected using development factors or other methods.

[DA06290]

factors would be applied to adjust for past and future changes in premium due to these external factors.

Calculate Indicated Overall Rate Change

The purpose of adjustments, development, and trending is to bring prior experience to a level comparable to the future rate's policy period. Based on the adjusted experience, an overall rate indication is calculated. In some cases, a new rate is calculated directly. However, in most cases, the indication shows a change from the current rate level, for example, an overall 2.7 percent increase.

Several different methods, such as the loss ratio method and the pure premium method, can be used to produce an indication. These methods depend on the amount and type of experience available.

Determine Territorial and Class Relativities

If rates vary by territory and/or class, they are reviewed after the calculation of the overall rate change. Further analysis is performed to determine territorial and/or class relativities. These relativities reflect the extent to which various subsets of insureds in a state deserve rates that are higher or lower than the statewide average rate. For example, in a territory with many congested highways, auto insurance rates might be 8.6 percent higher than the statewide average rate, while in a rural territory rates might be 20.2 percent lower. Similarly, a frame-constructed building has a different exposure to fire loss than a fire-resistive steel and concrete building, so different rates are warranted.

Territorial relativities can be determined by comparing the estimated loss ratio (or pure premium) for each geographic territory to the statewide average loss ratio (or pure premium). This comparison produces factors that are applied to the statewide average rate to reflect experience in each geographic territory. If a given territory has limited experience, its territorial loss ratios are likely to vary widely. Differences from the overall average rate must be supported by credible experience. If a class has only a few exposures, even very good (or very poor) experience will produce only minimal difference from the average rate; because of the limited exposures, the difference could be due to mere chance.

Class relativities are used to develop rates for each rating class. Class relativities are determined similarly to territorial relativities. Once class relativities have been determined, the insurer can prepare a rate table showing rates for each territory and each rating class.

Prepare and Submit Rate Filings

After data have been collected and adjusted, and after any territorial and class relativities have been determined, rate filings must be prepared. A rate filing is a document submitted to state regulatory authorities. The form for and the amount of information required in a filing vary by state.

Generally, the filing must include at least these seven items:

- Schedule of the proposed new rates
- Statement about the percentage change, either an increase or a decrease, in the statewide average rate
- Explanation of differences between the overall statewide change in rate and the percentage change of the rates for individual territories and/or rating classes (if any)
- Data to support the proposed rate changes, including territorial and class relativities
- Expense provision data
- Target profit provision included in the rates, if applicable, and any supporting calculations
- Explanatory material to enable state insurance regulators to understand and evaluate the filing

Depending on state law, formal approval of the filing by regulators might not be required. In some states, approval must be obtained before the rates are used. In other states, formal approval is not required by law, but many insurers prefer to obtain approval before use to avoid the possibility of having to withdraw the rates if regulators decide that rates do not meet statutory requirements.

Actuaries are best qualified to answer any technical questions that the regulators might raise. However, some insurers prefer to delegate most of the contact with regulators to the legal department or filing specialists and to involve actuaries only as needed.

If an advisory organization files rates or loss costs on behalf of an insurer, it handles any follow-up or negotiations. Generally, companies that use an advisory organization are assumed to adopt the filings made by that organization automatically. When loss costs are filed by an advisory organization, the insurer is responsible for filing its expense provisions, which would yield its final rates.

RATEMAKING DATA AGGREGATION METHODS

Understanding the premium and loss of a single insurance policy is straightforward, but an insurer must also know how to look at the combined results of policies that may have been written in different months or years. There are several standard ways of compiling loss data for review or for analyses of rates and reserves.

Insurers and rating organizations collect information about every premium and loss transaction. For ratemaking, reserving, and reporting purposes, the transactions during a specific period are compiled into useful aggregations that attempt to match losses with the premiums from the underlying coverage:

- Policy-year method
- Calendar-year method
- Accident-year method
- Report-year method

While the term "year" (12 consecutive months, not necessarily beginning January 1) is used throughout this section, any defined time period, such as month or quarter can be used.

Policy-Year Method

The policy-year method of aggregating data involves analyzing earned premiums, exposure units, and incurred losses associated with a particular group of policies that were issued during a specific twelve-month period—for example, all policies first issued from 1/1/X1 to 12/31/X1.

For year-long policies, the coverage period for this group spans two years because policies issued on 12/31/X1 expire one year later, on 12/31/X2. All premiums for a policy are linked directly to that policy, including the original premium; additional premiums; and return premiums resulting from premium audits, retrospective rating plans, policy changes, and similar transactions. Exposure units, incurred losses, and allocated loss adjustment expenses are also linked to the policies that cover them.

The policy-year method is the only ratemaking data collection method that exactly matches losses, premiums, and exposure units to a specific group of insureds. Because policy year defines a specific group of policies, most reinsurance contracts are on a policy-year basis.

Two major disadvantages apply to the policy-year ratemaking data collection method:

- It takes longer to gather data for this method than for the other methods.
- There is additional expense to gather data by policy year. The data used in the other methods are gathered in part as a byproduct of the insurer's accounting operations. Although this additional expense was once considered a major disadvantage of the policy-year method, automated recordkeeping has reduced the extra cost of compiling policy-year statistics.

Delays in data collection can be overcome partly by estimating the ultimate values of data for which final values are not yet available. However, potential errors in estimating such values reduce the "apples-to-apples" advantage of the policy-year method.

Calendar-Year Method

The calendar-year method involves aggregating data from accounting records to estimate earned premiums and incurred losses. An insurer's transactional accounting records show its written premiums and unearned premium reserves for a given calendar year. They do not, however, show information more directly relevant for ratemaking—earned premiums, incurred losses, or exposure units. This information must be approximated using accounting data.

Earned premiums for the calendar period must be calculated from the **written premiums** and **unearned premium** reserves.

Earned premiums = Written premiums for the year
+ (Unearned premiums at the beginning of the year
− Unearned premiums at the end of the year)

This formula provides a reasonably accurate estimate of the premiums earned from the coverage provided during the period. Computed this way, the earned premium might not reflect additional premiums or refunds resulting from premium audits or retrospective rating plans on previous policies, but the discrepancy should be relatively small for most insurers.

Under the calendar-year method of ratemaking data aggregation, incurred losses must also be estimated by formula:

Incurred losses = Losses paid during the year
+ (Loss reserves at the end of the year
−Loss reserves at the beginning of the year)

Written premiums

The total premium on all policies written (put into effect) during a particular period.

Unearned premiums

The portion of written premiums that corresponds to coverage that has not yet been provided.

The incurred loss formula sometimes results in inaccuracies because the estimated incurred losses for a given year might be distorted by changes in reserves for losses that occurred in previous years. Such inaccuracies can be substantial with liability insurance or types of insurance commonly involving delays between the date of loss occurrence and the date when resulting losses are paid. However, large inaccuracies are unlikely for insurance such as inland marine and auto physical damage, for which most losses are paid relatively quickly. For such insurance, calendar-year statistics might be sufficiently accurate.

Calendar-year data reflect how insurers must report their income on their financial statements. These data are available quickly, and compiling them involves little additional expense. However, insurer accounting records usually do not contain exposure unit data. Consequently, calendar-year data cannot be used alone in the pure premium ratemaking method unless exposure unit information is also collected separately.

Calendar year losses can arise due to changes in reserves for losses that occurred in previous years, and so might not reflect current experience alone. Therefore, the calendar-year method is the least accurate ratemaking data collection method. Further, calendar year losses are frequently not available at the desired level of detail. For instance, **bulk reserves** are not typically calculated at the class or territorial level.

Bulk reserves

Reserves set aside for future expected claim payments but not associated with any specific claim; include a provision for incurred but not reported (IBNR) claims, future development of known claims (beyond the carried case reserves), and potential reopening of claims that have been settled.

Accident-Year Method

The accident-year method uses the earned premium for the calendar period being reviewed, but calculates incurred losses for the given period using all losses and claims arising from insured events occurring during that period. The claims can be either open or closed; if they arose from an insured event that occurred during the specified period, they are included in incurred losses for that period.

Since accident-year losses arise only from insured events that occur during the period, they are not affected by changes in reserves for events that occurred in other periods. Therefore, the accident-year method eliminates the largest source of error inherent in the calendar-year method.

Under the accident-year method, neither earned premiums nor incurred losses are based as directly on a specific group of policies as they are with the policy-year method. The accident-year method achieves much of the accuracy of the policy-year method while preserving most of the economy and speed of the calendar-year method. The accident-year method is faster than the policy-year method because it does not wait for the policy year to be completed to collect data. However, accident-year data are slightly more expensive to compile than calendar-year data, because they require separate tabulation of loss data.

Because accident-year data are relatively easy to compile, and it is useful as a basis of projecting ultimate losses, it is required to be reported by line of business in the **Schedule P** of each company's Annual Statement.

Report-Year Method

The report-year method is similar to the accident-year method, except that claims are aggregated by when the claim was reported rather than when it occurred. Premiums used in this method are the same calendar-period earned premiums used with the accident year method.

Some insurance lines of business, such as medical malpractice and general liability, provide **claims-made coverage**. Aggregating by report year for these coverages has the same benefits accident-year aggregation has for standard coverages; it is available faster than policy year experience, and can be much more accurate than calendar year experience. Report-year data are also used in analyzing known (reported) claim experience separately from incurred but not reported (IBNR) experience.

As many insurers do not write claims-made coverages, report-year collection is the least common of the four loss aggregation methods.

Illustration

The exhibit illustrates five claims, indicating how each would be classified under the four ratemaking data collection methods. See the exhibit "Hypothetical Data to be Aggregated."

All policies in the "Hypothetical Data to be Aggregated" exhibit are one-year policies. Each claim is assigned to only one year under both the policy-year and accident-year methods, although the year might not be the same for both methods.

In the calendar-year method, loss payments for a single claim could be made over several successive calendar years. Consequently, the calendar-year method is unsuitable for collecting ratemaking data for liability and workers compensation insurance, because the delay in loss payment can be long and the loss reserves can be large relative to earned premiums. For those types of insurance, either the policy-year or the accident-year method should be used.

For fire, inland marine, and auto physical damage insurance, losses are paid relatively quickly, and loss reserves tend to be small relative to earned premiums. Hence, the calendar-year method may be satisfactory for ratemaking data collection, although it is still not as accurate as the other two.

A side-by-side comparison highlights the similarities and differences among the four methods of aggregating data. See the exhibit "Ratemaking Aggregation Methods Compared."

Schedule P

The NAIC Annual Statement Schedule that shows detailed historical information on paid and reserved losses and LAE.

Claims-made coverage

Coverage that is triggered by a claim alleging bodily injury or property damage that is made during the policy period, even if the claim arises from an event that happened before policy inception.

Hypothetical Data to be Aggregated

(1) Claim Number	(2) Date of Occurrence	(3) Policy Effective Date	(4) Date Claim Reported	(5) Original Loss Reserve	(6) Change in Reserve	(7) Date of Reserve Change	(8) Amount Paid to Close	(9) Date Paid	(10) Policy Year	(11) Calendar Year	(12) Accident Year	(13) Report Year	(14) Calendar-Year Reserve
1	7-1-X0	1-1-X0	2-1-X1	$100,000	—	—	$100,000	6-3-X2	20X0	20X1	20X0	20X1	$100,000
2	11-1-X1	12-15-X0	1-1-X2	200,000	—	—	200,000	9-1-X3	20X0	20X2	20X1	20X2	200,000
3	10-3-X0	2-4-X0	12-20-X0	100,000	+$200,000	3-1-X2	300,000	4-6-X3	20X0	20X0	20X0	20X0	$100,000
										20X2			200,000
4	9-13-X0	2-2-X0	3-14-X1	50,000	+100,000	4-4-X2	300,000	5-3-X3	20X0	20X1	20X0	20X1	50,000
										20X2			100,000
										20X3			150,000
5	12-1-X1	12-15-X0	1-10-X2	100,000	-50,000	3-1-X3	150,000	2-1-X4	20X0	20X2	20X1	20X2	100,000
										20X3			-50,000
											20X4		100,000

All policies are for one-year terms.

Notice how each claim is charged differently under the policy year, accident year, and calendar year:

- Policy years (Column 10) reflect the year in which the policy was effective.
- Calendar years (Column 11) reflect the year in which the loss was paid or reserves were changed.
- Accident years (Column 12) reflect the year in which the loss occurred.
- Report years (column 13) reflect the year in which the claim was first reported .

[DA03394]

Ratemaking Aggregation Methods Compared

Aggregation Method	Loss Data Analyzed	Premium Data Analyzed	Advantages	Disadvantages
Policy Year	Incurred losses that arise from policies written during period, including loss adjustment expenses. (Note: coverage period might span two calendar years.)	Exposure units, and premiums earned on policies written within year, including: • Initial premium • Additional premium • Return premium	Apples-to-apples exact matching of losses, premiums, and exposure units to a specific group of insured entities	• Longer delays in gathering statistics than in other ratemaking methods • Additional expense in gathering data that are used only for ratemaking
Calendar Year	Data used for accounting purposes. Incurred losses are calculated as: • Losses paid during the year regardless of when losses occurred, plus • Change in loss reserves (= total reserves at year end less total reserves at the beginning of the year)	Data used for accounting purposes. Earned premium calculated from: • Premiums written during calendar period, plus • Change in unearned premium during the period (unearned premiums at end of period less unearned premiums at beginning	• Statistics available immediately • Little expense involved in compiling data	• Accounting records do not contain exposure unit data. • Least accurate of the three ratemaking methods.
Accident Year	Losses for all accidents that occur during the period	Earned premiums calculated the same way as calendar-year method.	• Can be more accurate than the calendar-year method, because it uses incurred losses during a specific year • Faster than the policy-year method, because policy year need not be completed	• Neither earned premiums nor incurred losses are tied directly to a specific group of policyholders. • Accident-year data are slightly more expensive to compile than calendar-year data
Report Year	Losses for all accidents that are reported during the period	Earned premiums calculated the same way as calendar-year method.	• Can be more accurate than the calendar-year method, because it uses incurred losses during a specific year • Faster than the policy-year method, because policy year need not be completed	• Neither earned premiums nor incurred losses are tied directly to a specific group of policyholders. • Report-year data are slightly more expensive to compile than calendar-year data

RATEMAKING FACTOR VARIANCES FOR DIFFERENT TYPES OF INSURANCE

Ratemaking can vary widely by type of insurance. These variations can result from the characteristics of loss exposures, regulatory requirements, and other factors.

Major differences between ratemaking for different lines of business can be found in experience period, trending, large loss limitations, credibility, and increased limits factors.

Experience Period

Using an experience period of one to three years is common for auto insurance and other types of liability insurance. For fire insurance, a five-year experience period is used almost universally because it is required by law in many states. The experience for each of the five years is usually not given equal weight. The experience for the most recent years is given greater weight to promote rate responsiveness.

The experience period used for other property causes of loss, such as wind, is even longer—frequently twenty years or more. The purpose of such a long experience period is to avoid the large swings in rates that would otherwise result when a major hurricane, a series of major tornadoes, or another natural catastrophe strikes an area.

Three factors can be considered in determining the appropriate experience period: (1) legal requirements, if any; (2) the variability of losses over time; and (3) the credibility of the resulting ratemaking data. The second and third factors are related to some degree.

Trending

Trending practices also vary by type of insurance. Trending may be based on experience or external indices. Moreover, trending may be needed for premiums as well as losses.

For property insurance, loss claim frequency is low and generally stable, so trending may be restricted to claim severity. However, the average claim is not used to measure claim severity because the average property insurance claim may be distorted by infrequent large claims. Consequently, an external composite index, composed partly of a construction cost index and partly of the consumer price index, is used for trending.

For liability insurance, separate trending of claim severity and claim frequency is common because of the different factors that affect them. Economic inflation or deflation over the course of payments can affect the average cost of a claim (severity). Legislative, regulatory or other external changes, such as modification in rules governing claim settlement, can affect the number of losses (frequency).

In some lines, such as fire insurance, trending both losses and premiums is necessary. Losses are trended partly to reflect any effects of inflation on claim costs. For example, inflation can elevate property values, and people tend to increase the amount of property insurance purchased to reflect the increased values. This increases insurer premium revenue. Increases in amounts insured tend to lag somewhat behind inflation during certain periods. Consequently, insurers trend both losses and premiums and offset the growth in premiums against the growth in losses. Premiums are also trended in other types of insurance for which the exposure units are affected by inflation. Examples include workers compensation (which uses payroll as its exposure base) and some general liability insurance (which uses sales).

A special trending problem exists in workers compensation insurance. Because the benefits for such insurance are established by statute, legislation or a court decision can change the benefits unexpectedly. A law amendment factor is used to adjust rates and losses to reflect statutory benefit changes. Actuaries can estimate with reasonable accuracy the effects of a statutory benefit change on the losses that insurers will incur under their policies. Unlike other trending, rate changes in statutory benefits might apply to outstanding policies as well as new and renewal policies.

For equipment breakdown insurance, inspection and risk control services are a significant portion of the rate, often exceeding the pure premium component. In this case, trending is applied to the risk control expenses because they constitute such a large portion of the rate.

Large Loss Limitations

Unusual rate fluctuations could result from occasional large losses, whether from large individual losses or from an accumulation of smaller losses from a single event, such as a hurricane. In liability insurance, these fluctuations are controlled by using only basic limit losses in calculating incurred losses. **Basic limit** losses are losses capped at some predetermined amount, such as $100,000.

A similar practice is followed in workers compensation insurance ratemaking. Individual claims are limited to a specified amount for ratemaking purposes. Another limitation applies to multiple claims arising from a single event. Both limitations vary over time and by state.

Loss limitations also apply in ratemaking for property insurance. For example, when a large single loss occurs in fire insurance, only part of it is included in ratemaking calculations in the state in which it occurred. The balance is spread over the rates of all the states. The amount included in the state depends on the total fire insurance premium volume in that state, so it varies substantially by state.

Basic limit

The minimum amount of coverage for which a policy can be written; usually found in liability lines.

Catastrophe model

A type of computer program that estimates losses from future potential catastrophic events.

Most losses from catastrophic events, such as hurricanes, are excluded from ratemaking data and replaced by a flat catastrophe charge in the rates. The amount of the catastrophe charge is determined by catastrophe data collected over a long time period to smooth the fluctuations that would otherwise result. A **catastrophe model**, which incorporates past experience with scientific theory, is often used to calculate an appropriate charge for these potential losses.

Commercial insurers may also be required to quote a separate charge applicable to the terrorism loss exposure. Because past loss experience with terrorism losses in the United States has been extremely limited, terrorism ratemaking presents a special challenge.

Credibility

Credibility

The level of confidence an actuary has in projected losses; increases as the number of exposure units increases.

Credibility is a measure of the predictive ability of data. In ratemaking, the credibility of past loss data is important in projecting future losses. Fully credible ratemaking data have sufficient volume to provide an accurate estimate of the expected losses for the line, state, territory, and/or class being reviewed. The volatility of the loss data determines how much volume is needed to be fully credible—the higher the volatility, the more data are required to provide a reasonable projection of future losses. For example, a smaller amount of automobile liability experience is needed for full credibility than for fire insurance, because the larger number of claims per exposure and smaller average claim size leads to more stable results.

Credibility assumptions vary by type of insurance. In auto insurance, advisory organizations and some larger insurers consider the statewide loss data to be fully credible. That assumption might be inappropriate for some small insurers who base their rates solely on their own loss data. For territories and classes with loss data that the advisory organization determines are not fully credible, rates are calculated as a weighted average of the indicated rate for the territory or class and the statewide average rate for all classes and territories combined. The **credibility factor** is used as the weight in the weighted average. It indicates the amount of weight to give to the actual loss experience for the territory or class as compared with an alternative source—in this case, the statewide average loss experience. A credibility factor is a number between 0 (no credibility) and 1 (full confidence).

Credibility factor

The factor applied in ratemaking to adjust for the predictive value of loss data and used to minimize the variations in the rates that result from purely chance variations in losses.

For property insurance, because of the low average claim frequency, advisory organizations might determine that even the statewide loss data are not fully credible. In that case, a three-part weighted average could be used, combining the state loss data for the rating class, regional (multi-state) loss data of the rating class, and state loss data for a major group encompassing several rating classes. Again, credibility factors are used as weights.

The pure premiums for workers compensation insurance developed by the National Council on Compensation Insurance (NCCI) are composed of pure premium charges for medical and indemnity costs. Separate credibility standards exist for each of these categories.

Increased Limits Factors

Liability insurance coverage is provided at various limits of coverage. Actuaries use a number of ratemaking techniques for pricing coverage amounts in excess of the basic limit. Although it would be possible to develop separate rates for each limit of liability coverage offered, that approach would require credible ratemaking experience at each limit, as well as significant, often duplicative, efforts.

The most common approach to establishing rates for coverage greater than the basic limit is to develop **increased limits factors**. A base rate is first developed using losses capped at the basic limit. Increased limits factors can then be applied to the basic limit rate. For example, the additional charge to increase the general liability limit to $2 million for any one occurrence might be expressed as 70 percent of the basic coverage limit rate, producing an increased limits factor of 1.70.

Increased limit factor

A factor applied to the rates for basic limits to arrive at an appropriate rate for higher limits.

Charges to increase liability limits can, and frequently do, exceed 100 percent of the charge for basic coverage limits. Several reasons exist for the large increased limits factors for several lines of business, such as general liability and auto liability. First, the additional coverage purchased by the customer can be much higher than the basic limit. For example, in personal auto liability, the basic limit might be $50,000 per accident, but the customer purchases $1 million in coverage to protect his or her assets. Although loss severity does not increase uniformly with increased coverage limits, the exposure to loss is substantially greater at higher limits. Second, higher limits can also require a portion of the coverage to be reinsured, with the additional expense of reinsurance included in the rate. Finally, because large losses occur less frequently than small losses and take longer to settle, the variability of losses in higher coverage layers is greater than for the basic limit losses, and the credibility is lower. This greater variability requires a greater **risk charge** at higher levels of coverage.

Risk charge

An amount over and above the expected loss component of the premium to compensate the insurer for taking the risk that losses may be higher than expected.

LOSS RESERVES AND ANALYSIS

A matter of critical concern to an insurer is the holding of the appropriate amount of loss reserves.

Loss reserves for future claim payments are generally the largest liability on the insurer's balance sheet and a significant part of an insurer's financial condition. They represent the security that an insured's claim will be paid. Accurate estimation of these future liabilities provides the insurer with an understanding of the actual costs of business and ensures its ability to pay the claims in the future. Actuaries use various techniques to estimate the liability for these future payments.

Purpose of Loss Reserves

Insurers are required by law and good accounting practice to establish reserves for losses that reasonably can be assumed to have been incurred. These reserves are not just for reported claims but also for claims that have occurred but that have not yet been reported to the insurer. The reserves set aside part of current income (premiums) for the losses to be paid in the future.

Loss reserves are also needed to provide a complete picture of an insurer's financial status. Unlike manufacturers, insurers do not completely know their costs of doing business in advance of the sale of the product. Future payments on current claims may stretch out over years. An insurer must estimate these future payments in order to calculate its profit or loss.

The liability carried on an insurer's books for future payments on incurred claims is commonly called loss reserve. However, the liability is not just for payments of claimants' losses; the insurer is also responsible for future loss adjustment expenses (LAE). Such expenses include both allocated loss adjustment expenses (ALAE) and unallocated loss adjustment expenses (ULAE).

The responsibility for selecting the amount of loss reserves held by an insurer rests with the company's senior management. Actuaries and other professionals provide estimates of the liability (estimated unpaid claims) to management to assist them in this decision.

Types of Loss Reserves

The principal types of loss reserves established by insurers are case reserves and bulk reserves.

Case reserves are amounts that represent the estimated loss value of each individual claim. An insurer's claim department usually sets these reserves, but the actuarial department might assist with some complex claims. Case reserves are set according to the specific characteristics of each claim. When a claim is first reported, the claim representative's estimate might be based on very little information. Over time, as the specific characteristics of the claim become known, the case reserve becomes more accurate.

The claim department is responsible for setting case reserves on each of the individual claims. However, the insurer cannot identify specific claims with inadequate or excessive case reserves or predict which claims will reopen. Therefore, insurers make general provision for additional reserves, called bulk reserves (in contrast to case reserves). For some types of insurance, the bulk reserves can be a substantial part of an insurer's total liabilities.

The bulk (or aggregate) reserves can have three components:

- **Incurred but not reported (IBNR) reserves**
- Reserves for losses that have been reported but for which the established case reserves are inadequate (sometimes called IBNER (incurred but not enough recorded) reserves)
- Reserves for claims that have been settled and then reopened

Reserves specifically for unreported claims are sometimes called "pure IBNR." An example of a pure IBNR claim is a general liability claim for injuries suffered in a slip and fall inside an insured's premises, unknown to the insurer until a lawsuit is brought months after the accident. In practice, the term "IBNR reserves" is often used to mean all of the bulk reserves.

> **Incurred but not reported (IBNR) reserves**
> A reserve established for losses that reasonably can be assumed to have been incurred but not yet reported.

Importance of Accurate Loss Reserves

The purpose of loss reserve analysis is to determine whether the carried loss and loss adjustment expense reserves can be expected to adequately cover the losses that have been incurred but not yet been paid. Such analysis might be undertaken by a number of parties for various reasons:

- Management, as part of its analysis of costs of doing business
- The insurer's auditors, to determine whether the insurer's financial statements accurately indicate its financial condition and performance
- Rating agencies (such as A. M. Best or Standard & Poor's), on behalf of potential investors or creditors
- Regulators (on behalf of policyholders), to assure that claims will be paid

The National Association of Insurance Commissioners (NAIC) Annual Statement instructions require insurers to have their loss reserves certified by an **actuary** or another qualified professional. Those who provide such certification may be exposed to potential professional liability claims. Consequently, they ordinarily provide such opinions only after carefully analyzing the reserves.

> **Actuary**
> A person who uses mathematical methods to analyze loss data and develop insurance rates.

The effect of inaccurate loss reserves can be substantial. Loss reserves (including LAE reserves) often exceed the total surplus for an insurer and are usually a considerable multiple of the earnings in a year. A significant change in reserves for prior years not only affects the current year's profitability but can even risk the insurer's solvency.

An overestimation of loss reserves (higher than ultimately paid) can lower an insurer's financial strength ratings, reduce statutory limits on premiums that can be written, or lead to dissolution of an insurer. If loss reserves are underestimated, the insurer can become insolvent when it becomes apparent that the future payments will exceed the reserve level.

Analysis of Loss Reserves

Because of the size and potential effect of loss reserves, close attention is given to the estimation of these unpaid liabilities. The analysis is usually done by an actuary, using a variety of methods and techniques. In most cases, estimates are made of the ultimate losses to be paid on the exposures to date; the loss reserve is then estimated by subtracting payments to date. Sometimes separate projections of the reserve are required for known claims and for IBNR claims, and those results are added together.

ALAE reserves may be estimated with or separately from the loss reserve estimate. ULAE reserves are usually analyzed separately from those of loss and ALAE.

Among the most common methods used to estimate ultimate losses are these:

- Expected loss ratio method
- Loss development method
- Bornhuetter-Ferguson method

The expected loss ratio method uses a prior estimate of ultimate losses rather than current experience. It is often used when current experience is limited or of little predictive value, and in fact, the method ignores the experience to date.

The loss development method assumes that future changes in the loss will occur in a similar manner as in the past. This method assumes that the experience to date is an indicator of what future payments will be.

The Bornhuetter-Ferguson method uses parts of the other two methods. It accepts the experience to date (unlike the expected loss ratio method), but assumes that future results are independent of the current experience. The ultimate projection from this method is the sum of actual results to date plus expected future results. See the exhibit "An Illustration of Reserving Methods."

The selection of the appropriate method to be used depends on the data available, timing, and other characteristics of the experience reviewed. For example, it would usually be inappropriate to apply the loss development method to the experience of only the first week of a policy period.

Because the reserve analysis is an estimate of future events, there is inherent uncertainty in any reserve estimate. An actuarially sound reserve estimate should be based on reasonable assumptions using appropriate and generally accepted methodology. Even so, actuaries cannot and do not guarantee that actual future payments will be at or near the estimate.

An Illustration of Reserving Methods

An illustration may help clarify how the three common methods of estimating ultimate losses work. Assume Josh wishes to estimate the number of home runs Ethan will hit this season. Before the season starts, Josh looks at Ethan's record and finds that he has hit 40 home runs a year, spread about evenly through the season. Suppose that, after a quarter of the season has gone, Ethan has hit 15 home runs. How many home runs would Ethan be expected to hit for the whole season?

The expected loss method would stay with the initial estimate of 40 home runs. The 15 hit so far could be just a random fluctuation, which might be offset by a slump later in the season. The initial estimate remains.

The loss development method would note that Ethan usually hits 10 home runs in the first quarter and ends the season with 40 home runs, or four times the quarterly experience. Using this method would produce an estimate of 15 (home runs to date) × 4 = 60 home runs for the year. The estimate is based entirely on past patterns applied to current experience.

The Bornhuetter-Ferguson method combines these two approaches. For the three quarters of the year remaining, Ethan had been expected to hit 40 × ¾ = 30 home runs. Adding them to the 15 hit so far produces an estimate of 45 home runs for the year.

[DA06341]

Loss Development—a Closer Look

Because of the widespread use of the loss development method and underlying loss development triangles, it is useful to take a closer look at this method. Although most commonly used to project losses (both paid and reported) to ultimate values, this technique is also used to project allocated loss adjustment expenses, claim counts, and even premiums.

The loss development method involves four steps:

1. Compile the experience into a loss development triangle
2. Calculate the age-to-age development factors
3. Select the development factors to be used
4. Apply factors to experience to make projections

The loss development triangle is a table showing values for a specific group of claims at different points in time. The table is arranged so that it is easy to see values and changes of different groups at similar ages of development. The claims are usually grouped by accident year or policy year.

A simple example shows how the loss development triangle is created. Assume that accident year 20X1 has three claims, with payments made as shown. See the exhibit "Payments Made on Accident Year 20X1 Claims."

The payments at the end of each year can be summarized. See the exhibit "Cumulative Paid Loss as of Calendar Year-End."

Payments Made on Accident Year 20X1 Claims

Claim	Payment Made	Payment Amount
A	3/14/X1	$425
A	7/21/X2	$200
A	2/12/X3	$192
B	1/04/X2	$75
B	9/04/X2	$25
C	11/29/X2	$75

Paid as of 12/31/X1 = $425

Paid as of 12/31/X2 = Paid @ 12/31/X1 + Paid during 20X2

= 425 + (200 + 75 + 25 + 75)

= $800

Paid as of 12/31/X3 = Paid @ 12/31/X2 + Paid during 20X3

= 800 + 192

= $992

[DA06342]

By the end of 20X4, payments have also been made for later accident years, so a more complete table of payments can be assembled. See the exhibit "Cumulative Paid Loss as of Calendar Year-End, Multiple Years."

It is easier to compare the different years' experience at the same "age"; for example, comparing accident year 20X1 at the end of 20X1 to accident year 20X2 at the end of 20X2. Standard practice starts the age of a period from its start, so at 12/31/X1, the accident year 20X1 (which began January 1) is twelve months old.

Rearranging the experience so that the columns now are the age of the experience produces a loss development triangle: See the exhibit "Cumulative Paid Loss as of Year-End by Age."

This loss development triangle can be built up year after year. For analysis purposes, there should be enough data so that the amounts in the columns

Cumulative Paid Loss as of Calendar Year-End

Accident Year	Year-End 20X1	Year-End 20X2	Year-End 20X3	Year-End 20X4
20X1	$425	$800	$992	$992

[DA06343]

Cumulative Paid Loss as of Calendar Year-End, Multiple Years

Accident Year	Year-End 20X1	Year-End 20X2	Year-End 20X3	Year-End 20X4
20X1	$425	$800	$992	$992
20X2		450	750	870
20X3			500	850
20X4				600

[DA06344]

on the right do not change from the prior value; that is, there is no further development.

The second step, to calculate the age-to-age factors, is based on the information presented in the loss development triangle. The triangle provides an overview of how each accident year's losses develop over time. Comparison between years is easier by looking at the change from one evaluation period to the next. For example, at 24 months the losses paid for accident year 20X1 were 800, compared to 425 at 12 months. The ratio of the two values is 800/425 = 1.88; therefore, losses increased by 88 percent from 12 months to 24 months. This ratio is called an age-to-age factor. Similar factors can be calculated for each accident year's development, producing a loss development triangle of age-to-age factors. See the exhibit "Hypothetical Development of Loss Payments."

If the age-to-age factors down the column are relatively consistent, a pattern of development may be revealed that can be used to estimate how future development will occur.

The third step is selection of the loss development factors to be used. Assume that the average factors shown are a reasonable estimate of development. In an actual analysis, the factors selected might vary from the means. For example, if the accident-year multipliers indicated an increasing trend, the analyst

Cumulative Paid Loss as of Year-End by Age

Accident Year	After 12 Mos.	After 24 Mos.	After 36 Mos.	After 48 Mos.
20X1	$425	$800	$992	$992
20X2	450	750	870	
20X3	500	850		
20X4	600			

[DA06345]

Hypothetical Development of Loss Payments

	Months of Development			
Accident Year	12	24	36	48
20X1	$425	$800	$992	$992
20X2	450	750	870	
20X3	500	850		
20X4	600	992	992	

	Age-to-Age Development Factors		
Accident Year	12 to 24	24 to 36	36 to final
20X1	1.88	1.24	1.00
20X2	1.67	1.16	
20X3	1.70		
Average	1.75	1.20	1.00

[DA06346]

might use selected values higher than the mean. The expected development from each age to the final value can be derived by multiplying the factors together. See the exhibit "Expected Development Factors to Ultimate ."

Expected Development Factors to Ultimate

Expected development from 36 months to 48 months (final) =1.00

Expected development from 24 months to final
  = Expected development from 24 to 36 months × Expected development from 36 months to final
  = 1.20 × 1.00 = 1.20

Expected development from 12 months to final
  = Expected development from 12 to 24 months × Expected development from 24 months to final
  = 1.75 x 1.20 = 2.10

[DA06347]

The results are cumulative loss development factors that project from an age of development to a projected final value, or age-to-ultimate factors.

In the simplified example presented, the experience shows that there is no further development. In some cases, development may appear to continue beyond the last age for which there is experience. For example, liability claims may take many years to settle. An indication of further development is that factors for the most mature periods are still significantly different from 1.00. In such cases, a "tail" factor to account for this further development would have to be estimated using other information.

Finally, the ultimate development factors selected can be used to project immature loss data to full maturity. The respective factors multiply the losses to produce a projected ultimate loss. See the exhibit "Projected Ultimate Losses Using Development Factors."

Projected Ultimate Losses Using Development Factors

Accident Year	Paid Loss at 12/31/X4	Development Age at 12/31/X4	Factor to Ultimate	Projected Ultimate Losses
20X1	$992	48 mos.	1.00	992
20X2	$870	36 mos.	1.00	870
20X3	$850	24 mos.	1.20	1,020
20X4	$600	12 mos.	2.10	1,260

[DA06348]

An estimated loss reserve can be calculated by subtracting the current paid losses from the projected ultimate losses.

The loss development method does have limitations. Because it assumes that future experience will develop the same way it has in the past, any changes in business practices or external conditions could affect the usefulness of this method. Examples of such changes are changes in mix of business, policy limits purchased, and how case reserves are set. Also, large one-time events such as catastrophes would disrupt the historical pattern of development. There may be adjustments that can be made to the data, such as excluding catastrophe losses, which can correct for these different conditions. Other types of trends may be addressed by careful selection of the development factors. The power and usefulness of the development method more than offset these limitations in most circumstances.

SUMMARY

Actuaries are trained professionals who estimate the cost of risk for insurers. Major responsibilities for an insurer include ratemaking and estimation of unpaid liabilities and adequacy of loss reserves. Actuaries are also instrumental in developing predictive models, and perform other important functions for insurers. These functions can be performed within an insurer, an advisory organization, or a consulting firm.

Ratemaking is an important component of the overall insurance mechanism. From the insurer's perspective, rates should enable the insurer to be competitive and earn a reasonable profit. Insurers are also concerned about the stability, responsiveness, and reflect differences in risk exposure, as well as the potential to promote risk control. Rates should provide for unanticipated contingencies, such as actual losses being greater than projected. Ratemaking goals often conflict with each other, requiring compromise.

An insurance rate consists of three components: (1) an amount needed to pay losses and loss adjustment expenses (prospective loss costs), (2) an amount needed to pay expenses, such as acquisition expenses, overhead, and premium taxes (expense provision), and (3) an amount for profit and contingencies (profit and contingencies factor).

Common terms used in the ratemaking process are: exposure, earned exposure unit, pure premium, expense provision, loss adjustment expenses, profit and contingencies, and investment income.

Ratemaking is based on estimating losses from past coverage periods and then adjusting those losses for future conditions. However, past loss experience may not be completely known because not all covered losses are paid immediately. Because conditions are constantly changing, any delay between when data are collected and when they are used tends to reduce rate accuracy.

Other factors that affect ratemaking include changes in the cost of claims, the insurer's projected expenses, and the target level of profit and contingencies.

There are three ratemaking methods: the pure premium method, the loss ratio method, and the judgment method. The pure premium method involves calculating a pure premium, the amount needed to pay losses, and then adding an expense provision and applying a profit and contingencies factor. The loss ratio method determines a new rate by modifying an old rate, using a comparison of actual and expected loss ratios. The judgment method is used when little or no loss experience data are available for ratemaking and it relies heavily on the knowledge and experience of an actuary or underwriter.

The complexities of real-world ratemaking arise from variations in policyholders and loss exposures as well as from time-related changes in the insurance environment. The ratemaking process includes these steps:

1. Collect data
2. Adjust data
3. Calculate overall indicated rate change
4. Determine territorial and class relativities
5. Prepare rate filings and submit them to regulatory authorities as required

Insurers and rating organizations collect information about every premium and loss transaction. For ratemaking, reserving and reporting purposes, the transactions during a specific period are compiled into useful aggregations:

- Policy-year method
- Calendar-year method
- Accident-year method
- Report-year method

Ratemaking factors can vary significantly by type of insurance. These variations can result from the characteristics of loss exposures, regulatory requirements, and other factors. Some of the factors that can vary among types of insurance include these:

- Experience period
- Trending
- Large loss limitations
- Credibility
- Increased limits factors

An insurer's loss reserves provide for estimating future claim payments. Estimating the liabilities as accurately as possible is important for understanding the actual costs of business and ensuring the insurer's ability to pay the future claims. Actuaries use various techniques to estimate the liability for these future payments, including the expected loss ratio method, the loss development method, and the Bornhuetter-Ferguson method.

ASSIGNMENT NOTE

1. American Academy of Actuaries, www.actuary.org/becoming.asp (accessed August 9, 2010).

Direct Your Learning ▶▶

10

Reinsurance

Educational Objectives

After learning the content of this assignment, you should be able to:

▶ Describe reinsurance and its principal functions.

▶ Describe the three sources of reinsurance.

▶ Describe treaty reinsurance and facultative reinsurance.

▶ Describe the types of pro rata reinsurance and excess of loss reinsurance and their uses.

▶ Describe finite risk reinsurance and other methods that rely on capital markets as alternatives to traditional and non-traditional reinsurance.

▶ Describe the factors that should be considered in the design of a reinsurance program.

▶ Given a case, identify the reinsurance needs of an insurer and recommend an appropriate reinsurance program to address those needs.

▶ Explain how reinsurance is regulated.

Reinsurance

REINSURANCE AND ITS FUNCTIONS

A single insurer that sells a $100 million commercial property policy and a
$100 million commercial umbrella liability policy to the owners of a high-rise
office building may appear to be jeopardizing its financial stability. Insurers
who provide billions of dollars of property insurance in wind-prone Florida
and earthquake-prone California may seem similarly imperiled. However,
such transactions are possible when the insurers use reinsurance as a tool to
expand their capacity.

No insurer intentionally places itself in a situation in which a catastrophic
event could destroy its net worth. Additionally, insurance regulators attempt
to prevent insurers from being left in such a position. Reinsurance is one
way insurers protect themselves from the financial consequences of insuring
others. This section introduces basic reinsurance terms and concepts, including the principal functions of reinsurance.

Basic Terms and Concepts

Reinsurance, commonly referred to as "insurance for insurers," is the transfer
from one insurer (the **primary insurer**) to another (the **reinsurer**) of some
or all of the financial consequences of certain loss exposures covered by the
primary insurer's policies. The loss exposures transferred, or ceded, by the
primary insurer could be associated with a single subject of insurance (such as
a building), a single policy, or a group of policies.

An insurer that transfers liability for loss exposures by ceding them to a reinsurer can be referred to as the reinsured, the ceding company, the cedent, the
direct insurer, or the primary insurer. Although all these terms are acceptable,
"primary insurer" will be used to denote the party that cedes loss exposures to
a reinsurer.

Reinsurance is transacted through a **reinsurance agreement**, which specifies
the terms under which the reinsurance is provided. For example, it may state
that the reinsurer must pay a percentage of all the primary insurer's losses for
loss exposures subject to the agreement, or must reimburse the primary insurer
for losses that exceed a specified amount. Additionally, the reinsurance agreement identifies the policy, group of policies, or other categories of insurance
that are included in the reinsurance agreement.

Reinsurance

The transfer of insurance
risk from one insurer
to another through a
contractual agreement
under which one insurer (the
reinsurer) agrees, in return
for a reinsurance premium,
to indemnify another insurer
(the primary insurer) for
some or all of the financial
consequences of certain
loss exposures covered by
the primary's insurance
policies.

Primary insurer

In reinsurance, the insurer
that transfers or cedes all
or part of the insurance risk
it has assumed to another
insurer in a contractual
arrangement.

Reinsurer

The insurer that assumes
some or all of the potential
costs of insured loss
exposures of the primary
insurer in a reinsurance
contractual agreement.

Reinsurance agreement

Contract between the
primary insurer and
reinsurer that stipulates the
form of reinsurance and
the type of accounts to be
reinsured.

Insurance risk

Uncertainty about the adequacy of insurance premiums to pay losses.

Retention

The amount retained by the primary insurer in the reinsurance transaction.

The reinsurer typically does not assume all of the primary insurer's **insurance risk**. The reinsurance agreement usually requires the primary insurer to retain part of its original liability. This **retention** can be expressed as a percentage of the original amount of insurance or as a dollar amount of loss. The reinsurance agreement does not alter the terms of the underlying (original) insurance policies or the primary insurer's obligations to honor them. See the exhibit "Risk."

Risk

The Insurance Institute of America typically defines "risk" as uncertainty about the occurrence of a loss. However, risk has several other meanings that are useful in understanding reinsurance practices. In reinsurance, the term risk often refers to the subject of insurance, such as a building, a policy, a group of policies, or a class of business. Reinsurance practitioners use the term risk in this way and include it in common reinsurance clauses.

[DA05756]

Reinsurance premium

The consideration paid by the primary insurer to the reinsurer for assuming some or all of the primary insurer's insurance risk.

Ceding commission

An amount paid by the reinsurer to the primary insurer to cover part or all of the primary insurer's policy acquisition expenses.

Retrocession

A reinsurance agreement whereby one reinsurer (the retrocedent) transfers all or part of the reinsurance risk it has assumed or will assume to another reinsurer (the retrocessionaire).

Retrocedent

The reinsurer that transfers or cedes all or part of the insurance risk it has assumed to another reinsurer.

Retrocessionaire

The reinsurer that assumes all or part of the reinsurance risk accepted by another reinsurer.

The primary insurer pays a **reinsurance premium** for the protection provided just as any insured pays a premium for insurance coverage, but, because the primary insurer incurs the expenses of issuing the underlying policy, the reinsurer might pay a **ceding commission** to the primary insurer. These expenses consist primarily of commissions paid to producers, premium taxes, and underwriting expenses (such as policy processing and servicing costs, and risk control reports).

Reinsurers may transfer part of the liability they have accepted in reinsurance agreements to other reinsurers. Such an agreement is called a **retrocession**. Under a retrocession, one reinsurer, the **retrocedent**, transfers all or part of the reinsurance risk that it has assumed or will assume to another reinsurer, the **retrocessionaire**. Retrocession is very similar to reinsurance except for the parties involved in the agreement. The discussions of reinsurance in the context of a primary insurer-reinsurer relationship also apply to retrocessions.[1]

Reinsurance Functions

Reinsurance helps an insurer achieve several practical business goals, such as insuring large exposures, protecting policyholders' surplus from adverse loss experience, and financing the insurer's growth. The reinsurance that an insurer obtains depends mainly on the constraints or problems the insurer must address to reach its goals. Although several of its uses overlap, reinsurance is a valuable tool that can perform six principal functions for primary insurers:

- Increase large-line capacity
- Provide catastrophe protection

- Stabilize loss experience
- Provide surplus relief
- Facilitate withdrawal from a market segment
- Provide underwriting guidance

Depending on its goals, a primary insurer may use several different reinsurance agreements for these principal functions.

Increase Large-Line Capacity

The first function of reinsurance is to increase **large-line capacity**, which allows a primary insurer to assume more significant risks than its financial condition and regulations would otherwise permit. For example, an application for $100 million of property insurance on a single commercial warehouse could exceed the maximum amount of insurance that an underwriter is willing to accept on a single account. This maximum amount, or **line**, is subject to these influences:

- The maximum amount of insurance or limit of liability allowed by insurance regulations. Insurance regulations prohibit an insurer from retaining (after reinsurance, usually stated as net of reinsurance) more than 10 percent of its policyholders' surplus (net worth) on any one loss exposure.
- The size of a potential loss or losses that can safely be retained without impairing the insurer's earnings or policyholders' surplus.
- The specific characteristics of a particular loss exposure. For example, the line may vary depending on property attributes such as construction, occupancy, loss prevention features, and loss reduction features.
- The amount, types, and cost of available reinsurance.

Reinsurers provide primary insurers with large-line capacity by accepting liability for loss exposures that the primary insurer is unwilling or unable to retain. This function of reinsurance allows insurers with *limited* large-line capacity to participate more fully in the insurance marketplace. For example, a primary insurer may want to compete for homeowners policies in markets in which the value of the homes exceeds the amount the primary insurer can safely retain. Reinsurance allows the primary insurer to increase its market share while limiting the financial consequences of potential losses.

Provide Catastrophe Protection

Without reinsurance, catastrophes could greatly reduce insurer earnings or even threaten insurer solvency when a large number of its insured loss exposures are concentrated in an area that experiences a catastrophe. Potential catastrophic perils include fire, windstorm (hurricane, tornado, and other wind damage), and earthquakes. Additionally, significant property and liability losses can be caused by man-made catastrophes, such as industrial explosions, airplane crashes, or product recalls.

Large-line capacity

An insurer's ability to provide larger amounts of insurance for property loss exposures, or higher limits of liability for liability loss exposures, than it is otherwise willing to provide.

Line

The maximum amount of insurance or limit of liability that an insurer will accept on a single loss exposure.

The second function of reinsurance is to protect against the financial consequences of a single catastrophic event that causes multiple losses in a concentrated area. For example, an insurer might purchase reinsurance that provides up to $50 million of coverage per hurricane when the total amount of loss from a single hurricane exceeds the amount the insurer can safely retain.

Stabilize Loss Experience

An insurer, like most other businesses, must have a steady flow of profits to attract capital investment and support growth. However, demographic, economic, social, and natural forces cause an insurer's loss experience to fluctuate widely, which creates variability in its financial results. Volatile loss experience can affect the stock value of a publicly traded insurer; [2] alter an insurer's financial rating by independent rating agencies; cause abrupt changes in the approaches taken in managing the underwriting, claim, and marketing departments; or undermine the confidence of the sales force (especially independent brokers and agents who can place their customers with other insurers). In extreme cases, volatile loss experience can lead to insolvency.

Reinsurance can smooth the resulting peaks and valleys in an insurer's loss experience curve. In addition to aiding financial planning and supporting growth, this function of reinsurance encourages capital investment because investors are more likely to invest in companies whose financial results are stable.

Reinsurance can be arranged to stabilize the loss experience of a line of insurance (for example, commercial auto), a class of business (for example, truckers), or a primary insurer's entire book of business. In addition, a primary insurer can stabilize loss experience by obtaining reinsurance to accomplish any, or all, of these purposes:

- Limit its liability for a single loss exposure
- Limit its liability for several loss exposures affected by a common event
- Limit its liability for loss exposures that aggregate claims over time

The exhibit illustrates how reinsurance can stabilize a primary insurer's loss experience. See the exhibit "Stabilization of Annual Loss Experience for a Primary Insurer With a $20 Million Retention."

Provide Surplus Relief

Insurers that are growing rapidly may have difficulty maintaining a desirable capacity ratio, due to how they must account for their expenses to acquire new policies. State insurance regulation mandates that, for accounting purposes, such expenses be recognized at the time a new policy is sold. However, premiums are recognized as revenue as they are earned over the policy's life. When an insurer immediately recognizes expenses while only gradually rec-

Stabilization of Annual Loss Experience for a Primary Insurer With a $20 Million Retention

(1)	(2)	(3)	(4)
Time Period (Year)	Actual Losses ($000)	Amount Reinsured ($000)	Stabilized Loss Level ($000)
1	15,000	—	15,000
2	35,000	15,000	20,000
3	13,000	—	13,000
4	25,000	5,000	20,000
5	40,000	20,000	20,000
6	37,000	17,000	20,000
7	16,500	—	16,500
8	9,250	—	9,250
9	18,000	—	18,000
10	10,750	—	10,750
Total	$219,500	$57,000	$162,500

The total actual losses are $219.5 million, or an average of $21.95 million each time period. If a reinsurance agreement were in place to cap losses to $20 million, the primary insurer's loss experience would be limited to the amounts shown in the stabilized loss level column. The broken line that fluctuates dramatically in the graph below represents actual losses, the dotted line represents stabilized losses, and the horizontal line represents average losses.

Graph of Hypothetical Loss Data

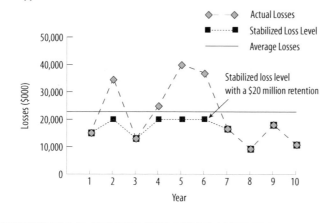

ognizing revenue, its policyholders' surplus will decrease as its capacity ratio increases.

Surplus relief

A replenishment of policyholders' surplus provided by the ceding commission paid to the primary insurer by the reinsurer.

Many insurers use reinsurance to provide **surplus relief**, which satisfies insurance regulatory constraints on excess growth. State insurance regulators monitor several financial ratios as part of their solvency surveillance efforts, but the relationship of written premiums to policyholders' surplus is generally a key financial ratio and one considered to be out of bounds if it exceeds 3 to 1 or 300 percent. Policyholders' surplus (also called "surplus to policyholders" or simply "surplus") is an insurer's net worth as reported on the financial statement prescribed by state insurance regulators. It represents the financial resource the primary insurer can draw on to pay unexpected losses.

Some reinsurance agreements facilitate premium growth by allowing the primary insurer to deduct a ceding commission on loss exposures ceded to the reinsurer. The ceding commission is an amount paid by the reinsurer to the primary insurer to cover part or all of a primary insurer's policy acquisition expenses. The ceding commission immediately offsets the primary insurer's policy acquisition expenses for the reinsured policies and often includes a profit provision, or an additional commission, if the reinsurance ceded is profitable.

Because the ceding commission replenishes the primary insurer's policyholders' surplus, the surplus relief facilitates the primary insurer's premium growth and the increase in policyholders' surplus lowers its capacity ratio.

Facilitate Withdrawal From a Market Segment

Reinsurance can also facilitate withdrawal from a market segment, which may be a particular class of business, geographic area, or type of insurance. A primary insurer may want to withdraw from a market segment that is unprofitable, undesirable, or incompatible with its strategic plan. When withdrawing from a market segment, the primary insurer has these options:

- Stop writing new insurance policies and continue in-force insurance until all policies expire (often referred to as "run-off")
- Cancel all policies (if insurance regulations permit) and refund the unearned premiums to insureds
- Withdraw from the market segment by purchasing portfolio reinsurance

To withdraw from a market segment, an insurer can stop writing new business or, to the extent permitted by applicable cancellation laws, cancel all policies in effect and return the unearned premiums to its insureds. However, these approaches can be unwieldy, expensive, and could create ill will among insureds, producers, and state insurance regulators. They also create uncertainty about the insurer's outstanding claims, which must be settled, and about new claims, which might continue to be filed even after the insurer ceases operations.

Another approach available to the primary insurer is to transfer the liability for all outstanding policies to a reinsurer by purchasing **portfolio reinsurance**. Portfolio reinsurance can facilitate withdrawal from a market segment and prevent the formation of ill will due to policy cancellation. It is an exception to the general rule that reinsurers do not accept all of the liability for specified loss exposures of an insurer.

In portfolio reinsurance, the reinsurer accepts all of the liability for certain loss exposures covered under the primary insurer's policies, but the primary insurer must continue to fulfill its obligations to its insureds. For example, the primary insurer may decide to use portfolio reinsurance to withdraw from the errors and omissions insurance market. In this situation, the reinsurer typically agrees to indemnify the primary insurer for all losses incurred as of, and following, the date of the portfolio reinsurance agreement. However, the primary insurer continues to pay claims to (or on behalf of) its insureds who are covered by the underlying insurance.

Portfolio reinsurance can be expensive, particularly if the portfolio has been unprofitable and is expected to incur additional losses for the reinsurer. In many states, portfolio reinsurance must be approved by the state insurance department.

Sometimes a primary insurer wants to completely eliminate the liabilities it has assumed under the insurance policies it has issued. This can be accomplished through a **novation**. A novation is not considered portfolio reinsurance because the substitute insurer assumes the direct obligations to insureds covered by the underlying insurance. Usually, the approval of state insurance regulators or the insured is required to effect a novation.

Provide Underwriting Guidance

Reinsurance may also provide underwriting guidance. Reinsurers work with a wide variety of insurers in the domestic and global markets under many different circumstances. Consequently, reinsurers accumulate a great deal of underwriting expertise. A reinsurer's understanding of insurance operations and the insurance industry can assist other insurers, particularly inexperienced primary insurers entering new markets and offering new products. For example, one medium-sized insurer reinsured 95 percent of its umbrella liability coverage over a period of years and relied heavily on the reinsurer for technical assistance in underwriting and pricing its policies. Without such technical assistance, certain primary insurers would find it difficult to generate underwriting profits from coverages with which they have limited expertise.

Reinsurers that provide underwriting assistance to primary insurers must respect the confidentiality of their clients' proprietary information. Reinsurers often learn about the primary insurer's marketing and underwriting strategies, but should not reveal insurer-specific information to other parties.

Portfolio reinsurance

Reinsurance that transfers to the reinsurer liability for an entire type of insurance, territory, or book of business after the primary insurer has issued the policies.

Novation

An agreement under which one insurer or reinsurer is substituted for another.

REINSURANCE SOURCES

The reinsurance market is international in scope, with many participants. In the United States, licensed insurers can market reinsurance unless prohibited by statute or charter. Few such prohibitions exist, and many primary insurers sell some reinsurance. If an insurer is too small to provide reinsurance on its own, it can participate in various reinsurance pools and syndicates.

Reinsurance can be purchased from three sources:

- Professional reinsurers
- Reinsurance departments of primary insurers
- Reinsurance pools, syndicates, and associations

Additionally, the reinsurance business has several professional and trade associations that serve member companies and provide information to interested parties.

Professional Reinsurers

Professional reinsurer

An insurer whose primary business purpose is serving other insurers' reinsurance needs.

Direct writing reinsurer

A professional reinsurer whose employees deal directly with primary insurers.

Reinsurance intermediary

An intermediary that works with primary insurers to develop reinsurance programs and that negotiates contracts of reinsurance between the primary insurer and reinsurer, receiving commission for placement and other services rendered.

The first source of reinsurance is **professional reinsurers**, which interact with other insurers either directly or through intermediaries as primary insurers do.

A reinsurer whose employees deal directly with primary insurers is called a **direct writing reinsurer**. However, most direct writing reinsurers in the U.S. also solicit reinsurance business through reinsurance intermediaries.

Reinsurance intermediaries generally represent a primary insurer, and work with that insurer to develop a reinsurance program that is then placed with a reinsurer or reinsurers. The reinsurance intermediary receives a brokerage commission—almost always from the reinsurer or reinsurers—for performing other necessary services in addition to placing the reinsurance, such as disbursing reinsurance premiums among participating reinsurers and collecting loss amounts owed to the insurer.

Although the variety of professional reinsurers leads to differences in how those reinsurers are used and what they can offer, some broad generalizations may be made about professional reinsurers:

- Primary insurers dealing with direct writing reinsurers often use fewer reinsurers in their reinsurance program.
- Reinsurance intermediaries often use more than one reinsurer to develop a reinsurance program for a primary insurer.
- Reinsurance intermediaries can often help secure high coverage limits and catastrophe coverage.
- Reinsurance intermediaries usually have access to various reinsurance solutions from both domestic and international markets.
- Reinsurance intermediaries can usually obtain reinsurance under favorable terms and at a competitive price because they can determine

prevailing market conditions and work repeatedly in this market with many primary insurers.

Professional reinsurers evaluate the primary insurer before entering into a reinsurance agreement because the treaty reinsurer underwrites the primary insurer as well as the loss exposures being ceded. In evaluating the primary insurer, the reinsurer gathers information about the primary insurer's financial strength by analyzing the primary insurer's financial statements or by using information developed by a financial rating service. Other information about the primary insurer may be obtained from state insurance department bulletins and the trade press.

Reinsurers also consider the primary insurer's experience, reputation, and management. The reinsurer relies on the quality of the management team, and a relationship of trust must underlie any reinsurance agreement. Whether it involves a one-time facultative agreement or an ongoing treaty agreement, the relationship between the primary insurer and the reinsurer is considered to be one of "utmost good faith." This is because each party is obligated to and relies on the other for full disclosure of material facts about the subject of the agreement. It would be considered a breach of this duty of utmost good faith if the primary insurer withheld material facts relevant to the reinsurer's underwriting decision, intentionally underestimated prior losses, or failed to disclose hazardous conditions affecting loss exposures.

Just as the reinsurer should evaluate the primary insurer, the primary insurer should evaluate the reinsurer's claim-paying ability, reputation, and management competence before entering into the reinsurance agreement.

Reinsurance Departments of Primary Insurers

Some primary insurers also provide treaty and facultative reinsurance, and the reinsurance departments of these companies serve as the second source of reinsurance.

A primary insurer may offer reinsurance to affiliated insurers, regardless of whether it offers reinsurance to unaffiliated insurers. To ensure that information from other insurers remains confidential, a primary insurer's reinsurance operations are usually separate from its primary insurance operations.

Many primary insurers are groups of commonly owned insurance companies. Intragroup reinsurance agreements are used to balance the financial results of all insurers in the group. The use of intragroup reinsurance agreements does not preclude using professional reinsurers.

Reinsurance Pools, Syndicates, and Associations

The third source of reinsurance is **reinsurance pools, syndicates, and associations**. These entities provide member companies the opportunity to participate in a line of insurance with a limited amount of capital—and a pro-

Reinsurance pools, syndicates, and associations

Groups of insurers that share the loss exposures of the group, usually through reinsurance.

portionate share of the administrative costs—without having to employ the specialists needed for such a venture. Whether a pool is a reinsurance device is determined by the organizational structure, the type of contract issued, and the internal accounting procedures. The terms pool, syndicate, and association are often used interchangeably, although there are some fine differences.

Reinsurance pool

A reinsurance association that consists of several unrelated insurers or reinsurers that have joined to insure risks the individual members are unwilling to individually insure.

In a **reinsurance pool**, a policy for the full amount of insurance is issued by a member company and reinsured by the remainder of the pool members according to predetermined percentages. Some pools are formed by insurers whose reinsurance needs are not adequately met in the regular marketplace, while others are formed to provide specialized insurance requiring underwriting and claim expertise that the individual insurers do not have. Reinsurance intermediaries also form reinsurance pools to provide reinsurance to their clients. A reinsurance pool may accept loss exposures from non-member companies or offer reinsurance only to its member companies. Some reinsurance pools restrict their operations to narrowly defined classes of business while others reinsure most types of insurance.

Syndicate

A group of insurers or reinsurers involved in joint underwriting to insure major risks that are beyond the capacity of a single insurer or reinsurer; each syndicate member accepts predetermined shares of premiums, losses, expenses, and profits.

In a **syndicate**, each member shares the risk with other members by accepting a percentage of the risk. These members collectively constitute a single, separate entity under the syndicate name. For example, syndicates are a key component of Lloyd's (formerly Lloyd's of London), an association that provides the physical and procedural facilities for its members to write insurance. Each individual investor of Lloyd's, called a "Name," belongs to one or more syndicates. The syndicate's underwriter, or group of underwriters, conducts the insurance operations and analyzes applications for insurance coverage. Depending on the nature and amount of insurance requested, a particular syndicate might accept only a portion of the total amount of insurance. The application is then taken to other syndicates for their evaluations.

Association

An organization of member companies that reinsure by fixed percentage the total amount of insurance appearing on policies issued by the organization.

An **association** consists of member companies that use both reinsurance and risk-sharing techniques. In many cases, the member companies issue their own policies; however, a reinsurance certificate is attached to each policy, under which each member company assumes a fixed percentage of the total amount of insurance. One member company is usually responsible for inspection and investigation, while a committee comprising underwriting executives from the member companies establishes the association's underwriting policy. Organizations of this type allow members to share risks that require special coverages or special underwriting techniques, and can increase the primary insurer's capacity to insure extra-hazardous risks.

Reinsurance Professional and Trade Associations

Unlike many primary insurers, reinsurers do not use service organizations such as Insurance Services Office (ISO) and the American Association of Insurance Services (AAIS) to develop loss costs and draft contract wording. However, the reinsurance field has several associations that serve member companies and provide information to interested parties.

Intermediaries and Reinsurance Underwriters Association (IRU)

The Intermediaries and Reinsurance Underwriters Association (IRU) was founded in 1967 and comprises intermediaries and reinsurers that broker or assume non-life treaty reinsurance. IRU publishes the *Journal of Reinsurance*, which discusses concepts and research affecting the reinsurance market. IRU conducts claim seminars, sponsors an internship program for college students, and holds conferences for members.[3]

Brokers & Reinsurance Markets Association (BRMA)

The Brokers & Reinsurance Markets Association (BRMA) represents intermediaries and reinsurers that are predominately engaged in U.S. treaty reinsurance business obtained through reinsurance brokers. BRMA seeks to identify and address industry-wide operational issues through various member committees and is described as a forum for treaty reinsurance professionals.

Of particular importance are BRMA's efforts in the area of reinsurance contract wording. The organization has compiled the *Contract Wording Reference Book*, which has become a benchmark for treaty reinsurance contracts. It is available on BRMA's Web site.[4]

Reinsurance Association of America (RAA)

The Reinsurance Association of America (RAA), headquartered in Washington, D.C., is a not-for-profit trade association of professional reinsurers and intermediaries. All members are domestic U.S. companies or U.S. branches of international reinsurers.

The RAA engages in many activities, serving its members and providing information on reinsurance issues to interested parties outside the industry. In addition to member advocacy and lobbying at both the state and federal levels, the RAA analyzes aggregate data and conducts seminars countrywide.[5]

REINSURANCE TRANSACTIONS

No single reinsurance agreement performs all the reinsurance functions. Instead, reinsurers have developed various types of reinsurance, each of which are effective in helping insurers meet one or more goals. A primary insurer often combines several reinsurance agreements to meet its particular needs. Each reinsurance agreement is tailored to the specific needs of the primary insurer and the reinsurer.

There are two types of reinsurance transactions: treaty and facultative.

Treaty reinsurance uses one agreement for an entire class or portfolio of loss exposures, and is also referred to as obligatory reinsurance. The reinsurance agreement is typically called the treaty.

Facultative reinsurance uses a separate reinsurance agreement for each loss exposure it wants to reinsure, and is also referred to as non-obligatory reinsurance.

Treaty Reinsurance

In treaty reinsurance, the reinsurer agrees in advance to reinsure all the loss exposures that fall within the treaty. Although some treaties allow the reinsurer limited discretion in reinsuring individual loss exposures, most treaties require that all loss exposures within the treaty's terms must be reinsured.

Primary insurers usually use treaty reinsurance as the foundation of their reinsurance programs. Treaty reinsurance provides primary insurers with the certainty needed to formulate underwriting policy and develop underwriting guidelines. Primary insurers work with reinsurance intermediaries (or with reinsurers directly) to develop comprehensive reinsurance programs that address the primary insurers' varied needs. The reinsurance programs that satisfy those needs often include several reinsurance agreements and the participation of several reinsurers.

Treaty reinsurance agreements are tailored to fit the primary insurer's individual requirements. The price and terms of each reinsurance treaty are individually negotiated.

Treaty reinsurance agreements are usually designed to address a primary insurer's need to reinsure many loss exposures over a period of time. Although the reinsurance agreement's term may be for only one year, the relationship between the primary insurer and the reinsurer often spans many years. A primary insurer's management usually finds that a long-term relationship with a reinsurer enables the primary insurer to be able to consistently fulfill its producers' requests to place insurance with them.

Adverse selection

The decision to reinsure those loss exposures that have an increased probability of loss because the retention of those loss exposures is undesirable.

Most, but not all, treaty reinsurance agreements *require* the primary insurer to cede all eligible loss exposures to the reinsurer. Primary insurers usually make treaty reinsurance agreements so their underwriters do not have to exercise discretion in using reinsurance. If treaty reinsurance agreements permitted primary insurers to choose which loss exposures they ceded to the reinsurer, the reinsurer would be exposed to adverse selection. **Adverse selection** occurs when the primary insurer decides to reinsure those loss exposures that have an increased probability of loss because the retention of those loss exposures is undesirable.

Because treaty reinsurers are obligated to accept ceded loss exposures once the reinsurance agreement is in place, reinsurers usually want to know about the integrity and experience of the primary insurer's management and the degree to which the primary insurer's published underwriting guidelines represent its actual underwriting practices.

Facultative Reinsurance

In facultative reinsurance, the primary insurer negotiates a separate reinsurance agreement for each loss exposure that it wants to reinsure. The primary insurer is not obligated to purchase reinsurance, and the reinsurer is not obligated to reinsure loss exposures submitted to it. A facultative reinsurance agreement is written for a specified time period and cannot be canceled by either party unless contractual obligations, such as payment of premiums, are not met.

The reinsurer issues a **facultative certificate of reinsurance** (or facultative certificate) that is attached to the primary insurer's copy of the policy being reinsured.

Facultative reinsurance serves four functions:

- Facultative reinsurance can provide large line capacity for loss exposures that exceed the limits of treaty reinsurance agreements.

- Facultative reinsurance can reduce the primary insurer's exposure in a given geographic area. For example, a marine underwriter may be considering underwriting numerous shiploads of cargo that are stored in the same warehouse and that belong to different insureds. The underwriter could use facultative reinsurance for some of those loss exposures, thereby reducing the primary insurer's overall exposure to loss.

- Facultative reinsurance can insure a loss exposure with atypical hazard characteristics and thereby maintain the favorable loss experience of the primary insurer's treaty reinsurance and any associated profit-sharing arrangements. Maintaining favorable treaty loss experience is important because the reinsurer has underwritten and priced the treaty with certain expectations. A loss exposure that is inconsistent with the primary insurer's typical portfolio of insurance policies may cause excessive losses and lead to the treaty's termination or a price increase. The treaty reinsurer is usually willing for the primary insurer to remove high-hazard loss exposures from the treaty by using facultative reinsurance. These facultative placements of atypical loss exposures also benefit the treaty reinsurer. For example, an insured under a commercial property policy may request coverage for an expensive fine arts collection that the primary insurer and its treaty reinsurer would not ordinarily want to cover. Facultative reinsurance of the fine arts collection would eliminate the underwriting concern by removing this loss exposure from the treaty. Often, the treaty reinsurer's own facultative reinsurance department provides this reinsurance. The facultative reinsurer knows that adverse selection occurs in facultative reinsurance. Consequently, the loss exposures submitted for reinsurance are likely to have an increased probability of loss. Therefore, facultative reinsurance is usually priced to reflect the likelihood of adverse selection.

- Facultative reinsurance can insure particular classes of loss exposures that are excluded under treaty reinsurance.

Facultative certificate of reinsurance

An agreement that defines the terms of the facultative reinsurance coverage on a specific loss exposure.

Primary insurers purchase facultative reinsurance mainly to reinsure loss exposures that they do not typically insure or on exposures with high levels of underwriting risk. Consequently, primary insurers use facultative reinsurance for fewer of their loss exposures than they use treaty insurance. Primary insurers that find they are increasingly using facultative reinsurance may want to review the adequacy of their treaty reinsurance.

The expense of placing facultative reinsurance can be high for both the primary insurer and the reinsurer. In negotiating facultative reinsurance, the primary insurer must provide extensive information about each loss exposure. Consequently, administrative costs are relatively high because the primary insurer must devote a significant amount of time to complete each cession and to notify the reinsurer of any endorsement, loss notice, or policy cancellation. Likewise, the reinsurer must underwrite and price each facultative submission. See the exhibit "Hybrids of Treaty and Facultative Reinsurance."

Hybrids of Treaty and Facultative Reinsurance

Reinsurers sometimes use hybrid agreements that have elements of both treaty and facultative reinsurance. The hybrid agreements usually describe how individual facultative reinsurance placements will be handled. For example, the agreement may specify the basic underwriting parameters of the loss exposures that will be ceded to the reinsurer as well as premium and loss allocation formulas. Although hybrid agreements may be used infrequently, they demonstrate the flexibility of the reinsurance market to satisfy the mutual needs of primary insurers and reinsurers. The two hybrid agreements briefly described next illustrate common reinsurance agreement variations.

- In a *facultative treaty*, the primary insurer and the reinsurer agree on how subsequent individual facultative submissions will be handled. A facultative treaty could be used when a class of business has insufficient loss exposures to justify treaty reinsurance, but has a sufficient number of loss exposures to determine the details of future individual placements.

- In a *facultative obligatory treaty*, although the primary insurer has the option of ceding loss exposures, the reinsurer is obligated to accept all loss exposures submitted to it. Facultative obligatory treaties are also called *semi-obligatory treaties*.

[DA05757]

TYPES OF REINSURANCE

Each reinsurance agreement negotiated between a primary insurer and reinsurer is unique because its terms reflect the primary insurer's needs and the willingness of reinsurers in the marketplace to meet those needs. Several forms of reinsurance have been developed to serve the functions of reinsurance and to help insurers meet their goals.

The two types of reinsurance transactions are treaty reinsurance and facultative reinsurance. These types can be further categorized based on the manner in which the primary insurer and the reinsurer divide the obligations under the reinsurance agreements. The principal approaches that reinsurers use to allocate losses are broadly defined as pro rata reinsurance and excess of loss reinsurance. These types of reinsurance reflect how the primary insurer and reinsurer will share premiums, amounts of insurance, and losses.

The exhibit shows the types of reinsurance and their relationships, and augments the description of the subcategories of pro rata and excess of loss reinsurance. In practice, a reinsurance agreement might contain several of the various types of reinsurance agreements to meet the specific needs of a primary insurer. Unlike primary insurance contracts, reinsurance agreements are not standardized. See the exhibit "Types of Reinsurance."

Pro rata reinsurance

A type of reinsurance in which the primary insurer and reinsurer proportionately share the amounts of insurance, policy premiums, and losses (including loss adjustment expenses).

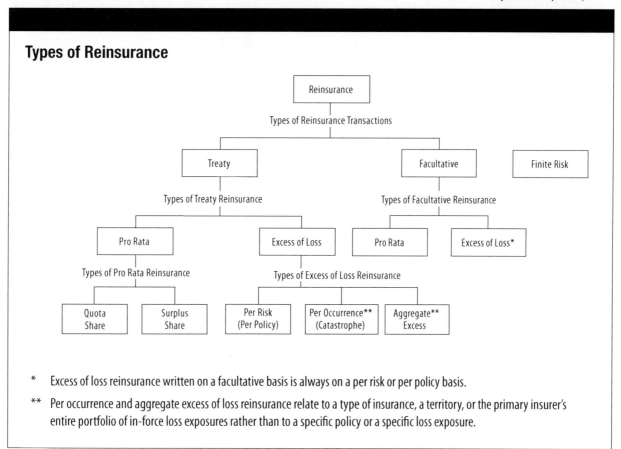

[DA05080]

Pro Rata Reinsurance

Under **pro rata reinsurance**, or proportional reinsurance, the primary insurer cedes a portion of the original insurance premiums to the reinsurer as a reinsurance premium. The reinsurer usually pays the primary insurer a ceding commission for the loss exposures ceded. The ceding commission reimburses the primary insurer for policy acquisition expenses incurred when the underlying policies were sold. In addition to policy acquisition expenses, insurers incur loss adjustment expenses. Loss adjustment expenses that can be related to a specific loss are usually shared proportionately by the primary insurer and the reinsurer.

The amount of insurance, the premium, and the losses (including loss adjustment expenses) are divided between the primary insurer and the reinsurer in the same proportions as the risk. For example, if the reinsurer covers 60 percent of the liability for each loss exposure the primary insurer insures, then the reinsurer would be entitled to 60 percent of the policy premiums and would be responsible for 60 percent of each loss. The amount of the ceding commission paid to the primary insurer is usually negotiated, and is taken from the reinsurance premium remitted to the reinsurer. When the ceding commission is a fixed percentage of the ceded premium with no adjustment for the primary insurer's loss experience, it is referred to as a **flat commission**.

The reinsurance agreement may also include a **profit-sharing commission**, or profit commission, which is negotiated and paid to the primary insurer after the end of the treaty year if the reinsurer earns greater-than-expected profits on the reinsurance agreement. The profit-sharing commission percentage is predetermined and applied to the reinsurer's excess profits; that is, the profits remaining after losses, expenses, and the reinsurer's minimum margin for profit are deducted. Profit commission is also called "contingent commission" because its payment is contingent on the reinsurance agreement's profitability.

Sometimes, as an alternative to the flat commission and profit-sharing commission, the ceding commission initially paid to the primary insurer may be adjusted to reflect the actual profitability of the reinsurance agreement. This type of commission is called a **sliding scale commission**, and could result in the commission being lower than the commission initially paid.

Pro rata reinsurance is generally chosen by newly incorporated insurers or insurers with limited capital because it is effective in providing surplus relief. Its effectiveness results from the practice of paying ceding commissions under pro rata treaties, a practice not common under excess of loss treaties.

Pro rata reinsurance can be identified as either quota share or surplus share. The principal difference between them is how each one indicates the primary insurer's retention.

Quota Share Reinsurance

The distinguishing characteristic of **quota share reinsurance** is that the primary insurer and the reinsurer use a fixed percentage in sharing the amounts of insurance, policy premiums, and losses (including loss adjustment expenses). For example, an insurer may arrange a reinsurance treaty in which it retains 45 percent of policy premiums, coverage limits, and losses while

Flat commission

A ceding commission that is a fixed percentage of the ceded premiums.

Profit-sharing commission

A ceding commission that is contingent on the reinsurer realizing a predetermined percentage of excess profit on ceded loss exposures.

Sliding scale commission

A ceding commission based on a formula that adjusts the commission according to the profitability of the reinsurance agreement.

Quota share reinsurance

A type of pro rata reinsurance in which the primary insurer and the reinsurer share the amounts of insurance, policy premiums, and losses (including loss adjustment expenses) using a fixed percentage.

reinsuring the remainder. Such a treaty would be called a "55 percent quota share treaty" because the reinsurer accepts 55 percent of the liability for each loss exposure subject to the treaty. Quota share reinsurance can be used with both property insurance and liability insurance, but is more frequently used in property insurance.

Most reinsurance agreements specify a maximum dollar limit above which responsibilty for additional coverage limits or losses reverts to the primary insurer (or is taken by another reinsurer). With a pro rata reinsurance agreement, that maximum dollar amount is stated in terms of the coverage limits of each policy subject to the treaty. For example, a primary insurer and a reinsurer may share amounts of insurance, policy premiums, and losses on a 45 percent and 55 percent basis, respectively, subject to a $1 million maximum coverage amount for each policy.

In addition to a maximum coverage amount limitation, some pro rata reinsurance agreements include a per occurrence limit, which restricts the primary insurer's reinsurance recovery for losses originating from a single occurrence. This per occurrence limit may be stated as an aggregate dollar amount or as a loss ratio cap. The per occurrence limit diminishes the usefulness of pro rata reinsurance in protecting the primary insurer from the effects of catastrophic events. Primary insurers exposed to catastrophic losses usually include **catastrophe excess of loss reinsurance** in their reinsurance programs.

Catastrophe excess of loss reinsurance

A type of excess of loss reinsurance that protects the primary insurer from an accumulation of retained losses that arise from a single catastrophic event.

The exhibit shows how the amounts of insurance, policy premiums, and losses would be shared between a primary insurer and a reinsurer for three policies subject to a quota share treaty. See the exhibit "Quota Share Reinsurance Example."

These observations can be made about quota share reinsurance:

- Because the retention and cession amounts are each a fixed percentage, the dollar amount of the retention and the dollar amount of the cession change as the amount of insurance changes. On policies with higher amounts of insurance, the primary insurer will have a higher dollar retention.

- Because the primary insurer cedes a fixed percentage under a quota share treaty, even policies with low amounts of insurance that the primary insurer could safely retain are reinsured.

- Quota share treaties are straightforward because of the fixed percentage used in sharing premiums and losses. The primary insurer can combine premium and loss amounts and determine the amounts owed to the reinsurer in premiums and owed by the reinsurer in losses.

- Because the primary insurer and the reinsurer share liability for every loss exposure subject to the quota share treaty, the reinsurer is usually not subject to adverse selection. The loss ratio for the reinsurer is the same as that of the primary insurer for the ceded loss exposures.

Quota Share Reinsurance Example

Brookgreen Insurance Company has a quota share treaty with Cypress Reinsurer. The treaty has a $250,000 limit, a retention of 25 percent, and a cession of 75 percent. The following three policies are issued by Brookgreen Insurance Company and are subject to the pro rata treaty with Cypress Reinsurer.

- Policy A insures Building A for $25,000 for a premium of $400, with one loss of $8,000.
- Policy B insures Building B for $100,000 for a premium of $1,000, with one loss of $10,000.
- Policy C insures Building C for $150,000 for a premium of $1,500, with one loss of $60,000.

Division of Insurance, Premiums, and Losses Under Quota Share Treaty

	Brookgreen Insurance Retention (25%)	Cypress Reinsurance Cession (75%)	Total
Policy A			
Amounts of insurance	$6,250	$18,750	$25,000
Premiums	100	300	400
Losses	2,000	6,000	8,000
Policy B			
Amounts of insurance	$25,000	$75,000	$100,000
Premiums	250	750	1,000
Losses	2,500	7,500	10,000
Policy C			
Amounts of insurance	$37,500	$112,500	$150,000
Premiums	375	1,125	1,500
Losses	15,000	45,000	60,000

Policy C
$150,000

Policy B
$100,000

Policy A
$25,000

25% / 75%

25% / 75%

25% / 75%

☐ Primary Insurer's Retention

▨ Ceded to the Reinsurer

[DA05081]

One type of quota share treaty, a variable quota share treaty, has the advantage of enabling a primary insurer to retain a larger proportion of the small loss exposures that are within its financial capability to absorb, while maintaining a safer and smaller retention on larger loss exposures.

Surplus Share Reinsurance

The distinguishing characteristic of **surplus share reinsurance** is that when an underlying policy's total amount of insurance exceeds a stipulated dollar amount, or line, the reinsurer assumes the surplus share of the amount of insurance (the difference between the primary insurer's line and the total amount of insurance). Surplus share reinsurance is typically only used with property insurance.

The primary insurer and the reinsurer share the policy premiums and losses proportionately. The primary insurer's share of the policy premiums and losses is the proportion that the line bears to the total amount of insurance. The reinsurer's share of the premiums and losses is the proportion that the amount ceded bears to the total. For example, if the line is $50,000 and the amount ceded is $200,000, the primary insurer would receive 20 percent ($50,000 ÷ $250,000) of the policy premium and pay 20 percent of all losses, while the reinsurer would receive 80 percent ($200,000 ÷ $250,000) of the policy premium and pay 80 percent of all losses.

The exhibit shows how a primary insurer and a reinsurer would share amounts of insurance, policy premiums, and losses under a surplus share treaty using the same three policies shown in the quota share treaty exhibit. See the exhibit "Surplus Share Reinsurance Example."

The reinsurance limit—the total limit or capacity—of a surplus share treaty is expressed in multiples of the primary insurer's line. A primary insurer with a nine-line surplus share treaty has the capacity under the treaty to insure loss exposures with amounts of insurance that exceed its retention by a multiple of nine. For example, if the line is $300,000 for a nine-line surplus share treaty, the primary insurer has a total underwriting capacity of $3 million, calculated as the $300,000 line, plus nine multiples of that $300,000 line. In addition to being expressed as a number of lines, the reinsurance limit of a surplus share treaty can also be expressed as an amount of insurance the reinsurer is willing to provide, such as $2.7 million ($300,000 multiplied by nine lines).

Surplus share reinsurance

A type of pro rata reinsurance in which the policies covered are those whose amount of insurance exceeds a stipulated dollar amount, or line.

Surplus Share Reinsurance Example

Brookgreen Insurance Company has a surplus share treaty with Cypress Reinsurer and retains a line of $25,000. The treaty contains nine lines and provides for a maximum cession of $225,000. Therefore, the retention and reinsurance provide Brookgreen with the ability to issue policies with amounts of insurance as high as $250,000. The following three policies are issued by Brookgreen Insurance Company and are subject to the surplus share treaty with Cypress Reinsurer.

- Policy A insures Building A for $25,000 for a premium of $400, with one loss of $8,000.
- Policy B insures Building B for $100,000 for a premium of $1,000, with one loss of $10,000.
- Policy C insures Building C for $150,000 for a premium of $1,500, with one loss of $60,000.

Division of Insurance, Premiums, and Losses Under Surplus Share Treaty

	Brookgreen Insurance Retention	Cypress Reinsurance Cession	Total
Policy A			
Amounts of insurance	$25,000 (100%)	$0 (0%)	$25,000
Premiums	400	0	400
Losses	8,000	0	8,000
Policy B			
Amounts of insurance	$25,000 (25%)	$75,000 (75%)	$100,000
Premiums	250	750	1,000
Losses	2,500	7,500	10,000
Policy C			
Amounts of insurance	$25,000 (16.67%)	$125,000 (83.33%)	$150,000
Premiums	250	1,250	1,500
Losses	10,000	50,000	60,000

Policy C
$150,000

Policy B
$100,000

Policy A
No participation
by the reinsurer

25%   75%

16.67%   83.33%

☐ Primary Insurer's Retention

▨ Ceded to the Reinsurer

[DA05082]

These observations can be made about surplus share reinsurance:

- The surplus share treaty does not cover policies with amounts of insurance that are less than the primary insurer's line. Many primary insurers use surplus share reinsurance instead of quota share reinsurance so that they do not have to cede any part of the liability for loss exposures that can be safely retained.

- The amount of insurance for a large number of loss exposures may be too small to be ceded to the treaty but, in the aggregate, may cause the primary insurer to incur significant losses that are not reinsured. For example, many homeowners policies in the same region that do not exceed the primary insurer's line could incur extensive losses from a single occurrence, such as a hurricane.

- Because the percentage of policy premiums and losses varies for each loss exposure ceded, surplus share treaties are more costly to administer than quota share treaties. Primary insurers must keep records and, in many cases, periodically provide the reinsurer with a report called a **bordereau**.

- Surplus share treaties may provide surplus relief to the primary insurer because the reinsurer usually pays a ceding commission for those policies ceded. Loss exposures with amounts of insurance that are less than the primary insurer's line are not reinsured, so a surplus share treaty typically provides less surplus relief than does a quota share treaty.

Bordereau

A report the primary insurer provides periodically to the reinsurer that contains a history of all loss exposures reinsured under the treaty.

Unlike the simplified example shown in the "Surplus Share Reinsurance Example" exhibit, many surplus share treaties allow the primary insurer to increase its line from a minimum amount to a maximum amount, depending on the potential loss severity of the exposed limit. For example, Brookgreen Insurance Company's surplus share treaty may allow the company to increase its line on a "superior" loss exposure from $25,000 to $50,000. In this case, the nine-line surplus share treaty would give Brookgreen Insurance Company the large line capacity to insure loss exposures with amounts of insurance as large as $500,000, which is calculated as the $50,000 line plus nine multiplied by the $50,000 line. The primary insurer's ability to vary its line also allows it to retain some loss exposures it may otherwise be required to cede. The flexibility provided by the reinsurer in the surplus share treaty is usually communicated to the primary insurer's underwriters through a **line guide**, or line authorization guide.

Line guide

A document that provides the minimum and maximum line a primary insurer can retain on a loss exposure.

When the total underwriting capacity of the primary insurer's surplus share treaty is insufficient to meet its large line capacity needs, the primary insurer can arrange for additional surplus share reinsurance from another reinsurer. When a primary insurer arranges more than one surplus share treaty, the surplus share treaty that applies immediately above the primary insurer's line is referred to as the first surplus. Other surplus share treaties are referred to in the order that they provide additional large-line capacity, such as second or third surplus treaties.

Excess of Loss Reinsurance

Excess of loss reinsurance (nonproportional reinsurance)

A type of reinsurance in which the primary insurer is indemnified for losses that exceed a specified dollar amount.

Attachment point

The dollar amount above which the reinsurer responds to losses.

In an **excess of loss reinsurance** agreement, also called "non-proportional reinsurance," the reinsurer responds to a loss only when the loss exceeds the primary insurer's retention, often referred to as the **attachment point**. The primary insurer fully retains losses that are less than the attachment point, and will sometimes be required by the reinsurer to also retain responsibility for a percentage of the losses that exceed the attachment point.

Excess of loss reinsurance can be visualized as a layer, or a series of layers, of reinsurance on top of the primary insurer's retention as illustrated in the exhibit. See the exhibit "How Excess of Loss Reinsurance Is Layered."

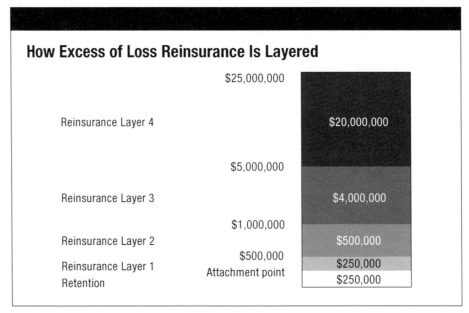

[DA05084]

An excess of loss reinsurer's obligation to indemnify the primary insurer for losses depends on the amount of the loss and the layer of coverage the reinsurer provides. The reinsurer providing the first layer of excess of loss reinsurance shown in the exhibit would indemnify the primary insurer for losses that exceed $250,000 (the attachment point) up to total incurred losses of $500,000. This reinsurer describes its position in the primary insurer's excess of loss reinsurance program as being "$250,000 in excess of (denoted as 'xs') $250,000." The reinsurer in the second layer of the excess of loss reinsurance program would indemnify the primary insurer for losses that exceed $500,000 up to total incurred losses of $1 million, or "$500,000 xs $500,000." Losses that exceed the capacity of the primary insurer's excess of loss reinsurance remain the primary insurer's responsibility unless otherwise reinsured. In the exhibit, loss amounts in excess of $25 million are the primary insurer's responsibility.

Excess of loss reinsurance premiums are negotiated based on the likelihood that losses will exceed the attachment point. The reinsurance premium for excess of loss reinsurance is usually stated as a percentage (often called a rate) of the policy premium charged by the primary insurer (often called the **subject premium** or underlying premium). Therefore, unlike quota share and surplus share reinsurance, the excess of loss reinsurer receives a nonproportional share of the premium.

Generally, reinsurers do not pay ceding commissions under excess of loss reinsurance agreements. However, the reinsurer may reward the primary insurer for favorable loss experience by paying a profit commission or reducing the rate used in calculating the reinsurance premium.

The primary insurer's attachment point is usually set at a level where claims that are expected are retained. However, if the primary insurer's volume of losses is expected to be significant, an excess of loss reinsurance agreement may have a low attachment point. This type of reinsurance agreement is sometimes referred to as a **working cover**. A working cover enables the primary insurer to spread its losses over several years. The primary insurer and the reinsurer anticipate that profitable years will offset unprofitable ones. Primary insurers selling a type of insurance with which they have little expertise may choose to purchase a working cover until they better understand the frequency and severity of losses that the portfolio for that particular type of insurance produces. Reinsurers typically require a working cover to contain an occurrence limitation of two or three times the reinsurance limit. This requirement prevents the working cover from being exposed to catastrophic events, such as an earthquake.

Sometimes a **co-participation provision** is contained within an excess of loss reinsurance agreement. The purpose of this provision is to provide the primary insurer with a financial incentive to efficiently manage losses that exceed the attachment point. A co-participation provision is usually denoted by specifying a percentage before the position of its layer. For example, if the fourth layer in the "How Excess of Loss Reinsurance is Layered" exhibit had a 5 percent co-participation provision, that layer would be specified as "95% of $20,000,000 xs $5,000,000."

In addition to indemnifying losses in a layer of coverage, the reinsurer's obligation may also extend to payment of loss adjustment expenses. Loss adjustment expenses are often a substantial insurer expense, especially for insurance for liability loss exposures. Therefore, excess of loss reinsurance agreements are usually very specific regarding how loss adjustment expenses attributable to specific losses are handled. In rare circumstances, they may be excluded from

Subject premium
The premium the primary insurer charges on its underlying policies and to which a rate is applied to determine the reinsurance premium.

Working cover
An excess of loss reinsurance agreement with a low attachment point.

Co-participation provision
A provision in a reinsurance agreement that requires the primary insurer to retain a specified percentage of the losses that exceed its attachment point.

the reinsurance agreement, but these are the two most common approaches to handling loss adjustment expenses:

- Prorate the loss adjustment expenses between the primary insurer and the reinsurer based on the same percentage share that each is responsible for the loss. This approach is commonly referred to as *pro rata in addition*.
- Add the loss adjustment expenses to the amount of the loss when applying the attachment point of the excess of loss reinsurance agreement. This approach is commonly referred to as *loss adjustment expenseincluded in the limit*.

If loss adjustment expenses are prorated, the primary insurer pays all of the loss adjustment expenses when the loss amount does not exceed the attachment point. If loss adjustment expenses are added to the loss amount, the reinsurer may have to pay a claim in which the loss amount alone does not exceed the attachment point. Primary insurers and reinsurers usually assess the potential for loss adjustment expenses independent of the actual loss potential when negotiating the excess of loss reinsurance agreement. Commonly, reinsurance agreements provide that loss adjustment expenses are prorated for property insurance and most types of liability insurance. However, excess of loss reinsurance covering liability insurance that usually involves substantial litigation often specifies that loss adjustment expenses are added to the amount of the loss when applying the attachment point. For instance, medical malpractice insurance often involves substantial loss adjustment expenses in the form of legal fees even if the claim can be settled with a nominal loss payment or no payment at all.

There are five types of excess of loss reinsurance, each of which usually has a specific use. See the exhibit "Five Types of Excess of Loss Reinsurance."

Five Types of Excess of Loss Reinsurance

1. Per risk excess of loss
2. Catastrophe excess of loss
3. Per policy excess of loss
4. Per occurrence excess of loss
5. Aggregate excess of loss

[DA05083]

Per risk excess of loss reinsurance

A type of excess of loss reinsurance that covers property insurance and that applies separately to each loss occurring to each risk.

Per Risk Excess of Loss

The first type of excess of loss reinsurance is **per risk excess of loss reinsurance**, which is often referred to as property per risk excess of loss and is generally used with property insurance. It applies separately to *each loss* occurring to *each risk*, with the primary insurer usually determining what constitutes one risk (loss exposure).

The exhibit indicates how a reinsurer would respond if the primary insurer defined three separate buildings under a per risk excess of loss reinsurance agreement as three separate risks. In this example, a tornado damaged all three buildings in one occurrence. Because each building is a risk, the attachment point and reinsurance limit apply separately to each. The attachment point and reinsurance limit are stated as a dollar amount of loss. See the exhibit "Example of Per Risk Excess of Loss Reinsurance Applying $950,000 xs $50,000."

Example of Per Risk Excess of Loss Reinsurance Applying $950,000 xs $50,000

Building Number	Loss Amount	Primary Insurer's Retention	Reinsurer's Payment
1	$ 500,000	$ 50,000	$ 450,000
2	350,000	50,000	300,000
3	700,000	50,000	650,000
Total	$1,550,000	$150,000	$1,400,000

[DA05686]

Per occurrence limits are commonly included with per risk excess of loss reinsurance agreements. A per occurrence limit restricts the amount that the reinsurer pays as the result of a single occurrence affecting multiple risks. Had a per occurrence limit of $1 million been imposed in the example in the exhibit, the reinsurer would have been responsible for only $1 million of losses (instead of $1.4 million) because the three losses arose out of the same occurrence (the tornado). Catastrophe excess of loss reinsurance is usually purchased in conjunction with per risk excess of loss reinsurance to protect the primary insurer from one occurrence affecting multiple risks.

Catastrophe Excess of Loss

The second type of excess of loss reinsurance is catastrophe excess of loss reinsurance, which protects the primary insurer from an accumulation of retained losses that arise from a single catastrophic event. It may be purchased to protect the primary insurer and its reinsurers on a combined basis but is more frequently purchased to protect the primary insurer on a net basis after all other reinsurance recoveries are made. Examples of catastrophic events include tornadoes, hurricanes, and earthquakes. Such events, especially major hurricanes, can result in losses totaling billions of dollars.

As with per risk excess of loss reinsurance, the attachment point and reinsurance limit for catastrophe excess of loss reinsurance are stated as dollar amounts of loss. The attachment point is subject to negotiation, but it is usually set high enough so that it would be exceeded only if the aggregation of losses from a catastrophe would impair the policyholders' surplus of a primary insurer. Additionally, losses exceeding the attachment point are usually subject to a co-participation provision.

Loss occurrence clause

A reinsurance agreement clause that defines the scope of a catastrophic occurrence for the purposes of the agreement.

Because the attachment point and reinsurance limit apply separately to each catastrophe occurring during a policy period, the catastrophe excess of loss reinsurance agreement defines the scope of a catastrophic occurrence through a **loss occurrence clause** (sometimes called an hours clause). The loss occurrence clause specifies a time period, in hours, during which the primary insurer's losses from the same catastrophic occurrence can be aggregated and applied to the attachment point and reinsurance limits of the catastrophe excess of loss reinsurance agreement. Such clauses usually specify a time period of 72 consecutive hours (three days) for hurricane losses and 168 consecutive hours (seven days) for earthquake losses. When making a claim against the catastrophe excess of loss reinsurance agreement, the primary insurer can usually choose the date and time when the period of consecutive hours commences to maximize the amount of recovery under the agreement. The exhibit provides an example of the operation of a loss occurrence clause in a catastrophe excess of loss reinsurance agreement and shows how a primary insurer can select the period of coverage to its advantage. See the exhibit "Example of the Operation of a Loss Occurrence Clause in a Catastrophe Excess of Loss Reinsurance Agreement."

Example of the Operation of a Loss Occurrence Clause in a Catastrophe Excess of Loss Reinsurance Agreement

Day	Losses	Period of Coverage Providing Maximum Recovery
1	$1,000,000	
2	1,000,000	
3	2,000,000	← $7,000,000
4	4,000,000	
Total	$8,000,000	

The total losses that could potentially be applied to the reinsurance agreement are $7 million if the seventy-two-hour period starts on the second day, as opposed to $4 million if the period had started on the first day.

[DA05087]

In this example, the primary insurer sustains $8 million in losses from a hurricane over a four-day period. The primary insurer has a $6 million xs $1 million catastrophe excess of loss reinsurance treaty with a loss occurrence clause that stipulates a period of seventy-two consecutive hours for a hurricane. In this simplified example, selecting the specific hour of the day that coverage begins is not an issue, and no co-participation provision applies. Given the distribution of losses over the four days, the primary insurer should elect to start the seventy-two-hour period on the second day to maximize its reinsurance recovery.

Payments from the reinsurer to the primary insurer for catastrophe losses reduce the reinsurance coverage limits available for future losses, but catastrophe excess of loss reinsurance agreements often include a provision requiring the primary insurer to pay an additional premium to reinstate the limits of the agreement after a loss. This provision allows the reinsurer to obtain additional premiums and gives the primary insurer confidence that sufficient limits are available should another catastrophe occur during the reinsurance agreement's term.

Primary insurers and their reinsurers usually do not anticipate that the catastrophe excess of loss reinsurance will be triggered every year. Catastrophe protection is purchased for the unlikely, but possible, event that may cause unstable operating results or that cannot be absorbed by the primary insurer's policyholders' surplus. A primary insurer's need for catastrophe reinsurance and the amount purchased depends on its catastrophe loss exposures. The "Catastrophe Excess of Loss Reinsurance Example" exhibit provides an example of how the amount of loss retained by the primary insurer and the amount of loss owed by the reinsurer are determined under catastrophe excess of loss reinsurance. See the exhibit "Catastrophe Excess of Loss Reinsurance Example."

Per Policy Excess of Loss

The third type of excess of loss reinsurance, **per policy excess of loss reinsurance**, is used primarily with liability insurance and applies the attachment point and the reinsurance limit separately to each insurance policy issued by the primary insurer, regardless of the number of losses occurring under each policy. The exhibit provides an example of how a reinsurer would respond under a $900,000 xs $100,000 per policy excess of loss treaty. In this example, three separate general liability policies issued by the same primary insurer incur losses from *separate events*. See the exhibit "Example of Per Policy Excess of Loss Reinsurance Applying $900,000 xs $100,000."

Per Occurrence Excess of Loss

Per occurrence excess of loss reinsurance, the fourth type of excess of loss reinsurance, is usually used for liability insurance. It applies the attachment

Per policy excess of loss reinsurance

A type of excess of loss reinsurance that applies the attachment point and the reinsurance limit separately to each insurance policy issued by the primary insurer regardless of the number of losses occurring under each policy.

Per occurrence excess reinsurance

A type of excess of loss reinsurance that applies the attachment point and reinsurance limit to the total losses arising from a single event affecting one or more of the primary insurer's policies.

Catastrophe Excess of Loss Reinsurance Example

Brookgreen Insurance Company (Brookgreen) decides to sell earthquake coverage in southern California but wants to limit its losses to approximately $1 million from any one earthquake. Brookgreen conducted a study and estimated that its maximum loss from any one earthquake, given its spread of earthquake loss exposures in southern California, would be $10 million. Brookgreen purchases catastrophe excess of loss reinsurance of 95 percent of $9,250,000 xs $750,000. If Brookgreen were to sustain a $10 million loss from an earthquake, it would retain $1,212,500 and the reinsurer would pay $8,787,500. These figures are calculated as follows:

Step 1—Determination of the loss amount exceeding the attachment point

Amount exceeding the attachment point	=	Amount of loss (subject to the reinsurance limit)	–	Retention
	=	$10,000,000	–	$750,000
	=	$9,250,000		

Step 2—Determination of the co-participation

Amount of co-participation	=	Amount exceeding the attachment point	×	Co-participation percentage
	=	$9,250,000	×	0.05
	=	$462,500		

Step 3—Determination of the amount of loss owed by the reinsurer

Amount owed by the reinsurer	=	Amount exceeding the attachment point	–	Amount of co-participation
	=	$9,250,000	–	$462,500
	=	$8,787,500		

Step 4—Determination of the amount retained by Brookgreen

Amount retained by Brookgreen	=	Retention	+	Amount of co-participation
	=	$750,000	+	$462,500
	=	$1,212,500		

[DA05088]

point and the reinsurance limit to the total losses arising from a single event affecting one or more of the primary insurer's policies.

The exhibit provides an example of how a per occurrence excess of loss treaty applies to the three policies used in the "Example of Per Policy Excess of Loss Reinsurance Applying $900,000 xs $100,000" exhibit. In the exhibit, a $100,000 attachment point applies to the total losses of the policies covering the same event, and there is a $4.9 million reinsurance limit. A per occurrence excess of loss treaty covering liability insurance usually has an

Example of Per Policy Excess of Loss Reinsurance Applying $900,000 xs $100,000

Primary Insurer has a $900,000 xs $100,000 per policy excess of loss treaty. The table below shows three policies for which Primary Insurer is indemnified by Reinsurer because the amount of loss arising out of each of the policies exceeds Primary Insurer's attachment point.

Policy	Loss Amount	Primary Insurer's Retention	Reinsurer's Payment
1	$ 300,000	$ 100,000	$ 200,000
2	500,000	100,000	400,000
3	600,000	100,000	500,000
Total	$1,400,000	$300,000	$1,100,000

[DA05094]

attachment point that is less than the highest liability policy limit offered by the primary insurer. See the exhibit "Example of Per Occurrence Excess of Loss Reinsurance Applying $4,900,000 xs $100,000."

Example of Per Occurrence Excess of Loss Reinsurance Applying $4,900,000 xs $100,000

Primary Insurer has a $4,900,000 xs $100,000 per occurrence excess of loss treaty. The table below shows how losses are accumulated to determine if the attachment point has been exceeded. Primary Insurer is indemnified by Reinsurer because the total amount of the loss arising out of all three policies exceeds Primary Insurer's attachment point.

Policy	Loss Amount	Primary Insurer's Retention	Reinsurer's Payment
1	$ 300,000		
2	500,000		
3	600,000		
Total	$1,400,000 =	$100,000 +	$1,300,000

[DA05095]

Clash cover, a type of per occurrence excess of loss reinsurance for liability loss exposures, can be provided for a combination of different types of liability insurance including auto liability, general liability, professional liability, and workers compensation. Clash cover has an attachment point higher than any of the limits of the applicable underlying policies.

Clash cover

A type of per occurrence excess of loss reinsurance for liability loss exposures that protects the primary insurer against aggregations of losses from one occurrence that affects several insureds or several types of insurance.

For example, a primary insurer could issue a workers compensation policy and a general liability policy with an each occurrence limit of $1 million. To obtain higher limits of coverage for an occurrence that may involve injury to both employees and nonemployees, a clash cover could be purchased in layers. If an explosion results in both workers compensation and general liability claims, the primary insurer would be covered by the clash cover because the claims arise from a single occurrence (the explosion). The clash cover retention is not in addition to the retention of any other applicable per occurrence excess of loss reinsurance; it is net of those retentions.

As another example, Brookgreen Insurance Company (Brookgreen) insures the general liability loss exposure of six contractors working on a single job site. Each of the six contractors' policies has a limit of $1 million. Brookgreen has per occurrence excess of loss reinsurance of $3 million xs $250,000. Brookgreen also has a clash cover of $3 million xs $1 million. An explosion injures employees and nonemployees. The injured parties are awarded damages that total $6 million from the six contractors' policies. The losses from this single occurrence are paid as indicated in the exhibit. See the exhibit "Application of a Clash Cover to One Occurrence Involving Multiple Claims."

Application of a Clash Cover to One Occurrence Involving Multiple Claims

Policy	Damages	Brookgreen Insurance Co. Retention	Per Occurrence Reinsurer	Clash Cover Reinsurer
1	$1,000,000	$ 250,000	$ 750,000	$ 0
2	1,000,000	—	1,000,000	0
3	1,000,000	—	1,000,000	0
4	1,000,000	750,000	250,000	0
5	1,000,000	—	Limit exhausted	1,000,000
6	1,000,000	—	—	1,000,000
Total	$6,000,000	$1,000,000	$3,000,000	$2,000,000

[DA05096]

Brookgreen exhausted its per occurrence excess of loss reinsurance retention ($250,000) with payment of the $1 million loss from Policy 1. The per occurrence excess of loss reinsurer paid the remaining losses until the per occurrence limit of $3 million was exhausted. Brookgreen paid the remaining $750,000 under Policy 4 to fulfill its $1 million retention under the clash cover. The clash cover reinsurer then paid the remaining losses.

Both catastrophe excess of loss reinsurance (for property insurance) and clash cover (for liability insurance) are also referred to as pure risk covers because they are expected to cover only rare events, not common claims covered by other excess of loss treaties.

Clash cover may be useful for types of liability insurance in which loss adjustment expenses are likely to be very high and the underlying per occurrence reinsurance limits include these expenses rather than pro rate them. Examples include professional liability (such as medical malpractice, directors and officers liability, and accountants professional liability) and expenses associated with environmental claims (for example, asbestos and pollution liability). Primary insurers also use clash cover when they want protection from extra-contractual damages and excess of policy limits losses.

Extra-contractual damages are damages awarded to an insured as a result of an insurer improperly handling a claim. This improper behavior is known as bad faith, and it implies that the insurer has failed to deal fairly with the insured. Damages awarded to an insured for an insurer's bad faith in claim handling are usually not considered to be a loss covered by the underlying policy and therefore are usually not subject to indemnification by a reinsurer unless the reinsurance agreement specifically provides coverage.

Excess of policy limits losses result when an insured sues an insurer for failing to settle a claim within the insured's policy limits when the insurer had the opportunity to do so. Excess of policy limits losses are also extra-contractual obligations of the insurer, but are usually distinguished from extra-contractual damages by reinsurers because they are covered losses that, as a result of a mistake of the primary insurer, exceed policy limits. As with other extra-contractual obligations, the reinsurance agreement specifies whether excess of policy limit losses are subject to indemnification by the reinsurer.

Aggregate Excess of Loss

The fifth type of excess of loss reinsurance is **aggregate excess of loss reinsurance**. This type of excess of loss reinsurance can be used for property or liability insurance and covers aggregated losses that exceed the attachment point and occur over a stated period, usually one year. The attachment point in an aggregate excess of loss treaty can be stated as a dollar amount of loss or as a loss ratio. When the attachment point is stated as a loss ratio, the treaty is called "stop loss reinsurance." With stop loss reinsurance, the primary insurer's retention may be a loss ratio of 90 percent, and the reinsurer would indemnify losses up to a loss ratio of 120 percent. The reinsurance agreement in this instance would specify the attachment point and reinsurance limit as "30% xs 90% loss ratio." The primary insurer retains responsibility for losses above a loss ratio of 120 percent.

Aggregate excess of loss treaties are less common and can be more expensive than the other types of excess of loss reinsurance. The treaty usually specifies an attachment point and reinsurance limit that does not result in the pri-

Extracontractual damages

Damages awarded to the insured as a result of the insurer's improperly handling a claim.

Excess of policy limits loss

A loss that results when an insured sues an insurer for failing to settle a claim within the insured's policy limits when the insurer had the opportunity to do so.

Aggregate excess of loss reinsurance

A type of excess of loss reinsurance that covers aggregated losses that exceed the attachment point, stated as a dollar amount of loss or as a loss ratio, and that occur over a specified period, usually one year.

mary insurer earning a profit on the reinsured policies when the policies were unprofitable overall. Most aggregate excess of loss treaties also contain a co-participation provision of 5 to 10 percent to provide the primary insurer with an incentive to efficiently handle claims that exceed the attachment point. See the exhibit "Aggregate Excess of Loss Reinsurance Example."

Aggregate Excess of Loss Reinsurance Example

Brookgreen Insurance Company (Brookgreen) offers liability insurance to a tavern. This general liability policy has an each occurrence limit of $1 million and a general aggregate limit (capping the number of per occurrence dollars the insurer will pay during the policy period) of $2 million.

Brookgreen purchases facultative per occurrence excess of loss reinsurance for this policy in excess of $500,000. This insurance protects Brookgreen against any loss above $500,000 but would not respond to any loss below $500,000. If the tavern suffered three separate losses of $450,000 each, Brookgreen would not recover from the reinsurer even though the total of all losses under the policy during the policy period exceeded $500,000.

Because of concern about aggregation of losses from this and similar loss exposures, Brookgreen decides to purchase a $7 million xs $3 million aggregate excess of loss treaty that is applicable to all of its liability insurance. This treaty further stabilizes losses by indemnifying Brookgreen for accumulations of losses exceeding $3 million. For example, Brookgreen insures a cosmetics manufacturer whose wrinkle cream causes an increase in susceptibility to skin cancer. Brookgreen settles a class action suit brought by customers who used the product for $15 million. Brookgreen's net loss is $8 million (the $3 million retention plus $5 million loss amount that exceeds the $7 million limit).

[DA05097]

Because of the stabilizing effect of aggregate excess of loss reinsurance on a primary insurer's loss ratio, it may be argued that it is the only type of rein-surance needed. However, aggregate excess of loss reinsurance has limited availability. When used, the aggregate excess of loss reinsurer usually expects to pay losses only after the primary insurer has been reimbursed under its other reinsurance agreements.

While a catastrophe excess of loss reinsurance agreement only protects against catastrophe losses (loss severity), an aggregate excess of loss reinsurance agreement provides the reinsured with broader protection. This is because the aggregate excess of loss reinsurance agreement includes catastrophes and unforeseen accumulations of non-catastrophic losses during a specified period (addressing both loss severity and loss frequency).

ALTERNATIVES TO TRADITIONAL REINSURANCE

While the demand for traditional reinsurance continues to evolve as the industry adapts to new economic and regulatory pressures, alternatives to traditional reinsurance have emerged.

Some types of risk, particularly catastrophe risk, cannot always be suitably addressed through traditional reinsurance. Alternatives to traditional reinsurance include finite risk reinsurance and instruments that use the capital market as a source for risk financing, such as insurance-linked securities and various exchange-traded products.

Finite Risk Reinsurance

Finite risk reinsurance is a nontraditional type of reinsurance in which the reinsurer's liability is limited (or "finite") and anticipated investment income is expressly acknowledged as an underwriting component. Because this type of reinsurance transfers a limited amount of risk to the reinsurer with the objective of improving the primary insurer's financial result, it is often called financial reinsurance.

Finite risk reinsurance can be arranged to protect a primary insurer against a combination of a traditionally insurable loss exposure and a traditionally uninsurable loss exposure. For example, the traditionally insurable loss could be building loss caused by an explosion, while the traditionally uninsurable exposure could be the possibility of loss due to economic variables such as product demand and market competition. It also effectively handles extremely large and unusual loss exposures, such as catastrophic losses resulting from an oil rig explosion or an earthquake.

A finite risk reinsurance agreement typically has a multi-year term (for example, three to five years). This allows the risk and losses to be spread over several years, while being subject to an aggregate limit for the agreement's entire term. With finite risk reinsurance, the primary insurer can rely on long-term protection and a predictable reinsurance cost over the coverage period, while the reinsurer can rely on a continual flow of premiums. Because of these benefits, both the primary insurer and the reinsurer tend to be flexible in negotiating the price and terms.

Finite risk reinsurance premiums can be a substantial percentage of the reinsurance limit (for example, 70 percent). This relationship between premium and reinsurance limit reduces the reinsurer's potential underwriting loss to a level that is much lower than that typically associated with traditional types of reinsurance.

Generally, finite risk reinsurance is designed to cover high severity losses. The reinsurer commonly shares profits with the primary insurer when it has favorable loss experience or has generated income by investing the prepaid

Finite risk reinsurance
A nontraditional type of reinsurance in which the reinsurer's liability is limited and anticipated investment income is expressly acknowledged as an underwriting component.

Capital market

A financial market in which long-term securities are traded.

Securitization of risk

The use of securities or financial instruments (i.e., stocks, bonds, commodities, financial futures) to finance an insurer's exposure to catastrophic loss.

Special purpose vehicle (SPV)

A facility established for the purpose of purchasing income-producing assets from an organization, holding title to them and then using those assets to collateralize securities that will be sold to investors.

Insurance derivative

Financial contract whose value is based on the level of insurable losses that occur during a specific time period.

Contingent capital arrangement

An agreement, entered into before any losses occur, that enables an organization to raise cash by selling stock or issuing debt at prearranged terms after a loss occurs that exceeds a certain threshold.

Insurance-linked security

A financial instrument whose value is primarily driven by insurance and/or reinsurance loss events.

Surplus note

A type of unsecured debt instrument, issued only by insurers, that has characteristics of both conventional equity and debt securities and is classified as policyholders' surplus rather than as a liability on the insurer's statutory balance sheet.

premium. This profit-sharing income can compensate the primary insurer for the higher-than-usual premium for finite risk reinsurance. The reinsurer will not assess any additional premium even if losses exceed the premium.

Capital Market Alternatives to Traditional and Non-Traditional Reinsurance

Capital markets have emerged as tools that primary insurers can use to finance risk as an alternative to insurance. Instead of purchasing reinsurance to cover its potential liabilities, the primary insurer uses traded security instruments to finance insurance risk.

Some of the capital market instruments are rooted in the concepts of **securitization of risk** and **special purpose vehicles (SPV)**, which allow primary insurers to exchange assets for cash. Others are based on **insurance derivatives** or **contingent capital arrangements**.

Although these products are expanding and evolving rapidly, these are among the methods most often used:

- Catastrophe bond—A type of **insurance-linked security** that is specifically designed to transfer insurable catastrophe risk to investors. A bond is issued with a condition that if the issuer suffers a catastrophe loss greater than specified amount, the obligation to pay interest and/or replay principle is deferred or forgiven. As long as catastrophe-related losses do not exceed the specified amount, investors earn a relatively high interest rate and receive a return of their principal. If catastrophe losses exceed the specified loss amount, the interest and/or principal forgone by bondholders is used to pay losses. Catastrophe bonds are typically issued by the SPVs of insurers, large reinsurers, or large corporations for any type of catastrophic insurable risk, such as hurricanes, earthquakes, and other adverse weather and environmental risks.

- Catastrophe risk exchange—A means through which a primary insurer can exchange a portion of its insurance risk for another insurer's. The exchange can be, for example, an Internet-based forum on which risks available for trade are advertised, negotiated, and completed. The insurance risk traded may differ by geographic area, type of property, or cause of loss insured against. A primary insurer with a geographic concentration of loss exposures can use a catastrophe risk exchange to reduce its losses from a single loss occurrence. A primary insurer can also diversify the kinds of property insured to make it less susceptible to heavy losses from a single cause of loss.

- Contingent surplus note—A **surplus note** that has been designed so a primary insurer, at its option, can immediately obtain funds by issuing notes at a pre-agreed rate of interest. A benefit of surplus notes is that they increase a primary insurer's assets without increasing its liabilities.

- Industry loss warranty (ILW)—An insurance-linked security that covers the primary insurer in the event that the industry-wide loss from a particular catastrophic event, such as an earthquake or hurricane, exceeds a predetermined threshold. The distinguishing characteristic of this instrument is that its coverage is triggered by industry losses as a whole, rather than only on the primary insurer's losses.

- Catastrophe option—An agreement that gives the primary insurer the right to a cash payment from investors if a specified index of catastrophe losses reaches a specified level (the **strike price**). The catastrophe loss index, such as that provided by Insurance Service Office's Property Claim Services, keeps track of catastrophe losses by geographic region, by cause of loss, and by time of occurrence.

- Line of credit—An arrangement in which a bank or another financial institution agrees to provide a loan to a primary insurer in the event the primary insurer suffers a loss. The credit is prearranged so that the terms, such as the interest rate and principal repayment schedule, are known in advance of a loss. In exchange for this credit commitment, the primary insurer taking out the line of credit pays a commitment fee. A line of credit does not represent any risk transfer; they simply provide access to capital.

- Sidecar—A limited-existence SPV, often formed as an independent company, that provides a primary insurer additional capacity to write property catastrophe business or other short-tail lines through a quota share agreement with private investors. Investors in the SPV assume a proportion of the risk and earn a corresponding portion of the profit on the primary insurer's book of business. The primary insurer charges a ceding commission and may receive a profit commission if the book of business is profitable.[6]

REINSURANCE PROGRAM DESIGN

A well-planned, well-executed reinsurance program plays a key role in meeting specific primary insurer goals. It can help stabilize loss experience while providing large-line capacity, catastrophe protection, and surplus relief. In a catastrophe, an effective reinsurance program can mean the difference between a primary insurer's survival or failure.

Many kinds of reinsurance exist, and, with rare exceptions, any primary insurer can find a combination of reinsurance agreements that meet its needs. Designing an optimal **reinsurance program** requires careful analysis of a primary insurer's needs, retentions, and reinsurance limits. Assistance in this could come from reinsurers, reinsurance intermediaries, and consultants.

Strike price

The price at which the stock or commodity underlying a call option (such as a warrant) or a put option can be purchased (called) or sold (put) during a specified period.

Reinsurance program

The combination of reinsurance agreements that a primary insurer purchases to meet its reinsurance needs.

Factors Affecting Reinsurance Needs

Primary insurers consider several factors to determine their reinsurance needs, all of which interact to increase or decrease a primary insurer's need for reinsurance:

- Growth plans
- Types of insurance sold
- Geographic spread of loss exposures
- Insurer size
- Insurer structure
- Insurer financial strength
- Senior management's risk tolerance

Growth Plans

A primary insurer that expects rapid premium growth is likely to need more reinsurance than a primary insurer that expects premium volume to remain stable or to decrease. There are three reasons for the need for additional reinsurance:

- Rapid growth can cause a drain on a primary insurer's policyholders' surplus. Pro rata reinsurance provides a replenishment of the primary insurer's policyholders' surplus because of the ceding commission paid by the reinsurer to the primary insurer.
- The loss ratio for a primary insurer's new business is likely to be less stable than the loss ratio for its established business, which has undergone renewal underwriting. This instability may be severe if the primary insurer is growing by selling types of insurance that it has not previously sold or by selling in markets in which it has no previous operating experience. For a rapidly growing primary insurer, new insurance sold may constitute a substantial part of total premium volume relative to renewals of existing policies. Consequently, the variability of the loss ratio on the new policies could cause instability in the primary insurer's overall loss ratio. Reinsurance, while not abrogating the total loss amount, limits the amount of this loss to the primary insurer's retention amount.
- Growth often entails expanding into markets with greater coverage requirements. To compete effectively in new markets, a primary insurer may have to offer coverage limits higher than it offered previously or insurance coverages it has not offered before. For example, a primary insurer may decide to enter the segment of the homeowners insurance market in which it must offer a personal umbrella with limits up to $2 million to match its competitors' products. Reinsurance enables primary insurers to provide larger amounts of coverage than they otherwise would be able to provide.

Pro rata reinsurance is the appropriate choice if a rapidly growing primary insurer needs only surplus relief. If the major concern is loss ratio stability or large line capacity, excess of loss reinsurance may be an appropriate choice.

While a primary insurer might reduce its long-term profits by entering into a reinsurance agreement because it has potentially ceded away profitable loss exposures, sacrificing these profits is a short-term strategy that enables the primary insurer to grow and possibly earn greater future profits.

Types of Insurance Sold

The types of insurance that a primary insurer sells are a major determinant of its reinsurance needs. The insurance products offered by primary insurers vary in loss stability, which affects the primary insurer's ability to project loss experience. A reinsurance program must be tailored to the loss characteristics of the insurance that the primary insurer sells.

Generally, primary insurers selling personal insurance need less reinsurance than those selling commercial insurance because personal insurance loss exposures need relatively lower coverage limits. Additionally, personal insurance loss exposures are more homogeneous and subject to fewer severe hazards than commercial insurance loss exposures. Because of the homogeneity among personal insurance loss exposures, the loss experience is usually more stable than that of commercial insurance loss exposures and therefore more predictable. Both personal and commercial insurance loss exposures are subject to catastrophic loss, but primary insurers usually address catastrophe reinsurance needs separately from reinsurance agreements designed only to smooth loss experience fluctuations.

Some types of insurance require a greater commitment of policyholders' surplus (capital) than do others. State insurance regulators use a risk-based capital system to establish an insurer's minimum capital requirements. This system has several components, but it gives the greatest weight to **underwriting risk**; some types of insurance require the insurer to maintain more policyholders' surplus than other types of insurance. For example, medical malpractice insurance is subject to severe losses that are difficult to forecast from past loss experience. A primary insurer selling medical malpractice insurance is therefore required to have sufficient policyholders' surplus to absorb unexpected fluctuations in losses. Using reinsurance that provides surplus relief can help primary insurers reduce demands on their policyholders' surplus.

The number of different types of insurance a primary insurer sells also affects its reinsurance needs. A primary insurer that sells several types of insurance is more diversified and therefore more likely to have a stable loss ratio than a primary insurer selling only a few types of insurance.

Underwriting risk

A measure of the loss volatility of the types of insurance sold by an insurer.

Geographic Spread of Loss Exposures

Another determinant of a primary insurer's reinsurance needs is the geographic spread of its loss exposures. A wide geographic spread may stabilize the insurer's loss ratio and minimize reinsurance needs, especially in property insurance. While no part of the world is completely immune to natural catastrophes, the nature of catastrophe loss exposures differs by geographic area and catastrophes seldom strike all geographic areas simultaneously. Consequently, if a property insurer's insured loss exposures are spread over a wide geographic area, poor loss experience in one area may be offset by good loss experience in another area during a given period.

Geographic diversification is an especially effective tool when property insurance is spread worldwide, but it can still be effective even if diversification is limited to the United States. For example, the West Coast is vulnerable to earthquakes, the South Atlantic and Gulf Coasts are vulnerable to hurricanes, and the middle of the country is vulnerable to tornadoes. However, these natural forces are not usually all at their worst in the same year.

Primary insurers selling property insurance in a single geographic area are especially vulnerable to fluctuations caused by catastrophe losses and need reinsurance to cover such losses. For example, devastating hurricanes that struck the South Atlantic and Gulf Coasts led to the insolvency of several insurers, including some that had been considered financially strong. These insurers had concentrations of loss exposures in the hurricane area and inadequate reinsurance to cover their losses.

Geographic diversification can also stabilize loss ratios for reasons other than limiting losses from natural catastrophe loss exposures. Insurance regulation, laws governing tort liability, law enforcement practices, and other factors affecting property or liability insurance losses vary by geographic area. Adverse changes in these factors in one geographic area may be offset by favorable developments in another if the loss exposures are geographically diverse.

Insurer Size

Insurer size is also an important determinant of reinsurance needs. Typically, small primary insurers need proportionately more reinsurance to stabilize loss ratios than large primary insurers. According to the law of large numbers, actual losses tend to approach expected losses as the number of loss exposures increases. Therefore, the loss ratio of a large primary insurer is likely to be more stable than the loss ratio of a small one even if the mix of business sold is identical.

Insurer Structure

The legal form of a primary insurer may affect its reinsurance needs. For example, stock insurers have more access to capital markets than mutual and reciprocal insurers. They may consequently be willing to accept less stability in their loss ratios and depend on capital markets to replace the policyholders' surplus depleted by adverse loss fluctuations. This could be risky, however, because the providers of capital may not look favorably on an insurer that has just sustained heavy losses.

Insurer Financial Strength

An insurer that is financially strong needs less reinsurance than a financially weaker one for two reasons. First, it does not need surplus relief to increase its premium capacity. Second, it needs less reinsurance to stabilize its loss ratio. A stronger surplus position enables the primary insurer to absorb more adverse loss ratio variations. The resulting lower reinsurance costs are an added advantage for a financially strong primary insurer.

One aspect of evaluating an insurer's financial strength involves assessing the stability and liquidity of its invested assets. If a primary insurer's strategy is to rely on its policyholders' surplus to absorb abnormal losses, that policyholders' surplus must be invested in assets that are readily marketable and not subject to wide fluctuations in market price. Otherwise, the primary insurer's financial resources may be insufficient to pay losses in a timely manner.

Because common stock may be marketable only at a substantial loss in an unfavorable market, a primary insurer that holds large amounts of it in an investment portfolio needs to be more heavily reinsured than one that holds short-term bonds. However, a large portfolio of long-term bonds could also sustain substantial market losses due to interest rate risk. A primary insurer that invests a large portion of its funds in wholly-owned subsidiaries needs to have a substantial reinsurance program because the stock of subsidiaries is not generally marketable.

Senior Management's Risk Tolerance

The decision of how much reinsurance and what types to buy is made by the primary insurer's senior management. Although the decision may be supported by statistical data and financial models, it usually reflects the senior management's risk tolerance, which is their willingness to assume risk. Senior management must be comfortable with the insurance risk assumed, particularly when setting retentions or changing the reinsurance program.

Senior management must be confident that other stakeholders are comfortable with the adequacy of the primary insurer's reinsurance program. For example, the reinsurance program should reflect the risk tolerance of the board of directors, stockholders, or policyholders in a mutual company. Senior management must be sensitive to those stakeholders' views.

The practical effect of any proposed reinsurance program changes on supervisors and underwriters must also be considered. For example, if treaty reinsurance is used to increase large-line capacity, then individual underwriters must adjust to the higher amounts of insurance that the primary insurer can now safely offer. If the underwriters are not comfortable with the additional large-line capacity available under the reinsurance treaty, they may continue to purchase facultative reinsurance when they do not need to. Those actions could negate the cost savings of the treaty.

Factors Affecting Retention Selection

The primary insurer's selection of its retention is an essential and sometimes complex step in designing a reinsurance program. Although the retention is based on the primary insurer's financial needs and the types of insurance that the primary insurer sells, it is also negotiable by the primary insurer and the reinsurer. Cost is always a factor in selecting a retention, and the cost of a reinsurance treaty usually increases as the size of the retention decreases.

In addition to cost, four factors are considered when selecting a retention:

- Maximum amount the primary insurer can retain
- Maximum amount the primary insurer wants to retain
- Minimum retention sought by the reinsurer
- Co-participation provision

Maximum Amount the Primary Insurer Can Retain

The first factor to consider in selecting a retention is the maximum amount that the primary insurer can retain. This amount is a function of two aspects: regulatory requirements and the primary insurer's financial strength.

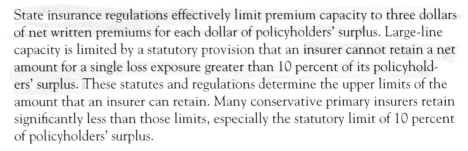

State insurance regulations effectively limit premium capacity to three dollars of net written premiums for each dollar of policyholders' surplus. Large-line capacity is limited by a statutory provision that an insurer cannot retain a net amount for a single loss exposure greater than 10 percent of its policyholders' surplus. These statutes and regulations determine the upper limits of the amount that an insurer can retain. Many conservative primary insurers retain significantly less than those limits, especially the statutory limit of 10 percent of policyholders' surplus.

Subject to the statutory and regulatory limits, a primary insurer's ability to retain loss exposures is also limited by its financial strength. An insurer should not retain loss exposures so large that the losses under a worst-case scenario can threaten its solvency. Determining the loss size that could threaten the primary insurer's solvency involves some judgment. The primary insurer must consider not only the losses within the retention of the possible reinsurance agreement, but also the retentions of closely related reinsurance agreements. For example, in setting the retention of a property per risk excess of loss treaty, potential retained losses under the related catastrophe excess of loss treaty must be considered and vice versa.

Maximum Amount the Primary Insurer Wants to Retain

The second factor to consider in selecting a retention is the maximum amount the primary insurer is willing to retain. Possible maximum retentions are rarely accepted. This may be partly because of the uncertainty of determining how much loss exposure can safely be assumed, and partly because of the conservatism of some managers.

In the case of publicly held stock insurance companies, market pressures may keep retentions well below the maximum that the insurer could legally or financially bear. Investors favor insurers that report growing, or at least stable, earnings. A primary insurer that assumes large retentions under its reinsurance agreements risks alienating investors because its earnings are likely to vary widely from year to year.

Minimum Retention Sought by the Reinsurer

The third factor to consider in selecting a retention is that reinsurers sometimes demand a minimum retention as a condition of providing reinsurance. This demand is especially likely for excess of loss treaties, particularly catastrophe treaties. The purpose of the minimum retention requirement is to encourage the primary insurer to implement sound risk control, underwriting, and loss adjustment practices. Occasionally, for profitable pro rata treaties, the reinsurer may seek a lower retention in order to participate more fully in the profitable business.

Co-participation Provision

The fourth factor in selecting a retention is the co-participation provision, which requires the primary insurer to participate in losses beyond the retention for risk control, underwriting, and loss adjustment reasons previously described.

Factors Affecting Reinsurance Limit Selection

Selecting treaty limits can be as complex as selecting retentions. There are five factors to consider in selecting treaty limits, which vary depending on the kind of treaty involved:

- Maximum policy limit
- Extra-contractual obligations
- Loss adjustment expenses
- Clash cover
- Catastrophe exposure

Maximum Policy Limit

The first factor to consider in selecting reinsurance limits is the maximum policy limit sold by the primary insurer. The maximum policy limit sold by the primary insurer may seem like a natural maximum policy limit for a treaty that applies separately to each policy because this practice would ensure coverage for any loss incurred. However, this may not be the most economical way to provide full reinsurance coverage. For example, if a primary insurer has many policies outstanding with limits of $500,000 or less and relatively few with limits between $500,000 and $1 million, setting the treaty limit at $500,000 and relying on facultative reinsurance to provide the remaining protection on the few larger loss exposures may be more economical than setting the reinsurance treaty limit at $1 million.

The limit for a stop loss treaty is stated as a loss ratio. Ideally, the limit should be set at the highest loss ratio that the primary insurer is likely to reach. Cost may force the primary insurer to settle for a lower limit, even if the reinsurer is willing to provide a higher limit.

Extra-Contractual Obligations

The primary insurer's potential exposure to extra-contractual obligations is the second factor to consider in selecting reinsurance limits. If a reinsurance treaty is to provide protection against extra-contractual damages and excess of policy limit losses, the reinsurance treaty limit should be substantially higher than the primary insurer's highest policy limit. Damages resulting from extra-contractual obligations may be several multiples of the highest coverage limit offered.

Loss Adjustment Expenses

The third factor to consider in selecting reinsurance limits is the potential magnitude of loss adjustment expenses. Loss adjustment expenses can be a significant loss component in per risk and per occurrence excess of loss treaties, depending on the type of underlying policy. Because loss adjustment expenses are generally added to the amount of loss and not pro rated between the primary insurer and reinsurer, loss adjustment expenses should be considered when selecting retentions and reinsurance limits. A primary insurer selling medical malpractice insurance, which has significant loss adjustment expenses, may exhaust the coverage provided by a casualty per occurrence excess of loss treaty with the loss adjustment expenses alone and have no reinsurance available to provide loss indemnification. Consequently, the primary insurer must carefully consider reinsurance limits and add an additional layer of reinsurance to accommodate the loss adjustment expenses.

Clash Cover

The primary insurer's potential exposure to multiple policies responding to the same occurrence is the fourth factor to consider in selecting reinsurance limits. Clash cover applies when claims from two or more policies arise as a result of the same occurrence. Clash cover limits should be set by considering the highest limits offered by the primary insurer and the perceived likelihood that multiple policies may be involved in a single occurrence.

Catastrophe Exposure

The fifth factor to consider in selecting reinsurance limits is the primary insurer's potential exposure to catastrophe losses. Selecting the limit for a catastrophe treaty is a more complex task than selecting limits for per risk excess of loss treaties because catastrophe losses involve an accumulation of losses arising from a single occurrence. The primary insurer's liability for such losses has no stated limit. The effective limit is set by the number and face amount of policies subject to losses by a single catastrophic occurrence that the primary insurer has in force in a geographic area. In the case of a hurricane, the area affected may cover hundreds of square miles.

Statistics on hurricanes have been collected for many years and show the paths that hurricanes have followed and the wind forces that have been involved. If an insurer has data on the loss exposures that it has previously assumed in a storm area, it can estimate future losses from a hurricane of a given intensity following a specified path. Insurers can do similar analyses for flood and earthquake losses because severe losses from those causes are likely limited to known flood zones and geological faults. Extensive data on the occurrence and intensity of floods, hurricanes, tornadoes, earthquakes, and other natural catastrophes are available from various government agencies such as the National Oceanic and Atmospheric Administration (NOAA) and other industry organizations. Catastrophe models that estimate catastrophe losses are also often used to help set treaty limits.

REINSURANCE PROGRAM DESIGN CASE STUDIES

To complete these case studies, the student should be familiar with these concepts:

- Reinsurance and its functions
- Treaty reinsurance and facultative reinsurance
- Types of pro rata reinsurance and excess of loss reinsurance and their uses
- Factors that should be considered in the design of a reinsurance program

The various ways in which the different types of reinsurance can be used to address a primary insurer's business constraints are best illustrated through case studies.

These case studies illustrate how reinsurance programs are applied to specific situations and how combinations of various forms of reinsurance are useful in property and liability insurance. The programs outlined are realistic for the circumstances shown, but are not necessarily the only appropriate reinsurance options for the hypothetical insurers.

Two caveats should be considered when reading these cases. First, reinsurance program design is a function of conditions in the reinsurance market and who is developing the program. Second, reinsurance program design is usually based on an in-depth analysis of several factors, such as the primary insurer's historical loss experience, financial condition, and types of insurance, as well as such subjective factors as senior management's aversion to risk.

The facts presented in these cases may be used to answer these questions:

- What factors lead Atley's reinsurance intermediary to recommend a reinsurance program that includes surplus relief and catastrophe protection?
- Why does Med-Mal's reinsurance intermediary recommend that Med-Mal purchase clash cover?

Atley Insurance Company

Two situations describe how Atley Insurance Company has used reinsurance to meet its objectives.

Situation 1

Atley Insurance Company has developed a program for insuring office condominiums that has proven to be very popular with its producers. One producer in particular has been aggressive in selling this program and is attempting to write accounts that need high property coverage limits. Atley is concerned about the rapid growth of this program and the negative consequences if Atley is unable to accept large accounts.

Atley and its reinsurers developed a reinsurance program that provides both large-line capacity and financing to aid future growth. The program consists of a four-line surplus share reinsurance treaty with Atley retaining $75,000. Two reinsurers participate in the program, each with two lines. Atley's underwriters must arrange facultative reinsurance for accounts with coverage limits that exceed $375,000 (the capacity of the four-line treaty). Atley's reinsurance program has a $1 million per occurrence limit. The exhibit illustrates how coverage limits, premiums, and losses will be shared on two of the accounts written under Atley's office program. The coverage limit of the first account is within the four-line treaty, and the second account exceeds the capacity of the four-line treaty. See the exhibit "Illustration of Situation 1."

Situation 2

Atley is concerned that its existing reinsurance program will not adequately handle its growing catastrophe exposure. Atley amends its reinsurance program by adding a catastrophe excess of loss reinsurance agreement that

Illustration of Situation 1

Account With Limits Within the Surplus Share Treaty

The Doctor's Office account has a policy limit of $200,000. Coverage, premiums, and losses would be retained by Atley and shared with its reinsurers as shown below.

Atley Reinsurance Program	Assumption of Liability	Percentage Assumption of Liability
Retention	$75,000	37.5
First Surplus Treaty (2 lines)	$125,000	62.5
Second Surplus Treaty (2 lines)		
Facultative Reinsurance ($750,000 Maximum)		
Total Assumption of Liability	$200,000	100.0

Account With Limits That Exceed the Surplus Share Treaty

The Chesterbrook Office Park account has property coverage needs of $650,000. Because the coverage needs of this account exceed the limits of Atley's surplus share treaty reinsurance program, Atley arranges facultative reinsurance that is also on a surplus share basis. Coverage, premiums, and losses would be retained by Atley and shared by its reinsurers as shown below.

Atley Reinsurance Program	Assumption of Liability	Percentage Assumption of Liability
Retention	$75,000	11.5
First Surplus Treaty (2 lines)	$150,000	23.0
Second Surplus Treaty (2 lines)	$150,000	23.0
Facultative Reinsurance	$275,000	42.0
Total Assumption of Liability	$650,000	100.0*

*This column actually totals 99.5. A primary insurer and its reinsurers would likely determine an exact percentage, but in this illustration we have not.

Assume that Doctor's Office and Chesterbrook Office Park both sustain substantial losses (50 percent) caused by a tornado. Atley's reinsurance program would respond as shown below.

Atley Reinsurance Program	Doctor's Office Account $100,000 Loss	Chesterbrook Office Park $325,000 Loss
Retention	$37,500	$37,375
First Surplus Treaty (2 lines)	$62,500	$74,750
Second Surplus Treaty (2 lines)		$74,750
Facultative Reinsurance		$136,500
Total	$100,000	$325,000*

*This column actually totals $323,375 because it uses the rounded percentages calculated previously.

[DA06161]

provides $5 million in excess of $750,000. (Atley's relationship with a faculta- tive reinsurer is sound, and Atley believes it can arrange facultative limits up to $750,000 for almost any account eligible under the office program.) The exhibit includes a substantially larger account and shows how this amended reinsurance program would respond to a catastrophe that affects all three risks. See the exhibit "Illustration of Situation 2."

Medical Malpractice Insurance Company

Medical Malpractice Insurance Company (Med-Mal) sells medical profes- sional liability insurance for physicians and surgeons in one state. Med-Mal insures physicians and surgeons statewide, but its policy portfolio is concen- trated in the state's two largest cities. Its medical professional liability policy has a $1 million limit that applies on a per occurrence and on an aggregate basis.

Med-Mal is concerned about an increase in the number of successful lawsuits against physicians and surgeons in the state. One significant loss for another insurer operating in the same state involved several surgeons who were insured under separate policies with the insurer and were successfully sued for injuries arising from a common incident. Because of this loss and the unfavor- able legal environment for medical malpractice insurance, Med-Mal wants to avoid potential catastrophic occurrences in which multiple insureds, with multiple limits of liability, would be involved in the same occurrence.

Med-Mal's reinsurance intermediary recommends per occurrence excess of loss reinsurance of $750,000 xs $250,000 to limit the effect of any one claim. Med-Mal's reinsurance intermediary also recommends that the reinsurance program address the possibility that more than one insured could be sued as the result of a single occurrence, and that extra-contractual damages or excess policy limits judgments could be awarded. The reinsurance intermediary suggests clash cover with a $500,000 attachment point (applies to the reten- tion after the per occurrence excess of loss treaty) to restrict the use of the clash cover to occurrences with more than one physician. It also suggests a $5 million limit to recognize the possibility of multiple insured doctors being involved in a common incident and/or the awarding of extra-contractual damages or excess policy limits judgments. See the exhibit " Application of Med-Mal's Reinsurance Program."

Illustration of Situation 2

In addition to the Doctor's Office account and the Chesterbrook Office Park account, Atley writes the Technology Office Complex account for $4 million.

Atley Reinsurance Program	Assumption of Liability	Percentage Assumption of Liability
Retention	$75,000	10.0
First Surplus Treaty (2 lines)	$150,000	20.0
Second Surplus Treaty (2 lines)	$150,000	20.0
Facultative Reinsurance ($750,000 Maximum)	$375,000	50.0
Total	$750,000	100.0
Catastrophe Excess ($5 million × $750,000)	$3,250,000	
Total Assumption of Liability	$4,000,000	

Had the tornado occurred and damaged 50 percent of Technology Office Complex as well, Atley's reinsurance program would have responded as shown below. The catastrophe excess of loss reinsurance applies net after other available reinsurance.

Atley Reinsurance Program	Doctor's Office Account $100,000 Loss	Chesterbrook Office Park $325,000 Loss	Technology Office Complex $2,000,000 Loss
Retention	$37,500	$37,375	$75,000
First Surplus Treaty (2 lines)	$62,500	$74,750	$150,000
Second Surplus Treaty (2 lines)		$74,750	$150,000
Facultative Reinsurance		$136,500	$375,000
Total	$100,000	$323,375	$750,000
Catastrophe Excess ($5 million × $750,000)			$1,250,000
Total	$100,000	$323,375	$2,000,000

Atley's reinsurance program includes a $1,000,000 per occurrence limit. The total losses under the reinsurance program, before the application of the catastrophe excess agreement, are $1,173,375, or $173,375 higher than the per occurrence limit. Atley's reinsurance program provides that the catastrophe reinsurer will include losses that exceed its per occurrence limit. The catastrophe reinsurer in this case will pay $1,423,375 ($1,250,000 plus $173,375).

[DA06162]

REINSURANCE REGULATION

As regulators have recognized how important properly placed reinsurance

Application of Med-Mal's Reinsurance Program

Med-Mal must pay a medical malpractice claim involving three surgeons insured under separate policies. The injured parties are awarded damages that total $2 million. The losses from this single occurrence are paid as indicated:

Policy	Damages	Med-Mal's Retention	Per Occurrence Reinsurer	Clash Cover Reinsurer
1	$500,000	$250,000	$250,000	$0
2	500,000	-----	500,000	0
3	$1,000,000	$250,000	Limit exhausted	$750,000
Total	$2,000,000	$500,000	$750,000	$750,000

[DA06163]

transactions are to the ongoing viability of insurers and their ability to pay claims under their policies, reinsurance regulations have become more stringent.

Reinsurers domiciled in the United States and alien reinsurers licensed in the U.S. are subject to the same solvency state regulations as primary insurers. Reinsurers are required to file financial statements with state regulatory authorities and to adhere to state insurance regulations regarding reserves, investments, and minimum capital and surplus requirements. They must also undergo periodic examination by the appropriate state authorities.

While the solvency tests for reinsurers are the same as those for primary insurers, the same requirements are not applied to unlicensed alien reinsurers because they are not within the jurisdiction of state (or federal) regulatory authorities. Concerns have been raised regarding possible insolvencies of some unlicensed alien reinsurers, but U.S. regulatory agencies can do little to prevent such insolvencies. Primary insurers and reinsurance intermediaries must rely on their own ability to detect impending insolvencies of unlicensed alien reinsurers.

Reinsurance rates are not regulated in the U.S, but the regulation of primary insurer rates could indirectly affect reinsurance rates to the extent that reinsurers receive a reinsurance premium based on the premiums of primary insurers. Thus, regulating the primary insurer's rates might place an effective ceiling on the amount the primary insurer can pay for reinsurance.

Reinsurance agreements are regulated to a slightly greater degree than reinsurance pricing. Because many reinsurers are not within the jurisdiction of state insurance regulators, regulation is aimed at the primary insurer rather than the reinsurer.

Contract Certainty

Until recently, regulatory requirements were aimed at ensuring that reinsurance contracts were signed within a reasonable period of time. Part of the National Association of Insurance Commissioners (NAIC) accounting for reinsurance rules, known as the "Nine-Month Rule," requires that the reinsurance contract be finalized, reduced to written form, and signed within nine months of the policy period's commencement.

Following extensive litigation regarding the World Trade Center losses that hinged on insurance policy wording that was not issued on a timely basis, regulatory efforts began focusing on the concept of contract certainty. Contract certainty generally requires the complete and final agreement of all terms between the insured and insurer by the time the contract is entered into, with contract documentation provided promptly thereafter. See the exhibit "Contract Certainty in the U.S. and Abroad."

Contract Certainty in the U.S. and Abroad

In the United States, the superintendent of the New York State Insurance Department issued Circular Letter 20 in October 2008 and a supplementary letter in January 2010 establishing the department's contract certainty expectations for insurance and reinsurance contracts. The department defined contract certainty as having documentation of all agreed terms of an insurance policy or reinsurance contract by the date of inception and issuing and delivering such policy or contract within thirty business days of inception of coverage. Proper contract documentation is defined to include a "binder, cover note, or similar documents, provided that it reflects all agreed terms and conditions to which the reinsurers have agreed." The supplement allows insurers and producers the flexibility to determine themselves the allocation of the thirty-business-day time period in order to meet contract certainty. Licensees had twelve months from the date of the Circular Letter to develop and implement practices assuring contract certainty in at least 90 percent of their policies and contracts. The department intends to use formal examinations, inquiries to licensees and information gathered from insureds to monitor.

Reinsurance regulators in other countries also have implemented rules and regulations based on the contract certainty concept. In England and Bermuda, for example, contracts must be final and certain on the contract's effective date. Australia, meanwhile, uses two benchmarks (the Two-Month Rule and Six-Month Rule) to achieve contract certainty.

Michael Moriarty, "Supplement No. 1 to Circular Letter No. 20 (2008)," State of New York Insurance Department, January 2010, www.ins.state.ny.us/circltr/2010/cl2008_20s1.pdf (accessed May 25, 2010). [DA06145]

Credit for Reinsurance Transactions

State insurance regulators have allowed primary insurers to take credit for a reinsurance transaction on their financial statements based on the reinsurer's authorization status and other conditions, rather than on the actual value of the economic benefit that the reinsurance transaction provides.

Consequently, state insurance regulators have adopted requirements that must be met for a reinsurance agreement to be treated as a reinsurance transaction.

Primary insurers are usually eager to take credit against their unearned premiums and loss reserves for premiums paid to and losses recoverable from reinsurers. The availability of those credits, referred to as credit for reinsurance, reduces the drain on the primary insurer's surplus from writing new business. Regulators motivate primary insurers to require some desirable clauses in their reinsurance agreements by withholding permission to take reserve credit for the reinsurance transaction unless the reinsurance agreements contain the specified clauses. However, a primary insurer that is willing to forgo the credit for the reinsurance transaction can enter into a reinsurance agreement that does not include them.

Some states permit the primary insurer to take the reserve credits only if the reinsurer is licensed in the state. Others permit the reserve credit if the reinsurer is licensed in any state. Finally, some states permit the reserve credit even if the reinsurer is not licensed anywhere in the U.S., provided the primary insurer obtains the state insurance department's permission before entering into the agreement. Reserve credit for reinsurance can also be permitted if reinsurance loss reserves are secured by a letter of credit or a trust fund.

Insolvency clause

A clause that is required in reinsurance agreements indicating that the primary insurer's bankruptcy does not affect the reinsurer's liability for losses under the reinsurance agreement.

The **insolvency clause**, which is required for the primary insurer to take credit for the reinsurance transaction, provides that the primary insurer's insolvency does not affect the reinsurer's liability for losses under the reinsurance agreement. The reinsurer pays the receiver or liquidator of the insolvent primary insurer for its creditors' benefit.

Intermediary clause

A clause that is required in reinsurance agreements indicating that the reinsurance intermediary is the reinsurer's agent for collecting reinsurance premiums and paying reinsurance claims.

More recently, some states have required an **intermediary clause** in reinsurance agreements under which the reinsurer assumes the credit risk that the reinsurance intermediary will be unable or unwilling to pay all of the premiums collected under its reinsurance agreements. The reinsurer also assumes the risk that the reinsurance intermediary will not transmit to the primary insurer all claim payments owed to the insurer. This clause is beneficial to primary insurers because courts have held in most cases that the reinsurance intermediary is the primary insurer's agent. In the absence of this clause, the risk of the reinsurance intermediary's insolvency would fall most often on the primary insurer rather than the reinsurer.

SUMMARY

Reinsurance is the transfer of insurance risk from one insurer to another through a contractual agreement under which the reinsurer agrees, in return for a reinsurance premium, to indemnify the primary insurer for some or all the financial consequences of the loss exposures covered by the reinsurance contract. Reinsurance performs these principal functions for primary insurers: increase large-line capacity, provide catastrophe protection, stabilize loss experience, provide surplus relief, facilitate withdrawal from a market segment, and provide underwriting guidance.

Reinsurance is available from professional reinsurers; reinsurance departments of primary insurers; and reinsurance pools, syndicates, and associations. A direct writing reinsurer is a professional reinsurer that deals directly with primary insurers. Reinsurers also may deal with primary insurers through reinsurance intermediaries. Some primary insurers also serve as reinsurers, either only to affiliates or to both affiliated and unaffiliated insurers.

Reinsurance pools, syndicates, and associations are groups of insurers that share the loss exposures of the group. Several reinsurance professional and trade associations serve member companies and provide information to interested parties.

The two types of reinsurance transactions are treaty reinsurance and facultative reinsurance.

Treaty reinsurance agreements provide coverage for an entire class or portfolio of loss exposures and involve an ongoing relationship between the primary insurer and the reinsurer. Treaty reinsurance agreements are usually obligatory; loss exposures must be ceded to and accepted by the reinsurer. Facultative reinsurance agreements insure individual loss exposures. Under a facultative agreement, the reinsurer is usually not obligated to accept the loss exposure submitted by the primary insurer.

Reinsurance agreements can be categorized as either pro rata (proportional) or excess of loss (nonproportional) reinsurance. Pro rata reinsurance involves the proportional sharing of amounts of insurance, policy premiums, and losses (including loss adjustment expenses) between the primary insurer and the reinsurer. Pro rata reinsurance can be either on a quota share basis or on a surplus share basis. With excess of loss reinsurance, the reinsurer responds to a loss only when the loss exceeds the primary insurer's retention (often referred to as the attachment point).

Finite risk reinsurance is a nontraditional type of reinsurance that can be arranged to protect a primary insurer against large and unusual loss exposures. Although premiums for finite risk reinsurance are typically higher than for other forms of reinsurance, the finite risk reinsurer usually shares profits with the primary insurer when it has favorable loss experience or has generated income by investing the prepaid premium. Organizations also can use capital markets to finance risk as an alternative to insurance and traditional reinsurance, particularly for catastrophe risk financing. Although the number of these products is increasing rapidly, the methods most often used are catastrophe bonds, catastrophe risk exchanges, contingent surplus notes, industry loss warranties, catastrophe options, lines of credit, and sidecars.

Reinsurance program design is a process through which primary insurers analyze their reinsurance needs to develop an optimal reinsurance program that meets their specific goals. In designing a reinsurance program, primary insurers or their reinsurers, reinsurance intermediaries, or consultants compare existing reinsurance agreements with ever-changing needs. To be effective, reinsurance programs must be flexible enough to meet known and anticipated needs. Designing a reinsurance program involves determining reinsurance needs, setting retentions, and setting limits.

Applying a reinsurance program to a specific situation requires understanding many characteristics of the primary insurer, such as its historical loss experience, financial condition, and the types of insurance it sells. Subjective factors such as senior management's aversion to risk must also be understood. A variety of reinsurance programs may be equally effective in a given scenario.

Reinsurers domiciled in the U.S. and alien reinsurers licensed in the U.S. are subject to the same solvency state regulations as primary insurers. However, these regulations do not apply to unlicensed alien reinsurers. Recent regulatory efforts have focused on contract certainty. Another key concern of state insurance regulators regarding reinsurance is the standards by which an insurer should be allowed to take credit for a reinsurance transaction. State insurance regulators have adopted requirements that must be met by a reinsurance agreement in order for a primary insurer to take reserve credit for the reinsurance transaction.

ASSIGNMENT NOTES

1. Many of the definitions of terms in this section were adapted from the Reinsurance Association of America's (RAA) *Glossary of Terms*. The RAA's Web site is www.reinsurance.org (accessed March 31, 2010).

2. Insurers that are publicly traded are usually referred to as "stock insurers" to differentiate them from "mutual insurers," which are owned by their policyholders.

3. Intermediaries and Reinsurance Underwriters Association, www.irua.com (accessed May 12, 2010).

4. Brokers & Reinsurance Markets Association, www.brma.org (accessed May 12, 2010).

5. Reinsurance Association of America, www.reinsurance.org (accessed May 12, 2010).

6. Definition adapted from Reinsurance Association of America, www.reinsurance.org (accessed June 15, 2010).

Direct Your Learning ▶▶

Insurer Strategic Management

Educational Objectives

After learning the content of this assignment, you should be able to:

▶ Describe the strategic management process.

▶ Explain how the Five Forces and SWOT methods can be used to analyze the environment in which an insurer operates.

▶ Explain how strategies are developed at the corporate, business, functional, and operational levels.

▶ Describe the strategic reasons, considerations, and approaches for insurers to expand their operations globally.

▶ Given information about an insurer's business strategies, conduct a SWOT analysis of its strategy.

▶▶

Insurer Strategic Management

11

STRATEGIC MANAGEMENT PROCESS

The strategic management process is critical to any organization's success. However, effective strategic management is especially important for insurers because they must distinguish themselves in a highly regulated business where products may not widely vary.

Organizations can be successful in the long term if they have effective strategies that efficiently deploy resources. Therefore, the heart of any successful business strategy is the alignment between the internal resources of the organization and external factors. This alignment allows an organization to create a sustainable competitive advantage.

The **strategic management process** involves three interdependent stages:

- Strategy formulation—creating a plan
- Strategy implementation—putting the plan into action
- Strategy evaluation—monitoring the results to determine whether the plan works as envisioned

Strategic management process
The process an organization uses to formulate and implement its business strategies.

Strategy Formulation

Strategy formulation depends on an organization's mission or value statements. Throughout the strategic management process, these statements should serve as a focal point for the organization's management and board of directors.

Mission and Vision Statements

A **mission statement** is a broad expression of an entity's purpose or goals, while reflecting the entity's character and spirit. The mission statement specifies the products or services the organization provides, its stakeholders, and what is important to the organization. Mission statements frequently refer to customers, shareholders, employees, and other corporate stakeholders. For insurers, mission statements frequently mention financial strength, customer service, and integrity.

Mission statements may also include, or be accompanied by, vision or value statements that provide additional information about company values or principles important to the organization. Values such as integrity, honesty,

Mission statement
A broad expression of an entity's goals.

customer focus, flexibility, and compassion are often included in these statements. See the exhibit "Example of Insurer Mission/Vision Statements."

Example of Insurer Mission/Vision Statements

STATE FARM INSURANCE

Our Mission, Our Vision, and Our Shared Values

State Farm's mission is to help people manage the risks of everyday life, recover from the unexpected, and realize their dreams.

We are people who make it our business to be like a good neighbor; who built a premier company by selling and keeping promises through our marketing partnership; who bring diverse talents and experiences to our work of serving the State Farm customer.

Our success is built on a foundation of shared values-quality service and relationships, mutual trust, integrity and financial strength.

Our vision for the future is to be the customer's first and best choice in the products and services we provide. We will continue to be the leader in the insurance industry and we will become a leader in the financial services arena. Our customers' needs will determine our path. Our values will guide us.

Source: http://www.statefarm.com/about/mission.asp (accessed June 22, 2010).

AMICA INSURANCE

Mission Statement

Amica's mission is to enhance the financial security of our customers by offering personal insurance protection and other related services at the lowest reasonable cost, consistent with sound financial management.

In accomplishing this mission, we are dedicated to the following principles:

Exceeding customer expectations by providing the highest quality service in the industry.

Offering superior products and services that respond to the needs of our customers.

Maintaining financial strength through sound business practices and the aggressive pursuit of efficient operations.

Promoting well-being, dedication, and professionalism in our employees by providing them with equal opportunity for personal growth and recognition in a pleasant, healthy, and safe work environment.

Adhering to the highest ethical, moral, and legal standards in our business and civic activities.

Source: http://www.amica.com/about_us/amica_advantage/missionStatement.html (accessed June 22, 2010).

[DA06246]

Strategy Formulation Steps

Considering the organization's mission and vision statements, board members and senior-level executives develop strategies through a three-step process. Although business theorists differ over the labeling and numbering of the steps (and some divide individual steps into more than one), strategy formulation has these basic components:

- Analysis of external and internal environments
- Development of long-term strategies and organizational goals
- Determination of strategy at different organizational levels

The first step of strategy formulation involves an internal analysis of the organization and an analysis of external factors including competitors, current and prospective customers' needs, the current and anticipated economy, and government regulations. Typically, a **SWOT analysis** may enable executives to determine how receptive the market would be to its products and services and its competitive position within the market. Opportunities can be categorized as those that "can" or those that "should" be pursued. With this approach, the framework for a strategic plan begins to emerge.

SWOT analysis

A method of evaluating the internal and external environments by assessing an organization's internal strengths and weaknesses and its external opportunities and threats.

The second step in the process involves development of long-term strategies and organizational goals to support the mission statement within the framework developed during the analysis step. An organization's goals should reflect an understanding of its identity, customers, and purpose. Companies establish these goals to set the priorities or direction for the organization, to establish a measurement of success, and to align its people and actions.

Normally, the chief executive officer (CEO) and executive officers will develop these strategies and goals, often with input from the board and operational-level managers. Depending on the organization, executives and others in management will then develop short-term financial objectives that are aligned with long-term strategies and goals.

The third step in strategy formulation is to determine strategies at different levels of the organization. This involves agreement on more specific action and delegation of responsibilities to achieve long-term strategies and goals. These strategies are based on an organization's core competencies, the competitive nature of the business, the potential customer base, and other factors. This step in the strategic management process involves formulating the "who," "what," and "when" responsibilities.

Strategy Implementation

The second stage of the strategic management process is strategy implementation, also called strategy execution. Strategy implementation is the process of making strategies work. In relation to the strategy formulation stage, this stage is more difficult to complete and requires more time.

Functional structure

An organizational structure in which departments are defined by the operation they perform.

Multidivisional structure

An organizational structure in which divisions are organized into separate profit centers.

Cost leadership

A business-level strategy through which a company seeks cost efficiencies in all operational areas.

The first consideration and a crucial component of strategy implementation is designing the structure of the organization. The most appropriate organizational structure for a company will be determined by its strategic goals. In a single-business company, a **functional structure** might be most suitable, with departments defined by the operation they perform for example. Examples of such departments would be claims, underwriting, and marketing and sales, among others. A diversified company is more likely to use a **multidivisional structure** to organize its operations and to segregate each division into separate profit centers.

Other possible structures organize company operations by region or by type of product or customer. A large insurer, for example, might have separate underwriting departments for commercial, marine, and personal lines insurance. This way, the expertise and resources required for specific customers is concentrated within the related department. Such an approach supports a differentiation strategy, in which the company seeks to provide unique products for specific market segments.

Structure can also determine the reporting relationships or the company's level of vertical differentiation, which is the extent to which an organization is stratified from its lowest to highest levels. Some companies are tall organizations, with many levels between functional-level positions and executive-level positions. Conversely, a flat organization has fewer levels from the top of the organization to the bottom. When following a **cost leadership** strategy, a flat organization helps to eliminate costs related to maintaining multiple reporting relationships within the company.

Companies should also decide what degree of centralization is needed to operate efficiently and to meet organizational goals. The degree of centralization determines whether authority is maintained at top levels of the organization or is delegated throughout headquarters, into regions, or even to the local level. For example, some insurers retain underwriting authority at the headquarters level, while others extend authority to local offices or to managing general agents. Their claim departments make similar decisions about whether claim-settling authority resides with home office claim staff or is extended to regional claim managers or local company adjusters.

Ultimately, the entire organization is responsible for successful strategy implementation. However, the plans for implementation begin with a filtering-down process, where organizational goals are communicated by top management. Often, managers at each successive level must "sell" organizational goals to their employees.[1] See the exhibit "Strategy Implementation Steps."

Strategy implementation and evaluation are intertwined—a company cannot achieve its goals if its strategies are not implemented effectively. Because of this, there must be a way to measure this effectiveness. Strategies also need to be continually evaluated and modified based on market, economic, and competitive conditions.

Strategy Implementation Steps

Mid-level managers are typically responsible for strategy implementation and may follow these five steps:

- Create a documented roadmap of the specific processes, tasks, and responsibilities necessary to disseminate the corporate strategies throughout the organization.

- Communicate information regarding the strategies clearly, frequently, and completely throughout the organization.

- Assign specific responsibilities, tasks, authority, and accountability throughout the organization.

- Allocate adequate resources for successful implementation. Resources include finances, staff, training, time, equipment, data, and technology.

- Manage variances between the goals and the mid-year results; make necessary adjustments to achieve the goals.

[DA06247]

Strategy Evaluation

Strategy evaluation, also called strategic control, provides a method for measuring a strategy's success. Control mechanisms allow management at each level to gauge the progress of the integration of established strategies into the organization's activities and toward achieving the goals that have been set. The control process has four steps:

1. Establish standards
2. Create and apply measurements
3. Compare actual results to standards
4. Evaluate and implement corrective actions if goals are not met

Following these steps provides a structured approach to strategy implementation. See the exhibit "Example of Steps in the Control Process Applied to an Underwriting Department."

Example of Steps in the Control Process Applied to an Underwriting Department

1. Establish standards—A combined ratio of under 100 was established as the standard. Combined ratios are usually readily available, which makes the ratio an appropriate and easily-applied standard.

2. Create and apply measurements—Measurement would consist of compiling all premium, expense, and loss data required to develop a combined-ratio figure for this individual office, as well as determining a format for reporting the data.

3. Compare actual results to standards—An inherent part of this process is for managers to communicate the importance of meeting this standard to all employees and to motivate them to do so. These premium, expense, and loss reports would then be used in comparing actual results to the established standard of a combined ratio under 100. If the standard has not been met, managers will need to determine the reason and then implement changes.

4. Evaluate and implement corrective actions if goals are not met—Depending on the results of this comparison, corrective actions might involve training initiatives for employees, strengthening communications with producers, examining marketing activities, or taking other corrective actions. If the goal has been met, management should reward and recognize all employees involved to provide motivation to achieve future strategic goals.

[DA06248]

These are categories of organizational controls that may be used to monitor goals:

- Financial controls—In the insurance industry, loss ratios, expense ratios, and combined ratios are financial controls typically used to evaluate overall corporate performance. They also measure the performance of business units, regional offices, and individual books of business. Other financial controls include stock price, return on investment formulas, cost/benefits analysis, or budget measurements.

- Operational or process controls—These include processes to monitor work flow, production processes, and customer service. In an insurance claims department, such controls could include the average cost of settlement, average case load per adjuster, or file turnover rates for individual adjusters.

- Human or behavior controls—This category includes rules, policies, and procedures that provide operating guidelines for employees within an organization, including measurement of individual performance.

As a result of evaluation, strategic plans may be reformed, and/or the manner in which they are implemented may need to be adjusted. The evaluation may indicate that results are off target in ways that cannot be addressed through moderate adjustments. Or it may reveal that the plan's concepts were not completely connected in the implementation stage which requires an adjustment to the implementation approach.

Unexpected outside economic forces also may make achievement of a strategic plan impractical or impossible. For example, significant events such as the September 11, 2001 terrorist attacks, Hurricane Katrina and related litigation, and the late 2000s recession required many insurers to revise strategic management plans.

THE FIVE FORCES AND SWOT METHODS OF ANALYZING THE ENVIRONMENT

An insurer's success depends on its ability to analyze changing environmental factors and influences and to formulate sound business strategies based on its analysis.

Insurers rely on the strategic management process to achieve long-term goals. Strategy formulation is a crucial component of the strategic management process and involves the interrelated steps of analysis of external and internal environments, development of long-term strategies and organizational goals, and determination of strategy at different organizational levels.

In the first step of the process, managers consider factors in both the general environment and the task environment. The general environment affects all businesses, regardless of the specific industry in which they operate, and includes demographic, sociocultural, legal, technological, economic, and global factors. The task environment, which includes an organization's customers, competitors, and suppliers, describes the environmental factors specific to the industry in which the organization operates. The task environment for an insurance company might include customers, competitors, suppliers, reinsurance providers, and regulators.

Many methods can be used to analyze the environment in which an organization operates. Two commonly used methods are the Five Forces Model and SWOT analysis.

The Five Forces Model

The widely used **Five Forces Model**, developed by Harvard Business School professor Michael E. Porter, deals with the external task, or competitive, environment and is often used to analyze customers, competitors and suppliers. Porter describes five forces that drive competition:

- Threat of new entrants
- Threat of substitute products or services
- Bargaining power of buyers

Five Forces Model
A method of evaluating the external environment in which a company operates. Involves assessing five forces that drive competition: threat of new entrants, threat of substitute products or services, bargaining power of buyers, bargaining power of suppliers, and rivalry among existing firms.

- Bargaining power of suppliers
- Rivalry among existing firms[2]

By analyzing these forces and their effect on the organization, managers can better understand their company's position in the industry. This increased understanding allows management to construct strategies that build a competitive advantage.

Threat of New Entrants

The threat of new entrants in a market is one force that drives competition, although the strength of this force depends on how difficult it is for outsiders to enter the market.. Barriers to entry include economies of scale, which contribute to lower overall costs by decreasing the unit cost of products as volume increases. Many insurers writing homeowners or personal auto policies have achieved economies of scale through technology. The standardized nature of personal insurance policies allows some insurers to use automated processes to issue large numbers of policies with relatively low overhead costs. These insurers have lower expenses than insurers relying on more labor-intensive processes, allowing them to charge lower premiums and thus raise barriers to entry for this market segment.

Insurers can also raise barriers to entry by offering unique products or services through the establishment of leadership in certain distribution methods (for example having a long-term relationship with producers, or creating an on-line direct application system known for its ease of use), or by having established advertising or group marketing programs. The ability for one insurer to access distribution channels in a marketing system can create barriers to entry for others and pose a competitive disadvantage for potential new entrants. For insurance products, the insurance distribution system and channel can be important components of the overall marketing plan.

State statute and regulatory policy can act as a barrier to entry if they deter potential entrants from considering the highly regulated insurance industry. Regulatory requirements within a given jurisdiction can also discourage insurers from entering certain states. For example, the state of Massachusetts once discouraged new entrants to the personal auto insurance market with state-made rates and restrictions on distribution.

Other potential barriers to entry include the presence of switching costs, cost disadvantages independent of scale, and the need to invest large amounts of capital for production facilities for research and development.[3] All of these conditions increase costs for potential entrants, raising the barriers for them.

Threat of Substitute Products or Services

A second force that drives competition is the threat of substitute products or services. This threat arises when products that are capable of performing the same function as those from another industry become widely available. This threat makes it difficult for any one seller to substantially increase prices and tends to hold down profits for all participants in the original industry.

The threat of substitute products or services to the insurance industry has been limited thus far, but remains an important force for insurers to consider. One example of such a threat is alternative risk transfer mechanisms including self-insured retention, formation of captive insurance companies, catastrophe bonds, and finite risk transfer. On a more limited scale, an example of such a threat is the state-run Florida Citizens Property Insurance Corporation (Citizens). Citizens, originally intended as a market of last resort, could pose a threat to private insurers to the extent that it seeks to compete with the private market.

Bargaining Powers of Buyers

The third force that drives competition is the bargaining power of buyers. When buyers have significant power, they can increase competition within an industry and demand lower prices. According to Porter, "consumers tend to be more price sensitive if they are purchasing products that are undifferentiated, expensive relative to their incomes, or of a sort where quality is not particularly important to them."[4] This force affects the insurance industry, principally in the personal insurance market, in which customers have exerted great pressure on insurers to lower prices and increase availability. The bargaining power of buyers is the reason that many government sponsored or mandated residual market plans were created. Auto assigned risk plans and property insurance plans (particularly those serving coastal markets) were created where the market would not support the prices needed for insurers to voluntarily offer coverage. Further, the bargaining power of buyers led to the explosive growth in a number of coastal property insurance plans and wind pools as property owners would not, or could not, pay rates sought by the private market.

The bargaining power of customers is also affected by the cyclical nature of the insurance business. In a soft market, many insurers vie for business and provide undifferentiated products. Insurance consumers have greater bargaining power and can negotiate for broader coverages at lower premiums. In a hard market, limited capacity results in rising prices and makes it difficult for customers to bargain for broader coverage.

When formulating strategy, companies should consider customer buying power. In some cases, insurers might decide not to enter markets where they feel pressure from buyer groups would inhibit their ability to be profitable.

Bargaining Power of Suppliers

A fourth force driving competition is the bargaining power of suppliers. In some industries, suppliers can exert power over companies by increasing prices, restricting supply, or varying product quality. For example, in the energy industry, oil-producing countries can exert tremendous power over the supply and price of petroleum products.

In the insurance industry, reinsurers are a supplier to primary insurers. Without access to reinsurance, many insurers would lack sufficient capacity to write certain types and amounts of insurance. Reinsurers are in a position to control the price and amount of capacity they provide depending on the market conditionsFor example, after consecutive years of devastating hurricanes in the United States (Charley, Francis, Ivan and Jeanne in 2004; Katrina, Rita and Wilma in 2005), reinsurers were faced with enormous losses and uncertainty as to whether or not losses might even be worse if post-Hurricane Katrina litigation resulted in an unanticipated expansion of coverage. At the same time, many insurers found that they had been underestimating worst-case loss scenarios. Such uncertainty in the marketplace generally results in tighter capacity, rising rates, and more restrictive terms. In this case, demand for reinsurance increased at the same time that reinsurers limited capacity, resulting in reduced capacity and higher rates for primary insurance.

Another example of the bargaining power of suppliers is the power exerted by auto manufacturers to mandate use of original equipment manufacturer (OEM) parts for auto physical damage repairs. Where suppliers have successfully limited the acceptance or use of less expensive non-OEM (aftermarket) parts, physical damage loss costs may increase for insurers.

Rivalry Among Existing Firms

Rivalry among existing companies is the fifth force that drives competition. Rivalry is reflected in pricing wars, aggressive advertising campaigns, and increased emphasis on customer service. Competitors are constantly striving to be at the top of their industry and to outperform other companies. This type of rivalry exists among personal lines auto insurers.

A high level of competition can be expected in industries having many companies, little product differentiation, or high exit costs. All of these characteristics are present in the insurance industry, making the market strongly competitive. While some insurers can use economies of scale to gain a competitive edge, the individual market share of insurers at the top of the market is still relatively small compared to that of other industries. No single insurer has enough market share to dominate the overall property-casualty market. For example, the leading property-casualty insurer's market share is only approximately ten percent.

SWOT Analysis

SWOT analysis, or situational analysis, is another method used to analyze the competitive environment. SWOT (Strengths, Weaknesses, Opportunities, and Threats) analysis allows organizations to consider both the general environment and the task environment. This method was devised by Albert S.

Humphrey, a business scholar and management consultant who specialized in business planning and change.

Strengths and Weaknesses

Identifying internal strengths and weaknesses involves consideration of financial, physical, human, and organizational assets.[5]Managers use SWOT analysis to determine the current state of their companies. These are some of the assets that management considers:

- Managerial expertise
- Available product lines
- Skill levels and competencies of staff
- Current strategies
- Customer loyalty
- Growth levels
- Organizational structure
- Distribution channels

It would be a strength if an organization has an executive training program that is considered an industry standard. If a company is having financial difficulty or is experiencing unfocused growth, it would be a weakness.In an insurance operation, an insurer that had been cutting prices to gain market share might identify loss of premium volume as a substantial weakness when an unanticipated rise in losses is projected as part of the SWOT analysis. Unfavorable loss results cause financial constraints.

For example, in 2002 several major property-casualty insurers conducted studies to determine the accuracy of reserves for asbestos-related claims. As a result of these studies, many of these insurers were required to increase their reserves significantly. These increases highlighted a key internal weakness for the insurers and had a negative effect on their earnings and stock prices.

Opportunities and Threats

Managers determine potential opportunities or threats by analyzing the external environment, including both general and task environment factor. One way to achieve this is through **trend analysis**, which identifies patterns related to specific factors in the past and then projects those patterns into the future to determine potential threats or opportunities. Insurers might determine opportunities and threats through trend analysis.Opportunities might be presented by new markets, possible acquisition targets, or a reduction in competition, while threats might include new competitors, an increase in competition levels, economic downturns, or changes in customer preferences.

For example, projection of various demographic trends might reveal new marketing opportunities or a shrinking market for an existing core product. See the exhibit "SWOT Analysis Table."

Trend analysis

An analysis that identifies patterns in past losses and then projects these patterns into the future.

SWOT Analysis Table

	Strengths	Weaknesses
Internal	List assets, competencies, or attributes that enhance competitiveness. Prioritize based on the quality of the strength and the relative importance of the strength.	List lacking assets, competencies, or attributes that diminish competitiveness. Prioritize based on the seriousness of the weakness and the relative importance of the weakness.
	Opportunities	**Threats**
External	List conditions that could be exploited to create a competitive advantage. Prioritize based on the potential of exploiting the opportunities.	List conditions that diminish competitive advantage. Prioritize based on the seriousness and probability of occurrence.
	Note strengths that can be paired with opportunities as areas of competitive advantage.	Note weaknesses that can be paired with threats as risks to be avoided.

[DA03626]

The approach used by organizations varies based on each company's needs. A company should not only identify strengths, weaknesses, opportunities, and threats, but should also thoroughly analyze how they affect its strategic plan.

Once the SWOT analysis has been completed, managers can develop strategies that position the company to gain a competitive advantage by leveraging organizational strengths and offsetting or reducing weaknesses. The company should also find ways to capitalize on identified opportunities and to neutralize existing threats.

DETERMINING STRATEGY AT DIFFERENT ORGANIZATIONAL LEVELS

Strategic plans encompass a variety of organizational activities. Because organizations vary widely, every organization requires its own approach. Strategies can be categorized based on the levels at which they are carried out within an organization, how they relate to the development stage of the organization, and how they align with the organization's overall business approach.

Different kinds of strategies are carried out at various levels within an organization. Strategies at all levels should be aligned to support the organization's overall mission and vision. On any given day, insurance professionals may participate in implementing multiple strategies simultaneously.

These are the most prevalent types of organizational strategies:

- Corporate-level strategy represents the highest strategy level for a diversified organization. It determines the types and potential profitability of businesses or activities the organization will undertake.

- Business-level strategy may be implemented by a single operation or, in the case of a diversified corporation, a strategic business unit (SBU). Managers develop strategies at this level to support the corporate-level strategy, to be competitive, and to respond to changes in the external environment.

- Functional-level strategy is carried out by individual departments performing specific organizational functions, such as marketing or underwriting.

- Operational-level strategy relates to a department's narrowly defined day-to-day business activities. Operational strategies include workflows and production processes.

[DA06291]

Corporate-Level Strategy

At the corporate level, the chief executive officer (CEO) and the executive team determine the businesses in which the company will be involved, allocate organizational resources properly, and coordinate strategies at all company levels to maximize profits. Corporate-level strategies are relatively long term, established for a five-year period and beyond.

Competitive advantage is reinforced when each department or unit in an organization creates value for the customer. In insurance operations, the marketing, underwriting, claim, customer service, and other departments must align to build value and to support corporate-level strategy in a continuous chain. This alignment can also provide additional advantages in the form of reduced operating expenses or increased differentiation of products and services through the interaction of various departments, such as marketing and underwriting.

Three generic corporate-level strategies are available for companies in a growth mode:

• Single business

• Vertical integration

• Diversification

There are different corporate-level strategies for companies in a decline mode, such as the bankruptcy, divestiture, turnaround, and harvest strategies.

Concentration on a Single Business

Based on a business environmental assessment, a company might determine that the best corporate-level strategy for it to pursue is concentration on a single business. By concentrating its efforts and resources on one industry, product, or market, a company can build distinctive competencies and gain a competitive advantage. Many property-casualty insurers pursue a single-business strategy, even though they write many types of insurance.

Concentrating on a single business, however, has some potential disadvantages. Most are related to missing opportunities to build a competitive advantage through either vertical integration or diversification into related areas.

Vertical Integration

Vertical integration strategy

A corporate-level strategy through which a company either produces its own inputs or disposes of its own outputs.

A **vertical integration strategy** can be either backward or forward. If an organization produces inputs for processing (such as an insurer printing policy forms in house instead of purchasing them from a printing supplier), it is backward integration. When an organization sells its product directly to the customer rather than through a wholesaler, it is called forward integration. Direct writer insurers are an example of forward integration being put to use.

Companies choose vertical integration to decrease expenses or increase efficiency. However, vertical integration could have an opposite effect due to a lack of expertise or the cost of resources in different stages of the production process.

Diversification

Diversification for the property and casualty insurance industry can be advantageous. Because the industry is affected by the weather cycles, diversifying into lines of insurance or financial products that are unaffected by the weather can help smooth the demand for both financial and human resources. Because the insurance underwriting cycle does not coincide with the general business cycle, some insurers may benefit from diversification into non-insurance businesses to offset lower insurer profits during troughs in the insurance profit cycle. In pursuit of diversification, companies can pursue either related or unrelated diversification strategies

Related diversification allows companies to gain economies of scope by sharing resources, such as the same distribution system or research and development facilities. For example, a property-casualty insurer may also provide life or health insurance and thus utilize its existing technology and agency system to grow its business while spreading risk. Another benefit of related diversification is the ability to leverage fixed expenses with additional revenues from diversified operations, resulting in a lower unit cost for each product or service offered. For example, insurers may enter into third-party administration of claims as some of their customers choose alternative risk financing approaches instead of traditional insurance. This allows the insurers to obtain additional revenue from their existing technology platforms, claim expertise, and other internal resources.

Related diversification strategy
A corporate-level strategy through which a company expands its operations into areas that are similar to its existing operations.

Unrelated diversification strategy (also referred to as conglomerate diversification strategy) involves acquiring companies that have no relationship to the existing business operations and is riskier than related diversification. The negative aspects of unrelated diversification include additional costs of coordinating the divergent businesses, a loss of synergy among business units, and diminishing returns from any economies of scale or scope. Companies that have succeeded with an unrelated diversification strategy excel at making the right types of acquisitions. These companies have also developed strong structure and control mechanisms to offset some of the difficulties stemming from managing an extensive and varied group of profit centers.

Unrelated diversification strategy
A corporate-level strategy through which a company expands its operations into areas that have no relation to its existing operations.

Decline Mode Strategies

All of the strategies discussed to this point involve companies operating in growing markets. However, some companies might not be growing, might be encountering substantial marketplace obstacles, or might have numerous internal weaknesses and external threats. The problems that these companies encounter could include decreasing profits, loss of market share, or changing economic conditions. When a company is operating in a market in which demand for its products or services is decreasing, it is in a decline mode and its strategic options are different than those of companies in a growth mode.

Corporate-level strategies for such companies are defensive. In the worst-case scenario, the company might determine that the only option is bankruptcy or liquidation. In bankruptcy, companies seek court protection from creditors to reorganize and improve their financial standing. If a company cannot recover from bankruptcy, it is liquidated and any remaining proceeds are used to satisfy outstanding obligations.

There are other corporate-level strategies that can be used in a decline mode. In the **harvest strategy**, for example, an insurer might sell real estate, such as office buildings, while it phases out an unprofitable line of insurance. In a **turnaround strategy**, an insurer might reorganize and reduce the number of offices and redundant administrative staff. In a **divestiture strategy**, an insurer will sell businesses or divisions to increase profits through the sale of assets or to reduce losses from unprofitable business. AIG provides an example of the divestiture strategy, having divested its stake in London City airport in 2008 and sold AIG Life of Canada and Hartford Steam Boiler in 2009.

Business-Level Strategy

Business-level strategies are developed at the business or division level by managers who are responsible for supporting the stated corporate-level strategy. These managers must find ways for their business units to be competitive and to respond to changes in the external environment. Business-level management also budgets for needed resources and coordinates the functional-level strategy within the division. The time frame for business-level strategies, sometimes referred to as tactical strategies, is three to five years in most organizations. There are three business-level strategies:

- Cost leadership
- Differentiation
- Focus

Cost Leadership

Cost leadership enables a company to charge a lower price for its products or services. It involves eliminating costs in every aspect of the operation, from product development and design to distribution and delivery. However, cost leadership involves more than just charging the lowest price in the industry. Even when prices for similar products are comparable, the cost leader can earn higher overall profits than its competitors because of its lower costs. Cost leaders can also better withstand prolonged price wars.

One requirement of a cost leadership strategy is that most products or services must be fairly standardized. Introducing varied types of products increases expenses and erodes any cost leadership advantages, so cost leaders do not tend to be first movers within an industry.

For insurers, price cutting might be limited by regulatory constraints. Insurers must closely examine the three components of an insurance rate (allowances for loss payments, expenses, and profit) to determine where costs can

Harvest strategy

A corporate-level strategy through which a company seeks to gain short-term profits while phasing out a product line or exiting a market.

Turnaround strategy

A corporate-level strategy through which a company rebuilds organizational resources to return to profitable levels.

Divestiture strategy

A corporate-level strategy through which a company sells off a portion of an operation, usually a division or profit center that is not performing to expectations.

be reduced. When evaluating how to decrease costs, insurers can consider reducing acquisition expenses by lowering producers' commissions, using a direct writer system for some or all of their marketing, or exploring alternative distribution channels.

Loss expenses can be reduced by streamlining claim adjusting processes, managing litigation expenses, or implementing cost containment practices, such as negotiation of repair or medical reimbursement rates with vendors. Underwriting expenses can be reduced by using expert computer systems or standardizing underwriting guidelines. Technology can automate processes, improve interaction among departments, and speed policy processing times. All of these efforts combine to execute the cost leadership strategy.

Differentiation

A successful **differentiation strategy** requires products and services that customers perceive as distinctive and that are difficult for rivals to imitate. Companies using this strategy must accurately determine the needs and preferences of their customers, or revenue and market share will be lost. Market share will also be lost if competitors can match or improve upon the product's unique features.

Insurers employing this strategy may choose to differentiate products or services to gain market share and to establish a competitive advantage. Insurers that offer special programs for commercial or homeowners insurance are examples. When an insurer writes only homeowners or personal auto insurance and targets multiple markets (such as teachers, retired persons, and military personnel), it is following a differentiation strategy. If an insurer offers a wide range of specialized coverages, but offers them only to municipalities, it is following a focus strategy.

Focus

A focus strategy involves concentrating on a group of customers, a geographic area, or a narrow line of products or services while using a low-cost approach or a differentiation strategy. The two types of this strategy are **focused cost leadership strategy** and **focused differentiation strategy**.

Many insurers follow one of the focus strategies. Niche marketing programs, which offer tailored coverages to specific groups of customers, are examples of focused differentiation. Alternatively, an example of a focused cost leadership approach is when an insurer that sells to a specific group of customers, such as retail hardware stores, and offers discounted commercial packages or automobile policies using standard forms. The use of standard forms is an important factor because any significant level of specialization increases costs and erodes profits.

Differentiation strategy

A business-level strategy through which a company develops products or services that are distinct and for which customers will pay a higher price than that of the competition.

Focused cost leadership strategy

A business-level strategy through which a company focuses on one group of customers and offers a low-price product or service.

Focused differentiation strategy

A business-level strategy through which a company focuses on one group of customers and offers unique or customized products that permit it to charge a higher price than that of the competition.

Functional-Level Strategy

Functional-level strategies are the plans for managing a particular functional area, such as finance, marketing, underwriting, actuarial, risk control, premium audit, and claims. These strategies establish how functional departments support the organization's business-level and corporate-level strategies. The time frame for these strategies is short term, usually one year.

Companies build value and competitive advantage through efficiency, quality, customer responsiveness, and innovation. Some combination of these factors must be incorporated into its activities at the functional level for a company to pursue either a cost leadership or differentiation strategy at the business level. For example, without efficiency and innovation, cost leadership cannot be attained. Similarly, quality and customer responsiveness must be included in the development, production, and marketing functions for a company to execute a differentiation strategy effectively.

In insurance operations, functional-level strategies specify how the underwriting, claim, actuarial, and other departments advance business-level strategies. For an insurer to be successful at garnering market share using a cost leadership strategy, it must become a highly efficient organization. For example, human resources, in cooperation with the underwriting, claim, customer service, and marketing departments, should find ways to improve productivity. The information technology department should provide innovative solutions to lower overall production costs and improve the speed of organizational communications, both internally and externally. Likewise, an insurer that is pursuing a differentiation strategy will consider innovation and quality at all functional levels to be critical to providing a distinctive product that meets the customer's needs.

Operational-Level Strategy

Operational-level strategies involve daily business processes and workflows, and are implemented at the department level to support the strategies of the functional, business, and corporate levels. For example, a claim office with a high volume of claims and a functional-level strategy to improve efficiency might decide to obtain more information through the claim reporting process in order to assign the claim properly and eliminate redundant communication with insureds. A premium auditing department, striving to achieve a functional-level budget strategy, might use pre-audit screening as an operational-level strategy to make the most effective use of resources to achieve its budget goals.

INSURERS' GLOBAL EXPANSION

Global competition is now a factor in virtually every industry. Advances in communication and transportation, international trade agreements to lower trade barriers, and growth in emerging markets have led many businesses to expand into global markets. Global investment and expansion in the insurance industry, both by insurers based in the United States entering foreign markets and by foreign insurers entering U.S. markets, have increased significantly in recent years and are likely to continue to do so.

Insurers are increasingly expanding operations to foreign markets. These four topics provide a basic understanding of why and how insurers engage in global expansion:

- Trends in global expansion
- Strategic reasons for global expansion
- Global market considerations
- Approaches to global expansion

Trends in Global Expansion

Global commerce has been growing since the end of World War II. During the past two decades, this growth accelerated as a result of numerous trade agreements throughout the world, advances in transportation and communication, the influence of the Internet, and financial innovation. The insurance market, like the markets in other industries, has become a global market where U.S. insurers compete in many other countries and where insurers domiciled in other countries compete in the U.S.

The U.S. experiences a trade deficit in global insurance trade that has increased steadily since 1995. In 1995 the deficit was approximately $1 billion, less than 1 percent of the U.S. global insurance trade. In 2006 the deficit was about $24.3 billion, almost 10 percent.[6] In 2006 foreign-owned insurers wrote 13.6 percent of the nonlife U.S. insurance premiums, and U.S. insurers ceded 53.1 percent of reinsurance premiums to foreign-domiciled entities.

Meanwhile, the U.S. also continued to increase exports of insurance with a 19 percent increase in 2006 (reinsurance comprised 60 percent of this total). However, in the same year, imports of insurance into the U.S. increased by 18 percent (reinsurance comprised 90 percent of the total).[7]

These statistics express the increased global competition within the international insurance industry. While there is greater competition for U.S. insurers from foreign insurers within the U.S. market, growth of the U.S. market has been slowing. From a low rate of growth of 2.1 percent for all insurance premiums (life and nonlife), to a decline of 7.8 percent in 2009, the U.S. market offers low growth potential along with increased competition.

As indicated in the chart in the exhibit, almost all of the premium growth in property and casualty insurance is occurring in emerging markets. For example, the Chinese nonlife market grew by 18.6 per cent in 2009. There is, therefore, a growth opportunity for U.S. insurers in global markets, especially in emerging markets. See the exhibit "Global Insurance Markets—2009."

Global Insurance Markets—2009

	Nonlife Premiums USD billion	Change v. 2008
Industrialized Countries	1486	-.6%
United States	647	-1.8%
Germany	127	1.0%
Japan	107	-2.0%
United Kingdom	92	-3.1%
France	89	0.9%
Italy	54	-2.5%
Hong Kong	3	6.1%
Emerging Markets	249	2.9%
Latin America and Caribbean	67	4.3%
Central and Eastern Europe	67	-7.5%
China	64	18.6%
India	8	1.6%
Other Asian Countries	3	
Middle East and Central Asia	22	4.7%
Africa	17	0.4%
World	1735	-0.1%

http://www.swissre.com/media/media_information/pr_sigma2_2010.html [DA06391]

Strategic Reasons for Global Expansion

Key strategic reasons why insurers pursue global expansion are revenue growth, financial stability, and building global competitiveness.

Revenue Growth and Financial Stability

Revenue growth is the primary reason that insurers look to global expansion. Some insurance markets, including the U.S, are considered mature markets, meaning that there are few new potential customers. In a mature market, competition for market share results in shrinking profit margins and companies will look for new opportunities for revenue growth. However, worldwide nonlife premium growth increased from $671 billion to more than $1.7 trillion between 1991 and 2009. Therefore, global markets, especially those in emerging economies (developing countries where the economy is growing rapidly) offer such growth opportunities.

Global expansion, particularly into emerging economy markets, also allows insurers to diversify operations and risks. Expanding into foreign markets has the benefit of allowing insurers to achieve these objectives:

- Greater stability during economic downturns—Spreading risks worldwide helps to counter the effects of economic downturn in a particular country. Furthermore, even in a worldwide recession, the potential for growth in emerging markets can offset loss of income from declines in premiums and investment returns. For example, in 2009, nonlife premiums dropped in the developed countries of the U.S., United Kingdom, and Japan, but increased in emerging markets.

- Diversification of risk—Spreading risk over a larger and more diverse base minimizes the impact of heavy losses in any one segment of the operation. This has long been the business model of international reinsurers who spread the risk of extreme natural catastrophes through globalization.

Global Competitiveness

Global expansion can increase an insurer's competitiveness in several ways. Through the growth from global expansion, an insurer may achieve economies of scale and efficiencies that allow it to compete more effectively in its domestic market as well as in the global market.

A global expansion strategy also provides an insurer with the technology and strategic resources to quickly expand into additional foreign markets or offer additional products when there is an opportunity. If an insurer waits to begin expansion until a market is developing, that insurer may lag behind other organizations that were more nimble in their ability to enter that market.

Insurers may also choose to expand in order to remain competitive in a specific specialty market. For example, an insurer specializing in mining risks or oil exploration may be better able to compete if it markets such coverage globally.

Global Market Considerations

Many companies pursue international growth strategies to build long-term financial strength. However, the decision to operate globally involves many variables. Management needs to determine the global markets to target, what products could be sold in other countries, what distribution channels should be used, and how regulations and government restrictions might affect global operations. Making these determinations is essential for an insurer to decide whether operating globally would improve its competitive advantage.

There are three key areas for an insurer to evaluate in making a strategic decision about expansion into a global market:

- Market analysis
- Economic considerations
- Political risks

Market Analysis

When a company is considering global expansion, it must analyze the insurance market in the country it plans to enter. Financial requirements, including capital and surplus, need to be evaluated. The company must also assess whether the potential return is worth the amount of capital that will need to be committed. Other factors include the ease of entry and the difficulty of withdrawal from the market. The competition from other insurers will also be included in this analysis. The insurer will consider whether it has any competitive advantage that it can use to provide leverage in the country where it plans to expand, such as a product offering that fits well in the market.

Distribution channels, the availability of producers, and underwriting practices are additional factors to analyze as well as whether these practices are compatible with the insurer's marketing and underwriting philosophy.

Other factors include cultural and language differences, and whether the insurer has the staff or can hire and manage the appropriate staff to overcome any linguistic or cultural barriers.

Economic Considerations

Insurers evaluating global expansion must also consider the host country's economic environment. Important considerations include the level of economic stability, monetary policies, the prevailing attitude toward foreign investors, and the potential for exchange-rate volatility. Other economic factors such as the country's gross domestic product or national income are also important, as is specific information including regulation, taxation, and premium tax requirements. Insurers will want to evaluate whether the country's economy is growing and whether there are any significant risks to economic growth on the horizon. For example, some countries that were growing rapidly may experience high levels of private and public debt that will restrain future growth potential.

Insurers need to have information regarding average personal income, disposable income, and the prevailing wages for various occupations in any country that is a potential market. This information is important, along with other demographic factors, to determine how many of the country's residents are potential consumers. Insurers also need to understand the wages they would need to pay employees in that country. Additionally, insurers considering expansion need to understand the laws and regulations that may affect them as potential employers.

Political Risks

Political risks are uncertainties faced by companies doing business in foreign countries that arise from the actions of host-country governments. These risks are greater in developing or emerging countries than in established countries with stable governments. Serious concerns include kidnap and ransom, terrorism, civil unrest, acts of war, revolution, and changes in government. Foreign nationals and their businesses can be at great risk in unsettled parts of the world. When considering global expansion, insurers often work with consultants who provide country reports or political risk scores to determine what political risks are present and how dangerous those risks are for foreign businesses.

Of greatest financial concern is the potential for the confiscation of business assets by a foreign government or other interference with the rights of ownership of corporate assets, such as confiscation of inventory. Expropriation occurs when a foreign government takes property without compensating its owners. This occurred in Cuba during the 1960s when many U.S. firms had business properties and inventory expropriated as part of Cuba's regime change. This can also occur when a cash-strapped government seeks to seize businesses that generate high returns.

Foreign governments might also nationalize a business and compensate the owners, usually at a lower rate than the market value of the assets. For example, in 1956 the government of India enacted legislation to nationalize insurance, resulting in the takeover of all insurers including several foreign companies.

Companies are also concerned when countries treat local businesses more favorably than foreign businesses regarding taxes, government contracts, or access to required financing. Insurers will also evaluate the nature and extent of regulation. Several countries prohibit nonadmitted insurance or have laws requiring insurance to be written by local insurers for designated classes of business. For example, China requires insurers to be licensed by the China Insurance Regulatory Commission (the CIRC) before they can write insurance in China.

Approaches to Global Expansion

Insurers who, after careful consideration, decide to expand into a global market may decide to form an alliance or joint venture with an existing insurer in that country, to merge with another insurer, to begin a new operation, or to acquire an existing foreign company.

- **Strategic Alliance**—Strategic alliances have the advantages of bringing together separate areas of expertise and of gaining a host-country

Strategic alliance

An arrangement in which two companies work together to achieve a common goal.

participant, who can access local markets and who is familiar with local laws, regulations, and customers. Such an alliance can provide a low-risk approach to quickly entering a new market. Strategic alliances include international licensing agreements (contractual agreement allowing one party to use another party's distribution system or trademark), and co-marketing/co-development agreements.

Joint venture

A specific type of strategic alliance in which companies share ownership, responsibilities, and management of a foreign venture.

- **Joint Venture**—A joint venture is a specific type of strategic alliance that involves shared ownership, shared responsibilities, and often joint management of the foreign venture. A joint-venture agreement brings together two companies to form a new organization that is legally separate and distinct from the parent companies, with its own management and directors. The most common form of joint venture occurs when a domestic company joins with a company from the country in which the operation is located. Joint ventures with governments or state-owned industries are referred to as public-private ventures and are common in India, China, Russia, and the former Soviet republics. Joint ventures allow companies to enter markets (both geographic and product markets) that would otherwise be beyond the reach of an individual company. For example, insurers wishing to expand into India commonly enter into joint venture agreements because India's law caps foreign direct investment for insurance.

Merger

A type of acquisition in which two or more business entities are combined into one.

- **Merger**—The advantage to merger is the ability to combine resources and reduce overhead expenses, allowing the new company to be more successful than the sum of the parties to the merger. International mergers carry a high degree of risk and are complicated by compliance with the regulations and antitrust laws of more than one country.

Subsidiary

A company owned or controlled by another company.

- Wholly Owned **Subsidiary**—Acquisition of, or formation of, a wholly owned subsidiary allows for direct ownership and control of assets in a foreign country. This presents the highest degree of business, political, and economic risk. Operating a subsidiary in a foreign country requires more capital than other methods of entering a foreign market, such as a joint venture, but also gives the domestic company greater control over operations. Acquiring an existing company generally results in faster entry into a market. However, establishment of a new company gives an insurer the greatest level of control over foreign affiliates because the parent company makes decisions about management, distribution channels, product mix, and other organization issues.

STRATEGIC MANAGEMENT CASE STUDY

A SWOT (strengths, weaknesses, opportunities, and threats) analysis can improve an insurer's planning process and the resulting outcome, particularly if those participating in the process represent a variety of perspectives and ask and find answers to difficult questions. It also may be used to evaluate whether an insurer's business strategies will contribute to its success.

A SWOT analysis can be used to examine an insurer's internal and external environment, and is frequently used in the strategic management planning process. The analysis is a step in action planning—not an end in itself. Results of SWOT analyses can change over time; therefore, the first step in the process of evaluation of business strategies should be to complete a current analysis. The current analysis can then be used to examine the insurer's business strategies, placing emphasis on any issues that have prompted the current evaluation. Strategies can then be evaluated to determine whether they are appropriate in guiding the insurer to meet its goals and objectives.

Case Facts

To evaluate an insurer's strategies, the reviewer or team of reviewers needs information about the insurer's strategic goals, as well as its internal and external environment. In addition, an understanding of the purpose of the evaluation will help narrow the review's focus.

Given background information on an insurer, the overall question to be answered is, "Will this insurer's current business strategies allow it to achieve its goals, or is a change required?"

Greenly Insurance Company—Internal and External Environment

Greenly Insurance Company (Greenly) is a sixty-year-old regional mutual insurance company authorized and operating in eight states. The company is headquartered in Pennsylvania, but maintains at least one satellite claims office in each state in which it writes.

Greenly writes only personal lines risks, with automobile insurance being the core of its business. Auto customers may be offered coverage in Greenly's "preferred" automobile insurance company, or in its "nonstandard" (high risk) company. The company offers generous discounts for drivers between the ages of thirty-five and sixty, based on the favorable loss ratios of this group. Greenly does not offer a rating discount based on longevity, although long-term households also show consistently favorable loss ratios.

The company's operations are consistent with core values it established sixty years ago: to protect policyholder assets, to gain customer loyalty, be a good corporate citizen, and to comply with all legal requirements. Throughout its existence, the company has enjoyed a consistently superior financial rating. A conservative investment strategy, favorable underwriting results, and conservative policy growth have allowed Greenly to maintain ample policyholder surplus even in years of high catastrophe losses and lackluster returns on investments. Greenly does not compete based on price, but rather on financial strength and core values.

Greenly uses independent agents to sell its products, and a monthly policyholder magazine accounts for the majority of its advertising. Greenly's customer-focused philosophy stresses personalized service to gain customer trust and loyalty. Therefore, Greenly's Web site does not provide quotes, direct purchase options, claim reporting, or premium payment options.

Over the past decade, the automobile insurance market has changed dramatically. Policyholders demand customer service, yet also want lower premiums. The line between "preferred" and "nonstandard" companies has blurred as the use of credit-based insurance scoring and other tools effective in predicting risk of loss have resulted in more refined pricing and increased use of rating tiers. More sophisticated coverage and rating options mean that insurers are able to rate and compete for segments of business that they may not have in the past.

Some automobile insurers invest millions of dollars annually in high-profile advertising. Celebrity spokespersons, mascots, special effects, and humor have led to name recognition for certain companies and remind consumers that they can easily switch companies. More than one-half of "Generation Y" insurance consumers (those born between 1977 and 1992) seek information from insurers' Web sites when shopping for automobile insurance, and those shoppers are almost twice as likely to seek an automobile insurance quote directly from a Web site as are Baby Boomers (those born between 1946 and 1964). At the same time, however, "Generation Y" shoppers are less likely than Baby Boomers to shop for new coverage based on price.[8]

Greenly Insurance Company—Goals

An organization's goals provide the overall context for what the organization seeks to achieve. Greenly's goals have remained fairly constant for many years, and it establishes metrics based on these goals annually:

- Maintain financial strength to protect insureds
- Build long-term customer loyalty and maintain high customer satisfaction by meeting customer needs
- Contribute to charitable community efforts through time and financial support
- Comply with legal requirements

Greenly Insurance Company—Business Strategies

Based on its goals of financial strength, customer loyalty and satisfaction, and charitable giving, Greenly has developed business strategies to direct its actions. See the exhibit " Greenly Insurance Company—Business Strategies."

Issues That Prompted the Evaluation

Greenly has failed to meet its automobile insurance written premium and policy growth goals for the past two years. Greenly's new business has declined steadily over the past few years and **retention ratios** of existing business have decreased at an even greater pace. After accounting for the impact of the

Retention ratio

The percentage of insurance policies renewed.

Greenly Insurance Company—Business Strategies

1. Financial Strength: We will protect our policyholders' security by maintaining financial strength. To accomplish this we will:
   - Increase policyholder surplus and maintain our superior financial rating
   - Achieve a combined ratio of 98% or less (automobile and homeowners)
   - Increase written premium by 5%
   - Gain a net increase of automobile policies in force by 2%

2. Customer Focus: We will commit to providing the outstanding customer service that our customers deserve and demand, and will strive to build long-term relationships with our policyholders. To accomplish this we will:
   - Offer quality products, while meeting or exceeding established product delivery goals
   - Increase average household longevity by providing consistently superior service
   - Achieve 98% customer satisfaction as expressed on post-claim settlement and annual policyholder renewal surveys

3. Technology and Data Management: We will provide the best service possible to our agents and policyholders by adopting current and efficient technologies intended to enhance our business. To accomplish this we will:
   - Safeguard all customer data
   - Expand use of data-driven products in the claims settlement process

4. Corporate Leadership: We will show leadership in the communities in which we operate through organizational effort and through the dedication of our employees. To accomplish this we will:
   - Dedicate our time and financial support to community activities
   - Encourage employee participation in community charitable efforts
   - Achieve a 50% positive response on recognition of our community efforts as measured by annual policyholder renewal surveys

[DA06385]

economic downturn, it has become clear that the negative trends likely stem from its current business practices.

A survey of Greenly's agents has revealed that Greenly insureds who were insured under their parent's policies seem increasingly less likely to stay with Greenly when they establish their own households. Further, many cited customer dissatisfaction with claims service as a primary reason for obtaining coverage elsewhere, despite the fact that post-claim surveys continue to show acceptable results. See the exhibit "SWOT Analysis Table."

SWOT Analysis Table

	Strengths	Weaknesses
Internal	List assets, competencies, or attributes that enhance competitiveness. Prioritize based on the quality of the strength and the relative importance of the strength.	List lacking assets, competencies, or attributes that diminish competitiveness. Prioritize based on the seriousness of the weakness and the relative importance of the weakness.
	Opportunities	**Threats**
External	List conditions that could be exploited to create a competitive advantage. Prioritize based on the potential of exploiting the opportunities.	List conditions that diminish competitive advantage. Prioritize based on the seriousness and probability of occurrence.
	Note strengths that can be paired with opportunities as areas of competitive advantage.	Note weaknesses that can be paired with threats as risks to be avoided.

[DA03626]

Case Analysis Tools and Information

To evaluate business strategies for Greenly Insurance Company, the reviewer or review team will need these:

- A current SWOT analysis
- The company's business strategies
- An explanation of the reason for the evaluation
- The company's goals and objectives that relate to the reason for the evaluation

Case Analysis Steps

Evaluating an organization's strategies involves a series of decision-making steps. Following these steps minimizes the effort required by focusing on the issues, strategies, and desired outcome:

1. Conduct a current SWOT analysis of the organization's internal and external environments

2. Determine the business strategies relevant to the business issue that generated the need for evaluation

3. Evaluate the relevant business strategies using the SWOT analysis

SWOT Analysis Process

One method of conducting a SWOT analysis is through a group activity that involves an organization's managers and is organized by a facilitator.

Brainstorming

- If the group is large, the facilitator may divide the managers into smaller groups to encourage participation.
- Through brainstorming, factors are listed under each of the SWOT headings.
- This activity will produce many factors randomly organized under each SWOT heading.

Refining

- To make the list easier to examine, similar items are clustered together.
- Items of high importance are noted under each of the SWOT headings.

Prioritizing

- Strengths are ordered by quality and relative importance.
- Weaknesses are ordered by the degree to which they affect performance and by their relative importance.
- Opportunities are ordered by degree and probability of success.
- Threats are ordered by degree and probability of occurrence.
- Strengths that require little or no operational changes and can be paired with opportunities are designated for potential action to maximize competitive advantages that entail low risk.
- Weaknesses that can be paired with threats are designated in the prioritized list for potential action to minimize consequences that entail high risk.

[DA03650]

Conduct a Current SWOT Analysis

The SWOT analysis is a methodical assessment of an organization and its business environment that usually is completed by those involved in planning and decision-making for the organization. While determination of strengths and weaknesses may be based on subjective criteria, the overall process allows for an objective view of the environments in which the organization operates.

The SWOT analysis of Greenly reveals that the company faces a high-risk threat because it has not kept pace with the needs of existing customers or the buying preferences of prospective customers. Customer satisfaction surveys may be unreliable because they are outdated and fail to ask the right questions, or fail to reach a broad enough audience. Further, the company's normal avenue of direct communication with policyholders, the monthly magazine, may have little impact on customer relations or loyalty.

A review of the survey questions asked and their target audience may reveal if such surveys need to be revised. For example, Greenly could be relying only on input from current satisfied customers rather than from former customers who may have left due to dissatisfaction, which would skew responses toward positive results. To prevent this, Greenly could utilize focus groups of current customers, former customers, and producers to determine how it is perceived and any areas needing improvement. See the exhibit "SWOT Case Table— Greenly Insurance."

Determine Business Strategies to Be Evaluated

The organization's business strategies are its long-term approach to attaining its goals and objectives. Because an organization's strategies can be extensive, it is helpful to narrow the focus of the examination by understanding the business issue that has prompted the evaluation. The strategies relevant to the issue can then be targeted for evaluation.

Which business strategies have contributed to the failure of Greenly to meet its customer satisfaction and loyalty goals and policy growth target?

Assuming that customers are leaving because they are either dissatisfied with the company's products, services or prices, the company may need to reevaluate its customer-focused strategy:

> 2. Customer Focus: We will commit to providing the outstanding customer service that our customers deserve and demand, and will strive to build long-term relationships with our policyholders. To accomplish this we will:
>
> - Offer quality products, while meeting or exceeding established product delivery goals
> - Increase average household longevity by providing consistently superior service
> - Achieve 98% customer satisfaction as expressed on post-claim settlement and annual policyholder renewal surveys

This goal seeks to meet the needs of customers, but fails to address identification of changes in the marketplace. The company's business strategies also lack commitment to respond to the changing needs or buying habits of insurance consumers.

Evaluate Relevant Business Strategies

After an organization's internal and external environments and its business strategies have been examined, the next step is to determine whether a change in course is required to achieve its goals.

Will the current business strategies for Greenly continue to be the most effective approach toward attaining its goals, or should its business strategies be changed?

SWOT Case Table—Greenly Insurance

Strengths	Weaknesses
Strengths are apparent in the organization's financial stability: • Superior financial rating and policyholder surplus • Branding based on customer satisfaction allows the company to focus on financial stability • Commitment to charitable efforts and community involvement • Established method of monthly communication with policyholders • Representation by independent agents fosters goal of customer loyalty (for example, trust and service) • Experienced employees	Weaknesses have emerged in the types of services that the organization has not developed and the needs it is not meeting: • Customer surveys are inadequate in measuring customer feedback • Technology in use has not kept pace with consumer demands/lack of development of Web site options for quotes and applications • Claim handling complaints increasing (distant locations may have resulted in inadequate oversight, training, or focus on company values) • Inadequate advertising/lack of branding • Reliance on products with few unique options/lack of new products (for example, "green" insurance options)

Opportunities	Threats
Opportunities provide potential actions that the organization can take to meet the needs of its current and potential policyholders. • Generation Y insurance consumers less sensitive to price—ability to target younger prospective policyholders based on factors other than price • Ability to enhance branding through focus on charitable and community involvement efforts • Ability to pilot discounts or incentives based on customer longevity • Claims staff can be retrained and customer evaluation materials can be revised to improve reliability of results • Ability to expand into additional states • Ability to pilot direct writing option, and internet-based partnership options with independent agents	Threats have surfaced as some are better positioned to meet the needs of the company's customers. • Current business is vulnerable to price leaders' advertising efforts, particularly of national writers • Agency force may lean toward better recognized brands or companies that advertise lower prices • Increasing percentage of consumers looking for direct purchase options and interactive Web site capability • Dissatisfaction with claims processes may damage the company reputation, particularly if dissatisfied customers tell others or if complaints are filed with state departments of insurance • Competitors offer more pricing options, reducing likelihood of declinations and nonrenewals and enhancing customer stability

Internal (left rows: Strengths, Weaknesses)

External (bottom rows: Opportunities, Threats)

Greenly's current customer-focused strategy will not lead to successful achievement of the company's growth goals. Greenly has committed to customer satisfaction, but has not devised an effective method of determining customer needs and opinions. Although the company is committed to soliciting feedback through renewal and post-claim surveys, those surveys may not be worded appropriately to invite the type of feedback needed for the company to truly evaluate its operations. For example, if the surveys only request feedback on current issues, the company will not have the benefit of hearing how customers believe the company has changed, improved, or even declined over time—or the benefit of hearing suggestions for the future. Perhaps even more important, Greenly has no established method of seeking input from former customers to determine why they left.

If the company revises its customer surveys and establishes additional methods of reaching out to current and former customer and agents, it may determine that additional changes are needed as well. For example, the company may wish to revise its business strategies to include opportunities identified to attract and retain policyholders and to help meet the company's goals. Such changes may include these:

- Redesign its Web site to add on-line quote capability or other interactive options
- Expand into a new state as a direct writer
- Implement a pilot program to test new products or coverage options
- Redesign the company magazine to emphasize new developments and to better target second-generation policyholders
- Refocus community involvement efforts on issues more likely to appeal to second generation policyholders and effectively promote those efforts
- Retrain claims staff to improve customer satisfaction

SWOT Case Correct Answer

The Greenly Insurance Company has failed to meet its automobile insurance written premium and policy growth goals for the past two years because customer satisfaction goals are not being met and lapse ratios are increasing. A SWOT analysis indicates that Greenly has not adequately identified or kept pace with the changing needs of customers.

Using that information to evaluate its business strategies, Greenly must revise its customer-focused strategy to meet its goals. As a well-capitalized company, Greenly is in a good position to implement changes, including updating technology and implementing pilot marketing programs designed to attract and retain business.

[DA06390]

SUMMARY

The strategic management process is employed by organizations to align external factors and internal resources to create a sustainable competitive advantage. Mission and value statements define a company's purpose and over-arching goals, and provide the framework for the strategic management process. The strategic management process includes strategy formulation, strategy implementation, and strategy evaluation. Implementation and evaluation phases are closely linked, and may reveal the need for adjustment to the strategic management plan.

The Five Forces Model can be used to thoroughly assess an organization's external environment by identifying factors related to customers, competitors, and suppliers. The "Five Forces" that drive competition are the threat of new entrants, the threat of substitute products or services, bargaining power of buyers, bargaining power of suppliers, and rivalry among existing firms. Evaluating these forces also helps management to better understand the organization's position within its industry.

A SWOT analysis can then be used to determine internal strengths and weaknesses related to the company's financial, physical, human, and organizational assets. An examination of the external environment is then conducted to determine opportunities and threats.

Strategy is planned and implemented at the organization's corporate, business, functional, and operational levels. Corporate-level strategies in a growing company include concentration on a single business, vertical integration, and either related or unrelated diversification. When a company is encountering a decreasing market, corporate management is faced with a different set of strategies from those available to a growing company. For organizations in a decline mode, bankruptcy or liquidation may be undertaken as a last resort. Other options are the harvest, turnaround, or divestiture strategies.

Business-level strategies are employed by divisional managers within the organization. These strategies include cost leadership, differentiation, and focus. At the functional level, strategies focus on integrating efficiency, quality, customer responsiveness, and innovation in each functional process or operation. Functional areas of insurers include marketing, underwriting, claim, risk control, premium audit, actuarial, and finance. Operational-level strategies are implemented at the department level to support the strategies of the functional, business, and corporate levels; these strategies focus on daily business operations.

The strategic reasons for global expansion include revenue growth and financial stability along with global competitiveness. However, there are significant risks associated with expanding into global markets, and insurers need to perform a market analysis and evaluate economic considerations along with political risks before deciding to expand into a global market. Insurers can enter a foreign market by forming a strategic alliance, joint venture, or merger with an insurer operating in that country. Alternatively, insurers can form a new company or acquire an existing one to establish a subsidiary in a new global market.

A SWOT analysis is a structured examination of an organization's internal and external environment as a prelude to action planning. When used to evaluate an organization's business strategies, the SWOT analysis focuses on the event that prompted the evaluation. The results of the business strategies relevant to the cause of the event are examined to determine whether those strategies will continue to be effective in achieving the organization's goals.

ASSIGNMENT NOTES

1. Robert Kreitner, Management Principles and Practices, 3rd edition (Atlanta: LOMA, 1997), p. 203.

2. Michael E. Porter, *Competitive Strategy: Techniques for Analyzing Industries and Competitors* (New York: The Free Press, 1980), p. 4.

3. Porter, *Competitive Strategy*, pp. 9-12.

4. Porter, *Competitive Strategy*, p. 26.

5. Kathryn M. Bartol and David C. Martin, *Management*, 3rd ed. (New York: McGraw-Hill Cos., Inc., 1998), p. 228.

6. U.S. Department of Commerce, *Survey of Current Business*, October 2007, pp. 114-115 and 132.

7. U.S. Department of Commerce, *Survey of Current Business*, pp. 114-115 and 132.

8. "Study: Overall Purchase Beats Price in Auto Insurance Satisfaction," Insurance Journal, May 2010, www.insurancejournal.com/news/national/2010/05/26/110212.htm (accessed July 15, 2010).

Index

Page numbers in boldface refer to pages where the word or phrase is defined.